# PEOPLE AND PRODUCTIVITY

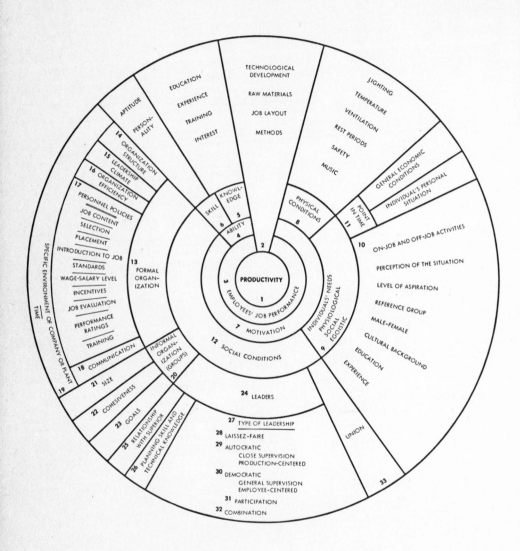

TECHNOLOGICAL
DEVELOPMENT

RAW MATERIALS

JOB LAYOUT

METHODS

LIGHTING

TEMPERATURE

VENTILATION

REST PERIODS

SAFETY

MUSIC

EDUCATION

EXPERIENCE

TRAINING

INTEREST

APTITUDE

PERSON-
ALITY

14 ORGANIZATION
STRUCTURE

15 LEADERSHIP
CLIMATE

16 ORGANIZATION
EFFICIENCY

17 PERSONNEL POLICIES

JOB CONTENT

SELECTION

PLACEMENT

INTRODUCTION TO JOB

STANDARDS

WAGE-SALARY LEVEL

INCENTIVES

JOB EVALUATION

PERFORMANCE
RATINGS

TRAINING

13 FORMAL
ORGAN-
IZATION

18 COMMUNICATION

SPECIFIC ENVIRONMENT OF COMPANY OR PLANT
TIME

19

21 SIZE

22 COHESIVENESS

23 GOALS

25 RELATIONSHIP
WITH SUPERIOR

26 PLANNING SKILL AND
TECHNICAL KNOWLEDGE

INFORMAL
ORGAN-
IZATION
(GROUPS)
20

KNOWL-
EDGE
5

ABILITY
4

6

SKILL

PRODUCTIVITY
1

3 EMPLOYEES' JOB PERFORMANCE

7 MOTIVATION

12 SOCIAL CONDITIONS

24 LEADERS

27 TYPE OF LEADERSHIP

28 LAISSEZ-FAIRE

29 AUTOCRATIC
CLOSE SUPERVISION
PRODUCTION-CENTERED

30 DEMOCRATIC
GENERAL SUPERVISION
EMPLOYEE-CENTERED

31 PARTICIPATION

32 COMBINATION

2

8

PHYSICAL
CONDITIONS

GENERAL ECONOMIC
CONDITIONS

INDIVIDUAL'S PERSONAL
SITUATION

POINT
IN TIME
11

10

ON-JOB AND OFF-JOB ACTIVITIES

PERCEPTION OF THE SITUATION

LEVEL OF ASPIRATION

REFERENCE GROUP

MALE-FEMALE

CULTURAL BACKGROUND

EDUCATION

EXPERIENCE

INDIVIDUALS' NEEDS
PHYSIOLOGICAL
SOCIAL
EGOISTIC
9

UNION

33

MAJOR FACTORS
AFFECTING
EMPLOYEES'
JOB PERFORMANCE
AND PRODUCTIVITY

NOTE:
For Explanation of the Mechanics of
This Diagram, Refer to the Six Points
Listed at the End of Chapter One.

# McGRAW-HILL SERIES IN MANAGEMENT

## KEITH DAVIS, Consulting Editor

# Robert A. Sutermeister

*Graduate School of Business Administration*
*University of Washington*

SECOND
EDITION **PEOPLE AND**
**PRODUCTIVITY**

*McGRAW-HILL Book Company*

*New York · St. Louis · San Francisco · London · Sydney*
*Toronto · Mexico · Panama*

# PEOPLE AND PRODUCTIVITY

*Library of Congress Catalog Card Number 69-14492*

**ISBN 07-062362**

0  DODO  7987654

# PREFACE

This book is written for the layman, the businessman, and the student.

Its unique contribution is the conceptual scheme or diagram on page ii. An attempt has been made to show in the diagram the most important factors which affect the performance of employees* and the productivity of a firm.

The values of the diagram are several:

(1) It will help the reader who is interested primarily in one segment of one of the concentric circles to maintain a proper perspective, realizing that there are many other segments of many other concentric circles which also have their influence on productivity. It will help the reader of research studies in the behavioral sciences to fit in the findings of one particular piece of research with findings of other pieces (even when they seem to be contradictory) and to see them in proper relation to each other.

(2) It will help the businessman to see what research findings are pertinent for his business and how they can be used by him, as well as to appreciate the complexity of human problems related to increased productivity. It will help executives in management development programs obtain a meaningful and integrated picture of current research and thinking in the broad behavioral science area.

(3) It will help the students of organizational behavior, informal groups, leadership, unions, sociology, psychology, human relations, personnel management, labor, production, engineering, general management, and other areas to relate their fields of interest to each other and to a goal of increased productivity.

The first nine chapters of the book are devoted to a brief explanation of the various segments of the diagram. A new chapter has been written, Chapter X, on the "Relationship between Satisfaction of Individuals' Needs and Motivation, Performance, and Productivity." In Chapter XI some of the interrelationships among the various segments and circles are considered, and the preceding chapters are summarized. In Chapter XII areas of the diagram which seem to hold the greatest importance for increased productivity in the future are indicated.

Several readings which appeared in the first edition have been deleted, and several new readings have been added. A great many articles which

---

* All employees, from the president to the machine operator or the clerk.

have appeared since the first edition and which relate closely to items discussed in the book have been referred to in the text or in footnotes.

The following list shows the numbers on the diagram which are explained in the various chapters of the book:

| Diagram Number | Chapter |
|:---:|:---:|
| 1 | I |
| 2–7 | II |
| 8 | III |
| 9 | IV |
| 10–11 | V |
| 12–19 | VI |
| 20–23 | VII |
| 24–32 | VIII |
| 33 | IX |

Throughout Chapters I to XII, the arabic numbers within parentheses indicate which segment of the diagram is being discussed.

The balance of the book consists of readings which have been cited in the chapters. Most of these readings report findings from empirical research that illustrate the effect of some segment of the diagram on productivity.

The reader may choose to read all the chapters first to get an integrated explanation of the diagram; or he may choose to read one chapter at a time, followed by any readings related to that chapter.

The conceptual scheme or diagram is, of course, tentative and subject to revision. In his choice of readings, the author has attempted to select the ones which (1) discuss a factor or factors with important bearing on productivity, (2) are readily understandable, and (3) represent, whenever possible, results of empirical research.

The author's interest in some of the areas of this book was stimulated by his attendance at a seminar in new developments in business administration, sponsored by the Ford Foundation. Time to begin the development of the diagram was provided by financial assistance from a Ford Foundation grant to the College of Business Adminstration.

The author is particularly indebted to the late Austin Grimshaw, Dean of the Graduate School of Business Administration, University of Washington, for his encouragement in this study, and to Professor Floyd Mann, Institute for Social Research, University of Michigan, for his suggestions. He would also like to acknowledge gratefully the suggestions which have been received from readers of the book, many of which have been incorporated in this new edition. It goes without saying that the shortcomings of the book can be attributed to the author alone.

*Robert A. Sutermeister*

# CONTENTS

# Chapter I

# PRODUCTIVITY AS A GOAL OF BUSINESS

In this book, increased productivity is assumed to be a primary goal of business.

From a national standpoint, various writers have advocated various goals. Many have stressed the necessity for increased productivity, forecasting that the labor force will increase much slower than the need for goods and services. Galbraith decries the further accumulation of gadgets we are persuaded we want and argues for "social balance." His feeling is that much more of our national income should go for parks, hospitals, and education; for things which emphasize human individuality, dignity, and worth; and for making life more pleasant and satisfying.[1] Kerr and Fisher take note of the conflict between "plant sociologists" who see stable operations and harmonious management of social systems as the task of management, and economists who see efficient management of productive resources as the end.[2]

From the standpoint of individual firms, this book also assumes increased productivity to be a primary goal. Other writers maintain that we must judge the efficiency of firms in terms of human costs of happiness and health. For example, Likert emphasizes the importance, in measuring organizational performance, of including measurements of human assets:

> Decentralization and delegation are powerful concepts based on sound theory. But there is evidence that, as now utilized, they have a serious vulnerability which can be costly. This vulnerability arises from the measurements being used to evaluate and reward the performance of those given authority over decentralized operations.
>
> This situation is becoming worse. While companies have during the past decade made greater use of work measurements and measurements of end results in evaluating managers, and also greater use of incentive pay in rewarding them, only a few managements have regularly used measurements that deal directly with the human assets of the organization—for example, measurements of loyalty, motivation, confidence, and trust. As a conse-

[1] John Galbraith, *The Affluent Society,* Houghton Mifflin Company, Boston, 1958, p. 280.
[2] "Plant Sociology: The Elite and the Aborigines" in M. Komarovsky (ed.), *Common Frontiers of the Social Sciences,* The Free Press of Glencoe, New York, 1957, p. 282.

quence, many companies today are encouraging managers of departments and divisions to dissipate valuable human assets of the organization. In fact, they are rewarding these managers well for doing so![3]

Georgopoulos and Tannenbaum[4] feel that "organizational effectiveness" is based on the "extent to which an organization, as a social system, fulfills its objectives without incapacitating its means and resources and without placing undue strain on its members." As criteria of effectiveness, they use not only organizational productivity, but also organizational flexibility and absence of intraorganizational strain or tension.

Some write of "higher profits" as the goal of business. This is normally the financial goal of a business, and productivity plays a major role in the determination of profit. Other factors, however, notably prices or market conditions, also affect profit. A firm in a monopoly or unusually favorable market position could increase profits without increasing productivity, or even while productivity is decreasing. This would be unusual. Most firms are vitally interested in increased productivity as a method for increasing profits or holding losses to a minimum. Moreover, with the economic recovery in Europe and Japan, and the growth of the European Common Market, the pressure of foreign competition is being felt increasingly in the United States and has forced many firms here to put greater emphasis on productivity if they wish to prosper or even, in some cases, to survive.

Thus, emphasis in this book is placed on productivity as a goal of business. The reader will note from the diagram inside the covers that Productivity (more accurately, increased productivity) is considered the bull's-eye of the target. "Productivity" is defined for our purposes as "output per man per hour, quality considered." If 20 units were produced by one man in one hour last month and 22 of the same units are produced by one man in one hour today, productivity has risen 10 per cent. If 20 units were produced last month and 20 units of higher quality are produced today, productivity has also risen, although the measurement of it is more difficult. The output per man per hour results not from man's effort alone but results jointly from all the factors of production used: labor, management, money, machines, raw materials, etc. When productivity is expressed as output per man per hour, it is done only for convenience. Productivity might also be expressed in terms of output per $1,000 invested, or output per 100 pounds of raw material, or output compared with any other input factor.

[3] "Measuring Organizational Performance," *Harvard Business Review*, vol. 36, no. 2, March–April, 1958, pp. 41–50. Quoted by permission of *Harvard Business Review*.

[4] "A Study of Organizational Effectiveness," *American Sociological Review*, vol. 22, no. 5, October, 1957, pp. 534–540.

In examining the diagram one should keep several points in mind:

1. The diagram consists of a series of concentric circles, each divided into segments. No attempt has been made to have the size of each segment reflect its relative importance. The importance of each segment would probably be different for each organization studied, for each department in the organization, and even for each individual employee with his own distinct needs.

2. The factors in each segment of each circle are deemed to affect or determine the factors in the corresponding segment of the next smaller circle.

3. The factors in each segment of each circle frequently affect and are affected by factors in some of the other segments in the same circle.

4. The factors in each segment of each circle may also affect factors in segments elsewhere in the diagram.

5. All the factors in the diagram are subject to change with time. The special importance of time in affecting Individuals' Needs (9) and Formal Organization (13) is indicated.

6. The numbers in the various segments of the diagram correspond to the figures in parentheses throughout Chapters I to XII.

The diagram indicates that greater productivity depends upon or is determined by technical factors (technological development, raw materials, job layout, and methods) and human factors (employees' job performance). Both of these are considered in the next chapter. .

# Chapter II

# TECHNICAL AND HUMAN CONTRIBUTIONS TO PRODUCTIVITY

## Technological Development (2)

We must recognize at once that Productivity (1) is not determined solely by how hard and how well people work. The technical factors play a role, sometimes an overwhelmingly important one,[1] sometimes a minor one.

The technical factors are all those other than employee performance which can affect output per man-hour. They include such factors as technological development (the machinery and equipment employees have to work with), the quality of raw materials, the layout of the work, and methods and techniques. In industrial plants, technological development will often be the most important factor influencing productivity, as illustrated in Figure 1. For example, Goodman in *Man and Automation*[2] cites the use of a tape to operate a machine tool which manufactures an aircraft spar. "The time taken by the conventional method was ten hours. By the computer method, ninety-two minutes were taken in planning time, and the actual tape-controlled machining time was fourteen minutes." In a department store, on the other hand, the degree of technology would have relatively little effect on productivity, except, perhaps, in the office if automatic equipment were in use. The segments in the diagram for a department store might be similar to those shown in Figure 2.

Other technical factors which have a bearing on productivity include ones such as:

The Plant: Its size, its capacity, the percentage of capacity utilized—all related to the ability to sell and distribute the product.
The Product: Its design, its quality (which may improve from year to year). This is related to research and development expenditures.

[1] The introduction of improved methods of working has shown increases in productivity ranging from 20 to 200 per cent, while the effect of supervision and group organization may be expected to lead to differences in productivity of 7 to 15 per cent. These results are reported in Michael Argyle, Godfrey Gardner, and Frank Coiffi, "Supervisory Methods Related to Productivity, Absenteeism, and Labor Turnover," *Human Relations,* vol. 11, no. 1, February, 1958, p. 24.
[2] Penguin Books, Inc., Baltimore, 1957, p. 52.

The Product Mix: If some items are produced more efficiently than others, the proportion in which they are combined will affect the overall productivity of the plant, without any change in the productivity of any individual item.

Plant and Job Layout: Work flow and methods.

Design of Machines and Equipment: To best match the limitations and capacities of people.

Degree of Integration of Production Processes: A plant which buys its raw materials partly processed will have a higher output of finished product per man-hour than the plant which starts from scratch. Moreover, a single highly integrated plant should have fewer man-hours spent for handling, sorting, shipping, etc., than two separate plants which are performing the same steps.

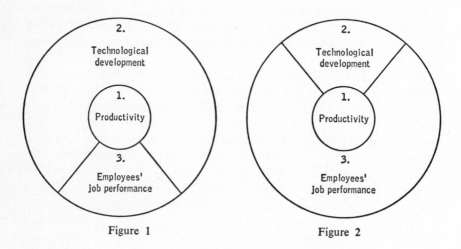

Figure 1                    Figure 2

Utilization of Power: Output per man-hour is usually increased with increased use of power.

Raw Materials: Quality of raw materials used and the continuity of their supply.

Percentage of Indirect Workers Employed: The firm with staffs of planners, quality control experts, industrial engineers, etc., should be able to devise methods which would result in greater output per man per hour.

Scientific Management: With its emphasis on better planning and coordination, simplified methods, standardization, time and motion study, reduced waste and spoilage, contributes notably to increased productivity; although in some cases, the employees' attitudes and performance prevent the attainment of the full potential for increased productivity which scientific management provides.

For convenience, all these technical factors are deemed to be included in segment 2 of the diagram, labeled "Technological Development—Raw

Materials—Job Layout—Methods."[3] There are some interrelations between this segment and segments 3 (Employees' Job Performance) and 7 (Motivation). If an employee has good materials, equipment, and tools to work with, he is likely to be encouraged to work harder than if he has inferior tools and materials.

### Employees' Job Performance (3)

So much for the technical side. Let's turn to the human side, or to Employees' Job Performance and its effect on productivity or output per man-hour. "Employees" includes executives and managers, supervisors, professional staff such as engineers and scientists, other white-collar workers, and blue-collar workers. Even if a plant has but one employee, his satisfactory performance is vital to the proper functioning of the machinery and equipment; and of course, in a company with many employees and little automation, productivity is likely to be determined largely by what the employees, rather than the machines, do.

The importance of human contributions to productivity has been stated by John Patton, President of John Patton Management Engineering Firm:

> Direct incentives will increase production 20–50% but "the ingredient I find in the excellent companies has a potential that overshadows the productivity increase achievable through industrial engineering techniques. When we learn to manage people, the increased productivity will be likened to the relationship of the water wheel to nuclear energy."[4]

Sometimes an improvement in technology is more than offset by changes for the worse on the human side of productivity, so that productivity which should go up actually goes down. An excellent example of this is the long wall method of coal mining in England, where the social and psychological consequences of the changed method offset the great technical improvement from mechanization.[5]

In the diagram, the human contributions to productivity, or Employees' Job Performance (3), are considered to result from Ability (4) and Motivation (7), or more accurately, Ability *times* Motivation. Thus, if a person had no motivation, he could be the most capable individual in the world,

[3] For a discussion of the link between technology and organizational characteristics, see Joan Woodward, *Industrial Organization: Theory and Practice,* Oxford University Press, London, 1965.

[4] Quoted in Alfred G. Larke, "Human Relations Research: Academic Woolgathering or Guide to Increased Productivity?" *Dun's Review and Modern Industry,* vol. 68, no. 1, July, 1956, pp. 42–44.

[5] E. L. Trist and K. W. Bamforth, "Some Social and Psychological Consequences of the Longwall Method of Coal-getting," *Human Relations,* vol. 4, no. 1, 1951, pp. 3–38.

but there would be no connection between his ability and his performance. Or, if a person had no ability, there could be terrific motivation, but there would be no connection between the motivation and the performance. Both ability and motivation are essential ingredients to good employee performance.

## Ability (4)

Ability is deemed to result from Knowledge (5) and Skill (6). Knowledge, in turn, is affected by education, experience, training, and interest. Skill is affected by aptitude and personality, as well as by education, experience, training, and interest.

## Motivation (7)

Motivation is here considered to result from the interacting forces in Physical Conditions of the job (8), Social Conditions of the job (12), and Individuals' Needs (9).

As we shall see, some of the forces are positive and contribute to motivation, improved employee performance, and increased productivity. They operate centripetally, working inward toward the bull's-eye on the diagram. Other forces are negative, reducing motivation, performance, and productivity. They operate centrifugally, or away from the target we have assumed for the firm. What actually happens to employees' performance, and through performance to productivity (unless offset by changes in the technical factors), depends on the relative strength of the multitudinous centripetal and centrifugal forces.

One might jump to the conclusion that an individual whose needs are being fairly well met will be motivated to improve his performance and contribute to greater productivity. This is an unwarranted assumption.[6] It may be true generally, but it is possible, as we shall see, for an individual's needs to be pretty well met, for him to be fairly well satisfied with his job and firm, and for him to have a fairly high level of morale[7] but to willfully restrict his output, not perform at his best, and in effect work against the company goal of increased productivity. The relation between

---

[6] For more detailed discussion of the relationship between individuals' needs and motivation, performance, and productivity, see Chap. X.

[7] "Morale" and "attitude" are not single dimensions. The author chooses to explain motivation not as resulting from morale or attitude but rather as the result of the interacting forces involved in Physical Conditions, Social Conditions, and Individuals' Needs. For an excellent article on various definitions of "morale," see Robert M. Guion, "Some Definitions of Morale," in "Industrial Morale (A Symposium): 1. The Problem of Terminology," *Personnel Psychology*, vol. 11, no. 1, Spring, 1958, pp. 59–61. Reprinted in E. Fleishman, *Studies in Personnel and Industrial Psychology*, The Dorsey Press, Inc., Homewood, Ill., 1961, pp. 301–304.

need satisfaction, morale, employees' job performance, and productivity is much too complex for us to assume that satisfaction of individuals' needs will automatically lead to better job performance and increased productivity.[8]

Chapter III will deal briefly with the physical conditions of the job; Chapters IV and V with individuals' needs; and Chapters VI, VII, VIII, and IX with the social conditions of the job.

[8] In fact, even the measurement of job performance is fraught with difficulties. Seashore, Indik, and Georgopoulos in "Relationships among Criteria of Job Performance," *Applied Psychology,* vol. 44, no. 3, June, 1960, p. 202, undertook a study of job performance in a delivery service firm. They selected five variables but did not propose that these five represented all aspects of performance: overall effectiveness, productivity, errors, accidents, and absences. They found that the first three criteria were internally consistent but that the last two were inconsistent with the first three and unrelated to each other. They concluded that "the relationships among certain different aspects of job performance are generally small, and that the size and direction of relationships are to a large degree unique to each population and situation, and somewhat different for organizations as contrasted to individuals. . . . These data are interpreted as contradicting the validity of 'overall job performance' as a unidimensional construct, and as a basis for combining job performance variables into a single measure having general validity."

# PHYSICAL WORKING CONDITIONS RELATIVELY UNIMPORTANT IN MOTIVATION

Industrial psychologists and human engineers have often stressed the importance of Physical Conditions on the job (8) to employee performance. Noise, lighting, music, rest periods, ventilation, temperature, humidity—all these and others have been seen as factors which could improve or impair employees' performance.[1] The Hawthorne plant studies originally focused on this area but were unable to demonstrate any relation between physical conditions and output; the studies were redirected toward the areas of social conditions, group attitudes, and individual reactions. Homans in his article on "The Western Electric Researches," page 73, describes in some detail the Hawthorne studies, the continuous increase in productivity irrespective of changing physical conditions of work, and the switch in direction by the researchers from physical conditions to attitudes of groups and individuals.

The subjective feelings of the employees and the way they view the physical changes, rather than the changes themselves, seem to influence motivation. Working conditions can, of course, affect the employees' comfort at work, but many are the examples of employees working under bad working conditions who have a high level of morale and, likewise, of employees working under the best physical working conditions who have low morale.[2]

This does not mean that management should ignore physical working conditions and make no effort to have them pleasant and comfortable. It does mean that if employees recognize that a job is unavoidably dirty or messy or hot and that management has done all it can to improve conditions, the poor conditions will not necessarily cause low morale of the employees. There may be some who will resign and seek jobs with

[1] Refer to Elton Mayo, "The First Inquiry," chap. 3 of *The Social Problems of an Industrial Civilization,* Harvard University Press, Cambridge, Mass., 1945, for an example of an increase in productivity when rest periods were introduced for people working a 50-hour week in a textile mill.

[2] See, for example, J. A. C. Brown, *The Social Psychology of Industry,* Penguin Books, Inc., Baltimore, 1954, pp. 192–194.

11

more pleasant conditions. But others will stay and be satisfied in the knowledge that management has done what it can to ameliorate the poor conditions.

In most working places today the physical conditions are good: temperature and ventilation are adequate; rest periods and coffee breaks are provided; lighting is good, etc. Thus, the presence of good physical working conditions in most plants and offices today is taken for granted and has little, if any, motivating force.[3]

[3] For reports of studies of fatigue, monotony, rest pauses, shift work, noise reduction, illumination, music, and their effects on human functioning and proficiency, see E. Fleishman, *Studies in Personnel and Industrial Psychology,* The Dorsey Press, Inc., Homewood, Ill., 1967, sec. 7, "Fatigue, Monotony, and Working Conditions," and sec. 9, "Engineering Psychology."

*Chapter* IV

# INDIVIDUALS' NEEDS

Although employees themselves may not be aware of different kinds and levels of needs, their needs may be considered of three major types: physiological, social, and egoistic. Maslow presents a theory in "A Theory of Human Motivation," page 83, which places needs in five categories: physiological, safety, love, esteem, and self-actualization. For our purposes, we shall consider physiological and safety needs combined under physiological; love as a social need; and esteem and self-actualization included under egoistic needs.

*Physiological needs* involve essentials such as air, water, food, housing, and clothing. These necessities must be at least partially fulfilled before a person gives much thought to other needs. They are met mainly through money and security on the job. As a person gets enough to eat, adequate clothing, and a roof over his head, he is inclined to place increasing emphasis on social and egoistic needs.

In our society, for people who have jobs, physiological needs are likely to be pretty well satisfied. A satisfied need is not a motivator of behavior.[1] Therefore, we cannot assume that more pay or more security will automatically lead to improved job performance. These traditional rewards of management provide little motivation because the struggle to satisfy subsistence work, and helping others and being helped.[3]

On the other hand, we cannot assume that more pay or more security won't lead to improved performance. A higher salary to the employee may fulfill an egoistic need for recognition and status. The point is, where pay and security are adequate to satisfy physiological needs, we must turn our attention more to the social and egoistic needs of individuals if we are to motivate them to better performance.

*Social needs* can be satisfied only by contacts with others, such as fellow employees, the supervisor, or friends off the job. Social needs include such group needs as friendship, identification with the group, teamwork, and helping others and being helped.[3]

[1] Douglas McGregor, *The Human Side of Enterprise,* McGraw-Hill Book Company, New York, 1960, p. 36.

[2] A. Zaleznik, C. R. Christenson, and F. Roethlisberger, *Motivation, Productivity, and Satisfaction of Workers,* Harvard Business School, Division of Research, Boston, 1958, p. 354.

[3] George Strauss and Leonard Sayles, *Personnel: The Human Problems of Management,* Prentice-Hall, Inc., Englewood Cliffs, N.J., 1960, p. 8.

13

In our society, a great many employees probably have very satisfying relations with other people on or off the job and thus fulfill their social needs pretty well. To the extent that social needs are satisfied, they do not motivate. If an individual's social needs are already satisfied, the establishment of congenial and satisfying work groups through such means as sociometry will not necessarily lead to better employee job performance and higher productivity.

*Egoistic needs* are those that an individual has for a high evaluation of himself, and include such needs as knowledge, achievement,[4] competence, independence, self-respect, respect of others, status, and recognition. To maintain a high estimate of ourselves, most of us never stop needing reassurance that we are held in esteem by others. Thus, if we satisfy our egoistic needs today, we continue to seek such satisfaction tomorrow and the day after. This differentiates egoistic needs from physiological and social needs which, when satisfied, cease to motivate. It can be argued that both the physiological and social needs are largely satisfied in our society for those who have jobs. The continuing satisfaction of egoistic needs, then, would seem to offer the best opportunity to motivate employees to better job performance.

It should be noted that some needs, of course, fall into more than one of the types mentioned. For example, money will purchase food and clothing and thereby fill a physiological need; at the same time, in our society, it can fill a need for status and recognition. A modest home can fill our physiological need for shelter; an elaborate home in a high-class neighborhood can fill an egoistic need for status and recognition. A college graduate receiving his first paycheck fills some physiological needs with it but probably also some egoistic needs of achievement, independence, and status.

Let us concentrate on egoistic needs. Chris Argyris points out that as we mature as individuals, we seek self-fulfillment more and more—an egoistic need.[5] Herzberg and others in "Motivation versus Hygiene," page 104, differentiate between motivation and hygiene and contend that some factors operate as satisfiers and some as dissatisfiers. If the dissatisfiers are eliminated, good hygiene results and conditions are produced under which the satisfiers, if present, can motivate. The satisfiers fulfill

---

[4] Much has been written about the "need for achievement" felt by many individuals in our society. See especially David C. McClelland, *The Achievement Motive,* Appleton-Century-Crofts, Inc., New York, 1953. The tendency or motivation to achieve success is a function of the need for achievement, the strength of expectancy or probability of achieving, and the incentive value of success. See John Atkinson, *A Theory of Achievement Motivation,* John Wiley & Sons, Inc., New York, 1966; also Bernard Indik, "Measuring Motivation to Work," *Personnel Administration,* November–December, 1966, pp. 39–44.

[5] Chris Argyris, *Personality and Organization,* Harper & Row, Publishers, Incorporated, New York, 1957, pp. 49–53.

the individual's egoistic needs for self-actualization. The mere absence of dissatisfiers, however, does not result in motivation.[6] Rensis Likert also emphasizes the importance of egoistic needs when he refers to the principle of supportive relationships which high-producing managers seem to be using.

> This provides the basis for stating the general principle which the high-producing managers seem to be using and which will be referred to as the *principle of supportive relationships.* This principle, which provides an invaluable guide in any attempt to apply the newer theory of management in a specific plant or organization, can be briefly stated: *The leadership and other processes of the organization must be such as to ensure a maximum probability that in all interactions and all relationships with the organization each member will, in the light of his background, values, and expectations, view the experience as supportive and one which builds and maintains his sense of personal worth and importance.*[7]

The area of egoistic needs assumes greater importance when we recognize that the educational level of employees in this nation is rising rapidly and that the number of white-collar and professional people is now greater than the number of blue-collar employees.[8]

[6] Successful results from using Herzberg's theory have been reported in his book *Work and the Nature of Man,* The World Publishing Company, Cleveland, 1966; in his "The New Industrial Psychology," *Industrial and Labor Relations Review,* vol. 18, no. 3, April, 1965, pp. 365–376; and in M. Scott Myers, "Who Are Your Motivated Workers?" *Harvard Business Review,* vol. 42, no. 1, January–February, 1964, pp. 73–88. A more recent article explaining his theory is Herzberg, "One More Time: How Do You Motivate Employees?" *Harvard Business Review,* vol. vol. 46, no. 1, January–February, 1968, pp. 53–62. See also Orlando Behling et al., "The Herzberg Controversy: A Critical Appraisal," *Academy of Management Journal,* vol. 11, no. 1, March, 1968, pp. 99–108.
Criticisms of Herzberg's theory have come from Arthur Kornhauser in *Mental Health of the Industrial Worker,* John Wiley & Sons, Inc., New York, 1965, who believes factors cannot be classified as "satisfiers" and "dissatisfiers"; from Martin G. Wolf, "The Relationship of Content and Context Factors to Attitudes toward Company and Job," *Personnel Psychology,* vol. 20, no. 2, Summer, 1967, pp. 121–132; and from Marvin D. Dunnette et al., "Factors Contributing to Job Satisfaction and Job Dissatisfaction in Six Occupational Groups," *Organization Behavior and Human Performance,* vol. 2, no. 2, May, 1967, pp. 143–174, which concludes that Herzberg's two-factor theory should be laid to rest. After a careful examination of Herzberg's theory and a review of research involving the theory, Robert House and Lawrence Wigdon conclude that the theory is an oversimplification. See "Herzberg's Dual Factor Theory of Job Satisfaction and Motivation: A Review of the Evidence and a Criticism," *Personnel Psychology,* vol. 20, no. 4, Winter, 1967, pp. 369–389.
[7] Rensis Likert, *New Patterns of Management,* McGraw-Hill Book Company, New York, 1961, chap. 8, "An Integrating Principle and an Overview." This chapter is reprinted in this book on pages 480 to 489.
[8] See Chap. V, pages 21–22, for further discussion on this point.

At the higher level of egoistic needs appear those for self-actualization or self-fulfillment. Such needs are often felt more strongly by professionals such as artists, doctors, and professors. Some writers feel that self-fulfillment needs are rarely activated for the average workers and that professors, for whom such needs may be quite active, are inclined to overstress their importance for all other workers.[9]

[9] See, for example, Edward Gross, *Industry and Social Life,* William C. Brown, Dubuque, Iowa, 1965, p. 143; and George Strauss, "Some Notes on Power Equalization," *The Social Science of Organizations,* Prentice-Hall, Inc., Englewood Cliffs, N.J., 1963, 47–48.

# Chapter V

# FACTORS AFFECTING INDIVIDUALS' NEEDS

It is important to recognize the wide diversity of factors which can influence the needs of a single individual.

## On-the-job and Off-the-job Activities

A *few* employees may have their needs well satisfied off the job and may work, not because they need the money or to fulfill social and egoistic needs, but because they have time on their hands or do not wish to appear parasitical or for some other reason.

A *larger group* of employees may find their social and egoistic needs satisfied off the job and may work only to be paid and satisfy their physiological needs. The job itself holds no interest and is merely a means to an end. They are active in the union or church or a hobby club and fulfill their social and egoistic needs in that manner.

For these groups there is likely to be a minimal relation between need satisfaction and job performance. This does not mean, however, that the employer should give up trying to motivate them: There are many ways (mentioned in Chapter XII) in which an employer can attempt to get these employees interested in their jobs so that they will gain some satisfaction of social and egoistic needs at their work.

*Most* employees derive need satisfaction on the job as well as off the job. Although the job provides the money and security to fill physiological needs, the social relations and opportunities for self-expression both on and off the job fill their social and egoistic needs.[1]

[1] For a discussion of the central life interests of industrial workers see Robert Dubin, "Industrial Workers' World: A Study of the Central Life Interests of Industrial Workers," *Social Problems,* vol. 3, no. 3, January, 1956, pp. 131–142. For a description of work-oriented, community-oriented, and indifferent persons, see Dubin, *The World of Work,* Prentice-Hall, Inc., Englewood Cliffs, N.J., 1958, pp. 255–258.

For a suggestion that perhaps we should forget about job satisfaction, devote our efforts to a shortening of the workweek, and then help people enjoy their leisure more (obtaining their need satisfaction from home and community life), see George Strauss, "Some Notes on Power Equalization," *The Social Science of Organizations,* Prentice-Hall, Inc., Englewood Cliffs, N.J., 1963, pp. 47–57.

## Perception of the Situation

Basic to an understanding of motivation is the recognition that a person or group responds to other people, situations, or issues as they are perceived, not as they actually are. This is such an important point that Stagner's entire chapter "Perception—Applied Aspects" has been included on pages 111 to 144.

"If a worker sees high (or low) productivity as a path to the attainment of one or more of his personal goals in the work situation, he will tend to be a high (or low) producer, assuming that his need is sufficiently high, or his goal is relatively salient, and that he is free from barriers to follow the desired path (high or low productivity)."[2]

## Level of Aspiration

The level of aspiration refers to the goal an individual sets for himself and attempts to achieve. If he sets his goal relatively low, his needs may be more easily satisfied. The individual feels himself successful if he meets or exceeds his own goal. Stagner, in his article "Level of Aspiration," page 144, points out that success in achieving one's goal usually leads a person to even higher aspiration.

## Reference Group

Related to the level of aspiration is the concept of reference group. "Reference groups are those groups with which an individual identifies or aspires to identify himself."[3] Thus, a new employee starting out on an assembly line in a factory may think of himself eventually as a supervisor or executive (supervisors and executives are his main reference group) and refuse to be governed by the standards and goals of the working group to which he currently belongs.

[2] B. S. Georgopoulos, G. M. Mahoney, and N. W. Jones, Jr., "A Path-Goal Approach to Productivity," *Journal of Applied Psychology,* vol. 41, no. 6, 1957, p. 353.

[3] For further discussion of reference groups, see Muzafer Sherif and Carolyn W. Sherif, *An Outline of Social Psychology,* Harper & Row, Publishers, Incorporated, New York, 1956, pp. 175–178.

For reports of a study "demonstrating that attitude change over time is related to the group identification of the person—both his membership group identification and his reference group identification," see Alberta E. Siegel and Sidney Siegel, "Reference Groups, Membership Groups, and Attitude Change," *Journal of Abnormal and Social Psychology,* vol. 55, 1957, pp. 360–364, reprinted in Cartwright and Zander (eds.), *Group Dynamics,* 2d ed., Harper & Row, Publishers, Incorporated, New York 1960, pp. 232–240.

## Male-Female

Up to 1940, women represented less than 25 per cent of all workers. In World War II the percentage rose to 36. After the war it dropped to 28, but by 1958 it had risen to 33.[4] Between 1960 and 1970 it is expected that women in the work force will increase by 25 per cent while men will increase by 15 per cent.[5] Thus the needs of women, as they may be different from those of men, must be considered. Herzberg[6] and others compiled the results of nine studies covering 10,000 employees. This compilation revealed that factors more important to women than to men included supervision, social aspects of the job, working conditions (including hours), and ease of work. Factors less important to women than to men included opportunity for advancement, company and management, wages, and intrinsic aspects of the job (excluding ease). Women and men thus weigh their needs differently. Women, for example, may be more inclined than men to seek praise and attention from their supervisors, and to want their supervisors to like them.

## Cultural Background

The standards of the society, the community, and the family in which an employee lives will greatly influence his perception of his needs.

If you focus on the social conduct of the person in a social position in an organization or even a small group, you are forced to take account of the cultural norms and groups to which he is sensitive. Whether you speak of job satisfaction, morale, the relative importance of economic and noneconomic incentives to work, types of leadership that make for high productivity, or what, you must go beyond the work group, beyond the organization, and into the community and society.[7]

Groups have motivating value. But the outside world (class, religion) gives workers their values. There is little chance that managers will improve performance by persuading workers of their own (managers') values.[8]

[4] *1958 Handbook of Women Workers,* U.S. Dept. of Labor, Women's Bureau, Bulletin 266, 1958.

[5] *Manpower—Challenge of the 1960s,* U.S. Dept. of Labor, 1960, p. 7.

[6] Frederick Herzberg et al., *Job Attitudes: Review of Research and Opinion,* Psychological Service of Pittsburgh, Pittsburgh, 1957, p. 52.

[7] Harold L. Wilensky, "Human Relations in the Workplace," in C. M. Arensberg et al., *Research in Industrial Human Relations,* Harper & Row, Publishers, Incorporated, New York, 1957, p. 45. Quoted by permission of the publisher.

See also Mason Haire et al., *Managerial Thinking: An International Study,* John Wiley & Sons, Inc., New York, 1967 (section on cultural background); and Lawrence Williams et al., "Do Cultural Differences Affect Workers' Attitudes?" *Industrial Relations,* vol. 5, no. 3, May, 1966, pp. 105–117.

[8] M. Komarovsky (ed.), *Common Frontiers of the Social Sciences,* The Free Press of Glencoe, New York, 1957, p. 331.

Allison Davis in his article "The Motivation of the Underprivileged Worker," page 149, points out how the behavior of the underprivileged worker is learned from the socioeconomic and cultural environment in which he lives and how he must be trained to work for increasing rewards.

The civil rights movement and problems of hard-core unemployment remind us that Negroes and members of minority groups have responded to their socioeconomic and cultural environment where job opportunities have been relatively scarce. They have seen little use in carrying on their education when they would be limited mostly to menial tasks. Their levels of aspiration consequently have been low for decades. Now an attempt is being made to give them new hope, to raise their levels of aspiration, and to make the realities match their hopes.

The background of an individual will affect his readiness to respond to authoritarian or democratic methods of leadership (29, 30). W. J. H. Sprott relates[9] the incident of a boy who was the son of an army officer and who preferred an autocratic leader to a democratic one.

An individual's cultural background will also affect the degree to which he conforms to group norms or deviates from them (23). For example, a person brought up on a farm, having worked hard and for long hours, might be more inclined in his first factory job to accept management's production goals rather than the goals of his work group. However, the person who has spent most of his life in factories might be more inclined to conform to the goals of his group rather than to the goals of management.

## Education

Other cultural factors influence employees' needs. The educational level of our citizens is constantly rising. Whereas in 1940 only 32 per cent of our population were graduated from high school and only 5.7 per cent from college, by 1967 this figure had risen to 60 per cent for high school and 12 per cent for college.[10] Undoubtedly education increases the strength of egoistic and status needs. Moreover, it is expected that employment of professional and technical personnel from 1964 to 1975 will increase 54 per cent, more than for any other group.[11] Peter F. Drucker's article "Managing the Educated," page 164, explores some

---

[9] In J. A. C. Brown, *The Social Psychology of Industry,* Penguin Books, Inc., Baltimore, 1954, p. 232.

[10] *Technology and the American Economy,* Report of the National Commission on Technology, Automation, and Economic Progress, February, 1966, p. 30, and "Education Attainment of Workers," *Monthly Labor Review,* vol. 91, no. 2, February, 1968, p. 28.

[11] *Ibid.*

of the implications for motivation of the higher educational levels and the rapidly increasing numbers in managerial, technical, and professional groups.

## Experience

An individual's experience in blue-collar, white-collar, professional, or executive jobs has an influence on the needs he feels. A study made by the Survey Research Center of the University of Michigan reported that

> Comparatively few of the blue-collar workers were dissatisfied with their jobs on the grounds that they afforded them no sense of personal fulfillment, whereas this was the major source of dissatisfaction for the professional and managerial groups. It would appear, the researchers conclude, that blue-collar workers either start out with minimal expectations of finding fulfillment in their jobs, or eventually become adjusted to the lack of it. Either way, they do not seem to be particularly frustrated about their situation. . . . Easily the most dissatisfied and frustrated of all the groups questioned were men engaged in clerical and white-collar occupations, well over half of whom said they would rather be doing some other kind of work—a clear indication that they expected to obtain some ego-satisfactions from working but were not finding them in their present jobs. . . . With more and more of the work force now moving into clerical occupations, the frustrations of the white-collar job may well become management's main area of future concern.[12]

An engineer or professor might attach more importance to his status and reputation among his fellows in other organizations than among those in the organization to which he is presently attached. Thus he might be devoting his major efforts not centripetally toward the organization's goal of productivity, but centrifugally to achieve status among his counterparts in other organizations.[13]

A modern professionally oriented manager will try to maximize his own lifetime income (in monetary and nonmonetary terms), and this

[12] Quoted by permission from *Personnel,* vol. 38, no. 2, March–April, 1961, pp. 5–6, which reported from Gerald Gurin et al., *Americans View Their Mental Health,* Basic Books, Inc., Publishers, New York, 1960.

For a study concluding that if we accept status quo values we should emphasize the social content of the job for blue-collar workers and the task-centered opportunities for white-collar workers, see Frank Friedlander, "Comparative Work Value Systems," *Personnel Psychology,* vol. 18, no. 1, Spring, 1965, pp. 1–28.

[13] For fuller discussion of "cosmopolitans" and "locals," see Alvin W. Gouldner, "Cosmopolitans and Locals," *Administrative Science Quarterly,* vol. 2, no. 3, December, 1957, pp. 282–292.

goal will often coincide with the firm's goals of increased productivity, but not inevitably.[14]

## Point in Time (11)

It was indicated previously that all the factors in the diagram might change over a period of time. Since it is especially important to recognize this in relation to needs of employees, segment 11 has been included in the diagram.

Needs of employees can vary with general economic conditions and changes in the business cycle. In times of depression, having a job and fulfilling his physiological needs may be the most important concern of the employee. Under these conditions poor morale and unsatisfied employee needs can go hand in hand with high productivity.[15] In times of rising living costs, getting higher wages to provide food and clothing for his family may be the predominant need—again a physiological one. In time of war, if survival is paramount, the physiological needs are likely to be of greatest importance. At other times, when one is reasonably well-assured of having and keeping a job which pays adequately to meet the physiological needs, the social and egoistic needs will probably be paramount.

Furthermore, the needs of employees change with time in their individual lives. At one period in life, family illness or an additional child may force placement of greater emphasis on money to satisfy physiological needs. At other times, recognition or opportunity for self-expression (egoistic needs) may be most important.

[14] R. J. Monsen, B. O. Saxberg, and R. A. Sutermeister, "The Modern Manager: What Makes Him Run?" *Business Horizons,* vol. 9, no. 3, Fall, 1966, pp. 23–24.

[15] For an example of such a situation, see W. J. Goode and Irving Fowler, "Incentive Factors in a Low Morale Plant," *American Sociological Review,* vol. 14, no. 5, October, 1949, pp. 618–624.

# Chapter VI

# SOCIAL CONDITIONS OF THE JOB: FORMAL ORGANIZATION

Since the Hawthorne experiments in the 1930s most research on employee motivation has concentrated on the area of social conditions in an organization and on their interactions with the needs of the employees. We have seen that Physical Conditions (8), while they can affect motivation and productivity, are usually of much less importance than Social Conditions. Although changes in an employee's performance can result from modification in Ability (4) or from forces outside the firm (10, 11), most changes probably can be attributed to alteration in social conditions and their effect upon his need satisfactions. In this book, the major factors which establish the Social Conditions in an organization are considered to be Formal Organization (13), Informal Organization or Groups (20), Leaders or supervisors (24), and the Union (33).

The formal organization of a firm vitally influences the social conditions of the job, which in turn play an important part in motivating employees toward either improved or impaired job performance. What is meant by formal organization? "Formal organization is that existing on paper (the logical relationships prescribed by the rules and policy of the company). . . ."[1]

Some of the classical assumptions of organization theory are that each position on the organization chart is occupied by a person who has a known and unchanging task, that formal authority is the central indispensable means of managerial control, that an individual should have only one boss (unity of command), that tasks should be broken down into specialized units, that there should be a division between line and staff functions, that the span of control (number of individuals supervised by one person) should be fairly small, and that responsibility and authority are equated.[2] Classical organization theory views an organization member

---

[1] J. A. C. Brown, *The Social Psychology of Industry*, Penguin Books, Inc., Baltimore, 1954, p. 94.

[2] Taken mostly from Douglas McGregor, *The Human Side of Enterprise*, McGraw-Hill Book Company, New York, 1960, pp. 15ff. See also chap. 2, "Classical Organization Theory," in J. G. March and H. A. Simon, *Organizations*, John Wiley & Sons, Inc., New York, 1958.

23

as a direct instrument to perform assigned tasks and as a "given" rather than a variable.[3]

How does formal organization affect the social conditions of the job?

It follows that the overall structure of a firm, its organization, influences the behavior of the individuals and groups contained in it. Just as the individual's acts can only be understood in relation to the group in which he is functioning, so the behavior of a group can only be understood in the context of the larger group to which it belongs.[4]

Management determines where men will work and what opportunities they will have to contact each other during the day. It also determines rates of pay, conditions of work, and the various symbols that are associated with each job. Given these basic elements, a sophisticated observer can predict the social relations that will exist within the organization long before the first employee enters the building.[5]

Recently organization theory has been defined to include the study of factors contributing to the effectiveness of the organization *and* of the individuals within the organization or group in terms of *both* productivity and satisfactions.[6]

Blake and Mouton in constructing their managerial grid (Figure 1) point out the need for simultaneous concern for production and people by calling for 9,9 style of management: the manager who seeks high output through the medium of committed people, and commitment achieved through mutual trust, respect, and a realization of interdependence.[7]

Argyris, in "A Basic Incongruency between the Needs of a Mature Personality and the Requirements of Formal Organization," page 177, points out the conflict between the goals of the formal organization (to make employees dependent, subordinate, and submissive) and the satisfaction of the individual's needs (particularly his egoistic needs for indepen-

[3] March and Simon, *ibid.*, p. 29.

[4] J. A. C. Brown, *op. cit.*, p. 123. Quoted by permission.

[5] George Strauss and Leonard Sayles, *Personnel: The Human Problems of Management,* Prentice-Hall, Inc., Englewood Cliffs, N.J., © 1960, p. 61. Quoted by permission of the publisher.

[6] American Institute for Research, *Planning for Progress, Proceedings of an AIR Planning Conference,* Pittsburgh, 1956, p. 27.

[7] Robert R. Blake and Jane S. Mouton, *The Managerial Grid,* Gulf Publishing Company, Houston, 1964, p. 10. Figure 1 is reprinted by permission of the publisher.

For a study of line workers in an electronics plant showing that higher-level needs such as achievement, autonomy, and recognition could be satisfied even though the jobs were highly structured, see William P. Sexton, "Organizational and Individual Needs: A Conflict," *Personnel Journal,* vol. 46, no. 6, June, 1967, pp. 337–343.

dence and self-esteem). Later in the same book he gives attention[8] to the ways in which management can decrease the degree of incongruency between the individual and the formal organization.

Douglas McGregor in his first selection, page 186, discusses "Theory X: The Traditional View of Direction and Control" and the assumptions it makes about motivation; in the second selection, page 194, he discusses "Theory Y: The Integration of the Individual and Organizational Goals."[9]

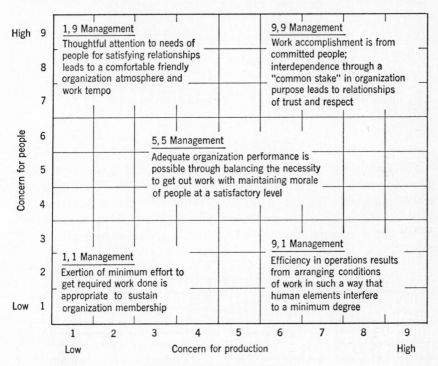

Figure 1. The Managerial Grid.

Some of the major factors affecting the Formal Organization are Organization Structure (14), Leadership Climate (15), Organization Efficiency (16), Personnel Policies (17), and Communication (18).

## Organization Structure (14)

Some recent writings concerning organization raise a question about the classical organization assumption about span of control that a super-

[8] Chris Argyris, *Personality and Organization,* Harper & Row, Publishers, Incorporated, New York, 1957, p. 237.

[9] For an excellent analysis of the ideas of Argyris and McGregor, as well as those of Robert N. McMurry, see Warren G. Bennis, "Revisionist Theory of Leadership," *Harvard Business Review,* vol. 39, no. 1, January–February, 1961, p. 27.

visor should have relatively few subordinates. Organizations which follow this practice tend to have a "tall" organization structure, or many layers between president and employees, which allows for rather close supervision (Figure 2).

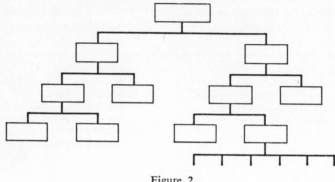

Figure 2

The question raised is whether a flat, decentralized organization structure (few layers between president and employees—see Figure 3) might not be preferable because it would give the subordinate more freedom to do the job in his own way, allow him to use more of his own initiative, permit him to become more self-reliant, and in general allow him to satisfy

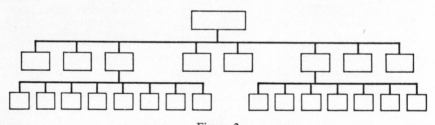

Figure 3

his egoistic needs. Worthy, in his article "Organizational Structure and Employee Morale," page 203, points out the advantages of the flat structure.

## Leadership Climate (15)

The "tone" or the "climate" established for the organization by the president and top officials affects both the organization and the perception of the organization by informal groups, leaders, unions, and individual employees. The best policies may contribute to poor social conditions on the job if they are not administered fairly. The best training of leaders in democratic methods of supervision may go for naught if the climate of the organization is authoritarian. "Attempts to change attitudes at one level without modifying the attitudes held by those at higher levels may cause serious confusion within the management hierarchy."[10]

A selection from Fleishman (included in Readings Related to Chapter VIII, page 380) points out that to a considerable extent, specific training of foremen in human relations is wasted unless the environment in the plant, including leadership climate, is also strong in human relations, and that the kind of supervisor a foreman has and the behavior of that supervisor influence the foreman's attitudes and behavior on the job more than the leadership training the foreman has received.

The degree of "participation" in any company depends upon the attitudes of top management or upon the leadership climate and whether "participation" is looked upon with favor or discouraged.

McGregor's two articles mentioned on page 25 spell out in detail two contrasting kinds of attitudes or climate that management might have: Theory X and Theory Y.

## Organization Efficiency (16)

If an organization is perceived by the supervisors and employees to be inefficiently run, it would be extremely difficult to motivate them to improve their job performance. One of the conclusions of Rice, in his study of an Indian textile plant, was that "irrespective of wages and working conditions, a work group will derive satisfaction from the efficient organization and performance of the task for which it has been organized, and an inefficient organization or performance will diminish the chances of satisfaction."[11]

## Personnel Policies (17)

Most employees when they first report for work to a new company are highly motivated and want to do the best possible job.[12] Numerous

[10] Raymond E. Miles, "Attitudes toward Management Theory as a Factor in Managers' Relationships with Their Superiors," *Journal of the Academy of Management,* vol. 7, no. 4, December, 1964, p. 313. See also A. J. M. Sykes, "The Effects of a Supervisory Training Course in Changing Supervisors' Perceptions and Expectations of the Role of Management," *Human Relations,* vol. 15, no. 3, August, 1962, pp. 227–243.

[11] A. K. Rice, "Productivity and Social Organization in an Indian Weaving Shed," *Human Relations,* vol. 6, no. 4, 1953.

Another author concludes that the workers' perception of the efficiency of management is closely associated with absenteeism. E. W. Holland in "Worker Attitudes and Industrial Absenteeism: A Statistical Appraisal," *American Sociological Review,* vol. 10, no. 4, August, 1945, pp. 503–510, listed eight attitudinal areas ranked according to the closeness of their association with absenteeism. The second most important of these eight was the Workers' Opinion of the Efficiency of Management.

[12] R. A. Sutermeister, "The First Day Makes the Difference," *Supervisory Management,* vol. 4, no. 1, January, 1959, pp. 2–10.

factors work toward retention or destruction of this positive motivation, and thus for or against improved job performance. Some of the important factors are personnel policies, which can be considered to include:

*Introduction to the Job.* Does the company have a job orientation program to show the employee the importance of his job, how it ties in with the end product, and to give him the information he needs to make a speedy adjustment to his new situation and the instruction necessary for him to perform his job well?

*Job Content.* Does the organization examine the content of each job and attempt to make it challenging and interesting to the employee? Can it "enlarge" the job where appropriate to give the employee a greater opportunity to satisfy his egoistic needs?

Walker and Guest in "The Man on the Assembly Line," page 218, raise the question: "To what degree can—or should—men be 'adjusted' to the new environment of machines, and to what degree is it possible to adjust or rebuild that environment to fit the needs and personalities of men?" This question emphasizes the interrelations on the diagram between job content (17), selection (also 17), knowledge (5), skill (6), physical environmental conditions (8), informal organization (20), leaders (24), organization structure (14), and perhaps other segments. Walker and Guest discuss possible changes in the content of jobs, job rotation, job enlargement, and opportunities for social interaction, which could bring the workers greater satisfaction.[13]

Louis Davis, in "Job Design and Productivity," page 239, advocates a new approach to job design to consider the three major basic variables of process, workers, and organization if intrinsic job satisfaction and increased productivity are to be attained.[14]

*Selection and Placement.* Does the organization have a good selection program to choose people with the proper abilities for the jobs they are to perform, and does it place them on the proper jobs where they are most likely to be able to meet their needs?

*Standards.* Does the organization make clear the standards it expects employees to meet or even, when appropriate, let the employees participate in a discussion of the goals to be established?

*Wage and Salary Level.* Are wages and salaries paid by this firm in line with those paid for similar jobs in the area?

*Incentives.* Does the firm pay incentive wages? Are they individual or group incentives? How are they perceived by the individuals, groups, and union?

[13] For a report of results of job enlargement in several different firms, see Robert H. Guest, "Job Enlargement—A Revolution in Job Design," *Personnel Administration,* vol. 20, no. 2, March–April, 1957, pp. 9–16. For another view of job enlargement based on interviews with 220 assembly line workers in a radio and television factory in Chicago, see M. D. Kilbridge, "Do Workers Prefer Larger Jobs?" *Personnel,* vol. 37, no. 5, September, 1960, pp. 45–48.

[14] See also Louis E. Davis, "The Design of Jobs," *Industrial Relations,* vol. 6, no. 1, October, 1966, pp. 21–45.

As we examine the rate-setting process and the economic results of incentive production we are forced to conclude that the connections between the symbols and the promised rewards are neither simple nor consistent. This does not mean that the piece-rate symbol will invoke no response. It does mean that the response will be importantly influenced by the context of human relations within which the symbol is offered.[15]

Harold F. Rothe raises the question, "Does Higher Pay Bring Higher Productivity?" (see page 253) and considers the types of money incentives which are likely to be effective in teaching employees new habits of greater productivity.[16]

*Job Evaluation.* Does the pay range for each job properly reflect the relative difficulty and responsibility of that job in comparison with other jobs so that the employee feels the pay range is fair?

*Performance Ratings.* Does the organization let each employee know how he is progressing, how he can improve, and what his opportunities for advancement are? Or, when appropriate, is the employee encouraged to set up his own performance goals and periodically judge how well he has met them in a problem-solving conference with his supervisor?

*Training.* If the organization is forced to hire employees who do not have adequate ability, does it provide a good training program for them? Does it train employees for supervisory and executive responsibilities? Do employees perceive the organization as a place where they can get ahead? Floyd Mann in "Studying and Creating Change—A Means to Understanding Social Organization" (see page 261) not only emphasizes the necessity for a good organization climate[17] if training of supervisors is to be effective but also stresses the desirability of feeding back results of surveys and research findings to supervisors in conferences as a means of creating and supporting changes.

Proper policies in these areas, applied with fairness, help set up a framework of social conditions within which employees are most likely to be able to satisfy not only their physiological needs but their social and egoistic needs, too.

[15] William F. Whyte, *Money and Motivation,* Harper & Row, Publishers, Incorporated, New York, 1955, pp. 208–209. Quoted by permission of the publisher.

[16] For more information on profit sharing, one of the types of incentive mentioned by Rothe, see the publications of the Council on Profit Sharing Industries, Chicago; of the Profit Sharing Research Foundation, Evanston, Ill.; and of the Center for Productivity Motivation, School of Commerce, University of Wisconsin, Madison, Wis. The Center for Productivity Motivation published *Solving Problems of Productivity in a Free Society* in 1962.

For an excellent more recent article, see Robert L. Opsall and Marvin D. Dunnette, "The Role of Financial Compensation in Industrial Motivation," *Psychological Bulletin,* vol. 66, no. 2, August, 1966, pp. 94–118. This article points out the need for more studies of the effects of money on employee behavior.

[17] See discussion of "Leadership Climate" on page 26.

## Communication (18)

The importance of communication in affecting employees' attitudes and motivating them to improved job performance has been well recognized, and almost every text on personnel management or human relations has a chapter on this subject. The purpose of communication is to achieve mutual understanding and thereby help establish the social conditions which will motivate the employees. Whether or not the purpose is achieved depends upon many factors, including the following:

1. The relations among those communicating. In the absence of a warm personal relationship and mutual trust and respect, giving more and better information is unlikely to improve communication. This is treated in Higham's "Basic Psychological Factors in Communication," page 278.
2. What is communicated.
3. The direction of the communication. It can be one-way from superior to subordinate; two-way, in which the subordinate listens to the superior and the superior in turn listens to the subordinate to make sure mutual understanding has been achieved; or several-way, in which there may be a group discussion and participation.
4. What network of communication is used. This affects the accuracy and speed of the communication as well as the morale of those communicating. Networks are discussed in Bavelas and Barrett, "An Experimental Approach to Organizational Communication," page 290.
5. What obstructions there are in the communication lines, such as unwillingness to listen and refusal to believe. These as well as content and feedback are discussed in Leavitt's "Communication: Getting Information from A into B," page 297.

## Specific Environment of the Company or Plant (19)

The organization structure (14), leadership climate (15), efficiency (16), personnel policies (17), and communication (18) are, of course, all subject to change with changing times and changing environmental conditions, whether physical, economic, political, or cultural.[18]

---

[18] See Abraham J. Siegel, "The Economic Environment in Human Relations Research," in C. M. Arensberg et al., *Research in Industrial Human Relations,* Harper & Row, Publishers, Incorporated, New York, 1957, chap. 6, pp. 86–99.

*Chapter* VII

# SOCIAL CONDITIONS OF THE JOB: INFORMAL ORGANIZATION

Just as the Formal Organization (13) vitally influences the social conditions of the job, so does the Informal Organization (20) or the informal groups of workers. Work is a social experience, and most workers can fulfill their social needs through membership in a small work group. The Informal Organization has its effect on the Formal Organization, on the Leader or supervisor, and on the individual employees constituting the group, and, in turn, the Informal Organization is influenced by all of these.

An individual employee can belong to several informal groups.[1] One is a group which has a common supervisor; another is a group engaged in a common task or function; another is a friendship clique, composed of employees who have a liking for each other;[2] another is an interest group of employees who "share a common economic interest and seek to gain some objective relating to the larger organization."

> Clusterings of workers-on-the-job all have these characteristics: they stem from the uniqueness of individual personality, which refuses to combine into larger "wholes" without changing those entities. The sum of a group of individuals is something more than the total of the constituents; it is a new organization, because most of the members (there are significant exceptions as we have noted) obtain satisfaction in gaining acceptance as a part of the group, and the group itself wields an influence over its members. . . .
>
> This observance of group-sanctioned behavior and attitudes "fills out"

[1] The following two paragraphs are taken from Leonard R. Sayles, "Work Group Behavior and the Larger Organization," in C. M. Arensberg et al., *Research in Industrial Human Relations,* Harper & Row, Publishers, Incorporated, New York, 1957, pp. 132, 144–145. Quoted by permission of the publisher.

[2] This type of group cohesiveness can be promoted by the use of sociometry, finding out workers' likes and dislikes toward other workers, and placing them in congenial work groups. Other types of group cohesiveness may have little to do with friendship or likes and dislikes (see Harold L. Wilensky, "Human Relations in the Workplace: An Appraisal of Some Recent Research," in Arensberg, *ibid.,* p. 48).

31

the rationally conceived organization. What is on paper an organization becomes a "living, breathing" social organism, with all the intricacies, emotions, and contradictions we associate with human relations. While no organization would long persist which did not provide its members with this opportunity for spontaneous "human relations," a major problem of the larger organization becomes one of successfully incorporating the small group.

J. A. C. Brown in "The Informal Organization of Industry," page 305, stresses the informal working group as the main source of social control in an organization.[3]

Three aspects of informal work groups will be considered briefly: Size (21), Cohesiveness (22), and Goals (23).

## Size of the Work Group (21)

It is an ancient sociological generalization . . . that size of immediate work group is negatively correlated with productivity, or job satisfaction, or regular attendance, or industrial peace—other factors being equal. This is due in part to the greater likelihood that primary relations (relations that are intimate, personal, inclusive, and experienced as spontaneous) are more likely to develop in small groups than in large groups. It is due in part also to the fact that the worker in the smaller group is likely to have more knowledge of the relations between effort and earnings, and this seems to increase his incentive to work.[4]

Although the small work group may have greater potential for improved employee performance and increased productivity, whether or not the potential is realized depends in large measure on the Cohesiveness and the Goals of the group.

## Cohesiveness of the Work Group (22)

A cohesive work group is one whose members will stick closely to group norms, whatever they are.[5] A cohesive group is likely to exhibit greater teamwork, gain greater social satisfaction from working together, and have higher morale and less turnover and absenteeism than a group which lacks cohesion.[6] A cohesive work group has great potential, then, for motivating employees to better performance or to poorer performance,

[3] For a point of view that "informal groups are not common among workers," especially at the lower organizational ranks, see Amitai Etzioni, *Modern Organizations*, Prentice-Hall, Inc., Englewood Cliffs, N.J., 1965, pp. 46–47.

[4] Wilensky, *op cit.*, p. 28. Quoted by permission of Harper & Row, Publishers, Incorporated, New York.

[5] George Strauss and Leonard Sayles, *Personnel: The Human Problems of Management*, Prentice-Hall, Inc., Englewood Cliffs, N.J., 1960, p. 177.

[6] *Loc. cit.*

depending upon the group's Goals (23). Seashore, in "Group Cohesiveness in the Industrial Work Group: Summary and Conclusions," page 330, discusses the relations between productivity, degree of cohesiveness, and employees' confidence in management; and points out that there is less variation in productivity within high cohesive groups than within low cohesive groups and that high cohesive groups differ (up or down) from the plant norm of productivity more frequently and in greater degree than low cohesive groups do.

That the cohesive work group can exert tremendous pressure on individuals in the group to conform to the group norms is effectively demonstrated by Asch in his article "Opinions and Social Pressures," page 335.[7] The cohesive group can ostracize individuals who refuse to conform to group norms. It can reward those who do with acceptance, friendship, and approval.

The Hawthorne studies showed that "the values and the customs of the group were more important to the individuals composing it than any cash benefits."[8]

In another study,[9] Zaleznik, Christensen, and Roethlisberger concluded that group membership or reward by the group was a major determinant of worker productivity and satisfaction, while reward by management had no noticeable motivation effect.

Van Zelst writes[10] of a cohesive work group which motivated its members to better performance because the work teams were sociometrically selected. Production increased 5 per cent among workers on a housing construction project when they had an opportunity to indicate their preferences for co-workers, and work teams were set up on that basis.

It must be remembered, however, that even if a group is highly cohesive, there may be some member(s) who does not accept the group goal because he has a different reference group or aspiration level, or a different cultural background, or for some other reason. For example, a "rate buster" may take pride in *not* being part of the work group.

[7] To see how a group held down the production of an individual worker, see a report of a Coch and French study at Harwood Manufacturing Co., in H. W. Hepner, *Perceptive Management and Supervision,* Prentice-Hall, Inc., Englewood Cliffs, N.J., 1961, p. 73. When the group was removed from this worker, her production jumped from about 45 to 92 units per hour. For additional evidence of a group exerting pressure on the individual to conform to group norms, see Donald Roy, "Selections from Quota Restriction and Goldbricking in a Machine Shop," *American Journal of Sociology,* vol. 57, no. 5, March, 1952, pp. 430–437.

[8] J. A. C. Brown, *The Social Psychology of Industry,* Penguin Books, Inc., Baltimore, 1954, p. 81.

[9] *Motivation, Productivity, and Satisfaction of Workers,* Harvard Business School, Division of Research, Boston, 1958, p. 352.

[10] "Sociometrically Selected Work Teams Increase Production," *Personnel Psychology,* vol. 5, no. 3, Autumn, 1952, pp. 175–185.

## Goals of the Work Group (23)

The potential in a small, cohesive work group can be used to support management's goals or to sabotage them.

A work group may be cohesive in maintaining low production standards, resisting change, hostility toward supervision and/or other groups, denying membership to newcomers, and demanding strict conformity of its membership. On the other hand, a cohesive work group may have high work standards, accept technological change, be friendly to other groups, cooperate with supervision, and have minimum unwritten codes on conformity for membership.[11]

The Goals of the work group will be influenced by the reaction of the members to their Leader or supervisor (24) and to the whole Formal Organization (13). The goals can be strongly influenced by the Union (33).[12] In fact, almost all the segments indicated on the diagram will have an influence on the goals which an informal group will adopt for its members. For example, there can be overwhelming pressure from outside the group itself toward conformity: threat of unemployment, recognized danger to survival (war, pending bankruptcy of the firm), etc.[13]

Where there exist informal organizations or groups with effective control over their members, the problem for management is clear. If it wishes to change human behavior, its attack must be made through the group.[14] As Seashore indicates in the work already cited,[15]

To assure a positive benefit to the organization from group cohesiveness the administrator might well take steps first to provide the basic conditions of equity and supportiveness which warrant employee confidence in management.

Thus, it is not enough for management to establish conditions (of Formal Organization, Leadership, relations with Union) in which employees can fulfill their physiological, social, and egoistic needs. Management must attempt to get the individual and the informal groups to work

[11] William H. Knowles, "Human Relations in Industry: Research and Concepts," *California Management Review,* vol. 1, no. 1, Fall, 1958, p. 92. Quoted by permission.

[12] Groups may purposely restrict output and reduce their goals as a union tool for bargaining with the employer. See Mason Haire, "Psychology and the Study of Business: Joint Behavioral Sciences," in Robert Dahl et al., *Social Science Research on Business: Product and Potential,* Columbia University Press, New York, 1959, p. 76.

[13] Wilensky, *op. cit.,* p. 35.

[14] Brown, *op. cit.,* p. 126.

[15] See pages 330 to 334.

toward the organization's goal, or toward the target of increased productivity. Perhaps "the essential task of management is to arrange organizational conditions and methods of operation so that people can achieve their own goals *best* by directing *their own* efforts toward organizational objectives."[16]

Stagner, in "Motivational Aspects of Industrial Morale," page 343, emphasizes that the organization should create a situation in which group and individual goals coincide to a maximum extent.

[16] Douglas McGregor, "Adventure in Thought and Action," *Proceedings of the Fifth Anniversary Convocation of the School of Industrial Management,* Massachusetts Institute of Technology, Cambridge, Mass., Apr. 9, 1957, pp. 23–30. Reprinted as "The Human Side of Enterprise" in Paul Pigors et al. (eds.), *Management of Human Resources,* McGraw-Hill Book Company, New York, 1964, p. 55.

# Chapter VIII

# SOCIAL CONDITIONS OF THE JOB: LEADERS

Leadership[1] has been defined as the process of influencing the activities of the organized group in its effort toward goal-setting and goal-achievement. The idea that there are certain character traits, or attributes of an individual, such as integrity, ambition, drive, loyalty, and judgment, which make him a leader has been seriously questioned:

Examination of this literature reveals an imposing number of supposedly essential characteristics of the successful leader—over a hundred, in fact, even after elimination of obvious duplication and overlap of terms. The search still continues in some quarters. Every few months a new list appears based on the latest analysis. And each new list differs in some respects from the earlier ones.

However, social science research in this field since the 1930s has taken new directions. Some social scientists have become interested in studying the behavior as well as the personal characteristics of leaders. As a result, some quite different ideas about the nature of leadership have emerged.[2]

The small group theorists have also markedly changed the interpretation of leadership. Particularly in the industrial setting, the traditional view of the leader in the past was of a charismatic individual possessing the trait of leadership. A great deal of research went, without much success, into attempts to identify these qualities of leadership in the interest of selection. . . . We now speak of the "emergent" leader, we distinguish between "headship" and "leadership," and we use "buddy ratings" to identify leaders. The pendulum has swung a long ways to one side, and the reverse trend is already discernible in the assessment field, in a return to the search for the qualities of leadership within the individual instead of the group. However, even as the pendulum swings back, it is more group-oriented, and the variables tend to deal with relations with others rather than decisiveness, forcefulness, and determination.[3]

---

[1] I. L. Heckmann and S. G. Huneryager, *Human Relations in Management,* South-Western Publishing Company, Cincinnati, 1960, p. 54.

[2] Douglas McGregor, *The Human Side of Enterprise,* McGraw-Hill Book Company, New York, 1960, p. 180. Quoted by permission of McGraw-Hill Book Company.

[3] Mason Haire, "Psychology and the Study of Business," quoted by permission of Columbia University Press from R. A. Dahl, M. Haire, P. F. Lazarsfeld, *Social*

Many now believe leadership to be an aspect of organization, with the leader's influence on the activities of the organized group depending upon the leader, the followers, and the particular situation. In terms of the diagram, a supervisor's influence with his group would operate within the limitations imposed by the Formal Organization, the Informal Organization, the Union, and the Needs of the individuals comprising the group.

It cannot be said that the "trait" approach to leadership has been completely abandoned. Haire in the quotation cited mentions that the pendulum may be swinging back toward traits, but toward traits that are group-oriented. Bavelas argues that

> The broad similarities which hold for a great number of organizations make it possible to say useful things about the kind of person who is likely to become a leader in any of these organizations. On various tests, persons who are leaders tend to be brighter, to be better adjusted psychologically, and to display better judgment. They tend to give more information, and to take the lead in summing up or interpreting a situation.[4]

Fiedler in a series of studies concludes that "psychologically distant leaders are more effective in promoting the productivity of task groups than are leaders with psychologically closer interpersonal relations" but that leadership traits (meaning leadership effectiveness traits, those which differentiate between the effective and the ineffective leaders) can become operative in influencing group productivity only when the leader has considerable power in the group.[5]

Major factors which seem to affect the leader's impact on his Group and on the Social Conditions of the job are his Relationship with his Superiors (25), his Planning Skill and Technical Knowledge (26), and the Type of Leadership (27) he employs.

## Relationship with Superior (25)

If a supervisor is to succeed in influencing the activities of his group, he must have a good relationship and carry some weight with his own superior. He may wish to assist employees in satisfying their needs and he may wish to use democratic or participative methods of supervision,

---

*Science Research on Business: Product and Potential,* Columbia University Press, New York, 1959, p. 77

[4] Alex Bavelas, "Leadership: Man and Function," *Administrative Science Quarterly,* vol. 4, no. 4, March, 1960. The first sentence is quoted from p. 494. The others are condensed from sentences on p. 492.

[5] Fred Fiedler, "The Leader's Psychological Distance and Group Effectiveness," in D. Cartwright and A. Zander (eds.), *Group Dynamics: Research and Theory,* 2d ed., Harper & Row, Publishers, Incorporated, 1960, pp. 604–605.

but if his recommendations to his superior on behalf of his subordinates are frequently or consistently turned down, he is likely to have little influence with his group. Pelz in his "Influence: A Key to Effective Leadership in the First-line Supervisor," page 349, points out that behavior on the part of a supervisor influential with his superior will have a quite different effect on subordinates from the same behavior by a supervisor who is not influential with his superior.

## Planning Skill and Technical Knowledge (26)

In a study of human relations in a railroad, it was concluded that supervisors of high-producing units more often assume management functions of supervising and planning and clearly differentiate their roles from the roles of the workers.[6] A supervisor who can plan his work well, who has good technical knowledge, and who can install better production methods can raise productivity without necessarily increasing group satisfaction.[7] According to the excerpts from Georgopoulos and Mann's "Supervisory and Administrative Behavior," page 359, supervisors require administrative competence, human relations competence, and technical competence; the particular mixture of these skills which will be most effective varies with the level in the organization as well as with the type of organization and the point in time.

## Type of Leadership (27)

A leader may influence "the activities of an organized group in its efforts toward goal-setting and goal-achievement" by using an approach to his subordinates which is Laissez-faire or free-rein (28), Autocratic (29), or Democratic (30), or by a Combination (32), using one approach at one time in one situation and other approaches at other times in other situations.

## Laissez-faire or Free-rein Leadership (28)

The laissez-faire leader is likely to give the group information, provide materials, and let the individuals or the group make their own decisions with little control and few limitations by the leader. This type of leadership is little used because "the net result is frequently disorganization or chaos,

[6] Daniel Katz et al., *Productivity, Supervision and Morale among Railroad Workers,* Survey Research Center, Institute for Social Research, University of Michigan, Ann Arbor, Mich., 1951, p. xi.

[7] Richard E. Andrews, *Leadership and Supervision,* Personnel Management Series, no. 9, U.S. Civil Service Commission, Washington, 1955, p. 17.

principally because this type of leadership permits different individuals to proceed in different directions."[8] However, as Auren Uris has pointed out, under certain conditions (such as with a group of scientists in an experimental laboratory) it will produce more successful results than either of the other two kinds of leadership. Under the right conditions, laissez-faire leadership could offer the greatest opportunities for subordinates to satisfy their egoistic needs.

## Autocratic Leadership (29)

An autocratic leader is likely to determine the policy for his group, make the decisions himself, and assume full responsibility, asking them only to be obedient in following his orders. Kahn and Katz in "Leadership Practices in Relation to Productivity and Morale," page 364, discuss the findings of the University of Michigan Survey Research Center relative to "close" and "general" supervision, "production-oriented" and "employee-oriented" supervision. Close supervision involves detailed instructions and frequent checking by the leader. Production-centered supervision involves an emphasis on techniques and processes rather than on people in attempting to attain high level and efficient production.

Fleishman in his "Leadership and Supervision in Industry," page 380, reports on Ohio State University studies[9] which differentiate "initiating structure" from "consideration." "Initiating structure" means that the leader organizes and defines the relation between himself and the members of his group, defines the role he expects each member to assume, and tries to establish well-defined patterns of organization, channels of communication, and ways of getting the job done. "Consideration" involves friendship, mutual trust, respect, and warmth between the leader and his group.

Autocratic leadership often involves close or restrictive supervision and production-oriented supervision. Does it also involve "initiating structure"? The Ohio research group found a low correlation between "consideration" and "initiating structure" and state that it is theoretically possible for a foreman to earn a high score in both.

It would probably be difficult for an employee with a high level of egoistic needs to satisfy them under autocratic leadership.

## Democratic Leadership (30)

A democratic leader is likely to encourage his followers to take part in setting goals and methods and to contribute ideas and suggestions.

[8] Heckmann and Huneryager, *op. cit.,* p. 49.
[9] These studies are also discussed briefly by Floyd Mann in Readings Related to Chapter VI, page 261.

"General" supervision means that the leader tries primarily to maintain good human relations and a smoothly running organization. He does not give detailed instructions or check frequently on his followers; he relies on their initiative and judgment; they have much freedom in planning their work.[10]

"Person-centered" or "employee-centered" supervision means that the leader indicates a personal interest in his followers and by his actions conveys the impression that he is fair, will keep his promises, and take the individuals' needs into account.[11] Generally, high-producing groups are to be found under leaders who employ general supervision and who are employee-centered[12] but who by no means overlook production.[13]

Certainly the democratic type of leadership seems to offer subordinates the best opportunity to satisfy their egoistic needs.

A democratic leader will carry out all aspects of his job in such a way as to indicate that he considers his subordinates important individual human beings, like himself, with ideas of their own and an eagerness to put their brains as well as their brawn to work when given a chance. Thus, the democratic leader will exercise great care in the everyday activities discussed in the following paragraphs.

*Introduction of new employee to his job:* to make sure he feels at home, understands the function he is to perform and its relation to the overall function of the department or firm, and knows his obligations and benefits as an employee.

*Job instruction:* to make sure the new employee thoroughly understands what his job is, what is expected of him, and that he is taught how to do his job in such a way that he grasps it fully and has confidence in his ability to perform it adequately.

*Directions:* so that the employee is motivated to the greatest extent to carry out his assignment. Sometimes the democratic supervisor may merely suggest that something ought to be done; at other times he may state a problem and request the employee to solve it; at all times he will be open to suggestions from the employee, exhibit an attitude so the employee is willing to ask questions if he does not fully understand the assignment.

*Recognition or appreciation:* to make sure the employee knows his good work has not gone unnoticed.

*Correcting mistakes:* to make sure the employee accepts the correction

[10] Rensis Likert and Samuel Hayes, Jr., *Some Applications of Behavioral Research,* UNESCO, Basle, Switzerland, 1957, p. 63.

[11] *Ibid.,* p. 57.

[12] This point is covered in the Kahn and Katz article, page 364.

[13] One study in a tractor company found that the most successful supervisors combined employee-centered and production-centered qualities. See Kahn's article in Readings Related to Chapter X, page 450.

willingly and is motivated to do better in the future. This involves a democratic approach of stating what the difficulty seems to be, giving the employee an opportunity to tell his side of the story, and oftentimes asking the employee for his own suggestions for avoiding the trouble in the future. In this way, a mistake is considered a mutual problem which supervisor and employee, working together, can discuss and solve.

*Hearing suggestions:* to make sure the employee realizes his ideas are wanted, to help the employee see for himself any "bugs," and to give him recognition when his idea is practical and is put to use.

*Handling complaints:* to make sure the employee gets a complete and fair hearing, that mythical grievances are nipped in the bud, and that real grievances are rectified promptly and without bitterness.

In the democratic type of supervision, the leader often consults with his followers and actively seeks their Participation (31) in decisions confronting the group.

Some of the advantages of the democratic type of leadership are: It seems better suited to the American people who have a democratic heritage and who enjoy a rather high level of education; and it gives greater freedom to the group yet retains control in the supervisor.

Possible disadvantages of democratic leadership are that it requires better coordination and communication and that the leader himself must be of a higher quality in order to deal with the intangibles and variables of group interaction.[14]

## Participation (31)

Davis defines participation as the "mental and emotional involvement of a person in a group situation which encourages him to contribute to group goals and share responsibility in them."[15]

Participation is widely used by democratic leaders, but it means different things to different people. Does participation mean that a supervisor lets his subordinates' votes determine the action to be taken? This might occur at one extreme in a continuum of leadership behavior. Often, however, participation means something different. It could mean that the leader, instead of just telling subordinates what his decision is, explains it to them and tries to get them to accept it as being correct and reasonable. Many times participation will mean the leader discusses a problem with the subordinates, gets their ideas and suggestions as to possible solutions with the pros and cons of each possibility, and then, after a full discussion,

---

[14] Keith Davis, *Human Relations in Business,* McGraw-Hill Book Company, New York, 1957, p. 170.
[15] *Ibid.,* p. 288.

himself decides what action to take.[16] Tannenbaum and Schmidt in "How to Choose a Leadership Pattern," page 395, demonstrate that the degree of participation may come at any point along a continuum between "boss-centered" leadership and "subordinate-centered" leadership.

Coch and French, in their article reproduced on pages 406 to 428, show the advantages of participation in overcoming resistance to change and increasing productivity.

From an examination of the diagram, it can readily be seen that participation does not necessarily and automatically lead to greater productivity. Participation, on the contrary, may have either a positive or negative effect on employee motivation, performance, and productivity. Does the employee whose participation is desired have an authoritarian or equalitarian background (10)?[17] How does he perceive the situation in which his participation is invited (10)? Does he have confidence in his leader (10)? Does he believe his leader carries influence up the hierarchy with *his* superior (25)? What is the attitude of the employee's group toward this participation (20)? Is the group working toward or against company goals (23)? How much time is available before a decision must be made (19)? What attitude does the union have toward participation by employees in decisions they will be asked to carry out (33)?

Tannenbaum and Massarik in "Participation by Subordinates in the Managerial Decision-making Process," page 428, have outlined conditions which they feel should exist if a leader is to have effective participation by his followers.

There *can* be many advantages to the use of participation by a leader. His followers may accept the final decision more readily, feel more responsibility for carrying it out, exhibit less resistance to change, set higher production quotas than management would, and have an opportunity to fulfill their egoistic needs—to become more mature and responsible with greater dignity and status.

Some possible disadvantages to participation are that it requires a high degree of skill on the part of the leader and that, once started, participation

[16] For a study showing how the individual satisfactions of employees increased significantly when changes were introduced into a firm under an autonomy program designed to increase the role of rank-and-file employees in the decision-making process, see Nancy C. Morse and Everett Reimer, "The Experimental Change of a Major Organizational Variable," *The Journal of Abnormal and Social Psychology,* vol. 52, no. 1, January, 1956, pp. 120–129.

[17] Victor H. Vroom in *Some Personality Determinants of the Effects of Participation,* Prentice-Hall, Inc., Englewood Cliffs, N.J., 1960, concludes that "authoritarians and persons with weak independence needs are apparently unaffected by opportunity to participate in making decisions" while "equalitarians . . . develop more positive attitudes toward their job and greater motivation for effective performance through participation (p. 60).

which gives the followers a greater feeling of responsibility and status could be discontinued only at the risk of damaging employee attitudes and production.

Another danger is that we become so enthusiastic about the benefits of participation that we view it as a cure-all and ignore or undervalue contributions made to the organization through industrial engineering and information and communication sciences.[18]

Participation raises some interesting questions. Is it possible to arrive at a group decision which is inferior to a decision the leader would have made by himself?[19] As automation increases, will the area in which it is possible for employees to participate steadily diminish? If a leader is now getting good results from using participation, will he get better results by using more participation?

Participation, properly used under the right conditions, can be an effective means of allowing employees to fulfill their egoistic needs and of motivating employees to improve their job performance and increase productivity.[20]

## Combination of Types of Leadership (32)

Many writers today agree that the knack of being a good leader is to analyze each situation and the people involved in it to decide which type of leadership (laissez-faire, autocratic, or democratic) is appropriate to the situation.[21] "Leadership" is not exercised in a vacuum but by a

[18] Harold J. Leavitt, "Unhuman Organizations," *Harvard Business Review,* vol. 40, no. 4, July–August, 1962, pp. 90–98.

[19] This question is discussed in Norman R. F. Maier, *Principles of Human Relations,* John Wiley & Sons, Inc., New York, 1952, chap. 10, "The Quality of Group Decisions as Influenced by the Discussion Leader."

[20] For an excellent discussion of participation, its critical elements, theories as to how it might increase motivation, and four possible dysfunctional aspects, see George Strauss, "Some Notes on Power Equalization," *The Social Science of Organizations,* Prentice-Hall, Inc., Englewood Cliffs, N.J., 1963, pp. 60–70.

A recent example of a productivity increase resulting from a switch from authoritarian to participative management is recited in Alfred Marrow et al., *Management by Participation,* Harper & Row, Publishers, Incorporated, New York, 1967.

Another recent case where participation has led to increased productivity, at Non-Linear Systems, is described in "Can Employees Manage Themselves?" *Dun's Review,* November, 1965, p. 59.

That participation will not inevitably lead to improved performance is borne out by a study of three executives with similar suborganizations where the performance of employees was approximately equal although one executive was autocratic, one was recessive, and one permissive. See James H. Mullen, *Personality and Productivity in Management,* Columbia University Press, New York, 1966.

[21] See, for example, Stanley Seashore, "Administrative Leadership and Organizational Effectiveness," in Likert and Hayes, *op. cit.,* pp. 68, 95; J. A. C. Brown,

given leader with a given subordinate or group of subordinates, in a particular leadership climate, with particular organizational limitations, with a particular informal group structure, etc.

An administrator in charge of a group of highly trained and competent scientists may well secure best results by using laissez-faire leadership much of the time. A foreman in charge of unskilled workers long used to autocratic leadership may discover that democratic methods don't produce the best results for that group. A supervisor of skilled workers or white-collar personnel may find that most of the time democratic methods bring the best results, but sometimes it is necessary for the supervisor to be autocratic. Thus, as Tannenbaum and Schmidt point out, "the successful manager of men . . . is one who maintains a high batting average in accurately assessing the forces that determine what his most appropriate behavior at any given time should be and in actually being able to behave accordingly."

With reference to the diagram, Argyris' words seem most fitting:

Effective leadership depends upon a multitude of conditions. There is no one predetermined, correct way to behave as a leader. The choice of leadership pattern should be based upon an accurate diagnosis of the reality of the situation in which the leader is imbedded. If one must have a title for effective leadership, it might be called *reality-centered leadership*. Reality-centered leadership is not a predetermined set of "best ways to influence people." The only predisposition that is prescribed is that the leader ought to first diagnose what *is* reality and then to use the appropriate leadership pattern. In making his diagnosis, he must keep in mind that all individuals see reality through their own set of colored glasses. The reality he sees may not be the reality seen by others in their own private world. Reality diagnosis, therefore, requires self-awareness and the awareness of others. This leads us back again to the properties of personality. A reality-oriented leader must also keep in mind the worth of the organization. No one can make a realistic appraisal if for some reason he weighs one factor in the situation as always being of minimal importance.[22]

And Georgopoulos and Mann, on the basis of their hospital study, add their voices in agreement:

*The Social Psychology of Industry,* Penguin Books, Inc., Baltimore, 1954, p. 221; D. A. Laird and E. C. Laird, *The New Psychology for Leadership,* McGraw-Hill Book Company, New York, 1956, p. 50; George Strauss and Leonard Sayles, *Personnel: The Human Problems of Management,* Prentice-Hall, Inc., Englewood Cliffs, N.J., 1967, p. 212; R. Dubin, G. C. Homans, F. C. Mann, and D. C. Miller, *Leadership and Productivity,* Chandler Publishing Company, San Francisco, 1965, p. 47.

[22] *Personality and Organization,* Harper & Row, Publishers, Incorporated, New York, 1957, p. 207. Quoted by permission of the author and of the publisher.

In summary, the preceding review of representative research concerning supervision and organizational effectiveness suggests that: (*a*) the behavior of those in leadership and supervisory positions in organizations can typically be related to various measures of organizational effectiveness, but the relationships that can be expected may vary depending on what aspects of supervision are involved and what criteria of effectiveness are used; (*b*) depending upon the nature and requirements of the organizational situation, and upon the needs, goals, and expectations of organizational members, a particular style of supervision, or a particular supervisory skill or characteristic, may have different consequences for organizational effectiveness and for different aspects of effectiveness; and (*c*) the combination of the technical, administrative, and human relations skills and practices of supervisory personnel that is most effective from the standpoint of organizational effectiveness will probably be different for different types of organizations, and even for different levels within the same organization.[23]

Even if there were irrefutable evidence that a type of supervision appropriate to the leader, the followers, and the situation would increase productivity, we would want to know to what extent. One study, dealing mainly with first-line supervisors, concluded that productivity would be increased thus no more than 15 per cent.[24]

Before we could attempt to predict the effect of the supervisor's style of leadership on the motivation of the employee, we would have to know a great deal about the employee (his perception, his background, his needs, even his expectation regarding supervisory behavior[25]); about the leadership climate of the formal organization; about the role of the informal group to which the individual belongs; and about the Union's influence on employees.

[23] From Basil S. Georgopoulos and Floyd C. Mann, *The Community General Hospital,* The Macmillan Company, New York, 1962, p. 447. Reprinted by permission.

[24] Michael Argyle et al., "Supervisory Methods Related to Production, Absenteeism, and Labor Turnover," *Human Relations,* vol. 11, no. 1, February, 1958, pp. 23–40. For a brief discussion of the possible significance of the 15 per cent figure, see George C. Homans, "Effort, Supervision and Productivity," in Robert Dubin et al., *Leadership and Productivity,* Chandler Publishing Company, San Francisco, 1965, pp. 57–58.

[25] Foa, who studied the relation of workers' expectations of supervisory behavior to satisfaction, concluded that satisfaction depends on whether the supervisor's attitude conforms with the workers' expectations. See "Relation of Workers' Expectations to Satisfaction with Supervisor," *Personnel Psychology,* vol. 10, Summer, 1957, pp. 161–168.

# Chapter IX

# SOCIAL CONDITIONS OF THE JOB: UNION

In an organization which has a very strong union, the diagram inside the covers might look like Figure 1. In an organization which has a rather ineffective union, the diagram might look like Figure 2. And, of course, if an organization has no union, that part of the diagram would be eliminated completely.

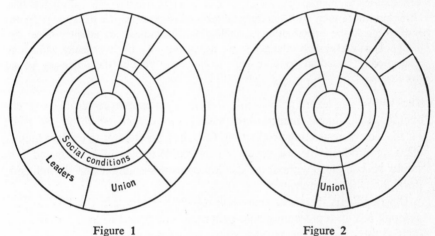

Figure 1                    Figure 2

A strong Union (33) can wield a tremendous influence on employee performance and on productivity. It can affect the individual's perception of his needs by telling satisfied employees that they are not being paid enough or are being cheated by the employer; or by telling them the employer is fair and honest and that the employees are getting a "good deal." The union can affect the technology in the firm by accepting new modern equipment and readily agreeing on the number of operators and their wages; or by refusing to allow a modern machine to start operation until union demands have been met. The union can affect the formal organization, its structure, climate, efficiency, and its communication effectiveness with employees. It can approve company policies on job content, selection and placement, job evaluation, performance ratings, training, etc., or oppose them. The union can affect the informal organization and its goals—whether it will work toward company goals or against them. It can affect the leaders, in extreme cases causing disliked supervisors

47

to lose their jobs. The union can cause a work shutdown as strategy to force the employer to meet its demands in negotiations. The union can favor participation by employees or oppose it.

Some of the restrictions unions can place on management and productivity have been listed by Wilensky:

> Economists have frequently criticized unions because union non-wage policies reduce incentives, limit productivity, or hamper technological change. The general lines of criticism can be summarized as follows: (1) By emphasizing and guaranteeing security through such devices as seniority, pensions, and grievance procedures, unions reduce the worker's incentive to work hard, and to strive for personal advancement. Unions also limit management's attempts to provide incentives through promotion on merit or incentive wage payment plans. (2) Unions often directly limit the amount of work performed on the job by means of working rules or informal pressures to restrict output. (3) Union rules (musicians, railroads) may require more men on a job than are needed to perform the work. (4) Unions may block the introduction of technological changes, or adopt policies designed to make such changes more expensive. (5) By interfering with management's "freedom to manage," unions may reduce the efficiency of an enterprise.[1]

The Union can exert a favorable influence on employee morale and cooperate with management in increasing production, or throw its force on the side of restricting production. Certainly no attempt to explain factors affecting productivity and employee job performance in a unionized firm would be complete without an examination of the union and its influence throughout the organization.

Developments in recent years indicate that unions will continue to play a strong role in representing blue-collar employees and will play an increasingly strong role in representing white-collar employees.

President Kennedy's Executive Order 10988, issued in January, 1962, encouraged Federal employees to engage in union activity. On the state and local level, the American Federation of State, County, and Municipal Employees has increased its membership significantly. Unions of engineers, nurses, and teachers are making new gains in their membership and are becoming increasingly militant. Some organizations which formerly were largely professional groups, such as the National Education Association and the American Nurses Association, have now embraced collective bargaining as a way of meeting their members' demands.

The exact forms which white-collar unions will adopt in the future cannot be foreseen, but they seem destined to become increasingly vital forces influencing employees' attitudes, need fulfillment, motivation, and productivity.

[1] Harold Wilensky, *Syllabus of Industrial Relations,* The University of Chicago Press, Chicago, pp. 116–117. Copyright 1954 by the University of Chicago. Quoted by permission.

# Chapter X

# RELATIONSHIP BETWEEN SATISFACTION OF INDIVIDUALS' NEEDS AND MOTIVATION, PERFORMANCE, AND PRODUCTIVITY

There is much discussion in the literature of the relationship between need satisfaction and motivation, employee performance, and productivity. Our analysis and the productivity diagram have recognized that *productivity* depends both on employee performance and on technology. We have recognized that *employee performance* depends both on motivation and ability of the employee. Thus, even though an individual is highly motivated, this motivation alone does not automatically lead to increased productivity. This much seems clear and can be illustrated as in Figure 1.

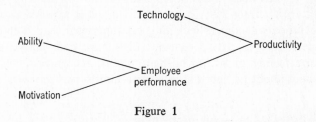

Figure 1

But the relationship between need satisfaction and motivation is not so clear. If the physical and social conditions of the job are such that employees satisfy their physiological, social, and egoistic needs,[1] will employees be motivated to improve performance? This important question can be illustrated as shown in Figure 2.

One is tempted to hypothesize that high level of need satisfaction would invariably produce a high level of motivation and low level of need satisfaction would invariably produce a low level of motivation. Such a neat

[1] Or at least the individuals perceive themselves to be on the way to satisfying them.

49

hypothesis has been exploded by studies which indicate that the opposite situation can exist: high need satisfaction accompanied by low motivation, or low need satisfaction accompanied by high motivation. Depending upon

Figure 2

the many different variables or factors present in a specific situation, then, any of the combinations shown in Figure 3 is possible.

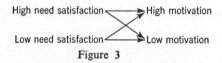

Figure 3

Let's consider in detail the various combinations.

## High Need Satisfaction—High Motivation

Assume an individual whose needs are well satisfied. If only his physiological and social needs have been activated, he is satisfied with his pay and his relations with others including his supervisor, and is highly motivated to perform well. If his egoistic needs have been activated, he has a continuing feeling of worthwhileness, status, recognition, and perhaps self-fulfillment about his job that motivates him to perform well.

## Low Need Satisfaction—Low Motivation

Assume an individual whose needs are not satisfied. If only his physiological and social needs have been activated, he is not satisfied with his pay or his relations with others, and may do just enough to get by yet still keep his job. If his egoistic needs have been activated, they have not been satisfied. He feels his efforts are not recognized or appreciated, his capabilities are not being utilized, and he is discouraged from giving his best efforts.

In connection with the preceding two combinations of factors, we might remind ourselves of the importance of the employee's perception by repeating the conclusion reached by Georgopoulos et al. quoted previously on page 18:

If a worker sees high (or low) productivity as a path to the attainment of one or more of his personal goals in the work situation, he will tend to be a high (or low) producer, assuming that his need is sufficiently high, or his goal is relatively salient, and that he is free from barriers to follow the desired path (high or low productivity).

## High Need Satisfaction—Low Motivation

Assume an individual whose needs have been activated at all levels (physiological, social, and egoistic) and are well satisfied. Under what circumstances might this be accompanied by low motivation rather than high?

Brayfield and Crockett in the excerpt from their article "Employee Attitudes and Employee Performance," page 441, emphasize that there is no necessary relationship between employees' attitudes and productivity, although employees whose needs are not reasonably well met may avoid the job situation entirely by having accidents, absenting themselves, or resigning.[2]

Many studies have demonstrated that a high level of need satisfaction and high morale do not necessarily assure high productivity. Kahn points this fact out effectively in "Productivity and Job Satisfaction," page 450, in which he reviews the research of the Survey Research Center at the University of Michigan and shows why it abandoned the use of satisfaction or morale indexes as variables intervening between supervisory and organizational characteristics on the one hand and productivity on the other.

One possibility explaining high need satisfaction and low motivation is that an individual's social and egoistic needs are satisfied largely off the job. He is a member of the school board, or a bowling expert, etc., and derives his social and egoistic need satisfactions from these activities. There may be no motivation for him to perform on the job any better than necessary to avoid discharge.

A second possibility is he may attain satisfaction of social and egoistic needs by being an important and esteemed member of an informal cohesive group whose goal is to restrict production. Thus his needs are well satisfied through his group membership, but his efforts are directed to working against the company goal of increased productivity. Arnold Tannenbaum in *Social Psychology of the Work Organization*[3] points out that an indi-

[2] For a discussion of the point that people quit their jobs because the jobs do not satisfy their needs, and also because the jobs keep the people from receiving satisfactions from other sources, see Ian C. Ross and Alvin F. Zander, "Need Satisfactions and Employee Turnover," *Personnel Psychology*, vol. 10, Autumn, 1957, pp. 327–338. Reprinted in E. Fleishman, *Studies in Personnel and Industrial Psychology*, The Dorsey Press, Inc., Homewood, Ill., 1961, pp. 259–267.

[3] Wadsworth Publishing Company, San Francisco, 1966, pp. 36–37.

vidual may be satisfied but this indicates little about his motivation to work—particularly when his satisfaction does not depend on the amount of effort he puts into his work.

A third possibility explaining high need satisfaction and low motivation is that an individual may have worked hard at first and made a favorable impression on his boss and now is coasting—doing just enough to get by. He is quite satisfied, enjoying pleasure and happiness, but has low motivation.[4] His behavior, of course, will be influenced by his level of aspiration. (A different individual, his needs also satisfied, might set up a new higher goal for himself and work toward the attainment of that goal, thus improving his job performance. Bellows maintains that worker satisfaction is a state of normal motivation or tension while worker dissatisfaction is a state of abnormal stress or tension.[5] Thus, continuing satisfaction of needs for many people may not mean a state of pure happiness but rather involve a tension motivating them on to greater achievement. In these cases, satisfaction of physiological, social, and egoistic needs may result in better performance and contribute to higher productivity.)

## Low Need Satisfaction—High Motivation

Assume an individual whose needs are not currently satisfied. His pay is low, he dislikes his job, perhaps dislikes his associates; but unemployment is high and he doesn't know where he could get another job. He works his hardest to keep from being fired. At least his physiological needs are being met through the weekly paycheck, and in times of widespread unemployment, social and egoistic needs become relatively unimportant for many people.[6]

A second combination of circumstances which provides low need satisfaction for an individual but high motivation occurs when the person hopes to satisfy his needs in the future. He is starting out as a beginner, perhaps, but has supervisors as a reference group. He may ignore restrictive goals of his present membership group, thus foregoing satisfaction of social needs now, and be guided more by goals of his supervisor, hoping himself one day to become a supervisor and at that time to satisfy his needs. As pointed out by March and Simon, present satisfactions are often less important in influencing behavior than perceived relations between present alternatives and future states.[7] Pelz and Andrews write

[4] Chris Argyris points out that human growth and productivity are not necessarily correlated with pleasure and happiness at all. See "Employee Apathy and Non-Involvement: The House That Management Built," *Personnel,* vol. 38, no. 4, July–August, 1961, p. 12.

[5] *Psychology of Personnel in Business and Industry,* Prentice-Hall, Inc., Englewood Cliffs, N.J., 1961, pp. 45–46.

[6] See footnote 15, page 22.

[7] *Organizations,* John Wiley & Sons, Inc., New York, 1958, chap. 3.

that effective scientists reported good opportunities for growth and higher status but were not necessarily satisfied,[8] and that "a certain amount of dissatisfaction, stemming from eager impatience, is perhaps inevitable in a healthy research atmosphere (though satisfaction generally characterizes high performance)."[9]

A third combination of circumstances where low need satisfaction is associated with high motivation could occur when the individual's needs are not satisfied but he belongs to a cohesive group whose production goals are high, and he is under constant pressure to conform to the expectations of his peers.

Another question must be faced in discussing the relationship between satisfaction of individuals' needs and motivation, performance, and productivity. If high need satisfaction under some circumstances is associated with high productivity, what is the causal relationship? Does high need satisfaction lead to high motivation and tend to increase productivity?

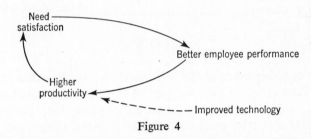

Figure 4

Or does increased productivity result in higher need satisfaction? Does the individual feel an egoistic need satisfaction of achievement by having improved the quantity or quality of his performance? Porter, in a study of dissatisfied managers, expresses his belief that it is the quality of the manager's performance which leads to his relative degree of dissatisfaction (compared with other managers holding the same types of positions).[10] Perhaps further research will support a hypothesis that improved performance and higher productivity in part result *from* need satisfaction and in part contribute *to* it, as shown in Figure 4.

Another element to be considered in this analysis is the reward—its magnitude and its frequency—which the individual receives as a result

[8] Donald Pelz and Frank Andrews, *Scientists in Organizations: Productive Climates for Research and Development,* John Wiley & Sons, Inc., New York, 1966, chap. 1.

[9] *Ibid.,* p. 139.

[10] Lyman W. Porter, "Organizational Profile of the Dissatisfied Manger," *Personnel Administration,* May–June 1965, p. 10. Bernard Bass also points out that productivity may influence satisfaction. See *Organizational Psychology,* Allyn and Bacon, Inc., Boston, 1965, p. 38. See also Victor Vroom, *Work and Motivation,* John Wiley & Sons, Inc., New York, 1964, pp. 181–185.

of his improved performance and increased productivity. If there is no recognition, monetary or nonmonetary, of his improved performance, his need satisfaction could diminish. If there is appropriate reward for his behavior, need satisfaction could increase and contribute to even better performance. Homans, furthermore, points out that the relationship between satisfaction and productivity depends on the *frequency* with which the activity is rewarded.[11] And March and Simon emphasize the *expected value of the rewards* as determining the individual's satisfaction (as well as probably raising his level of aspiration, which in turn may make him less satisfied). The relationship as they see it is illustrated in Figure 5.[12]

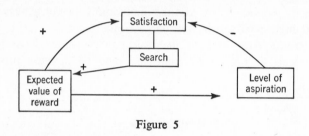

Figure 5

Another question concerns the importance of egoistic needs in the need hierarchy. With an ever-increasing part of our working population consisting of college-educated, technical, scientific, or professional people, egoistic needs such as desire for challenge, accomplishment, recognition, and self-fulfillment are becoming increasingly activated and important. For people of this type, let us state a *generalization,* but recognize that there can be many possible exceptions: The chances of motivating good employee performance and contributing to higher productivity over a period of time are greater if

1. Employees' physical and social needs are fairly well satisfied.
2. Employees' egoistic needs are activated.
3. Employees' egoistic needs are fairly well satisfied on a continuing basis or

[11] George C. Homans, *Social Behavior: Its Elementary Forms,* Harcourt, Brace & World, Inc., New York, 1961, p. 282. See also Edward Lawler III, "Antecedent Attitudes of Effective Managerial Performance," *Organization Behavior and Human Performance,* vol. 2, no. 2, May, 1967, p. 125.

[12] James G. March and Herbert A. Simon, *Organizations,* John Wiley & Sons, Inc., New York, 1958, p. 49. The figure is reproduced by permission of the publisher. Also see Lyman W. Porter and Edward E. Lawler III, "What Job Attitudes Tell about Motivation," *Harvard Business Review,* January–February, 1968, pp. 118–126; and Kae H. Chung, "Developing A Comprehensive Model of Motivation and Performance," *Academy of Management Journal,* vol. 11, no. 1, March, 1968, pp. 63–73.

Employees' egoistic needs are not being satisfied now but employees feel their present activities will lead to such need satisfaction in the future.[13]

[13] Compare with the conclusion of Robert L. Kahn in "Human Relations on the Shop Floor," in E. M. Hugh-Jones (ed.), *Human Relations and Modern Management,* North Holland Publishing Company, Amsterdam, 1958, p. 73, as follows:

We can predict, however, that an organization characterized by high productivity, and also by a strong wish of members to remain with its despite other choices, would necessarily be one which offered to its members relatively high levels of goal attainment and need satisfaction.

# Chapter XI

# COMPLEXITY OF INTERRELATIONS: A SUMMARY

The diagram includes some of the most important factors affecting employees' job performance and productivity. There are a large number of such factors. Most of them affect other factors in the diagram and are themselves affected by others. Thus there is an interdependency among them which is extremely complex. We cannot assume that a change in a factor in the outer circle will directly cause a change in employee job performance. More likely, a change in one factor in the outer circle would be accompanied by changes in other factors, so that any change in employees' job performance and ultimately in productivity would be the net result of all changes operating throughout the diagram.

There are, of course, other ways to show diagrammatically the complexity of the interrelations of various factors. James V. Clark in "Motivation in Work Groups: A Tentative View," page 461, demonstrates some relation between conditions in the work group's environment, motivation, satisfaction, productivity, and turnover-absenteeism, and speaks of factors which both release and constrain different motivations.

Mann and others[1] have shown graphically how a large number of measures relative to supervisory practices and characteristics, worker perception and satisfaction, and work group effectiveness are interrelated at one point in time.

In terms of the diagram used in this book, it is interesting to note that Likert, in his "An Integrating Principle and an Overview," page 480, cites as significant to the *high producing manager* such factors as technical resources (including time and motion study); supervisors with technical and planning skill; use of informal groups; use of participation; use of motives (such as ego, security, curiosity and creativity, and economic)—all in a cumulative and reinforcing manner; and attention to the needs and perceptions of all members of the organization.

Recognizing that the attainment of increased productivity is a complex phenomenon, we can readily see the superficiality of statements which

---

[1] F. Mann, Bernard P. Indik, and V. H. Vroom, *Productivity in Work Groups,* University of Michigan, Survey Research Center, Institute for Social Research, Ann Arbor, Mich., 1963.

57

attribute productivity changes to a change in one factor. In the left-hand column below are examples of the kinds of statements one sometimes hears. In the right-hand column are some of the assumptions which seem to be implied in the statements.

| *Statements* | *Apparent Assumptions* |
|---|---|
| If I want greater output per man-hour, I get it only through improved machinery and equipment. | The performance of employees is insignificant in importance. |
| Give me a worker with ability, and productivity will take care of itself. | Motivation is unimportant. |
| If our supervisors learn how to motivate, any workers are bound to turn in a good performance. | Workers' ability is unimportant. |
| Everybody knows that adopting a rest period will increase productivity. | Productivity is a function of physical working conditions. |
| The answer to all our problems is money. If we pay more in wages, we'll get greater productivity. | More money leads to greater satisfaction of physiological needs, which in turn leads to greater motivation. Social and egoistic needs do not have to be considered. |
| The answer to all our problems is participation. If we can train our supervisors to use participation, better employee performance is bound to result. | Organization structure, leadership, climate, attitudes of the informal group, the leader's relation with his superior, union attitude, individual employee's preference for autocratic or democratic supervision have no bearing on the success of participation. |
| All we need is another depression, with jobless men standing outside our plant, and worker performance will be maximized. | Union, groups, leaders, make no difference then. |
| If our supervisors are fair with employees and we know they are fair, the employee's perception of the situation is unimportant. | The important thing is the way matters actually are, not the way employees think they are. |
| If an individual employee has honesty and integrity, he will never work against the company goals—he will inevitably accept the company production standards as fair and reasonable. | All honest employees are automatically interested in the company goals and will not yield to pressure from fellow employees to restrict output. |
| If we train our first-line supervisors to use democratic methods when appropriate, we can count on them doing so. | It makes no difference that our higher executives use autocratic methods most of the time. |

| *Statements* | *Apparent Assumptions* |
|---|---|
| Our company believes in good pay and in establishing congenial work groups. This should be enough to call forth the best effort from any employees. | Egoistic needs of employees are unrelated to employees' performance. |
| We have the best group of personnel policies in this part of the country: selection, job evaluation, performance ratings, training. Our employees should appreciate these and do their best possible work. | The way policies are perceived by the employees, the way they are administered, the pressures of the leader, the informal group, and the union, the individual needs of employees do not affect employee performance. |

If management or supervisors have sometimes taken steps which they thought would improve employees' performance but didn't, the diagram should help them trace some possible reasons for the failure.

## Summary

Having recognized the superficiality of many statements about productivity which we have heard, let us now try to express verbally rather than digrammatically the complexities of productivity.

Productivity depends not just on employee performance; it also depends upon the state of technological development and the raw materials used.

Employee job performance depends not just on the ability of the employees; it depends also on their motivation.

Motivation of employees generally depends very little on physical work conditions, given a satisfactory minimum level of such conditions; it depends on social conditions in interaction with employees' needs.

A satisfied need is no motivator of behavior.

Physical job conditions in general in this country are good and have satisfied employees' needs for comfort and safety; as long as they remain satisfactory or good, they will have little or no motivating influence on employees. (The Hawthorne studies were unable to demonstrate any relation between physical conditions and output.)

Other physiological needs (met principally by money and security) are largely satisfied today in our country. Social needs are frequently satisfied. To the extent that physiological and social needs are satisfied, they do not motivate.

The largest remaining unsatisfied needs are the egoistic ones. Even if the egoistic needs are satisfied today, they demand continuing satisfaction and therefore never lose their motivating potential. Thus it is to the continuing satisfaction of these egoistic needs that management should devote major attention for a rapidly increasing number of employees.

Some employees may now be satisfying their egoistic (and even social) needs off the job. For them, social conditions which permit satisfaction of egoistic needs on the job are unlikely to motivate. Management would first have to arouse the employees' interest in their jobs so that they feel some egoistic needs in their work.

But even when employees seek satisfaction of some social and egoistic needs on the job, there are further complications. The employees may be members of a group which is small, cohesive, and has high morale; they may have an excellent attitude toward the group and find satisfaction of egoistic needs through the group. But satisfaction of the employees' egoistic needs is not enough. The group can have goals in opposition to management's goals. Thus, satisfaction of egoistic needs does not necessarily lead to improved employee performance from the company standpoint. High employee morale may accompany good employee job performance or poor performance. The problem then becomes one of management's getting the group to work toward management's goals for better employee job performance and increased productivity.

How can management get the group to work toward management's goals? Recent and current research give us some clues as this book has pointed out. It would seem that attention should be concentrated on Egoistic Needs and on the entire area of Social Conditions. The many facets of the Formal Organization, the Informal Organization or group, the Leader or supervisor, and the Union all play their important parts. Democratic leadership will often be effective, sometimes with a type of participation in which a group adopts for itself goals equal to or higher than those management would have set.

There are still two major problems. One is that of individual differences. If management succeeds in setting up social conditions which encourage the group to work with and not against the company, most employees in the group will usually conform to the group standards. However, there will often be one or more individuals whose perception of the situation or whose level of aspiration or whose reference group or whose cultural or experience background will not permit him to accept the goals of his present work group, and whose egoistic needs must be satisfied in some other manner if he is to be motivated toward improved job performance.

The other major problem, discussed in the preceding chapter, is that we cannot assume a positive correlation between need satisfaction and job performance always exists. It is possible for an individual's needs to be well-satisfied and his performance poor, or for his needs to be unsatisfied and his performance good. Such situations would appear to be temporary for most people. In the long run, the chances of achieving good employee performance and higher productivity are greater if the employees are obtaining a reasonable degree of need satisfaction or if they perceive their present activities as leading them toward need satisfaction in the future.

Chapter **XII**

# THE FUTURE AND
# THE CHALLENGE

*It is clear that the educational level of our citizens is constantly rising.*
The percentage of our population graduating from high school jumped,
between 1940 and 1966, from 32 to 60 per cent; and the percentage
graduating from college jumped from 5.7 to 11.8 per cent. College-educated people now represent one-third of all newcomers to the labor force.[1]

*It is clear that the number of white-collar workers exceeds the number
of blue-collar workers and is increasing at a faster rate.* Excluding farm
workers, the percentages in 1960 and estimated for 1975 are:[2]

|  | *1960* | *Estimated 1975* |
| --- | --- | --- |
| White-collar | 46.6 | 47.2 |
| Blue-collar | 39.7 | 37.2 |
| Service | 13.6 | 16.1 |

From 1964 to 1975 the number of blue-collar workers is estimated to
increase 4.4 million while the number of white-collar workers is estimated
to increase 11.7 million.[3]

*It seems clear that the number of professional and technical workers
will increase much more rapidly than any other group.* From 1964 to
1975 it is predicted that the number of professional and technical workers
will increase 54 per cent, clerical and sales workers over 30 per cent,
and service workers 35 per cent.[4]

There can be little doubt that nonmanual workers will play an increasingly greater role in our economy. Drucker has declared: "From now
on, our increases in productivity in this country will depend above all
on our ability to increase the productivity of the nonmanual worker."[5]

These increasing numbers of highly educated, nonmanual workers will
be seeking satisfaction of such egoistic needs as achievement, self-respect,
status, and recognition. If individuals are to be motivated to perform

[1] Peter F. Drucker, "Managing the Educated," in Daniel H. Fenn (ed.), *Management's Mission in a New Society,* McGraw-Hill Book Company, New York, 1956,
p. 164. (This article is included in the present volume on pages 164 to 176.

[2] National Commission on Technology, Automation, and Economic Progress, *Technology and the American Economy,* Washington, February, 1966, p. 30.

[3,4] *Loc. cit.*

[5] Drucker, *op. cit.,* p. 168.

Figure 1. Emerging Leadership and Administrative Patterns in Business Enterprises.

| Stage 1 | Stage 2 | Stage 3 |
|---|---|---|
| Charismatic domination (leadership) | Bureaucratic organization (professional leadership) | Task-oriented information systems and fluid organizations |

| | | |
|---|---|---|
| Strong top leader | Organizationally-created leader | Group leadership and decision |
| Strong owner influence | Indirect owner influence | Indirect owner influence |
| Non-rational | Highly rational | Highly rational |
| Hierarchy with informality of roles, positions | Formal roles, offices, and positions; strong hierarchy | Fluid structures; deemphasizes hierarchy |
| Arbitrary succession in hierarchy | Planned succession; assured careers and merit appointments | Weak hierarchy and more informal offices, positions |
| Loose functional units | Tight functional units | Task forces, teams, projects, and interfunctional activity |
| Situation oriented | Institutionally oriented | Systems and computer oriented |
| Emotional interpersonal relationships | Impersonal relationships | Colleagueship and personal relationships |
| Unstable; dependent on great leader | Stable and predictable | Stable, but less predictable |
| Resists specialization and routinization of decisions | Promotes specialization and routinization of decisions | Deemphasizes specialization and routinization of decisions |
| No organization charts | Strong dependence on charts | Deemphasizes charts |
| Handles emergencies and new situations well | Less flexible in emergencies and new situations | Slower and more uncertain in emergencies and new situations |
| Arbitrary reward systems | Planned reward systems | Rewards based on results |
| No participation in planning or decisions | Controlled participation | Meaningful participation in decisions and planning invited |
| Strong discipline with arbitrary rules | Strong discipline with fair rules | Deemphasis on rules and discipline |
| Moderately legalistic | Strongly legalistic | Permissive |
| Loyalty and conformity to leader | Loyalty and conformity to system and institution | Loyalty and conformity to profession and peer groups |

62

their best, they must have the opportunities to satisfy these needs. Watters in his article "Personnel Management: Future Problems and Opportunities," page 491, calls for the development of new concepts of organization and motivation to maximize the potential of our human resources in the future.

Dalton McFarland predicts that we are moving to the stage of "task-oriented information systems and fluid organizations," as explained in Figure 1.[6]

‣ Likert, in his "Human Asset Accounting," page 497, recommends that all financial reports of a firm include estimates of the current value of the human organization; this will end "the present practice of treating, with great precision, a fraction of the firm's assets and completely ignoring assets of roughly the same or greater magnitude." Any liquidation of human assets to achieve temporarily higher earnings would thus be detected readily.

What can we build upon to maximize the potential of our human resources in the future? What methods are already being used by management which are designed to permit satisfaction of egoistic needs by employees?

*Again the numbers refer to segments in the diagram inside the front and back covers.*

1. Discussion with employees (participation) about the need for *increased productivity.*

2. Discussion with the union and employees (participation) about the *technological* changes and opportunities for union and employees to make suggestions regarding them.

3. Discussion with the employee of his own *job performance* and helping him to improve it.

4. Selection of employees whose *abilities* can be fully utilized in this organization and whose needs can potentially be met under the social conditions existing in the firm.

8. Normal, decent *physical working conditions.*

9. Attempt by the organization to discover what the *needs* of its employees really are. This involves knowledge of their backgrounds, perceptions, goals, and expectations.

11. Recognition that employees' needs may change over *time.*

[6] Dalton E. McFarland, "Organizational Health and Company Efficiency," *MSU Business Topics,* Summer, 1965. Reprinted by permission of the publisher, The Bureau of Business and Economic Research, Division of Research, Graduate School of Business Administration, Michigan State University, East Lansing, Mich. See also Keith Davis, "Evolving Models of Organizational Behavior," *Academy of Management Journal,* vol. 11, no. 1, March, 1968, pp. 27–38; Paul R. Lawrence and Jay W. Lorsch, "New Management Job: The Integrator," *Harvard Business Review,* vol. 45, no. 6, November–December, 1967, pp. 142–151; and P. Slater and W. Bennis, "Democracy Is Inevitable," *Harvard Business Review,* vol. 42, no. 2, March–April, 1964, pp. 51–59.

14. A flat *organization structure,* under which considerable responsibility is placed on employees and they are given the leeway to use the initiative and ingenuity which they possess.

15. A company *climate* in which employee development and fulfillment of employee needs are looked upon as essentials which normally will contribute to increased productivity.

16. Overall *efficiency* of the organization so all employees can be proud of their association with it.

17. *a.* Careful attention to the *content* of jobs. Use of job enlargement or job rotation to increase interest and satisfaction of employees. Having work arranged in meaningful units.

*b.* Proper *placement,* or matching individuals with their particular needs to jobs in which those needs are most likely to be met.

*c. Wage and salary level* no lower than average for the community.

*d.* Use of financial *incentives* such as wage incentives, bonus plans, profit-sharing, or Scanlon plan only after consideration of union, informal organization, and employees' needs so that there is reasonable assurance that the use of incentives will help in motivating employees toward better job performance.

*e. Performance evaluation* carried out not as an act of judgment by the supervisor but perhaps as an act of self-appraisal by the employee, with counseling and coaching by the supervisor.

*f. Training* of employees, supervisors, and executives which takes into consideration the leadership climate of the firm and all the social conditions within which the trained person must function after his training is completed.

18. *Communication,* establishing a relationship of confidence, using proper channels, and providing for feedback.

21 Informal groups small enough in *size* to be supportive of their members.

22 *Cohesiveness* promoted, where appropriate, by sociometric selection of group members.

23. *Goals* of group determined through discussion and participation by group members with their supervisors.

26. Selection of leaders with necessary *technical skill and knowledge.*

27. Recognition of the various *types of leadership,* and the appropriateness of each type for various situations and various employees.

31. Knowledge of benefits and limitations of *participation* and its use, when appropriate, to create situations in which the employees can satisfy their egoistic needs.

33. Communication with the *union* and management's frequent use of participation by the union in an attempt to get union support for the management goal of increased productivity.

Which of these methods, and what other methods yet to be revealed through continuing research in the behavioral sciences and continuing experimentation by management,[7] can be utilized in the future to achieve

[7] For a plea for managers to become less "mechanistic" and to experiment with

increased productivity? Which of these methods, and what other methods, will be appropriate in the various parts of a particular organization, at a given time, with a particular informal group, composed of particular individuals, under a particular leader, and with a specific union situation?

This is the challenge of management!

---

conditions external to themselves, see Robert L. Katz, "Toward a More Effective Enterprise," *Harvard Business Review,* vol. 38, no. 5, September–October, 1960, especially p. 102.

# BIBLIOGRAPHY

Applewhite, Philip B.: *Organizational Behavior,* Prentice-Hall, Inc., Englewood Cliffs, N.J., 1965.

Arensberg, Conrad M., et al.: *Research in Industrial Human Relations,* Harper & Row, Publishers, Incorporated, New York, 1957.

Argyris, Chris: *Integrating the Individual and the Organization,* John Wiley & Sons, Inc., New York, 1964.

————: *Personality and Organization,* Harper & Row, Publishers, Incorporated, New York, 1957.

————: *Understanding Organizational Behavior,* The Dorsey Press, Inc., Homewood, Ill., 1960.

Atkinson, John: *A Theory of Achievement Motivation,* John Wiley & Sons, Inc., New York, 1966.

Barnes, Louis B.: *Organizational Systems and Engineering Groups: A Comparative Study of Two Technical Groups,* Harvard Graduate School of Business Administration, Division of Research, Boston, 1960.

Bass, Bernard M.: *Organizational Psychology,* Allyn and Bacon, Inc., Boston, 1965.

Beer, Michael: *Leadership, Employee Needs, and Motivation,* The Ohio State University Press, Columbus, Ohio, 1966.

Bell, Gerald D. (ed.): *Organizations and Human Behavior,* Prentice-Hall, Inc., Englewood Cliffs, N.J., 1967.

Bellows, Roger: *Psychology of Personnel in Business and Industry,* Prentice-Hall, Inc., Englewood Cliffs, N.J., 1961.

Bennis, Warren G.: *Changing Organizations,* McGraw-Hill Book Company, New York, 1966.

Berelson, Bernard, and Gary A. Steiner: *Human Behavior: An Inventory of Scientific Findings,* Harcourt, Brace & World, Inc., New York, 1964.

Blake, Robert R., and Jane S. Mouton: *The Managerial Grid,* Gulf Publishing Company, Houston, 1964.

Brown, J. A. C.: *The Social Psychology of Industry,* Penguin Books, Inc., Baltimore, 1954.

Browne, C. G., and Thomas S. Cohn: *The Study of Leadership,* The Interstate Printers and Publishers, Inc., Danville, Ill., 1958.

Cartwright, Dorwin, and Alvin Zander (eds.): *Group Dynamics: Research and Theory,* 2d ed., Harper & Row, Publishers, Incorporated, New York, 1960.

Carzo, Rocco, Jr., and John Yanouzas: *Formal Organization: A Systems Approach,* The Dorsey Press, Inc., Homewood, Ill., 1967.

Chruden, Herbert, and Arthur W. Sherman, Jr.: *Personnel Management,* 3d ed., South-Western Publishing Company, Cincinnati, 1968.

Dahl, Robert A., Mason Haire, and Paul F. Lazarsfeld: *Social Science Re-*

*search on Business: Product and Potential,* Columbia University Press, New York, 1959.

Davis, Keith: *Human Relations at Work,* McGraw-Hill Book Company, New York, 1967.

Dubin, Robert: *The World of Work,* Prentice-Hall, Inc., Englewood Cliffs, N.J., 1958.

————, George C. Homans, Floyd C. Mann, and Delbert C. Miller: *Leadership and Productivity,* Chandler Publishing Company, San Francisco, 1965.

Etzioni, Amitai: *Modern Organizations,* Prentice-Hall, Inc., Englewood Cliffs, N.J., 1965.

Faris, R. E. L.: *Handbook of Modern Sociology,* Rand McNally & Company, Chicago, 1964.

Fenn, Daniel H. (ed.): *Management's Mission in a New Society,* McGraw-Hill Book Company, New York, 1956.

Fisk, George (ed.): *The Frontiers of Management Psychology,* Harper & Row, Publishers, Incorporated, New York, 1964.

Flanagan, John C.: "Personnel Research and the Better Use of Human Resources," *Personnel,* vol. 35, no. 2, September–October, 1958.

Fleishman, Edwin A.: *Studies in Personnel and Industrial Psychology,* rev. ed., The Dorsey Press, Inc., Homewood, Ill., 1967.

Gellerman, Saul W.: *The Management of Human Relations,* Holt, Rinehart and Winston, Inc., New York, 1966.

Georgopoulos, Basil S., and Floyd C. Mann: *The Community General Hospital,* The Macmillan Company, New York, 1962.

Goode, Cecil E.: *Personnel Research Frontiers,* Public Personnel Association, Chicago, 1958.

Goodman, L. Landon: *Man and Automation,* Penguin Books, Inc., Baltimore, 1957.

Greenwood, William T.: *Management and Organizational Behavior Theories,* South-Western Publishing Company, Cincinnati, 1965.

Gross, Edward: *Industry and Social Life,* William C. Brown, Dubuque, Iowa, 1965.

Gurin, Gerald, Joseph Veroff, and Sheila Feld: *Americans View Their Mental Health,* Basic Books, Inc., Publishers, New York, 1960.

Haire, Mason: *Psychology in Management,* McGraw-Hill Book Company, New York, 1956.

————, Edwin E. Ghiselli, and Lyman Porter: *Managerial Thinking: An International Study,* John Wiley & Sons, Inc., New York, 1967.

Haynes, W. Warren, and Joseph L. Massie: *Management Analysis: Concepts and Cases,* Prentice-Hall, Inc., Englewood Cliffs, N.J., 1961.

Heckmann, I. L., and S. G. Huneryager, *Human Relations in Management,* South-Western Publishing Company, Cincinnati, 1960.

Hepner, Harry W.: *Perceptive Management and Supervision,* Prentice-Hall, Inc., Englewood Cliffs, N.J., 1961.

Herzberg, Frederick: *Work and the Nature of Man,* The World Publishing Company, Cleveland, 1966.

————, et al.: *Job Attitudes: Review of Research and Opinions,* Psychological Service of Pittsburgh, Pittsburgh, 1957.

————, et al.: *The Motivation to Work,* John Wiley & Sons, Inc., New York, 1959.

Hicks, Herbert G.: *The Management of Organizations,* McGraw-Hill Book Company, New York, 1967.

Homans, George C.: *Social Behavior: Its Elementary Forms,* Harcourt, Brace & World, Inc., New York, 1961.

Hugh-Jones, E. M. (ed.): *Human Relations and Modern Management,* North Holland Publishing Company, Amsterdam, 1958.

Huneryager, S. G., and I. L. Heckmann: *Human Relations in Management,* rev. ed., South-Western Publishing Company, Cincinnati, 1967.

Katz, Daniel, et al.: *Productivity, Supervision, and Morale in an Office Situation, Part I,* University of Michigan, Institute for Social Research, Ann Arbor, Mich., 1950.

Komarovsky, M. (ed.): *Plant Sociology: The Elite and the Aborigines,* The Free Press of Glencoe, New York, 1957.

Kornhauser, Arthur: *Mental Health of the Industrial Worker,* John Wiley & Sons, Inc., New York, 1965.

Kornhauser, W.: *Scientists in Industry: Conflicts and Accommodation,* University of California Press, Berkeley, Calif., 1962.

Lawrence, Paul R., et al.: *Organizational Behavior and Administration,* The Dorsey Press, Inc., Homewood, Ill., 1961.

Leavitt, Harold J.: *Managerial Psychology,* The University of Chicago Press, Chicago, 1958.

———— (ed.): *The Social Science of Organizations,* Prentice-Hall, Inc., Englewood Cliffs, N.J., 1963.

Likert, Rensis: *The Human Organization: Its Management and Value,* McGraw-Hill Book Company, New York, 1967.

————: *New Patterns of Management,* McGraw-Hill Book Company, New York, 1961.

————, and Samuel P. Hayes, Jr. (eds.): *Some Applications of Behavioral Research,* UNESCO, Paris, 1957.

Litterer, Joseph A.: *Organizations: Structure and Behavior,* John Wiley & Sons, Inc., New York, 1963.

McClelland, David C.: *The Achievement Motive,* Appleton-Century-Crofts, Inc., New York, 1953.

————: *The Achieving Society,* D. Van Nostrand Company, Inc., Princeton, N.J., 1961.

McGregor, Douglas: *The Human Side of Enterprise,* McGraw-Hill Book Company, New York, 1960.

————: *The Professional Manager,* McGraw-Hill Book Company, New York, 1967.

Mann, Floyd C., Bernard P. Indik, and V. H. Vroom: *Productivity in Work Groups,* University of Michigan, Survey Research Center, Institute for Social Research, Ann Arbor, Mich., 1963.

————, and Franklin W. Neff: *Managing Major Change in Organizations,* Foundation for Research on Human Behavior, Ann Arbor, Mich., 1961.

March, James G., and Herbert A. Simon: *Organizations,* John Wiley & Sons, Inc., New York, 1958.

Marrow, Alfred, et al.: *Management by Participation,* Harper & Row, Publishers, Incorporated, New York, 1967.

Maslow, A. H.: *Motivation and Personality,* Harper & Row, Publishers, Incorporated, New York, 1954.

Mayo, Elton: *The Social Problems of an Industrial Civilization,* Harvard Business School, Division of Research, Boston, 1945.

Megginson, Leon C.: *Personnel: A Behavioral Approach to Administration,* Richard D. Irwin, Inc., Homewood, Ill., 1967.

Miner, John B.: *Introduction to Industrial Clinical Psychology,* McGraw-Hill Book Company, New York, 1966.

Mullen, James H.: *Personality and Productivity in Management,* Columbia University Press, New York, 1966.

National Commission on Technology, Automation, and Economic Progress: *Technology and the American Economy,* Washington, February, 1966.

Pelz, Donald, and Frank Andrews: *Scientists in Organizations: Productive Climates for Research and Development,* John Wiley & Sons, Inc., New York, 1966.

Pigors, Paul, Charles A. Myers, and F. T. Malm (eds.): *Management of Human Resources,* McGraw-Hill Book Company, New York, 1968.

———, et al. (eds.): *Readings in Personnel Administration,* McGraw-Hill Book Company, New York, 1959.

Sayles, Leonard R., and George Strauss: *Human Behavior in Organizations,* Prentice-Hall, Inc., Englewood Cliffs, N.J., 1966.

Scott, William G.: *Human Relations in Management,* Richard D. Irwin, Inc., Homewood, Ill., 1962.

Seiler, John A.: *Systems Analysis in Organizational Behavior,* The Dorsey Press, Inc., Homewood, Ill., 1967.

Sherif, Muzafer, and Carolyn W. Sherif: *An Outline of Social Psychology,* Harper & Row, Publishers, Incorporated, New York, 1956.

Smith, Henry Clay: *Psychology of Industrial Behavior,* McGraw-Hill Book Company, New York, 1964.

Stacey, Chalmers, and Manfred F. DeMartino: *Understanding Human Motivation,* Howard Allen, Inc., Cleveland, 1958.

Stagner, Ross: *The Pyschology of Industrial Conflict,* John Wiley & Sons, Inc., New York, 1956.

———, and Hjalmar Rosen: *Psychology of Union-Management Relations,* Wadsworth Publishing Company, Inc., San Francisco, 1965.

Stogdill, Ralph M., and Alvin E. Coons: *Leader Behavior: Its Description and Measurement,* The Ohio State University Press, Columbus, Ohio, 1957.

Strauss, George, and Leonard Sayles: *Personnel: The Human Problems of Management,* Prentice-Hall, Inc., Englewood Cliffs, N.J., 1967.

Tannenbaum, Arnold: *Social Psychology of the Work Organization,* Wadsworth Publishing Company, Inc., San Francisco, 1966.

Vroom, Victor H.: *Motivation in Management,* American Foundation for Management Research, 1965.

————: *Some Personality Determinants of the Effects of Participation,* Prentice-Hall, Inc., Englewood Cliffs, N.J., 1960.

————: *Work and Motivation,* John Wiley & Sons, Inc., New York, 1964.

Whyte, William Foote: *Men at Work,* The Dorsey Press, Inc., Homewood, Ill., 1961.

————: *Money and Motivation,* Harper & Row, Publishers, Incorporated, New York, 1955.

Woodward, Joan: *Industrial Organization: Theory and Practice,* Oxford University Press, London, 1965.

Zaleznik, Abraham, C. R. Christenson, and Fritz Roethlisberger: *Motivation, Productivity, and Satisfaction of Workers,* Harvard Business School, Division of Research, Boston, 1958.

————, and David Moment: *The Dynamics of Interpersonal Behavior,* John Wiley & Sons, Inc., New York, 1964.

# READING RELATED TO CHAPTER III

## The Western Electric Researches*

### George C. Homans

Perhaps the most important program of research studied by the Committee on Work in Industry of the National Research Council is that which has been carried on at the Hawthorne (Chicago) Works of the Western Electric Company. This program was described by H. A. Wright and M. L. Putnam of the Western Electric Company and by F. J. Roethlisberger, now Professor of Human Relations, Graduate School of Business Administration, Harvard University, particularly at a meeting of the Committee held on March 9, 1938. These men, together with Elton Mayo and G. A. Pennock, both members of the Committee, had been intimately associated with the research.[1]

A word about the Western Electric Company is a necessary introduction to what follows. This company is engaged in manufacturing equipment for the telephone industry. Besides doing this part of its work, it has always shown concern for the welfare of its employees. In the matter of wages and hours, it has maintained a high standard. It has provided good physical con-

---

* From *Fatigue of Workers*, Reinhold Publishing Corporation, New York, 1941, pp. 56–65. Reprinted by permission.

[1] This research has been described in detail in a number of papers and in at least three books. The books are: Elton Mayo, *The Human Problems of an Industrial Civilization* (New York: The Macmillan Company, 1933); T. N. Whitehead, *The Industrial Worker*, 2 vols. (Cambridge: Harvard University Press, 1938); F. J. Roethlisberger and W. J. Dickson, *Management and the Worker* (Cambridge: Harvard University Press, 1939).

ditions for its employees; and it has tried to make use of every established method of vocational guidance in the effort to suit the worker to his work. The efforts of the company have been rewarded in good industrial relations: there has been no strike or other severe symptom of discontent for over twenty years. In short there is no reason to doubt that while these researches were being carried out, the morale of the company was high and that the employees, as a body, had confidence in the abilities and motives of the company management. These facts had an important bearing on the results achieved.

The program of research which will be described grew out of a study conducted at Hawthorne by the Western Electric Company in collaboration with the National Research Council, the aim of which was to determine the relation between intensity of illumination and efficiency of workers, measured in output. One of the experiments made was the following: Two groups of employees doing similar work under similar conditions were chosen, and records of output were kept for each group. The intensity of the light under which one group worked was varied, while that under which the other group worked was held constant. By this method the investigators hoped to isolate from the effect of other variables the effect of changes in the intensity of illumination on the rate of output.

In this hope they were disappointed. The experiment failed to show any simple relation between experimental changes in the intensity of illumination and observed changes in the rate of output. The investigators concluded that this result was obtained, not because such a relation did not exist, but because it was in fact impossible to isolate it from the other variables entering into any determination of productive efficiency. This kind of difficulty, of course, has been encountered in experimental work in many fields. Furthermore, the investigators were in agreement as to the character of some of these other variables. They were convinced that one of the major factors which prevented their securing a satisfactory result was psychological. The employees being tested were reacting to changes in light intensity in the way in which they assumed that they were expected to react. That is, when light intensity was increased they were expected to produce more; when it was decreased they were expected to produce less. A further experiment was devised to demonstrate this point. The light bulbs were changed, as they had been changed before, and the workers were allowed to assume that as a result there would be more light. They commented favorably on the increased illumination. As a matter of fact, the bulbs had been replaced with others of just the same power. Other experiments of the sort were made, and in each case the results could be explained as a "psychological" reaction rather than as a "physiological" one.

This discovery seemed to be important. It suggested that the relations between other physical conditions and the efficiency of workers might be obscured by similar psychological reactions. Nevertheless, the investigators were determined to continue in their course. They recognized the existence of the psychological factors, but they thought of them only as disturbing influences. They were not yet ready to turn their attention to the psychological factors themselves. Instead, they were concerned with devising a better way of eliminating them from the experiments, and the experiments they wanted to try by no means ended with illumination. For instance, there was the question of what was called "fatigue." Little information existed about the effect on efficiency of changes in the hours of work and the introduction of rest pauses. The investigators finally came to the conclusion that if a small group of workers were isolated in a separate room and asked to cooperate, the psychological reaction would in time disappear, and they would work exactly as they felt. That is, changes in their rate of output would be the direct result of changes in their physical conditions of work and nothing else.

The decision to organize such a group was in fact taken. A small number of workers was to be selected and placed in a separate room, where experiments were to be made with different kinds of working conditions in order to see if more exact information could be secured. Six questions were asked by those setting up the experiment. They were the following:

1. Do employees actually get tired out?
2. Are rest pauses desirable?
3. Is a shorter working day desirable?
4. What is the attitude of employees toward their work and toward the company?
5. What is the effect of changing the type of working equipment?
6. Why does production fall off in the afternoon?

It is obvious that several of these questions could be answered only indirectly by the proposed experiment, and several of them touched upon the "psychological" rather than the "physiological" factors involved. Nevertheless, all of them arose out of the bewilderment of men of experience faced with the problem of dealing with fellow human beings in a large industrial organization. In fact, one of the executives of the company saw the purpose of the experiment in even simpler and more general terms. He said that the experiment grew out of a desire on the part of the management to "know more about our workers." In this way began the experiment which is referred to as the Relay Assembly Test Room. With this experiment and the others that followed, members of the Department of Industrial Research of the Graduate School of Business Administration, Harvard University, came to be closely associated.

In April, 1927, six girls were selected from a large shop department of the Hawthorne Works. They were chosen as average workers, neither inexperienced nor expert, and their work consisted of the assembling of telephone relays. A coil, armature, contact springs, and insulators were put together on a fixture and secured in position by means of four machine screws. The operation at that time was being completed at the rate of about five relays in six minutes. This particular operation was chosen for the experiment because the relays were being assembled often enough so that even slight changes in output rate would show themselves at once on the output record. Five of the girls were to do the actual assembly work; the duty of the sixth was to keep the others supplied with parts.

The test room itself was an area divided from the main department by a wooden partition eight feet high. The girls sat in a row on one side of a long workbench. Their bench and assembly equipment was identical with that used in the regular department, except in one respect. At the right of each girl's place was a hole in the bench, and into this hole she dropped completed relays. It was the entrance to a chute, in which there was a flapper gate opened by the relay in its passage downward. The opening of the gate closed an electrical circuit which controlled a perforating device, and this in turn recorded the completion of the relay by punching a hole in a tape. The tape moved at the rate of one-quarter of an inch a minute and had space for a separate row of holes for each operator. When punched, it thus constituted a complete output record for each girl for each instant of the day. Such records were kept for five years.

In this experiment then, as in the earlier illumination experiments, great emphasis was laid on the rate of output. A word of caution is needed here. The Western Electric Company was not immediately interested in increasing output. The experiments were not designed for that purpose. On the other hand, output is easily measured, i.e., it yields precise quantitative data, and experience suggested that it was sensitive to at least some of the conditions under which the employees worked. Output was treated as an index. In short, the nature of the experimental conditions made the emphasis on output inevitable

From their experience in the illumination experiments, the investigators were well aware that factors other than those experimentally varied might affect the output rate. Therefore arrangements were made that a number of other records should be kept. Unsuitable parts supplied by the firm were noted down, as were assemblies rejected for any reason upon inspection. In this way the type of defect could be known and related to the time of day at which it occurred. Records were kept of weather conditions in general and of temperature and humidity in the test room. Every six weeks each operator was given a medical examination by the company doctor. Every day she was asked to tell how many hours she had spent in bed the night before and, during a part of the experiment, what food she had eaten. Besides all these records, which concerned the physical condition of the operators, a log was kept in which were recorded the principal events in the test room hour by hour, including among the entries snatches of conversation between the workers. At first these entries related largely to the physical condition of the operators: how they felt as they worked. Later the ground they covered somewhat widened, and the log ultimately became one of the most important of the test room records. Finally, when the so-called Interviewing Program was instituted at Hawthorne, each of the operators was interviewed several times by an experienced interviewer.

The girls had no supervisor in the ordinary sense, such as they would have had in a regular shop department, but a "test room observer" was placed in the room, whose duty it was to maintain the records, arrange the work, and secure a cooperative spirit on the part of the girls. Later, when the complexity of his work increased, several assistants were assigned to help him.

When the arrangements had been made for the test room, the operators who had been chosen to take part were called in for an interview in the office of the superintendent of the Inspection Branch, who was in general charge of the experiment and of the researches which grew out of it. The superintendent described this interview as follows:

> The nature of the test was carefully explained to these girls and they readily consented to take part in it, although they were very shy at the first conference. An invitation to six shop girls to come up to a superintendent's office was naturally rather startling. They were assured that the object of the test was to determine the effect of certain changes in working conditions, such as rest periods, midmorning lunches, and shorter working hours. They were expressly cautioned to work at a comfortable pace, and under no circumstances to try to make a race out of the test.

This conference was only the first of many. Whenever any experimental change was planned, the girls were called in, the purpose of the change was explained to them, and their comments were requested. Certain suggested changes which did not meet with their approval were abandoned. They were repeatedly asked, as they were asked in the first interview, not to strain but to work "as they felt."

The experiment was now ready to begin. Put in its simplest terms, the idea of those directing the experiment was that if an output curve was studied for a long enough time under various changes in working conditions, it would be possible to determine which conditions were the most satisfactory. Accordingly, a number of so-called "experimental periods" were arranged. For two weeks before the operators were placed in the test room, a record was kept of the production of each one without her knowledge. In this way the investigators secured a measure of her productive ability while working in the regular department under the usual conditions. This constituted the first experimental period. And for five weeks after the girls entered the test room no change was made in working conditions. Hours remained what they had been before. The investigators felt that this period would be long enough to reveal any changes in output incidental merely to the transfer. This constituted the second experimental period.

The third period involved a change in the method of payment. In the regular department, the girls had been paid according to a scheme of group piecework, the group consisting of a hundred or more employees. Under these circumstances, variations in an individual's total output would not be immediately reflected in her pay, since such variations tended to cancel one another in a large group. In the test room, the six operators were made a group by themselves. In this way each girl received an amount more nearly in proportion to her individual effort, and her interests became more closely centered on the experiment. Eight weeks later, the directly experimental changes began. An outline will reveal their general character: Period IV: two rest pauses, each five minutes in length, were established, one occurring in midmorning and the other in the early afternoon. Period V: these rest pauses were lengthened to ten minutes each. Period VI: six five-minute rests were established. Period VII: the company provided each member of the group with a light lunch in the midmorning and another in the mid-afternoon accompanied by rest pauses. This arrangement became standard for subsequent Periods VIII through XI. Period VIII: work stopped a half-hour earlier every day—at 4:30 P.M. Period IX: work stopped at 4 P.M. Period X: conditions returned to what they were in Period VII. Period XI: a five-day work week was established. Each of these experimental periods lasted several weeks.

Period XI ran through the summer of 1928, a year after the beginning of the experiment. Already the results were not what had been expected. The output curve, which had risen on the whole slowly and steadily throughout the year, was obviously reflecting something other than the responses of the group to the imposed experimental conditions. Even when the total weekly output had fallen off, as it could hardly fail to do in such a period as Period XI, when the group was working only five days a week, daily output continued to rise. Therefore, in accordance with a sound experimental procedure, as a control on what had been done, it was agreed with the consent of the operators that in experimental Period XII a return should be made to the original conditions of work, with no rest pauses, no special lunches, and a full-length working week. This period lasted for twelve weeks. Both daily and weekly output rose to a higher point than ever before: the working day and the working week were both longer. The hourly output rate declined somewhat but it did not approach the level of Period III, when similar conditions were in effect.

The conclusions reached after Period XII may be expressed in terms of another observation. Identical conditions of work were repeated in three different experimental periods: Periods VII, X, and XII. If the assumptions on which the study was based had been correct, that is to say, if the output rate were directly related to the physical conditions of work, the expectation would be that in these three experimental periods there would be some similarity in output. Such was not the case. The only apparent uniformity was that in each experimental period output was higher than in the preceding one. In the Relay Assembly Test Room, as in the previous illumination experiments, something was happening which could not be explained by the experimentally controlled conditions of work.

There is no need here to go into the later history of the test room experiment, which came to an end in 1933. It is enough to say that the output of the group continued to rise until it established itself on a high plateau from which there was no descent until the time of discouragement and deepening economic depression which preceded the end of the test. The rough conclusions reached at the end of experimental Period XII were confirmed and sharpened by later research. T. N. Whitehead, Associate Professor of Business in the Graduate School of Business Administration, Harvard University, has made a careful statistical analysis of the output records. He shows that the changes which took place in the output of the group have no simple correlation with the experimental changes in working conditions. Nor can they be correlated with changes in other physical conditions of which records were kept, such as temperature, humidity, hours of rest, and changes of relay type. Even when the girls themselves complained of mugginess or heat, these conditions were not apparently affecting their output. This statement, of course, does not mean that there is never any relation between output rate and these physical conditions. There is such a thing as heat prostration. It means only that, within the limits in which these conditions were varying in the test room, they apparently did not affect the rate of work.

The question remains: with what facts, if any, can the changes in the output rate of the operators in the test room be correlated? Here the statements of the girls themselves are of first importance. Each girl knew that she was producing more in the test room than she ever had in the regular department, and each said that the increase had come about without any conscious effort on her part. It seemed easier to produce at the faster rate in the test room than at the slower rate in the regular department. When questioned further, each girl stated her reasons in slightly different words, but there was uniformity in the answers in two respects. First, the girls liked to work in the test room; "it was fun." Secondly, the new supervisory relation or, as they put it, the absence of the old supervisory control, made it possible for them to work freely without anxiety.

For instance, there was the matter of conversation. In the regular department, conversation was in principle not allowed. In practice it was tolerated if it was carried on in a low tone and did not interfere with work. In the test room an effort was made in the beginning to discourage conversation, though it was soon abandoned. The observer in charge of the experiment was afraid of losing the cooperation of the girls if he insisted too strongly on this point. Talk became common and was often loud and general. Indeed the conversation of the operators came to occupy an important place in the log. T. N. Whitehead has pointed out that the girls in the test room were far more thoroughly supervised than they ever had been in the regular department. They were watched by an observer of their own, an interested management, and outside experts. The point is that the character and purpose of the supervision were different and were felt to be so.

The operators knew that they were taking part in what was considered an important and interesting experiment. They knew that their work was expected to produce results—they were not sure what results—which would lead to the improvement of the working conditions of their fellow employees. They knew that the eyes of the company were upon them. Whitehead has further pointed out that, although the experimental changes might turn out to have no physical significance, their social significance was always favorable. They showed that the management of the company was still interested, that the girls were still part of a valuable piece of research. In the regular department, the girls, like the other employees, were in the position of responding to changes the source and purpose of which were beyond their knowledge. In the test room, they had frequent interviews with the superintendent, a high officer of the company. The reasons for the contemplated experimental changes were explained to them. Their views were consulted and in some instances they were allowed to veto what had been proposed. Professor Mayo has argued that it is idle to speak of an experimental period like Period XII as being in any sense what it purported to be—a return to the original conditions of work. In the meantime, the entire industrial situation of the girls had been reconstructed.

Another factor in what occurred can only be spoken of as the social development of the group itself. When the girls went for the first time to be given a physical examination by the company doctor, someone suggested as a joke that ice cream and cake ought to be served. The company provided them at the next examination, and the custom was kept up for the duration of the experiment. When one of the girls had a birthday, each of the others would bring her a present, and she would respond by offering the group a box of chocolates. Often one of the girls would have some good reason for feeling tired. Then the others would "carry" her. That is, they would agree to work especially fast to make up for the low output expected from her. It is doubtful whether this "carrying" did have any effect, but the important point is the existence of the practice, not its effectiveness. The girls made friends in the test room and went together socially after hours. One of the interesting facts which has appeared from Whitehead's analysis of the output records is that there were times when variations in the output rates of two friends were correlated to a high degree. Their rates varied simultaneously and in the same direction—something, of course, which the girls were not aware of and could not have planned. Also, these correlations were destroyed by such apparently trivial events as a change in the order in which the girls sat at the workbench.

Finally, the group developed leadership and a common purpose. The leader, self-appointed, was an ambitious young Italian girl who entered the test room as a replacement after two of the original members had left. She saw in the experiment a chance for personal distinction and advancement. The common purpose was an increase in the output rate. The girls had been told in the beginning and repeatedly thereafter that they were to work without straining, without trying to make a race of the test, and all the evidence shows that they kept this rule. In fact, they felt that they were working under less pressure than in the regular department. Nevertheless, they knew that the output record was considered the most important of the records of the experiment and was always closely scrutinized. Before long they had committed themselves to a continuous increase in production. In the long run, of course, this ideal was an impossible one, and when the girls found out that it was, the realization was an important element of the change of tone which was noticeable in the second half of the experiment. But for a time they felt that they could achieve the impossible. In brief, the increase in the output rate of the girls in the Relay Assembly Test Room could not be related to any changes in their physical conditions of work, whether experimentally induced or not. It could, however, be related to what can only be spoken of as the development of an organized social group in a peculiar and effective relation with its supervisors.

Many of these conclusions were not worked out in detail until long after the investigators at Hawthorne had lost interest in the Relay Assembly Test Room, but the general meaning of the experiment was clear at least as early as Period XII. A continuous increase in productivity had taken place irrespective of changing physical conditions of work. In the words of a company report made in January, 1931, on all the research which had been done up to that date:

Upon analysis, only one thing seemed to show a continuous relationship with this improved output. This was the mental attitude of the operators. From their conversations with each other and their comments to the test observers, it was not only clear that their attitudes were improving but it was evident that this area of employee reactions and feelings was a fruitful field for industrial research.

# READINGS RELATED TO CHAPTER IV

## A Theory of Human Motivation*

### A. H. Maslow

## I. Introduction

In a previous paper (13) various propositions were presented which would have to be included in any theory of human motivation that could lay claim to being definitive. These conclusions may be briefly summarized as follows:

1. The integrated wholeness of the organism must be one of the foundation stones of motivation theory.

2. The hunger drive (or any other physiological drive) was rejected as a centering point or model for a definitive theory of motivation. Any drive that is somatically based and localizable was shown to be atypical rather than typical in human motivation.

3. Such a theory should stress and center itself upon ultimate or basic goals rather than partial or superficial ones, upon ends rather than means to these ends. Such a stress would imply a more central place for unconscious than for conscious motivations.

4. There are usually available various cultural paths to the same goal. Therefore conscious, specific, local-cultural desires are not as fundamental in motivation theory as the more basic, unconscious goals.

5. Any motivated behavior, either preparatory or consummatory, must be understood to be a channel through which many basic needs may be simultaneously expressed or satisfied. Typically an act has *more* than one motivation.

* From *Psychological Review*, vol. 50, pp. 370–396, 1943. Reprinted by permission of the American Psychological Association.

6. Practically all organismic states are to be understood as motivated and as motivating.

7. Human needs arrange themselves in hierarchies of prepotency. That is to say, the appearance of one need usually rests on the prior satisfaction of another, more prepotent need. Man is a perpetually wanting animal. Also no need or drive can be treated as if it were isolated or discrete; every drive is related to the state of satisfaction or dissatisfaction of other drives.

8. *Lists* of drives will get us nowhere for various theoretical and practical reasons. Furthermore any classification of motivations must deal with the problem of levels of specificity or generalization of the motives to be classified.

9. Classifications of motivations must be based upon goals rather than upon instigating drives or motivated behavior.

10. Motivation theory should be human-centered rather than animal-centered.

11. The situation or the field in which the organism reacts must be taken into account but the field alone can rarely serve as an exclusive explanation for behavior. Furthermore the field itself must be interpreted in terms of the organism. Field theory cannot be a substitute for motivation theory.

12. Not only the integration of the organism must be taken into account, but also the possibility of isolated, specific, partial or segmental reactions.

It has since become necessary to add to these another affirmation.

13. Motivation theory is not synonymous with behavior theory. The motivations are only one class of determinants of behavior. While behavior is almost always motivated, it is also almost always biologically, culturally and situationally determined as well.

The present paper is an attempt to formulate a positive theory of motivation which will satisfy these theoretical demands and at the same time conform to the known facts, clinical and observational as well as experimental. It derives most directly, however, from clinical experience. This theory is, I think, in the functionalist tradition of James and Dewey, and is fused with the holism of Wertheimer (19), Goldstein (6), and Gestalt Psychology, and with the dynamicism of Freud (4) and Adler (1). This fusion or synthesis may arbitrarily be called a "general-dynamic" theory.

It is far easier to perceive and to criticize the aspects in motivation theory than to remedy them. Mostly this is because of the very serious lack of sound data in this area. I conceive this lack of sound facts to be due primarily to the absence of a valid theory of motivation. The present theory then must be considered to be a suggested program or framework for future research and must stand or fall, not so much on facts available or evidence presented, as upon researches yet to be done, researches suggested perhaps by the questions raised in this paper.

## II. The Basic Needs

*The "physiological" needs.* The needs that are usually taken as the starting point for motivation theory are the so-called physiological drives.

Two recent lines of research make it necessary to revise our customary notions about these needs, first, the development of the concept of homeostasis, and second, the finding that appetites (preferential choices among foods) are a fairly efficient indication of actual needs or lacks in the body.

Homeostasis refers to the body's automatic efforts to maintain a constant, normal state of the blood stream. Cannon (2) has described this process for (1) the water content of the blood, (2) salt content, (3) sugar content, (4) protein content, (5) fat content, (6) calcium content, (7) oxygen content, (8) constant hydrogen-ion level (acid-base balance) and (9) constant temperature of the blood. Obviously this list can be extended to include other minerals, the hormones, vitamins, etc.

Young in a recent article (21) has summarized the work on appetite in its relation to body needs. If the body lacks some chemical, the individual will tend to develop a specific appetite or partial hunger for that food element.

Thus it seems impossible as well as useless to make any list of fundamental physiological needs for they can come to almost any number one might wish, depending on the degree of specificity of description. We can not identify all physiological needs as homeostatic. That sexual desire, sleepiness, sheer activity and maternal behavior in animals, are homeostatic, has not yet been demonstrated. Furthermore, this list would not include the various sensory pleasures (tastes, smells, tickling, stroking) which are probably physiological and which may become the goals of motivated behavior.

In a previous paper (13) it has been pointed out that these physiological drives or needs are to be considered unusual rather than typical because they are isolable, and because they are localizable somatically. That is to say, they are relatively independent of each other, of other motivations and of the organism as a whole, and secondly, in many cases, it is possible to demonstrate a localized, underlying somatic base for the drive. This is true less generally than has been thought (exceptions are fatigue, sleepiness, maternal responses) but it is still true in the classic instances of hunger, sex, and thirst.

It should be pointed out again that any of the physiological needs and the consummatory behavior involved with them serve as channels for all sorts of other needs as well. That is to say, the person who thinks he is hungry may actually be seeking more for comfort, or dependence, than for vitamins or proteins. Conversely, it is possible to satisfy the hunger need in part by other activities such as drinking water or smoking cigarettes. In other words, relatively isolable as these physiological needs are, they are not completely so.

Undoubtedly these physiological needs are the most prepotent of all needs. What this means specifically is, that in the human being who is missing everything in life in an extreme fashion, it is most likely that the major motivation would be the physiological needs rather than any others. A person who is lacking food, safety, love, and esteem would most probably hunger for food more strongly than for anything else.

If all the needs are unsatisfied, and the organism is then dominated by the physiological needs, all other needs may become simply non-existent or be pushed into the background. It is then fair to characterize the whole organism by saying simply that it is hungry, for consciousness is almost completely preempted by hunger. All capacities are put into the service of hunger-satisfaction, and the organization of these capacities is almost entirely determined by the one purpose of satisfying hunger. The receptors and effectors, the intelligence, memory, habits, all may now be defined simply as hunger-gratifying tools. Capacities that are not useful for this purpose lie dormant, or are pushed into the background. The urge to write poetry, the desire to acquire an automobile, the interest in American history, the desire for a new pair of shoes are, in the extreme case, forgotten or become of secondary importance. For the man who is extremely and dangerously hungry, no other interests exist but food. He dreams food, he remembers food, he thinks about food, he emotes only about food, he perceives only food and he wants only food. The more subtle determinants that ordinarily fuse with the physiological drives in organizing even feeding, drinking or sexual behavior, may now be so completely overwhelmed as to allow us to speak at this time (but *only* at this time) of pure hunger drive and behavior, with the one unqualified aim of relief.

Another peculiar characteristic of the human organism when it is dominated by a certain need is that the whole philosophy of the future tends also to change. For our chronically and extremely hungry man, Utopia can be defined very simply as a place where there is plenty of food. He tends to think that, if only he is guaranteed food for the rest of his life, he will be perfectly happy and will never want anything more. Life itself tends to be defined in terms of eating. Anything else will be defined as unimportant. Freedom, love, community feeling, respect, philosophy, may all be waved aside as fripperies which are useless since they fail to fill the stomach. Such a man may fairly be said to live by bread alone.

It cannot possibly be denied that such things are true but their *generality* can be denied. Emergency conditions are, almost by definition, rare in the normally functioning peaceful society. That this truism can be forgotten is due mainly to two reasons. First, rats have few motivations other than physiological ones, and since so much of the research upon motivation has been made with these animals, it is easy to carry the rat-picture over to the human being. Secondly, it is too often not realized that culture itself is an adaptive tool, one of whose main functions is to make the physiological emergencies come less and less often. In most of the known societies, chronic extreme hunger of the emergency type is rare, rather than common. In any case, this is still true in the United States. The average American citizen is experiencing appetite rather than hunger when he says "I am hungry." He is apt to experience sheer life-and-death hunger only by accident and then only a few times through his entire life.

Obviously a good way to obscure the "higher" motivations, and to get a lopsided view of human capacities and human nature, is to make the organism extremely and chronically hungry or thirsty. Anyone who attempts to make an emergency picture into a typical one, and who will measure all of man's goals and desires by his behavior during extreme physiological deprivation is certainly being blind to many things. It is quite true that man lives by bread alone—when there is no bread. But what happens to man's desires when there *is* plenty of bread and when his belly is chronically filled?

*At once other (and "higher") needs emerge* and these, rather than physiological hungers, dominate the organism. And when these in turn are satisfied, again new (and still "higher") needs emerge and so on. This is what we mean by saying that the basic human needs are organized into a hierarchy of relative prepotency.

One main implication of this phrasing is that gratification becomes as important a concept as deprivation in motivation theory, for it releases the organism from the domination of a relatively more physiological need, permitting thereby the emergence of other more social goals. The physiological needs, along with their partial goals, when chronically gratified cease to exist as active determinants or organizers of behavior. They now exist only in a potential fashion in the sense that they may emerge again to dominate the organism if they are thwarted. But a want that is satisfied is no longer a want. The organism is dominated and its behavior organized only by unsatisfied needs. If hunger is satisfied, it becomes unimportant in the current dynamics of the individual.

This statement is somewhat qualified by a hypothesis to be discussed more fully later, namely that it is precisely those individuals in whom a certain need has always been satisfied who are best equipped to tolerate deprivation of that need in the future, and that furthermore, those who have been deprived in the past will react differently to current satisfactions than the one who has never been deprived.

*The safety needs.* If the physiological needs are relatively well gratified, there then emerges a new set of needs, which we may categorize roughly as the safety needs. All that has been said of the physiological needs is equally true, although in lesser degree, of these desires. The organism may equally well be wholly dominated by them. They may serve as the almost exclusive organizers of behavior, recruiting all the capacities of the organism in their service, and we may then fairly describe the whole organism as a safety-seeking mechanism. Again we may say of the receptors, the effectors, of the intellect and the other capacities that they are primarily safety-seeking tools. Again, as in the hungry man, we find that the dominating goal is a strong determinant not only of his current world-outlook and philosophy but also of his philosophy of the future. Practically everything looks less important than safety (even sometimes the physiological needs which, being satisfied, are now underestimated). A man, in this state, if it is extreme enough and chronic enough, may be characterized as living almost for safety alone.

Although in this paper we are interested primarily in the needs of the adult, we can approach an understanding of his safety needs perhaps more efficiently by observation of infants and children, in whom these needs are much more simple and obvious. One reason for the clearer appearance of the threat or danger reaction in infants is that they do not inhibit this reaction at all, whereas adults in our society have been taught to inhibit it at all costs. Thus even when adults do feel their safety to be threatened we may not be able to see this on the surface. Infants will react in a total fashion and as if they were endangered, if they are disturbed or dropped suddenly, startled by loud noises, flashing light, or other unusual sensory stimulation, by rough handling, by general loss of support in the mother's arms, or by inadequate support.[1]

In infants we can also see a much more direct reaction to bodily illnesses of various kinds. Sometimes these illnesses seem to be immediately and *per se* threatening and seem to make the child feel unsafe. For instance, vomiting, colic or other sharp pains seem to make the child look at the whole world in a different way. At such a moment of pain, it may be postulated that, for the child, the appearance of the whole world suddenly changes from sunniness to darkness, so to speak, and becomes a place in which anything at all might happen, in which previously stable things have suddenly become unstable. Thus a child who because of some bad food is taken ill may, for a day or two, develop fear, nightmares, and a need for protection and reassurance never seen in him before his illness.

Another indication of the child's need for safety is his preference for some kind of undisrupted routine or rhythm. He seems to want a predictable, orderly world. For instance, injustice, unfairness, or inconsistency in the parents seems to make a child feel anxious and unsafe. This attitude may be not so much because of the injustice *per se* or any particular pains involved, but rather because this treatment threatens to make the world look unreliable, or unsafe, or unpredictable. Young children seem to thrive better under a system which has at least a skeletal outline of rigidity, in which there is a schedule of a kind, some sort of routine, something that can be counted upon, not only for the present but also far into the future.

---

[1] As the child grows up, sheer knowledge and familiarity as well as better motor development make these "dangers" less and less dangerous and more and more manageable. Throughout life it may be said that one of the main conative functions of education is this neutralizing of apparent dangers through knowledge, *e.g.,* I am not afraid of thunder because I know something about it.

Perhaps one could express this more accurately by saying that the child needs an organized world rather than an unorganized or unstructured one.

The central role of the parents and the normal family setup are indisputable. Quarreling, physical assault, separation, divorce or death within the family may be particularly terrifying. Also parental outbursts of rage or threats of punishment directed to the child, calling him names, speaking to him harshly, shaking him, handling him roughly, or actual physical punishment sometimes elicit such total panic and terror in the child that we must assume more is involved than the physical pain alone. While it is true that in some children this terror may represent also a fear of loss of parental love, it can also occur in completely rejected children, who seem to cling to the hating parents more for sheer safety and protection than because of hope of love.

Confronting the average child with new, unfamiliar, strange, unmanageable stimuli or situations will too frequently elicit the danger or terror reaction, as for example, getting lost or even being separated from the parents for a short time, being confronted with new faces, new situations or new tasks, the sight of strange, unfamiliar or uncontrollable objects, illness or death. Particularly at such times, the child's frantic clinging to his parents is eloquent testimony to their role as protectors (quite apart from their roles as food-givers and love-givers).

From these and similar observations, we may generalize and say that the average child in our society generally prefers a safe, orderly, predictable, organized world, which he can count on, and in which unexpected, unmanageable or other dangerous things do not happen, and in which, in any case, he has all-powerful parents who protect and shield him from harm.

That these reactions may so easily be observed in children is in a way a proof of the fact that children in our society feel too unsafe (or, in a word, are badly brought up). Children who are reared in an unthreatening, loving family do *not* ordinarily react as we have described above (17). In such children the danger reactions are apt to come mostly to objects or situations that adults too would consider dangerous.[2]

The healthy, normal, fortunate adult in our culture is largely satisfied in his safety needs. The peaceful, smoothly running, "good" society ordinarily makes its members feel safe enough from wild animals, extremes of tem-

[2] A "test battery" for safety might be confronting the child with a small exploding firecracker, or with a bewhiskered face, having the mother leave the room, putting him upon a high ladder, a hypodermic injection, having a mouse crawl up to him, etc. Of course I cannot seriously recommend the deliberate use of such "tests" for they might very well harm the child being tested. But these and similar situations come up by the score in the child's ordinary day-to-day living and may be observed. There is no reason why these stimuli should not be used with, for example, young chimpanzees.

perature, criminals, assault and murder, tyranny, etc. Therefore, in a very real sense, he no longer has any safety needs as active motivators. Just as a sated man no longer feels hungry, a safe man no longer feels endangered. If we wish to see these needs directly and clearly we must turn to neurotic or near-neurotic individuals, and to the economic and social underdogs. In between these extremes, we can perceive the expressions of safety needs only in such phenomena as, for instance, the common preference for a job with tenure and protection, the desire for a savings account, and for insurance of various kinds (medical, dental, unemployment, disability, old age).

Other broader aspects of the attempt to seek safety and stability in the world are seen in the very common preference for familiar rather than unfamiliar things, or for the known rather than the unknown. The tendency to have some religion or world-philosophy that organizes the universe and the men in it into some sort of satisfactorily coherent, meaningful whole is also in part motivated by safety-seeking. Here too we may list science and philosophy in general as partially motivated by the safety needs (we shall see later that there are also other motivations to scientific, philosophical or religious endeavor).

Otherwise the need for safety is seen as an active and dominant mobilizer of the organism's resources only in emergencies, *e.g.,* war, disease, natural catastrophes, crime waves, societal disorganization, neurosis, brain injury, chronically bad situation.

Some neurotic adults in our society are, in many ways, like the unsafe child in their desire for safety, although in the former it takes on a somewhat special appearance. Their reaction is often to unknown, psychological dangers in a world that is perceived to be hostile, overwhelming and threatening. Such a person behaves as if a great catastrophe were almost always impending, *i.e.,* he is usually responding as if to an emergency. His safety needs often find specific expression in a search for a protector, or a stronger person on whom he may depend, or perhaps, a Fuehrer.

The neurotic individual may be described in a slightly different way with some usefulness as a grown-up person who retains his childish attitudes toward the world. That is to say, a neurotic adult may be said to behave "as if" he were actually afraid of a spanking, or of his mother's disapproval, or of being abandoned by his parents, or having his food taken away from him. It is as if his childish attitudes of fear and threat reaction to a dangerous world had gone underground, and untouched by the growing up and learning processes, were now ready to be called out by any stimulus that would make a child feel endangered and threatened.[3]

The neurosis in which the search for safety takes its clearest form is in the compulsive-obsessive neurosis. Compulsive-obsessives try frantically to

---

[3] Not all neurotic individuals feel unsafe. Neurosis may have at its core a thwarting of the affection and esteem needs in a person who is generally safe.

order and stabilize the world so that no unmanageable, unexpected or unfamiliar dangers will ever appear (14). They hedge themselves about with all sorts of ceremonials, rules and formulas so that every possible contingency may be provided for and so that no new contingencies may appear. They are much like the brain injured cases, described by Goldstein (6), who manage to maintain their equilibrium by avoiding everything unfamiliar and strange and by ordering their restricted world in such a neat, disciplined, orderly fashion that everything in the world can be counted upon. They try to arrange the world so that anything unexpected (dangers) cannot possibly occur. If, through no fault of their own, something unexpected does occur, they go into a panic reaction as if this unexpected occurrence constituted a grave danger. What we can see only as a none-too-strong preference in the healthy person, *e.g.,* preference for the familiar, becomes a life-and-death necessity in abnormal cases.

*The love needs.* If both the physiological and the safety needs are fairly well gratified, then there will emerge the love and affection and belongingness needs, and the whole cycle already described will repeat itself with this new center. Now the person will feel keenly, as never before, the absence of friends, or a sweetheart, or a wife, or children. He will hunger for affectionate relations with people in general, namely, for a place in his group, and he will strive with great intensity to achieve this goal. He will want to attain such a place more than anything else in the world and may even forget that once, when he was hungry, he sneered at love.

In our society the thwarting of these needs is the most commonly found core in cases of maladjustment and more severe psychopathology. Love and affection, as well as their possible expression in sexuality, are generally looked upon with ambivalence and are customarily hedged about with many restrictions and inhibitions. Practically all theorists of psychopathology have stressed thwarting of the love needs as basic in the picture of maladjustment. Many clinical studies have therefore been made of this need and we know more about it perhaps than any of the other needs except the physiological ones (14).

One thing that must be stressed at this point is that love is not synonymous with sex. Sex may be studied as a purely physiological need. Ordinarily sexual behavior is multi-determined, that is to say, determined not only by sexual but also by other needs, chief among which are the love and affection needs. Also not to be overlooked is the fact that the love needs involve both giving *and* receiving love.[4]

*The esteem needs.* All people in our society (with a few pathological exceptions) have a need or desire for a stable, firmly based, (usually) high evaluation of themselves, for self-respect, or self-esteem, and for the esteem of others. By firmly based self-esteem, we mean that which is soundly based upon real capacity, achievement and respect from others. These

[4] For further details see (12) and (16, Chap. 5).

needs may be classified into two subsidiary sets. These are, first, the desire for strength, for achievement, for adequacy, for confidence in the face of the world, and for independence and freedom.[5] Secondly, we have what we may call the desire for reputation or prestige (defining it as respect or esteem from other people), recognition, attention, importance or appreciation.[6] These needs have been relatively stressed by Alfred Adler and his followers, and have been relatively neglected by Freud and the psychoanalysts. More and more today however there is appearing widespread appreciation of their central importance.

Satisfaction of the self-esteem need leads to feelings of self-confidence, worth, strength, capability and adequacy of being useful and necessary in the world. But thwarting of these needs produces feelings of inferiority, of weakness and of helplessness. These feelings in turn give rise to either basic discouragement or else compensatory or neurotic trends. An appreciation of the necessity of basic self-confidence and an understanding of how helpless people are without it, can be easily gained from a study of severe traumatic neurosis (8).[7]

*The need for self-actualization.* Even if all these needs are satisfied, we may still often (if not always) expect that a new discontent and restlessness will soon develop, unless the individual is doing what he is fitted for. A musician must make music, an artist must paint, a poet must write, if he is to be ultimately happy. What a man *can* be, he *must* be. This need we may call self-actualization.

This term, first coined by Kurt Goldstein, is being used in this paper in a much more specific and limited fashion. It refers to the desire for self-fulfillment, namely, to the tendency for him to become actualized in what he is potentially. This tendency might be phrased as the desire to become more and more what one is, to become everything that one is capable of becoming.

The specific form that these needs will take will of course vary greatly from person to person. In one individual it may take the form of the desire to be an ideal mother, in another it may be expressed athletically, and

[5] Whether or not this particular desire is universal we do not know. The crucial question, especially important today, is "Will men who are enslaved and dominated, inevitably feel dissatisfied and rebellious?" We may assume on the basis of commonly known clinical data that a man who has known true freedom (not paid for by giving up safety and security but rather built on the basis of adequate safety and security) will not willingly or easily allow his freedom to be taken away from him. But we do not know that this is true for the person born into slavery. The events of the next decade should give us our answer. See discussion of this problem in (5).

[6] Perhaps the desire for prestige and respect from others is subsidiary to the desire for self-esteem or confidence in oneself. Observation of children seems to indicate that this is so, but clinical data give no clear support for such a conclusion.

[7] For more extensive discussion of normal self-esteem, as well as for reports of various researches, see (11).

in still another it may be expressed in painting pictures or in inventions. It is not necessarily a creative urge although in people who have any capacities for creation it will take this form.

The clear emergence of these needs rests upon prior satisfaction of the physiological, safety, love and esteem needs. We shall call people who are satisfied in these needs, basically satisfied people, and it is from these that we may expect the fullest (and healthiest) creativeness.[8] Since, in our society, basically satisfied people are the exception, we do not know much about self-actualization, either experimentally or clinically. It remains a challenging problem for research.

*The preconditions for the basic need satisfactions.* There are certain conditions which are immediate prerequisites for the basic need satisfactions. Danger to these is reacted to almost as if it were a direct danger to the basic needs themselves. Such conditions as freedom to speak, freedom to do what one wishes so long as no harm is done to others, freedom to express one's self, freedom to investigate and seek for information, freedom to defend one's self, justice, fairness, honesty, orderliness in the group are examples of such preconditions for basic need satisfactions. Thwarting in these freedoms will be reacted to with a threat or emergency response. These conditions are not ends in themselves but they are *almost* so since they are so closely related to the basic needs, which are apparently the only ends in themselves. These conditions are defended because without them the basic satisfactions are quite impossible, or at least, very severely endangered.

If we remember that the cognitive capacities (perceptual, intellectual, learning) are a set of adjustive tools, which have, among other functions, that of satisfaction of our basic needs, then it is clear that any danger to them, any deprivation or blocking of their free use, must also be indirectly threatening to the basic needs themselves. Such a statement is a partial solution of the general problems of curiosity, the search for knowledge. truth and wisdom, and the ever-persistent urge to solve the cosmic mys·· teries.

We must therefore introduce another hypothesis and speak of degrees of closeness to the basic needs, for we have already pointed out that *any* conscious desires (partial goals) are more or less important as they are more or less close to the basic needs. The same statement may be made

---

[8] Clearly creative behavior, like painting, is like any other behavior in having multiple determinants. It may be seen in "innately creative" people whether they are satisfied or not, happy or unhappy, hungry or sated. Also it is clear that creative activity may be compensatory, ameliorative or purely economic. It is my impression (as yet unconfirmed) that it is possible to distinguish the artistic and intellectual products of basically satisfied people from those of basically unsatisfied people by inspection alone. In any case, here too we must distinguish, in a dynamic fashion, the overt behavior itself from its various motivations or purposes.

for various behavior acts. An act is psychologically important if it contributes directly to satisfaction of basic needs. The less directly it so contributes, or the weaker this contribution is, the less important this act must be conceived to be from the point of view of dynamic psychology. A similar statement may be made for the various defense or coping mechanisms. Some are very directly related to the protection or attainment of the basic needs, others are only weakly and distantly related. Indeed if we wished, we could speak of more basic and less basic defense mechanisms, and then affirm that danger to the more basic defenses is more threatening than danger to less basic defenses (always remembering that this is so only because of their relationship to the basic needs).

*The desires to know and to understand.* So far, we have mentioned the cognitive needs only in passing. Acquiring knowledge and systematizing the universe have been considered as, in part, techniques for the achievement of basic safety in the world, or, for the intelligent man, expressions of self-actualization. Also freedom of inquiry and expression have been discussed as preconditions of satisfactions of the basic needs. True though these formulations may be, they do not constitute definitive answers to the question as to the motivation role of curiosity, learning, philosophizing, experimenting, etc. They are, at best, no more than partial answers.

This question is especially difficult because we know so little about the facts. Curiosity, exploration, desire for the facts, desire to know may certainly be observed easily enough. The fact that they often are pursued even at great cost to the individual's safety is an earnest of the partial character of our previous discussion. In addition, the writer must admit that, though he has sufficient clinical evidence to postulate the desire to know as a very strong drive in intelligent people, no data are available for unintelligent people. It may then be largely a function of relatively high intelligence. Rather tentatively, then, and largely in the hope of stimulating discussion and research, we shall postulate a basic desire to know, to be aware of reality, to get the facts, to satisfy curiosity, or as Wertheimer phrases it, to see rather than to be blind.

This postulation, however, is not enough  Even after we know, we are impelled to know more and more minutely and microscopically on the one hand, and on the other, more and more extensively in the direction of a world philosophy, religion, etc. The facts that we acquire, if they are isolated or atomistic, inevitably get theorized about, and either analyzed or organized or both. This process has been phrased by some as the search for "meaning." We shall then postulate a desire to understand, to systematize, to organize, to analyze, to look for relations and meanings.

Once these desires are accepted for discussion, we see that they too form themselves into a small hierarchy in which the desire to know is prepotent over the desire to understand. All the characteristics of a hierarchy of prepotency that we have described above seem to hold for this one as well.

We must guard ourselves against the too easy tendency to separate these desires from the basic needs we have discussed above, *i.e.*, to make a sharp dichotomy between "cognitive" and "conative" needs. The desire to know and to understand are themselves conative, *i.e.*, have a striving character, and are as much personality needs as the "basic needs" we have already discussed (19).

## III. Further Characteristics of the Basic Needs

*The degree of fixity of the hierarchy of basic needs.* We have spoken so far as if this hierarchy were a fixed order but actually it is not nearly as rigid as we may have implied. It is true that most of the people with whom we have worked have seemed to have these basic needs in about the order that has been indicated. However, there have been a number of exceptions.

1. There are some people in whom, for instance, self-esteem seems to be more important than love. This most common reversal in the hierarchy is usually due to the development of the notion that the person who is most likely to be loved is a strong or powerful person, one who inspires respect or fear, and who is self confident or aggressive. Therefore such people who lack love and seek it, may try hard to put on a front of aggressive, confident behavior. But essentially they seek high self-esteem and its behavior expressions more as a means-to-an-end than for its own sake; they seek self-assertion for the sake of love rather than for self-esteem itself.

2. There are other, apparently innately creative people in whom the drive to creativeness seems to be more important than any other counter-determinant. Their creativeness might appear not as self-actualization released by basic satisfaction, but in spite of lack of basic satisfaction.

3. In certain people the level of aspiration may be permanently deadened or lowered. That is to say, the less prepotent goals may simply be lost, and may disappear forever, so that the person who has experienced life at a very low level, *i.e.*, chronic unemployment, may continue to be satisfied for the rest of his life if only he can get enough food.

4. The so-called "psychopathic personality" is another example of permanent loss of the love needs. These are people who, according to the best data available (9), have been starved for love in the earliest months of their lives and have simply lost forever the desire and the ability to give and to receive affection (as animals lose sucking or pecking reflexes that are not exercised soon enough after birth).

5. Another cause of reversal of the hierarchy is that when a need has been satisfied for a long time, this need may be underevaluated. People who have never experienced chronic hunger are apt to underestimate its effects and to look upon food as a rather unimportant thing. If they are dominated by a higher need, this higher need will seem to be the most

important of all. It then becomes possible, and indeed does actually happen, that they may, for the sake of this higher need, put themselves into the position of being deprived in a more basic need. We may expect that after a long-time deprivation of the more basic need there will be a tendency to reevaluate both needs so that the more prepotent need will actually become consciously prepotent for the individual who may have given it up very lightly. Thus, a man who has given up his job rather than lose his self-respect, and who then starves for six months or so, may be willing to take his job back even at the price of losing his self-respect.

6. Another partial explanation of *apparent* reversals is seen in the fact that we have been talking about the hierarchy of prepotency in terms of consciously felt wants or desires rather than of behavior. Looking at behavior itself may give us the wrong impression. What we have claimed is that the person will *want* the more basic of two needs when deprived in both. There is no necessary implication here that he will act upon his desires. Let us say again that there are many determinants of behavior other than the needs and desires.

7. Perhaps more important than all these exceptions are the ones that involve ideals, high social standards, high values and the like. With such values people become martyrs; they will give up everything for the sake of a particular ideal, or value. These people may be understood, at least in part, by reference to one basic concept (or hypothesis) which may be called "increased frustration-tolerance through early gratification." People who have been satisfied in their basic needs throughout their lives, particularly in their earlier years, seem to develop exceptional power to withstand present or future thwarting of these needs simply because they have strong, healthy character structure as a result of basic satisfaction. They are the "strong" people who can easily weather disagreement or opposition, who can swim against the stream of public opinion and who can stand up for the truth at great personal cost. It is just the ones who have loved and been well loved, and who have had many deep friendships who can hold out against hatred, rejection or persecution.

I say all this in spite of the fact that there is a certain amount of sheer habituation which is also involved in any full discussion of frustration tolerance. For instance, it is likely that those persons who have been accustomed to relative starvation for a long time are partially enabled thereby to withstand food deprivation. What sort of balance must be made between these two tendencies, of habituation on the one hand, and of past satisfaction breeding present frustration tolerance on the other hand, remains to be worked out by further research. Meanwhile we may assume that they are both operative, side by side, since they do not contradict each other. In respect to this phenomenon of increased frustration tolerance, it seems probable that the most important gratifications come in the first two years of life. That is to say, people who have been made secure and strong in the earliest years, tend to remain secure and strong thereafter in the face of whatever threatens.

*Degrees of relative satisfaction.* So far, our theoretical discussion may have given the impression that these five sets of needs are somehow in a step-wise, all-or-none relationship to each other. We have spoken in such terms as the following: "If one need is satisfied, then another emerges." This statement might give the false impression that a need must be satisfied 100 per cent before the next need emerges. In actual fact, most members of our society who are normal, are partially satisfied in all their basic needs and partially unsatisfied in all their basic needs at the same time. A more realistic description of the hierarchy would be in terms of decreasing percentages of satisfaction as we go up the hierarchy of prepotency. For instance, if I may assign arbitrary figures for the sake of illustration, it is as if the average citizen is satisfied perhaps 85 per cent in his physiological needs, 70 per cent in his safety needs, 50 per cent in his love needs, 40 per cent in his self-esteem needs, and 10 per cent in his self-actualization needs.

As for the concept of emergence of a new need after satisfaction of the prepotent need, this emergence is not a sudden, saltatory phenomenon but rather a gradual emergence by slow degrees from nothingness. For instance, if prepotent need A is satisfied only 10 per cent then need B may not be visible at all. However, as this need A becomes satisfied 25 per cent, need B may emerge 5 per cent, as need A becomes satisfied 75 per cent, need B may emerge 90 per cent, and so on.

*Unconscious character of needs.* These needs are neither necessarily conscious nor unconscious. On the whole, however, in the average person, they are more often unconscious rather than conscious. It is not necessary at this point to overhaul the tremendous mass of evidence which indicates the crucial importance of unconscious motivation. It would by now be expected, on a priori grounds alone, that unconscious motivations would on the whole be rather more important than the conscious motivations. What we have called the basic needs are very often largely unconscious although they may, with suitable techniques, and with sophisticated people become conscious.

*Cultural specificity and generality of needs.* This classification of basic needs makes some attempt to take account of the relative unity behind the superficial differences in specific desires from one culture to another. Certainly in any particular culture an individual's conscious motivational content will usually be extremely different from the conscious motivational content of an individual in another society. However, it is the common experience of anthropologists that people, even in different societies, are much more alike than we would think from our first contact with them, and that as we know them better we seem to find more and more of this commonness. We then recognize the most startling differences to be superficial rather than basic, *e.g.,* differences in style of hairdress, clothes, tastes in food, etc. Our classification of basic needs is in part an attempt to account for this unity behind the apparent diversity from culture to culture. No claim is made that it is ultimate or universal for all cultures. The claim is made only that it is relatively *more* ultimate, more universal, more basic, than the superficial conscious desires from culture to culture, and makes a somewhat closer approach to common-human characteristics. Basic needs are *more* common-human than superficial desires or behaviors.

*Multiple motivations of behavior.* These needs must be understood *not* to be *exclusive* or single determiners of certain kinds of behavior. An example may be found in any behavior that seems to be physiologically motivated, such as eating, or sexual play or the like. The clinical psychologists have long since found that any behavior may be a channel through which flow various determinants. Or to say it in another way, most behavior is multi-motivated. Within the sphere of motivational determinants any behavior tends to be determined by several or *all* of the basic needs simultaneously rather than by only one of them. The latter would be more an exception than the former. Eating may be partially for the sake of filling the stomach, and partially for the sake of comfort and amelioration of other needs. One may make love not only for pure sexual release, but also to convince one's self of one's masculinity, or to make a conquest, to feel powerful, or to win more basic affection. As an illustration, I may point out that it would be possible (theoretically if not practically) to analyze a single act of an individual and see in it the expression of his physiological needs, his safety needs, his love needs, his esteem needs and self-actualization. This contrasts sharply with the more naive brand of trait psychology in which one trait or one motive accounts for a certain kind of act, *i.e.,* an aggressive act is traced solely to a trait of aggressiveness.

*Multiple determinants of behavior.* Not all behavior is determined by the basic needs. We might even say that not all behavior is motivated. There are many determinants of behavior other than motives.[9] For instance, one other important class of determinants is the so-called "field" determinants. Theoretically, at least, behavior may be determined completely by the field, or even by specific isolated external stimuli, as in association of ideas, or certain conditioned reflexes. If in response to the stimulus word "table," I immediately perceive a memory image of a table, this response certainly has nothing to do with my basic needs.

Secondly, we may call attention again to the concept of "degree of closeness to the basic needs" or "degree of motivation." Some behavior is highly

[9] I am aware that many psychologists and psychoanalysts use the term "motivated" and "determined" synonymously, *e.g.,* Freud. But I consider this an obfuscating usage. Sharp distinctions are necessary for clarity of thought, and precision in experimentation.

motivated, other behavior is only weakly motivated. Some is not motivated at all (but all behavior is determined).

Another important point[10] is that there is a basic difference between expressive behavior and coping behavior (functional striving, purposive goal seeking). An expressive behavior does not try to do anything; it is simply a reflection of the personality. A stupid man behaves stupidly, not because he wants to, or tries to, or is motivated to, but simply because he *is* what he is. The same is true when I speak in a bass voice rather than tenor or soprano. The random movements of a healthy child, the smile on the face of a happy man even when he is alone, the springiness of the healthy man's walk, and the erectness of his carriage are other examples of expressive, non-functional behavior. Also the *style* in which a man carries out almost all his behavior, motivated as well as unmotivated, is often expressive.

We may then ask, is *all* behavior expressive or reflective of the character structure? The answer is "No." Rote, habitual, automatized, or conventional behavior may or may not be expressive. The same is true for most "stimulus-bound" behaviors.

It is finally necessary to stress that expressiveness of behavior and goal-directedness of behavior are not mutually exclusive categories. Average behavior is usually both.

*Goals as centering principle in motivation theory.* It will be observed that the basic principle in our classification has been neither the instigation nor the motivated behavior but rather the functions, effects, purposes, or goals of the behavior. It has been proven sufficiently by various people that this is the most suitable point for centering in any motivation theory.[11]

*Animal- and human-centering.* This theory starts with the human being rather than any lower and presumably "simpler" animal. Too many of the findings that have been made in animals have been proven to be true for animals but not for the human being. There is no reason whatsoever why we should start with animals in order to study human motivation. The logic or rather illogic behind this general fallacy of "pseudo-simplicity" has been exposed often enough by philosophers and logicians as well as by scientists in each of the various fields. It is no more necessary to study animals before one can study man than it is to study mathematics before one can study geology or psychology or biology.

We may also reject the old, naive, behaviorism which assumed that it was somehow necessary, or at least more "scientific" to judge human beings by animal standards. One consequence of this belief was that the whole notion of purpose and goal was excluded from motivational psy-

[10] To be discussed fully in a subsequent publication.

[11] The interested reader is referred to the very excellent discussion of this point in Murray's *Explorations in Personality* (15).

chology simply because one could not ask a white rat about his purposes. Tolman (18) has long since proven in animal studies themselves that this exclusion was not necessary.

*Motivation and the theory of psychopathogenesis.* The conscious motivational content of everyday life has, according to the foregoing, been conceived to be relatively important or unimportant accordingly as it is more or less closely related to the basic goals. A desire for an ice cream cone might actually be an indirect expression of a desire for love. If it is, then this desire for the ice cream cone becomes extremely important motivation. If however the ice cream is simply something to cool the mouth with, or a casual appetitive reaction, then the desire is relatively unimportant. Everyday conscious desires are to be regarded as symptoms, as *surface indicators of more basic needs.* If we were to take these superficial desires at their face value we would find ourselves in a state of complete confusion which could never be resolved, since we would be dealing seriously with symptoms rather than with what lay behind the symptoms.

Thwarting of unimportant desires produces no psychopathological results; thwarting of a basically important need does produce such results. Any theory of psychopathogenesis must then be based on a sound theory of motivation. A conflict or a frustration is not necessarily pathogenic. It becomes so only when it threatens or thwarts the basic needs, or partial needs that are closely related to the basic needs (10).

*The role of gratified needs.* It has been pointed out above several times that our needs usually emerge only when more prepotent needs have been gratified. Thus gratification has an important role in motivation theory. Apart from this, however, needs cease to play an active determining or organizing role as soon as they are gratified.

What this means is that, *e.g.,* a basically satisfied person no longer has the needs for esteem, love, safety, etc. The only sense in which he might be said to have them is in the almost metaphysical sense that a sated man has hunger, or a filled bottle has emptiness. If we are interested in what *actually* motivates us, and not in what has, will, or might motivate us, then a satisfied need is not a motivator. It must be considered for all practical purposes simply not to exist, to have disappeared. This point should be emphasized because it has been either overlooked or contradicted in every theory of motivation I know.[12] The perfectly healthy, normal, fortunate man has no sex needs or hunger needs, or needs for safety, or for love, or for prestige, or self-esteem, except in stray moments of quickly passing threat. If we were to say otherwise, we should also have to aver that every man had all the pathological reflexes, *e.g.,* Babinski, etc., because if his nervous system were damaged, these would appear.

It is such considerations as these that suggest the bold postulation that

---

[12] Note that acceptance of this theory necessitates basic revision of the Freudian theory.

a man who is thwarted in any of his basic needs may fairly be envisaged simply as a sick man. This is a fair parallel to our designation as "sick" of the man who lacks vitamins or minerals. Who is to say that a lack of love is less important than a lack of vitamins? Since we know the pathogenic effects of love starvation, who is to say that we are invoking value-questions in an unscientific or illegitimate way, any more than the physician does who diagnoses and treats pellagra or scurvy? If I were permitted this usage, I should then say simply that a healthy man is primarily motivated by his needs to develop and actualize his fullest potentialities and capacities. If a man has any other basic needs in any active, chronic sense, then he is simply an unhealthy man. He is as surely sick as if he had suddenly developed a strong salt-hunger or calcium hunger.[13]

If this statement seems unusual or paradoxical the reader may be assured that this is only one among many such paradoxes that will appear as we revise our ways of looking at man's deeper motivations. When we ask what man wants of life, we deal with his very essence.

## IV. Summary

1. There are at least five sets of goals, which we may call basic needs. These are briefly physiological, safety, love, esteem, and self-actualization. In addition, we are motivated by the desire to achieve or maintain the various conditions upon which these basic satisfactions rest and by certain more intellectual desires.

2. These basic goals are related to each other, being arranged in a hierarchy of prepotency. This means that the most prepotent goal will monopolize consciousness and will tend of itself to organize the recruitment of the various capacities of the organism. The less prepotent needs are minimized, even forgotten or denied. But when a need is fairly well satisfied, the next prepotent ("higher") need emerges, in turn to dominate the conscious life and to serve as the center of organization of behavior, since gratified needs are not active motivators.

Thus man is a perpetually wanting animal. Ordinarily the satisfaction of these wants is not altogether mutually exclusive, but only tends to be. The average member of our society is most often partially satisfied and partially unsatisfied in all of his wants. The hierarchy principle is usually empirically observed in terms of increasing percentages of non-satisfaction

---

[13] If we were to use the word "sick" in this way, we should then also have to face squarely the relations of man to his society. One clear implication of our definition would be that (1) since a man is to be called sick who is basically thwarted, and (2) since such basic thwarting is made possible ultimately only by forces outside the individual, then (3) sickness in the individual must come ultimately from a sickness in the society. The "good" or healthy society would then be defined as one that permitted man's highest purposes to emerge by satisfying all his prepotent basic needs.

as we go up the hierarchy. Reversals of the average order of the hierarchy are sometimes observed. Also it has been observed that an individual may permanently lose the higher wants in the hierarchy under special conditions. There are not only ordinarily multiple motivations for usual behavior, but in addition many determinants other than motives.

3. Any thwarting or possibility of thwarting of these basic human goals, or danger to the defenses which protect them, or to the conditions upon which they rest, is considered to be a psychological threat. With a few exceptions, all psychopathology may be partially traced to such threats. A basically thwarted man may actually be defined as a "sick" man, if we wish.

4. It is such basic threats which bring about the general emergency reactions.

5. Certain other basic problems have not been dealt with because of limitations of space. Among these are (*a*) the problem of values in any definitive motivation theory, (*b*) the relation between appetites, desires, needs and what is "good" for the organism, (*c*) the etiology of the basic needs and their possible derivation in early childhood, (*d*) redefinition of motivational concepts, *i.e.,* drive, desire, wish, need, goal, (*e*) implication of our theory for hedonistic theory, (*f*) the nature of the uncompleted act, of success and failure, and of aspiration-level, (*g*) the role of association, habit and conditioning, (*h*) relation to the theory of inter-personal relations, (*i*) implications for psychotherapy, (*j*) implication for theory of society, (*k*) the theory of selfishness, (*l*) the relation between needs and cultural patterns, (*m*) the relation between this theory and Allport's theory of functional autonomy. These as well as certain other less important questions must be considered as motivation theory attempts to become definitive.

## References

1. Adler, A.: *Social interest.* London: Faber & Faber, 1938.
2. Cannon, W. B.: *Wisdom of the body.* New York: Norton, 1932.
3. Freud, A.: *The ego and the mechanisms of defense.* London: Hogarth, 1937.
4. Freud, S.: *New introductory lectures on psychoanalysis.* New York: Norton, 1933.
5. Fromm, E.: *Escape from freedom.* New York: Farrar and Rinehart, 1941.
6. Goldstein, K.: *The organism.* New York: American Book Co., 1939.
7. Horney, K.: *The neurotic personality of our time.* New York: Norton, 1937.
8. Kardiner, A.: *The traumatic neuroses of war.* New York: Hoeber, 1941.
9. Levy, D. M.: Primary affect hunger. *Amer. J. Psychiat.,* 1937, **94,** 643–652.

10. Maslow, A. H.: Conflict, frustration, and the theory of threat. *J. abnorm. (soc.) Psychol.*, 1943, **38,** 81–86.

11. ————: Dominance, personality and social behavior in women. *J. soc. Psychol.*, 1939, **10,** 3–39.

12. ————: The dynamics of psychological security-insecurity. *Character & Pers.*, 1942, **10,** 331–344.

13. ————: A preface to motivation theory. *Psychosomatic Med.*, 1943, **5,** 85–92.

14. ————, & Mittelmann, B.: *Principles of abnormal psychology.* New York: Harper & Bros., 1941.

15. Murray, H. A., *et al.: Explorations in personality.* New York: Oxford University Press, 1938.

16. Plant, J.: *Personality and the cultural pattern.* New York: Commonwealth Fund, 1937.

17. Shirley, M.: Children's adjustments to a strange situation. *J. abnorm. (soc.) Psychol.*, 1942, **37,** 201–217.

18. Tolman, E. C.: *Purposive behavior in animals and men.* New York: Century, 1932.

19. Wertheimer, M.: Unpublished lectures at the New School for Social Research.

20. Young, P. T.: *Motivation of behavior.* New York: John Wiley & Sons, 1936.

21. ————: The experimental analysis of appetite. *Psychol. Bull.*, 1941, **38,** 129–164.

# Motivation versus Hygiene*

*Frederick Herzberg*
*Bernard Mausner*
*Barbara Bloch Snyderman*

Let us summarize briefly our answer to the question, "What do people want from their jobs?" When our respondents reported feeling happy with their jobs, they most frequently described factors related to their tasks, to events that indicated to them that they were successful in the performance of their work, and to the possibility of professional growth. Conversely, when feelings of unhappiness were reported, they were not associated with the job itself but with conditions that *surround* the doing of the job. These events suggest to the individual that the context in which he performs his work is unfair or disorganized and as such represents to him an unhealthy psychological work environment. Factors involved in these situations we call factors of *hygiene,* for they act in a manner analogous to the principles of medical hygiene. Hygiene operates to remove health hazards from the environment of man. It is not a curative; it is, rather, a preventive. Modern garbage disposal, water purification, and air-pollution control do not cure diseases, but without them we should have many more diseases. Similarly, when there are deleterious factors in the context of the job, they serve to bring about poor job attitudes. Improvement in these factors of hygiene will serve to remove the impediments to positive job attitudes. Among the factors of hygiene we have included supervision, interpersonal relations, physical working conditions, salary, company policies and administrative practices, benefits, and job security. When these factors deteriorate to a level below that which the employee considers acceptable, then job dissatisfaction ensues. However, the reverse does not hold true. When the job context can be characterized as optimal, we will not get dissatisfaction, but neither will we get much in the way of positive attitudes.

The factors that lead to positive job attitudes do so because they satisfy the individual's need for self-actualization in his work. The concept of self-actualization, or self-realization, as a man's ultimate goal has been

* From *The Motivation to Work,* John Wiley & Sons, Inc., New York, 1959, Chap. 12, pp. 113–119. Reprinted by permission of the publisher.

focal to the thought of many personality theorists. For such men as Jung, Adler, Sullivan, Rogers, and Goldstein the supreme goal of man is to fulfill himself as a creative, unique individual according to his own innate potentialities and within the limits of reality. When he is deflected from this goal he becomes, as Jung says, "a crippled animal."

Man tends to actualize himself in every area of his life, and his job is one of the most important areas. The conditions that surround the doing of the job cannot give him this basic satisfaction; they do not have this potentiality. It is only from the performance of a task that the individual can get the rewards that will reinforce his aspirations. It is clear that although the factors relating to the doing of the job and the factors defining the job context serve as goals for the employee, the nature of the motivating qualities of the two kinds of factors is essentially different. Factors in the job context meet the needs of the individual for avoiding unpleasant situations. In contrast to this motivation by meeting avoidance needs, the job factors reward the needs of the individual to reach his aspirations. These effects on the individual can be conceptualized as actuating approach rather than avoidance behavior. Since it is in the approach sense that the term motivation is most commonly used, we designate the job factors as the "motivators," as opposed to the extra-job factors, which we have labeled the factors of hygiene. It should be understood that both kinds of factors meet the needs of the employee; but it is primarily the "motivators" that serve to bring about the kind of job satisfaction and, as we saw in the section dealing with the effects of job attitudes, the kind of improvement in performance that industry is seeking from its work force.

We can now say something systematic about what people want from their jobs. For the kind of population that we sampled, and probably for many other populations as well, the wants of employees divide into two groups. One group revolves around the need to develop in one's occupation as a source of personal growth. The second group operates as an essential base to the first and is associated with fair treatment in compensation, supervision, working conditions, and administrative practices. The fulfillment of the needs of the second group does not motivate the individual to high levels of job satisfaction and . . . to extra performance on the job. All we can expect from satisfying the needs for hygiene is the prevention of dissatisfaction and poor job performance.

In the light of this distinction, we can account for much of the lack of success that industry has had in its attempts to motivate employees. Let us examine two of the more ubiquitous avenues through which industry has hoped to gain highly motivated employees: human-relations training for supervisors and wage-incentive systems.

As part of this era of human relations, supervisory training directed toward improving the interpersonal relationships between superior and subordinate has been widely incorporated into industrial-relations programs. These programs have been initiated with expectations of bringing about positive job attitudes and, hopefully, increased performance on the job. When we examine the results of our study, we find interpersonal relationships appearing in an exceedingly small number of the high sequences; in only 15 per cent of the low sequences are poor interpersonal relationships with the superior reported. The negligible role which interpersonal relationships play in our data tallies poorly with the assumption basic to most human-relations training programs that the way in which a supervisor gets along with his people is the single most important determinant of morale. Supervisory training in human relations is probably essential to the maintenance of good hygiene at work. This is particularly true for the many jobs, both at rank-and-file and managerial levels, in which modern industry offers little chance for the operation of the motivators. These jobs are atomized, cut and dried, monotonous. They offer little chance for responsibility and achievement and thus little opportunity for self-actualization. It is here that hygiene is exceptionally important. The fewer the opportunities for the "motivators" to appear, the greater must be the hygiene offered in order to make the work tolerable. A man who finds his job challenging, exciting, and satisfying will perhaps tolerate a difficult supervisor. But to expect such programs to pay dividends beyond the effects that hygiene provides is going contrary to the nature of job motivation. In terms of the approach-avoidance concept, the advocates of human relations have suggested that by rewarding the avoidance needs of the individual you will achieve the desired approach behavior. But a more creative design will not emerge from an engineer as a result of fair supervisory treatment. To achieve the more creative design, one or more of the motivators must be present, a task that is interesting to the engineer, a task in which he can exercise responsibility and independence, a task that allows for some concrete achievement. The motivators fit the need for creativity, the hygiene factors satisfy the need for fair treatment, and it is thus that the appropriate incentive must be present to achieve the desired job attitude and job performance.

The failure to get positive returns in both job attitudes and job performance from rewarding the avoidance needs of the individual is most clearly seen in the use of monetary incentives. We have listed salary among the factors of hygiene, and as such it meets two kinds of avoidance needs of the employee. First is the avoidance of the economic deprivation that is felt when actual income is insufficient. Second, and generally of more significance in the times and for the kind of people covered by our study, is the need to avoid feelings of being treated unfairly. Salary and wages are very frequently at the top of the list of factors describing answers to the question, "What don't you like about your job?" in morale surveys. They are at the middle of the list of answers to the question, "What do you want from your job?" We have explained this difference in emphasis by our distinction between factors that lead to job satisfaction and the factors that contribute to job dissatisfaction. Asking people what is important to them in their jobs will bring responses that we have classified as "motivators." The atmosphere of the usual morale survey encourages people to emphasize sources of dissatisfaction.

Where morale surveys have differentiated between dissatisfaction with amount of salary as opposed to the equity of salary, the latter looms as the more important source of dissatisfaction. In two consecutive morale surveys by the senior author, in which the employees were requested to illustrate their dissatisfaction or satisfaction with the various items on the morale questionnaire with critical incidents, the comments on the equity of salary greatly outnumbered the comments on the absolute amount of salary. All 1382 employees surveyed were at the supervisory level (21).

How then can we explain the success of the many employee motivational schemes that seem to rely directly on the use of wage incentives and bonuses? Reports on the Lincoln Electric Company of Cleveland, Ohio (37), and the George A. Hormel meat-packing plant at Austin, Minnesota (7), suggest good examples of the efficacy of money incentives for increasing production, job satisfaction, and company loyalty. But let us examine for a moment the nature of these programs and the nature of their success in the light of the findings presented here.

First, there are many other ingredients to these plans which are generally given less attention than they merit, ingredients that combine a large proportion of the factors that we have found to be motivators. The formation of Lincoln's Advisory Board and Hormel's Business Improvement Committee both resulted from attempts to increase job content and job responsibility by giving workers knowledge of, and responsibility for, operations and improvements. Both operate on the theory that the "boss" cannot know everything about all the work processes, that the workers are experts in their fields, and that their knowledge is of great value. Lincoln Electric, which is not unionized, has the additional advantage of being able to advance workers on the basis of merit, not seniority. James E. Lincoln, president of the company, says that "money is of relatively small importance. Beyond enough for our real needs, money itself is valued less for what it will buy than as an evidence of successful skill in achievement (37)." Money thus earned as a direct reward for outstanding individual performance is a reinforcement of the motivators of *recognition* and *achievement*. It is not hygiene as is the money given in across-the-board wage increases.

The Scanlon plan  is a system for involving employees of a company in the improvement of production by the distribution of savings in labor costs to all of the personnel of a participating company. This aspect of participation and of increased responsibility is the real secret of whatever success the Scanlon plan and its imitators have achieved. Lincoln Electric is implementing man's natural striving for self-realization. No man wants to be just a cog in a wheel. Lincoln says, "The most insistent incentive is the development of self-respect and the respect of others. Earnings that are the reward for outstanding performance, progress, and responsibility are signs that he is a man among men. The worker must feel that he is part of a worthwhile project and that the project succeeded because his ability was needed in it. Money alone will not do the job."

When incentive systems do not permit any of the motivators to operate, then any increase in performance or in apparent job satisfaction is misleading. For in these instances the removal of a decrement in performance by the elimination of job dissatisfaction is often mistakenly referred to as a positive gain in performance. That voluntary restriction of output is practiced on an enormous scale is common knowledge in industry (26, 27, 58). The existence of a standard of "a fair day's work" has been well documented in systematic studies by industrial psychologists and sociologists as well as industrial engineers. It is likely that poor hygiene will depress performance below the level of "the fair day's work." Correction of this poor hygiene, or the application of monetary incentives not related to motivators, may return performance to the norm. The improvement produced under these circumstances is actually far less than one could obtain were motivators to be introduced.

Are good job attitudes and company loyalty engendered by these incentive plans? The surface answer often seems to be yes. Employees in such companies will report that they like working for their companies, but the "liking" seems to be little more than the absence of disliking, their satisfaction little more than the absence of dissatisfaction. Blum reports on the Hormel packinghouse workers in this regard:

> If I had to summarize workers' feelings about the company in one sentence, I would repeat the words of a worker: "If a man is going to work for anybody else, it's hard to beat Hormel." It is the single most often heard expression in any conversation about the company. I have never heard a worker express an unconditional acceptance of the company as an organization to work for (7).

Are they really saying they like their work? Or are they merely saying that they have found a place to work in which life is not unbearable?

What is the evidence? According to Blum's report, shop talk is deafening by its absence when the work day is over. There seems to be a deliberate effort on the part of the employees to repress any mention of their jobs away from the plant. Contrast this with the unceasing shop talk reported by Walker in his study of steel workers at the National Tube Company of Ellwood City, Pennsylvania (56). His description of their jobs emphasizes the large number of motivators present. They are not running away from their work at the shift bell. They continue to live their jobs at home. The employees of Hormel seem to be psychologically running away from their jobs. Their extra effort, while it increases production, albeit probably not to the level of which they are capable, is not indicative of positive job attitudes. Rather it provides the means for escape from a job toward which their attitudes are little better than neutral. The sooner they finish the job, the sooner they can get away from it; the more money they can earn, the more effective their escape in pleasant living off the job. It is doubtful that the true production potential of these workers is being tapped; it is undeniable that the incentive system, along with other hygienic factors, serves to make their jobs tolerable.

The definition of *hygiene* and *motivation* and the relationship of these complexes of factors to the behavior of men at work has many implications for industrial practice. In the next section we try to explore these implications after setting the findings of our study in an historical background.

## References

7. Blum, F. A.: *Toward a Democratic Work Process.* New York: Harper, 1953.

21. Herzberg, F.: "An Analysis of Morale Survey Comments." *Personnel Psychol.,* 1954, 7 (2), pp. 267–275.

26. Horsfall, A. B., and C. M. Arensberg: "Teamwork and Productivity in a Shoe Factory." *Hum. Organization,* 1949, 8, pp. 13–25.

27. Hughes, E. C.: "The Knitting of Racial Groups in Industry." *American Sociol. Review,* 1946, 11, pp. 512–519.

37. Lincoln, J. F.: *Lincoln's Incentive System.* New York: McGraw-Hill, 1946.

56. Walker, C. R.: *Steeltown.* New York: Harper, 1950.

58. Whyte, W. F.: *Money and Motivation.* New York: Harper, 1955.

# READINGS RELATED TO CHAPTER V

## Perception: Applied Aspects*

*Ross Stagner*

The problem of industrial conflict is the problem of the perceptions of company executives, union officers, and rank-and-file workers, the ways in which they see themselves, and the prospects of achieving satisfaction for their motives within the framework of reality as they perceive it. In the foregoing chapter we have outlined some of the basic principles of the psychology of perception as they determine attitudes, values, and frames of reference for people in general. Let us now turn to a specific analysis of the situation as it relates to the three groups which we have identified as crucial for an understanding of the realities of industrial conflict and industrial cooperation.

At least three kinds of perceptions can be of decisive significance in union-management relations. One of them is *perception of persons*—what people on one side look like to people on the other side. Second, *perception of situations* is important. We can show how the same kinds of distortions identified in the generalized discussion already given can be found in a union-management context. And third, *perception of issues* is a significant part of the interaction. How the various groups perceive managerial policies, union activities, etc., can be very important in determining not only company-union relations but also public policy regarding this problem.

* Chap. 3 from *The Psychology of Industrial Conflict,* John Wiley & Sons, Inc., New York, 1956, pp. 53–88. Reprinted by permission of the publisher.

## Perception of Persons

From a psychological point of view, industrial conflict is first and foremost a matter of conflict between people. And the extent to which we fight with others depends to a substantial degree on how we perceive them. (Conversely, of course, we perceive persons differently if they frustrate us or satisfy us. This point will be developed in subsequent chapters.) Thus, it becomes important to ascertain whether executives and unionists perceive each other realistically. Do distortions in interpersonal perceptions affect the course of industrial relations? And if differences exist, how do they arise?

*Perceptual abstraction and differentiation.* Every percept is a complex experience involving a variety of elements and possessing characteristics enabling it to be differentiated from others. Thus the young child learns to *differentiate* objects on the basis of color, form, and size; and at a somewhat later age can *abstract* these qualities (e.g., classify all red objects together, all round objects together, etc.).

Perception of persons illustrates clearly these same processes. At a fairly early age children become aware of differences in dress (the policeman, the doctor, the waiter, etc.). Somewhat later we get evidence of recognition of differences in social role regardless of clothing. Conscious abstraction of categories of people probably is a fairly late (adolescent) development. Perceptual distortions occur when these differences in perceived traits are arbitrarily "loaded" in one direction, without regard to the "real" situation.

The evidence indicates that the earliest differentiations involve polarized, all-or-none judgments. For example, southern white children have been shown at first to have no prejudice as regards Negro children (perceive no difference); then they begin to develop a complete avoidance response (all perceived qualities "bad"). Only in later childhood and early adolescence does the white adult stereotype, with its inclusion of some desirable and some undesirable features, develop.

This process may be a necessary one in any kind of social perception. The typical executive seems to go through a developmental sequence in his perception of labor union officials. At first all are bad (frustrating, threatening figures). Later the executive begins to differentiate between individuals (some are better than others), and perhaps, even later, to differentiate within the individual (he has some features I don't like, but he has his good points too).

CHILDREN'S PERCEPTIONS OF LABOR AND MANAGEMENT FIGURES. We can verify the accuracy of the foregoing analysis, as regards children, by reference to a study by Haire and Morrison (1954). These investigators presented pictorial and verbal stimuli to 755 school children, ages 12–16.

They were interested first in differences related to the income status of the child's family. A few sample items are shown in Table 1.

**TABLE 1. Socioeconomic Differences among Children's Perceptions of Labor and Management Figures\***

| Item | Percentage of "Yes" Responses | |
|---|---|---|
| | High Economic Status | Low Economic Status |
| Photograph of people unloading a truck Caption reads: "These strikers are receiving food and clothing." | | |
| 1. Do they deserve help? | 48 | 76 |
| 6. Do you think they are bad people? | 22 | 7 |
| Photograph of a picket line—Telephone strike No caption. | | |
| 9. Are they good people? | 64 | 89 |
| 10. Would they be nice to talk with? | 43 | 71 |
| 12. Are they clean? | 39 | 54 |
| 13. Are these people smart? | 31 | 55 |

\* From Haire and Morrison (1954).

Inspection of this table indicates that children of upper economic background are more likely to see strikers as "bad," "dirty," etc. Of 57 items in the test, 38 gave differences significant at the 1% level or better. All of these indicate that lower economic status goes with more favorable perception of labor and union figures.

Particularly important for our purposes is the analysis of age differentials. We have already noted that perception of persons develops before perception of issues, and that discrimination of "good" and "bad" precedes awareness of other differential features. The Haire-Morrison data confirm these observations for union-management material. The younger children —roughly, 12 and 13 years old—are differentiated chiefly on items about the personal characteristics of workers and bosses. The older subjects— ages 14 to 16—give fewer distinctive responses to these purely personal items, although some differences persist; but they show differences on questions regarding issues, which do not appear at the earlier levels. This trend makes perfectly good sense in terms of the fact that an understanding of abstract issues by the age of 12 is rare, particularly if such issues have not been topics of specific indoctrination.

Thus, by the time the child is 12, he has already been slanted toward a pro-union or pro-management bias. From that point on, by selective learning and selective forgetting, he will as a rule become more and more disposed to see only those "facts" in a situation which fit in with his established attitudes.

This kind of perception influences the individual's evaluation of job opportunities. Table 2 shows how high school boys feel about jobs in relation to union membership. Active hostility to unions is clearly not large, but it does reflect the economic status of the family.

**TABLE 2. Attitudes of Boys toward Unions, by Occupation of Father**

| Father's Occupation | Attitude of Sons | |
|---|---|---|
| | Accept Unions* | Reject Unions† |
| Unskilled workers | 76% | 11% |
| Semiskilled workers | 77 | 11 |
| Skilled workers and foremen | 74 | 14 |
| Clerical, sales, and kindred workers | 63 | 28 |
| Farmers | 60 | 27 |
| Proprietors, managers, and officials | 61 | 30 |
| Professionals | 68 | 26 |

SOURCE: *Youth and the World of Work*, Social Research Service, Michigan State College, 1949.

* Adds together those preferring a job where one must join a union and those preferring a job where one can join a union if he wishes.

† Indicates those preferring a job where there is no labor union.

PERCEPTIONS OF COLLEGE STUDENTS. These observations suggest that persons friendly to unions perceive workers as having pleasant, desirable characteristics, whereas those disliking unions perceive workers as bad and threatening. Stagner (1950 *b*) reported on 50 college men who were consistently pro-union, and 50 who were consistently anti-union. These men checked a list of adjectives, first to show which they thought characteristic of factory workers, then for characteristics of business executives. A portion of the list is reproduced in Table 3.

**TABLE 3. Descriptions of Workers and of Executives by College Men***

| Adjective Checked | By Pro-union Men | | By Anti-union Men | |
|---|---|---|---|---|
| | For Exec. | For Worker | For Exec. | For Worker |
| Lazy | 10 | 10 | 3 | 20 |
| Aggressive | 46 | 23 | 49 | 23 |
| Ignorant | 6 | 6 | 3 | 25 |
| Violent | 8 | 7 | 3 | 13 |
| Kind | 26 | 37 | 36 | 34 |
| Sarcastic | 27 | 11 | 15 | 15 |
| Happy | 28 | 35 | 35 | 29 |
| Grasping | 39 | 15 | 29 | 16 |

* From Stagner (1950), by permission of the American Psychological Association. *N* = 50 for each group.

Table 3 shows consistent differences in the mental picture that the pro-union students and the anti-union students have of business executives. The pro-labor group tends to perceive the executives as grasping, sarcastic, and lacking in kindness, whereas the anti-labor students perceive the executive as having favorable characteristics. Conversely, the pro-labor students are prone to see the good side of the worker's personality, whereas the anti-labor students are likely, relatively at least, to characterize the worker as ignorant, violent, and lazy. We can hardly doubt that these mental pictures of the kinds of persons with whom they will be dealing in future years will have a profound influence on the policies and activities of these two groups of young men.

A STUDY OF EXECUTIVES AND UNIONISTS. The crucial question with regard to these perceptual differences, of course, is how they actually function in union-management relations. Let us consider first whether labeling a neutral person as an executive or as a union officer changes his perceived qualities. Haire (1955) tested 76 members of a Central Labor Council [1] and 108 representatives of management—mostly personnel managers and industrial relations men. The test materials consisted of two pictures and four descriptions. Each picture was that of an ordinary, middle-aged man. All four descriptions were virtually identical, though in slightly different words and arrangements. Two descriptions identified the picture as that of a "local manager of a small plant which is a branch of a large manufacturing concern." Two identified him as "Secretary-Treasurer of his union." Each description was paired with each picture for equal numbers of respondents. The men in the Central Labor Council were asked to look over a photograph and description, then check an adjective list to describe this person. The same was done by the group of executives. Since the photographs and descriptions were labeled half the time "manager" and half the time "union," we can ignore the specific pictures and see what adjectives were applied by each group. Some of the results are shown in Table 4. Haire offers the following generalizations regarding his study:

"The general impression of a person is radically different when he is seen as a member of management than when he is seen as a representative of labor.

"Management and labor each see the other as less dependable than himself.

"Management and labor each see the other as less appreciative of the other's position than he himself is.

"Management and labor each see the other as deficient in thinking, emotional characteristics and interpersonal relations in comparison with himself."

*Perception and the quality of union-management relations.* It seems

[1] The Central Labor Council is composed of delegates from local unions within a community. These men can therefore be assumed to be active unionists.

**TABLE 4. Traits Perceived as Applying to Photographs when Labeled Manager or Unionist***

|  | By Executives | | By Unionists | | p |
|  | Labeled Manager | Labeled Unionist | Labeled Manager | Labeled Unionist | |
|---|---|---|---|---|---|
| Dependability (conscientious, honest, responsible, etc.) | 252 | 176 | 200 | 231 | .01 |
| Seeing others' problems (considerate, cooperative, fairminded, etc.) | 123 | 47 | 93 | 137 | .01 |

* From Haire (1955), p. 210. Reprinted by permission of *Industrial and Labor Relations Review.*

plausible that the existence of these divergent perceptions would aggravate the real conflicts of interest which arise in union-management bargaining. A corollary of this idea is that, when the union-management relationship is full of conflict, each party will perceive "bad" traits in the other; whereas "good" labor-management conditions should be associated with perceptions of the opposing party as "good."

An early observational investigation into this question is that reported by Stagner (1948 *b*). In this study personal interviews were conducted with union officers and company officials to get some notion of the way in which they perceived each other. Marked agreement was observed between the general level of labor-management relationships and the kinds of reports obtained. For example, interviews at a company in which the general relationship was reported to be poor led to the following observations: "At one time ɪe (the executive) claims that his rank and file workers are all right, only the officers being bad. On other points, however, he says of the workers that 'They seem to lose sight of everyone else but themselves. No matter how you slice it, they still think they should have more.' He believes that 'workers are forced into the union, and once in it, a small group dominates the meetings so that only the desired few are allowed to speak.'"

An executive in another company, whose union officers had commented that he was "too stuck up" and they could not trust him, gave the following comments about the union: "I really don't see what good the union has done these fellows; they are just contributing money to the union." Under the Taft-Hartley Act he will have a chance to show the workers "where they have been led astray by some of the labor organizers." Regarding an annual wage, this executive says: "Of course, you have an awful lot of workers who are lazy. If you gave them an annual wage, it would take away the incentive to work." He then commented rather naively: "Why they should believe everything the union tells them and nothing management tells them is beyond me. *We pay them their wages.*" The perception of the worker as being lazy and likely to be corrupted by an annual wage, although the executive is not corrupted by an annual salary, is, of course, suggestive of some of the important elements in this man's frame of reference. Likewise, his notion that labor organizers are those who lead the workers astray is significant of the way in which he looks at certain kinds of situations.

In contrast to these descriptions of unfavorable perceptions by both union and company officials are reports from companies where relations were commonly said to be "good." In these establishments, executives saw their workers as "people like myself," and unionists described the boss as "a square shooter." We need no crystal ball to see the significance of such interpersonal perceptions for smooth-functioning contract negotiations and grievance settlements.

*The Illini City study.*[2] Finally, we can report on a comparison which makes use of quantitative estimates of the quality of the union-management situation. In the Illini City research, eight companies were ranked according to "attitudinal climate,"[3] using reports of proportions of conflict and cooperation in interviews with production workers. They were then ranked again by taking the proportion of favorable remarks that top managers made when interviewed about their union. The correlation of these rankings was +.74, a highly significant degree of agreement.

Since it seems unlikely that the views of hourly workers affected top executives, we incline to the following interpretation of these data: in some establishments top executives perceive the union and its officers as unreasonable, hot-headed, demanding, and irresponsible.[4] Their behavior toward the union is guided by these perceptions. This behavior sets off defensive and counterattacking responses by the union leaders. Thus workers (in plants where this sequence occurs) are correct in reporting more conflict between management and union. The reverse of this occurs where executives have favorable perceptions of the union.

*Cues, roles, and percepts.* Let us now relate these observations to the

[2] Frequent reference will be made in this book to *Labor-Management Relations in Illini City: Vol. 1. The Case Studies. Vol. 2. Explorations in Comparative Analysis.* Champaign, Illinois: Institute of Labor and Industrial Relations, University of Illinois, 1953, 1954. These volumes present extensive data of a comparative nature on eight union-management relationships, including considerable material of psychological character, along with economic, sociological and historical data on the companies and unions involved.

[3] For a more detailed treatment of this concept, see Chapter 12, pp. 398–403 [in *The Psychology of Industrial Conflict*].

[4] It is probable that these perceptions were in part realistic, but not wholly so. For example, the same union officers were perceived more favorably by executives in one company than by those in another; and the attitudinal climate of workers was more favorable in the former.

systematic view of perception outlined [previously]. Figure 1 diagrams a way of thinking about the perception of persons. The "real" individual has a number of social roles. In each of these he "emits" cues which reach the observer. However, the observer may be influenced by role A even though that role has been replaced by role B. The potency of specific cues in determining a percept depends on how they are "loaded" for a given observer. In Fig. 1[5] we suggest that Joe Jones has differentiable charac-

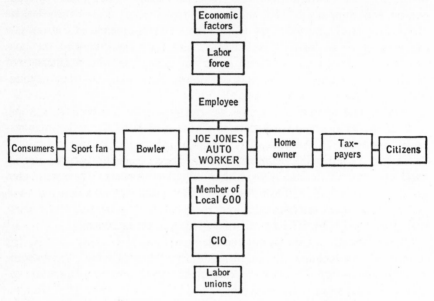

Figure 1. Abstracting different features of a perceived person.

teristics, such as being a worker, a bowler, a homeowner, and a union member. Which of these will play the major part in determining how Jones is perceived by Smith?

Obviously, the outcome depends substantially on characteristics within Smith. If he has been slanted by family background, college training, or prior experience to perceive unions as threatening, the cues from this role may overbalance everything and determine the perceived personality.

It is worth while, at this point, to note that many psychological errors derive from ill-founded generalizations based on these perceived characteristics.[6] In human relations we must deal with specific individuals, not

[5] This method of representing successive degrees of abstraction from a perceived "real" object has much in common with what Korzybski (1933) called the *structural differential,* later called the *abstraction ladder* by Hayakawa (1941). We have omitted any suggestion of the "real" object of physics, which Korzybski considered essential.

[6] For a more detailed analysis of the misunderstandings which derive from stereotypes and other errors in perception, see Ichheiser (1949).

consumers, or citizens, or unionists, as abstractions. Much of this book seems to lead to the opposite conclusion. We are engaged in locating those psychological traits that are reasonably common to executives, others that characterize unionists, and so on. But if we want to work successfully with Joe Jones, we need to perceive accurately his individual traits. To some extent what we have identified in the foregoing pages is indeed perceptual distortion. The manager's stereotyped picture of a unionist may have little in common with Jones's personality as observed by others. A knowledge of perception, then, warns us of a source of error that makes a sizable contribution to industrial conflict.

*Resistance to change of perceptions.* The extent to which one resists any attempt to modify his perceptions of another person is sometimes surprising. Psychologists, in their work with children, have often noted cases in which the child has a decidedly "unrealistic" picture of his father and, even when factual evidence is pointed out, refuses to change this perception. Thus, a boy who describes his father as stingy and denying pleasures to the son will, in the next breath, mention expensive gifts of objects or cash from the father. When this is pointed out, the son typically argues that this was just an attempt to bribe him into being friendly, or that the gift was tiny compared to what should have been given, and so on.

We are concerned, in our present context, with more generalized perceptions. Executives get pictures of what the average worker is like—as the worker gets a picture of the typical executive. These perceptions likewise tend to resist change, and they get in the way of improvements in union-management relations; for example, if one side does objectively change its tactics, this change may be denied or distorted by those on the other side.

An interesting experiment by Haire and Grunes (1950) illustrates this point in an ingenious way. Students were given the following instructions: "The object of the test is to determine the extent to which people are capable of sizing up a person from just a few facts about him. Below is a brief description of a certain working-man. Describe in a paragraph what sort of person you think he is. Indicate where possible which item gave you your impression of him."

| *Form I* | *Form III* |
|---|---|
| works in a factory | works in a factory |
| reads a newspaper | reads a newspaper |
| goes to movies | goes to movies |
| average height | average height |
| cracks jokes | cracks jokes |
| intelligent | strong |
| strong | active |
| active | |

It will be noted that the lists of items are identical except that Form I includes the item "intelligent." The descriptions based on Form III were quite uniform. The worker was seen as "A typical American joe, likeable and well-liked, mildly sociable, healthy, happy, uncomplicated, and well-adjusted in a sort of earthy way." The addition of "intelligent," however, complicates the task of the subjects; they must fit this item into a picture which is not congruous with the idea of an intelligent man.[7] Haire and Grunes identify four kinds of responses made by their subjects in dealing with this incongruous element: (1) denial of the existence of the elements; "he's intelligent, but not too much so." (2) Reinterpreting the attributes so that the conflict vanishes; "he is intelligent, but doesn't possess enough initiative to rise above his group" or "probably never had a college education, or he would do a bigger and better job than the work in a factory." (3) Allowing the new element to make a real change in the perception, sometimes with reference to his personality, sometimes about his job. "Because of his intelligence I think he is a little more interesting than the average;" or "this person is perhaps a foreman at the factory where he works, because for this position he would have to be intelligent." (4) Recognition of the incongruity but failure to resolve it; "the traits seem to be conflicting . . . most factory workers I have heard about aren't too intelligent." Of the four types of response, 5 used the first, 14 the second, 22 the third, and 3 the fourth. Thus it is clear that about half the group either refused to accept the information provided or twisted it so that it fitted into their stereotyped picture of the factory worker.

As Ichheiser (1949) has stated, "Once the image of another person . . . is fixed in our minds, we tend either to overlook all factors in the other person which do not fit in with our preconceived scheme; or else, we misinterpret all unexpectedly emerging factors in order to preserve our preformed misconceptions." Perceptual constancy is a powerful tendency in human thinking. Apparently we resist, in a variety of ingenious ways, "real facts" which would compel us to change our ways of perceiving the people immediately around us.

Is this fact important? Obviously it is. It means that executives are not inclined to notice when union officers change from hostility to a cooperative attitude, and unionists fail to see that management has shifted to efforts to get along with the union. A new union officer looks just like his predecessor to the director of industrial relations; a new company man looks just the same as the old one to the union committee.

---

[7] Actually, different subjects responded to Form I and Form III. However, it seems reasonably certain that the subjects receiving Form I developed the picture sketched by those subjects using Form III, and then had to modify their responses to take account of the item "intelligent."

## Perception of Situations

The point has been developed that people, faced with a concrete situation, magnify certain cues, suppress others, and distort some aspects of the situation to fit their personal prejudices and attitudes. This phenomenon as regards executives and unionists can be well-illustrated by another example from the study of Akron by Alfred W. Jones (1941). The following story, which was used as a basis for eliciting responses from the persons interviewed, relates to an actual situation which had developed just prior to Jones's investigation:

> The B. F. Goodrich Co. in early 1938 asked the workers in its plant in Akron, Ohio, to accept a wage cut and a longer working week. The company maintained that if the workers refused, some departments would have to be moved away from Akron, involving the removal of some four or five thousand jobs. They held that only in this way would they compete with the other rubber companies which already had a smaller proportion of their operations in Akron, where a strong union exists and maintains high wages. Assume that the Goodrich Co. can stay in business and continue to pay the old wages. They will not be able to make much money, if any, and they will not be able to pay much in dividends, but they will at least not be driven into bankruptcy. Assume also that if they move out of Akron they will be able to hire workers cheaper, make more money and pay more dividends, at least at first.
>
> The workers at a meeting held by the union refused to accept the wage cut.
>
> The company has the next move. What would you think of its *action* if the *company* should move these jobs away from Akron? [8]

It will at once be observed that the story offers numerous cues which can be interpreted by the respondent in a manner to fit his point of view. One set of cues relates to the welfare of the company as an organization, competitive advantage, wage cuts, higher dividends, absence of a strong union, etc. On the other hand, there are also certain cues which can be built up into an opposite perception, particularly the loss of four or five thousand jobs as far as residents of Akron are concerned, the fact that the company will not go bankrupt, etc. Each story was scored on a basis from 0 to 4, according to how emphatically the person answered against the company proposal or in favor of it. In this particular case 18 top executives in Akron companies received an average score of 3.7; only 2 out of the 18 gave answers deviating in any way from an emphatic assertion of the company's right to move under the conditions stated. In contrast to

[8] Jones (1941), p. 359. Reprinted by permission of the author.

this, a group of 167 members of the United Rubber Workers, CIO, received an average score of 0.4. Only 9% of this group gave any support to the proposal that the company move, and 89% vigorously rejected the proposal.

The differences in perception of the situation can be suggested by the following quotations, the first from a company executive: "This is not a moral question, but a matter of sheer business. The company owes nothing to the worker or to the town; *its only obligation* is to make money for the stockholders. If the management considers morals in this case, the stockholders ought to vote for a change in management." In contrast to this view which focuses completely on one set of elements in the story, we have the following quotations from members of the CIO: "The company in any town should be compelled to stay *if a lot of their workers have given it their very best years of faithful service.*" And again: "I know they can't make this cheaper elsewhere. The efficiency of Akron labor can overcome lower wages in other places by putting out a better product and more production per hour." Note that the persons who disapprove of the proposal are actually adding information which was not given in the story. They are so strongly involved in the situation that they are failing to distinguish between their own personal involvement in the problem and the specific facts which they were asked to respond to by the investigator. This, of course, is a very common process in the perception of conflict situations. People do not limit themselves to the known facts but add to the perception elements of their own needs, pressures, and emotions. The conflict between the two ways of viewing the situation was aptly characterized by an average citizen in his comment, "Of course, they have a right to move, but what they owe their workers and the community is *more important.*"[9] Each of us weights the various cues to produce a perception that fits our own point of view.

*Perceptions of employer rules.* Since there are so many other differences in perception of social objects, it is not surprising that employees differ in the way in which they perceive rules established by the employer. Oman and Tomasson (1952) demonstrate that supervisors differ from salesclerks in their beliefs as to what store rules exist, as to the frequency of violations of these rules, and as to punishments which would be meted out if violations occurred. Salesclerks also varied among themselves; it was found that many were carefully obeying requirements which were not store rules at all. Some of these differences were found to be due to variations at the executive level, some supervisors being more strict than others. Punishments also varied considerably. The personality of the supervisor contributed to differences at the salesclerk level.

The counterpart of this problem on the executive side, one which is

[9] The quotations are from Jones (1941), pp. 359, 176, 256, and 46. (Italics are ours.) Reprinted by permission of the author.

especially painful for foremen, is clear knowledge of the union contract. The number of grievances based upon contract violations by foremen, which arise from pure ignorance of contract provisions, is incredibly large. Many companies have resorted to conferences, quiz games, prizes, and other methods to induce their foremen to read the contract carefully. Even so, it is likely that men will misperceive provisions of which they disapprove, just as workers and stewards often "drop out" of the contract limitations which they do not like. Selective observation, selective learning, and selective forgetting all join in producing a distorted notion of contract requirements which contributes materially to industrial conflict.

*Perceptual differences in a crisis situation.* The foregoing considerations with regard to differences in the perceived facts in particular situations may be clarified and amplified by a consideration of a concrete example. The quotations given below are from the operating superintendent of a small textile factory and the organizer of the union which set up a local in this particular mill in the late 1930's. [The quotations are from much longer passages, Hartmann and Newcomb (1940).] The descriptions were written at the request of a psychologist who was personally acquainted with both these individuals and were prepared very shortly after the events in question. It will be instructive to note how very differently the two individuals perceive the same conflict situation.

For the sake of brevity we have eliminated rather long introductory statements from each of these accounts. For concrete context it should be understood that the mill had been non-union until quite recently, that the workers in the mill had submitted a petition for a pay increase which had been rejected and had then joined the union in a body. The union promptly demanded a pay increase, and the incident reflected in the following passages was the showdown on whether a strike would be called to enforce this union demand. Let us now consider first the comments of the superintendent with regard to this particular situation.

> The one thing that we seemed not to agree on was the method of *protecting ourselves from excessive union demands.* Some of the executives thought that we should bargain. It was reasoned that the phrase "collective bargaining" determined our course of action. It had never been my policy to bargain. *This seemed weak.* It is always wiser to know what you want to pay and then stand pat even though you lose the object of discussion. The next time either the buyer or the seller will change his price, and the purchaser has not paid too much nor has the seller lost on the sale. The same with help and jobs. *Every job has its correct value.* No job is worth more than it can earn for an employer when the best workman in the world is doing it at his best. *So often workers will be doing work that has no stabilized worth.* One man may get too much and others may get too little. When this is true, from experience I have found that the man who will be persuaded to pay too much for a job will always compensate by browbeating others to

work for less than they are worth. If a man is worth more money his employer should be proud to raise him before he expects it. On the other hand, it is shameful to raise an employee beyond his worth in order to keep him from getting a better job somewhere else. Because of this background, it seemed childish to fight for something lower than we were willing to pay and lower than we knew would be acceptable.

The union did extract a 5% increase. While we were doubtful about our ability to pay an increase, we were not brave enough to withstand a demonstration. When our help started one, we agreed to the 5% raise *just as the small school boy, when threatened with abuse, passes over his apple to the playground bully.*[10]

The superintendent has in many ways indicated his way of perceiving the industrial situation. First, we may note that he automatically assumes that any union demands are going to be "excessive." A 5 per cent wage increase plus one week's vacation with pay hardly seems to be an excessive demand, although, of course, this particular controversy arose at a time when American industry had not fully recovered from the depression. Secondly, we note the characterization of the union as if it were comparable to a "playground bully." This likewise reflects a particular way of perceiving the union. Third, we observe contradictions within the superintendent's account as he attempts to rationalize his policy. First he says, "It has never been my policy to bargain." Then he says, "The next time either the buyer or the seller will change his price," which obviously is a matter of bargaining. Furthermore, it is difficult to see how wages could be set by a process of give and take unless either the employer or the union were willing to change demands. Presumably the superintendent means that he wants all the changing to be done by the union. Similarly, the employer says, "Every job has its correct value," and then again he says, "So often workers will be doing work that has no stabilized worth." This contradiction suggests that the superintendent does not want to accept any criterion of the value of a job except his own personal judgment. Finally we observe the superintendent saying, "It seemed childish to fight for something lower than we were willing to pay and lower than we knew would be acceptable," and yet this is exactly what the superintendent did. He put up a rather lengthy struggle against granting the 5 per cent wage increase but eventually he did so. By his own criterion, therefore, he had behaved in a childish way.

The importance of these ways of perceiving the union, the proposed pay increase, the bargaining relationship between union and company, and the nature of the tactics to be employed lies, of course, in the implications they have for industrial relations policy. As long as a company executive has these particular ways of perceiving conflict situations involving the

---

[10] Hartmann and Newcomb (1940), pp. 170–172. Reprinted by permission of the Society for the Psychological Study of Social Issues. Italics are ours.

workers and the union, a certain amount of difficulty is almost inevitable. However, it is pleasant to be able to record that over a period of time this particular superintendent did modify his way of looking at the situation and came to perceive the union and the workers in a more favorable manner.

Union officials likewise perceive industrial conflict situations in terms of their own attitudes and values. The following passage is a description of this same crisis situation as written by the union organizer:

Another conference, at which this proposal (5% wage increase plus one week's vacation with pay) was made to the management, proved futile. The management's statement that further discussion of the question was useless was reported back to another union meeting. Their answer was brief: "We demand our terms within 48 hours; otherwise we give you authority to call a strike." The management's reply to this report was that they had given their last word. One of the officials, *shaky and white-faced*, was already busying himself *going through the motions* of preparing for a shutdown. But there was something *almost mystical in the way the workers saw through this bluff*. All the gestures which the management intended to impress us with their uncompromising readiness for war only had the effect of *intensifying the strike fever* "We know the old man; he can't bluff us," they said.

I asked for an hour in which to contact my regional office before taking final action. Actually, I did not consult the regional director, because *I felt perfectly sure of my ground.* . . . At the end of the hour I returned, met the negotiating committee and told them that we had no choice but to use the authority given us by the workers to call a strike. They left to lead out the workers in their several departments. Before their footsteps had died away, the official with whom we had conferred that morning rushed in, demanding to know what was going on. *I told him, as briefly and as calmly as I could. In a high state of emotion, he rushed out,* returning with another official, who also demanded what had happened. "Mr. Nelson, you are not being fair. Why didn't you notify me of this?" I replied that I had sat there for some time that morning, conferring with the only available representative of the management, and did not know that the management did not consider itself adequately represented. The second official then told me that the first one had taken an unauthorized position, and asked me if I would give him a few more minutes. . . . One of the officials rushed into the mill with the news that we were to confer again, and the workers agreed to return to their posts for a brief period, though it was too late to catch up with the workers of one of the skilled departments. When the news reached them, outside, they announced that they would not return until the management agreed to their terms.

In the half-hour that followed the management made an attempt to restrict the 5% increase to certain classes of employees, but this offer was refused. Finally the vice-president said, "We agree to your terms." [11]

[11] *Ibid.* Reprinted by permission of the Society for the Psychological Study of Social Issues. Italics are ours.

If we look at the italicized items in this quotation, we find many indications of perceptual distortions on the part of the organizer. For example, he says, "The official, *shaky and white-faced,* was already busying himself, *going through the motions* of preparing for a shutdown." Obviously the organizer had no way of knowing that the official was just "going through the motions." This is a way of protecting his own point of view against the possibility of a strike which might have been disastrous to this newly organized union. It is also relatively unlikely that the official was shaky and white-faced. These are perceptual devices in which people commonly indulge to reassure themselves as to the correctness of their position and the fact that they are not making a mistake in strategy. Had the company actually closed down operations and broken the union, it is likely that the organizer would have remembered this official as looking red-faced and aggressive, rather than white-faced and shaky.

Similarly, we note the gross exaggeration of the value of the union side of the case. "There was something *almost mystical* in the way the workers saw through this bluff." The attribution of superiority to one's own side and the denial of such perceptual acuity to the opponent is a widely used device for maintaining group solidarity and confidence in the rightness of one's position. The organizer asserts his own calmness and confidence, while representing management as confused and emotional. Such observations as these make it possible to underline our previous assertion that aspects of a situation which seem particularly important to one person are not even observed by another.

The foregoing examples help us to understand the common difficulty in resolving various kinds of grievances involving foreman-worker interactions. The account of what happened (as given by the worker) may seem to have little or no relationship to the account given by the foreman. Under these circumstances it may require a trained investigator to dig into the situation and find out, in a reasonably impartial way, what did occur. Many grievances, of course, are not significant enough to justify such detailed analysis. What is clear, however, is that we must avoid the tendency to jump to conclusions on the basis of a report given by one side of a particular controversy.

This observation has particular implications, furthermore, for evaluating newspaper reports, radio accounts, and similar communications with regard to controversial issues, strike incidents, etc. The kind of situation perceived (or at least described) by a reporter for the Chicago Tribune, for example, may have little in common with that observed by a reporter for the New York Times. In these cases crucial effects on public opinion result from particular kinds of distorted perceptions which are communicated through sources of public information.

**Perception of Issues**

In a sense, perceptions of persons and of situations make up the real total of information available to workers, executives, and union leaders in their day-to-day relationships. However, there is another way of approaching this problem of perception which has proved useful, and which should be given some consideration here. We have chosen to call this *perception of issues,* the individual's attitude as reflected in his broad generalizations about unions and management or in the positions he adopts when interviewed or presented with statements for endorsement. As we shall show, the attitudes so revealed are significantly related to the other, more direct kinds of perceptions.

A good example of an investigation indicative of differences in the perception of general issues regarding union-management relations can be found in the data gathered in the course of the Illini City investigation. In this case a series of ten opinion statements were presented to a substantial sample of the general public, union members, and management executives in Illini City. For the sake of simplicity we are reporting here only the percentage of the three groups which agreed with each of these statements. Table 5 shows that marked differences, particularly between union members and company executives, occur with regard to these opinions.

In purely quantitative terms, the largest difference between union and management opinion is with regard to the proposition "most labor trouble is caused by outside union organizers rather than by workers discontented with their wages and working conditions." Fifty-four per cent of the management group agreed with this statement, whereas only 14 per cent of the union members accepted it. This points to a very important difference in perception of real factory situations. The executive, for reasons which we have indicated in preceding pages, is disposed to perceive working conditions as good and, more specifically, as the best he can provide under the present circumstances. The workers, on the other hand, are likely to perceive working conditions in a much less favorable light. The executive is likely to perceive the outside union organizer as a troublemaker, an agitator who comes in and stirs up his otherwise happy and contented employees, whereas the workers themselves perceive the outside organizer as their agent who can stand up to the employer and talk to him without fear of being discharged. Thus the two sets of perceptions lead to totally different kinds of conclusions and behavior on the part of these two groups.

Other interesting differences between the two groups are, of course, with regard to management prerogatives, "Most unions interfere with an employer's right to run his business as he pleases," and with regard to the general benefits from unions which have accrued to workers and to the American people in general. It is significant, on the other hand, that virtual unanimity has been reached on certain points. For example, there are few agreements with "an employer is justified in firing an employee who joins a union." In this case, a sample of management taken in the early 1930's would undoubtedly have led to a sharply different response.

**TABLE 5. Union, Management, and Public Approval of Issues regarding Unions***

| | *Percentage Agreeing* | | |
| --- | --- | --- | --- |
| | *Public* | *Union* | *Management* |
| All strikes should be outlawed | 32 | 9 | 24 |
| Unions have been very helpful in raising the standards of living of the average worker | 85 | 97 | 82 |
| Most unions interfere with an employer's right to run his business as he pleases | 48 | 21 | 59 |
| Most strikes are caused by unfair tactics of employers | 28 | 29 | 7 |
| Unions have benefited the majority of the American people in the long run | 76 | 97 | 70 |
| An employer is justified in firing an employee who joins a union | 11 | 4 | 5 |
| Most labor trouble is caused by outside union organizers rather than by discontent of workers with their wages and working conditions | 43 | 14 | 54 |
| The right to strike is as justified as the right to own property | 53 | 74 | 46 |
| Very few workers are intelligent enough to deserve any voice in how industry is run | 26 | 22 | 32 |
| Management usually has to be forced by unions to raise wages or to improve working conditions | 49 | 58 | 34 |

* *Labor-Management Relations in Illini City*, Vol. 1, pp. 115–116. Reprinted by permission of the Institute of Labor and Industrial Relations.

*Trends in the perception of issues.* Since 1944, the Opinion Research Corporation has been maintaining a *Public Opinion Index for Industry*, which periodically questions a scientifically selected cross section of the public and of special groups such as union members, on significant issues. Charts prepared from their data on two issues are shown in Figs. 2 and 3.

The first chart shows trends on the question, "Do you think most companies try to pay higher wages as they prosper, or do you think they have to be forced to pay higher wages?" It is apparent that all three groups, public, manual workers, and union members, see management as becoming somewhat less stubborn.[12] The decline from 1944, however, is slight;

[12] Note that the Illini City sample of public and union seems a little kinder to management (Table 5). Various indices suggest that less hostility was manifested between management and unions there than in the larger industrial centers

about half of the public and three-fourths of union members still believe that management has to be forced to pay higher wages.

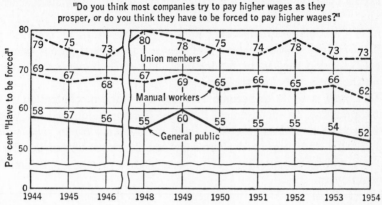

Figure 2. Trends of opinion regarding management's willingness to raise wages. (Data are from *Public Opinion Index for Industry,* used by permission of Opinion Research Corporation.)

The second chart reveals an even more clear-cut decline in perception of management hostility to unions. Only about 60% of unionists now see the companies as trying to break unions, and, for the general public, the

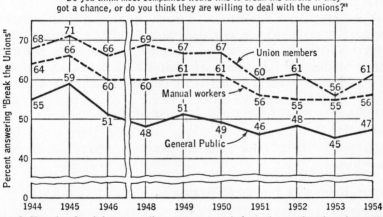

Figure 3. Trends of opinion regarding management's intention to break unions. (Data are from *Public Opinion Index for Industry,* used by permission of Opinion Research Corporation.)

figure is consistently below 50%. These trends seem to augur favorably for future union-management relations.

*Worker effort.* Perhaps a more touchy issue at present is that of worker productivity, or more precisely, of worker effort. In a 1947 survey[13] the

---

[13] Productivity and the Factory Worker, May, 1947.

*Public Opinion Index for Industry* reported on top executives' views of worker productivity, and also gave facts regarding the views of factory workers. The executives were heavily inclined toward the view that worker productivity had declined since the war, 66% agreeing with this view, and most of them blamed bad worker attitude for this drop. By contrast, only 28% of factory workers agreed that people had worked harder before the war (24% said they work harder now, and 40% thought the pace was about the same as before the war).

This issue is likely to become an important bone of contention as economic pressures on management increase. If competition and price resistance become important, executives will undoubtedly try to raise productivity levels. Both improved technology and increased output of effort by workers will be sought. Each of these is likely to evoke opposition from the employees. . . .

Under these conditions management raises the slogan, "a fair day's work"; and the union spokesman replies, "We'll give a fair day's work for a fair day's pay." Both of these clichés sound fine, but neither has operational meaning. The various kinds of perceptual distortions we have enumerated will cause the executive to perceive "a fair day's work" as a larger amount than will be perceived by workers and union leaders. The "facts" are not the same to the two sides of this controversy.

It is the failure to recognize this essential disagreement as to the "facts" which gives rise to such naive remarks as, "Determination of a 'fair day's work' is a problem of measurement through engineering and biometrics."[14] Technical procedures have long since been developed for measuring the physical work done, or the energy expended by the worker. But there is nothing in these devices which says that 1000 foot-pounds of work, or 2000 calories of energy, or any other physical measure, is a *fair* day's work. The judgment of what is fair inevitably implies a personal frame of reference. The frame of reference differs from person to person and from time to time. What workers would have considered "a fair day's work" in the early Lancashire textile mills would now be rejected on all sides as outrageous.

## Factors Related to Perceived Differences

We have sketchily reviewed, in this . . . chapter, some of the more important facts regarding differences in social perception. The data prove beyond any doubt that people differ in the way in which they perceive other persons, concrete situations, and abstract aspects of situations in the form of issues. Furthermore, these differences are systematic in the sense that executives and union members consistently show discrepancies in their way

[14] Joseph M. Juran. Management techniques for stimulating productivity. (p. 77, footnote) In: L. R. Tripp, Ed., *Industrial Productivity*. Industrial Relations Research Association, 1951.

of looking at objects which are significantly related to the work situation.

These perceptual differences can characteristically be reduced to three patterns: (1) the magnification of certain cues—stressing one aspect of a situation; (2) ignoring other cues—denying the presence, relevance, or importance of cues leading to disliked interpretations; and (3) distorting the significance of cues—asserting that this cue does not in fact have the meaning commonly attached to it. These three processes generally operate at the same time, and it is only by special techniques or by selected observations that we can separate them. Such a separation is not especially important for our purposes, and it will therefore be ignored. We are concerned with the over-all perception, which is usually based on a mixture of realistic evaluation of cues and distortions of the kinds suggested. The problem we must now consider is this: how do these differences arise?

A preliminary answer has, of course, been given early in this chapter. Haire and Morrison (1954) found that children of upper and lower income families show sharp differences in their perceptions of persons pictured in roles as strikers, workers, etc. We infer, then, that these children learned their percepts from their parents. But this is only a postponement of the answer. How did this divergence according to income arise in the first place?

The evidence indicates that differences in perception of social objects are related to a variety of factors. To what extent these correlated variables are casual influences cannot always be stated confidently. In some cases it is quite clear that the external condition is an independent variable which has influenced the person to develop a certain way of perceiving. In other cases people may join together, in groups, for example, because they see things similarly. . . .

For the present we are concerned with identifying some apparently important factors which are associated with differences in perception relevant to union-management problems. On the basis of the evidence to date, the following merit consideration: occupation and income status; group memberships; education and mass communications influences; personal experiences; and personal motives.

*Occupation and income.* [Previously] we developed an analysis of perception based on the principle of probability. The generalization was offered that cues are received from the external environment, and that each cue comes to be evaluated in terms of the probability that it will be accompanied by other cues. Thus the visual outline of a chair carries a high probability of certain contact and pressure cues, muscular relaxation, and so on. In social perception, emphasis was laid upon the extent to which the person observed has cue value for satisfaction or deprivation, goal achievement or frustration.[15] If we wish to understand the differences in

---

[15] A more rigorous analysis of these processes is offered [elsewhere].

perception of members of unions and of management, we must search for differences at this basic level.

Occupational differences in the perception of issues relevant to union-management problems can readily be demonstrated. Figure 4 shows how

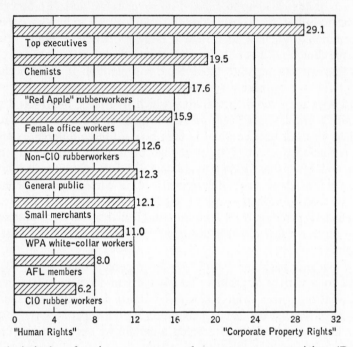

Figure 4. Attitudes of various groups toward corporate property rights. (Data are from Jones, 1941, p. 378, used by permission of Alfred W. Jones.)

various occupational groups in the city of Akron differed in their responses to Jones's interview situations. The chart confirms the fairly obvious expectation that top executives see most of these situations in a manner favorable to corporate property rights, whereas AFL and CIO members find little to value on the side of corporate property.

Similar differences, based upon the *Public Opinion Index for Industry* data (February 1954) are shown in Figs. 5 and 6. Figure 5 indicates the proportion of each occupational category holding that "companies have to be forced" to pay higher wages. Similarly, Figure 6 shows the proportions taking the position that "most companies would like to break the unions." In both charts, the proprietor-manager group is lowest, i.e., they see the company in a favorable light, whereas workers as a group, and especially union members, have the least favorable perception of the average company.

How does perceptual theory help us to understand the occurrence of these consistent and highly significant differences between groups? It seems

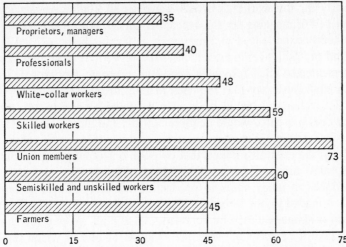

Figure 5. Opinions of various groups on management's willingness to raise wages. (Data are from *Public Opinion Index for Industry,* used by permission of Opinion Research Corporation.)

likely that each occupation involves certain regularities in contacts with situations, and in consequences following from contact with a specific object, person, or organization. For example, it is in the nature of the institution that top executives act in the name of the corporation whereas the rank-and-file production worker never takes action in the name of the

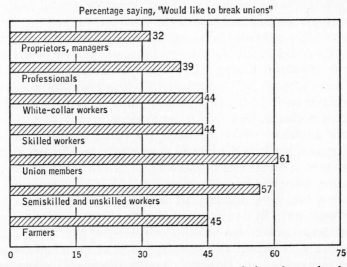

Figure 6. Opinions of various groups on management's intention to break unions. (Data are from *Public Opinion Index for Industry,* used by permission of Opinion Research Corporation.)

corporation. The idea that a corporation has certain "rights" therefore has little reality for the worker, whereas it evokes all kinds of associated experiences full of meaning for the executive. On the other hand, the worker has frequently experienced incidents such as layoffs, being evicted from a house, and protesting company actions—the very kinds of situations which Jones presented to elicit responses opposing corporate property rights. We can thus confidently say that the cues relating to one set of percepts had high reality value and would be heavily weighted by one group, whereas the other cues presented would be more realistic and more heavily weighted for the other group.

Similarly, the executive knows that corporations often give pay increases without union pressure (at least to white-collar workers and managers, and no doubt in many cases to production workers). Thus, to him, the situation is loaded in one direction. The production worker, who has probably been told many times by foremen, "That's all we pay for this job; you can take it or leave it," sees the situation as one in which the overwhelming preponderance of probabilities favors the view that management gives raises only when forced.

The needs of executives and workers in these situations also tend to load the probabilities in favor of divergent percepts. The executive sees in the situations presented by Jones a variety of frustrations and threats to his freedom of action (sit-down strikes, interference with corporate decisions, and the like). The probable consequences of such events are personal losses (in self-expression, and perhaps even in income). To the worker, the situations posed offer greater freedom of action and greater need satisfaction in the solutions which limit corporate property rights.

We have concentrated on occupational differences at the extremes. The charts show that professionals (lawyers, doctors, chemists) and white-collar workers tend to fall between executives and production workers in their views of industrial issues. The professional man, of course, is likely to have more contacts with the managerial group than with workers. He may therefore be inclined to adopt their views on such problems. The white-collar worker is, as a rule, in much closer contact with executives than is the production worker. However, the work situation of the white-collar employee is not so different as these results would seem to imply. Many students of white-collar employees hold that these differences in attitude reflect differences in status striving: the white-collar group not only are closer to "the boss" but they are more actively trying to rise in the socioeconomic scale. By accepting and repeating the views of top management, the clerical worker may unconsciously be trying both to be perceived as a member of the management group and to be accepted into this group.

*Direct economic effects.* How one perceives unions will presumably be in part a consequence of their immediate economic benefits or injury to oneself. Union members generally believe that the union has gained certain advantages for them which would not otherwise have been forthcoming (cf. Figure 5). Executives assert that they oppose the union because it will injure the company (and, implicitly, themselves) economically.

In a public opinion survey conducted as part of the Illini City study, we inserted a question designed to indicate whether a perception of such benefits or injuries was related to attitude toward unions. Table 6 shows

**TABLE 6. Attitudes to Unions as Related to Effect on Standard of Living**

"HAVE YOU FOUND THAT THE COMING OF UNIONS TO ILLINI CITY HAS AFFECTED YOUR STANDARD OF LIVING? IF SO, IN WHAT WAY?"

| *Public only:* Average Attitude to Unions* | *Response* | *Public* | *Union* | *Management* |
|---|---|---|---|---|
| | | *Percentage Responding* | | |
| 33.8 | Hasn't affected it | 41 | 20 | 53 |
| 38.8 | Raised it | 42 | 67 | 30 |
| 29.0 | Divided answer (helped some, hurt some) | 4 | 5 | 3 |
| 25.5 | Lowered it | 9 | 3 | 6 |

* For the attitude data, $p < .01$.

a consistent and meaningful relationship between answers to the question and the average attitude score (based on the ten items shown in Table 5). Those who say that the coming of unions has raised their standard of living are most favorable to unions (38.8), and those who believe the unions have lowered their living standard are most opposed (25.5). Among union members, 67 per cent believe that unions have helped them, whereas among managers only 30 per cent give this response (a very small proportion, it should be noted, say that unions injured them).

There is nothing surprising about these findings. They do, nevertheless, lend substance to the point already made, that uniformities in the perception of social objects arise as people perceive that a given object has beneficial or harmful effects. This is an elementary point which sometimes seems to be lost in the argument that most union members belong only because they are forced into joining. A man may be "forced" to take a job in a particular company (e.g., in a one-industry town) but, if he gets adequate benefits from this relationship, he will come to perceive the company favorably. The same is true, apparently, with regard to unions.

*Importance of group membership.* The foregoing kinds of explanation are decidedly incomplete and inadequate to the data. It will be noted, for example, in Fig. 4 that the "Red Apple" rubber workers (members of a company union) score 17.6 on favoring corporate property rights, whereas unaffiliated rubber workers score 12.6 and CIO rubber workers score 6.2. (Needless to say, these differences are statistically highly significant.) Clearly, then, any explanation of such generalized perceptual patterns which relies exclusively on objective experiences related to job and income status cannot be acceptable. Since there was a relatively high degree of homogeneity within each of these groups of rubber workers, and marked differences between groups, the evidence indicates that membership in certain groups influences one's way of perceiving relevant situations.

To some extent group membership operates through defining situations. As we note[d], many stimuli are ambiguous; adults must define for a child whether worms are edible or inedible, whether a swastika flag is to be hated or revered, and so on. Our standards of beauty in women, tastefulness in food, acceptability of economic and political institutions, all derive from the group in which we grow up.

Groups also modify the perceptions of new members. Numerous experiments on group discussion (cf. Festinger, 1950a; Lawson, 1954) show that minority members will shift their views of issues to agree with a majority.* It may be assumed that longer-enduring group membership, in which friendship and approval are more important to the individual, could modify attitudes even more. For example, a young man may join the executive staff of a large corporation. At that time he may feel that unions have their good points, that an FEPC law would be socially desirable, and that an excess-profits tax is both economically and politically sound. All around him, however, he will hear contrary views expressed. If he states his opinions, he will encounter signs of disbelief or disapproval. He will probably be told that such views are contrary to company policy. Implicitly if not explicitly, he will be told that promotion within the company is unlikely if he clings to these heresies. Soon he will change his verbalizations, and before long he will change his perceptions. He will explain apologetically that in the past he had not seen all the complexities of these problems.

The same process occurs when a new member joins a labor union. He will find a "universal" opinion about the company, the boss, working conditions, and so on, expressed by his companions—the phenomenon we have called "attitudinal climate." To the extent that he knows nothing of these conditions, he will tend to accept the definitions offered him; and, if he disagrees, he will be subjected to the social pressures described above, until he conforms or is ejected from the group. Thus, in some instances group membership will only strengthen and sharpen the influences normally to be expected in a given occupation. In other cases, especially where the occupational group is heterogeneous, people will cluster around leaders and will develop a shared frame of reference, a common way of viewing critical situations. This is true in the case of the rubber workers mentioned above; it would also apply to splits such as those between liberal and conservative Republicans and many other factional groupings not based on economic conditions.

REFERENCE GROUPS. Uniformities in social perception are not developed solely by membership in a group. A man may aspire to membership in a group (usually, of higher status than his present situation) and may adopt their views as a device for becoming more acceptable to them. Graduate students in psychology take on the views of the professors, and medical school students quickly learn not to endorse socialized medical plans. White-collar workers, aspiring to membership in the executive group, sometimes lean over backwards to see only the company's side of any controversy.

Since the United States is a country in which upward social and economic mobility is highly valued and believed to be fairly easy of attainment, conflict between a person's membership group and his reference group is not uncommon. In European cultures, where the average worker perceives no reasonable probability that he will ever move into a different socioeconomic stratum, this conflict seems to be less common. Such differences have a great deal to do with the failure of "labor party" proposals in this country.

Unions do not represent groups of high socioeconomic status, whereas management does. Thus it is not surprising to find that on many issues, "public" opinion resembles the views of management, though the economic status of the "public" is closer to the level of the union member. In Table 5, for example, the "public" sample is closer to management than to union opinion on 7 of the ten issues presented.[16] In two cases (outlawing strikes, firing an employee who joins a union) the public goes to a "management" position more extreme than the actual management sample. In no case does this occur for a pro-union statement.

*Ego-involvement.* We have already noted . . . that the individual's self or ego becomes a highly valued object of perception, and that associated groups may become ego-involved (part of the perceived ego). It can readily be deduced that any reference group with which the individual becomes ego-involved will have a powerful effect upon the perception of issues relevant to that group.

This is interestingly demonstrated in the study of pro-union and anti-union students and their perceptions of executives and workers (Table 3). These college men checked adjectives to describe the "typical" executive and factory worker; later, they checked from the same list of adjectives to describe themselves. In the anti-union group, self-description correlated with description of the executive quite well (.63) but, in the pro-union group, the corresponding figure was only .35. When self-description was correlated with that for factory worker, the figure for the pro-union group

---

[16] It is not implied that this is the sole cause of such opinion trends. Control of the mass media of communication by management may be more important. However, the higher status of management is unquestionably a significant variable here.

was .87, whereas it was only .68 in the anti-union group. Thus it appears that these students are already ego-involved, to some extent at least, with their respective reference groups, executives and factory workers.[17]

The stubborn resistance of social attitudes to change with experience depends in part upon perceptual constancy and in part upon ego involvement. Few of us willingly admit our own defects; similarly, we resist any admission that our views on social issues are erroneous. Thus it seems likely that any attitude will be protected to the extent that it has become ego-involved.

*Education and mass communications.* Uniformities of perception are also significantly increased by similarity in educational level. The various public opinion agencies have consistently revealed differences between persons of grade school, high school, and college training. Obviously these are contaminated to some extent by the occupational and income influences already described; thus, men of higher education tend to adopt a pro-business point of view, in part because they are more likely to be in managerial or professional positions than in production worker roles. By comparing groups of differing educational level within an occupation or income group, however, it has been possible to show that education is an independent determinant of opinion.

The public schools, as well as the colleges, have been partial in the union-management controversy particularly by omission. Even after 1950, few mentions of labor unions occurred in the typical high school curriculum, whereas courses in how to be a good business man have been common for a long time. Courses in how to suppress your individuality so that you will be more acceptable to an employer (this is often known as "improving" your personality!) have also been introduced into the schools.

The public school policies have, of course, been controlled mainly through school boards. These have normally been dominated by business and professional people. It is only since 1935 that unions have been successful in placing any of their members on such boards in significant numbers. With this increase in union-oriented board membership has come an increase in discussion of labor unions as a legitimate part of the high school program.

Boards of trustees of colleges and universities are still composed almost exclusively of business and professional people, high in the income scale. It is noteworthy that during the hectic period of union organization, 1935–1939, many college professors were discharged for pro-union sympathies and activities, whereas there is no evidence to indicate that any such pres-

----

[17] An important question is raised by these data because of the population studied. Why would any sizeable group of men from well-to-do families, students at an expensive college, adopt the worker reference group? Evidence of a somewhat impressionistic character indicated that it occurred because of conflict with the father, usually a successful executive; hence, rejection of executives as a reference group.

sure was ever exercised against a man with anti-union views. Thus college students tended to be exposed to influences somewhat loaded in the anti-union direction. This situation, fortunately, has been improved, although there are still occasional indications of its persistence.[18]

*Mass communications.* Pictures of unions and companies, of the corporation executive and the union leader, are communicated by newspaper stores, radio commentators, magazines, television, and so on. Since each of these enterprises is itself a business, often involving large amounts of capital, it is not surprising that the top executives see things as do top executives in most other corporations. And, since newspaper reporters, radio commentators, and others wish to receive salary increases and promotions, it is not surprising that some pro-management or anti-union bias creeps into their communications. Thus, for example, Sussman (1945) tallied 212 items on radio news programs between September and November, 1944. Of these, 21 per cent were simple factual items, 39 per cent were quoted opinions, and 40 per cent were the commentator's own opinions. As to favorableness of these items to unions, the tally was as follows:

| | |
|---|---|
| Favorable | 13.2% |
| Neutral | 8.4% |
| Balanced (both sides) | 15.0% |
| Unfavorable | 63.2% |

As Sussman remarks, "The presentation of labor in such an unfavorable way in the radio news can have two effects. It can foster an anti-labor psychology in the listening audience; and it can create a feeling in the ranks of labor that they simply do not have a chance for a fair hearing in the channels of mass communication."[19]

*Stereotypes in reporting.* Every act of reporting, like every act of perceiving, is a selective process. No reporter, no matter how conscientious, can report all the details of a controversial situation. What he will select and report will be a function, first of all, of his own frame of reference, and secondly, of official editorial policy. He will report chiefly those aspects which will please his superiors; and, if he reports material of which the editor disapproves, it will be censored before publication.

Some mass media even have detectable patterns of loading the communication with words evocative of stereotyped pictures in the minds of the readers. A widely quoted example of this is a study by Sargent (1939). He examined stories reporting presumably identical events, in the *New*

---

[18] For example, there have been allegations that professors were attacked as communists or "fellow travelers" when they were in fact only sympathetic to organized labor. Because "communist" is such an ambiguous term today, it is fairly easy for any anti-union person to perceive a pro-union professor as a communist.

[19] Sussman (1945), p. 214.

*York Times* and the *Chicago Tribune.* Some of the terms used in the *Times,* and the parallel terms from the *Tribune,* are shown in Table 7. For

**TABLE 7. Terms Used by the** *Chicago Tribune* **and by the** *New York Times* **in Reference to the Same Event***

| New York Times | Emotional Value | | Chicago Tribune |
| | *Times* | *Tribune* | |
| --- | --- | --- | --- |
| Progressive | +92 | −53 | Radical |
| Senate investigation | +57 | −38 | Government witch hunting† |
| Regulation | +32 | −53 | Regimentation |
| Maritime leader | +10 | −68 | Communist CIO leader |
| Labor organizer | +12 | −63 | Labor agitator |
| Home relief | +27 | −35 | The dole |
| Crop control | −02 | −55 | Farm dictatorship |
| Non-strikers | +08 | +60 | Loyal workers |
| Investigator | +23 | −22 | Inquisitor† |
| CIO chieftain | −33 | −72 | CIO dictator |
| Picketing | −50 | −55 | Mass picketing |

* Modified from Sargent (1939).

† These terms are not employed in stories relating to Senate investigations of which *Tribune* policy approves, such as those of Senator McCarthy of Wisconsin.

each word, its "emotional value" (composite judgments by 60 college students, who were not informed as to the source of the words) is also given. It is fairly clear that any reader of the *Tribune* got a picture of union labor and of the Roosevelt administration which would only re- motely resemble the picture communicated by the *Times;* and certainly the attitudes evoked by the *Tribune* would be decidedly anti-union. As a private organization the *Tribune* certainly has the right to do this; it must be presumed, nevertheless, that this policy has contributed its share to the misunderstandings between unions and companies in the Middle West.

To attempt to build a shared frame of reference among their members, labor leaders have started newspapers and even bought radio time. Within the period since World War II, attempts have begun to use the mass media to reach the public and build up more favorable pictures of unions. We have at present little indication as to the effectiveness of these efforts.

It is for the sake of building and maintaining a shared frame of refer- ence that union leaders keep alive the stories of mistreatment of workers by employers. The Homestead strike, the Ludlow massacre, Memorial Day, 1937, and other incidents are reviewed in mass meetings and in union communications material so that new union members will be able to see things as the "old-timers" in the movement see them. Management has not followed such tactics for a considerable time, but the hostility and suspicion generated will not be allowed to die out for years to come. Similarly, of course, executives judge unions more by what they used to be than by what they are today.

*Personal experiences.* Our discussion to this point has aimed at bringing explicitly into focus some of the factors which have made for group uniformities in perception. We have been concerned with the fact that large groups of people, who may be classified by occupation, or income, or education, or group affiliation, show relatively high agreement within the group, and marked disagreement with other groups, as regards important issues in union-management relations. Such influences as common work experiences, common environmental stimulation, common satisfactions and frustrations, similar educational experiences, and comparable mass communication exposures were identified as contributing to these intragroup uniformities and intergroup divergences.

But no group is completely homogeneous, and unanimous group decisions, whether in Russia or in the United States, are likely to be looked upon with suspicion. Each person encounters a variety of personal experiences which make his perception unique and different from others in his group. This means that occasionally a business man perceives unions as a help rather than a barrier; and some union leaders express opinions which would sound perfectly at home in an N.A.M. convention. In other words, we must not stress group uniformity to the point of losing sight of the unique individual. Our modern society tends to exalt the status of the group, and we often feel that individuals are too small to have social significance; but group policies are made by individuals, and new groups organize around leaders who offer new solutions for old frustrations. . . .

Individual variations in perception of industrial issues may arise in many ways; indeed, the fact that they are unique makes it difficult to classify them. However, we wish to call attention here to accidents of the individual biography—occurrences which do not fit into any of the group categories already indicated.

A young man, for example, may be building a home for his family. It is already costing more than he expected, and now he runs into an AFL building trades rule which costs him $20 for no reason at all that he can see (such as hiring an ironworker to lay the strip of iron over the opening of a fireplace). This may lead to hostility to unions in general (perceptual generalization). Or he may, on his first job, encounter a very severe and arbitrary foreman who is constantly scolding him for inefficient work but who gives him no training. This may generalize to all employers, even though such behavior is relatively unusual.

*Personal motives.* Every perception is potentially related to the satisfaction of motives. Physical objects are evaluated in terms of their value as food, sources of comfort or injury, etc. Other persons are perceived as threats, competitors, persons to be helped or to help us, to be loved or hated, approached or avoided.

Many of these perceptions are subject to motivational distortion. . . . Wishful thinking often causes us to "see" things as we would like them to be. The traveler lost in the desert sees water in the mirage; the lovesick youth sees evidence that his inamorata loves him, even though she is calmly indifferent to his presence. Paranoid individuals find evidence on all sides that they are persecuted.

Most of the uniformities in perception which are relevant to union-management conflicts are due to the broader causes sketched in the preceding pages: work situations, mass communications, and so on. However, it is fairly clear that some leaders of both unions and companies have a personal involvement in the controversy which goes beyond the kinds of influences described. Since these are both complex and relatively rare, we need not spend too much time on them. The following are examples:

1. A high school youth studied by Mandel Sherman (1935) was violently anti-communist. He perceived the communists as an immediate danger to the safety of the United States and to him personally. Detailed psychological study revealed that an unwise aunt had given the boy the impression that his birth had been the cause of his father's desertion. He felt that he had "broken up his mother's home." When he learned about "communists breaking up the home," he apparently solved his tremendous guilt feeling by projecting it onto the communists. Although labor unions are not specifically mentioned in Sherman's account, it is quite likely that this youth would also vigorously oppose unions, especially if he were in a role where this was appropriate.

2. A college man who took one of our tests for attitudes toward unions made an extremely favorable score. Upon closer check it was learned that he was also active in a student socialist group on campus. Detailed interviews revealed that his father was a wealthy man, president of a company manufacturing household appliances. The boy expressed violent hostility to his father, on the grounds—very possibly unrealistic—that his father was arbitrary and domineering. It became evident that his enthusiasm for labor and radical causes was an expression of this resentment. He rebelled against all authority—at the college, in government, and in industry. (Had he been in a union, he would probably have rebelled against union discipline too.)

Such instances, as we have stated, are relatively rare. It seems likely that they may account for certain instances of leadership, as in the case of a factory where management is vigorously anti-union. Only someone who is driven by these irrational inner needs may be willing to take the punishment involved in organizing a union. Later, such leaders may cause trouble for the union, and excuses must be devised for easing them out of important positions. . . . Management, too, has in some instances found it necessary to remove executives who were so irrationally hostile to unions that they could not accept normal collective bargaining relationships.

## Summary

Behavior is governed, not by "objective" facts, but by facts as perceived by individuals. In some respects it is true that each of us lives in his own private universe—each of us sees the world in a manner slightly different from anyone else. These differences give rise to the unique individual personality.

Social psychology, however, is interested in the behavior of groups. This depends upon uniformities in perception: members of one group see the facts in one way, members of an opposing group see them differently. The data show that executives and workers differ sharply as to the "facts" regarding many industrial situations and issues. Executives and union officers likewise differ; and it may be that in some instances there will be differences between workers and union officers.

Uniformities in perception arise from a variety of influences common to members of a group. These may include a common objective situation (tasks, problems, tools) with which the individual must come to terms; common education and communications, company and union newspapers, stories handed down by word of mouth, and the like; and common personal environments, in the form of other persons who accept a certain view of the facts and punish members of the group who do not accept this common frame of reference. In addition, unique personal experiences and personal motives may cause an individual to adopt a certain view of industry, even though he is not a member of the group concerned.

As we have progressed with this analysis, it has become clear that motivation is inextricably linked with perception. A variety of motives are involved in group membership, for example, as well as in the unique personal experiences mentioned. It is therefore important that we turn now to a consideration of the psychology of motivation, and find what light it throws upon these problems of group conflict.

## References

Festinger, Leon, et al.: 1950a. *Theory and Experiment in Social Communication.* Ann Arbor, Mich.: Institute for Social Research, 1950.

Haire, Mason: 1955. Role-perceptions in labor-management relations: an experimental approach. *Industr. Lab. Rel. Rev.,* **8** (2), 204–216.

Haire, Mason, and Willa Freeman Grunes: 1950. Perceptual defenses: processes protecting an organized perception of another personality. *Hum. Relat.,* **3** (4), 403–412.

Haire, Mason, and Florence Morrison: 1954. School children's perceptions of labor and management. (Unpublished m.s., University of California.)

Hartmann, George W., and Theodore Newcomb (eds.): 1940. *Industrial Conflict: A Psychological Interpretation.* New York: Cordon Co.

Hayakawa, S. I.: 1941. *Language in Action.* New York: Harcourt, Brace & Co.

Ichheiser, Gustav: 1949. Misunderstandings in human relations. *Amer. J. Sociol.*, **55**, 2 (2), 1–70.

Jones, Alfred W.: 1941. *Life, Liberty, and Property.* Philadelphia: J. B. Lippincott Co.

Korzybski, Alfred: 1933. *Science and Sanity.* Lancaster, Pa.: International Non-Aristotelian Library Publishing Co.

Lawson, Edwin D.: 1954. Attitude shift as related to palmar sweating in group discussion. Ph.D. thesis. University of Illinois.

Oman, Milton, and Richard F. Tomasson: 1952. Disparities in visualizing social norms. *Social Forces*, **30**, 328–333.

Sargent, S. Stansfeld: 1939. Emotional stereotypes in the *Chicago Tribune*. *Sociometry*, **2** (2), 69–75.

Sherman, Mandel: 1935. *Mental Hygiene and Education.* New York: Longmans, Green & Co.

Stagner, R.: 1948*b*. Psychological aspects of industrial conflict. I. Perception. *Pers. Psychol.*, **1**, 131–144.

Stagner, R.: 1950*a*. Psychological aspects of industrial conflict. II. Motivation. *Pers. Psychol.*, **3**, 1–16.

Stagner, R.: 1950*b*. Stereotypes of workers and executives among college men. *J. abnorm. soc. Psychol.*, **45**, 743–748.

Sussman, Leila W.: 1945. Labor in the radio news. *Journalism Quart.*, **22**, 207–214.

# *Level of Aspiration**

*Ross Stagner*

Since we are concerned with behavior of man in western culture, and specifically in industry in the United States, we must accept competitive impulses toward prestige and power as major considerations. We live in a society in which approximately 85 per cent of fathers say that they expect their sons to outdo their own achievements. The so-called "American dream" is that of the poor boy who rises to be a big business man, a famous inventor, or a great political leader. Children are urged to set goals above their present performance, and then work energetically to

* From chap. 4, "Motivation: Principles," *The Psychology of Industrial Conflict*, John Wiley & Sons, Inc., New York, 1956, pp. 105–109. Reprinted by permission of the publisher.

reach these goals. Such a projected or hoped-for future performance is known as the individual's *level of aspiration.*

The importance of aspirations is to be found chiefly in relation to social goals such as prestige and power. However, we can observe somewhat analogous phenomena at the simple biogenic level. Adolph (1941), for example, demonstrated that dogs when thirsty have a kind of quantitative notion of just how much water is needed to restore this particular equilibrium. Dogs were prepared with an esophageal fistula, so that water drunk fell out into a container and did not reach the stomach. (Needed water was later supplied through this same fistula.) The animals were then kept without water for specified numbers of hours, and the amount drunk was measured. Each animal took in almost exactly the amount required to restore his water balance, even though the liquid was not reaching his stomach and he therefore could not have any sensory feedback to inform him that he "had enough."

This kind of very simple, quantitative estimate of "how much I want" is quickly replaced by a socially determined craving for "something better" or higher in the scale of social values. Any house which provides shelter, warmth, and privacy might be said to satisfy biogenic needs. But people want houses which are attractive, in the right neighborhoods, and so on. We have already noted . . . that housing type is a fairly good predictor of attitude toward labor unions. The significant determinant, of

**TABLE 1. Economic Level of Aspiration as a Function of Current Status***

| Present Income Level | Occupation | Average Estimate† |
|---|---|---|
| Negroes | Farm labor | $1,000–1,499 |
| Poor | Miscellaneous labor | 1,500–1,999 |
| | Unemployed | |
| Lower middle | Factory labor | 2,000–2,499 |
| | Retired | |
| | Farm owners | |
| | White collar | 2,500–2,999 |
| | Housekeepers | |
| | Students | |
| | Miscellaneous | |
| | Proprietors | 3,000–3,499 |
| | | 3,500–4,499 |
| Upper middle | | 4,500–4,999 |
| | Professional | 5,000–5,499 |
| | Executives | |
| | | 5,500–5,999 |
| Prosperous | | 10,000–14,999 |

* *Fortune*, February, 1940. Reprinted by permission of the publisher. See also Centers and Cantril (1946).

† The lowest income that would satisfy a majority of persons in each group named.

course, is income; as people get more money, they acquire more expensive housing, and also take on more conservative views on economic affairs.

Goal setting in an industrial society characteristically takes the form of an orientation toward a certain status or position just a short distance "up" from the individual's present achievement. Just as the private must become a corporal before he can become a sergeant, so there is a ladder to success in the business world. Even in terms of income, the typical American sets his sights just a short distance from his present earnings (cf. Table 1) rather than "hitching his wagon to a star."

We can take this process into the laboratory and study it experimentally. The basic technique is to have the subject attempt some task (dart throwing, card sorting, solving anagrams, etc.). After he is given his score on the first trial, he is asked to estimate "how well you will do next time." It is assumed that the person setting a goal is revealing a generalized characteristic of his personality; that he gives some indication of how he sets goals in everyday life.

The results of a large number of investigations (cf. Gould, 1939) indicate that the typical American youth's response to the instructions given is to set a goal just a little in advance of his performance on the first trial. This is considered to indicate a realistic kind of motivation, in that the goal is reasonably probable of achievement. However, in any group there will be some who will set absurdly high aspirations—perhaps indicative of motivation so strong that it overpowers perception, distorting the situation so that it seems possible to attain so distant a goal. Conversely, there will generally be some youngsters who will actually estimate performance on the next trial *below* past performance; this is thought to reflect a need to avoid failure as being more powerful than the need to increase status (see, e.g., Gruen, 1945).

*Effect of success and failure.* One of the main reasons for taking a problem like this into the laboratory is to make possible manipulations of determining factors which cannot be controlled in everyday life. It was hypothesized that a series of successes would build up an expectancy of continued success, leading to higher aspirations; whereas a series of failures would lead to expectancy of failure, and hence to lowered aspiration. This has been confirmed by many investigators (cf. Gebhard, 1948). Since it is easy to manipulate scores on the performance task, the subject can be given successes and failures in any predetermined manner.

The results are in high agreement for almost all such studies. Success, with very few exceptions, leads to a rise in the reported aspiration. Failure, by contrast, leads to lowered aspirations, although these rarely become negative (predicting poorer performance than last time) except with maladjusted personalities. Failing individuals reduce their effort and attempt to get away from the experimental situation.

*Group norms.* The level of aspiration experiment provides an excellent opportunity for studying the role of perception in the process of energy mobilization. Suppose we introduce a reference group into the above design by telling our subject that he has just made a score higher than the average college senior. If the subject looks up to and respects college seniors, he gets a vigorous boost from such a report, and his level of aspiration increases. On the other hand, if the group is one upon which the subject looks with contempt, he does not perceive surpassing their record as anything important, and his level of aspiration does not change. By contrast, the report that he is below the norm of some "inferior" group usually releases a burst of energy and higher aspiration.

Another interesting problem arises where a dominance-submission relationship exists between the reference group utilized and the person being tested. Preston and Bayton (1941) presented Negro college students with an experiment of the type described. As a reference group, they introduced alleged Negro college norms, and found their subjects trying harder in order to surpass these figures. But when they introduced alleged White college norms, the effect was much less. They interpreted this as reluctance to set up, even in fantasy, a situation involving direct competition with the dominant White group. This may have some connection with the reluctance of workers to admit that they have any desire for managerial status. To be "aiming at" the boss's job might make him hostile, and he might retaliate in some unpleasant way. It may seem much safer to set only a low level of aspiration and say nothing of higher ambitions. Public opinion polls repeatedly indicate that about 20 per cent of manual workers think they have a chance to become a foreman. When the question is put in terms of wish to achieve this status, the percentage goes up to about 30, whereas, if the American competitive pattern were effective, the per cent aspiring to foreman's jobs ought to be at least 50, if not more. (However, Lipset and Bendix (1952) report that about 67 per cent of manual workers express a desire for a small business of their own. In this case. aspiring to the boss's job is not involved.)

*Income aspirations.* Because the dollar provides a convenient unit, comparisons of present income with aspiration level are fairly easy to make. However, if a person were asked, "how large an income would you like to have?" he might be tempted to use the sky as the limit. If asked how much he expects next year, he will be cramped by immediate realistic possibilities. A *Fortune* poll in 1940 seems to have struck a happy compromise between these two unsatisfactory approaches by asking, "What do you really think would be a perfectly satisfactory income for you?" Under these circumstances people gave an aspiration level which apparently reflected both motivation and present achievement. As Table 1 shows, aspiration rises steadily with present economic status—almost everyone tested felt that he could be content with "just a little more." The discrepancy between present status and aspiration ranges from a few hundred dollars at the bottom of the economic scale to a few thousand at the top. One might readily suspect that this is the familiar Weber law in perception, that the amount of increase in a stimulus which will be necessary for it to "look bigger" is a constant fraction of the starting stimulus.

*Importance.* The implications of these studies on aspiration level, as regards industrial motivation, are no doubt obvious. Let us note just a few. First of all, children and adolescents who have had an accumulation of "success" experiences have higher aspirations than those who have more "failure" experiences. Thus, children from upper class families, with advantages in home background, intelligence, education, etc., characteristically have higher aspirations than those from poorer homes. Even during school years some youngsters learn "not to hope for too much," whereas others are encouraged to try for higher accomplishments.

Stubbins (1950) has shown that a similar relationship holds for returning veterans. Those with higher vocational aspirations were more intelligent and better-educated. They had reached higher pay levels in the service, held postwar jobs of higher status, and had better jobs than their brothers. In other words, their higher aspirations could be considered as reflecting the successes that they have already experienced.

If we keep these observations in mind, we shall not be surprised at some of the dynamic differences observed in everyday industrial situations. The executive, with higher present attainment and a history of successes, will set his sights higher and strive for increasingly more income, power, and status. The worker, with a low income and probably some failures to look back upon, tends to hold his aspirations down and to strive for only fairly short-run, reasonably attainable goals. Such differences play an important part in producing the lack of mutual understanding between these groups, especially, the inability of many executives to understand the cautious, security-seeking behavior of the typical worker or union group.

### References

Adolph, E. F.: 1941. The internal environment and behavior: water content. *Amer. J. Psychiat.*, **97**, 1365–1373.

Centers, Richard, and Hadley Cantril: 1946. Income satisfaction and income aspiration. *J. abnorm. soc. Psychol.*, **41**, 64–69

Gebhard, Mildred E.: 1948. Effect of success and failure upon the attractiveness of activities as function of experience, expectation and need. *J. exp. Psychol.*, **38**, 371–388.

Gould, Rosalind: 1939. An experimental analysis of "level of aspiration." *Genet. Psychol. Monogr.*, **21**, 3–115.

Gruen, E. W.: 1945. Level of aspiration in relation to personality factors in adolescents. *Child Developm.*, **16**, 181–188.

Lipset, Seymour M., and Reinhard Bendix: 1952. Social mobility and occupational career patterns. *Amer. J. Sociol.*, **57**, 366–374, 494–504.

Preston, M. G., and J. A. Bayton: 1941. Differential effect of a social variable upon three levels of aspiration. *J. exp. Psychol., 29,* 351–369.

Stubbins, Joseph: 1950. Relationship between level of vocational aspiration and certain personal data. *Genet. Psychol. Monogr., 41,* 327–408.

# The Motivation of the Underprivileged Worker[*]

*Allison Davis*

If you ask Mr. Turner, the boss, why Phil Moore is a hard and skillful worker, Mr. Turner will answer, "Because Phil comes from good stock." If you ask the boss why Henry Spears, the Okie "immigrant," does poor work, he will reply, "Because he comes from bad stock."

When the boss says "bad stock," he usually means "bad" heredity, *i.e.,* innate inferiority. The boss, himself, has not learned that cultural environment and training are the chief reasons for the differences between the work habits of Phil and Henry. Like the average teacher or parent, the boss believes almost religiously that "blood will tell." His exaggerated belief in the scope of heredity will be made even clearer if the visitor asks him what he thinks of Negro, or Mexican, or Italian-American workers.

"Not much," he says cynically. "But after all, what can you expect of them? They all come from lousy stock, you know."

The boss is raising, in the natural fashion in which it daily recurs, the problem of heredity and environment. In his case the burden of proof rests upon this honest and no doubt well-intentioned man. For, until workers from little Italy, Okietown, and the Black Belt can be given environments similar to those from the "respectable" neighborhoods (that is to say, *equal chances* for developing their innate abilities), such workers cannot be judged scientifically, with regard to their comparative *hereditary* abilities. As Professor Jennings, the outstanding American geneticist, said in the *Biological Basis of Human Nature* more than a decade ago,

. . . bad living conditions often produce the same kind of results that bad genes do. Persons may become idle and worthless, insane, criminal, or

[*] From William F. Whyte, *Industry and Society,* McGraw-Hill Book Company, Inc., New York, 1946, chap. V, pp. 84–106. Reprinted by permission of the publisher.

tuberculous either through bad genes or through bad living conditions, or through a combination of both. So long as living conditions are bad we do not know what ills are due to bad genes.

The attitudes toward underprivileged groups, which I have described, are shared by most persons who have to train and supervise underprivileged workers in service and industry. As a rule, management has the attitudes, habits, and values of middle-class groups. Their attitudes toward, and standards for, work behavior are a part of their middle-class indoctrination. They are the result of the powerful motivation and the long processes of training, extending from early childhood through adult life, which the individual born into either the middle class or into the skilled working class receives in his family, in his social cliques, and in his social class.

The foreman's and the administrator's emphasis upon punctuality, responsibility, and the desire and drive to get ahead in life is part of their culture. They have *learned* all these traits. Not one of them has been inherited—through the foreman's or the vice-president's family, or his race, or his nationality. All these traits of the good worker, or good administrator, have had to be learned through training, family pressure, work opportunities, and through encouragement and reward on the job. To the foreman or the vice-president these traits and habits of his seem so integral to his behavior, so much a part of him, that he regards these virtues as entirely his *individual* achievement.

In fact, however, they are a part of his cultural environment, of the way of life, of the social environment with its social and economic rewards and punishments, in which he has been reared. They are part of a vast, overpowering group of social influences, of determinants of behavior, which have produced his own behavior and that of his family as well. His work habits, his ambition, his values, as well as the very disgust that he feels toward the habits of underprivileged workers, are chiefly the result of the family training, of the community standards and of the culture—the system of habits and attitudes—which he has learned.

Just as the members of the higher skilled working class and of management act in response to their culture, to their system of social and economic rewards, so do the underprivileged workers act in accord with their culture. The habits of "shiftlessness," "irresponsibility," lack of "ambition," absenteeism, and of quitting the job, which management usually regards as a result of the "innate" perversity of underprivileged white and Negro workers, are in fact *normal responses* that the worker has learned from his physical and social environment. These habits constitute a system of behavior and attitudes which are realistic and rational in *that environment* in which the individual of the slums has lived and in which he has been trained.

My purpose is to trace the origin of these work habits in the social and economic system of the communities in which the underprivileged worker has to live. I shall be specific and concrete. I shall not take time to indulge in sociological abstractions, but I shall try to deal with realities, with the habits of sleeping, of medical care, of joint communal living, of housing, of tavern and night-club life, of gambling, of sex, and of the social competition that the underprivileged worker learns from his slum environment.

The evidence will be taken from several studies of white and Negro working-class groups in the Chicago area, studies recently carried out by my colleagues and myself in The University of Chicago. They include evidence on 600 families, both white and Negro. Of these, 200 were middle class, and 400 were working class. In addition, the studies include intensive observation and interviewing of selected white and Negro working-class families in their homes, where they were observed several times a week throughout nearly a year. The intensive studies of Pearl, a white underprivileged worker, of Ruth, an even more underprivileged Negro worker, and of Clark, a lower class white worker, will be used to illustrate the findings of the statistical data on 600 families.

Pearl Elno, the white female worker, was born of old native stock in southern Indiana, the daughter of a coal miner. At the beginning of the great depression, her father came to Chicago to seek work, bringing his family. Here Pearl met Jim Elno, a young machinist, the son of a Polish laborer and a charwoman, and, like both his parents, extremely devoted to liquor in general and to schnapps in particular. At eighteen, Pearl married Jim Elno. Both youngsters were ambitious and smart. They were both good workers, anxious to buy a home of their own, and to get ahead in the world. Jim studied hard at his trade; and he bought a derby hat and a pair of spats—just to show his friends that he was a man who took himself seriously and intended to get somewhere in the world.

His young wife was always more practical and conscientious than Jim, and forced him to leave his mother's, set up a home of his own, and to work for goals more enduring than a derby and spats. All her efforts for a house of their own and for a decent standard of living were defeated, however, during the next 10 years, by the rapidly increasing number of their children. Jim was a Catholic, and Pearl was a very fertile woman. In 9 years, she bore seven children.

Unable to secure work during most of the thirties, and presented annually with a new baby by Pearl, Jim began to drink heavily. Any father who has had to come home to five, or six, or seven small children, and has had to try to live and sleep with them, crowded into a three-room flat, will sympathize with Jim, I imagine. During the depression, four children were born to the Elnos. They had to flee to steadily smaller and poorer apartments, and the children were reduced to half-starvation rations, which kept them sorely undernourished and chronically ill. Unemployment and their hopelessly large family wore away the determination and the morale of the parents, especially of Jim. They separated twice, and Jim deserted once but returned. He was arrested two or three times for panhandling while drunk. He beat his wife several times, when he was drunk. The Elnos and their seven little children were on the rocks and seemed headed for the bottom.

But Pearl still had her own parental family. Her father and mother, and her sisters, together with their husbands, formed a closely organized and loyal clan, which repeatedly rescued her and her seven children. The sisters took them in, when Jim was violently drunk, or when they were evicted for inability to pay the rent. They bought the children clothes, and helped feed them. Pearl's mother, still able to hold a job at sixty, borrowed money on her home to lend to Jim, when he was employed by the Works Progress Administration. She came up from southern Indiana repeatedly to care for the children, so that Pearl could work as a waitress, and as a machine operator, to help feed the children while Jim was unemployed. One of Pearl's sisters opened a tavern recently and employed the mother, who in turn helped Pearl's family. Both the sisters and mother thus have continued to help Pearl.

The history of the Elno family illustrates in part how the organization, and the typical experiences of the white working-class family, control the motivation of the lower class worker. First, its size is typical of working-class families, and it is an important factor in their motivation. We found the average number of children in white *middle-class* families in Chicago to be only 2.2. In white working-class families, the average number of children is 3.3. This is a tremendous difference; along with the lower incomes that go with these much larger families, it changes the nature of family relationships in the working class, the methods of child training, the standards of nutrition, of cleanliness, of education, and of sex behavior. The actual daily pressure of 5 to 10 hungry stomachs to fill, backs to clothe, and feet to cover forces the working-class parent to reduce his ambitions to this level of subsistence; to lower his sights as far as long-term planning and studying for better jobs and for finer skills are concerned; to narrow, limit, and shorten his goals with regard to the care, nutrition, education, and careers of his children.

This terrible pressure for physical survival means that the *child* in the average working-class family usually does not learn the "ambition," the drive for high skills, and for educational achievement that the middle-class child learns in his family. The working-class individual usually does not learn to respond to these strong incentives and to seek these difficult goals, because they have been submerged in his family life by the daily battle for food, shelter, and for the preservation of the family. In this sense, ambition and the drive to attain the higher skills are a kind of luxury. They require a minimum *physical security;* only when one knows where his next week's or next month's food and shelter will come from, can he and his children afford to go in for the long-term education and training, the endless search for opportunities, and the tedious apple polishing that the attainment of higher skills and occupational status requires.

Secondly, the Elno family's history illustrates the deprivations, the shocks of fortune, the drain of illness and malnutrition, as well as the social and psychological disorganization, that reduce the efficiency of the under-privileged worker. A society that pens families into this kind of physical and social environment actually cripples both the ability and the work motivation of its workers. If there is one thing that modern psychology makes clear, it is this: men cannot be motivated successfully to work hard, or to learn well, simply by putting the screws upon them. The starvation theory of wages may or may not have been abandoned in actual industrial practice, but it is certain that other theories of social punishment, and of economic pressure, other theories that men will work hard and well *only* when they are *compelled* to by economic or legal necessity are still very popular. But the analysis of our system of economic and social pres-tige, as well as the findings of psychologists, make it clear to any realist that men work hard and learn well only when they have been trained to work for increasing rewards.

To improve the underprivileged worker's performance, one must help him to learn *to want* and to be anxious to attain higher social goals for himself and his children. All one can get out of methods of starvation conditions in wages, or of threat and intimidations, is more of the same inferior work and more concealed resistance, as in the case of a man whipping a poorly trained mule. The problem of changing the work habits and motivation of people who come out of families like the Elnos' is far more complex than mere supervision and pressure. It is a problem of changing the goals, the ambitions, and the level of cultural and occupational aspiration of the underprivileged worker.

This change in his cultural motivation cannot be attained by getting him into the starvation box. For, as the Elno family illustrates, the average working-class family is a large economic unit, a clan of kin. They can de-pend upon *each other* for shelter and food in time of unemployment, or of reduced income, or of prolonged absenteeism, or when they simply quit the job. In this working-class culture, one may usually fall back upon his brothers, or sisters, or aunts, or nieces, or cousins for a bed and meals, in a way that middle-class people cannot. The middle-class adult person is ashamed to go to his relations or friends for food and shelter. "Respectabil-ity" prohibits such dependence. To avoid this embarrassing loss of "face," he will work harder, take more punishment of a mental and emotional kind on the job, and cling to the job more desperately than will the average lower class, underprivileged worker.

That is to say, the masses of working-class people, like the Elnos, can-not be frightened and forced into better work habits, simply through having the economic squeeze put on them, or through being threatened constantly with firing. Such threats do not intimidate them, as they do the middle-class clerk or schoolteacher, because the underprivileged worker is thoroughly accustomed to those conditions of life that middle-class people call "insecurity." Most important of all, he knows he can always "bunk in" with a relative, usually on his mother's side of the family, and he is certain that an extra plate will be filled for him and his, so long as his relatives have food. The harder the economic *noose* is drawn, the tighter the *protective* circle of the average working-class family is drawn. Thus economic intimidation is much less effective than with white-collar employees. Since most working-class people do not get the rewards of social and economic prestige in our society, they do not fear the loss of the job or the attendant loss of respectability in their communities nearly so deeply as do the white-collar workers.

One other example of this pattern of *group* economic help and solidarity should be included, before leaving the matter. In Negro families in the rural South, and generally in those which have migrated from the farms to Chicago, the circle of relations who help each other economically is even larger than in the average white working-class family. There are more children in these families; the average number of children in 300 Negro working-class families in the Chicago area is 4.9. The bonds of kinship, the closeness of feeling, and the number of mutual duties are also greater in the Negro working-class family, owing to its recent experiences as an integrated economic and social unit on the plantations.

There are also many broken white and Negro working-class families, of course. But these individuals, whose families have been scattered by death, disease, desertion, and immigration, are also provided with a communal group, which helps them in times of economic difficulty and illness. The life of Ruth, a Negro factory worker in Chicago, who was born in Mississippi, illustrates this point. Ruth's parents were unskilled workers, far below the Elnos in both education and opportunity for occupational training—at the very bottom of the economic hierarchy. The family came to Chicago in 1935. For a long time, they were unable to secure either work or relief. Both then, and later when the father was given a job as an unskilled laborer on WPA, Ruth, her four sisters and brother, and her parents lived in the large cellar of an old tenement on the South Side. The cellar had been divided into nine rooms, one for each family. There was no kitchen, only an open corner at the back of the cellar, with a small gas stove and a faucet. The nine families shared this corner as their "kitchen." But they had an organized, cooperative system of sharing, which went far beyond the joint use of the so-called "kitchen." They shared their small stocks of furniture, their bedclothes, and their wearing apparel. Most important of all, they shared their food and even their money. When a family was both out of work and off relief, the other families put their money and food into a communal "pot," in which the destitute family shared. This is a hard system to beat, for those who believe in the effectiveness of economic intimidation in making good workers. When workers can survive at this level, and still have the social support and approval of their friends, they can scarcely be threatened or starved into better work habits. They will have to be led, by the offering of concrete rewards of better job opportunities and wages and better treatment and status on the job.

In 1942, when Ruth was fifteen, her parents separated, and her mother remarried. This marriage forced Ruth out of her home at once. The next year she had to leave school and go to work. After she had to leave her home, but before she could obtain her working papers, Ruth lived, slept, and ate with the families of her working-class school friends. Often she had little sleep because there was no bed available, but she had a roof over her and at least a meal a day. She also shared the clothes of her school friends.

This communal, group living has persisted, even though Ruth has now been working for more than two years. She is a hard and powerful worker, who carries a man's load. Foremen pick her for heavy, driving jobs that not 1 woman out of 10 can stand. She likes to do this heavy work thoroughly, but she also finds it exhausting. Moreover, she is still very young, and she has no responsibilities except herself. Therefore, she stays off the job rather frequently and sometimes misses several days in succession. She can continue this habit, because she still has her group of friends, her large social clique, who are really her "adopted" family and who will give her shelter and food and lend her clothes whenever they have them. Therefore, Ruth disappears from the job even when she has *no* money. Keeping her broke, by paying her only every two weeks or every three weeks, will not keep her on the job. She can always "bunk in" with her group of friends. This is a typical experience of underprivileged workers, both male and female, and both in the South and in the North. Groups of people, who have *no families,* live together, share food, money, clothes, and beds, and also share their work; for example, trading their ironing for another person's washing or cleaning.

It scarcely needs to be emphasized that this is a way of life that is demoralizing to the individual's habits of work. It is not realized generally, however, that the problem of increasing the efficiency of the underprivileged worker always involves two major kinds of difficulties that must be attacked. First his cultural goals must somehow be raised; his ceiling of aspiration for education, for respectability, for skills, and for better training of his children must become high enough to motivate him to work harder. Such efforts to change their cultural habits and their social status are the driving force behind those relatively few workers who do rise above the slum environments that I have been describing. Because this problem of motivating the lower class worker to strive hard for more respectable and complex ways of life is the more difficult problem, it will be considered last here.

The other, more immediate, more tangible task for our society in improving the efficiency of the labor supply is that of improving the underprivileged worker's standard of living. Workers who live under the conditions that I have described suffer heavy penalties in loss of sleep, malnutrition, and disease, which in turn greatly reduce their efficiency. Worst of all, from the point of view of those who wish to change these poor work habits, the slum dwellers become accustomed and "adjusted" to their crippling standards of living. Like people in every class, every culture, they learn to regard their environment and their living habits as decent and satisfying. This is the circle that our society must break, in order *to increase the consciousness of economic needs among the masses of workers,* and thus lead to fuller production and better labor.

The miserable housing and recurrent homelessness of the underprivileged workers are the most costly of all drains upon his efficiency. A study of working-class Negroes in Chicago in 1944–1945 revealed that most of them had less than five hours' sleep per night. Children and adults must sleep three to five in a bed. Beds are usually filled day and night in Chicago's slums, as workers await their turn to sleep. The density of the population on the Negro South Side is the second highest in the United States.

Ruth sleeps in a kitchenette apartment rented by a mother with eight children. Ruth shares a bed with five other adolescents and children, sleeping crosswise the bed. She counts it a windfall when there are only three in the bed, and she may sleep lengthwise. A record of her hours of sleep was kept last winter, for two periods of two weeks each, one in November and one in January. She was in bed an average of 4½ hours out of each 24. During these 10 working days, she was absent 4. Her work was extremely heavy, so heavy that she was given a half hour's rest by the plant for each hour on the job. Without more sleep, she said, she could not stand the work even five days a week. She has been trying since Christmas to find a room to rent. Last fall she tried to find a kitchenette apartment, so that she could marry, but, as anyone who knows the South Side's residential "lock-in" understands, she had no chance.

Similar conditions prevail among white workers in many parts of the city, of course. In one large area restricted to whites on the South Side, the great majority of *families with children* live in single rooms, or in kitchenette apartments. No matter whether the people in these modern, urban ratholes in which human children and their parents must live are white or Negro the social and economic results are the same. The children are forced out into the streets, day and night; they are "movie children" or completely vagrant children. Life cannot be lived as a family group in these packed rooms; it has to be lived on the streets, in the motion-picture theaters, the taverns, the bars, and the night clubs. Under such unimaginable living conditions, all the effort, training, and money, which in the case of the middle-class worker goes into his home, is blocked and diverted to sex, recreation, and gambling. How can a worker be motivated to work to furnish or to improve his home, when he cannot get an apartment, or even a bed to sleep in? The most basic goal, the most powerful organizing control in our society, or in any Western society, is the establishment and maintenance of a living place and a home. A society, such as ours, that deprives great masses of the workers of this primary goal, deprives them thereby of the prime incentive, the most insistent drive for steady, determined work habits. In addition, it directly reduces their efficiency on the job by the steady drain of exposure, lack of sleep, and the diseases, such as tuberculosis, which are related to overcrowding.

The physical disabilities of underprivileged workers in Chicago are far more extensive than the favorite publicity concerning their lack of orange juice and milk, and the occasional ratbites, would suggest. Unemployment and inadequate income resulting in chronic malnutrition decrease both their physical resistance and their working efficiency. A series of recent scientific studies of the children of underprivileged workers, as contrasted with children of middle-class parents have revealed that the vitamin and chemical levels in the blood of working-class children are greatly below those of middle-class children and are seriously deficient. A study of the bone structure of children in two such groups, by means of X ray, revealed that these nutritional and other environmental deprivations of working-class people leave their marks upon the very bones, themselves. In Chicago, the rates of infection and death from tuberculosis are far higher among underprivileged working-class groups, both white and Negro, than among middle-class groups, as revealed by a survey made at the University of Illinois. At the same time, hospital and medical care is far more limited and is critically limited for Negroes.

For the employer, the most important consideration here is that the underprivileged worker becomes accustomed to these conditions; he learns to accept poor habits of nutrition and medical care and to accept physical impairment as a natural part of his life. Ruth, for instance, eats only one meal a day, even when doing heavy labor. She has never been to a physician, or an optician, or an ophthalmologist. Yet she is so nearsighted that she has to be within six inches of a newspaper or clock to read them; she is partly deaf from an early childhood accident, and she lived with a tubercular father for several years. But like Pearl, the white underprivileged worker, whose stamina is sufficient only for periods of a few weeks on a job, Ruth regards her physical impairment as "natural." She has not had the money nor the training requisite to secure good medical attention and to learn good health habits. Thus, both cultural attitudes toward nutrition and medical care, as well as severe limitations in housing and hospital facilities work together to reduce the efficiency of such workers. These social and economic drains accustom them to accept high absenteeism and chronic physical impairment as normal aspects of their work adjustment.

Education, as the underprivileged worker experiences it, likewise differs from the education of middle-class persons. It differs in its length, in its content, and in its value as a social and economic tool. In the Chicago area, the average number of grades completed by white *working-class* mothers is 8.6, whereas white middle-class mothers have completed an average of 14.2. White working-class fathers have finished the eighth (8.3) grade, on the average; by contrast, middle-class white fathers have completed an average of 16 grades. Among Negroes, the average for working-class parents is even lower, but is rapidly overtaking that for white workingmen.

On the whole, the Negro worker of the past generation in Chicago—that is, those who are grandparents now—was better educated than the white worker. Whereas 22.9 per cent of our sample of white working-class women in that generation had no schooling at all, only 11.1 per cent of the Negro working-class women had none. The proportion of both white and Negro working-class women who had finished grammar school was the same, 22 per cent. Among the working-class men of this older generation, the Negroes were nearly equal to the whites in years of schooling. Today, the Negro lower class workingman is practically on a par with the white worker with regard to grades completed in school. For example, if we consider those who have spent some time in high school, the proportion is higher among Negroes (34.8 per cent as compared with 32.7 per cent). For instance, in our *middle-class* Chicago sample, both white and Negro middle-class women had completed an average of 14 years in school. Negro middle-class men had completed 14.3 years, and white middle-class men 16.1 years. In the generation born since the First World War, moreover, Negroes have greatly increased their average level of schooling. In another decade, the Negro working class in the Chicago area probably will have a higher average grade attainment than the white working class. Their great handicap even now, in the fifteen to twenty year age group is the lack of opportunities for apprenticeship, from which they are barred generally by both management and unions.

Among the present adult generations of underprivileged workers, white or Negro, however, education has had little effect upon work habits. Nor does it "take" very successfully with the slum child of any color.

Whereas, for the skilled worker and the office person both their drive to work steadily and their interest in developing their skills are powerfully stimulated by their training in school, for the average underprivileged worker, on the other hand, our schools are unrealistic in their methods and in their attempts at motivation. Furthermore, the schools are staffed by highly protected middle-class persons, whose goals and whose economic opportunities are quite different from those of the families and children of the lower class. To the underprivileged adolescent, the words and the goals of his teacher—those words and goals to which middle-class adolescents react with respect and hard striving—mean very little. For the words of the teacher are not connected with the *acts of training in his home,* with the actual rewards in school, or with actual steps in moving toward a career, which alone can make the words effective in motivating him to learn good school habits. Thus our educational system, which next to the family is the most effective agency in teaching good work habits to middle-class people, is largely ineffective and unrealistic with underprivileged groups. Education fails to motivate such workers because our schools and our society both lack *real rewards* to offer underprivileged groups. Neither lower class children nor adults will work hard in school or on the job just to please the teacher or boss. They are not going to learn to be ambitious, to be conscientious, and to study hard, as if school and work were a fine character-building game, which one plays just for the sake of playing. They can see, indeed, that those who work hard at school usually have families that *already* have the occupations, homes, and social acceptance that the school holds up as the rewards of education. The underprivileged workers can see also that the chance of their getting enough education to make their attainment of these rewards in the future at all probable is very slight. Since they can win the rewards of prestige and social acceptance in their own slum groups without much education, they do not take very seriously the motivation taught by the schools.

The impact upon the underprivileged worker of the physical and cultural environment that I have been describing is represented by the case of Clark, a twenty-four-year-old white man, who was intensively studied by an interviewer in the department of education. In 1939 and 1940, Clark was living in basement rooms, bunking in with friends. As conditions became too crowded even for that level of society, or as Clark wore out his welcome, he moved from one such refuge to another. He ate what he could buy with the change he made on odd jobs and what his friends could give him. Except for a meal from his friends two or three times a week he lived on two or three nickel frankfurters or hamburgers a day. For clothes, he had one frayed suit made of shoddy and a ragged half-cotton overcoat. He also had two pairs of trousers and two or three shirts, which he left for a time with various friends, and which were all eventually stolen.

In the fall of 1940, Clark went to work as a machine operator in a defense plant. He continued to bunk in with friends for several months. With the wages he earned the first three or four months, he bought chiefly food and clothes, paid his debts to his friends, and got drunk on week ends. As time went on, he spent about 75 per cent of his income on clothes, liquor, night clubs, and house parties. Less than a week after payday, he usually had to borrow his carfare to get to work, and to depend upon his friends for his meals, as well as for a place to sleep.

This behavior was part of a practical cultural system, however. His friends also depended upon him for loans and food, when *he* had just been paid. Thus, they actually had developed a system of getting money every Friday or Saturday, instead of only every second week, on payday. Each worker's payday was in reality a payday that he shared with one or two friends. Thus each man had a payday every week. Their ideal was a payday every day, so that they would have ready cash always.

Like most of his group, Clark had a regular week-end bout of drunkenness and a series of parties. These lasted through Sunday night, so that he almost never went to work on Mondays. On other nights, he always stayed up until twelve or one o'clock. Since he had to be up by six in order to reach work on time, he averaged less than five hours per night, including week ends. He missed an average of 1½ days on the job, out of every week; sometimes because he did not have carfare or food; sometimes because his rest was too broken.

After about 15 months of work, Clark fell in love with a girl, and he began to take more interest in his job. He wanted to become a foreman, and began getting up at five o'clock in the morning, so as not to be late for work. He decided to marry the girl and for the first time began to "save" his wages, paying on furniture. He and the girl set out to find a place to live. Finally they discovered a tenement on the railroad tracks where the landlady agreed to rent them two rooms. They returned with their suitcases to discover that the landlady had decided she would rent only to men. In two months, they were unable to find any other place to live.

Clark is still living with his friends, four to a room, and has given up his plan to marry. He still spends almost all his wages on clothes, liquor, and recreation. He still misses at least three days on the job out of every two weeks. During the four years he has been working, however, there have been three periods when he improved his work habits, his punctuality, and his motivation. The first was when he wanted to marry, and actually was buying furniture, and looking for a home. The second period of improvement occurred later, when Clark was trying to become a foreman, in order to convince his girl's mother that he was not an "ignorant bum," as she claimed. The third period followed his first visit to a meeting of his union, and his resultant interest in winning status within the union. Each of these situations was a powerful stimulus to Clark's motivation on the job. From them, we can learn what makes him ambitious, and what can make him work more effectively.

First, however, what made him *fail* to work well? During these three periods when he actually wished to become an efficient worker and tried to change his habits, why did he gradually lose his drive and return to his old habits? The reasons seem clear enough. First, like Ruth, the colored worker, he was influenced powerfully by the fact that he had no home and was unable to find one. The effort of both these workers to find a home, so that they could marry, was blocked by our chaotic housing situation. A society in which a large proportion of the population cannot find a home— cannot even rent a home from the people who own them—is in this basic respect less well organized than most "primitive" societies. If people cannot find a place for themselves and for their families to live as a group, and to live fairly decently, according to their lights, their motivation to work hard is severely weakened. If the young adults cannot find a home, they usually cannot marry. Since marriage is one of the most powerful drives in motivating workers to accept responsibility and to "settle down," our housing situation is demoralizing to work habits.

Secondly, Clark failed in his hopeless desire to become a foreman, because both the habits he had learned and especially his lack of education made him unfit for this responsibility. He had gone only to the sixth grade, and he had not learned well what was taught in those grades. Like millions of underprivileged workers, he could barely write a sentence, even an ungrammatical sentence. Simple addition and subtraction were laborious problems for him. This educational handicap, plus the great mental and nervous strain created by the improvement of his habits (of his hours of going to bed and getting up, of his application to his work, of making time *every* day), is too great for 9 out of 10 individuals in his position to overcome.

Third, the same educational deficiencies and cultural habits, which prevented his improving his status in the plant, likewise made it impossible for him to attain any status in his union. The local, he found, was run by workers who were a step above him in social status, who were at the *top* level of lower class groups and sometimes were in the lower middle class. They had skills and habits with which he could not compete. He soon gave up this hope also, and thus his third powerful incentive to change his work habits was extinguished.

The most powerful of all the forces that keep him in his present way of life and of work are the pleasures that he actually can attain by following his underprivileged culture. He gets strong biological enjoyment. He spends a great deal of his nights in sexual exploration, since he does not have to go to work the next day. He lives in a social world where visceral, genital, and emotional gratification is far more available than it is in a middle-class world. Recreation, relaxation, and pure laziness from Friday night through Sunday night are extremely satisfying experiences. If such a week end leaves the worker too exhausted to get on the job Monday or even Tuesday and causes him to lose $10 or $15, it nevertheless is so organically rewarding that he will repeat the experience the following week end, or certainly the following payday.

Such are the emotional, the cultural, and the economic determinants of the work habits of the underprivileged worker. He lives in a different economic and social environment from that in which the skilled and the middle-class workers live. Therefore the behavior that he learns, the habits that are stimulated and maintained by his cultural group, are different also. The individuals of these different socioeconomic statuses and cultures are reacting to different realistic situations and psychological drives. Therefore their values and their social goals are different. Therefore, the behavior of the underprivileged worker, which the boss regards as "unsocialized" or "ignorant," or "lazy," or "unmotivated" is really behavior learned from the socioeconomic and cultural environments of these workers. In a realistic view, we must recognize it to be perfectly normal, a sensible response to the conditions of their lives.

If we wish to change these habits—and they are a great burden upon our production, because about one-third of our total population falls into this group—we must offer the underprivileged worker real rewards. They must be sufficiently powerful to repay him for the hard work and self-denial required to change his old habits, and to compete with the rewards of a physical kind that he already gets.

What are these real goals, for which he will work harder? The first is a place to live, a place that is not merely a kitchenette apartment, or a basement room, or a corner in a cellar, with three to six people to a bed. It has to be a place that appears desirable in the eyes of the underprivileged worker, a place he will "go for." Thus the first goal to be set before him, as a real, attainable probability is a permanent, decent home. This means a more permanent family life. This in turn means acceptance of responsibility and the setting up of long-term goals. And these require good, steady work.

A home, the rearing of a family, and the development of good work habits cannot be attained in a year or two. The underprivileged worker's goals are short term because his hold upon a job and upon clothes and upon food is short term. He knows well that he cannot establish a home, buy furniture, begin buying a house—all the endeavors that keep middle-class people busy and conscientious—in a year or two. He cannot educate his children, even through high school, on a few years of good wages. These basic social goals require a prospect of a steady job and good wages. This is what is meant by the words "economic and social security" to the middle-class person, namely, that there is an excellent chance that his work career and income will be steady and adequate to meet his standard of living. This is the kind of security possessed by middle-class people.

For the worker, short periods of good wages and plentiful jobs do not take the place of this security. One cannot change his way of living, or buy a home, or educate his children on this kind of income. To have a chance to develop stable habits of living, which means good work habits, people must have a stable job. The underprivileged worker is perfectly realistic when he asks, "Why should I try to save and get a little ahead in these times, when I'll be back on relief, anyhow, in a year or two?"

All this is to say that our society must offer the underprivileged worker a fair prospect, a better chance than he now has, of improving his status. It must convince him that he can secure a better life by hard work, and he can be convinced only when he *sees* a fair number of underprivileged *people like himself* getting reasonably secure jobs, a place to live, and a chance for promotion. I am *not* saying that society has to provide every such worker with permanent tenure and homeownership, and likewise make him a foreman, in order to motivate him to work harder. But I am saying that the underprivileged worker will not improve unless he finds that there is a chance of his getting the basic social and economic rewards that I have mentioned. He must be given the realistic hope that the game is worth the candle. If he *does change* his work habits, if he does become ambitious, if he does begin to crave respectability, then industry and society must have the homes and steady jobs and education to offer him in return for this great effort.

We see that middle-class people work like beavers and have an insistent conscientiousness. They have the craving for respectability to drive them, and the hope of a better home, or better job, or higher status for their children to pull them. In order to make underprivileged people anxious to work harder and willing to bear more responsibility on the job, our industry, business, and government must convince them that they can get more out of life than they now get. This means that our system of production must expand so as to offer a larger proportion of the working class steadier jobs, good wages, and a decent place in which to live and to rear a family. Otherwise, a third or more of our white and Negro labor supply will become increasingly demoralized. In a society where even wars are won by the side with the largest skilled labor supply and the most efficient industrial structure, this is a vital consideration. In the future, our survival as a nation very likely will depend upon what happens to this one-third of our labor supply.

# Managing the Educated*

*Peter F. Drucker*

For the first time in our history—or indeed in the history of any country—managerial, professional, and technical employees have become the largest group in our work force. They not only outnumber all other white-collar groups, but they have even overtaken manual working groups, especially the machine workers.

Equally significant, for the first time in our history, and again for the first time in the history of any country, people with a high degree of education—that is, people who have finished high school—constitute more than half of our total labor force, including those employed in agriculture.

This trend is certain to accelerate sharply. The number of managerial, professional, and technical employees is growing at the rate of 10% each year—three times as fast as the total population. The number of machine workers, on the other hand, has not grown at all since the end of World War II and is indeed beginning to shrink not only in its proportionate importance but even in absolute numbers. Today managerial, professional, and technical people are one fifth of the American population at work. Fifteen or twenty years hence they are likely to constitute two fifths, perhaps even one half. This would mean that every other American gainfully employed would work as a manager, professional, or technician.

The development of an "educated society" is going to come even faster, for the people who do not have a high school education are to be found predominantly among the older population. Among those under 50, high school graduates already account for something like three quarters of the total. College-educated people, who 30 years ago were still so insignificant in number as almost to escape statistical notice, are a full third of all the newcomers to the labor force, so that 20 years hence 1 out of every 3 peo-

* From Dan H. Fenn (ed.), *Management's Mission in a New Society,* McGraw-Hill Book Company, Inc., New York, 1956, pp. 163–178. Reprinted by permission of the publisher.

NOTE: Mr. Drucker is a consultant on business policy and management organization. He is also Professor of Management at the Graduate School of Business, New York University, and author of many well-known books and articles on American society and business management.

ple gainfully employed in this country is likely to have attended college, if not graduated.

Here is a basic change in the structure of this country and of our economy. In times of economic swings and of international crisis little attention has been paid to it, for other events seize the headlines. Yet it is so important in the long run, and perhaps even in the short run, that it may prove to be more significant than any other single change. Surely its impact on us in business and management will be both profound and long-lasting. It challenges basic axioms of business management and business economics. It creates new opportunities and new problems for management. And it will force us into basic new thinking about organizational structure, authority and responsibility, and the relation of people working together in an organization.

A good many managers today are familiar with the management of highly educated people in special organizations like research laboratories or design-engineering departments. All of us know that these groups pose a good many new problems. Indeed, our meetings and our magazines are full of discussions on how one manages research people, how one makes a human being out of a Ph.D. in mathematics, and how one goes about managing the professional in an organization.

Yet very little of this, I am afraid, is really relevant to the basic problems we face, or is really concerned with them. For the essence of the big change—and we are well past the mid-point in it—is not that we have to learn how to organize highly educated people for special work outside or next to the traditional business organization. The essential point is that tomorrow, if not today, more and more of the people in the normal traditional organization, in the day-to-day operations of a business, are going to be people with very high education; people who work with their minds rather than their hands; people who do everyday "line" work rather than special "long-hair" work and yet who are different in their background, their expectations, and the way they work from the people who did these line jobs yesterday.

Specifically, we face major new situations in three areas: (1) the economics of business enterprise, (2) the personnel management and the personnel behavior of the great bulk of our employees, and (3) basic organization. I shall try to outline some of the directions we can already see in each of these three areas.

*New economic outlook.* Economists will undoubtedly be busy for many years trying to analyze the causes, lessons, and characteristics of the recession of 1957–1958. One of the most important lessons we can already define:

In the industries that were hard-hit—especially the manufacturers of durable consumer goods and their main supplier, the steel industry—production dropped faster between the summer of 1957 and the spring of 1958 than it ever has in any major industry during a comparable period in our history (faster even than during the 1937–1938 slump). In some companies it dropped 50% or so. Yet employment fell only 20%. Actually, while we headlined the unemployment news, the real story should have been the tremendous crisis resistance of our employment. And, much more important, personnel costs hardly fell at all. They too showed almost complete recession resistance, which, of course, explains why profits in these industries tended to disappear altogether. This is simply a manifestation of the great structural change in our labor force, the structural change which has made the "production worker," that is, the machine operator, increasingly secondary, and those employees more important whom the accountants call "nonproduction workers," that is, the white-collar employees and especially the managerial, professional, and technical employees.

The industries that were particularly hard-hit by the recession are among the ones that have changed the least in their employment structure during the last ten years. They are essentially old-fashioned in the composition of their labor force, compared, for instance, with the chemical industry, the petroleum industry, or the paper industry. Yet even their manufacturing employment dropped much more slowly than production, and total employment fell even more slowly—as evidenced by the personnel costs. Also, employment fell the most in respect to low-income labor; it barely moved in respect to high-income labor. In other words, even in these industries labor costs have ceased to be elastic; they have become more or less fixed.

It is important to stress that this happened in industries which in their production concepts are industries of yesterday rather than industries of tomorrow. They also rank with those firms that have the highest average age in the work force. Thus, they are still much closer to yesterday's labor structure, both in respect to job and educational background, than the growth industries in our economy like electronics, chemistry, and so on. Yet even in these industries, which could have been expected to behave pretty much in the traditional pattern—could have been expected to decrease employment at least as fast as production and labor costs at the same rate as production—employment proved highly inelastic and total personnel costs even more so.

I submit that this is the "normal" in an economy in which managerial, professional, and technical employees are the largest single group. If you add to this group the foremen, craftsmen, and highly skilled workers, you have 22 million employed people, out of a total of 64 or 65 million, whose employment is of necessity highly stable. Or to put it more accurately: the need for these people does not fluctuate directly with the volume of production, and to a very large extent their employment is tied more to the expectation of future production than to current orders. These are, in other words, people who are employed not according to the number of pieces or the number of hours worked but rather according to the expected capacity. And in the majority of cases they have to be on the payroll regardless of the present volume of business—partly because they are needed as long as the business operates at all, partly because they represent too much of an investment, too much of a "capital resource," to be discharged.

This is in sharp, indeed irreconcilable, contrast to the axioms of the economists. Every economist still assumes that business adjusts to short-term fluctuations in the economy by laying off or hiring people. They disagree whether this adjustment is the way out of a recession or whether it is the cause of recessions and depressions, but they all still believe in the phenomenon itself. It is quite clear, however, that this is no longer true. Though this would have been clear even without the lesson of the recession, since it follows from the structure of our labor force, the economic dip served to dramatize the change. So the economists—and let me add the accountants too—would be well advised to assume that business cannot adjust at all by varying labor costs; that labor costs, for any short-term period, can be considered fixed, determined by future expectations rather than by present volume of business. In many industries—a conspicuous example would be retailing—this is indeed already an established fact. Yet we lack economic theory for such a situation. As a result, we do not really understand it.

We also lack business policy for it. It is obvious that what I have just said spells out great fluctuation of profit, since it is the only factor left that can give. This is one of the functions of profit in a free enterprise economy. If we cannot adjust easily to short-term fluctuation by adjusting labor costs, the leverage on profits must become conspicuously greater, as indeed it proved to be during the recent recession. We need, therefore, a financial policy which starts out with the assumption of high year-to-year fluctuations in actual profits, and which therefore focuses on a rate of return over a cyclical period—over a wide range of fluctuations—rather than on annual profits. We need instruments of financial analysis and control for such a new situation. And we need to think through our capital investments with much greater sophistication, instead of simply basing them on the idea that today's expected rate of return will actually be realized in any one year during the life of the new investment.

But there is another and perhaps even more important implication in this new economic situation. The rise of our economy was based on the steady increase in the productivity of the direct, manual producer, the farmer, and the machine operator. Incidentally, most of us in business are not sufficiently aware of the tremendous contribution the increase in farm productivity has made to our economic growth. During the last 30 years the annual step-up in productivity on the farm was at least of the order of 6% per year—twice that of manufacturing industry. In very large measure our economic growth and our capacity to produce can be credited to this progress.

There is reason to believe that the main increase in agricultural productivity is over. There is still a very substantial number of farmers with substandard productivity, farmers who are indeed marginal in every sense of the word. They may account for almost one third of our farm population. But even if all of them left farming—and over the next 20 years most of them will—it would not materially decrease our farm production or farm productivity, since these marginal farmers contribute almost nothing to the supply of foods and industrial raw materials for our economy. All the flight from the farm will contribute is additional workers for industry, and workers who unfortunately are precisely the kind we need the least: unskilled and very largely uneducated people.

We can expect, by contrast, very sharp productivity increases in the manufacturing industries, simply as a result of increased mechanization and automation. But these increases may be largely an illusion. We will indeed have dramatic upswings in output per man-hour of production workers. But the very fact that our managerial, professional, and technical groups have been growing so much faster than the total economy indicates that we can obtain these productivity increases of the machine operator only by adding nonmanual workers. In other words, I would submit that all evidence today, both that derived from an analysis of the over-all figures and that derived from any study of an individual company's shift to automation, indicates that increased automation only shifts the demand for labor from the machine operator and his manual work to the highly educated man and his mind work, but does not result in actual increase in the over-all productivity of the business or of the economy.

What I am saying is simply that from now on our increases in productivity in this country will depend above all on our ability to increase the productivity of the nonmanual worker. Two thirds of our total labor force in 1956 were not working with their hands—the managerial, professional, and technical workers; the clerical and sales people; the workers in service work; and finally the supervisors. Yet no one even knows how one measures the productivity of people in this kind of work. All we can measure today is the productivity of people who work with their hands to produce a physical output. No one, I am afraid, would claim that the productivity of these mind workers has gone up appreciably. Certainly such data as we have do not indicate that there has been a great increase. Since their numbers have gone up at least as fast as total production of goods and services, one must deduce that the productivity has at best remained the same.

This I submit is the primary challenge to American management. First, here is our major inflationary factor. The wages of these people go up, or are pushed up by the union contracts of industries in Detroit and Schenectady. You may or may not agree that the manufacturing worker should have received the full benefit of higher productivity; but whatever you would like to believe, over a long period of time manufacturing productivity has risen roughly parallel to manufacturing wages. The major inflationary factor is the nonmanufacturing workers' income, which goes up along with manufacturing workers' incomes but without any noticeable increase in productivity. Because of its impact, this is a bigger responsibility than the cost control of a business, for we are talking here about the cost control of the American economy.

The productivity of these people can, to a substantial extent, be increased in the way that we have increased the productivity of the manual worker: by the investment of capital in machinery. This is certainly true in clerical and other office work, where automation will undoubtedly have a major impact and where it may be more important and have greater results than in the factory. This may also be true for the very substantial number of people who are engaged in selling—where automation may not mean so much in terms of use of machinery but certainly will bring great changes because of the planning and systematizing of work that it demands.

But for the managerial, professional, and technical people, and they are the real core of the problem and the real opportunity, capital investment in machinery—in physical tools—is not going to mean much. Their work is not physical; it is work of the mind. The only way to increase their productivity is to increase the output and the effectiveness of the mind. This can be accomplished only if we succeed both in making each of these men more productive in his own right and then in making his contribution more effective throughout the entire company.

*Future personnel problems.* This leads me to my second major topic: the management of highly educated people at work. Let me say again that I am not talking about the management of highly educated people in special programs such as research. I am talking about highly educated people in the ordinary, everyday, line organization.

Our concepts of personnel management were largely formed around World War I or shortly thereafter. They grew essentially out of experience in working with machine operators of very limited education. The famous Hawthorne experiments, for instance, were conducted with people who had, on the average, barely finished grade school. I think there is serious reason to doubt that tomorrow's employee will conform to the image upon which our current personnel management practices depend.

What are the expectations of people who have sat on school benches for at least 12, if not for 16 years, and, however little they may have learned otherwise, have learned to expect to work with their minds and to apply thinking, concept, system, and theories to their jobs? What are the expectations of people who have, as a matter of course, been given an education which only a short generation ago was reserved for a very small, essentially upper-class group? What work, opportunities, and treatment do they expect?

Is "scientific management," as the term is commonly understood, at all applicable to them, let alone "scientific" for them? Is it right to try to make the job as simple, repetitive, or highly organized as we possibly can? I doubt it.

Let me say that we have evidence that people who now come out of school expect something different from what we offer them. I do not want to attempt to define "automation." I do not want to argue whether we mean by this the substitution of machine for manual labor or a new concept of the organization of work by system and process. It is already fairly clear that the major driving force in the development is neither machines nor concepts but the changed educational structure of our work population.

People who have spent 12 or 16 years in formal education are not attracted to the job of a preautomated factory, least of all to the assembly line, which socially, if not technologically, is already obsolete. They are looking for jobs in which they can exercise what they have learned—that is, jobs in which they can work by using their minds—and they are looking for jobs in which they have the opportunities of educated people for better pay, advancement, and chances to make a contribution. The assembly line as we have known it cannot survive in this country—there is plenty of evidence that the young people in Detroit, Flint, or Schenectady simply do not want assembly-line jobs and will take them only as a last resort and with a deep consciousness of frustration and defeat.

Another new problem turns around the mobility of this kind of worker. To the old laborer, who at best had a manual skill but no education, mobility was a threat. Even in this, the most mobile country in the world, he was much more afraid of losing a job than he was attracted by better opportunities elsewhere. Stability of employment and job security ranked highest in his priorities.

Is this still likely to be true of today's and tomorrow's worker with his high degree of education and his conceptual training and skill? I doubt this very much. We see today in the electronics industry, for instance, a revival of the itinerant specialist in the tradition of the exceedingly highly skilled trades of old, like the printing business of 50 or 100 years ago. We see young men with a specialty who simply look on a job as an opportunity to ply their craft, who could not care less for job security, and who are almost unbelievably mobile. This is very much more characteristic of tomorrow's most important employees than fear of job loss, attachment to a job, and the resulting very low mobility of today's or yesterday's worker. This poses a very real problem for us in management, and it is a problem which we are not attacking by trying to keep down turnover rates. We have to think through how we can best make use of such workers, who are inherently mobile, who know a good deal of the world and are at home everywhere, and whose contribution to us very largely consists of their mobile and easily transported knowledge and skill.

The real problem of managing people at work, however, is not to satisfy their expectations. It is to think through the demands on them. What should we expect from people who are highly educated and who work as managers, professionals, and technicians? We have, during the last 30 or 50 years, increasingly tended to talk about "average jobs." "Scientific management" is focused on finding the "standard job," or the amount of work that can reasonably be expected of everyone. This, I am afraid, is the wrong way to make demands on tomorrow's worker. There we shall have to make demands for extraordinary performance, for performance that contributes not the minimum but the optimum, for performance that steadily pushes the limitations outward and reaches for new contributions and new excellence. Otherwise we can never expect to obtain the benefit of the great, almost revolutionary, change in the structure of our work force and of our work. And this in turn quite obviously means very real changes in the way we structure and define jobs.

Above all, however, we must recognize that this new worker cannot be supervised and that his performance cannot be easily measured. He can only be motivated. He must reach for excellence. He must want to contribute. He must try to develop himself, his capacity, and his contribution. All we can do is pay him. The supervision that we could give to the manual worker simply cannot be applied effectively to people who have to contribute their knowledge, conceptual skill, imagination, and judgment.

While we have been talking a great deal about motivation these last 20 or 30 years, we know very little about it—and I do not believe that many of us would claim that we even apply the little we know. The comments made in Mr. Zaleznik's chapter [in *Management's Mission in a New Society*] are most interesting in this regard.

*The new organization.* The greatest challenge, however, may well come to our concept of organization. Let me give you an illustration—intentionally taken from the armed forces rather than from business. If you look at a modern air base, you will find on it, in addition to a fairly small number of flying personnel, a very large complement of highly trained professional and technical people who exercise judgment. In rank they may be quite low. The crew chief in charge of the maintenance of a group of planes, for instance, is a master sergeant—and will never be more than that. Yet who "commands" the crew chief? Who can give him orders? The commanding general of the base can remove the crew chief, demote him in rank, or overrule him. But he cannot "command" him. The crew chief decides whether a plane is airworthy, what has to be done to put it in shape, and how long it will take. In other words, he exercises judgment, and he has a high degree of final authority within his field.

Or take the meteorologist. Again there is a ceiling on his rank—he is rarely more than a captain or a major, and will not rise higher. Yet while he works within a highly specialized area, his sphere of concern is the entire base rather than a part of it. He is a "specialist" with a "general" sphere of authority and responsibility. Again, who can "command" him?

It is his professional judgment and knowledge to which he is really responsible rather than a superior officer. He can be removed, and he can be overruled, but he cannot be commanded.

You could go through the entire base and pick out one technical or professional function after the other and say exactly the same thing about it. Yet the commanding general has a final decision and a final responsibility. He does "command"—and the difference in performance between a mediocre and an outstanding commanding general is still the most important and the one truly decisive "variable" in the performance of the whole base. The general is not just a "coordinator," nor does he just listen to his functional people and synthesize their judgment and advice. He has real, final authority. And yet, except in a merely formal sense, he can hardly be said to be over all these people. He has a *different* job to do rather than a higher job.

On the chart, of course, none of this is shown. The chart shows the line of command from the general on down as it has always existed. And, in polite fiction, every one of these men exercises delegated authority—though the Air Force, smarter in this than most businesses, realizes that these people do not do part of the general's work but do their own work. The reality of organization we can muddle through, though no one is very happy with the way we do it. But we do not really understand what we are doing, nor do we really understand how to organize such a system.

This is the new organization, in which highly educated people contribute theoretical and conceptual knowledge, through responsible judgment, for a joint effort. This is the organization of an educated society, the organization in which the bulk of the people are managerial, professional, or technical. And this organization does not answer to our traditional organization concept and indeed cannot be organized on this basis.

Our organization concepts, no matter how refined, are all really variations on the traditional organization of a fighting force as it first emerged well over 3,000 years ago—in China, in Egypt, and then, shortly after the Trojan War, in Greece. It was an organization which succeeded in bringing together fairly large numbers of people for unskilled, repetitive, drilled work. When we began to build large-scale business organizations some 75 years or so ago, we simply took the prevailing concepts of military organization and adapted them. The principle of such an organization was authority, and the basic problem was to make responsibility commensurate with authority. To this day, the relationship of authority to responsibility is central to our concept of organization.

For the new organization of highly educated people, authority and responsibility may well be the wrong principles of organization. It may well be that we will have to learn to organize not a system of authority and responsibility—a system of command—but an information and decision system—a system of judgment, knowledge, and expectations.

Let me say that this does not involve a greater emphasis on human relations. In fact, we cannot solve the organizational problems we face by an emphasis on relations between people. We cannot, for instance, solve them by emphasizing the informal organization as against a formal one. We need a formal organization that is focused on the new reality. This will have to be an objective focus on the work to be done, the risks to be taken, the decisions to be made, and the actions to follow therefrom, rather than a focus on the relations between people.

We have some tools for this—but only the beginning. Even the little we have indicates that we may well face very radical changes—changes aimed not at making the central decision-making authority less effective but at making it more effective and, at the same time, at building the organization according to the need for information, judgment, decision, and execution rather than according to the hierarchical concept of command and response. This is anything but easy or painless. We may have to learn to consider authority, responsibility, rank, and reward as four separate and distinct variables to be merged in a configuration, rather than as synonyms for the same thing. We may even have to learn to look at an organization as a process (and as one that corresponds to organic biological processes) rather than as merely a mechanism; in other words, as something in which there is no "higher" or "lower," but only a "different."

*Other problems.* I could discuss a good many other things. For instance, what impact will this change in the basic structure of our work force and of our work have on the labor union? Here is a major institution of American life, a major power center, and a major element in our society and our economy. Historically, it has been able to embrace only yesterday's worker, the manual machine operator. Will it succeed in reaching tomorrow's worker? Or will it become essentially stagnant and sterile? It is perhaps not irrelevant that, in sharp contrast to 25 years ago, the age structure of the labor union is today a good deal older than that of the work population in general. In other words, labor is becoming an institution of the old rather than the cause of the young.

Another area for discussion is the way in which we direct our personnel efforts. What emphasis, for instance, do we still give to the first-line supervisor and to labor relations in our management thinking, even though these are the tasks and priorities of the past rather than of tomorrow? It is possible that tomorrow we will have two employee groups, distinguished primarily by sex. It may be that the women will provide the bulk of our unskilled labor force, both of machine tenders and unskilled service workers, whereas the men will do the new work, the managerial, professional, and technical work. Here is a change for which we are totally unprepared and which would introduce some very serious tensions and problems into American life and business.

There is also the question whether this shift in the basic structure of the

American population is likely to result in basic changes in demand; whether there will be a move, for instance, from more durable consumer goods, which have a high-status importance for the low-income groups, to more community satisfactions, such as education, which have a high-status importance for the managerial, professional, and technical group.

But I think I have said enough to indicate that we face very real problems, enough to substantiate my own conviction that the shift in the structure of American society and in the jobs in American business is, in retrospect, the really fundamental event of these last years, rather than the recession on which so much of our attention has been focused. And I think I have also said enough to show why I do not believe that I am writing about something in the future; the challenges and the opportunities are already here, and they demand thinking, understanding, and action from business and management.

## Questions and Answers[1]

FROM THE FLOOR: In England we have found the typical organizational structure breaking down under conditions of very rapid change, whether in growth or in rapid technological advance. A recent study of about eight or ten electronics firms in England has shown that under conditions of rapid change the old hierarchy breaks down. Then either the firm becomes chaotic and gives up working in this sphere, or people relax and say, "Well, we have got to get the job done, so the heck with the formalities."

Once the organization relaxes this way, you release a sudden and terrific enthusiasm and you are off. When you get over the stage where the line hierarchy feels uncertain, unstable, and by-passed, you begin to move. And when things clear up, the line men find that they don't have to worry about their jobs; they still are needed in the organization!

One other point on this matter of autocratic command: we have been looking into this, and we have decided that to get the job done when you have educated people in your work force, you have to give people a chance to use their brains and training. We have come around to saying that we don't command, but are aiming at a catalytic organization.

MR. DRUCKER: Since I am so unsympathetic to this point of view, I hesitate to comment! First, I don't think I was talking of autocratic management. Very few of us in this room would believe in it. Let us forget how many practice it; we don't believe in it. Still, we do have an authority structure because of the responsibility involved—an authority not just of position but of knowledge, which is not unimportant and has its own responsibility—so this is not, I think, the problem.

---

[1] Businessmen present at the panel session on which this chapter is based raised certain questions which brought about the interplay of ideas reported more or less verbatim in this section.

The issue is not only one of methods; it is one of basic organizational structure, too. Good methods may release a tremendous enthusiasm, but they only release *real* enthusiasm if the mess was unspeakable before! What you do need is a new kind of organization to cope with rapid growth and change. This implies a very considerable degree of conceptual rigidity, though not of organizational rigidity. You cannot create it by sitting down and being nice to everyone or discussing it together. You can create it only by analyzing a very difficult society and building the machinery for that society.

It is quite conceivable that a wave of enthusiasm will carry you a considerable way. All our electronics people have been through what you are discussing, but every one of them has run out of enthusiasm within three years and been up against the hard fact of the need for organized management if they are to have a solid operation in which people can work independently and yet together. But what do they have to know to do this? What do they have to tell? Whom do they have to tell? Who makes these decisions? These are not riddles that you can solve by being enthusiastic. I love enthusiasm, but it burns out.

FROM THE FLOOR: Do you think this new group, in establishing its status symbols, will bring a change in the direction of production output, and thereby meet some of the shortcomings Mr. Canham pointed out?

MR. DRUCKER: Leaving aside any discussion of values and looking at the economy as an economist, I think you can anticipate some changes in detail. If you ask me what is going to be the main growth industry in the next ten years, I would say, "Obviously education is."

If you ask which industry in our country has shown the greatest growth in the last ten years, I may surprise you. It happens to be paper-book publishing, not aircraft or television. On a percentage basis, that has been our most rapidly growing industry, and the record industry is second. I am not saying that these two will replace the washing machine, but I am saying that it is very likely that we are seeing a shift of priority in demand preferences.

FROM THE FLOOR: If the major problem in management in the years to come will be managing the educated, do you think it is possible that we could get some help on how to proceed from institutions like universities which already manage the educated?

MR. DRUCKER: I think we have to learn to look for lessons wherever we can find them. The institution which has the most experience and can teach us the most things not to do is the hospital! We can learn a lot from such groups as the engineering department of a defense contractor. But a university would not teach us very much, because essentially its structure is so different. Basically, most universities consist of individual scholars working in one house but not actually working together.

FROM THE FLOOR: What do we do with the large group of people in the next ten years who have been forced to grow beyond their capacity, and are now being pushed by this group of experts for their jobs?

MR. DRUCKER: I think this is going to be a very real problem. We have it in our first-line supervision in many places. Our first-line supervision in many industries today is the oldest age group, and the least educated. They have dead-end jobs. It isn't polite to say it, but it is true. And what about the hordes of narrow specialists who have suddenly seen their jobs expand beyond their abilities? These people are perfectly adequate to do the job of yesterday and perhaps even of today. Can we give them an understanding of the new knowledge that is hammering in on them? Obviously management development programs would not be flourishing if the problem were not acute. You can't fire them, and you can't retire them yet, not for 20 more years. We have to make them effective, somehow, or live it out. The real question is now to make their successors tomorrow, who *may* well have the education, much better.

# READINGS RELATED TO CHAPTER VI

## A Basic Incongruency between the Needs of a Mature Personality and the Requirements of Formal Organization*

*Chris Argyris*

Bringing together the evidence regarding the impact of the formal organizational principles upon the individual, it is concluded that there are some basic incongruencies between the growth trends of a healthy personality and the requirements of the formal organization. If the principles of formal organization are used as ideally defined, employees will tend to work in an environment where (1) they are provided minimal control over their workaday world, (2) they are expected to be passive, dependent, and subordinate, (3) they are expected to have a short time perspective, (4) they are induced to perfect and value the frequent use of a few skin-surface shallow abilities and, (5) they are expected to produce under conditions leading to psychological failure.

All these characteristics are incongruent to the ones *healthy* human beings are postulated to desire. . . . They are much more congruent with the needs of infants in our culture. In effect, therefore, organizations are willing to pay high wages and provide adequate seniority if mature adults

---

\* From "The Formal Organization," *Personality and Organization*, Harper & Row, Publishers, Incorporated, New York, 1957, chap. 3, pp. 66–75. Reprinted by permission of the author and the publisher.

will, for eight hours a day, behave in a less than mature manner! *If the analysis is correct, this inevitable incongruency increases as* (1) *the employees are of increasing maturity,* (2) *as the formal structure* (based upon the above principles) *is made more clear-cut and logically tight for maximum formal organizational effectiveness,* (3) *as one goes down the line of command, and* (4) *as the jobs become more and more mechanized* (i.e., take on assembly line characteristics).

As in the case of the personality developmental trends, this picture of formal organization is also a model. Clearly, no company actually uses the formal principles of organization exactly as stated by their creators. There is ample evidence to suggest that they are being modified constantly in actual situations. However, those who expound these principles would probably be willing to defend their position that this is the reason that human relations problems exist; the principles are not followed as they should be.

In the proposed models of the personality and the formal organization, we are assuming the extreme of each in order that the analysis and its results can be highlighted. Speaking in terms of extremes helps us to make the position sharper. In doing this, no assumption is made that all situations in real life are extreme (i.e., that the individuals will always want to be more mature and that the formal organization will always tend to make people more dependent and passive all the time). In fact, much evidence is presented in subsequent chapters to support contrary tendencies.

The model ought to be useful, however, to plot the degree to which each component tends toward extremes and then to predict the problems that will arise. . . .

It is not difficult to see why some students of organization suggest that immature and even mentally retarded individuals would probably make excellent employees. There is little documented experience to support such a hypothesis. One reason for this lack of information is probably the "touchiness" of the subject. Examples of what might be obtained if a systematic study is made may be found in a recent work by Brennan.[1] He cites the Utica Knitting Mill, which made arrangements during 1917 with the Rome Institution for Mentally Defective Girls to employ 24 girls whose mental ages ranged from six to ten years. The girls were such excellent workers that their employment continued after the war emergency ended. In fact the company added forty additional mentally defective girls in another of their plants. The managers praised the subnormal girls highly.

In several important reports, they said that "when business conditions required a reduction of the working staff," the hostel girls were never "laid off" in disproportion to the normal girls; that they were more punctual, more regular in their habits, and did not indulge in as much "gossip and levity." They received the same rate of pay, and they had been employed successfully at almost every process carried out in the workshops.

In another experiment, the Works Manager of the Radio Corporation Ltd. reported that of five young morons:

> The three girls compared very favourably with the normal class of employee in that age group. The boy employed in the store performed his work with satisfaction. . . . Although there was some doubt about the fifth child, it was felt that getting the most out of him was just a matter of right placement.

In each of the five cases, the morons were quiet, respectful, well-behaved, and obedient. The Works Manager was especially impressed by their truthfulness, and lack of deceit or suppression of the facts. A year later, the same Works Manager was still able to advise that,

> In every case, the girls proved to be exceptionally well-behaved, particularly obedient, and strictly honest and trustworthy. They carried out work required of them to such a degree of efficiency that *we were surprised they were classed as subnormals for their age.*[2] Their attendance was good, and their behavior was, if anything, certainly better than any other employee of the same age.

Let us now turn to the literature to see if there are illustrations of the points made regarding the dependence and subordination created by the nature of formal organization and its impact upon the individuals. Unfortunately, there are not many available studies that focus on the impact of the formal organization on the individuals (holding the leadership variable "constant").

Probably the best available evidence of the impact of formal organization based upon unity of command and task specialization is the experimental work on communication by Bavelas[3] and Leavitt,[4] which is confirmed by Heise and Miller[5] and Shaw and Rothchild.[6] They focus on the question—can the structure of certain patterns of communication result in significantly better performance than others? Their results clearly imply that in a structure where one individual has a "central" position in the communications network and thereby is able to control communications, as would an executive in a plant, he will probably be chosen the leader and have the best morale in the group. The individuals who depend upon him (e.g., supervisors) will tend to have lower morale, feel more frustrated, confused, and irritated at others along the network. Guetzkow and Simon confirm these results, and through the use of more refined experimental procedure they show strong evidence to support the hypothesis that of all communications structures tried, the "wheel"[7] created initially the *least* organizational problem for the group, thereby permitting the group to organize itself most quickly in order to solve a particular problem.[8]

Further indirect evidence is provided by Arensberg,[9] who "revisited" the famous Hawthorne Studies. He noted that many of the results reported about the relay assembly experiments occurred *after* the girls were placed in a work situation where they were (1) made "subjects" of an "important" experiment, (2) encouraged to participate in decisions affecting their work, (3) given veto power over their supervisors to the point where, as the girls testify, "we have no boss." Clearly these conditions constitute a sweeping shift in the basic relationship of modern industrial work where the employee is subordinate to people above him.

Bakke's study of the unemployed worker[10] includes much evidence that the workers are clearly aware of the differences in the degree of authority and control manifested by themselves and their boss. His evidence suggests that independently of the personality of the boss, the workers perceived their boss as someone with power to achieve his goals; a power which they did not believe they had. For example, one worker defines the boss as someone who, "When he decides to do something, he can carry it through." Another states, "Some birds have got enough (authority) and stand high enough so that what they say goes . . . and anybody who can do that won't be found very often to be what you might call a worker."[11]

Blau,[12] in a study of the departmental structure in a federal enforcement agency, reports that even when deliberate attempts were made to minimize the social distance between leaders and subordinates and where leaders tried to use a "democratic" approach, the supervisors frequently but inadvertently lapsed into behavior more appropriate to the formal authoritarian relationships with the subordinates. Thus, the impact of the formal structure influences leadership behavior toward being more "autocratic" even when there exist informal norms emphasizing a more egalitarian climate and when the leaders consciously try to be more "democratic."

Not only do the supervisors "slip" into more directive leadership, but the subordinates "slip" into dependent, submissive roles even if the supervisor requests their increased participation. As one subordinate states, "Lots of times, I've differed with the supervisor, but I didn't say anything. I just said, 'Yes,' with a smile, *because he gives the efficiency rating.*" Blau continues:

> Bureaucratic authority is *not* based on personal devotion to the supervisor or on respect for him as a person but on an adaptation necessitated by his rating power. The *advancement chances of officials and even their chances to keep their civil service jobs depend on the rating they periodically receive from their superior.* . . . The group's insistence that the supervisor discharge his duty of issuing directives—"That's what he gets paid for" —serves to emphasize that their obedience to them does *not* constitute submission to his will but *adherence, on his part as well as theirs, to abstract principles* which they have socially accepted.[13]

In comprehensive reviews of the literature Gibb,[14] Blau[15] and Bierstedt[16] conclude that it is important to differentiate between formal leadership (headship or authority) based upon formal organization and informal leadership (leadership). For example, Gibb states:

> . . . leadership is to be distinguished, by definition, from domination or headship. The principal differentia are these: (i) Domination or headship is maintained through an organized system and not by the spontaneous recognition, by fellow group members, of the individual's contribution to group goals. (ii) The group goal is chosen by the head man in line with his interests and is not internally determined by the group itself. (iii) In the domination or headship relation there is little or no sense of shared feeling or joint action in the pursuit of the given goal. (iv) There is in the dominance relation a wide social gap between the group members and the head, who strives to maintain this social distance as an aid to his coercion of the group. (v) Most basically, these two forms of influence differ with respect to the *source* of the authority which is exercised. The leader's authority is spontaneously accorded him by his fellow group members, the followers. *The authority of the head derives from some extra-group power which he has over the members of the group, who cannot meaningfully be called his followers. They accept his domination on pain of punishment, rather than follow. The business executive is an excellent example of a head exercising authority derived from his position in an organization through membership in which the workers, his subordinates, satisfy many strong needs. They obey his commands and accept his domination because this is part of their duty as organization members and to reject him would be to discontinue membership, with all the punishments that would involve.*[14]

Carter,[17] in some recent controlled field experiments, points up the importance of the power and status inherent in the formal organizational structure by an interesting study of the behavior of "emergent" vs. "appointed" leaders. He concludes that appointed leaders tend to support their own purposes, defend their proposals from attack, express their own opinions, and argue—all *less* than emergent leaders. Apparently, the data suggests, because the appointed leader feels that he has power and status, he feels less need to defend his position than does an emergent leader.

Fleishman's[18] descriptions of leadership training also point up the degree of dependence and leader-centeredness of a subordinate upon his boss. He reports that subordinates tend to use the same leadership style that their boss tends to use regardless of the training they receive.

Probably no review of the literature would be complete without mentioning the classic work of Max Weber on the study of bureaucracy.[19,20] It is important to keep in mind that Weber conceived of bureaucracy (formal organization) as "the most efficient form of social organization ever developed."[21] He maintained that bureaucracy was one of the characteristic forms of organization of all modern society, finding wide expression in industry, science, and religion, as well as government.[22] In fact, it may be said that he saw no difference between socialism and capitalism, since the fundamental characteristic of both was (a particular kind of) formal organization. "If Marx said that the workers of the world had nothing to lose but their chains by revolting, Weber contended that they really had nothing to gain."[23] It remained for Merton to try to balance the "rosy" picture that Weber painted about bureaucracy. At the outset of this work, Merton, in clear and concise terms, describes some of the essential conditions of formal organization. Again we note the emphasis made here on the inherent authoritarian power structure of the formal organization which is independent of the leadership pattern of the person holding the power position.

> Authority, the power of control which derives from an acknowledged status, inheres in the office and not in the particular person who performs the official role. Official action ordinarily occurs within the framework of preexisting rules of the organization. The system of prescribed relations between the various offices involves a considerable degree of formality and clearly defined social distance between the occupants of these positions. Formality is manifested by means of a more or less complicated social ritual which symbolizes and supports the "pecking order" of the various offices. Such formality, which is integrated with the distribution of authority within the system, serves to minimize friction by largely restricting (official) contact to modes which are previously defined by the rules of the organization . . .[24]

Charles Walker, Robert Guest,* and Arthur Turner have been studying the impact of the assembly line (an example of a highly specialized aspect of organizational structure) and of the management upon the workers. Their findings show the degree and kind of impact of the mass production type of organizational structure upon the employee, independent of the personality of the management. Walker and Guest report that about 90 per cent (of 180) workers dislike their actual job because of its mechanical pacing, repetitiveness, minimum skill requirements, minute subdivision of work, and surface mental attention. Their results show that the degree of dislike for the job increased in proportion to the degree to which the job embodies mass production characteristics[25] and to the degree to which the employees are dependent upon management. These results have been confirmed in another study by the same team.[26]

Turner, in an article based upon the second study mentioned above, expands on the impact of the assembly line. The employees especially dislike the mechanical pacing of the assembly line which (1) decreases their control over their own activities, (2) makes them dependent, subordinate, and passive to a machine process, and (3) leads them to forget quality production and aspire to an acceptable minimum quantity output. Turner[27] points out that the men dislike the necessity to work at a job that requires

* [Walker and Guest's article "The Man on the Assembly Line" is reprinted in this volume, pages 218–238.—Ed.]

only a minimum skill, and forces them, through repetitiveness, to continue using only a minimum skill. These findings are understandable since these requirements run counter to the needs of relatively mature human beings. Finally, the characteristics of impersonality and anonymity also inveigh against the needs of "ego integrity" and feelings of self worth.

Indirect evidence comes from two studies of organization reported by the writer. In both organizations the employees' degree of morale with the company increased as the degree of directive leadership decreased. Passive leadership (i.e., leadership that seldom contacts the employees) minimized the pressure from above and permitted the employees to feel more "self-responsible" (i.e., they could be their own boss). Over 91 per cent of the respondents (total group sampled about 300) reported that passive leadership (i.e., "we hardly ever talk with the boss") permits them to be their own boss and thereby reduces the potential pressure from above. However, the same number of employees also reported they still feel pressure from the very way the work and the companies are organized. For example, a bank teller states,

> I don't know what I would do if Mr. B. supervised us closely. The pressure would be terrific. As it is, I hardly see him. He leaves me alone and that's fine with me. But don't get me wrong. It isn't that I don't feel I haven't got a boss. I have one. *I know I will always have one, if it's Mr. B. or Mr. X.*[28]

Some trade union leaders are aware that the formal organization places the workers in dependent and dissatisfying situations. Many report that the process of management (independent of the personality of the leader) carries with it certain "inevitable" dislikes by the workers, because the workers view management (who represent the formal organization) as the ones who place them in dissatisfying work situations. This may be one reason that many trade union leaders do not aspire to gain political control over the management.

Mr. Green, for example, said, "The line of distinction between the exercise of the rights of labor and of management must be scrupulously observed. The philosophy which some have advanced that labor should join with management in the actual management of the property could not and cannot be accepted."[29] Mr. Murray agrees when he states, "To relieve the boss or the management of proper responsibility for making a success of the enterprise is about the last thing any group of employees would consider workable or even desirable."[30]

The fears implied by these two labor leaders exist as facts in countries like Norway, England, and Holland. The trade union leaders in these countries are partially or indirectly responsible for the economic health of the country (because the party identified with labor has strong political power). It is not uncommon to see trade union leaders "selling" work study, scientific management, and increased productivity to the workers.[31] Many workers feel that their national leaders are closer in outlook with management than with their own members.[32] In short, the American trade union leaders may realize that because of the impact of the nature of formal organization, even if they were perfect administrators, they still would have human problems with the employees.

## Summary

On the basis of a logical analysis, it is concluded that the formal organizational principles make demands of relatively healthy individuals that are incongruent with their needs. Frustration, conflict, failure, and short time perspective are predicted as resultants of this basic incongruency.

Empirical evidence is presented to illustrate the rational character of the formal organization and to support the proposition that the basic impact of the formal organizational structure is to make the employees feel dependent, submissive, and passive, and to require them to utilize only a few of their less important abilities.

In the next chapter [of *Personality and Organization*], empirical evidence is amassed to illustrate the existence in the employee of the predicted frustration, conflict, failure, and short time perspective and to show some of the resultants of these factors.

## References

1. Brennan, Mal: *The Making of a Moron* (New York: Sheed and Ward, 1953), pp. 13–18.

2. Mr. Brennan's emphasis.

3. Bavelas, Alex: "Communication Patterns in Task-Oriented Groups." Chapter X in *The Policy Sciences* (ed.) by D. Lerner and H. L. Lasswell (Palo Alto: Stanford University Press, 1951), pp. 193–202. ———, "A Mathematical Model for Group Structures," *Applied Anthropology*, Vol. VII, 1948, pp. 16–30.

4. Leavitt, H. J.: "Some Effects of Certain Communication Patterns on Group Performance," *Journal of Abnormal Social Psychology*, Vol. 46, 1951, pp. 38–50.

5. Heise, G. C., and Miller, G. A.: "Problem-Solving by Small Groups Using Various Communications Nets," *Journal of Abnormal Social Psychology*, Vol. 46, 1951, pp. 327–335.

6. Shaw, Marvin E., and Rothchild, Gerard H.: "Some Effects of Prolonged Experience in Communication Nets," *Journal of Applied Psychology*, Vol. 40, No. 5, October, 1956, pp. 281–286.

7. A "wheel" structure is similar to the structure that is created by the use of the principles of chain of command and space of control. One individual becomes the "boss" of the structure.

8. However, they also point out that once the other structures "got going," they were as efficient (in terms of time required to achieve the task) as the wheel. Guetzkow, Harold, and Simon, Herbert A.: "The Impact of Certain Communication Nets upon Organization and Performance in Task-Oriented Groups," *Management Science,* Vol. 1, April–July, 1955, pp. 233–250.

9. Arensberg, Conrad M.: "Behavior and Organization: Industrial Studies," (eds.) John H. Rohrer and Musafer Sherif, *Social Psychology at the Cross-roads* (New York: Harper, 1951), p. 340.

10. Bakke, E. Wight: *Citizens Without Work, op. cit.,* p. 90.

11. *Ibid.,* p. 91.

12. Blau, Peter M.: *The Dynamics of Bureaucracy* (Chicago: University of Chicago Press, 1955), pp. 167 ff.

13. *Ibid.,* pp. 172–173.

14. Gibb, Cecil A.: "Leadership," in *Handbook of Social Psychology* (ed.), Gardner Lindzey (Reading, Mass.: Addison-Wesley, 1954), pp. 887–920. (Italics mine.)

15. Blau, Peter M.: *Bureaucracy in Modern Society* (New York: Random House, 1956).

16. Bierstedt, Robert: "The Problem of Authority," in Morroe Berger, Theodore Abel, and Charles H. Page (eds.), *Freedom and Control in Modern Society* (New York: Van Nostrand, 1954), pp. 67–81.

17. Carter, Launor: "Leadership and Small Group Behavior," in M. Sherif and M. O. Wilson (eds.); *Group Relations at the Crossroads* (New York: Harper, 1953), p. 279.

18. Fleishman, Edwin A.: "The Description of Supervisory Behavior," *Journal of Applied Psychology,* Vol. 37, No. 1. Although I was unable to obtain it, E. F. Harris' thesis is also reported to include valuable data. It is entitled, "Measuring Industrial Leadership and Its Implications for Training Supervisors," Ph.D. thesis, Ohio State, 1952. It should be pointed out that Fleishman's study was not limited to the impact of the formal structure It includes leadership patterns.

19. Weber, Max: *The Theory of Social and Economic Organization,* A. M. Henderson (tr.) and Talcott Parsons (ed.) (New York: Oxford, 1947).

20. For an interesting discussion of Weber's and others' work, see Merton, Robert K., Gray, Ailsa P., Hackey, Barbara, and Selvin, Hanan C.: *Reader in Bureaucracy* (Glencoe, Illinois: The Free Press, 1952).

21. Gouldner, Alvin (ed.): *Studies in Leadership* (New York: Harper, 1950), p. 75.

22. *Ibid.,* p. 57.

23. *Ibid.,* p. 58.

24. Merton, Robert K.: "Bureaucratic Structure and Personality," *Social Forces,* 1940, printed also in *Studies in Leadership, op. cit.,* pp. 67–68.

25. Walker, Charles R., and Guest, Robert H.: *The Man on the Assembly Line* (Cambridge: Harvard University Press, 1952).

26. Personal communication. Publication in progress.

27. Turner, Arthur N.: "Management and the Assembly Line," *Harvard Business Review,* September–October, 1955, pp. 40–48.

28. Argyris, Chris: *Organization of a Bank, op. cit.,* and *Human Relations in a Hospital, op. cit.*

29. *New York Sun,* December, 1954.

30. Lewisohn, Sam: *Human Leadership in Industry* (New York: Harper, 1945).

31. Ruttenberg (one of the originators of the idea of the Guaranteed Annual Wage, while an economist for the CIO Steel Workers and now a plant president) insists that if "pay by the year" becomes effective the employees must take on management responsibilities. *Harper's,* December, 1955, pp. 29–33.

32. Argyris, Chris: *An Analysis of the Human Relations Policies and Practices in England, Norway, Holland, France, Greece, and Germany,* OEEC, Dept. of Management Reports, Paris, France, 1955.

# Theory X: The Traditional View of Direction and Control*

*Douglas McGregor*

Behind every managerial decision or action are assumptions about human nature and human behavior. A few of these are remarkably pervasive. They are implicit in most of the literature of organization and in much current managerial policy and practice:

1. *The average human being has an inherent dislike of work and will avoid it if he can.* This assumption has deep roots. The punishment of Adam and Eve for eating the fruit of the Tree of Knowledge was to be banished from Eden into a world where they had to work for a living. The stress that management places on productivity, on the concept of "a fair day's work," on the evils of featherbedding and restriction of output, on rewards for performance—while it has a logic in terms of the objectives of enterprise—reflects an underlying belief that management must counteract an inherent human tendency to avoid work. The evidence for the correctness of this assumption would seem to most managers to be incontrovertible.

2. *Because of this human characteristic of dislike of work, most people*

* From *The Human Side of Enterprise,* McGraw-Hill Book Company, Inc., New York, 1960, chap. 3, pp. 33–44. Reprinted by permission of the publisher.

*must be coerced, controlled, directed, threatened with punishment to get them to put forth adequate effort toward the achievement of organizational objectives.* The dislike of work is so strong that even the promise of rewards is not generally enough to overcome it. People will accept the rewards and demand continually higher ones, but these alone will not produce the necessary effort. Only the threat of punishment will do the trick.

The current wave of criticism of "human relations," the derogatory comments about "permissiveness" and "democracy" in industry, the trends in some companies toward recentralization after the postwar wave of decentralization—all these are assertions of the underlying assumption that people will only work under external coercion and control. The recession of 1957–1958 ended a decade of experimentation with the "soft" managerial approach, and this assumption (which never really was abandoned) is being openly espoused once more.

3. *The average human being prefers to be directed, wishes to avoid responsibility, has relatively little ambition, wants security above all.* This assumption of the "mediocrity of the masses" is rarely expressed so bluntly. In fact, a good deal of lip service is given to the ideal of the worth of the average human being. Our political and social values demand such public expressions. Nevertheless, a great many managers will give private support to this assumption, and it is easy to see it reflected in policy and practice. Paternalism has become a nasty word, but it is by no means a defunct managerial philosophy.

I have suggested elsewhere the name Theory X for this set of assumptions. . . . Theory X is not a straw man for purposes of demolition, but is in fact a theory which materially influences managerial strategy in a wide sector of American industry today. Moreover, the principles of organization which comprise the bulk of the literature of management *could only have been derived from assumptions such as those of Theory X*. Other beliefs about human nature would have led inevitably to quite different organizational principles.

Theory X provides an explanation of some human behavior in industry. These assumptions would not have persisted if there were not a considerable body of evidence to support them. Nevertheless, there are many readily observable phenomena in industry and elsewhere which are not consistent with this view of human nature.

Such a state of affairs is not uncommon. The history of science provides many examples of theoretical explanations which persist over long periods despite the fact that they are only partially adequate. Newton's laws of motion are a case in point. It was not until the development of the theory of relativity during the present century that important inconsistencies and inadequacies in Newtonian theory could be understood and corrected.

The growth of knowledge in the social sciences during the past quarter century has made it possible to reformulate some assumptions about human nature and human behavior in the organizational setting which resolve certain of the inconsistencies inherent in Theory X. While this reformulation is, of course, tentative, it provides an improved basis for prediction and control of human behavior in industry.

## Some Assumptions about Motivation

At the core of any theory of the management of human resources are assumptions about human motivation. This has been a confusing subject because there have been so many conflicting points of view even among social scientists. In recent years, however, there has been a convergence of research findings and a growing acceptance of a few rather basic ideas about motivation. These ideas appear to have considerable power. They help to explain the inadequacies of Theory X as well as the limited sense in which it is correct. In addition, they provide the basis for an entirely different theory of management.

The following generalizations about motivation are somewhat oversimplified. If all of the qualifications which would be required by a truly adequate treatment were introduced, the gross essentials which are particularly significant for management would be obscured. These generalizations do not misrepresent the facts, but they do ignore some complexities of human behavior which are relatively unimportant for our purposes.

Man is a wanting animal—as soon as one of his needs is satisfied, another appears in its place. This process is unending. It continues from birth to death. Man continuously puts forth effort—works, if you please—to satisfy his needs.

Human needs are organized in a series of levels—a hierarchy of importance.* At the lowest level, but preeminent in importance when they are thwarted, are the physiological needs. Man lives by bread alone, when there is no bread. Unless the circumstances are unusual, his needs for love, for status, for recognition are inoperative when his stomach has been empty for a while. But when he eats regularly and adequately, hunger ceases to be an important need. The sated man has hunger only in the sense that a full bottle has emptiness. The same is true of the other physiological needs of man—for rest, exercise, shelter, protection from the elements.

A satisfied need is not a motivator of behavior! This is a fact of profound significance. It is a fact which is unrecognized in Theory X and is, therefore, ignored in the conventional approach to the management of people. I shall return to it later. For the moment, an example will make the point. Consider your own need for air. Except as you are deprived of it, it has no appreciable motivating effect upon your behavior.

* [For a more detailed explanation of the hierarchy of needs, see A. H. Maslow, "A Theory of Human Motivation," reprinted in this volume, pages 83–103.—Ed.]

When the physiological needs are reasonably satisfied, needs at the next higher level begin to dominate man's behavior—to motivate him. These are the safety needs, for protection against danger, threat, deprivation. Some people mistakenly refer to these as needs for security. However, unless man is in a dependent relationship where he fears arbitrary deprivation, he does not demand security. The need is for the "fairest possible break." When he is confident of this, he is more than willing to take risks. But when he feels threatened or dependent, his greatest need is for protection, for security.

The fact needs little emphasis that since every industrial employee is in at least a partially dependent relationship, safety needs may assume considerable importance. Arbitrary management actions, behavior which arouses uncertainty with respect to continued employment or which reflects favoritism or discrimination, unpredictable administration of policy—these can be powerful motivators of the safety needs in the employment relationship at every level from worker to vice president. In addition, the safety needs of managers are often aroused by their dependence downward or laterally. This is a major reason for emphasis on management prerogatives and clear assignments of authority.

When man's physiological needs are satisfied and he is no longer fearful about his physical welfare, his social needs become important motivators of his behavior. These are such needs as those for belonging, for association, for acceptance by one's fellows, for giving and receiving friendship and love.

Management knows today of the existence of these needs, but it is often assumed quite wrongly that they represent a threat to the organization. Many studies have demonstrated that the tightly knit, cohesive work group may, under proper conditions, be far more effective than an equal number of separate individuals in achieving organizational goals. Yet management, fearing group hostility to its own objectives, often goes to considerable lengths to control and direct human efforts in ways that are inimical to the natural "groupiness" of human beings. When man's social needs—and perhaps his safety needs, too—are thus thwarted, he behaves in ways which tend to defeat organizational objectives. He becomes resistant, antagonistic, uncooperative. But this behavior is a consequence, not a cause.

Above the social needs—in the sense that they do not usually become motivators until lower needs are reasonably satisfied—are the needs of greatest significance to management and to man himself. They are the egoistic needs, and they are of two kinds:

1. Those that relate to one's self-esteem: needs for self-respect and self-confidence, for autonomy, for achievement, for competence, for knowledge
2. Those that relate to one's reputation: needs for status, for recognition, for appreciation, for the deserved respect of one's fellows

Unlike the lower needs, these are rarely satisfied; man seeks indefinitely for more satisfaction of these needs once they have become important to him. However, they do not usually appear in any significant way until physiological, safety, and social needs are reasonably satisfied. Exceptions to this generalization are to be observed, particularly under circumstances where, in addition to severe deprivation of physiological needs, human dignity is trampled upon. Political revolutions often grow out of thwarted social and ego, as well as physiological, needs.

The typical industrial organization offers only limited opportunities for the satisfaction of egoistic needs to people at lower levels in the hierarchy. The conventional methods of organizing work, particularly in mass production industries, give little heed to these aspects of human motivation. If the practices of "scientific management" were deliberately calculated to thwart these needs—which, of course, they are not—they could hardly accomplish this purpose better than they do.

Finally—a capstone, as it were, on the hierarchy—there are the needs for self-fulfillment. These are the needs for realizing one's own potentialities, for continued self-development, for being creative in the broadest sense of that term.

The conditions of modern industrial life give only limited opportunity for these relatively dormant human needs to find expression. The deprivation most people experience with respect to other lower-level needs diverts their energies into the struggle to satisfy *those* needs, and the needs for self-fulfillment remain below the level of consciousness.

Now, briefly, a few general comments about motivation:

We recognize readily enough that a man suffering from a severe dietary deficiency is sick. The deprivation of physiological needs has behavioral consequences. The same is true, although less well recognized, of the deprivation of higher-level needs. The man whose needs for safety, association, independence, or status are thwarted is sick, just as surely as is he who has rickets. And his sickness will have behavioral consequences. We will be mistaken if we attribute his resultant passivity, or his hostility, or his refusal to accept responsibility to his inherent "human nature." These forms of behavior are *symptoms* of illness—of deprivation of his social and egoistic needs.

The man whose lower-level needs are satisfied is not motivated to satisfy *those* needs. For practical purposes they exist no longer. (Remember my point about your need for air.) Management often asks, "Why aren't people more productive? We pay good wages, provide good working conditions, have excellent fringe benefits and steady employment. Yet people do not seem to be willing to put forth more than minimum effort." It is unnecessary to look far for the reasons.

Consideration of the rewards typically provided the worker for satisfying his needs through his employment leads to the interesting conclusion that most of these rewards can be used for satisfying his needs *only when he leaves the job*. Wages, for example, cannot be spent at work. The only contribution they can make to his satisfaction on the job is in terms of status differences resulting from wage differentials. (This, incidentally, is one of the reasons why small and apparently unimportant differences in wage rates can be the subject of so much heated dispute. The issue is not the pennies involved, but the fact that the status differences which they reflect are one of the few ways in which wages can result in need satisfaction in the job situation itself.)

Most fringe benefits—overtime pay, shift differentials, vacations, health and medical benefits, annuities, and the proceeds from stock purchase plans or profit-sharing plans—yield needed satisfaction only when the individual leaves the job. Yet these, along with wages, are among the major rewards provided by management for effort. It is not surprising, therefore, that for many wage earners *work is perceived as a form of punishment* which is the price to be paid for various kinds of satisfaction away from the job. To the extent that this is their perception, we would hardly expect them to undergo more of this punishment than is necessary.

Under today's conditions management has provided relatively well for the satisfaction of physiological and safety needs. The standard of living in our country is high; people do not suffer major deprivation of their physiological needs except during periods of severe unemployment. Even then, social legislation developed since the thirties cushions the shock.

But the fact that management has provided for these physiological and safety needs has shifted the motivational emphasis to the social and the egoistic needs. Unless there are opportunities *at work* to satisfy these higher-level needs, people will be deprived; and their behavior will reflect this deprivation. Under such conditions, if management continues to focus its attention on physiological needs, the mere provision of rewards is bound to be ineffective, and reliance on the threat of punishment will be inevitable. Thus one of the assumptions of Theory X will appear to be validated, but only because we have mistaken effects for causes.

People *will* make insistent demands for more money under these conditions. It becomes more important than ever to buy the material goods and services which can provide limited satisfaction of the thwarted needs. Although money has only limited value in satisfying many higher-level needs, it can become the focus of interest if it is the only means available.

The "carrot and stick" theory of motivation which goes along with Theory X works reasonably well under certain circumstances. The *means* for satisfying man's physiological and (within limits) safety needs can be provided or withheld by management. Employment itself is such a means, and so are wages, working conditions, and benefits. By these means the individual can be controlled so long as he is struggling for subsistence. Man tends to live for bread alone when there is little bread.

But the "carrot and stick" theory does not work at all once man has reached an adequate subsistence level and is motivated primarily by higher needs. Management cannot provide a man with self-respect, or with the respect of his fellows, or with the satisfaction of needs for self-fulfillment. We can create conditions such that he is encouraged and enabled to seek such satisfactions for himself, or we can thwart him by failing to create those conditions.

But this creation of conditions is not "control" in the usual sense; it does not seem to be a particularly good device for directing behavior. And so management finds itself in an odd position. The high standard of living created by our modern technological know-how provides quite adequately for the satisfaction of physiological and safety needs. The only significant exception is where management practices have not created confidence in a "fair break"—and thus where safety needs are thwarted. But by making possible the satisfaction of lower-level needs, management has deprived itself of the ability to use the control devices on which the conventional assumptions of Theory X has taught it to rely: rewards, promises, incentives, or threats and other coercive devices.

The philosophy of management by direction and control—*regardless of whether it is hard or soft*—is inadequate to motivate because the human needs on which this approach relies are relatively unimportant motivators of behavior in our society today. Direction and control are of limited value in motivating people whose important needs are social and egoistic.

People, deprived of opportunities to satisfy at work the needs which are now important to them, behave exactly as we might predict—with indolence, passivity, unwillingness to accept responsibility, resistance to change, willingness to follow the demagogue, unreasonable demands for economic benefits. It would seem that we may be caught in a web of our own weaving.

Theory X explains the *consequences* of a particular managerial strategy; it neither explains nor describes human nature although it purports to. Because its assumptions are so unnecessarily limiting, it prevents our seeing the possibilities inherent in other managerial strategies. What sometimes appear to be new strategies—decentralization, management by objectives, consultative supervision, "democratic" leadership—are usually but old wine in new bottles because the procedures developed to implement them are derived from the same inadequate assumptions about human nature. Management is constantly becoming disillusioned with widely touted and expertly merchandised "new approaches" to the human side of enterprise. The real difficulty is that these new approaches are no more than different tactics—programs, procedures, gadgets—within an unchanged strategy based on Theory X.

In child rearing, it is recognized that parental strategies of control must be progressively modified to adapt to the changed capabilities and characteristics of the human individual as he develops from infancy to adulthood. To some extent industrial management recognizes that the human *adult* possesses capabilities for continued learning and growth. Witness the many current activities in the fields of training and management development. In its *basic* conceptions of managing human resources, however, management appears to have concluded that the average human being is permanently arrested in his development in early adolescence. Theory X is built on the least common human denominator: the factory "hand" of the past. As Chris Argyris has shown dramatically in his *Personality and Organization,* conventional managerial strategies for the organization, direction, and control of the human resources of enterprise are admirably suited to the capacities and characteristics of the child rather than the adult.

In one limited area—that of research administration—there has been some recent recognition of the need for selective adaptation in managerial strategy. This, however, has been perceived as a unique problem, and its broader implications have not been recognized. As pointed out in this and the previous chapter [of *The Human Side of Enterprise*], changes in the population at large—in educational level, attitudes and values, motivation, degree of dependence—have created both the opportunity and the need for other forms of selective adaptation. However, so long as the assumptions of Theory X continue to influence managerial strategy, we will fail to discover, let alone utilize, the potentialities of the average human being.

## References

Allen, Louis A.: *Management and Organization.* New York: McGraw-Hill Book Company, Inc., 1958.

Bendix, Reinhard: *Work and Authority in Industry.* New York: John Wiley & Sons, Inc., 1956.

Brown, Alvin: *Organization of Industry.* Englewood Cliffs, N.J.: Prentice-Hall, Inc., 1947.

Fayol, H.: *Industrial and General Administration.* London: Sir Isaac Pitman & Sons, Ltd., 1930.

Gouldner, Alvin W.: *Patterns of Industrial Bureaucracy.* Glencoe, Ill.: Free Press, 1954.

Koontz, Harold, and Cyril O'Donnell: *Principles of Management.* New York: McGraw-Hill Book Company, Inc., 1955.

Maslow, Abraham: *Motivation and Personality.* New York: Harper & Brothers, 1954.

Urwick, Lyndall: *The Elements of Administration.* New York: Harper & Brothers, 1944.

Walker, Charles R.: *Toward the Automatic Factory*. New Haven, Conn.: Yale University Press, 1957.

Whyte, William F.: *Money and Motivation*. New York: Harper & Brothers, 1955.

Zaleznick, A., C. F. Christensen, and F. J. Roethlisberger: *Motivation, Productivity, and Satisfaction of Workers*. Cambridge, Mass.: Harvard University Press, 1958.

# Theory Y: The Integration of Individual and Organizational Goals[*]

*Douglas McGregor*

To some, the preceding analysis will appear unduly harsh. Have we not made major modifications in the management of the human resources of industry during the past quarter century? Have we not recognized the importance of people and made vitally significant changes in managerial strategy as a consequence? Do the developments since the twenties in personnel administration and labor relations add up to nothing?

There is no question that important progress has been made in the past two or three decades. During this period the human side of enterprise has become a major preoccupation of management. A tremendous number of policies, programs, and practices which were virtually unknown thirty years ago have become commonplace. The lot of the industrial employee —be he worker, professional, or executive—has improved to a degree which could hardly have been imagined by his counterpart of the nineteen twenties. Management has adopted generally a far more humanitarian set of values; it has successfully striven to give more equitable and more generous treatment to its employees. It has significantly reduced economic hardships, eliminated the more extreme forms of industrial warfare, provided a generally safe and pleasant working environment, *but it has done all these things without changing its fundamental theory of management*. There are exceptions here and there, and they are important; nevertheless, the assumptions of Theory X remain predominant throughout our economy.

[*] From *The Human Side of Enterprise*, McGraw-Hill Book Company, Inc., New York, 1960, chap. 4, pp. 45–57. Reprinted by permission of the publisher.

Management was subjected to severe pressures during the Great Depression of the thirties. The wave of public antagonism, the open warfare accompanying the unionization of the mass production industries, the general reaction against authoritarianism, the legislation of the New Deal produced a wide "pendulum swing." However, the changes in policy and practice which took place during that and the next decade were primarily adjustments to the increased power of organized labor and to the pressures of public opinion.

Some of the movement was away from "hard" and toward "soft" management, but it was short-lived, and for good reasons. It has become clear that many of the initial strategic interpretations accompanying the "human relations approach" were as naïve as those which characterized the early stages of progressive education. We have now discovered that there is no answer in the simple removal of control—that abdication is not a workable alternative to authoritarianism. We have learned that there is no direct correlation between employee satisfaction and productivity. We recognize today that "industrial democracy" cannot consist in permitting everyone to decide everything, that industrial health does not flow automatically from the elimination of dissatisfaction, disagreement, or even open conflict. Peace is not synonymous with organizational health; socially responsible management is not coextensive with permissive management.

Now that management has regained its earlier prestige and power, it has become obvious that the trend toward "soft" management was a temporary and relatively superficial reaction rather than a general modification of fundamental assumptions or basic strategy. Moreover, while the progress we have made in the past quarter century is substantial, it has reached the point of diminishing returns. The tactical possibilities within conventional managerial strategies have been pretty completely exploited, and significant new developments will be unlikely without major modifications in theory.

## The Assumptions of Theory Y

There have been few dramatic break-throughs in social science theory like those which have occurred in the physical sciences during the past half century. Nevertheless, the accumulation of knowledge about human behavior in many specialized fields has made possible the formulation of a number of generalizations which provide a modest beginning for new theory with respect to the management of human resources. Some of these assumptions were outlined in the discussion of motivation [on page 188]. Some others, which will hereafter be referred to as Theory Y, are as follows:

1. *The expenditure of physical and mental effort in work is as natural as play or rest.* The average human being does not inherently dislike work. Depending upon controllable conditions, work may be a source of satisfaction

(and will be voluntarily performed) or a source of punishment (and will be avoided if possible).

2. *External control and the threat of punishment are not the only means for bringing about effort toward organizational objectives. Man will exercise self-direction and self-control in the service of objectives to which he is committed.*

3. *Commitment to objectives is a function of the rewards associated with their achievement.* The most significant of such rewards, e.g., the satisfaction of ego and self-actualization needs, can be direct products of effort directed toward organizational objectives.

4. *The average human being learns, under proper conditions, not only to accept but to seek responsibility.* Avoidance of responsibility, lack of ambition, and emphasis on security are generally consequences of experience, not inherent human characteristics.

5. *The capacity to exercise a relatively high degree of imagination, ingenuity, and creativity in the solution of organizational problems is widely, not narrowly, distributed in the population.*

6. *Under the conditions of modern industrial life, the intellectual potentialities of the average human being are only partially utilized.*

These assumptions involve sharply different implications for managerial strategy than do those of Theory X. They are dynamic rather than static: They indicate the possibility of human growth and development; they stress the necessity for selective adaptation rather than for a single absolute form of control. They are not framed in terms of the least common denominator of the factory hand, but in terms of a resource which has substantial potentialities.

Above all, the assumptions of Theory Y point up the fact that the limits on human collaboration in the organizational setting are not limits of human nature but of management's ingenuity in discovering how to realize the potential represented by its human resources. Theory X offers management an easy rationalization for ineffective organizational performance: It is due to the nature of the human resources with which we must work. Theory Y, on the other hand, places the problems squarely in the lap of management. If employees are lazy, indifferent, unwilling to take responsibility, intransigent, uncreative, uncooperative, Theory Y implies that the causes lie in management's methods of organization and control.

The assumptions of Theory Y are not finally validated. Nevertheless, they are far more consistent with existing knowledge in the social sciences than are the assumptions of Theory X. They will undoubtedly be refined, elaborated, modified as further research accumulates, but they are unlikely to be completely contradicted.

On the surface, these assumptions may not seem particularly difficult to accept. Carrying their implications into practice, however, is not easy. They challenge a number of deeply ingrained managerial habits of thought and action.

## The Principle of Integration

The central principle of organization which derives from Theory X is that of direction and control through the exercise of authority—what has been called "the scalar principle." The central principle which derives from Theory Y is that of integration: the creation of conditions such that the members of the organization can achieve their own goals *best* by directing their efforts toward the success of the enterprise. These two principles have profoundly different implications with respect to the task of managing human resources, but the scalar principle is so firmly built into managerial attitudes that the implications of the principle of integration are not easy to perceive.

Someone once said that fish discover water last. The "psychological environment" of industrial management—like water for fish—is so much a part of organizational life that we are unaware of it. Certain characteristics of our society, and of organizational life within it, are so completely established, so pervasive, that we cannot conceive of their being otherwise. As a result, a great many policies and practices and decisions and relationships could only be—it seems—what they are.

Among these pervasive characteristics of organizational life in the United States today is a managerial attitude (stemming from Theory X) toward membership in the industrial organization. It is assumed almost without question that organizational requirements take precedence over the needs of individual members. Basically, the employment agreement is that in return for the rewards which are offered, the individual will accept external direction and control. The very idea of integration and self-control is foreign to our way of thinking about the employment relationship. The tendency, therefore, is either to reject it out of hand (as socialistic, or anarchistic, or inconsistent with human nature) or to twist it unconsciously until it fits existing conceptions.

The concept of integration and self-control carries the implication that the organization will be more effective in achieving its economic objectives if adjustments are made, in significant ways, to the needs and goals of its members.

A district manager in a large, geographically decentralized company is notified that he is being promoted to a policy level position at headquarters. It is a big promotion with a large salary increase. His role in the organization will be a much more powerful one, and he will be associated with the major executives of the firm.

The headquarters group who selected him for this position have carefully considered a number of possible candidates. This man stands out among them in a way which makes him the natural choice. His performance has been under observation for some time, and there is little question that he possesses the necessary qualifications not only for this opening but for an even higher position. There is genuine satisfaction that such an outstanding candidate is available.

The man is appalled. He doesn't want the job. His goal, as he expresses it, is to be the "best damned district manager in the company." He enjoys his direct associations with operating people in the field, and he doesn't want a policy level job. He and his wife enjoy the kind of life they have created in a small city, and they dislike actively both the living conditions and the social obligations of the headquarters city.

He expresses his feelings as strongly as he can, but his objections are brushed aside. The organization's needs are such that his refusal to accept the promotion would be unthinkable. His superiors say to themselves that of course when he has settled in to the new job, he will recognize that it was the right thing. And so he makes the move.

Two years later he is in an even higher position in the company's headquarters organization, and there is talk that he will probably be the executive vice-president before long. Privately he expresses considerable unhappiness and dissatisfaction. He (and his wife) would "give anything" to be back in the situation he left two years ago.

Within the context of the pervasive assumptions of Theory X, promotions and transfers in large numbers are made by unilateral decision. The requirements of the organization are given priority automatically and almost without question. If the individual's personal goals are considered at all, it is assumed that the rewards of salary and position will satisfy him. Should an individual actually refuse such a move without a compelling reason, such as health or a severe family crisis, he would be considered to have jeopardized his future because of this "selfish" attitude. It is rare indeed for management to give the individual the opportunity to be a genuine and active partner in such a decision, even though it may affect his most important personal goals. Yet the implications following from Theory Y are that the organization is likely to suffer if it ignores these personal needs and goals. In making unilateral decisions with respect to promotion, management is failing to utilize its human resources in the most effective way.

The principle of integration demands that both the organization's and the individual's needs be recognized. Of course, when there is a sincere joint effort to find it, an integrative solution which meets the needs of the individual *and* the organization is a frequent outcome. But not always— and this is the point at which Theory Y begins to appear unrealistic. It collides head on with pervasive attitudes associated with management by direction and control.

The assumptions of Theory Y imply that unless integration is achieved *the organization will suffer*. The objectives of the organization are *not* achieved best by the unilateral administration of promotions, because this form of management by direction and control will not create the commitment which would make available the full resources of those affected. The lesser motivation, the lesser resulting degree of self-direction and self-control are costs which, when added up for many instances over time, will more than offset the gains obtained by unilateral decisions "for the good of the organization."

One other example will perhaps clarify further the sharply different implications of Theory X and Theory Y.

It could be argued that management is already giving a great deal of attention to the principle of integration through its efforts in the field of economic education. Many millions of dollars and much ingenuity have been expended in attempts to persuade employees that their welfare is intimately connected with the success of the free enterprise system and of their own companies. The idea that they can achieve their own goals best by directing their effort toward the objectives of the organization has been explored and developed and communicated in every possible way. Is this not evidence that management is already committed to the principle of integration?

The answer is a definite no. These managerial efforts, with rare exceptions, reflect clearly the influence of the assumptions of Theory X. The central message is an exhortation to the industrial employee to work hard and follow orders in order to protect his job and his standard of living. Much has been achieved, it says, by our established way of running industry, and much more could be achieved if employees would adapt themselves *to management's definition* of what is required. Behind these exhortations lies the expectation that of course the requirements of the organization and its economic success must have priority over the needs of the individual.

Naturally, integration means working together for the success of the enterprise so we all may share in the resulting rewards. But management's implicit assumption is that working together means adjusting to the requirements of the organization *as management perceives them.* In terms of existing views, it seems inconceivable that individuals, seeking their own goals, would further the ends of the enterprise. On the contrary, this would lead to anarchy, chaos, irreconcilable conflicts of self-interest, lack of responsibility, inability to make decisions, and failure to carry out those that were made.

All these consequences, and other worse ones, *would* be inevitable unless conditions could be created such that the members of the organization perceived that they could achieve their own goals *best* by directing their efforts toward the success of the enterprise. If the assumptions of Theory Y are valid, the practical question is whether, and to what extent, such conditions can be created. To that question the balance of this volume is addressed.

## The Application of Theory Y

In the physical sciences there are many theoretical phenomena which cannot be achieved in practice. Absolute zero and a perfect vacuum are examples. Others, such as nuclear power, jet aircraft, and human space flight, are recognized theoretically to be possible long before they become feasible. This fact does not make theory less useful. It it were not for our theoretical convictions, we would not even be attempting to develop the means for human flight into space today. In fact, were it not for the development of physical science theory during the past century and a half, we would still be depending upon the horse and buggy and the sailing vessel for transportation. Virtually all significant technological developments wait on the formulation of relevant theory.

Similarly, in the management of the human resources of industry, the assumptions and theories about human nature at any given time limit innovation. Possibilities are not recognized, innovating efforts are not undertaken, until theoretical conceptions lay a groundwork for them. Assumptions like those of Theory X permit us to conceive of certain possible ways of organizing and directing human effort, *but not others*. Assumptions like those of Theory Y open up a range of possibilities for new managerial policies and practices. As in the case of the development of new physical science theory, some of these possibilities are not immediately feasible, and others may forever remain unattainable. They may be too costly, or it may be that we simply cannot discover how to create the necessary "hardware."

There is substantial evidence for the statement that the potentialities of the average human being are far above those which we typically realize in industry today. If our assumptions are like those of Theory X, we will not even recognize the existence of these potentialities and there will be no reason to devote time, effort, or money to discovering how to realize them. If, however, we accept assumptions like those of Theory Y, we will be challenged to innovate, to discover new ways of organizing and directing human effort, even though we recognize that the perfect organization, like the perfect vacuum, is practically out of reach.

We need not be overwhelmed by the dimensions of the managerial task implied by Theory Y. To be sure, a large mass production operation in which the workers have been organized by a militant and hostile union faces management with problems which appear at present to be insurmountable with respect to the application of the principle of integration. It may be decades before sufficient knowledge will have accumulated to make such an application feasible. Applications of Theory Y will have to be tested initially in more limited ways and under more favorable circumstances. However, a number of applications of Theory Y *in managing managers and professional people* are possible today. Within the managerial hierarchy, the assumptions can be tested and refined, techniques can be invented and skill acquired in their use. As knowledge accumulates, some of the problems of application at the worker level in large organizations may appear less baffling than they do at present.

Perfect integration of organizational requirements and individual goals and needs is, of course, not a realistic objective. In adopting this principle, we seek that degree of integration in which the individual can achieve his goals *best* by directing his efforts toward the success of the organization. "Best" means that this alternative will be more attractive than the many others available to him: indifference, irresponsibility, minimal compliance, hostility, sabotage. It means that he will continuously be encouraged to develop and utilize voluntarily his capacities, his knowledge, his skill, his ingenuity in ways which contribute to the success of the enterprise.[1]

Acceptance of Theory Y does not imply abdication, or "soft" management, or "permissiveness." As was indicated above, such notions stem from the acceptance of authority as the *single* means of managerial control, and from attempts to minimize its negative consequences. Theory Y assumes that people will exercise self-direction and self-control in the achievement of organizational objectives *to the degree that they are committed to those objectives.* If that commitment is small, only a slight degree of self-direction and self-control will be likely, and a substantial amount of external influence will be necessary. If it is large, many conventional external controls will be relatively superfluous, and to some extent self-defeating. Managerial policies and practices materially affect this degree of commitment.

Authority is an inappropriate means for obtaining commitment to objectives. Other forms of influence—help in achieving integration, for example —are required for this purpose. Theory Y points to the possibility of lessening the emphasis on external forms of control to the degree that commitment to organizational objectives can be achieved. Its underlying assumptions emphasize the capacity of human beings for self-control, and

---

[1] A recent, highly significant study of the sources of job satisfaction and dissatisfaction among managerial and professional people suggests that these opportunities for "self-actualization" are the essential requirements of both job satisfaction and high performance. The researchers find that "the wants of employees divide into two groups. One group revolves around the need to develop in one's occupation as a source of personal growth. The second group operates as an essential base to the first and is associated with fair treatment in compensation, supervision, working conditions, and administrative practices. *The fulfillment of the needs of the second group does not motivate the individual to high levels of job satisfaction and . . . to extra performance on the job.* All we can expect from satisfying [this second group of needs] is the prevention of dissatisfaction and poor job performance." Frederick Herzberg, Bernard Mausner, and Barbara Bloch Snyderman, *The Motivation to Work.* New York: John Wiley & Sons, Inc., 1959, pp. 114–115. (Italics mine.)

the consequent possibility of greater managerial reliance on other means of influence. Nevertheless, it is clear that authority *is* an appropriate means for control under certain circumstances—particularly where genuine commitment to objectives cannot be achieved. The assumptions of Theory Y do not deny the appropriateness of authority, but they do deny that it is appropriate for all purposes and under all circumstances.

Many statements have been made to the effect that we have acquired today the know-how to cope with virtually any technological problems which may arise, and that the major industrial advances of the next half century will occur on the human side of enterprise. Such advances, however, are improbable so long as management continues to organize and direct and control its human resources on the basis of assumptions—tacit or explicit—like those of Theory X. Genuine innovation, in contrast to a refurbishing and patching of present managerial strategies, requires first the acceptance of less limiting assumptions about the nature of the human resources we seek to control, and second the readiness to adapt selectively to the implications contained in those new assumptions. Theory Y is an invitation to innovation.

## References

Brown, J. A. C.: *The Social Psychology of Industry*. Baltimore: Penguin Books, Inc., 1954.

Cordiner, Ralph J.: *New Frontiers for Professional Managers*. New York: McGraw-Hill Book Company, Inc., 1956.

Dubin, Robert: *The World of Work: Industrial Society and Human Relations*. Englewood Cliffs, N.J.: Prentice-Hall, Inc., 1958.

Friedmann, Georges: *Industrial Society: The Emergence of the Human Problems of Automation*. Glencoe, Ill.: Free Press, 1955.

Herzberg, Frederick, Bernard Mausner, and Barbara Bloch Snyderman: *The Motivation to Work*. New York: John Wiley & Sons, Inc., 1959.

Krech, David, and Richard S. Crutchfield: *Theory and Problems of Social Psychology*. New York: McGraw-Hill Book Company, Inc., 1948.

Leavitt, Harold J.: *Managerial Psychology*. Chicago: University of Chicago Press, 1958.

McMurry, Robert N.: "The Case for Benevolent Autocracy," *Harvard Business Review*, vol. 36, no. 1 (January–February), 1958.

Rice, A. K.: *Productivity and Social Organizations: The Ahmedabad Experiment*. London: Tavistock Publications, Ltd., 1958.

Stagner, Ross: *The Psychology of Industrial Conflict*. New York: John Wiley & Sons, Inc., 1956.

# Organizational Structure and Employee Morale*

*James C. Worthy*

## 1. Introduction

This discussion will review some of the findings of the research conducted by Sears, Roebuck and Co. in the field of employee attitudes and morale. This research is an integral part of our company's personnel program; its primary purpose is to assist executives in their efforts to maintain sound and mutually satisfactory employee relationships. Such relationships are conceived by our management not only as a positive good in themselves but as an essential condition for the continued economic success of the enterprise.

We have had 12 years of experience in the formal study of employee morale. During that period our surveys have covered over 100,000 employees, working in several hundred different company units both in Sears, Roebuck proper and in a number of other organizations as well. Types of employees covered include sales and clerical personnel, manual and professional workers, supervisory employees, and executives. The size of units surveyed has ranged from fewer than 25 employees to more than 10,000. Many different types of units have been surveyed, including retail stores, mail order plants, factories, warehouses, and offices. The geographical distribution of employees covered would correspond rather well with the geographical distribution of the U.S. population. By the same token, the communities in which units surveyed have been located cover practically the full range of sociological and cultural categories to be found in this country, except the small town and the rural.

## 2. Methods of Study

Time does not permit any detailed account of our survey methods; however, some brief explanation is necessary if only to indicate the extent to which confidence can be reposed in our findings.

* From *American Sociological Review*, vol. 15, pp. 169–179, April, 1950. Reprinted by permission of the publisher.

Our original surveys were based solely on questionnaires, which were answered anonymously by employees. The questions covered a great variety of subjects—practically every subject, in fact, which we thought likely to have any influence on employee attitudes. In other words, the questionnaires had the simple, straightforward purpose of finding out how well employees liked their jobs, what their attitudes were toward supervision and management, and what factors in their employment situation might be contributing to dissatisfaction or poor working relationships. We assumed that when we had learned these things we would be able to take specific action to correct specific problems and thus restore peace and harmony where any lack thereof was found to exist.

We did find certain things that were susceptible of direct management action, but we also found many things that were difficult to take hold of. It soon became apparent that we were dealing with an infinitely complex system of influences and relationships, and not with a simple system of logical cause and effect. We began to question the adequacy of questionnaires and found, as we analyzed thousands of employee responses, that we could not even be sure we were asking the right questions or asking them in the right way.

Finally, there were real difficulties in attempting to analyze the significance of questionnaire responses. What was a "good" score on a certain point? Was a 65% "favorable" response to a question about employee discount policy equivalent to a 65% "favorable" response to a question about wage rates? Beyond certain relatively superficial points, there was often great uncertainty as to just what the tabulation of responses meant and what, if anything, could or should be done about it.

We have handled this problem by developing quite a different type of questionnaire and by supplementing it with other techniques (notably interviewing). Instead of covering a great many specific points, the questionnaire we now use seeks only to determine the general "feeling tone" of employees with respect to six key aspects of their working environment: (1) the company in general, (2) the local organization, (3) the local management, (4) immediate supervision, (5) fellow employees, and (6) job and working conditions. Ten items are included under each of these headings on which employees can express varying degrees of satisfaction or dissatisfaction. In scoring, we are not concerned with responses to each particular item in the questionnaire, but rather with the *general tendency* of responses in each of the six areas. In this respect, the questionnaire is patterned after the familiar "interest" or "personality" schedules used in psychological testing. As with such schedules, our questionnaire results can be expressed in "profiles." Furthermore, we have enough "cases" (i.e., units surveyed) to be able to translate raw scores into percentiles, thus greatly facilitating the process of interpretation and comparative analysis. As our survey people gain more experience in relating different types of profiles to concrete situations, they are developing real skill in using questionnaire results as a diagnostic tool.

The function of the questionnaire is not, however, to secure detailed information, but rather to "take the temperature" of an organization and its various subdivisions, to determine whether the general level of morale is high or low, and to point out areas of stress and strain which may be tending to undermine cooperative working relationships. In other words, by means of the questionnaire, we are able to locate problem departments and to identify the general nature of employee dissatisfactions. Only within broad limits, however, does the questionnaire tell *why* morale may be low. The real task of determining the "why" falls to a team of carefully trained interviewers. Because the questionnaire has already indicated the general nature and location of problems, the interviewing team is able to concentrate its time and energies on those departments and employee groups most requiring attention.

Surveys are conducted by members of the company's regional personnel staffs, with technical direction and coordination from the national personnel office in Chicago. (Administrative control of survey activities is strictly a regional responsibility.) People conducting the surveys receive special training in non-directive interviewing and in certain aspects of sociological and anthropological theory which we have found to contribute meaningfully to understanding the problems of organizations. In large part, they are trained by the case method, not only through studying reports dealing with "classic" situations (of which by this time we have a fair variety) but also through participating directly in survey work under the tutelage of experienced survey personnel.

In this connection, it should be noted that the entire survey program makes extensive use of clinical methods, not only for training younger practitioners, but for analyzing the significance of survey results and for working out necessary corrective measures with the executives responsible for the operating units involved. The participation of line executives, with their intimate and long-standing knowledge of their organizations, in these "clinical sessions" has contributed greatly to both the pragmatic value of the survey program and the growth of knowledge and understanding on the part of survey personnel. Valuable as our extensive statistical data has been and is, most of the insights and hypotheses which the program has produced have been an outgrowth of this clinical approach.

Thus, the scope of our survey program has broadened significantly since its inception 12 years ago. We have found that there is more to good morale than high wages and pleasant working conditions (although these are of unquestioned importance). We have learned that effective leadership involves more than "winning friends and influencing people" (although social skill is an essential ingredient of executive capacity). It has gradually become clear that to understand what might be taking place within any particular working group we must have some knowledge of a variety of factors both internal and external to the group itself, and that, above all, we must have some dynamic conception of the manner in which these factors relate themselves one to the other and to the total situation of which each is an influencing and influenced part.

The scope of the surveys has thus been broadened to include the functioning of the organization as a whole and the entire pattern of technical processes and formal and informal relationships which comprise it. To the extent permitted by practical operating considerations, community and regional factors are likewise taken into account. In recognition of this broader scope, our surveys are no longer known as "*morale* surveys" but as "*organization* surveys." Determining the level of morale has ceased to be an end in itself and is now useful chiefly as a means for diagnosing the problems of an organization. Above all, our survey teams seek to deal not merely with the superficial manifestations of problems, but with the basic influences which have created the problems.

Surveys are concerned not merely with discovering the nature and origin of difficulties; their primary purpose is problem-solving. To this end, the survey team attempts to give the local manager a more complete picture of his organization and the way it is functioning, and to help him understand the various factors operative in his particular situation and their effects, not only on the attitudes and behavior of his people, but on the efficiency with which his organization is functioning. With this clearer picture of his organization, the manager is in a better position to take constructive action directed at the root of his problem rather than its superficial symptoms. However, the long-range objective of the survey program is not so much to correct immediate situations as to assist in developing the kind of organizations that can solve their own problems. A survey has failed in this essential purpose unless it leaves the particular store, plant, or department stronger and more self-reliant than it was before.

Our survey program is thus primarily an administrative device; its chief function is to assist local executives in doing a better job of handling the problems of their organizations. However, the surveys have also provided highly useful information about certain fundamental problems of human relations. One of the responsibilities of the research and planning staff of the national personnel office is the constant analysis and evaluation of survey data and the development of working hypothesis based on these data. Time will not permit any general review of our findings to date, but I would like to indicate some of the general directions of our current thinking.

### 3. A Problem of Integration

One line of thought on which we are working is the possibility of developing a typology of the malfunctioning of organization which can be useful in studying social groups as the typologies used by psychiatrists are useful in studying the malfunctioning of personality. This possibility was first suggested by the frequency with which the questionnaire "profiles" tended to form themselves into patterns with which we began to grow familiar. Our interviewing, likewise, attested that certain types of problems tended to occur in fairly well organized syndromes. For instance, we have found that certain kinds of difficulties typically follow changes in key management staff. We can usually predict not only what difficulties are likely to occur but the exact sequence in which they are likely to appear.

A typology of the malfunctioning of organization would be useful not only for scientific purposes but for administrative purposes as well, for with it could be developed a symptomatology by which problem situations could be diagnosed and acted upon more rapidly and more accurately. As already pointed out, our survey program is primarily an administrative device. Useful as it has been for this purpose, it has certain unwieldy features because sometimes it has to go a rather long way around to reach a fairly simple conclusion. For administrative purposes, we would be far better off if we had a group of people (preferably our administrators themselves) skilled at recognizing and diagnosing symptoms and dealing with the problem thus defined according to whatever therapy had been found useful for that particular type of difficulty.

It would be even more useful to be able to predict with reasonable accuracy the probable consequences of a given event or a given set of circumstances and to set in motion early a series of moves designed to minimize any adverse possibilities. We are able to do precisely this on a number of counts (for instance, cases of key executive changes) and our success here encourages us in our efforts to broaden the area in which we can predict with confidence.

As to our survey program as a whole, we are, as things stand now, somewhat in the position the medical profession would be in if the physician had to give a basic metabolism to determine whether a patient had a cold in the head. To continue the analogy, if we had a workable symptomatology (no matter how tentative), we could recognize the head cold and treat it accordingly. On the other hand, if the symptoms in the case indicated a more dangerous or more complicated disability, we could always apply our equivalent of the basic metabolism or such other procedure as the circumstances might require.

Any typology of malfunctioning must relate, of course, to the underlying dynamic system and not merely to the symptoms. All of our research testifies to the frequency with which the identical symptom can arise from entirely different factors. In one context, complaints over wages can be a danger signal; in another, merely an indication of the normal desire of everyone to be making a little bit more than he is. Sometimes, complaints over wages can really be complaints over wages; at other times, they can be merely a convenient target against which to direct verbalizations of resentment that arise out of situations that have little to do with wages. Because of the unreliability of symptoms taken in isolation we have found it more and more useful to think in terms of syndromes. The fact that our questionnaire is so constructed as to yield results in the form of profiles has greatly aided this purpose.

The psychiatrists have found the concept of *integration* a useful one around which to organize their ideas about personality and its disorders. We think a similar concept, related to group phenomena, could form the basis of a useful typology of the malfunctioning of organization. Certainly, the degree of integration (internal and external) of any organization relates very directly to the underlying dynamic factors in operation. One type of failure of integration leads to one type of difficulty which is different from that likely to arise from another type of failure of integration. Moreover, the methods for dealing with the two sets of circumstances are likely to differ, although often many of the superficial symptoms may be identical.

The scope of this paper does not permit a systematic exposition of the concept of integration. One of its aspects, however, is suggested by consideration of the problem of size of the organizational unit. Our researches demonstrate that mere size is unquestionably one of the most important factors in determining the quality of employee relationships, the smaller the unit the higher the morale, and vice versa. It is clear that the closer contact between executives and rank and file prevailing in smaller organizations tends to result in friendlier, easier relationships. To employees in such units the "big boss" is not some remote, little-known, semi-mythical personage but an actual, flesh and blood individual to be liked or disliked on a basis of personal acquaintance.

In broader terms, the smaller organization represents a simpler social system than does the larger unit. There are fewer people, fewer levels in the organizational hierarchy, and a less minute subdivision of labor. It is easier for the employee to adapt himself to such a simpler system and to win a place in it. His work becomes more meaningful, both to him and to his associates, because he and they can readily see its relation and importance to other functions and to the organization as a whole. The organization operates primarily through the face-to-face relationships of its members and only secondarily through impersonal, institutionalized relationships. The closer relations between the individual employee and the top executive in such a situation are only one aspect—but an important one—of the relatively simple and better-integrated social system of the smaller organization.

The importance of both external and internal integration is emphasized by other findings of our surveys. One of the most suggestive of these is that morale tends to be substantially lower in the large, industrialized metropolitan centers and higher in the smaller and less complex communities. For closely related reasons, morale tends to be lower in the Eastern sections of the country and higher in the West and South. Likewise, the simpler the industrial base of the community and the more homogeneous its population, the higher the level of employee morale.

These factors obviously relate, by various means, to the social characteristics of employee groups, and these social characteristics have an important bearing on the problem of integration. In certain cities of the south, a high percentage of employees grew up in small towns or in the country. Often their first job, after migrating to the "big city," is with our company. A great many of these young people have had religious upbringing which, together with parental admonitions, emphasizes the rightness of hard work for its own sake and the moral obligation of the employee to give his employer a full day's work for a fair day's pay.

Employees of units in large metropolitan centers, particularly those located in the East, are likely to have somewhat different social characteristics. Instead of coming from smaller towns and rural communities, most of them are likely to have originated within the metropolitan area itself. Likewise, many of them are likely to be the children or grandchildren of foreign-born stock whose personalities have been strongly molded by the special circumstances and the influences of growing up within ethnic communities. The marked tendency toward lower morale among employees drawn from such groups seems, in part at least, to reflect the high degree of social disorganization characteristic of the great metropolitan agglomerations.

An important element of this disorganization is the tendency for sharp cleavages to develop between different groups comprising the community, and one of the most significant of these cleavages is that between workers and management. Where the rank and file members of an organization have been drawn largely from working class homes in which factory employment has been the chief means of family support for two or three generations, their patterns of thinking and systems of value will be those of the urban working class. One characteristic of their way of life, growing out of their family and neighborhood experiences and traditions, is often a latent or overt distrust of the employer and a strong tendency to identify their security and well-being with their fellow-workers and not with the employer. The management of an organization employing large numbers of people with this type of background is thus likely to involve complications seldom encountered in what is sometimes described as the "less mature" regions of the country.

The problem, however, is by no means an insuperable one. No better testimony is needed than the survey showings of many of our own company units. Despite the fact that in some locations employees may be drawn from backgrounds representing all that is worst in social disorganization, morale in many such units is unusually high. A thoroughgoing urban working class background on the part of the rank and file is significant chiefly because it tends to create attitudes and values which do not correspond fully with those usually characteristic of management and executive groups, and because this difference in outlook frequently leads to *mutual* misunderstanding and lack of confidence. Under these circumstances, not only are management's action and motives frequently misinterpreted by the rank and file, but management itself is often at a loss as to ways and means by which it can effectively mobilize the interest and cooperation of employees in achieving the aims of the enterprise.

This gap can be bridged—and our surveys provide striking proof of that fact—by *skillful and understanding leadership operating in an organizational structure which facilitates rather than inhibits effective integration.* Both leadership and structure are of crucial importance. The structural aspect, however, has received relatively less attention. Moreover, there are a number of curious and significant interrelations between type of structure and character of leadership that will bear close investigation.

## 4. Organizational Structure

The results of our research suggest that over-complexity of organizational structure is one of the most important and fundamental causes of poor management-employee relationships in our modern economic system, and that until this problem is faced and corrected no substantial improvement in those relationships is likely to be possible.

In viewing many business enterprises, one cannot but be impressed by the number of different departments and sub-departments into which they are divided, and the extent to which the activities of both individuals and groups have been highly specialized. In a very large number of cases, employees perform only elementary, routine functions because jobs have been broken down "scientifically" into their most elementary components. The resulting specialization undoubtedly has certain advantages, such as requiring less skilled people, shorter training time, etc. In many cases, however, the process has been carried to such extremes that jobs have little inherent interest or challenge; operations have been reduced to the simplest possible repetitive level and the worker makes nothing he can identify as a product of his own skill.

One has the feeling of division of labor having gone wild, far beyond any degree necessary for efficient production. Peter F. Drucker, in a penetrating analysis, has pointed out that over-specialization is not an inevitable consequence of mass production, and that, "The traditional assembly line is simply a piece of poor engineering judged by the standards of human relations, as well as those of productive efficiency and output." [1]

[1] Peter F. Drucker, "The Way to Industrial Peace," *Harper's Magazine,* November, 1946.

The evidence of the studies conducted in our own company strongly support this conclusion, for we have found that where jobs are broken down too finely we are more likely to have both low output and low morale. Conversely, the most sustained efforts are exerted by those groups of employees who perform the more complete sets of tasks (e.g., salesmen, supervisors, master mechanics, etc.), and they likewise exhibit the highest levels of morale and esprit de corps.

The sharp trend toward over-specialization in our economy has not been limited, of course, to individual jobs. Just as particular activities have been broken down into their simplest possible components and each component assigned to a different person, so many *operations* (often after having been highly "simplified") have been separated out of the broader complex of activities of which they are a part and set up as specialized and semi-independent organizational entities. While over-specialization of individual jobs is serious enough, this over-specialization of the functions of entire departments and sub-departments has even more far-reaching consequences.

For one thing, it brings together in one place large numbers of employees on the same job level (and that level is likely to be fairly low where there has been any considerable over-specialization of individual jobs). This is another way of saying that the size of the administrative unit has been greatly expanded. Let us suppose an organization which performs three essential functions, A, B, and C. Let us suppose further that the volume of output requires three units of each function. Under these circumstances the organization could be set up in either of two ways:

1. It could be set up in three divisions, each function (A, B, and C) being represented in each division and each division, therefore, being a relatively independent administrative entity.

2. On the other hand, the organization could be set up in three *functional* divisions, one division having all three A units, another all three B units, and the third all three C units. In this case, none of the three divisions has any independence; each can operate only in closest coordination with the other two. Under the first alternative, there are really three administrative units; under the second only one, and that, by definition, three times as large.

This second type of arrangement is typical of much modern organization practice, both in industry and government. It is assumed that this separation and specialization of activities will permit better supervision, make possible smoother scheduling, and generally improve efficiency. There may be a certain spurious efficiency in this kind of organization but it is likely to have many off-setting liabilities.

One of the most serious of these liabilities is the fact that it so greatly expands the size of the administrative unit. Much of industry's present vast scale of operation is required not so much by economic or technical factors as by an unhappy and unnecessary principle of organization. The experience of many companies, of which my own is one, demonstrates that it is entirely possible to have many of the economic and technical advantages of large size without sacrificing too many of the essential human advantages of small size.

A further liability of over-functionalization is the fact that, from the standpoint of the individual employee, it tends to destroy the meaning of the job. He and those around him are working at highly specialized tasks which have meaning to management because they are a necessary part of a total process. But the worker cannot see that total process; he sees only the small and uninteresting part to which he and his fellows are assigned. In a real sense, the job loses its meaning for the worker—the meaning, that is, in all terms except the pay envelope.

Thus a very large number of employees in American industry today have been deprived of the sense of performing interesting, significant work. In consequence, they have little feeling of responsibility for the tasks to which they are assigned. Management in its efforts to maintain production in face of the resulting apathy is likely to resort to increasing supervisory pressure, but this procedure only creates more resistance on the part of employees. Sometimes the resistance is only passive, in the sense that employees fail to respond to the pressure or find means of avoiding it. Under certain circumstances, however, it can take more active form and lead to the creation of resistance groups in which employees band together (commonly through union organization) to exert a corresponding pressure against supervision and management.

Over-functionalization thus requires close and constant supervision at the work level to maintain production. Furthermore, the supervisors themselves must be closely supervised and controlled to assure the necessary degree of coordination between the many different units into which the organization has been subdivided. In a simpler type of organization structure, coordination can usually be achieved on a fairly informal basis because there are fewer artificial barriers in the form of departmental separations and lines of authority.

Where the work of the organization is broken down into so many functional divisions, however, cooperation can no longer be achieved spontaneously. After all, each functional unit was set up as a distinct entity in order that it might achieve a more efficient system. Each unit, therefore, tends to operate primarily in terms of its own systems rather than in terms of the needs of the other departments with which it must cooperate. Each unit becomes jealous of its own prerogatives and finds ways to protect itself against the pressure or encroachments of others. Conflict develops on the employee as well as the supervisory level, thus forcing an extra load on higher levels of management who must be constantly reconciling differences.

In order to achieve the necessary degree of coordination and cooperation between administratively separated functions, management is thus forced not only to build up an elaborate hierarchy of many supervisory levels, but to institute a wide variety of formal controls. Unfortunately, these controls are themselves often a source of conflict, because the individual supervisor or manager is under strong compulsion to operate in such a manner as to make a good showing in terms of the particular set of controls to which he is subject, and often he can do so only at the expense of impairing the service he is expected to render to other departments. This conflict is particularly acute when two closely related functions report up two different administrative lines and operate under two different systems of standards and controls.

The management of organizations which have been over functionalized to the extent characteristic of much of modern business imposes a severe burden on the top administrative staff. Functions and activities have been so subdivided and specialized that no individual unit can operate except in closest coordination with others, and the system is often so complex that this coordination cannot take place spontaneously. If it is to occur at all, it must occur on the basis of specific administrative action from the top, which requires the development of a specialized staff to assist the top administrator.

This growth of staff complicates the situation still further, because an inevitable consequence is the elaboration of formal controls of various kinds to permit the staff to perform the functions and exercise the responsibilities which have been delegated to it or which it gradually assumes in an effort to strengthen its own position or extend its own authority. The result is a gradual undermining of the line organization for the benefit of the staff, an impairment of flexibility and adaptability, and a weakening of the effectiveness of the entire organization.

An objective appraisal suggests that to too large an extent work processes have been analyzed from a strictly "rational" or mechanical point of view with too little attention to the human factors involved. As a result, functions have been separated out of their context and set up as semi-independent activities. Necessary collaboration and cooperation between the units thus artificially separated becomes possible only through an elaborate system of controls and a complicated administrative hierarchy. Under these circumstances, management necessarily becomes strongly centralized, despite the frequently expressed concern of business leaders over the need for greater delegation of authority and responsibility. Too often, this is simply impossible because the nature of the organization structure makes effective decentralization impossible. For much the same reason, such organizations often require from their top administrators a high degree of driving pressure to hold the system together and make it operate with a reasonable degree of efficiency.

Where this is the case, executives and supervisors down the line quite understandably tend to pattern their own methods after those of their superiors. In many cases the copying may be done unskillfully and in such a way as to exaggerate the worst features of the pressure methods. As a result, supervisory methods at the middle and lower levels of over-functionalized organizations are often crude and inept.

Furthermore, the degree of pressure often required from the top is likely to create an atmosphere of anxiety and apprehension within the executive and supervisory group. This atmosphere tends to amplify the severity of pressure as it moves downward in the organization, so that even a moderate amount of pressure at the top is often greatly magnified by the time it reaches the lower levels. Attitudes of mind characterized by fear and apprehension are not particularly conducive to real skill in managing and leading subordinates. Above all, poor supervisory techniques at the lower levels of an organization generally reflect the experience and type of supervision to which the supervisors themselves have been subjected over the years and which they have come to accept as normal and expected behavior.

The significant point in all this, however, is that the over-complex, over-functionalized organization structure is likely to require the driver type of leader; the over-use of pressure as a tool of supervision is thus related primarily to the character of the structure and only secondarily to the character of the individual at the head of it. (On the other hand, it is recognized that the personality of the top man may have a great deal to do with the kind of organization structure he sets up. This entire problem of the reciprocal relationships between structure and personality should be studied carefully.)

## 5. Systems Compared

The most striking feature of the over-elaborate type of organization structure is its lack of integration, a deficiency which can be only partially and very unsatisfactorily overcome by driving pressure from the top. Our studies suggest that this type of structure is not only bad human relations but equally unsound from a standpoint of productive efficiency. Our studies also suggest that alternative systems of organization are conceivable and eminently practical.

For one thing, we seriously question the necessity for much of our present high degree of over-specialization and over-functionalization. The so-called "scientific management movement" which has given such impetus in this direction is based to a considerable extent on an extremely inadequate conception of human motivation and social organization. It has tended to approach the problems of management from an almost purely mechanistic point of view and has tried to organize human efforts in much the same way an engineer might design a machine. Much of our present over-specialization is based on this type of thinking.

However, the experience of a number of companies indicates that individual jobs and departmental functions need not be broken down to this degree in order to achieve productive efficiency. Quite the contrary; their experience has been that both efficiency and morale are best served by keeping specialization to a minimum. The experience of these companies likewise indicates that organization structures and administrative hierarchies can be vastly simplified, thus making possible a far higher degree of decentralization of authority and responsibility.

In the course of our survey work we have had an opportunity to study a fairly wide variety of organization structures. We have been struck by the sharp contrasts between otherwise comparable units which differ mainly in the complexity of their organizational structure and in the degree to which authority and responsibility are effectively decentralized to those farther down the line. A review of some of these contrasts may be instructive.

In the more elaborate and complex organizations, the individual supervisor or executive is subject to constant control and direction and has little opportunity to develop the qualities of initiative and self-reliance. In systems characterized by extensive management decentralization, primary reliance is placed on the personal initiative and capacity of the people in the organization. There is usually a conspicuous lack of detailed supervision and of formal controls, and executives and supervisors (and to a large extent rank and file employees) enjoy considerable freedom in the way they accomplish their jobs.

They are judged primarily by their results, not on the details of the way they get those results. This concentration on end-results rather than on system and controls, together with management's alertness to recognize and reward good results, develops initiative and self-reliance and generates a far more powerful driving force than could ever be imposed from the top down. This pattern of administration not only gets today's job done better but permits the individual to grow and develop in a way that is impossible in more centralized systems. Furthermore, it contributes strongly to morale because employees work in an atmosphere of relative freedom from oppressive supervision and have a sense of individual importance and personal responsibility which other types of arrangements often deny them.

A number of highly successful organizations have not only paid little heed but have gone directly counter to one of the favorite tenets of modern management theory, the so-called "span of control," which holds that the number of subordinate executives or supervisors reporting to a single individual should be severely limited to enable that individual to exercise the detailed direction and control which is generally considered necessary. On the contrary, these organizations often deliberately give each key executive so many subordinates that it is impossible for him to exercise too close supervision over their activities.

In this type of organization structure, the individual executive is thrown largely on his own to sink or swim on the basis of his own ability and capacity. He cannot rely to more than a limited extent on those above him, and these superiors, by the same token, cannot too severely restrict, through detailed supervision and control their subordinates' growth and development.

Not all individuals can function effectively in this type of set-up. It requires a very large measure of self-confidence and personal capacity. The system tends to weed out those who lack these qualities in adequate degree. Those who are able to adapt to this type of organization, however, are likely to be not only better executives but also the type of people who can build and maintain teamwork and cooperation and a high level of employee morale, not so much because they consciously attempt to do so but because these results are a natural by-product of their ways of operating and a reflection of their own personalities.

On the other hand, in organizations characterized by many levels of supervision and elaborate systems of controls, the individual not only has little opportunity to develop the capacities of self-reliance and initiative but the system frequently weeds out those who do. Furthermore, those who survive in this type of organization are often likely, by virtue of the very qualities which enabled them to survive, to have personalities and ways of operating which do not make for greatest skill in building employee teamwork and cooperation.

An organization with few layers of supervision and a minimum of formal controls places a premium on ability to stimulate and lead. The driver type of executive, who functions through maintaining constant pressure and whose chief sanction is fear cannot operate as effectively in such an organization. In the more simple types of organization structures, where management has been effectively decentralized, an executive accomplishes results and moves to higher levels of responsibility chiefly to the extent that he is able to secure the willing, enthusiastic support of his colleagues and subordinates; he does not have the "tools" (with which a more centralized system would to some extent provide him) to accomplish the result in any other manner. The outcome is not only a higher level of accomplishment but, at the same time, a more satisfying type of supervision and a higher level of employee morale.

## 6. Conclusion

Our studies have shown that employee morale and operating efficiency are closely related to the degree the organization is integrated. Integration is not necessarily achieved, however, when the organization meets the requirements of machine-logic. As a matter of fact, what may appear to be logical from a purely technical standpoint may run directly counter to the personal and social demands of employees. We have seen a number of organizations which have a logical technology, division of labor, and hierarchy of control but which are badly disorganized from the standpoint of the actual working relationships of the people involved. Such organizations are well-integrated only on paper. In actual fact, they are irritating and frustrating from the standpoint of employees and inefficient, trouble some, and costly from the standpoint of management.

Our research indicates that two trends in particular are making effective integration difficult and contributing to the progressive deterioration of management-employee relations. One is the trend toward increasing size of the administrative unit; the other, the trend toward increasing complexity of organizational structure. Both trends appear logical in terms of widely held theories of business organization, but in both cases improvements in mechanical efficiency are at some point over-balanced by losses in the willingness and ability of employees to cooperate in the system. Moreover, the larger, more complex organizations are likely to become unadaptive and rigid, and to find it difficult to meet the requirements of economic and social change.

Intelligent planning on the part of management in setting up the formal structure of organizations can do much to improve the quality of human relations in industry. Flatter, less complex structures, with a maximum of administrative decentralization, tend to create a potential for improved attitudes, more effective supervision, and greater individual responsibility and initiative among employees. Moreover, arrangements of this type encourage the development of individual self-expression and creativity which are so necessary to the personal satisfaction of employees and which are an essential ingredient of the democratic way of life.

# The Man on the Assembly Line*

### Charles R. Walker
### Robert H. Guest

"There are a lot of good things about my job. The pay is good. I've got seniority. The working conditions are pretty good for my type of work. But that's not the whole story. . . . You can't beat the machine. They have you clocked to a fraction of a second. My job is engineered, and the jigs and fixtures are all set out according to specifications. The foreman is an all right guy, but he gets pushed, so he pushes us. The guy on the line has no one to push. You can't fight that iron horse."—*Worker on an assembly line, interviewed by the authors.*

"Machines alone do not give us mass production. Mass production is achieved by both machines *and* men. And while we have gone a long way toward perfecting our mechanical operations, we have not successfully written into our equation whatever complex factors represent man, the human element."—*Henry Ford II, in a talk before the American Society of Mechanical Engineers, shortly after he was made President of the Ford Motor Company.*

The principal social and psychological problems connected with mass production and human nature have been stated many times and in many different forms. Their importance in an age of advancing technology is hardly in dispute. The question has become rather: What shall we do about them?

Here are a few of the common problems. Since individuals react very differently to industrial occupations, what are the personality characteristics of those who adjust quickly to—and appear to thrive on—mechanically paced and repetitive jobs? What, on the other hand, are the personality characteristics of those who suffer mentally and physically on such jobs—and who therefore tend to perform them badly? Can the adjust-

* From *Harvard Business Review*, vol. 30, no. 3, pp. 71–83, May–June, 1952. Reprinted by permission of the publisher.

ment problem, in other words, be solved by selection? Or is the modern work environment simply *wrong* for the normal human being?

Or to take an engineering and management approach: In the present state of the mechanical arts, what part of a worker's skill and power can the engineer build into a machine? What must he leave out? Precisely how and to what extent in the most mechanized sectors of our economy does the human equation still affect quantity and quality?

Or again, granted that the principles of mass production such as breakdown of jobs into their simplest constituent parts are sound and vital to efficient manufacture, have we yet found how to combine these principles with equally well authenticated principles of human behavior?

Or taking still another approach, if a man spends a third of his life in direct contact with a mass-production environment, why should we not consider important (to him and to society) the hours of living time he spends inside the factory—as important and valuable, for example, as the product he produces which is consumed outside the factory? We talk of a high standard of living, but frequently we mean a high standard of consumption. Man consumes in his leisure, yet fulfills himself not only in his leisure but in his work. Is our mass-production work environment making such fulfillment more difficult?

A short way to sum up these and a great many more questions is: To what degree can—or should—men be "adjusted" to the new environment of machines, and to what degree is it possible to adjust or rebuild that environment to fit the needs and personalities of men?

### Need for Systematic Study

Despite the tremendous contribution of mass-production methods to the productiveness of the economic system under which we live, and notwithstanding the fact that editors, philosophers, and propagandists have long speculated and written about the beneficent or injurious effects of highly mechanized jobs on human behavior, there has been singularly little systematic effort to discover "whatever complex factors represent man, the human element" in the mass-production method as such. The relatively small number of studies which have been made of assembly-line and other types of repetitive work have been mostly laboratory experiments, not explorations of experience in actual industrial plants.

A notable exception is the series of monographs which for some 25 years have been published from time to time under the auspices of the British Medical Council on the effects of mechanization and the repetitive job on productivity and *mental* fatigue. Even these, however, have only touched occasionally on the subject of assembly lines, and have never at all—to the best of our knowledge—dealt specifically with that advanced sector of a mass-production economy, the final assembly line of a plant making a large, complex product like automobiles.

*Survey of automobile assembly plant.* For these reasons the authors undertook two years ago an exploratory survey of a modern automobile assembly plant.[1] This is intended as the first of a series of studies designed to define more clearly the several "human equations" involved in assembly work, to prepare and sharpen tools of research, and to look for proximate and empirical answers to the more acute practical problems posed for men and management.

In this article we shall emphasize how an assembly line looks and feels to the men who work on it, rather than its importance to the engineers who designed it, the executives who manage it, or the public who buys its product.

In order to preserve the anonymity of those who freely supplied information—managers, workers, and union leaders—the plant in question has been called Plant X. Over a period of months 180 workers were interviewed in their homes about all phases of their life on "the line." These workers constituted a substantial—and representative—sample of the total number of productive workers in the plant.

Nearly 90 per cent of the men working at Plant X came from jobs where the pace of work was not machine-governed in a strict sense, and from jobs over 72 per cent of which were not repetitive. In short, the area from which they were recruited had few mass-production factories. One might say, then, that these men were like the majority of workers who in the past 30 years have made the transition from occupations characteristic of the first industrial revolution to work environments characteristic of a mass-production era. Their attitudes should be all the more revealing.

Most people, in thinking about an assembly line and the workers on it, focus only on the effect of the line on what a man does hour by hour, even minute by minute, with his mind and his muscles. Any serious study of the human effects of the mass-production method, however, must extend its field of vision. For the method not only impinges directly on a man's immediate or intrinsic job but molds much of the character of the in-plant society of which he is a part, including both his relations with his fellow workers and his relations with management. Accordingly we shall discuss the impact of the mass-production method not only directly but indirectly on human nature.

*Definition of mass-production method.* But what is the "mass-production method?" We must have a definition if our discussion and our findings are to be understandable.

Although the methods of mass production or, more accurately and specifi-

[1] The full details of this survey are being published in book form, *The Man on the Assembly Line,* by the Harvard University Press (June 1952).

cally for our purposes, the methods of *progressive manufacture* have been defined and discussed in different ways by different writers, it is agreed by nearly everyone that these methods derive from at least two fundamental and related ideas: (a) standardization and (b) interchangeability of parts.

Given these basic ideas, plus the accurate machining methods which make them applicable to manufacture, Ford was able to work out and apply the three following additional "principles" of progressive manufacture: (c) the orderly progression of the product through the shop in a series of planned operations arranged so that the right part always arrives at the right place at the right time; (d) the mechanical delivery of these parts and of the product as it is assembled to and from the operators; and (e) a breakdown of operations into their simple constituent motions.[2]

Let us look now at how these principles translate themselves into job characteristics from the standpoint not of the engineer but of the man on the assembly line. In the first place, most automobile assembly jobs are *mechanically paced* (especially those on the main line). In the second place, since the engineer has broken the jobs down into simple and separate elements and assigned only a few to each man, they are clearly *repetitive*. Among other characteristics of most jobs are these: they have a low skill requirement, permit work on only a fraction of the product, severely limit social interaction, and predetermine for nearly every worker any use he may make of tools and methods.

Taken together, automobile assembly-line jobs exemplify all these characteristics, but not every job exemplifies all of them. Put another way, in spite of many common characteristics, automobile assembly jobs are far from being equal—either as to the quantity or quality of job content or as to the satisfaction or dissatisfaction which workers derive from them. They differ both in the number of the several assembly-line characteristics they exemplify and in the degree of impact of any one characteristic. An understanding of this point must mark the beginning of any serious inquiry into the relation of human behavior to assembly-line work.

### Attitude toward Jobs

But that is enough of making distinctions. Now let the men on the assembly line tell us themselves about their jobs, and tell us also what they like and what they do not like about them. Here are six jobs by way of illustration: two on the main moving line, one off the main line but on a moving conveyer, one off the main line and not on a moving conveyer, one repair job on the line, and one utility job on the line. These six will illustrate at least the principal differences in human impact of mass-production as-

[2] This is a rephrased and slightly more explicit statement of the three principles of mass production as set down in "Mass Production" by Henry Ford in the *Encyclopaedia Britannica,* Fourteenth Edition, Vol. 15, pp. 38–39.

sembly-line jobs. (It should be remembered, however, that these six are not representative of the distribution of jobs in the whole plant, where one-half the jobs are on the *main moving assembly line*. Specifically the distribution of jobs in our sample was as follows: main assembly line, 86; subassembly on moving belt, 28; subassembly not on moving belt, 38; repairmen, 14; utility men, 11; and other, 3.)

*On the main moving line.* Here is the way the assembler of the baffle windbreaker in the trim department describes his job:

> As the body shell moves along the line, I start putting on a baffle windbreaker (two fenders fit on it) by putting in four screws. Then I put nine clips at the bottom which hold the chrome molding strip to the body. On another type of car there is a piece of rubber which fits on the hood latch on the side and keeps the hood from rattling. I drill the holes in the rubber and metal and fit two screws in. Also I put four clips on the rubber in the rear fender. On another type of body, I put the clips on the bottom molding, and in the trunk space I put two bolts which hold the spare tire clamp. I repeat these things all the time on the same types of car.

How does this man's job measure up in terms of some of the characteristics we have mentioned, particularly pace and repetitiveness?

To begin with, the job is on the main line and the worker rides along on the conveyer, completing his cycle of operations in less than two minutes while the conveyer is moving over a distance of about 30 feet. He then walks to his starting point and begins over again. In short, his pace is directly determined by the moving belt. On the other hand, he is sometimes able to work back up the line and so secure a breather for himself.

The job is clearly repetitive, but there is some element of variety since between five and ten operations are required to complete the job cycle. There are also different models to be worked on. Comparing the repetitiveness of this job with that of other assembly jobs, it is somewhere in the middle range—far less repetitive than a single-operation job and far more repetitive than the job of a repairman.

Similarly, in the matter of skill it is in the middle as assembly-line jobs go. Because of the number of parts handled, learning time is slightly longer than that for many assembly jobs. The worker reported that it took him a month to do the job properly. As for the expenditure of physical energy, it is a light job.

*Also on the main moving line.* Or consider the job of the worker who installs toe plates and who performs operations typical of short-cycle, on-the-main-line jobs:

> I put in the two different toe plates. They cover the holes where the brake and clutch pedals are. I am inside the car and have to be down on the seat to do my work. On one kind of car I put in the shift lever while another man puts in the toe plates.

While doing his job this man rides along in the car and must complete the job before he is carried too far. After finishing his work cycle he returns to his station, climbs into another car, and begins another installation. Thus his pace is strictly governed by the moving line. This particular worker told the interviewer that he did not mind the pace.

Such a job which demands but two operations in a two-minute cycle is highly repetitive. Only slight variety is introduced when the man installs a shift lever instead of a toe plate on certain cars.

The job demands very little skill and has a learning period of just two days. Although the worker gets in and out of the car 20 or 30 times an hour, his expenditure of physical energy on the actual assembly operation is slight.

*Off the main line but on a moving conveyer.* The job of a seat-spring builder is typical of those off the main line but on a moving belt:

> I work on a small conveyer which goes around in a circle. We call it a merry-go-round. I make up zig-zag springs for front seats. Every couple of feet on the conveyer there is a form for the pieces that make up the seat springs. As that form goes by me, I clip several pieces together, using a clip gun. I then put the pieces back on the form, and it goes on around to where other men clip more pieces together. By the time the form has gone around the whole line, the pieces are ready to be set in a frame, where they are made into a complete seat spring. That's further down the main seat cushion line. The only operation I do is work the clip gun. It takes just a couple of seconds to shoot six or eight clips onto the spring, and I do it as I walk a few steps. Then I start right over again.

This job is clearly paced by a moving conveyer quite as much as if it were on the main line. A comment by the worker regarding his previous job emphasized the point: "I liked the piecework system on my old job. If I wanted to stop for a few minutes, I could. You can't do that here."

As for variety, there is none. The job is highly repetitive, consisting of one set of operations repeated every few seconds on a part which is standard for all models.

The skill requirement is minimum. This worker gave two days as his learning time, with a few days more "in order to do it like I do it now."

As for physical energy, the job would probably be rated as light since the worker guides an automatic hand gun. But there is considerable fatigue because the worker performs the operation standing up.

The worker's over-all estimate of the job is typical. As to what he liked about the job, he mentioned good pay, steady work, and good working hours—in that order of priority. As to what he disliked, he said that he could not set his own pace, that he did not have interesting work, and that his job was physically tiring.

*Off the main line but not on a moving conveyer.* We turn to a blower-defroster assembler who works off the main line and not on a moving belt:

I work at a bench on blower defrosters. The blowers come in two parts. I take one part and attach the blower motor to it. I then connect the fan to the motor shaft. Then I take the other half on the air pipe and put two parts together with fourteen screws. I test the motor to see if it works, and if it does, I put in a fifteenth screw which grounds it to the pipe. The materials are brought to me and put in a pile by a stock chaser. After I finish, I put each assembled blower on one of six shelves.

Here is an example of a job where pace is only indirectly determined by the main line. The worker must keep his shelves stocked with a supply of blower defrosters, but he has some choice of pace in doing so. He may work fast and "build up a bank," then slow down and take a breather. Or he may choose to work quite steadily. The demands of the stock-chaser who brings him materials and takes away the finished assembly are the determinants of his work pace, rather than the moving conveyer.

There is not much variety since there are only three operations. However, a slight variation is introduced through differences in models. The worker called his job completely repetitive but said he did not mind it.

His job operations require a minimum of skill: "I learned it in a couple of hours, though it took me about a week to get up speed." He does not move around, and the materials he handles are light, so very little physical energy is demanded.

Summing up his job, this worker gave good bosses, good pay, and good working conditions as his first three reasons for liking the job. He mentioned only one thing he disliked: "I cannot do different things."

*Repairman.* Here is a job description by a repairman in the car-conditioning section of the chassis department:

I work in a pit underneath the final line. The cars move along over the pit. On the previous assembly operations, the inspectors for the under parts of the car have indicated where parts were missing or damaged or not properly attached. There are any number of things which can be wrong, and they are usually different for each car. Sometimes we have a run of the same thing which we have to work on until they get at the bug earlier in assembly operations. The shock absorbers may be bad, gas line in wrong, brake lines or spring attachments off. I fix whatever I see checked by the inspector. The others in the pit do the same thing. I just work down the line until I get it cleared up. Sometimes I have to work down a long way on one thing. Other times it's just a simple problem on a number of different things.

This worker is on the main line, but his pace is not strictly governed by the moving conveyer. "We don't feel the pressure of the line since we don't have to do just one thing in a given area and length of time."

The variety the job offers is derived from the nature of the work. "There are any number of things which can be wrong, and they are usually different for each car. . . . There is something different all the time."

As for skill, the job as repairman requires manual skill and mechanical experience. A garage repairman's job would be a good preparation. (The man whose job description is given here had, in fact, worked as a repairman in a garage before coming to Plant X.)

The job varies between light and medium-heavy work, with the expenditure of physical energy called for changing appreciably from job to job and from day to day.

The worker's personal satisfaction with his job was clear. He gave as three reasons for liking the job: "I can set my own pace, I have good working conditions, and I have steady work." He also commented favorably on being able to "use my brains," "do different things," and "choose how the job is to be done."

*Utility man.* A utility man in the chassis department describes his job as follows:

> I work on the whole length of that part of the chassis line beginning with motor drop up to where the wheels are mounted. My job is to fill in wherever I am needed. A man might be absent or away from the job or may need help on the job.
>
> We start where the motor is lowered onto the frame (motor mount). The clutch assembly is installed and hooked up. Then the exhaust system is attached and the bolts tightened. The clutch assembly bolts and the motor mount bolts are also tightened. In the next area on the line the brake chambers are filled and bled.
>
> Off to the side, the subassembly men put the steering column together. The steering post and the Pittman arm assembly are put in. Further down the line, men put in air cleaners and inject hydraulic fluid for the transmission.
>
> Next, the brakes are tested and the clutch linkage hooked up. The bumper brackets are put on; a serial number is attached next; and then the bumper brackets are tightened up. Finally, the chassis is sprayed, mounted on wheels, and moved on toward body drop. All in all, about 28 men work on these jobs, each man with his own special operation. I go on each of these jobs, depending on where I am needed most. It is different each day. Some of the jobs are hard to learn, so when I take over one on which I haven't had much experience, it's hard to keep up. I have been learning how to do the work ever since I've been in the plant. I can never learn everything because new changes are always being made.

The pace of this utility man's work, since it is on the main line, is as strictly governed as that of any assembly worker. In certain ways he may feel the pressure more acutely than some of those for whom he substitutes since he has less practice on any single job than its regular holder.

To compensate him, however, there is plenty of variety, for, as he points out, he shifts about among 28 different jobs. Notice how in describing his many tasks this utility man gives a very clear account of a whole segment of assembly operations in the chassis department.

Notice, too, the character of a utility man's skill. It is the sum of many little skills of many repetitive jobs. The learning time is six months to a year. The worker said: "Sometimes I walk up and down checking the line. I ask questions of the different men. I rarely stay on the same job more than a couple of days." That his job is not easy is suggested by an additional comment.

Some days you feel like learning, other days you don't. On jobs that take time to learn, you get disgusted because it's hard to keep up. A utility man, when on a job, has more trouble keeping up than the regular man.

This man mentioned good pay, steady work, and good bosses as the three main reasons for liking his job, in that order. Other items bearing on the immediate job which he liked were "having interesting work, having to use my brains, doing many different things," as in the case of the repairman, and also "talking with others." He had only one complaint about the job: that it was "physically tiring."

*Summary of attitudes toward jobs.* In all of this classification of the automobile assembly workers' jobs, we have clearly been concerned not with an engineering analysis but with factors which have an effect on satisfaction or dissatisfaction with the immediate job. Mechanical pace, repetitiveness, minimum skill requirement, and the other factors were all found reflected in attitudes and feelings.

These examples underline some of the commonest facts and feelings which are part of the daily experience of the productive worker in an assembly plant. To recall a few:

1. Contrary to popular belief, all jobs on an assembly line are not alike, either in skill, variety, learning time, or the degree of satisfaction or dissatisfaction which they offer the average wage earner.
2. There are definite ways on certain jobs to get a break or a breather, such as "working back up the line," or "bank building."
3. There is a general, though not a unanimous, desire to move from highly paced jobs to jobs which are less highly paced, and "off the line."
4. It is evident from the statements of the six workers—which for illustrative purposes we have selected from 180—that other factors such as good pay, a good foreman, and a secure job must be considered in appraising the total index of a worker's satisfaction or dissatisfaction.

## Major Reactions of Workers

Looking over the range of factors connected with their immediate jobs by all the men interviewed, we see that the two which were given greatest prominence were (a) mechanical pacing and (b) repetitiveness.

*To mechanical pacing.* We asked no direct attitude questions on the first and central characteristic of any automobile assembly plant—the moving conveyer—but nearly every worker expressed his opinions about it when describing his job, when talking about the company, or at some other point in the interview. These free-association comments on pace as governed by the moving conveyer showed that: (1) A large majority of the workers regarded the moving line or belt as an undesirable feature of the job. (2) A small minority expressed themselves as enjoying the excitement of the moving line.

Following are typical comments of workers who were highly critical of the line:

> The bad thing about assembly lines is that the line keeps moving. If you have a little trouble with a job, you can't take the time to do it right.

> On the line you're geared to the line. You don't dare stop. If you get behind, you have a hard time catching up.

> The line speed is too great. More men wouldn't help much. They'd just expect more work out of an individual. There's an awful lot of tension.

> I don't like rushing all the time. . . . I don't mind doing a good day's work, but I don't like to run through it.

> The work isn't hard; it's the never-ending pace. . . . The guys yell "hurrah" whenever the line breaks down. . . . You can hear it all over the plant.

In contrast, a minority liked the challenge and excitement of keeping up with the line:

> I do my job well. I get some satisfaction from keeping up with a rapid-fire job. On days when the cars come off slowly, I sometimes get bored.

> I get satisfaction from doing my job right and keeping up with the line.

> It makes you feel good . . . when the line is going like hell and you step in and catch up with it.

*To repetitiveness.* Turning now to the job characteristic, repetitiveness, our findings are that: (1) A majority of the workers were critical of the repetitive character of their jobs. (2) A minority preferred the repetitive character of their work or were indifferent to it. (3) A large number of workers compared on-the-line jobs unfavorably with off-the-line jobs, because off-the-line jobs offered more variety.

We found we were able to correlate the number of operations a man performed (which can serve as a rough measure of repetitiveness) with expressions of interest or lack of interest in his job. The number of operations performed on any given job was determined not by direct questioning but by analysis of the job descriptions. The workers, however, were asked directly: "Would you say your job was very interesting, fairly interesting, not at all interesting?" The correlation with number of operations was as follows:

| Operations Performed | Very or Fairly Interesting | Not Very or Not at All Interesting |
|---|---|---|
| 1 | 19 | 38 |
| 2–5 | 28 | 36 |
| 5 or more | 41 | 18 |

In the column of workers giving a positive rating to "interest," the number of workers increases as the number of operations increases. In other words, there is a tendency for interest in work to vary directly with the number of operations performed.

Following are typical comments of those men who were critical of the repetitive nature of their jobs:

> I dislike repetition. One of the main things wrong with this job is that there is no figuring for yourself, no chance to use your brain. It's a grind doing the same thing over and over. There is no skill necessary.

> I'd rather work for a small company any day. They're interested in doing good work, and they are willing to allot enough time for it. The assembly line is no place to work, I can tell you. There is nothing more discouraging than having a barrel beside you with 10,000 bolts in it and using them all up. Then you get a barrel with another 10,000 bolts, and you know every one of those 10,000 bolts has to be picked up and put in exactly the same place as the last 10,000 bolts.

> I'd like to do different things on this job. I get bored. It's the same thing all the time. Cars always coming down the line endlessly every time I look up.

> I would like to perform different operations, but I do the same thing all the time. I always know what I'm going to do when I come in. There's nothing to look forward to like there was on my old job.

> The monotony is what I don't like. It's pretty noisy, but you get used to that. I'd never get used to the monotony. I dislike the plant for this reason.

> It's not a matter of pace. It's the monotony. It's not good for you to get so bored. I do the same thing day after day; just an everlasting grind.

> The job gets so sickening—day in and day out plugging in ignition wires. I get through with one motor, turn around, and there's another motor staring me in the face.

A minority of workers who declared that they were indifferent to or preferred doing the same thing over and over again commented as follows:

I keep doing the same thing all the time, but it doesn't make any difference to me.

Repeating the same thing you can catch up and keep ahead of yourself. I like the routine. You can get in the swing of it.

We do the same thing all the time, but I don't mind it really.

I like doing the same thing all the time. I'd rather stay right where I am. When I come in in the morning, I like to know exactly what I'll be doing.

I like to repeat the same thing, and every car is different anyway. So my job is interesting enough.

Explanation of why this minority group either preferred or was indifferent to the factor of repetitiveness in contrast to the majority of workers in our sample would appear to lie in the pattern of their individual personalities. An investigation of the psychological characteristics of men who react this way is clearly suggested. We sought but found no other unique characteristics in the group as regards education, age, or any of the other categories of information we used.

### Effect of Human Equation

In the introductory paragraphs of this article we reviewed some of the typical questions on which it was hoped research into the human equation of assembly-line work might throw light, including some of special interest to both the production manager and the engineer: What part of a worker's skill and power can the engineer build into a machine? What must he leave out? Precisely how and to what extent in the most mechanized sectors of our economy does the human equation still affect quantity and quality?

*Influence of workers on quality.* So far as assembly lines go, there is still a widespread belief on the part of *outsiders* that the machine has completely taken over and that on mechanized conveyer-line jobs the individual has no influence on quality. There is also a belief widely held by *insiders* (employers and production managers) that, even though the quality of individual performance on a mechanized job may still be important for the final product, the average worker no longer cares or gets satisfaction from doing a good job.

In Plant X, both beliefs were shown to be unfounded.

As many as 79 men in the sample of 180 felt that it was difficult to sustain the kind of quality performance which was expected of them or which they themselves wanted to sustain. To most of the 79, *this was a discouraging and negative feature of the job.*

About half the workers felt it was possible to do the kind of quality job expected of them. Few of these workers, however, had jobs which were strictly line-paced. Rather they included mostly repairmen, utility men, workers on off-line jobs, or men on the line who had longer time cycles or greater freedom to move up and down the line. Typical comments among this group were:

> No time limit is set on my job, so I can do it right. I get satisfaction out of really fixing a job. I can usually get this, but sometimes the company doesn't want the cars fixed as well as I'd like to.

> I get satisfaction and quality because I have time to complete my job right.

> I never let a car go by with my number on it unless it is done right. Maybe some of the men on the line don't get quality.

> You can take time to get quality. It's not like on the line when you have to rush so much. And I get satisfaction. It makes me feel good when I put out a good day's work and get no kickbacks.

The effects of poor-quality work on job satisfaction were reflected in many of the comments of men on conveyer-paced jobs:

> The cars come too fast for quality. It's quantity instead of quality. I'm doing the best I can, but could do a neater job slower.

> On an assembly line you just do it once; if it's wrong, you have no time to fix it. I get no satisfaction from my work. All I do is think about all the things that went through wrong that should have been fixed. My old job was nothing like this.

> I try to do quality work, but I'm too rushed. This keeps me from getting pleasure from the work. They say "haste makes waste," and they're getting plenty of both.

> I'd rather do less work and do it right. How can you get quality when they don't give you time? The "quality" signs they have mean nothing.

These comments tend to show that the characteristics or components of the assembly man's immediate job do have a significant bearing upon the quality of the product, and that mass production restricts rather than eliminates the "human factor" as a determinant of quality for any given part or for the total product. Most workers were conscious of this fact. For a substantial number, inability to put out quality was a source of irritation while putting out quality was a source of job satisfaction.

## Constructive Measures by Management

Are there any measures that management can take to modify on-the-job conditions of work in the interest of greater efficiency and of increased satisfaction for the individual operator?

One answer to this question may be sought in the elements of satisfaction or of compensation which some workers already found in their jobs. To begin with, it should be remembered that there was a minority of workers who preferred or were indifferent to repetitiveness and mechanical pacing. Presumably by improved methods of recruiting and selection this minority could be increased. Then there were a number of men who found their immediate jobs on and off the line satisfying—actually all the repairmen and utility men interviewed with one exception. The only measures needed here are protective—to make sure that the content of these jobs is not diluted.

This still leaves the majority of the production workers. Here the clue to constructive action lies in the fact that many of them reacted favorably to particular features of their jobs:

1. Social interaction breaking the monotony
2. Enough operations on their particular jobs to give variety
3. Opportunity to work back up the line and get a breather
4. Opportunity to build up a bank and get a breather
5. Opportunity to alternate one set of operations with another set of a substantially different character
6. Opportunity to alternate jobs with other workers within the same section
7. A long time cycle encompassing a larger number of operations than usual and of a more interesting character

A practical directive for management would appear to be exploration of the possibility of extending these and other desirable features, so that more assembly men could share in them. The degree of that extension would necessarily vary with the special circumstances—physical and organizational—of individual plants, and with the ingenuity of management; but there would be few plants where something could not be done in this direction.

Detailed discussion of such measures is beyond the scope of this article, but the tenor of our thinking may be indicated by reference to two of the seven features to which Plant X workers reacted favorably.

*Job rotation.* Take Number 6—alternation of jobs between workers, a technique often called "rotation." At Plant X we were struck with the unusually high degree of job satisfaction expressed by the members of one work group under a particular foreman. With the permission and encouragement of their foreman, the men were working under a system of job rotation. It was to this system that the members of the group ascribed their relatively high job satisfaction. And to the same system the section foreman owed in part a smoothly running and efficient work unit. Top plant management is now encouraging a more widespread application of this practice.

In connection with any system of job rotation the question immediately comes to mind: Since it requires some effort to learn several jobs instead of one, will not the worker—unless he is exceptional—object? Many managers seem to find it difficult to get workers to change jobs frequently.

The best answer to this question about worker resistance is the pragmatic one. In certain sectors on the line at Plant X rotation *is* working. Moreover, in other industries and on other types of assembly lines the practice of rotation is steadily gaining ground. For most people learning to do something new is hard work, and it is only undertaken when an adequate reward is held out. For a considerable number of assembly-line workers the rewards of variety and of possessing a repertory of skills will be sufficient.

Of course, some resistance to an experiment in rotation is to be expected. The key to the situation lies, we suggest, in the word "experiment." Where rotation has been successfully installed on other types of assembly lines, it has usually been started as an experiment, with management guaranteeing to the work group or to any single individual a return to stationary assignments if desired—and rarely have the workers wished to return.

Another question is: Will the work be done as well or as fast under job rotation? The answer for the Plant X section which practices it is an affirmative. For other work groups in other industries with which the authors are familiar, the answer has also been "yes." Of course there are work situations where job rotation appears either altogether impractical or less efficient. But always the real test is in the over-all and long-term performance of the group. Gains in quality and a drop in turnover or absenteeism may balance some decrease in output, if it occurs.

*Job enlargement.* Or consider Number 7—a long-time cycle encompassing a larger number of operations than usual and of a more interesting character, sometimes called "job enlargement." Here is a concept and a practice that has proved successful in decreasing monotony without impairing efficiency in certan sectors of other industries. We here suggest that it be introduced experimentally into automobile assembly work.

Job enlargement is simply the recombining of two or more separate jobs into one. Certain plant managers in other industries have been finding that a law of diminishing returns applies to the subdivision of jobs and that a recombination of certain fractured parts has increased efficiency. This points toward a lengthening of time cycles. Job enlargement in the sense in which we suggest it does not mean turning automobile assembly back into the hands of master mechanics with one worker assigned to the assembly of one car. It does mean paying greater attention to psychological and social variables in the determination of time cycles and, by the same token, paying more attention to the *content* of individual jobs.

To one unfamiliar with assembly-line work experience, the difference between a job with five operations and a job with ten, or between a job taking two minutes to perform and a job taking four minutes, might seem a matter far too trivial to concern anyone. Our data have shown that this is not true. Management has a vital interest in such matters; the proper assignment of time cycles throughout an assembly plant will make an important difference in the efficiency of the plant. As for the worker, one of the most striking findings of this study is the psychological importance of even minute changes in his immediate job experience.

At the risk of oversimplification, the point may be summarized this way: Other things being equal, the difference between a satisfied and a dissatisfied worker may rest on whether he has a ten-operation or a five-operation job.

## Relationship among Workers

Another place to look for possibilities of improvement is in the area of indirect influences—the impact of mass-production methods on the plant's social structure. Ever since the early studies of Elton Mayo, it has been widely accepted that the character of the "work group" frequently exercises a decisive influence on a worker's efficiency—not to mention on his satisfaction on the job. How did the technology of the automobile assembly line affect the grouping of men at Plant X?

Most workers are located along the "main line" according to the particular manpower requirements of each segment of the assembly process. Each operator works in a limited area completing his own operations independently of others as the car is carried by the conveyer down the line. A particular individual may talk with the men immediately around him, but these men cannot be said to comprise a bona fide work group in the usual sense of the term. Take as an illustration the polishing line. Figure 1 shows in diagrammatic form an actual interaction pattern of a left-front-door polisher, Worker E.

The ten men from A to J comprise a work group of which Worker E is a part, and he has some social contact with all the other nine. His really close contacts, however, are only with C, D, F and G. Note that these four workers comprise a group—*but only from E's point of view*. As to the social relationship pattern of G, his immediate group would consist of E, F, H and I; it would not include C and D, who were clearly members of E's group. Further variations occur, for example, when a line makes a bend or loop and brings men in different sections closer together. Thus each man, because of the nature of conveyer operations, has a slightly different circle of associates from that of the man next to him. So it goes along the entire stretch of a line, a line well over two miles long.

In our interviews these men exhibited little of what the sociologist would call "in-group awareness." Rarely, for example, did they talk about "our team" or "our group" or "the men in our outfit." Instead, the following remark was typical: "I've been here over a year, and I hardly know the first names of the men in the section where I work."

In sharp contrast, however, to the majority of line workers, a minority

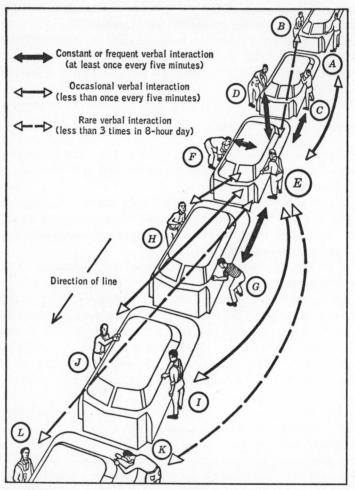

Figure 1. Social Interaction Pattern of Typical Main Assembly Line Worker— Polisher, Paint Department.

—principally off-line operators—worked on bona fide teams or crews; that is, they were members of a close working group, were functionally interdependent, and frequently assisted their fellows or exchanged operations with them. On charting the interaction pattern of such groups it was found that the frequency of conversational exchange was high and constant for nearly all members of the group. Of greater significance, the group exhibited a marked *esprit-de-corps* not found among the bulk of line operators.

It is clear that the present technology of an automobile assembly line limits social interaction and does not lend itself to the arrangement of men in bona fide teams or crews. It is suggested, however, that in the design of *new* plants, and at periods of retooling or of layout revisions, an effort be made to maximize the opportunities for social interaction and for team relationships.

## Relations with Management

Still another area of social relationships—that of worker to supervisor —is crucial to an intelligent understanding of social organization.

The formal organizational structure of the various production departments in Plant X was similar to that found in many plants. In interviews with workers we came to know the quality of relationship between workers and supervisors.

*Foremen.* Qualitative comments by the men about their foremen suggested a relatively informal and friendly relationship on the part of the majority. The average foreman had from 15 to 25 men under him, and talking between worker and foreman was generally frequent, friendly, and informal. The sort of remarks one hears about any good foreman were also heard here, as for example: "Our foreman is a real good guy. We're lucky. If he got into trouble, the whole department would back him right up."

There were criticisms of foremen, but usually these were not directed at the individual. Rather they were aimed at the "line" and the role the foreman had to play with reference to the line. As one man said: "After all, the foreman has to be a pusher, and nobody likes to be pushed. He's got to hold his job. If he doesn't push, somebody else will get his job."

Often men exonerated foremen for "pushing" since they recognized that the compulsion of line production was not the fault of the foremen. One man put it this way: "I guess you'd say the foreman gets along with the men. But they don't need a foreman. *The line is the foreman.* You have to keep up with the line."

*Higher supervisors.* An interesting finding which came out of the study was the relationship, or lack of it, between workers and management above the foreman level. The 180 men in our sample were asked to indicate contacts with supervisors in their department at the general foreman and department-head levels. Only 59 reported that they talked with their general foreman as often as once a week; 15 put it at one to three times a month; and 88 said less than once a month. Contact between workers and upper departmental supervisors was even less, with 70% saying they spoke with their department heads less than once a month. (Departments ranged in size from 200 to 400.)

It is significant in this connection that in a steel fabricating plant which we recently studied the workers talked far more frequently with supervisors above the foreman level. There the nature of the process and the high degree of worker skills made for a closer relationship. It was an everyday experience to find a superintendent in charge of 400 men talking with an individual worker or group of workers. He did this because the technical and skilled judgment of the individual worker was important in the production process.

On the automobile assembly line, on the other hand, because of the high degree of mechanization and fractional assembly there appears to be less need for supervisors to discuss production matters with individual workers. Management relies on the judgment of the engineer, not the worker. Thus the basic factor which determines the rate and quality of worker-supervisor interaction is the technology of mass production.

### Impact on Wage Structure

Not the least important secondary effect of the mass-production method has been its impact on the wage structure. A leveling of workers' skills has inevitably resulted in a narrowing of differentials between wage grades, in contrast to industries where the latest mass-production methods have not been applied. For example, in the steel fabricating plant which we investigated—a seamless tube mill—the differential between the rates of the lowest and of the highest paid workers was over a dollar an hour. At Plant X, however, the differential between the lowest paid and the highest paid was around 10 cents for the major categories of production workers, and over half the workers in the production departments received exactly the same hourly wage.

It is obvious that changes in skill levels and in wage categories affect what the wage administrator calls the "system of job progression." Before the application of mass-production methods most industries had many well-defined steps in their ladders of promotion. Mass-production methods, while often raising the general level of wages and bringing other benefits, have knocked out a good many rungs in these promotion ladders. To turn again to the steel mill for contrast: there were as many as seven or eight steps from laborer to roller, each one associated with progressively higher wages, skills, and prestige.

This system of promotion, with its connotations of growth, incentive, and progress, has been weakened or virtually eliminated on the assembly line. Almost any assembly worker can—and some do—say: "There are hundreds of jobs like mine, not much better, not much worse. The differences are so slight—or seem so slight to management—that I am interchangeable." Consequently, to escape a resulting sense of anonymity as much, perhaps, as to escape monotony, the average worker at Plant X does not aspire to climb into another slightly better production job, but rather into a utility man's job or a repairman's job or out of production altogether, where he can be recognized, and where also he can recognize himself, as an individual.

Most of the benefits of the mass-production method are obvious and have often been celebrated. If we are to continue to enjoy them and to expand and refine the method, we should understand more fully its impact on the traditional organization of industry. Surely the problems as well as the promises of mass production are worthy of study.

## Conclusion

It is obviously impossible in a single article to do more than sketch some of the problem areas in the broad field of relations between mass production and human nature. Concerning the direct impact of the method on the individual we made a few empirical suggestions and tried to point out at least one direction in which management might seek practical solutions.

But what can be said about the *indirect* impact of mass production on human nature through the character of work groups, the wage structure, and the promotion system? In a negative sense, at least, all these phenomena appear to be related: At Plant X they tended to increase the workers' sense of anonymity within the production enterprise of which they were functional parts. In fact, one way to express the net result of these several influences might be to say that little sense of membership in a common work community existed. (Our evidence showed that to some extent membership in the union gave the worker the feeling of personal identity and "belonging" which neither the shop nor relations with management supplied.)

It seems to us significant that the average worker appeared to be oppressed by this sense of anonymity *in spite of the fact that he declared himself well satisfied with his rate of pay and the security of his job*. The answer to this problem in the most general terms would appear to be a program designed to re-create the sense *and also* the reality of a bona fide work community. And for such a program to be successful we believe that both union and management would have to agree on the measures to be taken.

A comment by a man on the line will suggest the nature of the problem more clearly than many paragraphs of exposition:

> There is a different feeling in this plant. It's much bigger than people around here have ever seen. It's just like the kid who goes up to a grown-up man and starts talking to him. There doesn't seem to be a friendly feeling. At the plant I used to work in there was a different feeling. Everyone spoke to everyone else. . . . Nobody goes to other departments in this plant. The understanding could be better—happier and much easier. Here a man is just so much horsepower.

Perhaps the human needs in Plant X are merely an expression in more explicit terms of the needs of our industrial civilization. The problem of reintegrating the several faculties of man into a significant unity presents itself in many fields—in industry, science, and government, to name but three—in an age of overspecialization.

It is striking that throughout the survey of Plant X both union and management agreed with the authors that the more basic problems to be explored were not those connected with a particular plant, industry, or corporation. Rather they were problems related to technological and organizational trends common to modern industry. Both agreed that modern American civilization as we know it rests upon mass-production principles quite as much as upon the natural resources of the United States. The attitude of both, therefore, was a simple and heartening one: *Since these problems exist, let us get all the facts we can. In time we shall be able to solve them*

As Saint-Exupéry, the French aviator and author wrote:

The Machine is not an end. . . . It is a tool . . . like the plough.

If we believe that it degrades Man, it is possibly because we lack the perspective for judging the end results of transformations as rapid as those to which we have been subjected. What are two hundred years in the history of the Machine when compared with two hundred thousand years in the history of Man? We have scarcely established ourselves in this country of mines and of central electricity. It is as if we had hardly begun to live in the new house that we have not yet finished building. Everything has changed so rapidly around us: human relations, conditions of work, customs. . . . Every step in our progress has driven us a little further from our acquired habits, and we are in truth pioneers who have not yet established the foundations of our new country.[3]

[3] Antoine de Saint-Exupéry, *Terre des Hommes* (Paris, Gallimard, 1939), p. 58.

# Job Design and Productivity*

*Louis E. Davis*

It has long been taken for granted that specialization is the organizing principle of modern industry and the mainspring of its phenomenal productivity. However unfortunate some of the by-products of specialization, they have been accepted by and large as necessary evils. Better to put up with them, it seemed, than to attempt remedies which might impair efficiency and thus jeopardize the material gains of industrialization.

But are these actually the alternatives today? In the light of recent research and experiment, it appears to be high time to re-examine the issue. Has specialization perhaps been carried too far—to the point where productivity is *adversely* affected? Are fatigue, tension, low morale, absenteeism, turnover, and other causes of inefficiency actually the result of over-specialization? Can increases in productivity be achieved by *reversing* the principle of specialization?

## Specialization and Job Design

The approach to these questions has always been blocked by the assumption—accepted implicitly by management, engineers, and social scientists alike—that *the content of each job in an organization is fixed by the requirements of the production process and the organization structure* and therefore cannot be altered without jeopardizing economic efficiency.

It is this assumption which has persistently biased the judgment of both experts and laymen and ruled out the possibility of an objective approach to the problems created by specialization. Engineers and industrial managers have designed jobs on the basis of this assumption, and their concepts and methods of job design, reinforced by the economists', have set the pattern of industrial organization.

In its classical form, then, job design incorporates the principles of specialization, repetitiveness, reduction of skill content, and minimum impact

* From "Job Design and Productivity: A New Approach," *Personnel*, vol. 33, pp. 418–430, 1957. The author wishes to express his appreciation to Dr. Ralph R. Canter for his collaboration in developing the concepts and supervising the experiments reported in this paper. [Reprinted in the present volume by permission of the American Management Association.]

of the worker on the production process. The basic criteria for job design are minimizing immediate cost and maximizing immediate productivity.

Social philosophers, it is true, have long deplored the dehumanizing effects of this type of job design—monotony, the lack of mental stimulus, rigid adherence to job specifications and standards of output, and, not least, a hierarchical social order in which subordinates depend upon their superiors for the satisfaction of basic needs and aspirations. Whether the worker subjected to such a life experience could ever become a responsible citizen in a free democratic society seemed open to question.

Although the social scientists, beginning with Mayo, were the first to put to the test some of the basic assumptions of industrial society, they too took for granted the critical assumption that job content is fixed by technology, and hence focused their investigations for the most part on other aspects of the work situation, leaving job content to be prescribed by the engineer.

More to the point, therefore, are the criticisms being made today of the concept of job design itself.[1]

Drucker has argued, for example, that the use of the worker as a single-purpose machine tool is poor engineering and a waste of human resources. As he states the case:

> The principle of specialization is productive and efficient. But it is very dubious, indeed, whether we yet know how to apply it except to machinery. There is first the question of whether "specialization" as it is understood and practiced today is a socially and individually satisfying way of using human energy and production—a major question of the social order of industrial society.[2]

Or as Walker, even more boldly, has suggested:

> We are only at the threshold of a scientific understanding of man's relation to work and especially his relation to the new technological environments within which much of the work of the modern world is being performed.[3]

It may well be, then, that society has bowed too soon to the expert in accepting the principle of specialization as inviolate. Once the critical as-

---

[1] See, for example, J. C. Worthy, "Organizational Structure and Employee Morale," *American Sociological Review*, Vol. 15, No. 2, April, 1950, p. 169; C. R. Walker and R. H. Guest, *The Man on the Assembly Line* (Cambridge, Mass.: Harvard University Press, 1952); F. L. Richardson and C. R. Walker, *Human Relations in an Expanding Company* (New Haven, Conn.: Yale University Press, 1948); R. H. Guest, "Men and Machines: An Assembly-line Worker Looks at His Job," *Personnel*, Vol. 21, 1955, p. 496. [See pages 203 and 218 in this volume for the Worthy article and an article by Walker and Guest.—Ed.]

[2] P. F. Drucker, *The New Society* (New York: Harper & Bros., 1950), p. 171.

[3] C. R. Walker, "Work Methods, Working Conditions and Morale," in A. Kornhauser *et al.* (ed.), *Industrial Conflict* (New York: McGraw-Hill, 1954), p. 358.

sumption of fixed job elements is put to the test, it may prove to be invalid and the traditional concepts of job design may have to be reformed.

It is from this point of view that current trends in job design will be analyzed in this article and the outlines of a new approach to the problem presented.

*Current approaches to job design.* Job design[4] is a phase in production planning which follows the planning and design of product, process, and equipment. It specifies the content of each job and determines the distribution of work within the organization.

This simple definition of job design does not take into consideration the many choices open to the job designer in specifying the content of a particular job. Generally speaking, however, the job design process can be divided into three phases:

1. The specification of individual tasks.
2. The specification of the method of performing each task.
3. The combination of individual tasks into specific jobs to be assigned to individuals.

The first and third determine the content of a job while the second indicates how the job is to be performed. It is possible, therefore, to distinguish between the design of *job content*—content design—and the design of job methods—*methods design*. There is a large body of knowledge about methods design—it is the subject of a specialized branch of industrial engineering, called methods engineering[5]—but relatively little information about content design.

According to a recent survey,[6] however, it is the prevailing practice in designing the content of industrial jobs to rely upon the criterion of minimizing immediate costs, as indicated by minimum unit operation time. To satisfy the minimum-cost criterion, the following rules are generally applied:[7]

*In specifying the content of individual tasks:*

1. Specialize skills.
2. Minimize skill requirements.
3. Minimize learning time.

[4] This and other technical terms used hereafter are defined in the Appendix to this article.

[5] L. E. Davis, "Work Methods Design and Work Simplification," *Progress in Food Research,* Academic Press, Vol. 4, 1953, p. 37.

[6] L. E. Davis *et al.,* "Current Job Design Criteria," *Journal of Industrial Engineering,* Vol. 6, No. 2, 1955, p. 5.

[7] See, for example, H. G. Thuesen and M. R. Lohmann, "Job Design, Parts I and II," *Oil and Gas Journal,* Vol. 41, Nos. 35–36; H. B. Maynard *et al., Methods-Time Measurement* (New York: McGraw-Hill, 1948).

4. Equalize workloads and make it possible to assign full workloads.

5. Provide for the workers' satisfaction (no specific criteria for job satisfaction are known to be in use, however).

6. Conform to the layout of equipment or facilities or, where they exist, to union restrictions on work assignments.

*In combining individual tasks into specific jobs:*

1. Limit the number and variety of tasks in a job.
2. Make the job as repetitive as possible.
3. Minimize training time.

In contrast with this *process-centered approach,* another concept of job design has been developed in recent years—the *worker-centered approach* which emphasizes the participation of the worker in certain areas of decision making as a way of giving meaning to the work situation.

Representative of this approach are the group planning method and job enlargement. In group planning,[8] a team of workers participates in deciding the content of the various jobs to be performed by members of the team. In job enlargement,[9] the job is specified in such a manner that the worker performs a longer sequence or a greater variety of operations and may be responsible as well for testing the quality of his work, setting up and maintaining his equipment, and controlling his own production rate.

There is a third approach which combines the process-centered and worker-centered approaches. In job rotation, for example, the operator is assigned a series of jobs to be performed in rotated order.[10] This method is often used to counteract the unfavorable effects of process-centered job designs in circumstances where the basic job specifications cannot be altered for one reason or another.

*Some criticisms.* These new approaches to job design—the outgrowth of social science research and experiment in industry—may be welcomed on the whole as a step in the right direction.[11] By calling attention to the

[8] E. A. Woodhead, "Jobs Break-Down Under Group Study Plan," *Electrical World,* Vol. 120, No. 4, 1943.

[9] C. R. Walker, "The Problem of the Repetitive Job," *Harvard Business Review,* Vol. 28, No. 3, 1950; E. J. Tangerman, "Every Man His Own Inspector, Every Foreman His Own Boss at Graflex," *American Machinist,* Vol. 7, No. 3, 1953, p. 7; J. D. Elliott, "Increasing Office Productivity Through Job Enlargement," *AMA Office Management Series,* No. 114, 1954, p. 3.

[10] A. Wood and M. L. Okum, "Job Rotation Plus That Works," *American Machinist,* Vol. 96, No. 9, 1946.

[11] They have been greeted with enthusiasm in many quarters. See, for example, "Broadening the Job," *Time,* Vol. 63, April 12, 1954, p. 100; D. R. Wright, "Job Enlargement," *Wall Street Journal,* March 11, 1954, p. 1; D. Wharton, "Removing Monotony from Factory Jobs," *American Mercury,* October, 1954, p. 91; J. K. Lagemann, "Job Enlargement Boosts Production," *Nation's Business,* Vol. 42, No. 12, 1954, p. 34.

critical role of the worker himself in the modern industrial system, they have challenged some of the basic premises of traditional job design.

A strong word of caution is in order, however. Most, if not all, social science research in industry, as was pointed out earlier, has been based on the assumption that the contents of a job are technically inviolate. If this assumption is invalid, as it may well be, the research findings cannot be accepted without question.

Given this basic limitation, it is not surprising that most of the recent experiments in job design have been haphazard—a kind of trial-and-error attempt to remedy the defects of completely "engineered" job specifications. As yet, there has been relatively little systematic analysis, under controlled conditions, of the actual relationship between job content and other variables (long-term cost, productivity, motivation, and so on). Hence, in the absence of adequate theories of job design and experimental evidence to back them up, the doctrine of minimum costs still holds the field.

There are, however, three pioneering studies of job design to which this criticism does not apply. Since these investigations focused on actual job content and were carried out under controlled conditions, they may serve as models for future research in this area.

The first of these is the study made by Walker and Guest of the Institute of Human Relations at Yale University,[12] one of the first systematic investigations into the consequences of job specialization. Using depth interviews to explore workers' experiences on automobile assembly line jobs, the investigators analyzed the effects of mass production technology on job satisfaction and human relations.

*Job design on the assembly line.* The characteristic principles of mass production technology are defined in the study as follows:

1. Standardization.
2. Interchangeability of parts.
3. Orderly progression of the product through the plant in a series of planned operations at specific work stations.
4. Mechanical delivery of parts to work stations and mechanical removal of assemblies.
5. Breakdown of operations into their simple constituent motions.

The study focuses on the consequences of these principles as translated by the engineer into specific job designs—that is, the resulting gains and costs, both social and economic, for workers and for the company. Looking first at the gains, it is evident that the "engineered" job has yielded

[12] C. R. Walker and R. H. Guest, *The Man on the Assembly Line* (Cambridge, Mass.: Harvard University Press, 1952); Walker and Guest, "The Man on the Assembly Line," *Harvard Business Review,* Vol. 30, No. 3, 1952, p. 71; Guest, "Men and Machines," *Personnel,* May, 1955. [The *Harvard Business Review* article is reprinted in this volume, pages 218–238.—Ed.]

high levels of output per man-hour at low cost, providing profits for the company and a relatively low-priced product for the public.

In examining the social costs, however, some disturbing facts come to light. These can be summed up in the one overwhelming fact that the workers despise their jobs. This dissatisfaction does not seem to arise from the circumstances usually considered important by management such as pay, security, working conditions, pension plan, and supervision—the workers regarded these as satisfactory on the whole—but from certain features of job design:

1. *The anonymity of the individual worker* (what has been referred to previously as the principle of "minimum impact of the worker on the production process"). This is a consequence of designing *out* of the job virtually everything that might be of personal value or meaning to the worker. Specifically:

   a. The worker has no control over his work pace.

   b. His job is highly repetitive, having been broken down into the simplest motions possible.

   c. There is little or no need for skill because of the simple movements required.

   d. Methods and tools are completely specified and the worker has no control over them or any changes made in them.

   e. Because he never works on more than a small fraction of the product, the worker does not see the final results of his work, has no identity with the product, and cannot estimate the quality of his contribution to it.

   f. Since the job requires only surface attention, the worker does not become really absorbed in his work.

   g. The geographic arrangement of the production line severely limits social interactions. Men on the line work as individuals rather than as a work group, and the lack of group awareness seems to reinforce the feeling of anonymity.

2. *The depersonalization of the job,* as evidenced in the lack of job progression vertically. Since tasks have been simplified, skill differences between jobs are practically eliminated. Very few workers in the study had experienced any substantial change in job classification during a period of 12 to 15 years.

The manager and the engineer, of course, may feel that these social costs are more than justified by the gains for the company and the consumer. This, however, is not the point. Granting that low unit cost production—or minimum total economic cost, which amounts to the same thing—is the fundamental requirement for progress and well-being in an industrial society, the main question is this: Is the method of job design chosen by the engineer the *optimum* one for achieving minimum total economic cost *which includes social costs by definition?*

The question implies, of course, that the engineer's criteria for measuring the effectiveness of job design are inadequate, and this inference is strongly supported by the evidence of this study. As Walker and Guest point out, turnover was high; the quality of performance was far from optimum; and labor-management relations were in a constant state of tension.

*An experiment in redesigning jobs.* The second study to be examined,[13] one of the first controlled experiments on job design in an industrial plant, was aimed at investigating how productivity could be improved by altering job content. The experiment was designed to test the hypothesis that higher economic productivity could be achieved by:

1. Increasing the number of tasks in a job.
2. Combining tasks that (a) have similar technological content and skill demands; (b) are sequentially related in the technical process; (c) include final activities in the process or sub-process; (d) increase worker responsibility by enlarging the area of decision-making concerning the job; and (e) increase the opportunity for the worker to perceive how his contribution is related to the completion of the work process.

Two major criteria were chosen for analyzing the effectiveness of these modifications in job design: quantity of production per man-hour, and quality of work. Certain measures of attitude and satisfaction were also used.

The experimental setting was a manufacturing department of a unionized company on the West Coast. The department had been the subject of detailed engineering study for some years and its activities were organized according to the latest engineering practices. A similar department in the same company was used as a control group to permit monitoring of plant-wide changes which might affect employee attitudes and performance.

At the start of the experiment, the product—a hospital appliance—was being made on an assembly line at which 29 of the department's 35 members worked, the rest of the workers being engaged in supplying the line and inspecting the product. The 29 line workers were unskilled women with an average of four-and-a-half years' experience on the line (the range was from one to seven years approximately).

Each job on the line consisted in performing one of nine operations (these had similar skill requirements and technological content) as well as inspection in the form of rejecting defective parts. The operations were spaced at stations along the conveyor line, and the women rotated between hard and easy stations every two hours. Since the conveyor line set the pace, the workers were not responsible for the rate of output, and job rotation in effect eliminated any individual responsibility for the quality of output.

[13] A. R. N. Marks, "An Investigation of Modifications of Job Design in an Industrial Situation and Their Effects on Some Measures of Economic Productivity," Ph.D. dissertation, University of California, 1954. This study was under the direction of Dr. R. R. Canter and the author.

The experiment was divided into four phases (the details are given in Table 1):

1. *Line Job Design.* The original assembly line job, used as a reference base.
2. *Group Job Design.* In this modification, the conveyor is eliminated and the workers set their own pace. Otherwise, the operations are the same as above.
3. *Individual Job Design No. 1.* Workers perform all nine operations at their own stations, control the sequence of assembly, procure supplies, and inspect their own product.
4. *Individual Job Design No. 2.* Job content is the same as in (3) but workers are located in the main production area.

The changes in productivity resulting from the modifications in job design may be seen in Figure 1. In Group Job Design which eliminated con-

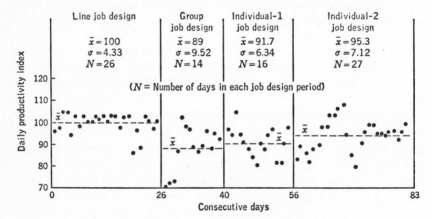

Figure 1.   Average Daily Productivity Indexes.

veyor pacing, productivity fell markedly below the Line Job Design average, indicating how conveyor pacing maintained output. The introduction of Individual Job Design, however, raised productivity above the Group Job Design average.

Although productivity under Individual Job Design did not reach the Line Job Design norm of 100, the level actually achieved is nonetheless impressive in view of the fact that the workers had only six days' experience on Individual Job Design No. 2 (only two days' experience on Individual Job Design No. 1), whereas they had an average of over four years' experience on Line Job Design. Moreover, the daily averages shown in Figure 1 do not reflect the trend resulting from consecutive days of experience with the modified job designs since workers were assigned to the experimental designs on an overlapping basis. The data given in Figure 2, however, showing the average output of the whole group for *each successive day* of the trial period, indicate that the trend was consistently upward

**TABLE 1. Experimental Conditions for the Modification of Job Designs**

| Type of Job Design | Purpose | Criteria | Locations | Number of Workers | Total Number of Days Assigned | Number of Days Each Worker Assigned | Production Method |
|---|---|---|---|---|---|---|---|
| Line Job Design | Obtain reference base of job design where separate tasks are performed on rotated basis. | Quantity, quality, some measures of attitude and satisfaction. | Main department | 29 | 26 | 26 | Workers rotate among nine stations on belt conveyor, performing minute specified operations at pace of conveyor. |
| Group Job Design | Eliminate conveyor pacing. Other conditions same as above. | Quantity, quality. | Adjacent room | 29 | 14 | 2 | Workers rotate among nine individual stations using batch method. |
| Individual Job Design No. 1 | Give workers experience on experimental job design. | Quantity, quality. | Adjacent room | 29 | 16 | 2 | Workers perform all nine operations at own stations, plus inspection and getting own supplies. |
| Individual Job Design No. 2 | Obtain measure of experimental job design. | Quantity, quality, some measures of attitude and satisfaction. | Main department | 21 | 27 | 6 | Same as Individual Job Design No. 1. |

and that, on the sixth day, the group achieved an average productivity *higher* than that reached under Line Job Design.

An examination of the dispersion of points about the averages in Figure 1 reveals an even more significant result. The narrow dispersion about the

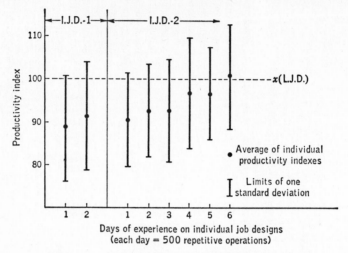

Figure 2.   Average Individual Productivity Indexes.

average for Line Job Design reflects the fixed work pace imposed by the line—workers could not deviate from this pace unless there were absences on the line. On the other hand, when the workers set their own pace, individual differences came into play, as indicated by the wide dispersion about the average for the three experimental designs, and some individual performances were as much as 30 to 40 per cent higher than the Line Job Design average.

The superiority of the experimental job designs is demonstrated further in the quality data shown in Figure 3. (The number of kinked assemblies produced gave a direct measure of workmanship since the quality of parts and sub-assemblies was not involved.) Beginning with a high level of quality under Line Job Design, quality levels rose with the removal of conveyor pacing. Under Individual Job Design, when responsibility for quality was placed in the hands of the workers, quality levels rose still higher, kinked assemblies dropping to one-fourth of the original value.

It was concluded that Individual Job Design, besides bringing about improvements in productivity and quality, had:

1. Increased the flexibility of the production process.
2. Permitted identification of individual deficiencies in productivity and quality.
3. Reduced the service functions of the department such as materials delivery and inspection.

4. Developed a more favorable attitude toward individual responsibility and effort—after experience with Individual Job Design, workers disliked the lack of personal responsibility characteristic of Line Job Design.

The third piece of research, a study carried out in an Indian textile mill, highlights the importance of the organizational component in job design.[14]

*An Indian textile mill.* The research problem was posed by the fact that the mill's production was unsatisfactory although new equipment had re-

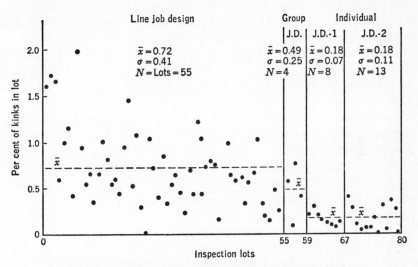

Figure 3. Percentage of Kinked Assemblies in Consecutive Lots.

cently been installed and work loads assigned on the basis of an intensive study by engineers.

In reviewing job designs, it was found that existing worker-machine assignments produced organizational groupings and interaction patterns which mitigated against continuity of production. In one room containing 240 looms, for example, 12 activities were organized as follows:

| | |
|---|---|
| A weaver tended approximately | 30 looms |
| A battery filler | 50 looms |
| A smash-hand | 70 looms |
| A gater, cloth carrier, jobber, and assistant jobber | each 112 looms |
| A bobbin carrier, feeler-motion fitter, oiler, sweeper, and humidification-fitter | each 224 looms |

Since these activities were highly interdependent, the utmost coordination was required to keep production going.

[14] A. K. Rice, "Productivity and Social Organization in an Indian Weaving Shed," *Human Relations,* Vol. 6, No. 4, 1954, p. 297.

Each weaver came into contact with five-eighths of a battery filler, three-eighths of a smash-hand, one-quarter of a gater, and one-eighth of a bobbin carrier

After a study of travel and communication patterns, the work groups were reorganized so that all of the workers who were interdependent became part of the same work group. Each group was then made responsible for the operation and maintenance of a specific bank of looms—a geographic rather than a functional division of the weaving room which produced regular interaction among individuals whose jobs were interrelated. As a result of these changes, efficiency rose from an average of 80 per cent to an average of 95 per cent after 60 working days, and the mean per cent of damage dropped from 32 per cent to 20 per cent. In those parts of the weaving shed where job design remained unchanged, efficiency dropped to 70 per cent, finally rising again to 80, and damage continued at 32 per cent.

*Some basic questions.* The results of these investigations underscore the criticism made earlier of the usual approaches to job design. Relying as it does on extremely narrow criteria, traditional job design has often failed to yield the gains in efficiency which have been anticipated. On the other hand, it has produced a host of *unanticipated* and disturbing secondary effects—monotony, dissatisfaction, resistance, and even obstruction. These failures have often been laid to the "contrariness" of human nature, but this is merely another way of saying that, given the current state of knowledge, the effects of job design are unpredictable.

Yet when jobs have been manipulated or redesigned in order to enlarge job content or personal responsibility, even within a given state of technology, *reduced costs have been reported as well as gains in productivity and morale.* These results could not have been achieved on the basis of the classical theory of job fractionalization.

In short, the traditional concepts and methods of job design have obviously failed to provide satisfactory answers to two fundamental questions:

1. What criteria should guide the design of jobs?
2. What criteria should be used to evaluate the effectiveness of job designs?

If adequate criteria for job design are to be developed, research and experiment toward this end must be based on the following conditions:

1. A recognition of the limitations of the traditional minimum-cost criterion.
2. A new approach to job design which encompasses not only the technical requirements of production but the organizational requirements, the social elements in the work situation (the individual's relationship with fellow workers and with management), and the interaction between the human and the technological imperatives of the job.

**3.** The formulation of explicit theories of job design which will permit prediction. This requires systematic analysis of how specific changes in job content affect productivity, morale, and other variables.

**4.** Validation of these theories by experimental evidence gathered under controlled conditions so that causal factors can be identified and general principles established.

*A new approach.* Since many of the flaws in job design can be traced to the inadequacies of the minimum-cost criterion, what is needed is a criterion of *total economic cost* which takes account of the multi-dimensional character of job design and includes relevant long term changes for economic, engineering, organizational, social, psychological, and physiological costs.

To determine how such costs are to be measured poses, of course, some formidable research problems. Among the variables that would have to be measured are the following:

Labor turnover and absenteeism.
Learning time.
Flexibility of work skills.
Quality deficiencies and production bottlenecks associated with job performance.
Grievances and interpersonal conflicts arising out of job and process requirements.
Organizational rigidities.
Service requirements such as supervision and inspection, engineering, maintenance, and personnel services.
Other overhead costs.

These considerations dictate a new approach to job design—the *job-centered approach*—which goes beyond the process-centered and worker-centered approaches. The job-centered approach operates on the premise that a job cannot be adequately designed without taking into account all three of the basic variables—process, worker, and organization—as well as the variables arising from their interaction, and that changing any of these in isolation may affect economic productivity—that is, total economic-cost—adversely.[15]

It is hoped that this approach will point the way for future research and lay the basis for a more satisfactory theory of job design.

*The outlook for research.* Research and experiment must reflect the multi-dimensional character of job design. While job content remains the focus of research, other variables should be included in experimental de-

[15] L. E. Davis and R. R. Canter, "Job Design," *Journal of Industrial Engineering,* Vol. 6, No. 1, 1955, p. 3. See also L. R. Sayles, "Human Relations and the Organization of Work," *Michigan Business Review,* November, 1954, p. 21; R. H. Guest, "A Neglected Factor in Labor Turnover," *Occupational Psychology,* October, 1955.

signs, and certainly the range of data required is such as to call for a problem-centered, research-team approach by engineers, psychologists, sociologists, anthropologists, economists, and others.

Job design research can be expected to pay off in a number of areas: For management, in re-examining organizational designs, reward systems, control devices, communications, and the administration of the personnel function; for the engineering sciences, in improving design theories and methods in every area—product, process, equipment, plant layout, control systems, and so on; and for the social sciences, in re-evaluating human relations, programs, leadership methods, personnel techniques, communication networks, and organizational design at all levels.

The need for more effective job design, though urgently felt at present, will become even more acute as our economy moves into the era of automation. The introduction of automatic equipment makes rigorous demands on job design theory and methods in determining what processes should be automated, how automation systems should be designed, and how the human links in the control system should be related.

Even where automation is not applicable—and only a small number of jobs relative to the total will actually be transformed by automation—the design of non-automated jobs, either in automated plants or elsewhere, will be a critical factor in maintaining operations and meeting competition.

Hence—despite the popular illusion that automation will solve most of our problems by making the machines do the work—job design will remain a central problem for industry not only in the area of production and clerical jobs but, in view of the requirements of functional organization, at supervisory and managerial levels as well.

## Appendix

### Definitions of terms

1. *Job:* The structure of tasks assigned to an individual together with the work methods and the setting. The *content* of a job comprises the following:

a. *Work Content:* The assigned series of tasks which arise from the requirements of the technical process or the equipment used or from traditionally established needs.

b. *Methods Content:* The specification of the ways in which the work activities are to be performed, including tools, equipment, and location. It is often referred to as methods design.

c. *Organization Content:* The organizational setting in which the assigned tasks are to be carried out—for example, the location of the job in a work group, hierarchical relations, and so on.

d. *Personal Content:* The factors in the job that affect personal behavior, growth, motivations, etc.

2. *Job Design:* The process of specifying the content of a job (work, methods, organizational, and personal content) in terms of a job definition or a job description.

3. *Total Economic Cost:* The total cost of producing a unit of product or service. In addition to the immediate charges for labor, materials, overhead, and so on, it includes the relevant long-term charges for economic, engineering, organizational, social, psychological, and physiological costs.

4. *Economic Productivity:* Productivity measured on the basis of total economic cost—that is, direct productivity modified by the addition of appropriate overhead or hidden charges stemming from absenteeism, labor turnover, quality failures, inflexibility, and so on.

5. *Minimum Cost:* The cost of producing a unit of product or service which includes only the immediate charges for direct labor, materials, and overhead.

# Does Higher Pay Bring Higher Productivity?*

*Harold F. Rothe*

In practically all companies today, the preferred method of inducing employees to work faster, or better, or both, is to offer them more money. The particular inducement used may take any one of a variety of forms—group or individual incentive systems, merit increases, length-of-service increases, bonuses, commissions, profit-sharing plans, to name but a few. But whatever incentive is offered, its underlying rationale is the belief that workers are spurred to greater efforts by the prospect of higher earnings.

In actual fact, there is remarkably little experimental evidence to support this view. This is not to say, of course, that money is not an effective motivator *per se*. Any company paying substandard wages eventually learns that, though people may not work for money alone, they are seldom particularly receptive to the idea of working for less than they can earn in a similar job elsewhere. But this is hardly the point at issue. The question to be resolved is not so much whether people work primarily for money, or even whether they work better for more money. What we really want to know is which financial inducements can be relied upon to increase productivity and which cannot. Or, to put the question another way, how can money be used to motivate employees to produce more?

Actually, "motivate" is hardly the right word to use in this connection.

* From *Personnel,* vol. 37, pp. 20–27, July–August, 1960. Reprinted by permission of the American Management Association.

Expressed in its simplest psychological terms, a "motive" is an inner urge toward something—food, drink, recognition, security, and the like. The external object that satisfies the need—a hot dog, a milk shake, a pat on the back, insurance—is an "incentive." Thus, money, strictly speaking, is an incentive, and our question would be more properly phrased: How can money be used to incentivate employees to produce more? Rather than fall back on this barbarism, however, let us continue to say "motivate," remembering that when we offer people something over and above their base wages or salaries, it is their incentives, not their motives, that are being changed.

## Some Classic Studies

Before coming to grips with our main question, it may be pertinent to review here some research findings about the effectiveness of money as a reward. One study, for example, that compared college freshmen of equal ability but varying economic status found that the students who needed money received better grades than those who were financially secure. The researchers concluded that the hope of winning scholarships stimulated the needy students to work harder.

In another study, conducted in a school for the unemployed in England, four girls who were paid by the day stitched on canvas for two months to establish a production standard. After a six months' interval, they returned to stitch for five weeks under a wage incentive system. Though they had presumably lost some skill in the meantime, the girls exceeded their old standard from the first week onward.

Still another study found that children learned to read better when rewards of candy, toys, or money were held out to them. Though candy was the most effective incentive, money could be, and always was, exchanged for candy, and so it too was effective.

While all these studies apparently showed that money motivated people, none of them can be considered in any way definitive. They are too academic and cover too short a time span and too few persons. As a group, however, they do suggest that money can be an effective incentive to produce more.

On the other hand, an English factory study similar to the ones described above showed that this is not necessarily so. Here, a group of young girls was employed threading needles for older girls to use. The girls threaded an average of 96 dozen needles a day and were paid on a day rate. When a piece-rate system was installed, their average dropped to 75 dozen needles. Then a new system was introduced: When the girls reached a daily standard of 100 dozen, they were allowed to go home. Production immediately jumped; the girls reached their quota on an average of two-and-one-half hours early each day.

The explanation in this case was simple: Money had no incentive value in this situation because the girls' parents were taking all their earnings. The chance to get out of work early, on the other hand, had a real appeal to them and hence was a real incentive.

The evidence offered by industrial engineers, though taken from more pertinent situations than these classic studies, is equally inconclusive and even more likely to involve oversimplification. In his book, *Lincoln's Incentive System,* J. F. Lincoln tells how his plant's productivity increased over the years after the introduction of an incentive system and a profit-sharing bonus. Concluding that piecework is the only proper way of paying for production, he advises management to study the job in question, set the best method of doing it, establish a price for the job, and stick to it regardless of what happens to earnings.

Unfortunately, this kind of study does not really demonstrate the effect of any one variable like money. It merely shows that over a period of years productivity, pay, and sales went up, prices went down, and so forth. With so many variables to take into account, it is impossible to determine what effect a particular one might have had, especially over an extended period of time.

## Maybe It's Not the Money

The Hawthorne studies covered a shorter period and were more limited in scope than most industrial engineering studies. There it was found that small groups of employees increased their production under varying working conditions and pay systems. All incentive system brought about greater productivity—or was accompanied by greater productivity—than a time system, and when one group was later put back on a day rate, its production fell off. There were indications, however, that the increased production under the incentive system was a result not of the system itself but of the reduction in the size of the work group from a whole department to only four or five employees.

This explanation receives some support from an English study that found small work groups producing about 6 per cent more than large work groups, regardless of the pay system. If we subtract this figure from the 15–30 per cent productivity increase at the Hawthorne plant, we are left with 9–24 per cent to be accounted for by other factors, including the pay system. The Hawthorne researchers noted that the effects of different wage systems were completely entwined with other variables in the situation and agreed that there was therefore no real evidence that the productivity increases were due to wages alone.

A similar experiment in an English candy factory, carried out around the same time as the Hawthorne studies, pointed up another factor modifying the effects of wage incentives. The ten girls studied rotated on five operations. For nine weeks, each girl was paid a straight day rate, and production was roughly constant; for the next 15 weeks, a competitive bonus system was used, and production increased 46 per cent; for the final 12 weeks, an individual piece rate was in effect, and production increased another 30 per cent. Interestingly enough, however, the production rate on one of the five operations—unwrapping poorly wrapped pieces of candy—showed no change throughout the entire study, simply because the girls disliked this particular task. Here again, more money was not necessarily an infallible spur to greater productivity.

Still another factor that can reinforce or counteract the effect of wage incentives cropped up in a study conducted in the boot and shoe industry. Out of 454 comparisons made in 43 English factories, 430 found piece workers producing at a higher rate than day workers. In fact, piece workers produced about twice as much as day workers. Pitting these averages against American figures, however, the researchers discovered that not only did American workers in both categories far outproduce their English counterparts, but American day workers came much closer to the production rates of the English piece workers. It seems likely that the substantial increase in productivity that accompanied the incentive systems in England was as much a function of the way the work had been reorganized before the incentive systems were installed as of the incentives themselves. (Incidentally, the work was as well organized for the average American day worker as for the average English piece worker.)

To summarize thus far, the evidence from empirical studies indicates that while financial incentives do seem to result in greater productivity, their precise influence is impossible to determine. Productivity is clearly affected also by such factors as the size of the work group, the inherent nature of the task, the organization of the work, the nature of the incentive system itself, and perhaps the length of time involved. There are undoubtedly still others, such as union-management attitudes and collective bargaining agreements, whose effect has not yet been fully analyzed.

## Evidence from Surveys

The conclusions drawn from these empirical and quasi-experimental studies of incentive systems are supported by the findings of various surveys. Thus, in 1948, the Dartnell Corporation surveyed 117 companies with incentive systems. The respondents agreed that their systems had resulted in lower unit costs, higher productivity, higher morale, and lower absenteeism. (Needless to say, these were merely the opinions of the participating companies, and there is no way of knowing how far they were actually based on objective data.)

Another survey, of 514 incentive plans, which was carried out in 1953, found that production had increased about 38.99 per cent, labor costs had decreased about 11.58 per cent, and take-home pay had increased about 11.76 per cent. Like the industrial studies, however, this survey could not measure the exact contribution of the wage incentive itself.

Though our discussion thus far has centered on formal wage incentive systems, principally because these have been so extensively studied, there are, of course, other supplements to base pay that might be mentioned here. Profit-sharing plans, for example, are often regarded in this country as a kind of incentive system. In other countries, however, they are not considered to be incentives, and no evidence has yet been adduced that entitles us to conclude that profit sharing results in greater productivity. In fact, a worldwide survey carried out by the Australian Government in 1947 found that profit sharing had no effect on output and efficiency. Though companies with profit-sharing plans may be happy with them, their main benefit seems to be that they induce employees to stay with the company, not necessarily to work harder.

Industrial research, then, throws little light on the question: Does more money spur employees to greater effort—and if so, what kind of inducement constitutes the most effective means of increasing productivity? To answer this question, and to formulate a set of basic principles as a guide for action, we must employ an entirely different approach. We must begin by asking ourselves: When an employer offers some financial inducement to his employees in the hope of raising their productivity, what actually is he trying to do?

Analysis of this question will quickly show that, in effect, the employer is trying to change the employees' behavior. He is trying to *teach them a new habit*—the habit of producing at a faster rate, or perhaps at a higher level of quality. The effectiveness of the inducements he offers will depend, therefore, on how far they fulfill the requirements that must be met if learning is to take place.

What are these requirements—the basic conditions of the learning process? The following simple formulation should be adequate for our purposes here, as well as acceptable to the various schools of psychological thought, regardless of their differences on more specific points:

Learning proceeds better—faster, more accurately, and so forth—when

The learner is motivated—when he has a need for something.

There is an incentive appropriate to the motive. For the traditional rat in the maze, food is an effective incentive only if he is hungry; drink, only if he is thirsty. Similarly, for the English girls threading needles, money was an ineffective incentive, but time off was highly effective.

The learner intends to learn. The teacher should gratify his intention by keeping him informed of his progress. There must be an awareness of the relationship between the activity and its motive and incentive.

The learner understands what he is supposed to be learning—a principle that we implicitly recognize by instituting indoctrination programs.

The reward immediately and invariably follows the successful completion of the task, while failure is equally certain not to be rewarded.

In summary, then, the learning process requires that there be (1) a *motive,* even if it is only the intent to learn; (2) *understanding* of what is to be learned; and (3) an *incentive* that is *appropriate* to the motive, recognized as being *related* to the action, and *certain* of being applied *immediately* as soon as the correct action has been successfully completed.

The accompanying table represents an attempt to apply these criteria to various types of financial incentives. (Two criteria—motivation and understanding—have been omitted as being applicable to all types.) Though the table clearly shows which incentives meet the necessary criteria and which do not, some explanatory notes on each type of incentive may be helpful.

*1. Merit increases.* These are usually given at a predetermined review date and thus are not associated with any particularly good piece of work. In fact, the employee seldom perceives any relation between his work and the increase, except that someone may tell him that he has done a good job over the past year. In the case of an employee's talking his boss into a

**How Various Types of Financial Incentives Meet Conditions Required for Increasing Productivity**

| Type of Incentive | Conditions Required for Increasing Productivity | | | |
|---|---|---|---|---|
| | Appropriate to Intent | Related to Some Behavior | Immediate upon Behavior | Certain upon Behavior |
| Merit increases | Possibly | Possibly | Possibly | Possibly |
| Negotiated increases | Possibly | No | No | No |
| General increases | No | No | No | No |
| Productivity increases | Possibly | Possibly | No | No |
| Cost-of-living increases | No | No | No | No |
| Length-of-service increases | No | No | No | No |
| Profit-sharing plans | Possibly | Possibly | No | No |
| Bonuses and commissions | Yes | Yes | Possibly | Yes |
| Individual incentive plans | Yes | Yes | Yes | Yes |
| Group incentive plans | Yes | Yes | Yes | Yes |

raise, the performance record is even less relevant. The employee is being rewarded for his persuasiveness, not his performance. He need not even have intended to do well in his job, though he no doubt intended to get a raise.

Then, too, merit increases are usually determined by the supervisor's opinions of the employee's performance, which may not be objectively sound. (A recent study using the "critical incident" technique found that supervisors forgot even important actions by their subordinates within one or two weeks.) Since merit ratings may, and generally do, bear little relationship to actual performance, there is little or no reason to expect the raises to have any influence on output. As a matter of fact, employees may come to expect a periodic raise and become bitter if they don't get it, or don't get it on time, or don't get as much as they expected.

As they are usually administered, then, merit increases do not meet the four criteria of an effective incentive. They can work, though—if they are given soon after an outstanding accomplishment, if the employee is told the reason for the increase, and if, on the other hand, his undesirable actions are immediately pointed out to him as grounds for the withholding of a raise.

*2. Negotiated increases.* It would be unrealistic to expect an increase in production to follow a negotiated wage increase, which does not recognize either the group's or the individual's productivity and whose timing is determined by quite another set of factors. There is no certainty under this system, either: negotiations during a period of rising employee productivity do not necessarily result in an increase, whereas negotiations during a period of low productivity sometimes do result in an increase. The behavior that is really being rewarded here is skill or power in negotiating, but not productivity. Moreover, sharp labor-management conflict in the course of negotiations is likely to result in an immediate lowering of productivity.

Individually negotiated increases usually take the form of a contract such as salesmen have and include some sort of bonus or commission. For this reason, they ought really to be considered as individual incentive systems and hence will not concern us here.

*3. General increases.* General increases, whether or not they are won by negotiation, have the same defects as negotiated increases: they bear no relation to what the employees are doing or to their intent, since the poor producer is rewarded as well as the good producer; and, of course, they are neither immediate nor certain upon good performance. The only possible source of increased productivity under this system is a slight temporary feeling of gratitude on the part of the employees.

*4. Productivity increases.* Despite their name, productivity increases are, most commonly, negotiated general increases with no necessary relation to the contributions of the beneficiaries. A company might raise its productivity through better tooling or better design, thereby achieving lower costs regardless of the actions of its labor force. These gains would then be passed on to employees who might have had nothing at all to do with the increase in output. This kind of increase thus has no relation to employees' intentions or behavior, it is not applied immediately upon their performing some desirable action, and it is not certain.

*5. Cost-of-living increases.* Though they seem at first glance to be ethically "right," cost-of-living increases are basically inequitable and, unless accompanied by greater productivity, inflationary. In any event, as the table shows, they are totally ineffective in assuring productivity. Actually, they are nothing but negotiated general increases.

In passing, it may be said that the increases we have been examining may, of course, have a strong and direct effect on the company's productivity—by forcing the employer to develop better products or methods, or buy better tools and equipment, in order to offset the cost of the increase. Needless to say, this is not the direct effect he is seeking, and should not be equated with an actual increase in the productivity of the employees.

6. *Length-of-service increases.* Though often valuable in reducing labor turnover, these increases bear no more than a coincidental relation either to productivity or to the intent to produce more. They do have immediacy and certainty, but the achievement they reward—ten years of service, for instance—is altogether irrelevant to productivity.

7. *Profit sharing.* Since profit-sharing plans bear some relationship to the productivity of individual employees, if only remotely, it can be presumed that employees will want to produce more in order to share in greater profits. Under most plans, however, the rewards are granted only once a year and thus lack immediacy. They also lack certainty, though the employees often have some idea whether or not things are going well for the company.

These plans could be more effective if the connection between performance and reward were made clearer by a more frequent distribution of the profits—perhaps quarterly instead of annual. One defect, however, would still remain: the individual employee's performance does not determine his share of the pie.

8. *Bonuses and commissions.* These two forms of compensation are sufficiently alike to be treated together. For our purpose, the term "bonus" means extra payment for extra results, such as a salesman might get, rather than, say, a Christmas bonus, which is usually a form of profit sharing. Bonuses and commissions need not be related to profits, but they *are* related to some activity, and are, obviously, appropriate to the intent to make more money by producing more. In general, the reward is sure to follow the results, and it comes soon after. These forms of compensation meet, or can easily be made to meet, the four requirements of an effective incentive.

9. *Individual and group incentive plans.* Incentive plans score on all four criteria: the incentive is directly related to performance and to the intent to earn more by producing more; the rewards are certain, and they come quickly.

To make group incentives wholly satisfactory on the first two criteria, the size of the group may need adjusting. As was noted earlier, small groups are usually more productive than large groups. In small groups the individual's contribution is more apparent, and there is more room for his intent to produce to come into play. Industrial engineers usually equate the group with an operational unit, which may actually be quite large. To achieve the optimum operation of an incentive plan they might do well to make the group as small as timekeeping and other control activities will permit.

# Studying and Creating Change: A Means to Understanding Social Organization*†

*Floyd C. Mann*

Social organizations are functioning entities with interdependent structures and processes. They are not fixed, static structures, but rather continuously moving patterns of relationships in a much larger field of social activity. To understand what their essential elements and dimensions are, what it is that gives an organization its unity, it is necessary to study and create social change within organizational settings.

Relatively little is known about organizational change. Social scientists stress the study of the dynamic in social systems, but few[1] accept the risks involved to gain the knowledge and skills needed to create and measure changes in functioning organizations. This is not surprising, for research within large-scale organizations is at such an early stage that the social scientist knows little about how (1) to gain access to these research sites, (2) to initiate and sustain organizational change, and (3) to measure such changes. We have only begun the systematic codification of the working knowledge and skills necessary for the researcher to get into, and maintain himself within, the social science laboratories of functioning organizations.[2] Systematic, quantitative measurement of change processes in complex or-

* From Arensberg et al., *Research in Industrial Human Relations*, Harper & Row, Publishers, Incorporated, New York, 1957, chap. 10, pp. 146–167. Reprinted by permission of the publisher.

† Drs. Rensis Likert, Daniel Katz, Robert Kahn, and Norman R. F. Maier have made especially helpful suggestions concerning the organization and presentation of this material. They can, of course, in no way be held responsible for the shortcomings which remain.

[1] For an account of a conspicuous exception to this, see N. C. Mare and E. Reimer, "The Experimental Manipulation of a Major Organizational Variable," in *Journal of Abnormal and Social Psychology* (1956).

[2] F. Mann and R. Lippitt, eds., "Social Relations Skills in Field Research," *Journal of Social Issues*, VIII, No. 3 (1952).

ganizational settings is in its infancy. Longitudinal studies are rare—social scientists seldom attempt to obtain more than a single "before" and "after" measurement and are often content to try and decipher findings from *ex post facto* study designs. The actual steps and skills necessary to initiate and sustain changes within an organization are not only relatively unknown, but there is even some suspicion that knowledge of social action and an ability to engineer change are not appropriate for the social scientist.

While social scientists are not spending any sizable proportion of their time in learning how to change interpersonal and intergroup relations in functioning organizations, a wide variety of practitioners are. These include at the one extreme the consultants or the "operators" who take over organizations which are failing and rebuild them, and at the other extreme, the "human relations" trainers. Most of these men know very little theoretically about processes of organizational, attitudinal, and behavioral change, but they do know a great deal intuitively about the problems of changing people in an organization. This is especially true of the training men.

This suggests that there should and can be a closer working relationship between those concerned with actually *changing* organizational structure and processes and those researchers concerned with *understanding* organizational change. Social scientists have not begun to take advantage of their opportunities for learning about organizations from those in the "practicing professions"—those who are *doing*.[3] Observations and systematic measurements around the practitioner's efforts to alter systems of relationships in organizations can provide the researcher with valuable insights into the dynamics of organization. Gaps in knowledge become excruciatingly apparent; new sources of data and problems for research emerge. In turn, social scientists can contribute to practitioners by helping them assess what effect their actions as change agents have. Most practitioners—and especially those trainers who are concerned with changing the human relations skills of supervisors—have very little systematic, and no quantitative, evidence on the success of their efforts to create changes in individuals or organizations. It seems clear that there is a broad basis for cooperation here. Systematic studies of the work of those attempting to change the way things are done in an organization may contribute to our understanding of social organizations. And developments in measurement and the procedures used by researchers to understand organizations better may contribute to the working knowledge of trainers and others in the "practicing professions."

In this chapter we will focus on the description and evaluation of several different types of procedures designed to change interpersonal and intergroup relations in complex organizations. We will first look at two human relations training programs whose effects have been systematically and

[3] Donald Young, "Sociology and the Practicing Professions," *American Sociological Review*, XX (December 1955), pp. 641–648.

quantitatively studied. Then we will describe briefly the development and evaluation of a change procedure with which we are experimenting to increase the understanding, acceptance, and utilization of survey research findings. At the close of the chapter these two specific types of procedures for creating change in organizational settings are contrasted as a first step in identifying facets of change processes which merit greater experimentation and in providing insights into the structure and functioning of organizations.

## Changing Interpersonal Relations through Training Supervisors

Recurrent opportunities for social scientists to study a change process within an organizational setting are provided by human relations training programs for supervisors. As change procedures, these programs are formal, rational, purposeful efforts to alter institutional behavior. In contrast to the day-to-day attempts of management to bring about change, they are bounded in time and organizational space, and are thus easily studied intensively.

Because of the several historical developments described [elsewhere], management by the late forties began to be convinced that training might be useful for their supervisors, and there has since been a wholesale adoption of human relations training programs. While there was and still is a remarkable range in the content, methods, and settings of these programs, nearly all of them have centered around improving supervisory skills in dealing with people—either as individuals or in face-to-face groups. They are frequently directed at teaching the supervisor how to work with an employee as an individual, occasionally at working with employees as members of a small group, but only rarely at understanding and working within the complex social system of the large corporation or factory. Another way of saying this is that the courses have drawn heavily from psychology, to a lesser extent from social psychology, and usually not at all from sociology.

There are no commonly agreed-upon ways by which these programs can be described. The following headings are, however, useful: objectives, content, methods, setting, training leader, and training unit. For example, the objectives of these programs are usually very general and quite ambitious: "to assist supervisors in developing the skills, knowledge, and attitudes needed to carry out their supervisory responsibilities," or "to improve morale, increase production, and reduce turnover." Their contents usually include human nature, personality, motivation, attitudes, and leadership, and other information about relevant psychological principles and research findings may also be included. More often than not the methods of training are some variant of the "lecture-discussion method." The settings are frequently in a classroom away from the job. The trainers are generally staff men whom the trainee did not know before the training; the trainees, first-line supervisors or foremen meeting with other supervisors from other parts of the organization.

Few systematic, quantitative studies have been made to investigate the effectiveness of these programs.[4] This is not to say that there has been no interest in evaluation. Any review of the literature will indicate many such attempts and many testimonials about the relative advantages of different procedures of training. Mahler and Monroe[5] reported a number of "evaluative studies" after reviewing the literature and conducting a survey of 150 companies known to have training programs. While these studies almost without fail acclaim the many benefits of such training, few of them meet more than a fraction of the requirements necessary for a rigorous test of the basic underlying assumptions.

What are these assumptions? In general, they are that training supervisors in human relations will result in changes in the supervisors' attitudes and philosophy, that these changes will be reflected in their behavior toward employees on the job, that this changed behavior will be seen by the employees, and that they will in turn become more satisfied with their work situation, then more highly motivated, and, ultimately, more productive workers.

While there is a good deal of evidence that human relations training programs do meet part of these assumptions—e.g., they do appear to change the verbal veneer of supervisors—there are few scientifically rigorous, quantitative studies which have demonstrated that these changes in what supervisors *know* affect their attitudes and behavior as seen or experienced by their subordinates. Few studies show that human relations training of supervisors is related to changes in the attitudes or productivity of employees under those supervisors.

It is not possible to make a complete review of these studies here. A review of the findings from several recent, major evaluative studies will, however, provide a good deal of evidence concerning the effectiveness of certain types of training programs. The findings will certainly emphasize the need for more systematic, quantitative research to assess the most effective combinations of content, methods, settings, training units, and trainers.

*The Canter-Tyler studies.* In 1949, Canter[6] developed a human relations training course for first-line supervisors in the home offices of a large insurance company. The three objectives of the course were "(1) to establish facts and principles concerning psychological aspects of behavior and group

[4] A nonquantitative, but extraordinarily thorough and insightful study of foreman training was made by A. Zaleznik, *Foreman Training in a Growing Enterprise* (Boston: Graduate School of Business Administration, Harvard University, 1951).

[5] W. R. Mahler and W. H. Monroe, *How Industry Determines the Need for and Effectiveness of Training,* Personnel Research Section Report 929 (Washington: Department of the Army, 1952).

[6] R. R. Canter, "A Human Relations Training Program," *Journal of Applied Psychology,* XXXV (February 1951), pp. 38–45.

functioning to enable supervisors to become more competent in their knowledge and understanding of human behavior; (2) to increase supervisors' capacities for observing human behavior; and (3) to present personality adjustment concepts to aid in integration of achievements made in the first two objectives." This training was designed to provide a foundation of information on which to build later through additional practice and "technique" training. Specific content was primarily psychological: human nature, personality, motivation, attitudes, leadership, and group structure. Method was lecture-discussion. The training occurred in the conference rooms of the company; Canter himself was the trainer. The trainees were eighteen supervisors whose superiors had participated in a preliminary run for executives. The course was presented in ten two-hour weekly sessions.

To determine the influence of this training, Canter employed a battery of paper-and-pencil questionnaires and tests which were given before and after training to two groups of supervisors: an experimental group of eighteen from one department who received the training, and a control group of eighteen from two other departments who did not receive training. The two groups were similar in type of work performed, age (about thirty), education (thirteen years), and proportion of men and women. While the control group had more years of service with the company (7.5 and 4.6, respectively) and higher mean scores on a mental alertness test, the statistical technique used in the final analysis did not require prematched individuals or groups.

Six tests, yielding a total of twelve separate scores, were used. (1) General Psychological Facts and Principles; (2) "How Supervise"; (3) General Logical Reasoning; (4) Social Judgment Test; (5) Supervisory Questionnaire; and (6) Test for Ability to Estimate Group Opinion. The major findings were that the trained supervisors obtained mean scores on all tests better than would have been predicted on the basis of the performance of the untrained group alone. For five out of the twelve measures, the differences were statistically significant at the 5 per cent level; for two other measures, differences were significant at the 10 per cent level. Other important conclusions were that trained supervisors became more similar in abilities measured by the tests and more accurate in estimating the opinions of employees in their departments, but not their sections. It was also found that those holding highest scores initially gained the most on all measures except the Test of Ability to Estimate Group Opinion, where the opposite result was obtained.

While Canter assumed in his design that cognitive training—i.e., an ability to understand human relations concepts and principles—would have to precede any behavioral training in supervisory skills, practices, and attitudes, Tyler[7] designed a companion study to measure any changes in em-

---

[7] B. B. Tyler, "A Study of Factors Contributing to Employee Morale" (Master's thesis, Ohio State University, 1949).

ployee morale which might be attributed to this training. Her morale surveys indicated improvement in employee morale scores for *both* the experimental and control departments. Morale improved by an average of 11 points per section (range 2–25 points) in five of seven sections in the experimental group, and decreased slightly in two others. "In the control groups, morale increased in eight of the nine sections by an average of 14 points (range 5–32 points). The decrease in the other section was seven points. The only category which showed a somewhat consistent change among sections was 'supervision' on which scores for over half of the sections decreased." After warning the reader of the possible effect of the before-test experience, she notes: "Undoubtedly, the difference in change in morale between the control and the experimental groups is not large enough to be significant" (page 47). Canter, however, points out that in Tyler's study "morale was quite high initially, which might account for the lack of any improvement in the experimental department over the control."

The strength of the Canter-Tyler studies is that they used both *before* and *after* measures for experimental and control groups. Canter's use of multiple criteria against which to evaluate the various sub-goals of the training program is also noteworthy. The use of Tyler's perceptual and employee morale measures in conjunction with Canter's attitudinal and cognitive measures permits an evaluation of the course's effectiveness at two levels: the supervisor's intent, and his on-the-job performance. The findings from this combination of studies make it obvious that classroom learning does not guarantee the translation of such learning into job performance. It should be remembered, however, that Canter did not set out to change supervisors' skills and practices, but only their understanding of human relations concepts and ideas.

*Fleishman-Harris studies.* Working with the education and training staff of a large company manufacturing trucks and farm machinery, Fleishman[8] developed a study design and a battery of research instruments for measuring the continuing effectiveness of leadership training. The general objectives of this training[9] were to change understanding, attitudes, habits, and skills of foremen by giving them solid foundation in four basic areas of industrial knowledge. These areas were personal development, human relations, economics, and company operations. The method was primarily lecture-discussion. The training staff included full-time instructors, former supervisors, and part-time university faculty. The training was given to foremen who were taken from a wide variety of operations and plants and sent to a central school in Chicago for two weeks of eight-hours-a-day intensive development.

[8] Edwin A. Fleishman, "Leadership Climate, Human Relations Training, and Supervisory Behavior," *Personnel Psychology*, VI (Summer 1953), pp. 205–222. [Refer also to "Leadership and Supervision in Industry," pages 380–395 of this volume.—Ed.]

[9] Charles L. Walker, Jr., "Education and Training at International Harvester," *Harvard Business Review*, XXVII (September 1949), pp. 542–558.

To determine the effects of this course on foremen from one motor-truck plant who had taken this training, Fleishman employed an *ex post facto* design with four groups of about thirty each. One group had not received the training; the other three had, 2–10, 11–19, and 20–29 months earlier. The groups were alike on a number of background characteristics: age (early forties), education (eleven years), length of service (sixteen years), supervisory experience (seven years), size of work group (about twenty-eight), and supervisory experience with present work group (six years). Seven paper-and-pencil questionnaires were used to obtain opinion, expectation, and perceptual data about leadership practices from the trainees, their superiors, and their subordinates. This battery gave Fleishman an opportunity to investigate the differences between supervisory beliefs as reported by the foreman himself and supervisory practices as reported by his employees, and to explore the interaction of training effects with the supervisor's "leadership climate." Each questionnaire contained two independent leadership dimensions which had been identified by factor analysis: "consideration"—the extent to which the supervisor was considerate of the feelings of employees; and "initiating structure"—the extent to which the supervisor defined or facilitated group interactions toward goal attainment.

The results obtained by giving attitude questionnaires to foremen on the first and last days of their training in Chicago provide evidence of how the topics stressed in this leadership training affected these two dimensions. The results obtained from these before and after measures showed a significant increase in "consideration" (.05 level) and an even more marked decrease in "initiating structure" (.01 level). The on-the-job effects of the training, however, appeared to be "minimal." "The training did not produce any kind of permanent change in either the attitudes or behavior of the trained foremen." The employees under the most recently trained foremen actually saw them as *less* considerate than the employees under the untrained foremen saw their superiors. This statistically significant finding was supported by other trends toward more structuring and less consideration by those foremen who had the training. Thus, while the human relations approach was stressed in the course and understood at least well enough to be registered as an opinion change on a paper-and-pencil questionnaire, it was not evident in what trained foremen said they did, or what their employees saw them doing in the actual work situation.

The most important variable found to affect leadership was the climate within which the foreman worked. In fact, the kind of superior under whom the foreman operated seemed "more related to the attitudes and behavior of the foremen in the plant than did the fact that they had or had not received the leadership training."

These results, showing that the training was not meeting its objective of making foremen more human-relations oriented in the plant, left two alternatives open: redesign the course, or initiate an intensive criterion study relating supervisory behavior to group effectiveness. The latter alternative was chosen, and Harris[10] designed a study in the same plant to investigate (1) the relationship between these two dimensions of leadership behavior and various measures of work efficiency, and (2) the effects of a training course planned as a brief refresher for the central school training in Chicago. It is the findings from this second objective in which we are primarily interested here.

The course, lasting one week, was given at a small nearby college. The effects were evaluated by field experimental design with before and after measures for experimental and control groups. Two groups of thirty-one foremen were established through matching on a number of variables, including length of time since attending the central school (almost three years), scores on before measures (including leadership climate), and other personal factors. One group was given the training. Questionnaires, similar to Fleishman's, were used to obtain information from employees and foremen about the foremen's attitudes and behavior.

Harris used several different methods of analyzing his findings. His most rigorous method indicated there were no statistically significant differences in the foremen's own leadership attitudes or the workers' descriptions of their foremen's behavior—before and after this additional refresher course. The only significant difference he found was a decrease in the degree to which the foremen in the *control* group showed structuring in their leadership behavior as described by their employees. Building on Fleishman's gradual decreases in structuring and increases in consideration the longer the foreman is back on the job, Harris suggests this finding might be interpreted to mean that the refresher course may have "tended to retard a general decrease in structuring."

Harris and Fleishman[11] in analyzing the data from both of their studies in the same plant have uncovered one finding which tends to qualify the general, completely negative conclusion of their findings regarding the effectiveness of this training. This finding concerns the stability of leadership patterns of individual foremen who did not have the training in contrast to those foremen who had the training. They find there is *less* stability in the pre-post measures for the foremen who had the training than for those foremen who did not have training. This suggests that the courses had markedly different effects on different foremen, and that "large individual shifts in scores occur in both directions." They conclude that their research findings show no significant changes in *group* means among trained foremen and that future research should be directed toward investigating personal and situational variables which interact with the effects of training.

[10] E. F. Harris, "Measuring Industrial Leadership and Its Implications for Training Supervisors" (Doctoral thesis, Ohio State University, 1952).

[11] E. F. Harris and E. A. Fleishman, "Human Relations Training and the Stability of Leadership Patterns," *Journal of Applied Psychology*, XXXIX (February 1955), pp. 20–25.

At best, these two studies suggest that this type of training has little or no general effect on the behavior of foremen in the plant. At worst, they suggest that the unanticipated consequences of separating foremen from their work groups and making them keenly aware of their role in management more than offset the anticipated consequences of making the foremen more considerate of employees as human beings. Fleishman's finding that *leadership climate* appeared to be a better predictor than *training* of foremen's plant attitudes and behavior underscores the importance of considering the constellation of expectation patterns in which the trainee is embedded. Training which does not take the trainee's regular social environment into account will probably have little chance of modifying behavior. It may very well be that human relations training—as a procedure for initiating social change—is most successful when it is designed to *remold the whole system of role relationships of the supervisor.*[12]

The findings from these four studies suggest that trainers, researchers, and others interested in social change need to rethink what forces are necessary to create and sustain changes in the orientation and behaviors of peoples in complex systems of relationships. There is a good deal of evidence that management and trainees are enthusiastic about these training courses in general. Management's enthusiasm may be an index of whether the training will continue, but it does not indicate whether training is achieving changes in behavior. And while trainee satisfaction and acceptance may be important as an antecedent to learning, these factors do not indicate whether the training will produce attitudinal and, more significantly, on-the-job behavioral changes.

It should be stressed that the criterion which has been used here for measuring the effects of human relations training is not easily met. There is ample quantitative evidence in the preceding studies that supervisors' information about, and verbal understanding of, human relations principles can be increased. There is much less evidence that these courses have an effect on the trainee's on-the-job behavior as seen by those working under him. And the hard fact remains that there are no quantitative studies which indicate that these courses in leadership affect workers' job satisfactions or motivations.

## Feedback: Changing Patterns of Relationships between Superiors and Subordinates by Using Survey Findings

Long-range interest in the actual varying of significant variables in organizations has necessitated that members of the Human Relations Program of the Institute for Social Research, University of Michigan, not only

[12] For a full account of these two studies combined, see E. A. Fleishman, E. F. Harris, and H. E. Burtt, *Leadership and Supervision in Industry* (Columbus: Personnel Research Board, Ohio State University, 1955).

study existing programs for training and changing people in organizations, but that we *develop* new techniques for changing relationships, and that we learn how to *measure* the effects of such changes within organizations. As a result, we have invested a good deal of professional effort in exploring the effectiveness of different procedures for changing attitudes, perceptions, and relationships among individuals in complex hierarchies without changing the personnel of the units. The latter is an important qualification, for we have found that the changes in subordinates' perceptions and attitudes which follow a change in supervisory personnel are frequently of a much larger order than those generated by training or other procedures for changing the attitudes or behavior of incumbents.

*Exploratory and developmental phase.* One procedure which we developed and subsequently found to be effective in changing perceptions and relationships within organizations has been called "feedback." This change process evolved over a period of years as we[13] tried to learn how to report findings from human relations research into organizations so that they would be understood and used in day-to-day operations. Work began on this process in 1948 following a company-wide study of employee and management attitudes and opinions. Over a period of two years, three different sets of data were fed back: (1) information on the attitudes and perceptions of 8000 nonsupervisory employees toward their work, promotion opportunities, supervision, fellow employees, etc.; (2) first- and second-line supervisor's feelings about the various aspects of their jobs and supervisory beliefs; and (3) information from intermediate and top levels of management about their supervisory philosophies, roles in policy formation, problems of organizational integration, etc. We had several aims in this exploratory phase: (1) to develop through first-hand experience an understanding of the problems of producing change; (2) to improve relationships; (3) to identify factors which affected the extent of the change; and (4) to develop working hypotheses for later, more directed research.

The process which finally appeared to maximize the acceptance and utilization of survey and research findings can be described structurally as an interlocking chain of conferences. It began with a report of the major findings of the survey to the president and his senior officers, and then progressed slowly down through the hierarchical levels along functional lines to where supervisors and their employees were discussing the data. These meetings were structured in terms of organizational "families" [14] or

---

[13] A number of people contributed to the design of this feedback process during its developmental phase. They included Sylvester Leahy, Blair Swartz, Robert Schwab, and John Sparling from the Detroit Edison Company, and Rensis Likert, Daniel Katz, Everett Reimer, Frances Fielder, and Theodore Hariton from the Survey Research Center.

[14] F. Mann and J. Dent, "The Supervisor: Member of Two Organizational Families," *Harvard Business Review*, XXXII (November–December 1954), pp. 103–112.

units—each superior and his immediate subordinates considering the survey data together. The data presented to each group were those pertaining to their own group or for those subunits for which members of the organizational unit were responsible.

Members of each group were asked to help interpret the data and then decide what further analyses of the data should be made to aid them in formulating plans for constructive administrative actions. They also planned the introduction of the findings to the next level. The meetings were typically led by the line officer responsible for the coordination of the subunits at a particular level. Usually, a member of the Survey Research Center and the company's personnel staff assisted the line officer in preparing for these meetings, but attended the meetings only as resource people who could be called upon for information about the feasibility of additional analyses.

These meetings took place in the office of the line supervisor whose organizational unit was meeting, or in the department's own small conference room. All of the survey findings relative to each group were given to the leader and the members of his organizational unit; they decided what to consider first, how fast to work through each topic, and when they had gone as far as they could and needed to involve the next echelon in the process.

This feedback change procedure was developed in an organization where a great amount of effort had already been invested in the training of management and supervisors. During the war the company had participated in the various J-programs sponsored by the War Manpower Commission, and more important, during the several years we were experimentally developing the feedback process, Dr. Norman R. F. Maier was working with all levels of management to improve their understanding of human relations and supervision.[15] The supervisors with whom we were working to increase their understanding of their own organizational units therefore had a great deal of training in the application of psychological principles to management.

Our observations of the feedback procedure as it developed suggested that it was a powerful process for creating and supporting changes within an organization.[16] However, there was no quantitative proof of this, for our work up to this point had been exploratory and developmental.

*A field experiment in accounting departments.* In 1950, when eight accounting departments in this same company asked for a second attitude and opinion survey of their seventy-eight supervisors and eight hundred em-

---

[15] For a thorough description of this training, see N. R. F. Maier, *Principles of Human Relations* (New York: Wiley, 1952).

[16] F. Mann and R. Likert, "The Need for Research on Communicating Research Results," *Human Organization*, XI (Winter, 1952), pp. 15–19.

ployees, we[17] had an opportunity to initiate the steps necessary to measure the effects of this organizational change process. The questionnaires used in this resurvey were similar to those used in 1948 and provided the basis for a new cycle of feedback conferences. The general plan for the handling of these new resurvey data was to let everyone in the departments—employees and department heads—see the over-all findings for eight accounting departments combined as soon as they were available, and then to work intensively on their use in *some* departments, but not in others until there had been a third survey.

While our objective was to test the effectiveness of the basic pattern of feedback developed during the preceding two years, we encouraged department heads and their supervisors to develop their own variations for reporting data to their units and maximizing their use in the solution of problems. After the all-department meetings had been concluded, the chief executive of the accounting departments held a meeting with each department head in the experimental group. At this meeting, the findings for the department head's unit were thoroughly reviewed. The findings included comparisons of (1) changes in employee attitudes from 1948 to 1950, (2) attitudes in that department with those in all other departments combined, and (3) employees' perceptions of supervisory behavior with supervisory statements about their behavior. Department heads were encouraged to go ahead with feedback meetings as soon as they felt ready, tentative next steps were discussed, and assistance from the researchers and the company personnel staffs was assured. Four departments launched feedback activities which were similar to each other in purpose but somewhat different in method. The programs varied in duration (13–33 weeks), in intensity (9–65 meetings), and in the extent to which nonsupervisory employees were involved in the process. During the eighteen months that these differences were unfolding, nothing was done in two of the remaining four departments after the first all-departments meetings. This was done so they might be available as "controls." Changes in key personnel eliminated the remaining two departments from any experimental design.

A third survey of attitudes was conducted in these departments in 1952 after the natural variations in the feedback programs had run their courses. In 1950 and 1952 surveys were then used as "before" and "after" measurements, the four departmental programs as "experimental variations," with the two inactive departments as "controls."

Our findings indicate that more significant positive changes occurred in employee attitudes and perceptions in the four experimental departments than in the two control departments. This was based on two measures of

[17] F. Mann and H. Baumgartel, *The Survey Feedback Experiment: An Evaluation of a Program for the Utilization of Survey Findings,* Survey Research Center, University of Michigan, mimeographed, 1954, 8 pp.

change: (1) a comparison of answers to sixty-one identical questions which were asked in 1950 and 1952, and (2) a comparison of answers to seventeen "perceived change" questions in which employees had an opportunity to indicate what types of changes had occurred since the 1950 survey. In the experimental group, a fourth of the sixty-one items showed relative mean positive changes, significant at the .05 level or better; the change for another 57 per cent of the items was also positive in direction, but not statistically significant. Major positive changes occurred in the experimental groups in how employees felt about (1) the kind of work they do (job interest, importance, and level of responsibility); (2) their supervisor (his ability to handle people, give recognition, direct their work, and represent them in handling complaints); (3) their progress in the company; and (4) their group's ability to get the job done. The seventeen perceived-change items were designed specifically to measure changes in the areas where we expected the greatest shift in perceptions. Fifteen of these showed that a significantly higher proportion of employees in the experimental than in the control departments felt that change had occurred. More employees in the experimental departments saw changes in (1) how well the supervisors in their department got along together; (2) how often their supervisors held meetings; (3) how effective these meetings were; (4) how much their supervisor understood the way employees looked at and felt about things, etc. These indicate the extent to which the feedback's effectiveness lay in increasing understanding and communication as well as changing supervisory behavior.

Comparisons of the changes among the four experimental departments showed that the three departments which had the two feedback sessions with their employees all showed positive change relative to the control departments. The change which occurred in the fourth was directionally positive. but it was not significantly different from the control departments. In general, the greatest change occurred where the survey results were discussed in both the departmental organizational units *and* the first-line organizational units. The greater the involvement of all members of the organization through their organizational families—the department heads, the first-line supervisors, *and* the employees—the greater the change.

*Implications of these findings.* The basic elements of this feedback process described above are not new. They involve (1) the orderly collection of information about the functioning of a system, and (2) the reporting of this information into the system for (3) its use in making further adjustments.

Work by Hall [18] and others who have had considerable practical experience with the use of information about a system for creating change show

[18] Milton Hall, "Supervising People—Closing the Gap Between What We Think and What We Do," *Advanced Management,* XII (September, 1947), pp. 129–135.

a similarity in both action steps and basic approach. This suggests there are certain psychological and sociological facts which must be taken into consideration in attempting to change the attitudes and behavior of an *individual* or a *group of individuals* in an *organizational setting*.

1. Attitudes and behavior of an individual are functions of both basic personality and social role. *Change processes need to be concerned with altering both the forces within* an individual and the forces in the *organizational situation* surrounding the individual.

2. Organizations, as systems of hierarchically ordered, interlocking roles with rights and privileges, reciprocal expectations, and shared frames of reference, contain tremendous forces for stability or change in the behavior of individuals or subgroups. Change processes need to be designed to harness these forces for creating and supporting change. *As forces already in existence, they must first be made pliable, then altered or shifted, and finally made stable again to support the change.*

3. Essentially, unilateral power and authority structures underlie the hierarchical ordering of organizational roles. *Expectations of the superior are therefore more important forces for creating change in an individual than the expectations of his subordinates.* Also, those with a direct authority relationship —line superiors—have more influence than those without direct authority— staff trainers.

4. The attitudes, beliefs, and values of an individual are more firmly grounded in the groups which have continuing psychological meaning to him than in those where he has only temporary membership. The supervisor's role of interlocking the activities of two organizational units requires that he have continuing membership in two groups: (a) the organizational unit directed by his superior in which he is a subordinate along with his immediate peers; and (b) the organizational unit for which he is responsible. *Change processes designed to work with individual supervisors off the job in temporarily created training groups contain less force for initiating and reinforcing change than those which work with an individual in situ.*

5. Information about the functioning of a system may introduce a need for change. This is especially true when the new data are seen as objective and at variance with common perceptions and expectations. Change processes organized around objective, new social facts about one's own organizational situation have more force for change than those organized around general principles about human behavior. *The more meaningful and relevant the material, the greater the likelihood of change.*

6. Involvement and participation in the planning, collection, analysis, and interpretation of information initiate powerful forces for change. Own facts are better understood, more emotionally acceptable, and more likely to be utilized than those of some "outside expert." *Participation in analysis and interpretation helps by-pass those resistances which arise from proceeding too rapidly or too slowly.*

7. Objective information on direction and magnitude of change—knowledge

of results—facilitates further improvement. *Change processes which furnish adequate knowledge on progress and specify criteria against which to measure improvement are apt to be more successful in creating and maintaining change than those which do not.*

## Comparison of "Classroom" Human Relations Training and Organizational Feedback

This is only a partial listing of the points with which a scientifically based technology of social change in organizational settings will have to be concerned  Our conceptualization and the identification of the relevant individual and organizational variables and their interrelationship is at a primitive stage. The systematic quantitative investigation of the effectiveness of different change procedures has scarcely begun. Even at this early date, however, a comparison between the structure and process of feedback and "classroom" human relations training as two different types of change procedures may be a useful exercise. It may help identify variables or facets of change processes which merit greater experimentation and investigation both by the practitioners and by those researchers interested in organizational change. By a "classroom" human relations program we mean a training which would consist of a series of classroom-like meetings in which supervisors from many different points of the organization meet to listen to a presentation of psychological principles which a trainer from the personnel department thinks they ought to know about and be ready to use on the job after a brief discussion following the training. This kind of training experience differs from the feedback process in a number of respects. These differences are stated to keep the comparisons reasonably brief and to sharpen the contrasts.

1. What are the objectives?
   *"Classroom" Training*—Improve supervisor-subordinate relations through changing the supervisors' understanding of human behavior, attitudes, and skills.
   *Organizational Feedback*—Improve organizational functioning through changing understanding, attitudes, and behavior among all members of the organization.
2. What is the setting in which change is being attempted?
   *"Classroom" Training*—Trainees are taken off the job and out of the network of interpersonal relationships in which they normally function for training in an "encapsulated" [19] classroom-like situation.
   *Organizational Feedback*—Change is attempted as a regular part of the day's work in established organizational relationships.
3. What is the informational content?

[19] M. Haire, "Some Problems of Industrial Training," *Journal of Social Issues,* **IV,** No. 3 (1948), pp. 41–47.

*"Classroom" Training*—General psychological principles of human behavior, case materials, or data from outside the training group and often the organization, only occasionally using problems from the group's own experience.

*Organizational Feedback*—Objective quantitative information about attitudes, beliefs, and expectations of the trainees themselves, or the subordinates in their own organization.

4. What is the method?

*"Classroom" Training*—Lectures, presentations, films, skits, and occasionally role-playing followed by discussion on how to apply what has been learned back on the job.

*Organizational Feedback*—The progressive introduction of new information about the problems within the groups for which the trainees are responsible. Group discussions of the meaning and action implications of the findings, followed by group decisions on next steps for changing or handling the situation.

5. Who are the trainees?

*"Classroom" Training*—First-line supervisors and foremen whose superiors may have, but more often have not, had the course.

*Organizational Feedback*—Everyone in the organization from the top down[20]—the president, top management, intermediate and first-line supervision, *and* employees.

6. What is the training unit?

*"Classroom" Training*—An aggregate or collection of individual supervisors from different departments throughout the organization. A functional conglomerate without continuing psychological meaning for the individuals. Frequently seen as a "group" simply because the individuals are in close spatial proximity to one another.

*Organizational Feedback*—An organizational unit whose members have an organizational function to perform and whose members (a superior and his immediate subordinates) have continuing psychological meaning perceptually and behaviorally to one another as a team or family.

7. Who is the change agent?

*"Classroom" Training*—An outsider—an expert. a staff man—who has no direct, continuing authority or power over the trainee and few recurrent opportunities to reinforce the training.

*Organizational Feedback*—The organizational unit's line supervisor, who is given some help through pre- and post-meeting coaching by the expert outsider.

8. How is the pace or rate of change set?

*"Classroom" Training*—The trainer sets the pace, attempting to gear the training to average trainee's ability to comprehend and assimilate the material.

*Organizational Feedback*—The members of the group move from one topic to another as they are ready for the next step.

[20] N. R. F. Maier, "A Human Relations Program for Supervision," *Industrial and Labor Relations Review,* I (April, 1948), pp. 443–464.

9. How long does the change process continue?
   *"Classroom" Training*—A fixed number of days or weeks, seldom less than 16 or more than 80 hours.
   *Organizational Feedback*—No fixed length of time, the change procedure usually continues over a period of months—6 to 24 months.
10. How much tension is there?
    *"Classroom" Training*—Usually relatively little, most trainees feel they already know a good deal about human behavior and how others feel.
    *Organizational Feedback*—Frequently considerable, as objective information and particularly the differences between supervisory beliefs and practices come into a focus so sharp that complacency is shattered and the security about what is social reality is shaken.
11. What assumptions are made about attitudes and how they are changed? [21]
    *"Classroom" Training*—The primary assumption is that the trainee does not know certain facts, that his previous organization of relevant information will be altered when he understands the new facts. Attitudes are seen as a function of the range of information available to the trainee; they are changed by altering cognitive structure.
    *Organizational Feedback*—Here the assumptions are that the trainee already has satisfying ways of seeing things and relating to others, that attitudes and behavior can be changed only by altering their motivational bases. Norms of psychologically relevant groups are seen as more important determinants of attitudes than cognitive processes.
12. How is effectiveness of the change measured?
    *"Classroom" Training*—Usually by informal comments of trainees, occasionally by interviews or questionnaires with the trainees after the training.
    *Organizational Feedback*—By changes in employees' perception of their supervisor's behavior.

The differences drawn between these two types of procedures for creating change in an organizational setting may not be as marked as presented here. Human relations training programs do vary tremendously from company to company and from time to time. There is no single pattern. Since we know little about the frequency of different species of human relations training programs, the specific mix of content, method, setting, etc., which we used as the basis of our contrast may no longer be found in organizations. Our comparison aimed to emphasize the extent to which various characteristics of change processes vary on the basic dimension of *motivation for change.*

Different contents, different methods, different settings, different training units, and different change agents contain different motivational impacts for change. What constitutes the most effective combination for changing behavior in organizations is not known. Few practitioners have really done any bold experimenting; almost none have combined measurement and

[21] I. Sarnoff and D. Katz, "The Motivational Bases of Attitude Change," *Journal of Abnormal and Social Psychology,* XLIX (January, 1954), pp. 115–124.

experimenting to search for the most significant dimensions and variables in change processes. This is an area in which there is a great need for social experimentation and social invention.

In the social sciences, as in the physical sciences, invention plays a crucial role. Inventions in social technology—skills and processes for creating change—and innovations in measurement both contribute speedily to progress in understanding social phenomena. The responsibility of experimenting with different methods of measuring change and with new procedures for investigating the interrelationship of functioning organizational processes rests heavily with the students of social organization. The rate at which knowledge about organization is developed will probably be closely correlated to the rate at which we try new approaches to the study of problems in this area.

# Basic Psychological Factors in Communication\*

## T. M. Higham

A celebrated authority on Canon law and mediaeval Universities, Dr Hastings Rashdall, was one of those who could ride, but not understand a bicycle. One day, for example, having had a puncture in his front tyre, he was found vigorously pumping up the back one; when a passer-by pointed this out to him, he remarked, "What? Do they not communicate?" I sometimes wonder whether, in our present-day eagerness to "put people in the picture," we do not behave rather like Dr Rashdall, strenuously pumping in information at one end of a firm, in the hopeful expectation that it will somehow find its way to the other. Perhaps we too ride, but cannot understand.

In the last few years, a great deal has been written on this topic of "communications," mainly to the effect that communication must be "two-way," a comment of unstartling originality, as anyone familiar with the derivation of the word must realise. Today you can hardly open one of the many journals, English or American, in the personnel field, without finding some

\* Reprinted, by permission of the Editor, from *Occupational Psychology*, vol. 31, pp. 1–10, 1957, the quarterly journal of the National Institute of Industrial Psychology, 14, Welbeck Street, London, W.1.

article on the subject, or some review of the latest authoritative work on it; there is even a "Communications Training Center" in existence, and one firm, at any rate, now has its "Communications Manager"; Technical Colleges, Evening Institutes and other organisations run courses in clear expression, and the art of speaking or writing; you can be trained in running a meeting or leading a conference. Training Officers and others make increased use of visual and other aids, as a help in putting their teaching across; industries make use of suggestion schemes, joint consultative committees, broadcast address systems and similar devices to try to ensure that information reaches to all levels in the business and is fed back again to the top. But, as P. H. Cook (1951) has said:

> There is as yet no firmly-established theory of communication which can provide guiding principles guaranteeing that effective communications will be achieved. As a result much communication practice is dependent on unconfirmed hypotheses, personal hunches and techniques and tricks of doubtful merit.

The nearest approach to a theory of communications has probably come from students of cybernetics and information theory. The new science of "Communication Engineering," as Professor Meredith (1955) pointed out recently, is so highly developed that "we are strongly tempted to use it as a ready-made frame of reference, and to fit all our ideas about communication into this frame." That I believe to be a mistake—not so much because it is difficult to see what relevance a man-made machine has in considering the problems of a God-made man, but rather because, in everyday life, at home, in industry, in social life generally, the problems of communication (that is, of the transmission of ideas and attitudes) between people and groups are not those which can be solved, or even greatly understood, by means of a knowledge of information theory. Until such time as a machine is developed which can not only interpret information, but also convey its like or dislike of its informant, I believe we should do well to stick to our knowledge of human and animal psychology in trying to understand the problems and workings of communication between individuals and groups.

In most of the studies of communication between individuals and groups which I have come across, scant recognition is given to what is, perhaps, the one fact which we do know from experience about it—that if a person dislikes or mistrusts us, he is not likely to be receptive to what we have to say, and his version of our words is likely to be distorted by his personal opinions of us, or his preconceived notions about our motives. For that reason a study of communication could well begin with an examination of the problems of the reception of information—that process by which we perceive what is said against a background of who says it. It is there that the work of animal psychologists, and the many experimental studies of perception, can help us.

The experiments of Schelderup-Ebbe (1935) with hens, Maslow (1936) with apes, and Lorenz (1954) with dogs have shown clearly that a sizing-up process goes on when two animals meet, which subsequently merges into a dominance-submission relationship. Of these, the most vivid is probably Lorenz's description of the encounter of two adult male dogs.

> Two adult male dogs meet in the street. Stiff legged, with tails erect and hair on end, they pace towards each other. The nearer they approach, the stiffer, higher and more ruffled they appear, their advance becomes slower and slower. . . . They do not make their encounter head to head, front against front, but make as though to pass each other, only stopping when they stand at last flank to flank, head to tail, in close juxtaposition. Then a strict ceremonial demands that each should sniff the hind regions of the other. Should one of the dogs be overcome with fear at this juncture, down goes his tail between his legs and he jumps with a quick, flexible twist, wheeling at an angle of 180 degrees, thus modestly retracting his former offer to be smelt. Should the two dogs remain in an attitude of self-display, carrying their tails as rigid as standards, then the sniffing process may be of a long protracted nature. All may be solved amicably and there is still the chance that first one tail and then another may begin to wag with small but rapidly increasing beats and then this nerve-racking situation may develop into nothing worse than a cheerful canine romp.

Apart from the fact that such encounters take place primarily on a symbolic level, is the encounter between two humans so very different? When two individuals meet for the first time, there is usually a rather more refined process of "sniffing over"—an interchange of neutral information (the weather, for example, or a search for mutual acquaintances) which serves the same purpose. An attempt to set up a dominance-submission relationship also emerges on some occasions, as Maslow (1937) has shown. Pear (1955) has explored with skill the part played by voice and social differences in the same situation. The fact that this process may be going on belov the level of consciousness is a further factor: there are still, for example, some managers who sit with their backs to the light, in a chair just a little higher than that of their visitors, and continue to write after someone enters their office; but luckily their numbers are dwindling. But these, unlike the Admiral's gold braid and the peacock's tail, are more often than not unconscious ways of conveying an impression of importance. None the less, their effect on recipients is much the same.

What has not yet been satisfactorily demonstrated is the opposite of that —the approach or manner which makes for confidence and an easy reception. If there are mannerisms which tend to put the recipients of information in a subordinate position, by conveying an attitude of superiority, are there other ways in which an atmosphere of trust and confidence can be built up without loss of status by either party?

If we recall the two dogs sniffing each other over, I believe we can say that such a situation is possible—and in fact many well-trained interviewers and counsellors are creating such a situation every day. Every interviewer is taught to "put the candidate at his ease"—in other words to make him receptive, whether it be to questions about himself or to advice and guidance. The exact ways in which this is done vary, but the essential part has been well put by Oldfield (1941):

> The adoption of an appropriate *general attitude* at the outset of the inter-view is a matter of greater importance than the maintenance of an effort to *behave* appropriately throughout its course. As an eminent psychologist remarked apropos this question, "each interview is a world to itself. One hour I am a schoolmaster, the next a parson."

It seems clear that to ensure good reception, you must create the right atmosphere. This is, perhaps, the one pre-requisite for effective communication. Where it does not exist, communication will be difficult, and all that is said is likely to be distorted. A further complication is that two people, or two groups, rarely if ever meet with what is called an "open mind." Each comes together, instead, with preconceived ideas about the other, and about the other's preconceived ideas about them.

During the preliminary "sniffing over," any small clues that can be fitted into the pre-existing picture will be readily grasped. The ingenious experiments of Asch (1946) demonstrate this point neatly. It will be remembered that he read two lists of personality traits to two different groups of people. The first group's list was "Kind, Wise, Honest, Calm, Strong." The second group's list was "Cruel, Shrewd, Unscrupulous, Calm, Strong." The last two epithets in both lists were the same. After hearing the lists, separately, the two groups were told, "Suppose you had to describe this person in the same manner, but without using the terms you heard, what other terms would you use?" The first group, who heard the list "Kind, Wise, Honest, Calm, Strong," gave the following synonyms for "calm"—soothing, peaceful, gentle, tolerant, mild-mannered. But the second group, who heard "Cruel, Shrewd, Unscrupulous, Calm, Strong," produced synonyms for "calm" like cold, frigid, calculating. Similar results were got from the two groups with synonyms for "strong"—the first group listing such terms as fearless, helpful, just, forceful; the second group giving ruthless, over-bearing, hard, inflexible, dominant. Both groups on hearing the first few epithets, got a fixed idea about the sort of person described; the later terms were merely fitted into the existing pattern.

This is not merely an academic point, illustrated by carefully controlled laboratory experiments; it is a very real factor in communication, simply because "the past in the worker's mind," as Zweig (1952) calls it, is so strong and potent a factor in his reactions. The truth of that is seen in the study made recently by the Acton Society Trust (1952) of communications in the coal mining industry. In an attempt to raise the output of coal, many attempts were made to tell the miners why a higher output was necessary; pamphlets, magazines, even a personal letter from the then Prime Minister, Mr. Attlee, were employed. But, as the report makes clear:

> The mere provision of information . . . does not reduce proneness to prejudice . . . it does not succeed in modifying the underlying attitude of mistrust upon which credulity seems to be based.

In a later report, *Management under Nationalisation,* the Trust (1953) quote the comment of an Area Manager in the Coal Industry, pointing out that he:

> can never forget that the (Coal) Board's biggest headache is the attitude of the miners and their misconceptions about the work the Board and its staff perform, and, perhaps most important, about the need for economic efficiency.

Then follows the comment of the Area General Manager:

> We have issued booklets, but nobody bothered to read them. We had a few questions when we started joint consultative committees, but even these have now petered out. We have tried to put explanations into the minutes and put them up on the notice-board, but nobody bothered to read them. It is no use trying to put it over at the lodge meetings of the union, for only a few miners attend them. This is really our major difficulty, how to put this information across and how to rid the minds of the men of misconceptions.

The pathetic notion that you can improve communications by giving more and better information should surely be allowed to die a natural death; you will not get any reception if you are not trusted; but if relations are good, then there is a good chance that what you say will be received, and that you will get co-operation in return.

But even where trust and mutual confidence do exist, that tendency to come to an interview, meeting or conference with preconceived notions is still found, and we cannot afford to forget that the same situation is almost always seen in different ways by different people, depending on their personal capacities, inclinations and background. Zangwill's (1937) experiment on "Aufgabe" showed the importance of that. Two groups of subjects were shown, separately, a vague, ill-determined ink-blot. They were not told what it represented, but one group was told that it might be like an animal; and the second group was told that it might resemble a landscape. Both groups drew and described what they had seen. The first group all drew cats, rabbits, or similar animals, while the second group drew mountains and hills. The same stimulus confronted both groups, but their preconceived ideas about it determined their reactions to it.

I believe, therefore, that in trying to understand human communication, we would be well advised to study the basic mental processes that underlie so much of everyday human behaviour—the study of perception in particular, and the many experiments on "Aufgabe" and attitude formation.

But further problems arise. Suppose that a person to whom we wish to communicate something has sniffed us over, asking unconsciously, "Is he friendly, can I trust him?" and decided that he is disposed to listen to us, we still need to know whether what we say will be understood, and if so, whether, at a later date, it will be recalled or repeated accurately. So I would suggest that comprehension and recall are legitimate subjects for research and study when considering human communications.

Both of these, as it happens, have been studied fully in recent years. I should like, therefore, only to point out a few of the researches or experiments which seem to me to throw light on how we succeed or fail in comprehending information and recalling it accurately.

Bartlett (1951) has suggested that one of the chief functions of the mind, when it is active, is "filling up gaps"; that is, it is constantly trying to link new material into the pattern of older material, in order to make it meaningful. Our minds seem to prefer the simple and regular to the complex and irregular, and to organise what is received into tidy, meaningful bundles. That is why it is so difficult to get a new idea across; for a new idea has to be fitted into the existing structure in the mind, and it is often quite a struggle to do so. A simple demonstration of that difficulty was given by Wertheimer; to give you an example of it, suppose you look at these four words:

MAN   TABLE   KNIFE   CLOTH

You can, without much difficulty, form some kind of mental picture out of them. If I add the word TROLLEY, you can probably fit that in quite easily to your already established picture. But if I now add the words:

SURGEON   BLOOD   ANAESTHETIC

you will probably have a few puzzled moments before you are able to re-organise the picture in your mind. The meaning of the isolated words changes as the pattern alters, so that the table, once laid for a meal, with a knife handy for cutting a cake, becomes an operating table, with the knife poised over the man who a few moments earlier was sitting down to his tea.

Our mental habits persist and may help or hinder us; they will only do the former if we can link what we have to say on to what our listeners already know; for in that way, the new can be assimilated to the old.

But there is more to comprehension than mental habits; the interest of the subject matter and our own intelligence are also involved. Some idea of the extent of these factors can be seen in two very detailed and careful experiments carried out by the BBC Audience Research Department (1950, 1951, 1952).

The first of these researches was an attempt to assess the intelligibility of a series of Forces Educational Broadcasts; the second was concerned with the comprehensibility of the five minute programme "Topic for Tonight" which follows the 10 o'clock news. What was particularly striking about both these researches was that they demonstrated that understanding was largely based on intellectual capacity—not perhaps a very new finding, but an interesting one because it showed the extent to which comprehension relies on intelligence. To quote from the report:

> It would seem that the talk which is couched at a level of difficulty appropriate to the top third of the population can rarely convey much to people of even average intelligence and little or nothing to the backward quarter (of the population).

But something else came out of the first research too; that was the finding that, apart from intellectual capacity, comprehension was "profoundly influenced by the extent to which (people) are interested in the subject, or have their interest in it aroused. The greater the listeners' interest, the greater their understanding is likely to be, and vice versa." This factor of interestingness was more important for intelligibility than any factor of style, language, and delivery. Certainly, such factors as limiting the number of main points, providing clear summaries, a lucid and lively style, concrete treatment, and the illustration of abstract points all *make for* intelligibility —the research proved that—but they do not *guarantee* intelligibility; they only come into play if the talk is interesting in the first place.

Although these studies are of great value in showing just how complicated a matter it is to get information across that will be remembered with any accuracy, a broadcast talk is not the same as face-to-face contact; there are, unfortunately, to my knowledge, no scientific studies of the intelligibility of personal talks to an audience as compared with broadcast talks. The nearest approach to such an investigation is the series of experiments conducted by Lewin (1947) on the respective values of lectures and group discussions in changing food habits. It will be remembered that the latter proved far more effective because the audience participated in a decision. They were, in fact, "ego-involved." I should like to suggest that it is that factor of ego-involvement which lies behind the importance of interest in the subject matter of a talk, which was so well shown in the BBC researches.

Some years ago, I carried out some experiments on the transmission of rumour (Higham, 1951). The method I used was to get someone to recount a short tale to a second person, who repeated it to a third, and so on;

each version of the story was recorded on a recording machine, so that a permanent record was available; by those means the successive reproductions could be analysed to see what changes had taken place in the narrative. I used different types of story and different groups of subjects; one day, quite by accident (as I must admit), I made up a short tale about a professor discussing the prospects of his students in their forthcoming examinations; I tried this out on just such a group of his students as might be involved in this sort of discussion. To my surprise, I found that reproduction of the story showed few changes and comparatively small loss of detail, whereas all the other stories produced many changes and a great loss of content with successive reproductions. Applying an appropriate statistical technique, I found that such a result was unlikely to have happened by chance. The explanation was that the students were personally involved in the story; it was about something that affected their interests; and for all they knew it might have been true, or a prophetic warning! Because of this personal interest they remembered it better.

Joint Consultation, particularly through Works' Councils, shows this sort of thing well: matters which management thinks of burning interest are passed by almost without comment; but if an announcement is made that the price of tea in the canteen is going up, discussion is animated and prolonged. People will show most interest in things which concern them personally, or which are linked to their basic needs; that is perhaps why discussion methods seem to be more successful in bringing about change than are formal lectures, for if you take part in a discussion you become involved in it, and it means more to you.

None the less, I think we would be unwise to neglect the importance of the personal factor even in the comprehension of information. For, as many will testify, a good speaker can arouse interest in his audience, even if he breaks every known rule of lecturing. Professor Meredith (1950) has given an excellent example of this in a talk he gave some time ago:

I am not a theologian, but I was once privileged to attend, at a weekend conference, a lecture by a professor of theology. It was twenty-five years ago and it is still vivid to me today. The subject was Amos, of whom I previously knew precisely nothing. By the end of the lecture I had not only a dynamic impression of the character and message of the prophet but also a clear and colourful picture of the contemporary economic, political, and social structure of the people of Israel. The professor used no notes. He padded round the room, with his hands behind his back, and wearing felt slippers. From time to time he raised one foot to scratch the calf of the other leg. Now and then he looked at one or other of us directly in the eyes, with a kind of challenging glare. At other times he gazed through the window into the extreme distance, as if looking at Palestine, and describing what he saw, taking our gaze with him. I recall that he pronounced Jahweh with the sort of sound one makes in clearing one's throat.

Later Professor Meredith gives his views on why the professor of theology, and other lecturers he had heard, succeeded in communicating to their listeners. He says:

> You can wander about, you can indulge in irritating mannerisms, you can hem and haw, you can remain glued to a desk, you can twiddle your fingers, you can commit all the crimes on the statute book (the latter would make entertaining reading if someone would write it: "The Deadly Sins of the Lecture Theatre"), and you can get away with all of them if only you have the one supreme virtue. What is that virtue? The name I would give it is *vitality*. This was the common factor in all my remembered lectures.

I suggested earlier that the recall of information was a part of the process of communication which could well be studied. Indeed it has been thoroughly explored, notably and perhaps primarily by Sir Frederic Bartlett (1932) whose book *Remembering* is still the classic on that subject. Later work by Allport and Postman (1948) and others on rumour has supported these earlier findings. The factors of interest and personal involvement, which I mentioned earlier, are important in recall, because we tend to remember better and more accurately those things in which we have been personally interested; but with matters less personal, or less interesting, our minds tend to transform what we have heard, until our final recollection may be quite different from what actually took place. This is an important factor in two way information, because if, for example, a Works' Council holds a meeting, it is attended by delegates from different sections of the organisation, who have to report back to their constituents; and it is in this reporting back that mistakes and falsifications—albeit involuntary ones— are apt to occur.

Another BBC experiment has shown the importance of some other factors in recall as well. This experiment (1954) was about the immediate memory of a feature programme, one of the "This is the Law" series, in which the script was enlivened by dramatisation, and by being cast in the form of a continuous story. In addition the subjects were all personally invited to the BBC to take part in the experiment. Under such conditions about 80 per cent of the story was recalled accurately, with the same variations according to intelligence, occupation, etc. as had been found previously. What is interesting, though, is that the material—a connected story, dealing with everyday people and incidents in everyday language—"lent itself to quick and easy assimilation." But illustrations and dramatisations cannot just be left to make their point; as Vernon has pointed out (1946) they must be related to the subject matter as a whole, otherwise the point is apt to be forgotten.

Here, as in the other aspects of communication which I have touched on, much work remains to be done. So much of what passes for "communication theory" (in the non-engineering sense) is based on hunches and prejudices that further careful experiments are needed. It is the importance of the personal factor in communication that particularly needs to be examined. Simply because we almost all have to live and work among other human beings, we all tend at times to be like the character in Shaw's "Fanny's First Play," who was asked to comment on a production. "You don't expect me to know what to say about a play," she said, "when I don't know who the author is, do you?"

If subjective evidence is acceptable, we have the testimony of teachers, sages and others over the centuries, that people tend to weigh up who we are before listening to what we have to say.

St. Thomas Aquinas warned his pupils "Non respicias a quo sed quod sane dicetur memoriae recommenda." Dr Johnson said of someone, "What you have to say about Aristotle tells me very little about Aristotle, but a great deal about you." Emerson put it more forcefully, "What you are sounds so loudly in my ears that I cannot hear what you say." In many speeches, talks, and other forms of communication, it is often the character of the man that shows through the words he uses, as for example in Sir Winston Churchill's war-time speeches. What is said, and how it is said, often matter less than who says it. As Lord Rosebery said of William Pitt the Elder:

> It is not merely the thing that is said, but the man who says it that counts, the character which breathes through the sentences.

There needs to be some degree of warmth in a personal relationship for real communication to exist. When people in conference or consultation have built up stable and firm relationships, then communication is not only easier but, usually, better. As Sir Geoffrey Vickers (1954) has put it:

> Consider how much easier it is to communicate on a standing committee, the members of which are used to deliberating together, than on an ad hoc committee which has never met before. Consider also, how, if the atmosphere of a conference begins to deteriorate, all the experienced members will set to work to put it right again, that is, to recreate the mutual attitudes without which it is a waste of time to confer.

So I should like to suggest to you that successful communication will come about by careful placement of key-men—men, that is, who command trust and respect, who are sympathetic and intelligent; they are your eyes and ears, the people through whom information will flow to you and from you. As to most operatives, the foreman, not the Board of Directors, *is* the firm, it means careful selection and training of your supervisors. On a higher level, it means equally careful selection and training of junior staff. But a fundamental attitude of "consistent and fair treatment of employees, pursued in good times and bad, and humour and common sense in day to day relationships," as John Marsh of the Industrial Welfare Society put it recently, is not something you can just lay on; it is not a technique; it springs from qualities of character and personality, which is why selection is so important. As Marsh (1954) says:

> The fully fashioned personnel or welfare service cannot be effective unless the foreman—who is "the firm" to most employees—is efficient, just and consistently humane in his leadership. One knows of instances where the results of years of patient endeavour in building up morale have been dissolved within a few hours of a manager losing his temper. All this goes to show that there are no final answers to human relations questions.

And if at times we tend to forget that last sentence, and to think that we really have at last found the means to cure the human ills of industry once and for all—and judging by the rise and fall in the popularity of such means to that end as welfare schemes, joint consultation, communications and co-partnership, at times we all do think that—then we would do well to remember the warning of Sir Thomas More:

> It is not possible for all things to be well unless all men are good, which I think will not be for these many years.

## References

Acton Society Trust (1952): *The Worker's Point of View*. London: Acton Society Trust, 39, Welbeck Street, W.1.

Acton Society Trust (1953): *Management under Nationalisation*. London: Acton Society Trust.

Allport, G. W., and Postman, L. (1948): *The Psychology of Rumour*. New York: Holt.

Aquinas, St. Thomas (?1260): *De modo studendi*. Oxford: Blackfriars.

Asch, S. E. (1946): Forming Impressions of Personality. *J. Abnorm. Soc. Psychol.*, **41**, 258–290.

Bartlett, F. C. (1932): *Remembering*. London: Cambridge University Press.

Bartlett, F. C. (1951): *The Mind at Work and Play*. London: Allen and Unwin.

Belson, W. A. (1952): *An Inquiry into the Comprehensibility of "Topic for Tonight."* Audience Research Department Report. London: British Broadcasting Corporation.

Cook, P. H. (1951): *The Productivity Team Technique*. London: Tavistock Institute of Human Relations.

Higham, T. M. (1951): The Experimental Study of the Transmission of Rumour. *Brit. J. Psychol. (General Section)* **42**, 42–55.

Lewin, K. (1947): Frontiers in Group Dynamics (II). *Hum. Rel.*, **1**, 143–153.

Lorenz, K. (1954): *Man Meets Dog*. London: Methuen.

Marsh, J. (1954): Human Relationships in Industry. *Financial Times*, 30 September.

Maslow, A. H. (1936): The Dominance Drive as a Determiner of the Social and Sexual Behavior of Infra Human Primates I-IV. *J. of Genet. Psychol.* **48** and **49.**

Maslow, A. H. (1937): Dominance-feeling, Behavior and Status. *Psychol. Rev.* **44,** 404–429.

Meredith, G. P. (1950): The Art of Lecturing. *Brit. Med. J.,* 26 August.

Meredith, G. P. (1955): The Flow of Information. *Occup. Psychol.,* **29,** 99–103.

Nias, A. H. W. and Kay, H. (1954): Immediate Memory of a Broadcast Feature Programme. *Brit. J. Educ. Psychol.,* **24,** 154–160.

Oldfield, R. C. (1941): *The Psychology of the Interview.* London: Methuen.

Pear, T. H. (1955): *English Social Differences.* London: Allen and Unwin.

Schelderup-Ebbe, T. (1935): The Social Behaviour of Birds. In Murchison, C., *A Handbook of Social Psychology.* Worcester: Clark University Press.

Silvey, R. (1951): The Intelligibility of Broadcast Talks. *Public Opinion Quarterly,* Summer.

Vernon, P. E. (1946): An Experiment on the Value of the Filmstrip in the Instruction of Adults. *Brit. J. Educ. Psychol.,* **16,** 149–162.

Vernon, P. E. (1950): *An Investigation into the Intelligibility of Broadcast Talks.* Audience Research Department Report. London: British Broadcasting Corporation.

Vickers, C. G. (1954): Human Communication. *Brit. Management Rev.,* **12,** 71–79.

Zangwill, O. L. (1937): A Study of the Significance of Attitude in Recognition. *Brit. J. Psychol.,* **28,** 12–17.

Zweig, F. (1952): *The British Worker.* London: Penguin Books.

# An Experimental Approach to Organizational Communication*

*Alex Bavelas*
*Dermot Barrett*

*The improvement of industrial communication has come to be recognized generally as an important part of management's "unfinished business." However, management's growing interest in the subject of communication, implemented by the results of current research, gives promise of continuing improvement in this field. This article details some of the laboratory experiments in communication which are now in progress and their possibilities for further development.*

Communication as a critical aspect of organization has been attracting more and more attention. If one may judge from articles and speeches, much of the current thinking on communication centers around categories of problems which arise in day-to-day operations—"getting management's point of view to the workers," "stimulating communication up the line as well as down," "obtaining better communication with the union," "establishing more effective communication within management, and especially. with the foremen." Knowing how such questions usually arise, it is not surprising that their discussion invariably resolves itself into considerations of *content* and *technique:* on the one hand, analyses of what management ought to be saying to the worker, the union, the foreman; on the other hand, descriptions of devices which can best say it—bulletin boards, letters, films, public address systems, meetings, etc. In its extreme form this approach becomes one of searching for a specific remedy for a specific ill. Helpful and practical as this may be, it is doubtful that such activity can lead to the discovery and understanding of the basic principles of effective organizational communication. Breakdown and other difficulties at some point of a communication system are often only superficially related to the local conditions which appear to have produced them. They may, rather, be

* From *Personnel*, vol. 27, no. 5, pp. 366–371, March, 1951. Reprinted by permission of the American Management Association.

cumulative effects of properties of the entire communication system taken as a whole. But what are these properties, if, indeed, they exist?

*Formal and informal systems.* An organizational system of communication is usually created by the setting up of formal systems of responsibility and by explicit delegations of duties. These categories include statements, often implicitly, of the nature, content, and direction of the communication which is considered necessary for the performance of the group. Students of organization, however, have pointed out repeatedly that groups tend to depart from such formal statements and to create other channels of communication and dependence. In other words, informal organizational systems emerge. One may take the view that these changes are adaptations by the individuals involved in the direction of easier and more effective ways of working, or, perhaps, not working. It is no secret that informal groups are not always viewed by managers as favorable to the goals of the larger body. Also, it is by no means obvious that those informal groupings which evolve out of social and personality factors are likely to be more efficient (with respect to organizational tasks) than those set up formally by the managers. Altogether, if one considers how intimate the relations are between communication channels and control, it is not surprising that the managers of organizations would prefer explicit and orderly communication lines.

*Is there "one best way"?* Unfortunately, there seems to be no organized body of knowledge out of which one can derive, for a given organization, an optimal communication system. Administrative thinking on this point commonly rests upon the assumption that the optimum system *can* be derived from a statement of the task to be performed. It is not difficult to show, however, that from a given set of specifications one may derive not a single communication pattern but a whole set of them, all logically adequate for the successful performance of the task in question. Which pattern from this set should be chosen? The choice, in practice, is usually made either in terms of a group of assumptions (often quite untenable) about human nature, or in terms of a personal bias on the part of the chooser. The seriousness of this situation is illustrated by the following example.

Let us assume that we have a group of five individuals who, in order to solve a problem, must share as quickly as possible the information each person possesses. Let us also assume that there are reasons which prevent them from meeting around a table, and that they must share this information by writing notes. To avoid the confusion and waste of time of each person writing a message to each of the others, a supervisor decides to set up channels in which the notes must go. He strikes upon the pattern shown in Fig. 1.

In this arrangement each individual can send to and receive messages from two others, one on his "left" and one on his "right." Experiments actually performed with this kind of situation show that the number of mistakes made by individuals working in such a "circle" pattern can be reduced by fully 60 per cent by the simple measure of *removing one link,* thus making the pattern a "chain" as shown in Fig. 2. The relevance of such a result to organization communication is obvious, simple though the example is. The sad truth, however, is that this phenomenon is not clearly

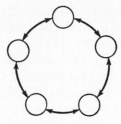

Figure 1

derivable either from traditional "individual psychology" or from commonly held theories of group communication.

*An integral process of organization.* Perhaps some headway can be made by approaching the general problem from a somewhat different direction. In the affairs of organizations, as well as in the affairs of men, chance

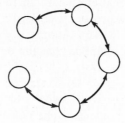

Figure 2

always plays a part. However good a plan may be, however carefully prepared its execution, there is a point beyond which the probability of its success cannot be increased. With the firmest of intentions, agreements and promises may be impossible to carry out because of unforeseen events. Nevertheless, an organization whose functioning is too often interrupted by unforeseen events is looked upon with suspicion. Bad luck is an unhappy plea, and it may well be that the "unlucky" organization is more to be avoided than the simply incompetent one. On the other hand, few things about an organization are more admired and respected than the ability to "deliver" despite widely varying conditions and in the face of unusual difficulties.

In a very broad sense, it may be argued that the principal effort of organizational activities is the making of favorable conditions for the achievement of certain goals. In other words, an effort is made to increase, as much as the economics of the situation will permit, the probabilities of succeeding. This is the essence of the manager's job. The development of training and selection programs, the improvement of methods and the specification of techniques, the organization of research and development activities, the designation of responsibility and the delegation of duties—all these processes have one organizationally legitimate purpose: to increase the chances of organizational success. Upon this point rest almost all of the notions by which we are accustomed to evaluate organizations—in part or as a whole.

An organization is, in short, a social invention—a kind of "machine" for increasing certain sets of probabilities. (Which sets of probabilities are given to it to increase, which it chooses, how freely and by what means will not be discussed here. These problems, although they lie well within the scope of this subject, are outside the range of this paper. We will confine ourselves to a consideration of the process by which an accepted set of probabilities is optimized.) Probabilities of success are increased, however, only by taking relevant and appropriate actions. For the manager, these actions reduce in most instances to the gathering and evaluating of information in the form of reports, schedules, estimates, etc. It is entirely possible to view an organization as an elaborate system for gathering, evaluating, recombining, and disseminating information. It is not surprising, in these terms, that the effectiveness of an organization with respect to the achievement of its goals should be so closely related to its effectiveness in handling information. In an enterprise whose success hinges upon the coordination of the efforts of all its members, the managers depend completely upon the quality, the amount, and the rate at which relevant information reaches them. The rest of the organization, in turn, depends upon the efficiency with which the managers can deal with this information and reach conclusions, decisions, etc. This line of reasoning leads us to the belief that communication is not a secondary or derived aspect of organization—a "helper" of the other and presumably more basic functions. Rather it is the essence of organized activity and is the basic process out of which all other functions derive. The goals an organization selects, the methods it applies, the effectiveness with which it improves its own procedures—all of these hinge upon the quality and availability of the information in the system.

*Patterns of communication.* About two years ago a series of studies was begun whose purpose was to isolate and study certain general properties of information handling systems. The first phase of this research program[1] is directed at a basic property of all communication systems, that of connection or "who can talk to whom."

This property of connection can be conveniently expressed by diagrams.

[1] These studies are supported jointly by the Rand Corporation and the Research Laboratory of Electronics at M.I.T.

The meaning of the picture in Fig. 3 is obvious. Individuals A and B can send messages to C but they can receive messages from no one; C and D can exchange messages; E can receive messages from D, but he can send messages to no one. The pattern shown in Fig. 3, however, is only one of the many that are possible. A group of others is shown in Fig. 4. An ex-

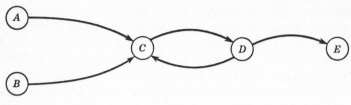

Figure 3

amination of these patterns will show that they fall into two classes, separated by a very important difference. Any pair of individuals in each of the patterns d, e, and f can exchange messages either directly or indirectly over some route. No pair of individuals in each of the patterns a, b, and c can exchange messages. Patterns like a, b, and c obviously make any coordi-

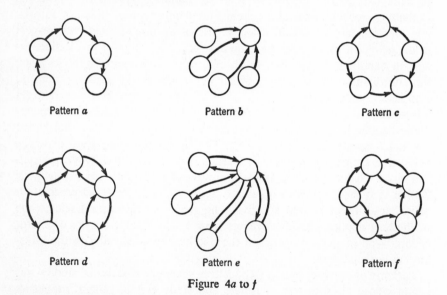

Figure 4a to f

nation of thought or action virtually impossible; we will be concerned from this point on only with patterns like d, e, and f.

Since the individuals in any connected pattern like d, e, and f can share ideas completely, should we expect that the effectiveness of individuals in performing group tasks or solving group problems would be the same in patterns d, e, and f except for differences in ability, knowledge, and per-

sonality? Should we expect differences in quality and speed of performance? Is it likely that the individuals working in one pattern would show
significantly better morale than the individuals working in a different pattern? Sidney Smith and Harold J. Leavitt conducted a series of experiments[2] which yielded very definite answers to these questions. An experimental design was used which made it possible to equate the difficulty of
the tasks which the groups performed, and which permitted the cancelling
of individual differences by randomizing the assignment of subjects to patterns. Also, the experiment was repeated with different groups enough
times to establish the consistency of the results. A brief summary of the
findings is given in Fig. 5. The use of qualitative terms in Fig. 5 in place

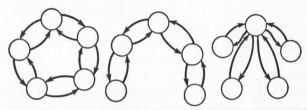

| Speed | slow | fast | fast |
|---|---|---|---|
| Accuracy | poor | good | good |
| Organization | no stable form of organization | slowly emerging but stable organization | almost immediate and stable organization |
| Emergence of leader | none | marked | very pronounced |
| Morale | very good | poor | very poor |

Figure 5

of the quantitative measurements which were actually made blurs the comparison somewhat, but it gives a fair picture of the way these patterns
performed. Since the original experiments were done by Smith and Leavitt, this experiment has been repeated with no change in the findings.

The question very properly arises here as to whether these findings can
be "explained" in the sense of being related to the connection properties
of the patterns themselves. The answer to this question is a qualified yes.
Without developing the mathematical analysis, which can be found in Leavitt's paper, the following statements can be made:

For any connected pattern, an *index of dispersion* can be calculated.
Relative to this index, there can be calculated *for each position in each
pattern* an *index of centrality,* and an *index of peripherality.* The data suggest strongly that the rapidity with which organization emerges and the
stability it displays are related to the gradient of the indices of centrality

[2] Harold J. Leavitt reports these experiments in detail in the January, 1951, issue
of the *Journal of Abnormal and Social Psychology.*

in the pattern. In Fig. 6 these indices are given for each position. It should be added at this point that in the patterns in which leadership emerged, the leader was invariably that person who occupied the position of highest centrality.

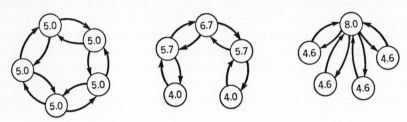

Figure 6

The index of peripherality appears to be related strongly to morale. In Fig. 7 the indices of peripherality are given by position. Those individuals who occupied positions of low or zero peripherality showed in their actions as well as in self-ratings (made at the end of the experiments) that

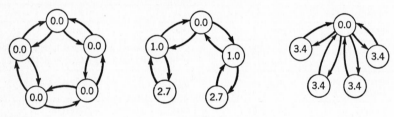

Figure 7

they were satisfied, in high spirits, and generally pleased with the work they had done. Those individuals who occupied positions of high peripherality invariably displayed either apathetic or destructive and uncooperative behavior during the group effort, and rated themselves as dissatisfied and critical of the group's operation.

A word of caution should be given concerning the slow, inaccurate, but happy "circle" pattern. Subsequent experiments by Sidney Smith indicate that this pattern possesses unusual abilities for adaptation to sudden and confusing changes of task—a quality lacking in the other two patterns.

*A promising field for research.* Clearly, these experiments are only the beginning of a long story. The findings, although they promise much, settle nothing; but they do suggest that an experimental approach to certain aspects of organizational communication is possible and that, in all probability, it would be practically rewarding. As the characteristics of communication nets and their effects upon human performance *as they occur in the laboratory* become better understood, the need will grow for systematic studies of actual operating organizations. The job of mapping an existing net of communications even in a relatively small company is a complicated and difficult one, but it is not impossible. Some work is beginning on the development of field methods of observation. The importance of bridging the gap between the simple, directly controlled experiment and the very complex, indirectly controlled social situation cannot be overestimated.

# Communication: Getting Information from A into B*

## Harold J. Leavitt

People begin, modify, and end relationships by communicating with one another. Communication is their channel of influence, their mechanism of change. In industrial organizations it has become popular recently to communicate about communication—to talk and write about the importance of communication in problem solving. The talk about communication is appropriate because communication is indeed a critical dimension of organization.

Unfortunately, though, much of the talk has been either nonsensical or unusable. For one thing, the word "communication" has been used to mean everything from public speaking to mass merchandising. For another, most of the talk has been hortatory rather than explanatory. Managers are urged to use "two-way" communication, because it is "better" (what does "better" mean?) than one-way communication. The fad has extended to "three-way" communication, again without evidence or precise definition.

The purpose of this chapter is to describe some major dimensions of the communication process, to examine what can be meant by "better" or "worse" communication, and to relate the idea of communication to the ideas of interpersonal influence and behavior change.

*Some dimensions of communication.* Sometimes there are advantages to asking simple-minded questions. They can help to strip away some of the confusing gingerbread surrounding an idea so that we can see it more objectively.

Suppose we ask, simple-mindedly, what are the things that can happen

* From *Managerial Psychology*, The University of Chicago Press, Chicago, 1958, chap. 9, pp. 118–128. © 1958 by the University of Chicago. Reprinted by permission

when A talks to B? What is involved in two people's talking to one another?

First, A usually talks to B *about something*. The process has a content. They talk baseball or they talk business or they talk sex. The content is what usually hits us first when we tune in on a conversation. Content of communication, in fact, is what psychologists and businessmen alike are usually thinking about when they think about human relations.

We can see subclasses within content too. We can differentiate categories of content like, for example, *fact* and *feeling*.

Other things, quite independent of what is said, take place when A talks to B. Some conversations take place in the presence of a great deal of *noise;* others are relatively noiseless. In this context "noise" means things that interfere with transmission. We can encounter channel noise like the static on a telephone line that makes it hard for B to hear what A is saying. We can also usefully think of psychological noises, like B's thinking about something else, so that again it is hard for him to hear what A is saying; or like B's being so afraid of A that it is hard for him to hear what A is saying. Language or code noise may make it hard for B to hear: he doesn't understand the words A is using in the way A understands them.

All sorts of noise can occur independently of content. We can find noisy or noiseless communications about *any* content. We also can usually observe that A, in the presence of noise, is likely to communicate more *redundantly*—to repeat his message in the hope that B will be able to hear it better the second time or to say the same thing in a different way. Redundancy is one of the most common weapons for combating noise. It is "inefficient" in the sense that repetition is wasteful of time and energy. It is "efficient" in the sense that, so long as noise exists, it helps to push the content through.

Besides the content and noise dimensions of conversation between A and B, a third dimension is the *communication net*. Usually we think of A to B conversation as a direct one; but many such conversations, especially in organizations, are mediated through other people. One thing an organization chart is supposed to tell us is that A can speak to B only through C or D. As a later chapter will show, the structure of the net a particular organization uses can have a lot to do with the speed and accuracy of members' talking to one another.

One more dimension of the process is worth noting, especially since it has been ridden so hard in recent managerial literature. It is the *direction* of communication—its one-wayness or two-wayness. Again it is an independent dimension. No matter what A and B may be talking about, no matter how much static may be involved, no matter what the network, A may talk to B this way: $A \rightarrow B$; or this way: $A \leftrightarrows B$. A can talk and B can only listen, i.e., one-way communication; or A can talk and B can talk back, i.e., two-way communication.

This last aspect of the process, one-wayness versus two-wayness, gets special attention in the remainder of this chapter. Is two-way communication really better? What does "better" mean? Better for what and for whom? When?

*One-way versus two-way communication.* In its simplest essentials our problem is to clarify the differences between these two situations: (1) One person, A, talking to another, B, *without* return talk from B to A; versus (2) conversation from A to B *with* return conversation from B to A. The differences can be clarified best by testing one method against the other. Here is such a test situation:

The pattern of rectangles shown here is an idea you would like to tell some B's about. Suppose you try to communicate it *in words* to a half-dozen of your friends who are sitting around your living room:

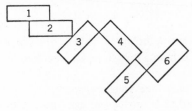

Figure 1

Assume that the rectangles touch each other at "sensible" places—at corners or at midpoints along the line. There are *no* touch points at any unusual places. All the angles are either 90° or 45° angles; there are no odd ones. This pattern of rectangles is an idea comparable perhaps to a complicated set of instructions you may have to give to a subordinate or to the definition of a policy that you would like to pass along or to the task of explaining statistical quality control to a sales manager. This idea can be communicated to others under (1) one-way or (2) two-way conditions.

If you are the communicator, these are your *one-way* instructions:

1. Turn your back on your audience so that you cannot get visual communication back.
2. Give the audience blank sheets of paper, so that they can listen and draw exactly what you are communicating. Ask them to try to draw as accurate a picture of the pattern of rectangles as possible.
3. Describe the pattern of rectangles to them *in words* as fast as you can. The audience is not permitted to ask questions, or laugh, or sigh, or in any other way to communicate back to you any information about what it is receiving.

This game is a good parlor game, if you can find some people to try it on. Try it, time it, and then check the accuracy of your communication by determining whether or not your audience has drawn what you have described. If they received what you tried to send, so their pictures match the test picture, then you have communicated. To the extent that their pictures do not match the one in the drawing, you have not communicated.

Two-way communication can be tested for contrast in the same way. The same rules apply, and here is a similar test pattern:

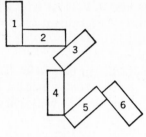

Figure 2

This time the basic job is the same, to describe the pattern verbally so that the people who are listening can draw it. But here are the differences:

1. This time you may face your audience.
2. They are allowed to interrupt and ask you any questions they want to at any time they want to.

Try it this way and time it. The differences between what happened the first time and what happened the second time are the differences between one- and two-way communication. (The order in which the two methods are used does not matter.)

Under experimental conditions these findings have emerged from this game: (1) One-way communication is considerably *faster* than two-way communication. (2) Two-way communication is *more accurate* than one-way, i.e., more people in the audience correctly reproduce the drawing under two-way conditions. (3) The receivers are more sure of themselves and make more correct judgments of how right or wrong they are in the two-way system. (4) The sender finds himself feeling psychologically under attack in the two-way system, because his receivers pick up his mistakes and oversights and *let him know about them.* The receivers may make snide remarks about the sender's intelligence and skill, and, if the receivers are trying very hard and taking the task seriously, they may actually get angry at the sender, and he at them. (5) The two-way method is relatively noisy and disorderly—with people interrupting the sender and one another, with the slowest man holding up the rest, and so on. The one-way method, on the other hand, appears neat and efficient to an outside observer, but the communication is less accurate.

Such a demonstration points out both the advantages and the costs of one-way and of two-way communication. If *speed* alone is what is important, then one-way communication has the edge. If *appearance* is of prime importance, if one wishes to look orderly and business-like, then the one-way method again is preferable. *If one doesn't want one's mistakes to be recognized,* then again one-way communication is preferable. Then the sender will not have to hear people implying or saying that he is stupid or that there is an easier way to say what he is trying to say. Of course, such comments may be made about him whether he uses one-way or two-way communication, but under one-way conditions he will not have to listen to what is said, and it will be harder for anyone to prove that mistakes were made by A rather than B. *If one wants to protect one's power,* so that the sender can blame the receiver instead of taking blame himself, then one-way communication is again preferable. The sender can say: "I told you what to do; you just weren't bright enough to get the word." If he uses two-way communication, the sender will have to accept much of what blame there is, and it will be apparent to all that he deserves some of it; *but he will also get his message across.*

Those are the major differences between one- and two-way communication. They are differences that most people are aware of implicitly. If a person gets a chance to ask questions, to double check what he might have missed, then he can make sure he has gotten exactly what he is expected to get. On the other hand, if he must only sit and listen, he may or may not get the word, and he is likely to feel frustrated and uncertain about what he does get. Moreover, that bit of frustration and uncertainty is likely to grow because he has no way of making sure of things he isn't sure of.

To put it another way, one-way communication is not likely to be communication at all. It is more likely to be talk. One can talk by passing words out into the air. Those words don't become communication until they enter meaningfully into somebody else's head.

Of course, it is simple for a communicator to claim that his responsibility is only to pass a message along, that the receiver's responsibility is to make sure that he understands it. But this is not a very adequate claim. If one really were to argue through the question of who is responsible for the success of communication, one would certainly conclude that communication is largely the communicator's responsibility. For if the communicator's job is to communicate—and if to communicate he must get his message into the receiver—then his responsibility cannot end until the receiver has received. And he cannot be sure that the receiver has received until he gets confirming feedback from the receiver. On the other hand, the location of responsibility becomes a far less significant issue when one perceives communication as a two-party process to begin with.

A partial definition of communication is now possible. First, to communicate is to shoot information *and* to hit a target with it. Shooting alone is not communicating. Second, to have more than chance probability of hitting a target requires that the sender get feedback from the target about the accuracy of his shots.

If an artilleryman had to fire over a hill at an invisible target, he would have to fire blind and hope that by luck one of his shells would land on the target. He would spray the area with shells and go away, never being certain whether he had or had not destroyed his objective. But by the simple addition of a spotter standing on the hilltop, the likelihood of accurate shooting can be greatly increased. The spotter can feed back to the gunner information about the effects of the gunner's own shots. "Your last shot was a hundred yards short. The second was fifty yards over." And so on. The advantage is obvious, and it is precisely the advantage of two-way over one-way communication—the communicator can learn the effects of his attempts to communicate and can adjust his behavior accordingly. Like the learning machine we discussed [previously], the decision maker needs inputs as well as outputs to correct his own behavior.

With our definition of communication, the issue of one- and two-way communication in industry can be cast somewhat differently than is usual. For now one encounters apparent conflict between the short-run efficiency of two-way communication and the long-run need to maintain power and authority at various levels of the hierarchy. Two-way communication makes for more valid communication, and it appears now that more valid communication results not only in more accurate transmission of facts but also in reorganized perceptions of relationships. Authority, for example, may under ideal conditions of two-way communication cease to serve as a sufficient protection for inadequacy. The dictum that a well-informed citizenry is democracy's protection against autocracy may also be applicable to the well-informed staff or the well-informed employee. And though "democracy" may connote things desirable in governments, its connotations for industrial organizations in our society are far from clear.

*Communication about novel and routine problems.* [Previously], when our focus was on individual learning and problem solving, we pointed out that people *learn,* they use their memories of past problems to solve similar present ones.

Correspondingly, it is obviously true that if the problem in the experiment on two-way communication had been a familiar instead of a novel one, the results might have been quite different. A, for instance, could probably have communicated the English alphabet accurately and rapidly through one-way communication alone. In fact, it has been shown that if we use two-way communication on these rectangle problems again and again with the same group, *communication soon becomes one-way* anyhow. People stop asking questions. They don't have to. They have learned the code; so A and B understand one another.

From the point of view of speed and accuracy, then, one could make this tentative generalization. Two-way communication improves the accurate communication of previously uncoded or insufficiently coded ideas. But two-way communication contributes considerably less to accuracy *after* the code has been clarified—after new problems have been programed and routinized. Coupling this generalization with the notion that new problems occur more frequently in upper organizational echelons, we can also tentatively conclude that two-way communication is more useful within the management group than further down the line.

But let's not ignore two major constraints. First, one-way communication affects morale as well as speed and accuracy and *may* therefore be worth discarding for that reason alone. And, second, to what extent is it true in a particular plant to say that managers face more new problems per week than salesmen? Or employment interviewers? Or lathe operators in a job shop?

*What gets communicated?* One aspect of the content problem deserves mention here, although it will be dealt with more fully later. The problem is that people usually communicate more than information to the target; they communicate feelings as well as facts. Suppose the artillery spotter, instead of simply announcing where the last shell had landed, decided to add a few typically human comments of his own. Suppose the spotter said to the gunner: "Look, you stupid s.o.b., your last shot was three hundred yards over. Where the hell did you learn to shoot?" That kind of communication of unsolicited information will complicate the psychological picture, just as will the communication of inaccurate information, sometimes causing the now frustrated gunner to change his target from the farmhouse to the spotter. . . .

*In summary.* Communication is a primary tool for effecting behavior change. We can isolate at least four independent dimensions of the communication process: content, noise, network characteristics, and direction.

One-way communication has some advantages in speed over two-way. It also has the advantage of protecting the sender from having to recognize his own faults. Two-way communication has the advantages of greater accuracy and greater feelings of certainty for the receiver. But two-way communication involves some psychological risks to the defenses of the sender.

# READINGS RELATED TO CHAPTER VII

## The Informal Organization of Industry*

### J. A. C. Brown

C. I. Barnard has pointed out that all large organizations may be thought of as having been built up from a number of smaller groups. These small groups vary in size, but average about eight or ten people, the number being determined by the fact that problems of communication become greater as the size of a group increases. Since it is impossible to hold a primary group together in the absence of adequate face-to-face communication, there is a tendency for it to break up or subdivide after it has reached a certain critical size. This process resembles in many respects the cell-division which may be observed under the microscope in the tissues of animals or plants—in this case, too, the cell increases in size until its internal metabolism can no longer be effectively maintained, and, when this stage is reached, it subdivides into two daughter cells. A group of more than ten or twelve people is likely to divide in a similar manner, since, beyond this size, intimate face-to-face contacts between all its members can no longer be maintained. (It is significant, as Gordon Rattray Taylor notes, that throughout history we find that groups of just this size have been formed under circumstances in which high morale was important—the twelve disciples, the cricket eleven, the Communist cell, the army section, and so on.) But the groups which result from this process, assuming that they do not wish to separate altogether, can only be kept in communication by setting up another organization with executive functions. That is to say,

* From *The Social Psychology of Industry,* Penguin Books, Inc., Baltimore, 1954, chap. 5, pp. 124–156. Reprinted by permission of the publisher.

the leaders of the unit groups must not only be members of their own work-ing units—they must also join together to form an executive unit which acts as a sort of nervous system in maintaining contact between the individual groups. In biology this phenomenon may also be observed, when, at a certain stage of evolution, single-celled animals or plants no longer sub-divide and go their own way but group together in colonies which require a nervous system in order that the collection of cells may function as a sin-gle unit creature. "This simultaneous contribution to two organizations by a single act appears to be the critical fact in all complex organizations; that is, the complex is made an organic whole by it" (C. I. Barnard). When all the unit groups of which a large organization is composed subordinate their purposes to a common goal, we may describe the organization as well-integrated, but if the units are in conflict with each other or try to dominate each other or attain independence of the parent organization, the state of affairs is described as showing a tendency to segmentation. All groups or combinations of groups represent an equilibrium between inte-gration and segmentation, and every large organization has to face the same dilemma: that unit groups must be permitted to preserve their indi-vidual identity as much as possible, and that, on the other hand, their individual identity must be reduced to such an extent that all may work together towards a common goal.

The small natural unit groups we have been discussing are what we have already described as "primary" or "face-to-face" groups, whilst the larger bodies within which they function (the factory, the combine, etc.) are de-scribed as "secondary" groups. In the former, the individual members are interrelated by a network of personal relationships which may be of any type or degree, but, whether the feeling is liking, disliking, or indifference, each member has a more or less clearly defined attitude towards every other member. The latter are altogether more formal, and the attitude of individ-ual members towards the secondary group is likely to be determined by the degree to which its goals coincide, or conflict with, those of their own primary group. Edmund Burke tells us that "to love the little platoon we belong to in society, is the first principle of public affections," a statement which carries the implication that all the individual's deepest feelings take place within the bounds of the primary groups of which he is a member; he cannot, as it were, love, hate, or feel any other emotion at first hand towards the state, the army, the Church, or the large industrial concern, which only arouse emotions in so far as their goals are seen to coincide, or clash with, those of his primary groups. It will be seen, then, that if the worker feels that the interests of his firm clash with those of his primary group (in this instance, his working-group), no amount of propaganda or pleading or "discipline" will cause him to develop feelings of loyalty towards that firm. A situation will arise similar to that in the "bank-wiring" room of the Hawthorne works in which the working-group went its own way and acted according to its own social norms which did not correspond with the interests of the factory as a whole. *The primary group is the instrument of society through which in large measure the individual acquires his attitudes, opinions, goals, and ideals; it is also one of the fundamental sources of discipline and social controls.* Although some of the individual's attitudes and ideals are acquired actually within the primary group, others come from his culture or subcultures—to a considerable extent, however, it is through the primary group (and especially the family) that these are enforced and handed on. Moral controls are . . . partially enforced by the superego, but (a) the superego does not cover the whole field of morals but only a few fundamental regulations (e.g., prohibiting incest or murder), and (b) the power of the superego to influence behaviour varies greatly from one person to another. Outside these fundamental regulations, it is the social pressure of the primary group which, in most people, becomes the instrument of discipline and moral control. It is, of course, also the source of certain controls such as those in the "bank-wiring" room relating to "rate-busting," "chiselling," and "squealing," which, although not moral controls in the ordinary sense of the word, were based on a code of behaviour suited to the circumstances in which the group was placed. The primary group then, is the most potent influence in regulating the individual's behaviour.

What we have just said has two important implications for industry:

1. In attempting to change human behaviour (within the peripheral regions of the personality, at least), the attack must be made through the medium of the group rather than through the individual. Thus F. M. Thrasher, a sociologist who made a study of gangs of delinquent boys in Chicago, found that it was impossible to deal with these boys individually, but, when the social norms of the gang were altered, the behaviour of its members also changed. This point, however, will be dealt with more fully at a later stage.

2. It is most important that the manager should realize that the informal working group is the main source of social control, that he should endeavour to exercise legitimate control through such groups, and that he should avoid breaking them up. The common belief of management that such groups are subversive in their nature and always act according to the psychology of the mob is based on the dangerous misapprehension that any individual or group with opinions different from those of management must necessarily be in the wrong. The average strike, for example, is *not* based on "mob psychology" or "bad morale"—on the contrary, it is usually carefully planned and can only be successful if it is based on very good morale. The reason why the manager thinks the strikers' morale is "bad" is because it does not happen to coincide with *management* interests, but how glad he would be if the same amount of energy and enthusiasm were shown by the workers towards the goals of industry! In short,

the actions of the well-integrated primary group are likely to be disciplined, controlled, and, in relation to the situation as seen by the group, fairly logical. The wise manager should hesitate to criticize until he has asked himself whether he has treated his employees fairly, and whether he has taken the trouble to explain the situation fully to them and allowed them to discuss it fully with him.

What is known as a crowd or mob is entirely different from either primary or secondary group-formations, and, in fact, can only exist in their absence. The characteristic feature of the mob is that no personal inter-relationships exist between its members. Everyone remains virtually anonymous and lost in the mass. Indeed, it is this quality of anonymity which is largely responsible for the phenomena of "mob psychology." It is precisely because the members of a crowd are unknown to each other with no loyalties or any form of primary group control that these phenomena occur. It is, therefore, in the type of firm where Mayo's "rabble hypothesis" has almost become a reality, in which labour is casual, disintegrated, and unorganized, that the management have most reason to be concerned. A crowd, to quote Dr Karl Mannheim in *Man and Society,* "has as yet no social aim or function, so that the conduct of the individual cannot be determined by his function in it or regulated by the mutual control of its members, for these members have not as yet entered into personal relationships. The effect of the crowd on the individual is purely contagious; it does not subordinate his impulses to functional tasks . . The reason why we behave as we do in a crowd is that the inhibitions connected with our family, or neighbours, our work, are cast aside; and in the anonymity of the mass, sober citizens throw stones and scared employees fire on the police." The groups we have been discussing are the opposite of this. They are not temporary associations—they have some degree of permanence. They have particular aims and a definite structure. Their size is limited and their members are known. Within such a group, each member has a specific function and relationships with other members.

Although it is in general the case that primary groups, for the reasons given, are small in size and the larger secondary group is likely to be more formal, purposeful, and rational, Ellsworth Faris has made the observation in his book *The Nature of Human Nature* that there are some large social groups, usually of a political or religious nature, which show many of the characteristics of the primary group. Thus the Society of Friends, although in no sense of the word a face-to-face group, manages to preserve some of the intimacy of personal relationship which is found in the primary group. There is, therefore, no abrupt point of distinction between primary and secondary groups. But the contrast remains a valid one; the secondary group tends to be organized for a formal purpose (in the case of the factory, for the production of goods), its structure is more or less rationally designed towards that end, and its members are not all intimately known to each other. The primary group may have a specific practical goal, and, when in pursuit of that goal will organize itself logically to that end, but essentially it is based on social satisfactions and personal choice, and, quite apart from any practical goal, it seeks to maintain itself as a unity. When a secondary group no longer has a practical function, it tends to disintegrate, but for the primary group its own existence is an adequate goal. Charles H. Cooley, who, more than twenty years ago, was the first to study this problem, has given the classical description of the primary group in his book *Social Organization,* which is less well-known than it deserves to be in this country:

> By primary groups I mean those characterized by intimate face-to-face association and co-operation. They are primary in several senses, but chiefly in that they are fundamental in forming the social nature and ideals of the individual. The result of intimate association, psychologically, is a certain fusion of individualities in a common whole, so that one's very self, for many purposes at least, is the common life and purpose of the group. Perhaps the simplest way of describing this wholeness is by saying that it is a "we"; it involves the sort of sympathy and mutual identification for which "we" is the natural expression. One lives in the feeling of the whole and finds the chief aims of his will in that feeling.
>
> It is not to be supposed that the unity of the primary group is one of mere harmony and love. It is always a differentiated and usually a competitive unity, admitting of self-assertion and various appropriative passions; but these passions are socialized by sympathy, and come, or tend to come, under the discipline of a common spirit. The individual will be ambitious, but the chief object of his ambition will be some desired place in the thought of the others, and he will feel allegiance to common standards of service and fair play. So the boy will dispute with his fellows a place on the team, but above such disputes will place the common glory of his class and school.

Cooley gave as typical examples of primary groups the family, the playgroups of children, and the neighbourhood group of elders in the village community; to these, as has already been noted, we must add the "natural" work-group which is the basic unit of informal organization in the factory. The informal organization of industry, however, does not consist solely of the primary working-group, and may be said to exist at five separate levels:

1. The total informal organization of the factory, viewed as a system of interlocking groups of all types.
2. Large groups which generally arise over some particular issue of internal politics within the factory (e.g., the question of union or non-union labour, whether or not to employ foreign workers). A diffuse group of this sort may extend throughout all the departments of the factory, and is generally described as a "crowd" or a "gang."
3. The primary group formed more or less on the basis of a common job in

the same part of the factory. Relationships between members are more or less intimate and they are likely to work, dine, and talk together. The group in this case is usually described as a "clique."

4. Groups of two or three particularly intimate friends who may be members of larger cliques.

5. Isolated individuals who rarely participate in social activities.

As Miller and Form have pointed out, there is a special technique in studying the informal organization of a factory (or, for the matter of that, of a school or orphanage). In the first place, it must be remembered that no amount of study of individual people will be likely to give much information; *the unit of observation is the social relationship rather than the individual.* Roethlisberger and Dickson, who did much of the pioneering work at the Hawthorne plant, started with the false assumption that it was necessary to study each individual in order to get a picture of the group, until they finally came to realize that the group was a unit in its own right and could not be understood as the mere sum of the reactions of its individual members. In other words, the behaviour and opinions of the members as isolated individuals may be different from their behaviour and opinions when they come to be integrated into a group. Examples of this phenomenon will be given later, but for the moment it may be accepted that this is a fundamental axiom of social psychology. (It need hardly be said that no modern social psychologist believes in the old concept of the "group mind" which was at one time used as an explanation of why group behaviour was more than the mere sum of individual behaviours of group members. The explanation lies, of course, in the changing patterns of interrelationships within the group.) Secondly, it is necessary for the investigator to note which actions are spontaneous and which are determined by formal considerations relating to the performance of the job. If, for example, the investigator interpreted the frequent visits of one worker to another in a distant part of the factory as based on friendship when, in fact, the visit was part of the job, his interpretation of the informal organization of the firm would go far astray. It is useful, therefore, to distinguish between those actions which are fundamentally technical, those which are sociotechnical, and those which are purely social. Thus the actions of a coal miner when drilling a hole in which he places an explosive charge are strictly technical, as are those of an operative at his machine or a chemist at his bench. Whether, under these circumstances, the worker is single or married, black or white, Protestant, Catholic, or Jew, is largely irrelevant. The only social aspect of his job in this sense is the social status or significance that others assign to it since the worker's performance of his job may depend on his reaction to its social status. When, however, technical behaviour involves social interaction, we may speak of sociotechnical behaviour. For example, the operative must "clock in," go to the cloakrooms to change, report to his supervisor, engage in a certain minimum of conversation with his mates on technical matters, teach a new worker the job, call for his wages at the end of the week, and attend a union meeting periodically. All of these actions, although social in the sense that they involve social interaction, are in effect part of the job. This sociotechnical behaviour shades gradually into the purely social—the social interaction which takes place on a basis of purely personal interest in people as people. Clearly technical and sociotechnical behaviour is an aspect of formal organization, whereas social behaviour belongs to the informal structure of the factory. It is with the latter that we are here concerned. Having distinguished between these different types of behaviour and directed his attention towards social relationships rather than individuals, the social psychologist or sociologist will then proceed to note how the group members react towards each other—only secondarily will he concern himself with what they are producing or servicing. He will listen to what they say, or avoid saying, what they do, or avoid doing, and observe the extent to which saying and doing coincide with each other. The ideas, beliefs, and attitudes on which members agree or disagree will also be noted. Lastly, he will try to discover how far these observations remain stable or alter with changing situations. While carrying out his investigations, he must take care to remain, so far as is possible, outside the group. He must not himself become a factor in the situation he is observing. If it is impossible not to become involved, he must attempt to analyse his relationship towards the group as he would any other person's.

In what we are now about to discuss it should be remembered that what is being described is the behaviour of informal groups, not mere mobs of people The extent to which the behaviour to which we refer may be observed in a given factory or industry will depend on the extent to which informal groups have been allowed to form within it. For although there is no factory which is completely lacking in any form of social life, there are many circumstances at the present day which militate against a closely-integrated society. When labour turnover is high for whatever reason and casual labour is readily accepted there is little opportunity for primary groupings to arise except in the small nucleus of semi-permanent employees which is found in almost every factory. It seems likely that the tendency to employ part-time female labour may sometimes have a similar effect; for women who are primarily housewives working in order to get a little extra money are unlikely to develop a close interest in factory affairs. When a worker enters a job with the awareness that he or she is likely to be permanently employed with the firm, he will wish to make a success of it and will probably take a real interest in the social life of the firm. But this rarely applies to casual or part-time labour, and sometimes (although by no means always) the same might be said of young women full-time workers who may regard their job as in the nature of a stopgap between school and marriage. When people feel strongly about their firm, even if the feeling is anger or resentment, there is always the possibility of redirecting their emotions, but when for reasons largely external to the factory they are indifferent, the problem is more difficult to solve. The attitude of shrugging the shoulders and leaving to get another job elsewhere often found amongst this type of worker poses a serious problem for industrial morale. But, as has already been pointed out, this is simply one aspect of a more general state of affairs, which is the "rootlessness" of modern society, the constant shifting of populations from one place to another. The small town or village community of which the factory is an integral part and within which the whole factory staff have lived most of their lives is becoming less common. As Mayo puts it: "No longer does the supervisor work with a team of persons he has known for many years or perhaps a lifetime—he is a leader of a group of individuals that forms and disappears almost as he watches it." Under these circumstances, morale is bound to be low and social life negligible, since nobody stays long enough, or cares sufficiently to attempt to improve working conditions either socially or technically. When a job is regarded as merely a temporary one, why should the worker bother to change its conditions?

It seems likely, then, that well-integrated groups and a genuine social life are most likely to be found under the following circumstances:

1. In skilled trades (since the skilled worker is less likely to become a casual labourer).
2. Where the factory is situated in a relatively small and long-established community.
3. Where casual and part-time labour is not employed, and in firms where a seasonal incidence of work does not necessitate the frequent taking-on and putting-off of large numbers of workers.

Closely-integrated groups are most likely to be found amongst skilled or semi-skilled workers (who take an interest in their job and tend to remain at it), married men (who require stability in their job), and elderly women (to whom the social contacts mean a great deal). It is, of course, possible to create good morale under almost any circumstances, but it is only fair to recognize that even the best management may find some of these problems very difficult to deal with.

The most detailed account of group structures is that based on the work of the American sociologist J. L. Moreno whose book *Who Shall Survive?* initiated a new approach to certain aspects of social psychology. Moreno describes his technique as "sociometry," and the charts which illustrate the patterns of social interaction within a group as "sociograms." Briefly, he classifies the basic attitudes which people may show towards each other as attraction, repulsion, and indifference (compare this with the classification of the psycho-analyst Karen Horney: moving towards people, moving against people, and moving away from people), and the members of the group to be studied are asked to indicate those with whom they would, or would not, like to associate. Their choices are then paired and ranked and the members are regrouped in terms of their preferences. Moreno's early work was carried out at the New York Training School for Girls which he had been asked to investigate because poor morale and lack of discipline had been causing trouble. This school is a closed community with a population of five or six hundred girls living in sixteen cottages each with a "housemother" in charge. It was arranged that each girl should list the five others with whom, in order of preference, she would like to share the cottage. Although it was impossible to satisfy all demands, it was found that there were many mutual choices, and the final results appear to have been excellent both in terms of improved morale and general satisfaction. Housemothers were also to be chosen, and as new girls came to the institution each housemother who had vacancies in her cottage was asked to interview them separately. The housemother and the girls were both asked to make first and second choices, and the girls were placed accordingly. However, it is unnecessary to discuss the details of this particular case, which, as is the purpose of most of Moreno's work, was primarily psychotherapeutic in intention. What is important is the information obtained about the basic types of sociological nuclei on which informal organizations are founded. Five principal types of nucleus were noted:

1. The most elementary and clear-cut nucleus was the mutual first choice of two or more individuals amongst themselves. This might be represented by couples, triangles, squares, circles, or other more complex figures.

2. Non-mutual choices capable of being represented by chains of any number of individuals (e.g., A chooses B, B chooses C, C chooses D, and so on).

3. The configuration described by Moreno as a "star," resulting from the clustering of a large number of choices around a single individual, who might in turn respond by mutual attraction, indifference, or repulsion.

4. A grouping of great practical importance was that of the powerful as opposed to the popular individual. Thus a popular individual might be the object of a large number of choices both within his own group and from people relatively isolated from the rest of the community, but, in spite of this, he might have very little influence owing to the limited contacts of his admirers. On the other hand, an individual chosen by only a few popular members might have a powerful influence through the extensive connexions of the people to whom he is a centre of attraction.

5. Lastly, there are the isolated individuals chosen by nobody although they may have chosen a few other persons. Such individuals are frequently maladjusted, and may be the source of maladjustments in their group. In Moreno's terminology, they may form the focal point of cleavages of an inter-personal sort. The reason for this is that such an individual is cut off by his isolation from the currents of feeling by which the behavior standards of the group are impressed on each member, and, when no such pressures are felt, he is like a ship in the fog without radar to guide it.

These nuclear structures are, of course, interrelated, and they overlap to form an immensely complex system, each member being a part of numerous structures in varying degrees of intensity and completeness. The "over-chosen" members are not merely popular in the superficial sense—they are the protagonists of the needs and desires of large numbers of the population.

> They are the members who are the most wanted participants and who have earned this choice status because they act in behalf of others with a sensitivity of response which does not characterize the average individual in the community (chosen to an average extent). They are found to be the individuals who see beyond the narrow circumference of their own personal needs into the wide range of needs of their fellow-citizens. They are the individuals who go farthest in relating themselves to others and in translating the needs of others into effective outlets. (Helen Jennings in the article "Sociometry" contained in the *Encyclopedia of Psychology,* edited by Philip L. Harriman.)

The structure of a group is not static but is rather a dynamic network of forces, which, at varying tempos, is always changing. Members may leave the group and be replaced by others, or events may occur which alter the prestige of particular members. Above all, the structure of the group may change according to the tasks with which it is confronted. For example, a number of people on a camping trip may be organized around a leader who is the best-liked and most popular individual (in the ordinary sense of the word) within the group. But if the party is lost in the mountains, the leader who comes to the fore is the man with knowledge of the countryside and the ability to take the others back to their base. The other members will spontaneously organize themselves around his leadership in accordance with their usefulness in the specific situation. Moreno has pointed out that the choice of the girls at the New York State Training School as to who they would wish as housemates was not always the same as their choice when they were seeking workmates. An individual isolated with respect to the one situation might be found popular in the other. "The community is found to produce many varieties of leadership—varieties which represent the manifold, diverse needs of its many interacting participants. Similarly many varieties of isolation are revealed." (Helen Jennings.) It follows that there is no such thing as a "natural" or "universal" leader in the popular meaning of the phrase—a good leader is the man or woman who is most fitted to take charge in a given situation. Leadership is not a psychological trait which can be investigated as if it were a property of the individual—it is always a function of the situation and the nature of the group. This point is well illustrated in J. M. Barrie's play *The Admirable Crichton,* which describes how an aristocratic family with a butler named Crichton is marooned on a desert island. Within a short time, the butler has assumed leadership because of his qualities of resourcefulness and his special knowledge, and the other members of the party have willingly restructured themselves around him. Crichton is the man whose potentialities and knowledge fit the new situation. In industry, however, situations do not change quite so dramatically—the possible situations are limited in number. In the formal sense, the leader of a working-group is the supervisor or foreman, who, in ordinary circumstances, is likely to be accepted as leader for the purposes of the job. In so far as he is a good supervisor, he will try to see to it that he is accepted willingly as the appropriate leader in that situation, rather than as one who has forced himself on the group by virtue of his formal authority. But if trouble should arise, the accepted leader may be what is popularly known as an "agitator" —possibly a group member who is ordinarily ignored or teased as an eccentric or extremist. Other frustrated or resentful men may surround him as the nucleus of the new structure. It is quite possible for a leader who has been voluntarily chosen to be one of the most unpopular men in the group, as happened, for instance, in a certain factory where the supervisors felt their position to be threatened, and their authority undermined, by management. In this case, the man who was regularly elected as chairman of the supervisors' group was a blustering bully who was heartily disliked by most of the others. Yet he was unanimously elected on each occasion since he alone was capable of standing up to the management. Similarly, as we have already noted, a man of the agitator type who is almost insanely suspicious of management intentions *and is recognized to be so* by his fellow-workers may be elevated to a position of leadership when discontent has become general. It often appears that the leader's core personality shows those traits or attitudes which environmental influences have temporarily produced in the peripheral personalities of the led. An excellent example of this observation in the political field was the rise of the Nazi party in Germany. The German people, suspicious and resentful after the Treaty of Versailles, chose as a leader the man Hitler, who was from the psychiatrist's standpoint a paranoiac—a man mentally sick with suspicion and resentment. His henchmen possessed in large measure the same traits—Streicher, Himmler, and Hess were obviously mentally sick paranoid individuals, and around this nucleus of fanatics there came to be attached such opportunists as Goering, Ribbentrop, and the rest.

Under more normal circumstances, the members of a group in industry come together for such obvious reasons as that they are employed on the same job, are of similar nationality or regional origin, or of about the same age, sex, or seniority in the firm. Most of all, they come together because they are placed near each other in the workshop. This is especially the case if mobility is limited by the nature of the job. Since spatial proximity is so important, it follows that to a considerable extent the formal working-group and the informal group coincide. On the other hand, there is a good deal of overlapping. For example, a number of supervisors may create their own informal group, and, although separated during working hours, may meet in the canteen at meal-times or socially after work. Similarly young people or older workers or those who have been many years with the firm may form cliques which do not coincide with the group in which they happen to work. So each worker may be a member of more than one group within the factory and in each his status may be different, the important man in one context being relatively insignificant in another.

An individual's status is based on the degree to which he contributes to the purposes of his group, and since to the members of the primary working-group there are many purposes other than the production of goods, it follows that there are also many sources of status. A man's status may derive from his skill with certain tools, his knowledge of a particular process, his generosity, his ability to make others laugh, or his reputation as a first-aider who knew the correct treatment when an accident occurred. In the informal working-group, as in the small village, even the idiot has a certain status and "belongs." Within the face-to-face group individual traits are readily observed and become common knowledge, but in the larger secondary group, largely because of defective communication, status cannot so readily be assigned.

> In modern industry the man in one department has little idea of what the man in another does, and how far it contributes to the common purpose. In particular, the manual worker cannot understand what it is that the office staff does, nor the factory hand what the farmer does. (Gordon Rattray Taylor, *Are Workers Human?*)

Under these circumstances, people have to depend on external signs of status which comes to mean status within the formal organization of the firm. A man tends to be assessed by his salary, by his position in the hierarchy, by the size of his desk, by the canteen in which he has his meals, and so on. The amount of significance which is attached to such matters in the average factory is really amazing, and many liberal-minded observers, previously unacquainted with industry, and from brief war-time experience convinced that the army is somewhat undemocratic and authoritarian, are astonished to find on entering certain factories that by comparison the army begins to appear as a tolerant, just, and relatively democratic institution. As Dr Tredgold has noted:

> In the army, for instance, which even nowadays some regard as undemocratic, generals and lieutenants do eat together—and wash their hands together; and though units have sometimes three different messes some firms have six or seven. Badges of rank in industry are not sartorial (or less obviously so) but take the form of the size of the desk (and often the largest desk had the least on it); the size and texture of the carpet; the size (and gilding) of the letters of the name outside the office door; the number (and

even the colour) of the telephones; and, of course, the accessibility of the person. (*Human Relations in Modern Industry.*)

Or, to take another example, Gordon Rattray Taylor tells us that in the Civil Service the practice of having external badges of status has become institutionalized, and "elaborate regulations prescribe at what level in the hierarchy one may have a desk-lamp, a padded armchair, and, finally, a strip of carpet in one's office." In the more authoritarian type of factory, the new recruit to management is likely to have some embarrassing moments when he is attempting to discover where he may wash, dine, or park his car, and black looks will follow him whenever he makes a slip. Management personnel will fight for the right to a telephone, a carpet, a place in the executives' canteen or car-park, not because they want these things in themselves, but because of their social significance. Yet the same people often cannot understand why the worker in the manufacturing department of their firm should object to using the cloakroom belonging to the warehouse whilst building operations are taking place! In every factory there are jobs which appear to the outsider (and often to management) to be "the same" both in pay and official status, but are regarded by the workers concerned as at quite different levels of social significance. Thus in certain restaurants, those who handle fish are considered to be lower in status than those who handle meat, although both may receive the same wages. Dr Tredgold quotes the case of a lavatory cleaner who threatened to leave because she was asked to clean ovens in a canteen; in this factory the job of lavatory cleaner ranked higher than that of oven cleaner in the informal estimate of the workers. The main reason was that the former, in addition to being a cleaner, had charge of certain materials such as soap and toilet rolls, and had the authority to move out other workers when she considered that they had been talking or smoking too long in the lavatory. Strangely enough, many of these traditional prestige-ratings are completely unknown to those in authority, who, as a result, may unwittingly make mistakes which seem quite shocking to the workers. The worker may be just as upset when he is moved to another job at the same pay, but with a lower prestige-rating, as is the director who finds the new management trainee in the lavatory reserved for executives. It frequently happens that workers who, for reasons of redundancy, or because of bad health, are moved to another job at the same pay but with lower informal status become deeply resentful. Indeed the status situation is one of the commonest causes of strikes. So, too, individual factories or whole industries vary in the prestige with which they are associated in the minds of workers. A steel-worker or coal-miner expected to work in a canning factory would be just as indignant as a doctor who was asked to work as a male nurse. It should be one of the first principles of good management to ensure that people do not have their self-esteem injured by any action which may lower their status in relation to that of others. Status, it must be remembered, may be lowered not only by demoting a person from one level to another which is held in lower esteem, but also by taking some action which, by raising the relative prestige of one group, indirectly lowers that of another. . . . Many industrial disputes have indicated that workers are more concerned with how their wages compare with those of others than with what the amount happens to be in absolute terms. An economist writes:

> Every study of industrial workers has shown that wage rates are not uppermost in their minds. Differences in wage rates between various jobs are very close to the workers' hearts because they establish prestige. But absolute wage rates are only rarely very important. They matter a great deal—they may indeed be the most important thing—in an economy very close to subsistence, that is, in the very early stages of industrialization. They also count in inflation, when incomes never quite catch up with prices. But otherwise wage rates do not rank very high among the workers' concerns. (Peter Drucker, *The New Society*.)

The concepts of "status," "rôle," and "prestige" are often confused. Generally speaking, status implies a position within a group, rôle the appropriate behaviour which goes with that position, and prestige is something more personal which the individual brings to his status and rôle. A doctor, for example, will always have a certain amount of respect from the mere fact of his official status as a physician, but he may have more or less prestige depending on whether he is a good or bad physician. The distinction is important, since a popular fallacy about promotion is based on this confusion between status and prestige. It is simply not true to say, as is often done, that everybody wants promotion in the sense of higher formal status. What people *do* want is a position in which it is possible to increase in prestige. Thus the average skilled craftsman does not want to become a supervisor or a factory manager—he wants to become a better craftsman *and recognized as such*. That is to say, he wishes to feel that if he does his job well the fact will be recognized, not only financially, but also in terms of increased privileges.

Status is sub-divided by anthropologists into the two types of "intrinsic" (or "functional") status, and "derived" (or "non-functional") status. In the former, the person commands deference on the basis of skill, knowledge, or physical attributes—he is the good craftsman or the knowledgeable first-aider; in the latter, rank and prestige are derived from occupying a certain position or office in the formal hierarchy—the chairman or factory manager or supervisor clearly come into this class. From the present point of view, it is simpler to regard intrinsic status as that belonging to the informal organization of the factory, and derived status as belonging to the formal organization. While the two may often be combined, they are not necessarily related. It has been suggested that modern industry should restore functional prestige to work, and avoid non-functional, derived, or artificially-created prestige—that status, privileges, and pay should correspond to the real contribution made. But this cannot be done until each individual with improved communication is enabled to understand the value of the contribution each other individual makes to the whole. The great advantage of functional or intrinsic status is that it contains room for all: "respect for father as the bread-winner does not take away from respect for mother, whose claims are based on different grounds. The best dentist in the community is not the less respected because someone else is the best ploughman." (Gordon Rattray Taylor, *Conditions of Happiness.*) For this reason, functional status leads to less rivalry and more satisfaction than derived status based on power or wealth. Another defect of derived status systems is that, under conditions in modern times, they tend to be what is described as "mobile." That is to say, except when derived status is based on birth as in the Middle Ages, it is always possible to move down, as well as up, the hierarchy. Money and power are as easily lost as they are difficult to gain, and their possessor has little security of tenure in his position. With functional status, on the other hand, the individual will always be given credit for what he has achieved in the past, even when he is no longer capable of his former skill. The only way in which functional status may be lost is when the holder behaves in such a way as to forfeit the respect of others. We have noted that in the informal group status is essentially functional. But, for practical purposes, what really matters in industry is not whether status is functional or non-functional; the important point is whether it is accepted by the majority of employees or not. The supervisor who manages to get himself accepted and respected by his working-group has, in effect, transformed his status from non-functional to functional. He is both the formal and the informal leader of the group, and holds his position not only by virtue of authority from above but also by the willing acceptance of those below.

Whilst the working-group rewards its members by giving them status and function, or, what amounts to the same thing, emotional security and self-respect, it also expects the individual member to conform to its customs. These customs may involve the general ideology of the group as a whole, or they may relate to the behaviour expected of an individual occupying a particular status. Conformity may be enforced by ridicule, "sending to Coventry," or sometimes even by violence; but these sanctions are rarely needed as the group member is usually much too concerned lest he should lose the respect of his comrades. Miller and Form describe the case of a labourer who came to work wearing a light grey felt hat instead of the old cloth cap generally worn at the job. On the first occasion, the rest of the workers teased him, asking him whether he thought he was the boss, but on the second day their reaction was more violent. On the third day, the man came to work in the generally accepted style of head-gear. A similar situation arose when a lorry-driver wore a white shirt and tie to work. In these instances the men concerned were not behaving according to the general concept of what constituted normal behaviour within the group. Great pressure is often brought to bear in order to ensure that those in a particular status-position fulfil their rôle in what is deemed to be a proper manner. It is, for example, not always appreciated when someone in authority tries to behave as an "ordinary" individual. Gordon Rattray Taylor tells how a popular managing director who came to work in a battered old car was thought to be "letting the firm down." People who complain that doctors give themselves airs and consider themselves different from other men and women are often the first to complain that the doctor is being "unprofessional" when he tries to behave as an "ordinary" person.

Nearly all informal industrial groups insist on members doing their fair share of the work (i.e., a fair proportion of the work done by the group collectively). This is part of a more general rule that no member shall profit at the expense of any other. Likewise promotion through undue influence is disapproved of, not because it is "unfair" in the wider meaning of the term, but because it is disloyal to the group. On the other hand, should the group have gained an unfair advantage over other groups (e.g., by violating company regulations), the member who reported this would be strongly censured by his mates. The individual member is protected only where the formal organization is concerned, and when he breaks the rules of the informal organization his action will be generally resented. Some of the common rules of the informal working-group have already been described in the last chapter,* but, as Professor Florence has pointed out, it should not be thought that these rules are peculiar to workers or people in industry. Any small and closely-knit group, whether the family, a group of schoolboys in a Public School, or a group of mill-girls, is almost certain to object to the member who tells tales on another member to someone outside the group, to the member who fails to do his fair share of the work, and to the member who does too much and thereby shows the others up. The industrial working-group usually has a fairly clear estimate of what, in the circumstances, is considered to be a "fair day's work," and it tends to keep production within the range of the average worker. This type of restriction of production is, therefore, based on factors within the group and on the relationship, good or bad, which the group feels to exist between itself and the firm as a whole. When it is felt that the weaker members are unlikely to be penalized and that the firm is fair in its dealings with the workers, restriction of production due to these causes will come to an end. But, of course, many restrictive practices have little to do with conditions within the individual firm, being related to economic and political factors largely outside the control of the management. These will be

* [of *The Social Psychology of Industry*—ed.]

dealt with elsewhere. In many jobs the exact methods of keeping production within the bounds set by the group have been standardized—for example, informal rules may decide that the worker should lift two pieces of material of a certain size or weight, and only one piece of another size or weight in each lifting operation. Even workers who are unorganized by a trade union are likely to have rules of this sort, and detailed examples of such practices will be found in S. B. Mathewson's *Restriction of Output Among Unorganized Workers* (Viking Press, 1931). Mathewson and his co-workers took jobs as machine-operators, labourers, and in other occupations, living with working people in their home environments, and found that, apart from the restrictive practices which are part of trade-union policy, the most frequent reasons given by the unorganized worker for such practices were rate-cutting, fear of unemployment, excessive speeding-up, and resentment at management.

But it would be a mistake even in the worst factory to regard the informal organization of the working-group solely in the light of the intention of the workers to resist company policy. Miller and Form show that if the "you're-not-paid-to-think-do-what-you're-damn-well-told" policy of some old-fashioned managers were carried out in detail by the workers, the firm would soon find it impossible to carry on business:

> Without the assistance of informal organization, formal organization would often be ineffective. This is frequently the case when managers try to determine every detail in production. They are too far removed from production to envisage many of the problems that arise. Yet frequently they give orders on the basis of presumed knowledge. If their orders were completely obeyed, confusion would result and production and morale would be lowered. In order to achieve the goals of the organization workers must often violate orders, resort to their own technique of doing things, and disregard lines of authority. Without this kind of systematic sabotage much work could not be done. This unsolicited sabotage in the form of disobedience and subterfuge is especially necessary to enable large bureaucracies to function effectively. (*Industrial Sociology.*)

The culture of industrial groups derives from many sources: from class origins, occupational and technical sources, the atmosphere of the factory which forms their background, and, finally, from the specific experiences of the small informal group itself. Some of its more important manifestations may be classified as (a) occupational language, (b) ceremonies and rituals, and (c) myths and beliefs.

It is well known that different trades have to make use of a great variety of technical terms in the course of their work. But it is not always recognized how far this process of language-making may become institutionalized. . . . at this point we need only mention the more important sources of occupational language. Such deviations from standard English derive not merely from the use of specialized technical terms peculiar to a given trade, but also from the use of argot (i.e., substitutes for words in daily use), and certain usages based on class differences. Thus many words used by the chemist, by the engineer, or in other specialized trades or occupations are strictly technical in that no everyday word exists to replace them. On the other hand, the words "bulkhead," "starboard," and "port," used by seamen are, properly speaking, argot, since they might be replaced by the everyday words "wall," "right-hand," and "left-hand" sides. Whereas technical words are obviously necessary, the use of argot mainly serves the function of creating group solidarity and as a means of identifying individual members. In addition, class-differences are evident in the different use made by working-class men of "blasphemous" or "obscene" expressions. This is not to say that such expressions are uncommon among the middle-classes, but, by and large, the latter swear and blaspheme under more rigidly defined situations. The factory manager or the average clerical worker will use such expressions at a convivial gathering of men, or under emotional pressure, but ordinarily he will not use them as an everyday jargon. When the factory manager uses an obscene one-syllable word to describe a colleague, it will generally be supposed that his opinion of his colleague is, for the moment at any rate, low. But amongst workers such words have a more everyday use which almost empties them of any derogatory significance and they may often be used as terms of endearment. It has been suggested by some serious-minded psychologist that swearing in the working-classes is a response to conditions of tension and frustration, but it is obviously difficult to test the validity of this hypothesis. The language of the working-group is derived, then, from these three sources, with additions from regional sources in the form of dialect.

All well-integrated groups, whether in the Australian Bush, the South Sea Islands, or a London factory have certain ceremonies and rituals which may be classified as initiation rites, rites of passage, and rites of intensification. Initiation rites for the novice who is joining the working-group may take such forms as teasing or ridiculing him, asking him to do favours or run errands for group members, or sending him for such non-existent tools as a "left-handed monkey wrench." The (mainly unconscious) function of such behaviour is to demonstrate to the newcomer his inferiority and ignorance in relation to the superiority of the group members, as a consequence of which the morale of the latter is raised simultaneously with the desire of the former to become fully initiated. The novice's attitude towards the group is tested, and his resourcefulness or lack of it made clear. A recent case in the newspapers described how members of the women's services who became attached to a certain air-force station were "initiated" by having their blouses pulled up and being stamped on the upper abdomen with the rubber stamp ordinarily used for the station correspondence. (It is not, of course, suggested that this primitive rite is in general use in the

Royal Air Force.) Such initiation ceremonies closely resemble those of primitive tribes, although they are obviously less elaborate in content. They carry the implication that, if full membership of the group were too easily attained, it would not be worth having. Rites of passage are the ceremonies carried out when a group member is promoted, demoted, or sacked—when, in other words, he is about to leave the group. "The function of the ritual may be to manifest group identification and loyalty, to ease the process of separation from the group, to emphasize the finality of the social rupture, or merely to indicate that all past animosities are forgiven and forgotten." (Miller and Form.) They may take such forms as shaking hands, giving a party, speech-making, joking, giving absurd advice, and so on. Between the rites of arrival and departure there are the rites of intensification— ceremonies which have the purpose of demonstrating the solidarity of the group. The unity of the group may be demonstrated by the way members wear their caps, the way they address each other, the informal meetings to smoke and talk in the cloak-rooms, the private jokes whose significance is lost to outsiders, the dining together at lunch in the canteen, and, on special occasions, the drinking together at factory outings, the parties at Christmas and the New Year, and on other holidays and feast-days. It may be thought that too much is being made of such everyday happenings in the life of any industrial group, and that to compare them with the rites and customs of primitive tribes is absurd. But the important point is that, however attenuated the form these ceremonies may take, no group worthy of the name ever assumes that membership is a mere matter of walking into it. There is no integrated or coherent social group which does not make something of a ceremony of the arrival or departure of members or take part in ceremonies which, in effect, indicate its distinctness from any other group. Nor is there any group worthy of the name which does not regard itself as superior to, or at any rate different from, every other group. There always exists the awareness of what the anthropologist would call the "in-group" and the "out-group." The reasons for this are fairly obvious, since, if an individual's status, prestige, or pride of position come to a considerable extent from the groups of which he is a member—from his family, his working-group, his factory, and, in a lesser degree, from the larger secondary groups of the city, the county, and the nation, then clearly the more important these groups are, the greater is his own personal prestige. His attitude towards his own in-group will be that of the Old Testament writer whose feeling towards his religion or his tribe was expressed in the words: "I would rather be a door-keeper in the house of my God than a dweller in the tents of wickedness." This fact has two very important implications for the manager in industry. Firstly, it implies that every man or woman has a great desire to "belong" within a group and to be able to take a pride in it. This "belongingness" and pride of membership is one of the social goods which the firm is in a position to supply, and, when the firm is one with a great name in the world or even in the local community, the manager has a great asset on his side. Gordon Rattray Taylor shows very clearly the appallingly ineffectual use to which this asset has been put by some firms. He writes:

> I have only once met an employee of (a certain very famous motor-car factory), but I am perfectly sure that most of the men who work there state the fact with a certain pride. It is therefore almost a miracle of bad management that employers have managed to kill pride in the factory's achievements to the extent that they have.

Large concerns such as Unilever Ltd who hold frequent exhibitions of their products at each of their individual factories have discovered the astonishing enthusiasm and interest shown by the workers when they are "put in the picture," to use the modern jargon which signifies improved communications. In the Ford factory at Dagenham, the visit of Henry Ford, Jr., aroused the greatest enthusiasm amongst the workers who crowded round him to shake hands or ask for autographs. Admittedly, this aspect of industrial relations is an aspect which, in itself, will not take us very far, but the failure to recognize its existence does demonstrate how some managements have become so stupefied by their own propaganda, their ideology of the unwilling worker and the carrot and the stick, that they are quite incapable of observing human nature and using their own common sense.

The second implication of this attitude of the worker towards his in-group relates to the problem of filling jobs of low status, of getting people who will do the lowly and dirty work. This, again, is a problem which has, in large measure, been created by management. For, if the manager begins by stating the problem in the form: "This is a nasty job, a job fit only for a simpleton—how can I find anyone stupid enough to do it?", he is completely forgetting the quite obvious fact that the lowliness or nastiness of a job are subjective estimates, and that what really matters is the prestige of the job, and, even more important, the prestige of the group for which the job is to be done. A doctor or a nurse, for example, or a sanitary inspector, have to do some things which would disgust the most unskilled casual labourer who did not see these actions in their social context. Yet the status and prestige of such people is generally high. But when the supervisor or factory manager puts a man in a "dirty" job with the, probably unspoken, implication: "I'm sorry to have to ask you to do this job, but, after all, you are the most unskilled and dullest person I can find, so you must do it," he is by his attitude lowering the prestige of the job to such a degree that nobody in their senses *would* wish to have anything to do with it. The supervisor or manager of this type would no doubt feel that the job of lavatory cleaner was insignificant and dirty, but the woman who was doing the work, as we saw in the case quoted a few pages back, thought it a very important piece of work and was insulted at the idea that she might be asked to clean ovens in the canteen. The Sanitary Orderly in the army who has to clean out the latrines would hardly feel flattered if it were suggested to him that he was in a position similar to that of the Untouchables in India who do the same task. In point of fact (and this is something else in which industrial management might profitably study army methods), he is given lectures on sanitation and dirt-borne diseases, taught the best methods of doing his job, and therefore considers himself a highly-skilled man doing important work. It is, therefore, foolish on the part of the manager to go round his factory assessing jobs as childish, dirty, or mean on the basis of his own subjective estimates; for, in doing so, he is only further lowering the status of those who do them. At the same time, he should see to it that no job is *unnecessarily* dirty or dangerous, since, although few people object to work which is unavoidably dirty or dangerous, they will certainly not forgive the sort of unpleasantness which indicates neglect of their interests on the part of management.

Above all, it is the prestige of his working-group and his position in it which will influence the worker's attitude to such jobs. If the prestige of his group is high and he is satisfied in his membership of it, the type of work he has to do becomes a minor consideration. The late Professor Mannheim told how a friend of his who dealt with the problem of refugees had great difficulty in finding an occupation for elderly ladies who had seen better days, and resented doing any work which they considered a social come-down. But he managed to form them into co-operative squads to go round cleaning hospitals and schools. As individuals, they would never have dreamed of consenting to do such menial work. But as members of a group they did it enthusiastically. Because each lady was sure of the approval of the members of her group—and would actually have lost this approval by refusing to go along—she could afford to ignore any possible comment by outsiders.

Myths and beliefs are based on the need both to justify the actions of the group and to understand what is going on in the world surrounding it. In part, they are also an attempt to maintain group solidarity by recalling the traditions of the past. The myths may be those of a whole class—management and workers, sociologically speaking, both possess their own mythology—or they may be those of the individual factory or working-group based on its own experiences. Although in many industries the working-group is much less stable than in former times, it is still possible to hear older employees telling of the fabulous strength or skill of a former member of the group, of how, in the "old days" factory outings were not the petty affairs they have now become when everybody drinks lemonade and behaves as if he were on a Sunday-school outing. In those days group members (long transformed into giants of virtue or depravity) are alleged to have *really* enjoyed themselves and, although they got roaring drunk, were able to be back on the job the next day as if nothing had happened. But nowadays people are soft, they are unable to carry their drink, and, even after such a minor celebration, have to keep running to the Medical Department for aspirins. Or so the mythology goes. Meanwhile, the senior executives recount their own private mythology: "Ah yes, X was a hard man, but he was just—management stood no nonsense in those days. Why, I remember . . ."—and so on. But there is a more general mythology common to managers as a class which takes the form of such beliefs as that they have reached their position by reason of personal merit alone, that workers are lazy, shiftless, and stupid when they are not cunning, that the "carrot and the stick" are the only incentives, that "a little dose of unemployment would cure all our present troubles," and that the natural relationship is that of master and man. Workers, too, have a more general mythology which similarly explains how managers reached their present position (although in a less flattering version), how the workers are always being "done down," how everything is done for ulterior motives of profit, how management requires little or no skill and could be done equally well, or even better, by any group of workers, and so on. It is not for a moment suggested that all managers or all workers share these ideologies; they simply represent general trends in the thought of their respective classes which may, or may not, be fully accepted by individual members. Nor is it suggested that all of these beliefs on either side are necessarily untrue— but they have not been adopted on rational grounds. They are attitudes which are basically emotional in origin, although they may be based on beliefs which were true enough in a particular situation or at a particular time in history. A dangerous aspect of any such mythology or emotionally-held system of beliefs is that, to the individual who holds it, it is capable of explaining everything. Since all experiences are seen in terms of that frame of reference, it never fails to satisfy. S. I. Hayakawa shows in his *Language in Action* how, for example, the mythology of anti-semitism is capable of convincing the holder of anti-semitic prejudices that he is always correct in his beliefs. He can explain all the actions of Mr Miller, who is a Jew, somewhat as follows:

> If Mr Miller succeeds in business, that "proves" that "Jews" are "smart"; if Mr Johansen succeeds in business it only proves that Mr Johansen is smart. If Mr Miller fails in business, it is alleged that nevertheless he has "money salted away somewhere." If Mr Miller is strange or foreign in his habits, that "proves" that "Jews don't assimilate." If he is thoroughly Ameri-can—that is, indistinguishable from other natives—he is "trying to pass him-self off as one of us." If Mr Miller fails to give to charity, that is because "Jews are tight"; if he gives generously, he is "trying to buy his way into society." If Mr Miller lives in the Jewish section of the town, that is because

"Jews are so clannish"; if he moves to a locality where there are no other Jews, that is because "they try to horn in everywhere." In short, Mr Miller is condemned no matter who he is or what he does.

Although this example is taken from outside industry, it is easy to see how it applies to the relationships between workers and management. If either side of industry relies on a set of fixed ideas, whether they are those of Adam Smith and Ricardo or Karl Marx and Engels, they will never be able to see reality in any other terms and each new experience will merely serve to fix their ideas more firmly. Professor W. J. H. Sprott, although in a different context, has given some useful advice about the place of theories or systems of belief which might well be taken to heart by both sides of industry: "Theories are not utterances of absolute truth, they are useful devices for understanding. If a theory ceases to be useful, we cast it aside and turn to another; theories are to be *used* rather than believed in." (*General Psychology*.)

The systems of belief or ideologies we have been discussing show the following characteristics:

1. They are functionally equivalent to wrong theories (although not neces· sarily wrong in every detail).
2. They are not changed by the possession of correct knowledge.
3. Even extensive first-hand experience is unlikely to change them.
4. They influence the individual's actions.
5. They form a more or less coherent whole which cannot be altered item by item.
6. The sentiments of management towards workers (or vice versa) are determined less by the knowledge of the individual manager or worker than by the sentiments which prevail in the social atmosphere which surrounds him.

The last item in this list of characteristics is, perhaps, worth further elaboration. What it means is that, in general, each member of management within the factory tends to be seen first of all as an official in the service of a set-up which may be regarded as pleasant or hateful by the worker. Only much later, or perhaps never, is he seen as an individual in his own right. For example, the factory physician in a "problem" factory will find that he is no longer regarded as someone who is out to help others regardless of their official status or whether they are considered as good or bad workers, but rather as a supporter of the hated management. This may be so even when he is himself regarded by management with suspicion as being too progressive or democratic. Thus a doctor who has had the interesting experience of working in more than one firm may find that, although he treats all his patients in all of the factories in the same way, in one firm he is regarded with affection and trust whereas in another he is looked on with suspicion and resentment. In short, the way he is regarded by the employees does not depend solely, as is so often thought, upon his personal qualities as an individual; on the contrary, it tends to be a function of the atmosphere obtaining in the firm. Similarly, the good manager in the bad firm is often regarded with as much suspicion as the bad manager; whatever good he may do is interpreted in terms of the prevailing attitude of suspicion. The atmosphere of the factory is, therefore, immensely important since it determines the way in which any act within its boundaries is interpreted by the employees. Thus, to the worker, almost everything in the factory with a bad atmosphere is regarded as bad or done with ulterior motives. If the sick worker is sent to a convalescent home, it is to "shut him up" and forestall possible criticism (and, of course, it sometimes is); if the long-service worker is given a presentation, it is because "so he bloody well should be" after working there; if an employee is stood a drink by one of the managers at some social function, the employee comes to be regarded as a "ruddy crawler." Or, to quote an example given in another book by the present writer, the welfare worker in a factory may be surprised to find something like the following situation:

> In two factories there are Welfare departments which may lend a worker money when he is in need of it. In each the Welfare department is equally well fitted out, in each the Welfare worker is equally pleasant and anxious to help. But the response of the workers who have been given loans is very different in each case. Of course, if you ask them, they will be polite and assume a grateful air, but a little more questioning makes it evident that in one factory the worker is really grateful and happy, in the other he is secretly resentful and angry. Why? The answer lies in the fact that one factory is autocratic, the other democratic in structure. A loan from the autocratic factory arouses resentment, since one dislikes being obliged to someone who is feared and hated. But if one belongs to a democratic group, a "we" group, the loan comes from one's associates and is welcome. All relationships in a resentful factory are tainted with resentment. (J. A. C. Brown, *Psychology*.)

(In point of fact, the above account is probably incorrect in so far as it infers that an autocratic factory *necessarily* leads to the state of affairs described. That an autocratic set-up is likely to lead to such attitudes is certain, but a great deal depends on the social background of the firm and whether or not the autocracy is accepted by the employees. In the democratic state of modern times the worker is less and less likely to accept autocracy within the factory.)

Most of what we have said in this chapter has been concerned with the informal organization of industrial workers, and little or nothing has been said about the informal organization of management. Reasons why little research has been done in this direction have already been given . . . , but, in point of fact, there is little difference between the informal organizations of the two groups. There are the same cliques which in some cases have a disruptive effect on the total structure and in other cases seem to oil the wheels and make things flow more smoothly. One may see the same fight for status and the same tendency to squeeze out the man whose face does not fit. In some firms the general tone of senior management is friendly (this may be quite genuine or a mask to conceal deep-seated tensions), and one may see the chairman simply by walking into his office. The chairman would be deeply hurt if one did not sit on his desk and smoke and everyone is "Alf," "Bob," and "George." At its best, to work in a firm like this may be very pleasant. Does one want a seat booked on the train to Birmingham? Old George can "fix" it through the traffic department. Or some information concerning income-tax forms? Well, Alf can help you there. Even if, in some firms, there is a hint of what Lin Yutang describes as "old roguery" about these goings-on, the cheerful wink accompanying the deed deprives it of any sense of guilt. Lunch is accompanied by some ragging, some mild obscenity, or even conversation about classical music, politics, and literature. In yet another firm one is all too aware that "life is real and life is earnest!" A request to see the chairman may result in an interview within two or three weeks (depending, of course, on one's position in the hierarchy), and the chairman expects to be called "Sir" whilst his visitor gets the impression that he is expected to stand rigidly to attention. Here every manager has two sets of opinions —those he tells to his equals and those he reserves for his superiors (official and non-official opinions). At lunch, one's words, if not one's thoughts, are pure and non-controversial, and although the usual amount of "fiddling" goes on the guilty ones are fearful and feel guilty indeed. Such attitudes of management in the individual factory are set by those in authority, and their importance lies in the fact that, for better or worse, they ultimately penetrate right down the line: "Good morale (or bad morale) is not a quality that wells up from below—it is something that trickles down from above."

# Group Cohesiveness in the Industrial Work Group: Summary and Conclusions*

*Stanley E. Seashore*

Prior research on the characteristics of groups has suggested that the variable group cohesiveness is of considerable consequence in relation to the functioning of the group and the behavior of the individual members. The variable has been explored principally in laboratory experiments with groups of small size, although there is a rich literature of anecdote and careful observation with respect to the cohesiveness of "natural" groups in industry and in other kinds of social settings.

For the present investigation, group cohesiveness was conceptualized as attraction of members to the group in terms of the strength of forces on the individual member to remain in the group and to resist leaving the group.

The objective of this study has been to explore in an industrial situation some of the facilitating conditions and consequences of group cohesiveness. The research hypotheses were as follows:

1. Members of high cohesive groups will exhibit less anxiety than members of low cohesive groups with respect to matters relevant to group activities or the group setting.

2. The degree of cohesiveness within a group determines the power of the groups to create forces towards uniformity of behavior among members (group standards).

3. In the case of a cohesive group subjected to forces toward an uncertain or unobtainable goal imposed by an external agent, the point of equilibrium of forces toward and away from the goal (group standard) will be a function of the perceived supportiveness of the external agent.

4. The degree of cohesiveness developed in a group will be a function of the

* From *Group Cohesiveness in the Industrial Work Group,* The University of Michigan Press, Ann Arbor, Mich., 1954, chap. 7, pp. 97–102. Reprinted by permission of The Institute for Social Research, University of Michigan.

attractiveness of the members of the group as determined by the prestige of the members.

5. The degree of cohesiveness developed in a group will be a function of the attractiveness of the members of the group as determined by the degree of similarity among members of the group.

6. The degree of cohesiveness developed in a group will be a function of opportunities for interaction among members of the group.

The study design uses the correlational technique, with group cohesiveness treated as the independent variable, and measures of anxiety, productivity standards, member similarity, member prestige, and opportunity for interaction as dependent variables. The data are drawn from a population of 228 groups (formally designated work sections in a machinery factory) ranging in size from 5 to over 50 members. The data were obtained through a questionnaire completed by all members of these groups, 5,871 in number.

The major findings relevant to the hypotheses outlined above were as follows:

1. Members of high cohesive groups exhibit less anxiety than members of low cohesive groups, using as measures of anxiety: (a) feeling "jumpy or 'nervous'," (b) feeling under pressure to achieve higher productivity (actual productivity held constant), and (c) feeling of lack of support from the company. The hypothesis was not clearly supported in the case of a fourth measure of anxiety, namely, report of frequent worry about certain work-related matters such as earnings, lay-off, etc., although a majority of these findings were in the predicted direction and one (out of eight) was statistically significant.

2. High cohesive groups have less variation in productivity among members than do the low cohesiveness groups. This is regarded as confirmation of the existence of a more effective group standard in the high cohesive condition.

3. High cohesive groups differ more frequently and in greater amount than low cohesive groups from the plant norm of productivity. These deviations are towards both high and lower productivity.

4. The direction of deviation of group productivity (i.e., towards higher or lower productivity) is a function of the degree to which the larger organization (the company) is perceived by group members to provide a supportive setting for the group.

5. The prediction regarding degree of group cohesiveness and similarity among members was not confirmed, using as measures, similarity in age and similarity in educational level.

6. Group cohesiveness is positively related to the degree of prestige attributed by the group members to their own jobs.

7. Group cohesiveness is positively related to opportunity for interaction as measured by (a) size of group, and (b) duration of shared membership on the job.

8. The findings with respect to group standards (2, 3, and 4, above) using actual productivity as the measure, were not confirmed when an alternative

measure of group productivity standard (perceived level of reasonable productivity) was used.

In addition to these findings, which relate directly to the research hypotheses, there were several theoretical and methodological by-products which seem worth a passing note. These are summarized below with suggestions for their interpretation.

1. Homans (24) makes the distinction between group norms (actual behavior) and group standards (ideal behavior). He further holds that there is likely to be a discrepancy between the two and that within a group there will be greater uniformity with respect to the verbalized standard of behavior than with respect to the behavioral norm. Our data do not support this conception; actual productivity is found to have about the same variability within groups as is perceived reasonable productivity. Both differ from the formal company standard of 100 per cent, which very few employees appear to accept even as an ideal level of productivity. It seems more useful to conceptualize group standards in terms of group-induced uniformities of behavior regardless of whether the behavior in question is overt physical behavior, verbal behavior, or private attitudinal response. This does not deny the utility of Homans' conception in a context of societal norms and the precedence of behavior change over ideal change.

2. Schachter, et al., (52) in an experiment on group cohesiveness and productivity found differential group cohesiveness to be related to differential degrees of change in group productivity when the group induction was in a negative direction, i.e., towards lower productivity, and when there were external forces towards higher productivity. On the other hand, the differences in degree of cohesiveness of the group had no apparent effect when the group induction was in a direction consistent with external forces towards higher productivity. He gives a rationale leading to the hypothesis that positive group induction would have been accepted by the members, differentially in high and low cohesive groups, if the restraining forces against higher productivity had been of greater magnitude than his experimental conditions provided. Our findings are that the hypothesized relationship between cohesiveness and productivity holds for both positive and negative directions of group induction. This offers some confirmation for his formulation of the matter.

3. We have encountered the finding, not statistically significant but consistent for four sets of data, that under conditions of relatively low group cohesiveness, perception of a high degree of support from the company is coincident with low productivity standards while low support is coincident with high production. This result is paralleled by findings from other studies: for example, several studies relating productivity to employee attitudes toward the company suggest that high-producing employees may tend to be more critical of the company and its policies (29, 30). We are inclined to interpret this finding with reference to primary group processes, and hypothesize that in the absence of the security provided by a primary group, the insecure employee will experience greater anxiety regarding his fulfillment of company demands and will tend to adopt productivity standards which are relatively high in order to mini-

mize this anxiety; in the opposite case—an employee feeling relatively secure in relation to the company—this additional force towards higher productivity will be minimized.

4. We assumed in designing this study that formally-designated section-shift groups, so designated for accounting purposes, would in fact function to some degree as primary social groups. This seemed a rather large assumption considering the fact that the "groups," for the most part, are of a size greater than is ordinarily considered to be optimum or "natural" for primary groups, and in view of the fact that there is no assurance that conditions of physical proximity and sub-group formation would permit the section-shift units to function as groups. The assumption, however, appears to be supported by the fact of significant findings which stem from group-related influences. To a significant degree, the formal units of organization in this factory—and presumably in other factories—function as effective social units. This enlarges considerably the convenience and potential scope of future research on group processes in industrial settings.

We opened this report with the general assertion that the behavior of people in large formal organizational settings cannot be understood unless we take into account the forces generated by their association in primary groups. We specifically set out to determine whether these group associations were relevant factors in the mental health and adjustment of the individual with reference to his work, and in the determination of standards of productivity.

The formulation of our research hypotheses stemmed in part from prior research focussing upon the problems of organization management and the problems of the individual seeking a satisfactory way of life in a society characterized by the association of people in large organizations. Our manner of thinking about the problem—the choice of concepts, and the development of relationships to be tested—was drawn largely from the field theoretical approach which views the individual's behavior in terms of a dynamic field of forces exerting influence upon the individual, with the direction and magnitude of these forces determined in part by social interaction and specifically by interaction within the primary group.

We emerge from this study with some new ideas, but mainly with considerably increased respect for some old ones. We see demonstrated in a typical social setting the dependence of the individual upon his primary associations for feelings of security and the reduction of his anxieties. We see the primary group as a source of potent influences which may or may not be marshalled in support of the goals of the larger organization. We come to a conception of group cohesiveness—the attraction of the group for the members—as a facilitating factor which determines the amount of influence a group has, but not necessarily the direction or the goal toward which the group influences operate. We see the variable, group cohesiveness, as being of sufficient importance so that its effects are measurable; they are measurable even in a complex setting in which the formal social structure is designed to ignore or even suppress group effects and in which there are strong factors, such as individual mobility, multiple group membership, out-plant associations, problems of reliable measurement, and others, which tend to obscure primary group effects.

Finally, we observe that some, at least, of the factors determining the degree to which group cohesiveness is developed, are external to and prior to group formation. The work group is more likely to become cohesive if administrative actions are designed with these ends: (1) to lend prestige to the group members, (2) to structure the organization so that there is provision for groups of relatively small size, and (3) to maintain a continuity in group membership over a period of time.

The administrator of an organization may draw from these findings some hints regarding policy and action. It is clear that the association of employees in cohesive groups may generate influences that are or may be of considerable consequence to the success of an organization. With respect to employee morale—in the context of anxieties at work—the cohesive work group appears to have a favorable influence. But with respect to productivity the positive value of cohesiveness in the work group appears to be contingent upon the administrator's success in developing among the employees a feeling of confidence and security in the management of the organization. The popular admonition to supervisors that they should develop a cohesive team, if carried out indiscriminately, may merely lend force to the divisive influences within the larger organization. To assure a positive benefit to the organization from group cohesiveness the administrator might well take steps first to provide the basic conditions of equity and supportiveness which warrant employee confidence in management. A policy of "divide and conquer," as expressed in an emphasis on man-to-man relationships and suppression of group processes, may be partially effective; but the greater gains appear to lie in a policy to "unite in common cause," as expressed in the positive emphasis upon the formation of cohesive work teams.

## References

24. Homans, G. C.: *The Human Group*. New York: Harcourt, Brace, 1950.

52. Schachter, S., Ellertson, N., McBride, D., and Gregory, D.: "An experimental study of cohesiveness and productivity," *Human Relations*, 1951, **4,** 229–238.

29. Katz, D., Maccoby, N. and Morse, N. C.: *Productivity, Supervision and Morale in an Office Situation*. Ann Arbor, Mich.: Survey Research Center, 1950.

30. Katz, D., Maccoby, N., Gurin, G. and Floor, L. G.: *Productivity, Supervision and Morale Among Railroad Workers*. Ann Arbor, Mich.: Survey Research Center, 1951.

# Opinions and Social Pressure*

*Solomon E. Asch*

That social influences shape every person's practices, judgments and beliefs is a truism to which anyone will readily assent. A child masters his "native" dialect down to the finest nuances; a member of a tribe of cannibals accepts cannibalism as altogether fitting and proper. All the social sciences take their departure from the observation of the profound effects that groups exert on their members. For psychologists, group pressure upon the minds of individuals raises a host of questions they would like to investigate in detail.

How, and to what extent, do social forces constrain people's opinions and attitudes? This question is especially pertinent in our day. The same epoch that has witnessed the unprecedented technical extension of communication has also brought into existence the deliberate manipulation of opinion and the "engineering of consent." There are many good reasons why, as citizens and as scientists, we should be concerned with studying the ways in which human beings form their opinions and the role that social conditions play.

Studies of these questions began with the interest in hypnosis aroused by the French physician Jean Martin Charcot (a teacher of Sigmund Freud) toward the end of the 19th century. Charcot believed that only hysterical patients could be fully hypnotized, but this view was soon challenged by two other physicians, Hyppolyte Bernheim and A. A. Liébault, who demonstrated that they could put most people under the hypnotic spell. Bernheim proposed that hypnosis was but an extreme form of a normal psychological process which became known as "suggestibility." It was shown that monotonous reiteration of instructions could induce in normal persons in the waking state involuntary bodily changes such as swaying or rigidity of the arms, and sensations such as warmth and odor.

It was not long before social thinkers seized upon these discoveries as a basis for explaining numerous social phenomena, from the spread of opinion to the formation of crowds and the following of leaders. The so-

* From *Scientific American*, vol. 193, no. 5, pp. 31–35, November, 1955. Reprinted with permission. Copyright © 1955 by Scientific American, Inc. All rights reserved.

ciologist Gabriel Tarde summed it all up in the aphorism: "Social man is a somnambulist."

When the new discipline of social psychology was born at the beginning of this century, its first experiments were essentially adaptations of the suggestion demonstration. The technique generally followed a simple plan. The subjects, usually college students, were asked to give their opinions or preferences concerning various matters; some time later they were again asked to state their choices, but now they were also informed of the opinions held by authorities or large groups of their peers on the same matters. (Often the alleged consensus was fictitious.) Most of these studies had substantially the same result: confronted with opinions contrary to their own, many subjects apparently shifted their judgments in the direction of the views of the majorities or the experts. The late psychologist Edward L. Thorndike reported that he had succeeded in modifying the esthetic preferences of adults by this procedure. Other psychologists reported that people's evaluations of the merit of a literary passage could be raised or lowered by ascribing the passage to different authors. Apparently the sheer weight of numbers or authority sufficed to change opinions, even when no arguments for the opinions themselves were provided.

Now the very ease of success in these experiments arouses suspicion. Did the subjects actually change their opinions, or were the experimental victories scored only on paper? On grounds of common sense, one must question whether opinions are generally as watery as these studies indicate. There is some reason to wonder whether it was not the investigators who, in their enthusiasm for a theory, were suggestible, and whether the ostensibly gullible subjects were not providing answers which they thought good subjects were expected to give.

The investigations were guided by certain underlying assumptions, which today are common currency and account for much that is thought and said about the operations of propaganda and public opinion. The assumptions are that people submit uncritically and painlessly to external manipulation by suggestion or prestige, and that any given idea or value can be "sold" or "unsold" without reference to its merits. We should be skeptical, however, of the supposition that the power of social pressure necessarily implies uncritical submission to it: independence and the capacity to rise above group passion are also open to human beings. Further, one may question on psychological grounds whether it is possible as a rule to change a person's judgment of a situation or an object without first changing his knowledge or assumptions about it.

In what follows I shall describe some experiments in an investigation of the effects of group pressure which was carried out recently with the help of a number of my associates. The tests not only demonstrate the operations of group pressure upon individuals but also illustrate a new kind of attack on the problem and some of the more subtle questions that it raises.

A group of seven to nine young men, all college students, are assembled in a classroom for a "psychological experiment" in visual judgment. The experimenter informs them that they will be comparing the lengths of lines. He shows two large white cards. On one is a single vertical black line— the standard whose length is to be matched. On the other card are three

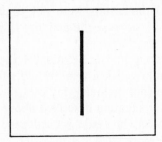 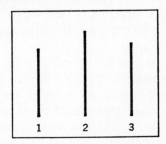

Figure 1. SUBJECTS WERE SHOWN two cards. One bore a standard line. The other bore three lines, one of which was the same length as the standard. The subjects were asked to choose this line.

vertical lines of various lengths. The subjects are to choose the one that is of the same length as the line on the other card. One of the three actually is of the same length; the other two are substantially different, the difference ranging from three quarters of an inch to an inch and three quarters.

The experiment opens uneventfully. The subjects announce their answers in the order in which they have been seated in the room, and on the first round every person chooses the same matching line. Then a second set of cards is exposed; again the group is unanimous. The members appear ready to endure politely another boring experiment. On the third trial there is an unexpected disturbance. One person near the end of the group disagrees with all the others in his selection of the matching line. He looks surprised, indeed incredulous, about the disagreement. On the following trial he disagrees again, while the others remain unanimous in their choice. The dissenter becomes more and more worried and hesitant as the disagreement continues in succeeding trials; he may pause before announcing his answer and speak in a low voice, or he may smile in an embarrassed way.

What the dissenter does not know is that all the other members of the group were instructed by the experimenter beforehand to give incorrect answers in unanimity at certain points. The single individual who is not a party to this pre-arrangement is the focal subject of our experiment. He is placed in a position in which, while he is actually giving the correct answers, he finds himself unexpectedly in a minority of one, opposed by a unanimous and arbitrary majority with respect to a clear and simple fact. Upon him we have brought to bear two opposed forces: the evidence of his senses and the unanimous opinion of a group of his peers. Also, he must declare his judgments in public, before a majority which has also stated its position publicly.

The instructed majority occasionally reports correctly in order to reduce the possibility that the naive subject will suspect collusion against him. (In only a few cases did the subject actually show suspicion; when this happened, the experiment was stopped and the results were not counted.) There are 18 trials in each series, and on 12 of these the majority responds erroneously.

How do people respond to group pressure in this situation? I shall report first the statistical results of a series in which a total of 123 subjects from three institutions of higher learning (not including my own, Swarthmore College) were placed in the minority situation described above.

Two alternatives were open to the subject: he could act independently, repudiating the majority, or he could go along with the majority, repudiating the evidence of his senses. Of the 123 put to the test, a considerable percentage yielded to the majority. Whereas in ordinary circumstances individuals matching the lines will make mistakes less than 1 per cent of the time, under group pressure the minority subjects swung to acceptance of the misleading majority's wrong judgments in 36.8 per cent of the selections.

Of course individuals differed in response. At one extreme, about one quarter of the subjects were completely independent and never agreed with the erroneous judgments of the majority. At the other extreme, some individuals went with the majority nearly all the time. The performances of individuals in this experiment tend to be highly consistent. Those who strike out on the path of independence do not, as a rule, succumb to the majority even over an extended series of trials, while those who choose the path of compliance are unable to free themselves as the ordeal is prolonged.

The reasons for the startling individual differences have not yet been investigated in detail. At this point we can only report some tentative generalizations from talks with the subjects, each of whom was interviewed at the end of the experiment. Among the independent individuals were many who held fast because of staunch confidence in their own judgment. The most significant fact about them was not absence of responsiveness to the majority but a capacity to recover from doubt and to re-establish their equilibrium. Others who acted independently came to believe that the majority was correct in its answers, but they continued their dissent on the simple ground that it was their obligation to call the play as they saw it.

Among the extremely yielding persons we found a group who quickly reached the conclusion: "I am wrong, they are right." Others yielded in order "not to spoil your results." Many of the individuals who went along suspected that the majority were "sheep" following the first responder, or that the majority were victims of an optical illusion; nevertheless, these suspicions failed to free them at the moment of decision. More disquieting were the reactions of subjects who construed their difference from the majority as a sign of some general deficiency in themselves, which at all costs they must hide. On this basis they desperately tried to merge with the majority, not realizing the longer-range consequences to themselves. All the yielding subjects underestimated the frequency with which they conformed.

Which aspect of the influence of a majority is more important—the size of the majority or its unanimity? The experiment was modified to examine this question. In one series the size of the opposition was varied from one to 15 persons. The results showed a clear trend. When a subject was confronted with only a single individual who contradicted his answers, he was swayed little: he continued to answer independently and correctly in nearly all trials. When the opposition was increased to two, the pressure became substantial: minority subjects now accepted the wrong answer 13.6 per cent of the time. Under the pressure of a majority of three, the subjects' errors jumped to 31.8 per cent. But further increases in the size of the majority apparently did not increase the weight of the pressure substantially. Clearly the size of the opposition is important only up to a point.

Disturbance of the majority's unanimity had a striking effect. In this experiment the subject was given the support of a truthful partner—either another individual who did not know of the prearranged agreement among the rest of the group, or a person who was instructed to give correct answers throughout.

The presence of a supporting partner depleted the majority of much of its power. Its pressure on the dissenting individual was reduced to one fourth: that is, subjects answered incorrectly only one fourth as often as under the pressure of a unanimous majority [see Fig. 2c]. The weakest persons did not yield as readily. Most interesting were the reactions to the partner. Generally the feeling toward him was one of warmth and closeness; he was credited with inspiring confidence. However, the subjects repudiated the suggestion that the partner decided them to be independent.

Was the partner's effect a consequence of his dissent, or was it related to his accuracy? We now introduced into the experimental group a person who was instructed to dissent from the majority but also to disagree with the subject. In some experiments the majority was always to choose the worst of the comparison lines and the instructed dissenter to pick the line that was closer to the length of the standard one; in others the majority was consistently intermediate and the dissenter most in error. In this manner we were able to study the relative influence of "compromising" and "extremist" dissenters.

Again the results are clear. When a moderate dissenter is present, the

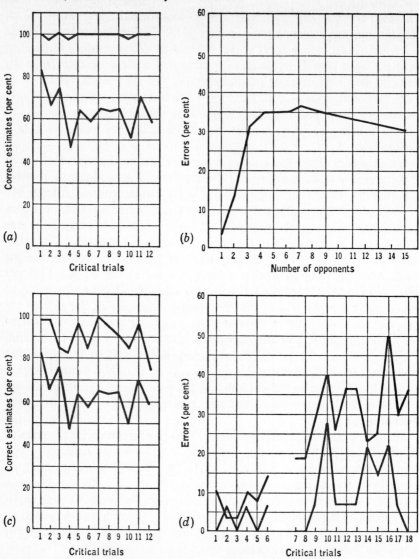

Figure 2. (*a*) ERROR of 123 subjects, each of whom compared lines in the presence of six to eight opponents, is plotted in the [lower] curve. The accuracy of judgments not under pressure is indicated in [the upper curve].

(*b*) SIZE OF MAJORITY which opposed them had an effect on the subjects. With a single opponent the subject erred only 3.6 per cent of the time; with two opponents he erred 13.6 per cent; three, 31.8 per cent; four, 35.1 per cent; six, 35.2 per cent; seven, 37.1 per cent; nine, 35.1 per cent; 15, 31.2 per cent.

(*c*) TWO SUBJECTS supporting each other against a majority made fewer errors [*upper curve*] than one subject did against a majority [*lower curve*].

(*d*) PARTNER LEFT SUBJECT after six trials in a single experiment. The [upper right-hand] curve shows the error of the subject when the partner "deserted" to the majority. [lower right-hand] shows error when partner merely left the room.

effect of the majority on the subject decreases by approximately one third, and extremes of yielding disappear. Moreover, most of the errors the subjects do make are moderate, rather than flagrant. In short, the dissenter largely controls the choice of errors. To this extent the subjects broke away from the majority even while bending to it.

On the other hand, when the dissenter always chose the line that was more flagrantly different from the standard, the results were of quite a different kind. The extremist dissenter produced a remarkable freeing of the subjects; their errors dropped to only 9 per cent. Furthermore, all the errors were of the moderate variety. We were able to conclude that dissent *per se* increased independence and moderated the errors that occurred, and that the direction of dissent exerted consistent effects.

In all the foregoing experiments each subject was observed only in a single setting. We now turned to studying the effects upon a given individual of a change in the situation to which he was exposed. The first experiment examined the consequences of losing or gaining a partner. The instructed partner began by answering correctly on the first six trials. With his support the subject usually resisted pressure from the majority: 18 of 27 subjects were completely independent. But after six trials the partner joined the majority. As soon as he did so, there was an abrupt rise in the subjects' errors. Their submission to the majority was just about as frequent as when the minority subject was opposed by a unanimous majority throughout.

It was surprising to find that the experience of having had a partner and of having braved the majority opposition with him had failed to strengthen the individuals' independence. Questioning at the conclusion of the experiment suggested that we had overlooked an important circumstance; namely, the strong specific effect of "desertion" by the partner to the other side. We therefore changed the conditions so that the partner would simply leave the group at the proper point. (To allay suspicion it was announced in advance that he had an appointment with the dean.) In this form of the experiment, the partner's effect outlasted his presence. The errors increased after his departure, but less markedly than after a partner switched to the majority.

In a variant of this procedure the trials began with the majority unanimously giving correct answers. Then they gradually broke away until on the sixth trial the naive subject was alone and the group unanimously against him. As long as the subject had anyone on his side, he was almost invariably independent, but as soon as he found himself alone, the tendency to conform to the majority rose abruptly.

As might be expected, an individual's resistance to group pressure in these experiments depends to a considerable degree on how wrong the majority is. We varied the discrepancy between the standard line and the other lines systematically, with the hope of reaching a point where the error of the majority would be so glaring that every subject would repudiate it and choose independently. In this we regretfully did not succeed. Even when the difference between the lines was seven inches, there were still some who yielded to the error of the majority.

The study provides clear answers to a few relatively simple questions, and it raises many others that await investigation. We would like to know the degree of consistency of persons in situations which differ in content and structure. If consistency of independence or conformity in behavior is shown to be a fact, how is it functionally related to qualities of character and personality? In what ways is independence related to sociological or cultural conditions? Are leaders more independent than other people, or are they adept at following their followers? These and many other questions may perhaps be answerable by investigations of the type described here.

Life in society requires consensus as an iu.'ispensable condition. But consensus, to be productive, requires that each individual contribute independently out of his experience and insight. When consensus comes under the dominance of conformity, the social process is polluted and the individual at the same time surrenders the powers on which his functioning as a feeling and thinking being depends. That we have found the tendency to conformity in our society so strong that reasonably intelligent and well-meaning young people are willing to call white black is a matter of concern. It raises questions about our ways of education and about the values that guide our conduct.

Yet anyone inclined to draw too pessimistic conclusions from this report would do well to remind himself that the capacities for independence are not to be underestimated. He may also draw some consolation from a further observation: those who participated in this challenging experiment agreed nearly without exception that independence was preferable to conformity.

# Motivational Aspects of Industrial Morale*

*Ross Stagner*

Morale, I think, must always be defined in terms of an individual-group relationship; it is an index of the extent to which the individual perceives a probability of satisfying his own motives through cooperation with the group. Obviously, then, there is no such phenomenon as morale *in general;* the state of an individual's morale must be gauged relative to some specific group, such as his company, his informal work group, or his union.

Morale, to me, is not a meaningful term if the individual is seeking individual goals through individualistic action. At least from the subjective or *phenomenal* view, if he does not perceive himself as a member of a group, the term morale simply is not relevant. Of course, he may be *objectively* a member of a group, as when he is an employee of a company; and so from an external point of view, we may speak of his morale as a part of the employing organization. In this case, if he is acting in a purely individualistic fashion, we must conclude that his morale is low. Nevertheless, as Brayfield and Crockett[1] have recently emphasized, his productivity may be high. Morale and efficiency have a complex, not a linear relation.

High morale exists when the individual perceives himself as a member of a group, and perceives a high probability of achieving both individual and group goals through a course of action. He consciously seeks to achieve the goals of the group because these are important to him—they have become individual goals—or because they provide a *pathway* to his own personal goals which are not related to the group.

When we attempt to apply motivational analysis to the problem so de-

* From *Personnel Psychology,* vol. 11, pp. 64–70, 1958. Reprinted by permission of *Personnel Psychology.*
[1] A. H. Brayfield and W. H. Crockett, "Employee Attitudes and Employee Performance," *Psychological Bulletin,* Vol. 52, 1955, pp. 396–424. [Partially reprinted in this volume, pages 441–449.—Ed.]

fined, we find that there are three separate phases to be examined: (a) the individual's private goals; (b) the group goals; and (c) the perceived relationship between these sets of goals.

An extended treatment of individual goals would be out of place here. Let me say only that I consider the lists of common motives so widely used to be both inaccurate and misleading. Motivation is properly a *state of energy-mobilization* oriented toward some perceived or imagined goal-object or goal-situation. Thus an individual may have an infinity of motives, and his motives are constantly subject to change as the incidence of deprivation and satiation make some goals *more* or *less* attractive. It is useful to classify goals into categories and to observe that, in a specific individual's life-history, he has shown a tendency to mobilize more energy in behalf of income, or power, or prestige; this gives us something better than chance prediction as to his future motivations. But, as is obvious in industrial situations, the same goal—e.g., more money—may serve security, prestige or power needs.

The differences between individuals, and especially between classes of individuals, e.g., executives, workers, and union officials, arise from other than internal motivational tensions. As I have pointed out elsewhere,[2] one major determinant is the perceived probability of success. Executives have a history of successful achievement, which makes them willing to take chances, since they are optimistic as to the outcome. Workers more often perceive their probabilities of success as low when they take a chance; hence we say they are "security-oriented."

A second consideration which is important with reference to the concept of individual goals is that these goals are often group-determined. The executive sets many facets of corporate policy in terms of group norms; the group here may be composed of his associates in the company, or of industrialists in general. The worker is influenced by informal work groups, by his family group, and by the union. The union leader is influenced by his members and by other union executives. Hence the difference between individual and group goals may seem to get blurred even before we have started using the two terms. However, I think we can say that, in the instances I have cited, the individual seeks the goal for purely personal satisfaction; he has merely accepted the *group definition* of what is good for him. Goodwin Watson used to define Utopia as a place in which a person was paid for doing work which he would have enjoyed doing even if unpaid. By contrast, George Orwell, in *1984,* depicted a society in which the individual was so manipulated that he wanted to do that which society compelled him to do. These two situations get alarmingly close to one another in some writings. Perhaps we can establish a criterion

[2] Ross Stagner, *Psychology of Industrial Conflict* (New York: John Wiley & Sons, 1956).

for differentiation by saying that in Utopia, the person is the independent variable; in *1984,* society is the independent variable.

A further clarification of the relationship I want to emphasize may be achieved by a more precise analysis of the concept of *group goal.* This is a slippery concept, because it tends to become associated with the old group-mind fallacy. Obviously, I will maintain that *only* individuals mobilize energy on behalf of goals. In a phenomenal frame of reference, however, we know that groups *seem* to have goals and *seem* to work (more or less vigorously) to attain them. I suggest that the resolution of this paradox derives from perception. If members of a group perceive it as a unit, and perceive it as striving for a goal, this gives us a phenomenological basis for treating group goals as real.

This definition differs, I realize, in some respects from tradition. I am proposing, essentially, that a decision at the top does not establish a group goal unless the members accept it. The goal chosen by the leader becomes a group goal *when* the members perceive it as the goal of their group and perceive the group as making efforts to attain it. Notice that I am still not stating that any specific member is making efforts to accomplish this purpose.

We come now to the question of morale. Morale, as I see it, derives from the person's perception of himself as a component of this group-unit, and perception of his goals as being identical to or contiguous with the group-goals as defined. Let me illustrate this latter relationship by diagramming some of the principal possibilities:

1. The achievement of the group goal and the individual goal is a single process (see Figure 1). E.g., the worker turns out a product which meets com-

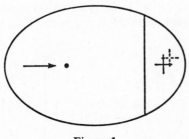

Figure 1

pany specifications at low cost, and he is proud of his work. The union leader wins a contract which protects his members and also protects him. Morale is at a maximum when the group goal and the individual goal are seen as identical.

2. The two goals are closely associated (see Figure 2). E.g., a group of

workers raise their team output and receive bonus payments. The union leader wins a contract which brings a pay raise to his members and more prestige for himself.

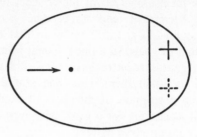

Figure 2

3. The attainment of the group goal is a necessary precondition of the individual goal (see Figure 3). E.g., a corporation executive helps expand sales,

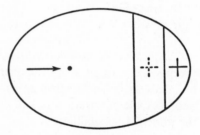

Figure 3

expects more pay and status. The union leader tries to organize more workers, and expects a rise in prestige and status.

4. Group and individual goals are perceived as separable and as attainable independently (see Figure 4). In this case a worker may produce at a high rate,

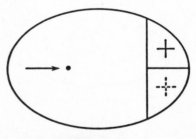

Figure 4

and ignore the informal group goal of security. His morale as a group member is low, even though his output is high. The union leader accepts a job as foreman, fails to pursue the union goal of strong organization. His morale as a union member is low.

Obviously, each of these examples is oversimplified, since there may be several individual goals and even varying group goals involved; especially, the person may be a member of overlapping groups and hence subject to conflicting group goals. These latter will be effective accordingly as the person perceives them to be compatible with his own goals.

Let me consider for just a moment the question of how this analysis relates to studies of job satisfaction. Instead of speaking of a single personal goal, we should more accurately conceive of the individual as seeking numerous rewards in the industrial situation. The situation may be one in which some of these goals are barred from achievement by company policy or by the nature of the situation (see Figure 5). Job satisfaction in

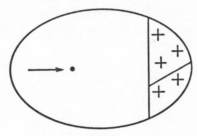

Figure 5

such cases will be determined by the relative importance *as perceived by the employee* of the satisfactions achieved and those not achieved or perceived as unattainable. Questionnaires often try to get at these employee perceptions. If his over-all evaluation is negative, we can predict that his morale in relation to the company will suffer; that is, he cannot attain an acceptable level of individual goal achievement while cooperating with the company. However, this may or may not raise his morale as a member of the union Our dual allegiance studies[3] indicate that, on the average, those workers who are hostile to the company are also dissatisfied with the union.

These last examples suggest that wherever the individual perceives a substantial separation of group goals and individual goals, morale will suffer. This is true even though the person may outwardly seem to conform to the group policy. He still feels attracted to his individual goals, and some of his energy will be directed to them, not to the group goal.

The task of the person who wishes to raise morale within an organization, therefore, is to create situations in which group and individual goals coincide to the maximum extent possible. Work and social role assignments which separate these two are asking for trouble. The classical instance in this connection is that of the executive who believes—and behaves as if—workers desire only money. This attitude encourages attempts on the part

[3] Ross Stagner *et al.*, "Dual Allegiance to Union and Management (A Symposium)," *Personnel Psychology*, Vol. 7, pp. 41–80.

of the workers to get more money without cooperating in the goal-seeking activity of the company. They want more pay without doing more for the company—a fine example of the motivation the executive has attributed to them. But when the work-situation is made intrinsically satisfying, this conflict does not arise.

The union leader who knows he is dealing with a political institution and recognizes the importance of getting "a little something for everybody" in a settlement has, by and large, done a better job of morale-engineering than the corporation executives. The unions have been fairly ingenious in devising ways by which individuals obtain feelings of satisfaction of a personal nature through group action. Management, by and large, has neglected this approach. As far as I can see, this is not a necessary consequence of any psychological law. I do think, however, that it represents the major challenge to managerial skill and wisdom at the present time.

# READINGS RELATED TO CHAPTER VIII

## Influence: A Key to Effective Leadership in the First-line Supervisor[*]

*Donald C. Pelz*

The spotlight these days is very much on the first-line supervisor. The reasons are obvious—and good ones. The first-line supervisor is the most direct link between employees and management. On him hangs much of the responsibility for seeing that employees understand and support the goals adopted by management. And in turn he is responsible for seeing that the employees' difficulties and complaints get transmitted up the line and that these problems get solved. Much management attention has therefore been concentrated on this link. Are your employees unhappy or unproductive? The popular panacea is: Put your first-line supervisors through another training course.

But what is this flood of training supposed to accomplish? How is the effective supervisor supposed to act? Everyone has his opinion on this score, and numerous studies have been conducted, but there still is no clear-cut answer based on scientific evidence. This problem has therefore occupied a central position in several studies conducted at the University of Michigan's Survey Research Center as part of its Human Relations Program.

Since the start of the program, we have been forced more and more to a major realization: that the question we started with—what are the

* From *Personnel*, vol. 29, pp. 209–217, 1952. Reprinted by permission of the American Management Association,

methods for effective supervision?—may not have any one answer! This doesn't mean that there are no rules for supervision. Rather, it means that before we can give an answer we must know what kind of an organization it is that we are dealing with and *what kind of relations the individual supervisor and his group have to the organization.* To talk of "good supervision" or "poor supervision" as if the supervisor and his group existed in a social vacuum may be meaningless.

To put it in technical terms, the surrounding organization and the way the group fits into the organization may "condition" the way in which the behavior of the supervisor affects his employees. It is likely that a great many organizational factors can act as "conditioners" of supervisory leadership. The focus of this article is on just one of these organizational factors: what we can call the supervisor's *power* or, more accurately, his *influence within the department.* How much weight does the supervisor swing? Is he simply a work leader who passes on instructions from higher-ups? Or is he an influential person whose opinions are respected and sought by his superiors? Our findings to date show that the low-influence supervisor may have to behave rather differently toward employees from the high-influence supervisor, if maximum employee morale is to be achieved.

## The Drama of Research

But we are jumping ahead of the story. The idea just expressed has emerged only after long and tedious searching. Discovery of scientific truth is a little like discovering the culprit in a detective novel. You are faced at first with a meaningless jumble of tangled facts. Only after a long search, full of ventures up blind alleys, do you finally piece together a systematic explanation in which many facts fit together and reinforce each other. Instead of looking for "whodunit," of course, you are looking for "whatduzit"—what are the factors, the conditions, the elements in the situation that produce the tangle of facts which you have observed?

One of your difficulties is that very likely you will have not one culprit but many, and all will be at work affecting the data you are trying to explain. Another major difficulty is that your culprits may be so many "undercover agents"; unless you suspect they are there, and go out to find them, you may never know that they exist. That was the case with our crucial factor of supervisory "power or influence," which was uncovered only rather late in the specific investigation reported here.

## The Setting of the Investigation

This particular search had its beginning in 1948, and the results to be described were not achieved until three years later. As part of the Human Relations Program, we were invited by the Detroit Edison Company to undertake a study of its employees' attitudes. The company employs well over 10,000 people and provides Detroit and the surrounding areas with electric power and other utilities. Its employees perform a wide range of functions, such as constructing and operating power plants, building and maintaining power lines, reading meters, collecting money, conducting electrical research, and many other office and manual jobs. Some 8,000 nonsupervisory employees filled in a paper-and-pencil questionnaire; all supervisory and managerial personnel in the company were given a personal interview.

The Detroit Edison Company has encouraged and supported several scientific studies of this and other material. One of these studies was the problem tackled by the author: What attitudes and behavior in the first-line supervisor lead to greater employee satisfaction? We were especially interested in employee satisfaction regarding the supervisor himself, but we were also interested in satisfaction regarding the job, fellow-employees, and the company in general.

We were concerned with a number of supervisory behaviors. For example, to what extent should the supervisor involve his employees in the decision-making process, if employee satisfaction and job performance are to be of the highest? This area is part of what is often referred to as "democratic supervision."

Another part of the same concept is what might be called the supervisor's "equalitarian philosophy." Should the supervisor remain dignified and aloof? Or should he mingle freely with his employees as a social equal? These behaviors are indicative of the "social distance" between the supervisor and his group. What degree of social distance has the best effect on employee attitudes?

A third problem, somewhat similar to these, is the matter of "identification" with management or with employees. In the case of conflicts between what management wants and what the employees want, does the supervisor go to bat for management or does he go to bat for the employees? These and many other aspects of supervisory behavior toward employees and toward superiors were explored in personal interviews, and quantitative measures of them were obtained.

## Installment No. 1: Looking into Effective Supervision

The first installment of our detective story was begun with no expectation that other installments would follow. It was intended to answer questions, not to raise them. It was designed, specifically, to answer the following single question: What are the characteristics of effective supervisors —effective, that is, in term of high employee satisfaction? The method selected in an attempt to find the answer was a simple one. A criterion of effective leadership was chosen in terms of the work group's "over-all satisfaction" (you might, loosely, call it "group morale"). A measure of over-all satisfaction was obtained by combining seven satisfaction items answered by each employee, and group averages were then computed. Forty high-satisfaction and 30 low-satisfaction groups were pulled out, and their supervisors were compared. We inspected differences between these two sets of supervisors in terms of 50 items of information obtained from interviews with them, expecting to find a number of items which distinguished between the two sets of supervisors. The items on which they differed might therefore be said to account in part for the high or low satisfaction within their groups.

The tantalizing fact was that only 6 out of the 50 items showed differences large enough to be trustworthy—technically, large enough to be "statistically significant at the 5 per cent level of confidence." This was hardly more than we should expect solely from chance. Firm conclusions cannot be based on so insubstantial a foundation.

What was wrong? What psychological or sociological culprits were concealing the clear-cut facts we had hoped to find?

## Installment No. 2: A New Strategy

If you take a close look at the method used in the first analysis, you find a hidden assumption there. Implicitly, we were assuming that a certain leadership practice will produce high employee satisfaction in *all* groups. But sober and common-sense reflection shows that this assumption is not necessarily true. For example, self-reliant employees will probably enjoy a supervisor who thrusts responsibility upon them; dependent employees will probably dislike a supervisor who does this. These two reactions will simply cancel each other out if all employees are thrown together, as was the case in the first analysis.

In Installment No. 2 of our detective story, then, a different strategy was used. Here different types of employees and different types of situations were studied separately rather than being thrown together. We tried to anticipate what types of employees or situations would react in different ways to the same supervision. For example, men and women were studied separately; those performing white-collar or office work were treated apart from those doing blue-collar or manual work; those in small work groups (10 employees or under) were studied separately from those in large work groups, and so on.

This approach paid off. The relationships between supervisory behaviors and employee attitudes emerged much more clearly. Trustworthy or statistically significant results were now approximately seven times as numerous as chance alone would yield. But now many of the relationships seemed contradictory!

For example, there was the supervisory measure of "taking sides with employees in cases of employee-management conflicts." In small work groups, employees thought more highly of the leader who took their side in cases of conflicts with management. But, in large white-collar work groups, employees were significantly *less* satisfied with such a supervisor; they preferred the supervisor who sided with management. Other supervisory measures showed similar contradictory results.

Why? What was there about the large work group situation that produced some relationships apparently opposite to those found in small work groups?

## An "Undercover Agent" Uncovered

It seemed likely that some factors which we had not attempted to measure up to now were producing these puzzling results. A number of candidates for this "undercover agent" role were suggested. One of the most promising was the idea of the first-line supervisor's *power or influence within the department*. While new to this particular study, such a factor had been hinted at in one of the previous studies conducted under the Human Relations Program. In the home office of a large insurance company, it was possible to locate a number of "high-producing" work groups and a number of "low-producing" groups. The supervisors of these groups were compared on a number of items (in a manner similar to that used in our own first analysis). For example, what practice did the supervisor follow in recommending promotions for his employees?

It was found that the supervisors of high-producing work groups in the insurance company played one of two roles in the promotion process. Either they made recommendations which generally went through, or they made no recommendations at all. In contrast, the supervisors of low-producing work groups often recommended promotions, but these generally did not go through. To recommend promotions was not, as such, related to high employee productivity. A more basic factor seemed to be operating—the supervisor's power within the department. The high-producing supervisors were more realistic about their power; they entered the promotion process only when they could influence the outcome.

Could such a factor of power or influence within the department be partly responsible for the contradictory effects obtained in our second analysis? It seemed a worth-while avenue to explore.

The whole area of the first-line supervisor's power or influence seems to be a critical one. One effect of the centralization of business, of piling up supervisory layer on top of supervisory layer, is inevitably to take away power or control from the lower levels of supervision. And one of the arguments given in favor of decentralization is that in relatively small organizations the immediate supervisors (and all other supervisors) have more control over the destiny of their respective groups.

But it was one thing to suspect activity on the part of this undercover agent called "power" or "influence," and another thing actually to locate and measure it. We searched through the supervisory data hoping to find items that would yield a measure of the supervisor's influence within the department. Three items seemed to do this: the amount of *voice he felt he had in his superior's decisions,* the amount of *autonomy* he had with respect to his superior (as indicated by the nonfrequency of contact with the superior), and his *salary* (a general indication of his status, level of responsibility, etc.). These three items were combined into a single measure which we called "influence."

## A Theory of Influence

Kurt Lewin was fond of saying that "nothing is so practical as a good theory." A theory is like the detective's "reconstruction of the crime." It forces the researcher to piece the facts together to see if they jibe with each other, to find out if there are missing parts, and to determine where to look for the crucial facts that may solve the mystery. A good theory, like a useful reconstruction, is not a complete picture. It leaves out a great many facts, but it highlights the essential ones. The particular theory of influence that seemed to fit the present situation looked like this:

1. Employees (and for that matter the members of any group) will think well of the leader who helps them to satisfy their needs, to achieve their goals.
2. If a supervisor (or any group leader) has considerable influence within his organization, then when he behaves so as to help employees toward their goals, he will achieve concrete benefits for them. Consequently, their satisfaction regarding him will increase. Not his good intentions, but his actual accomplishments, are what pay dividends in employee satisfaction.
3. We must also recognize that the supervisor's power can be used to harm as well as to help employees. Sometimes the supervisor is mainly a disciplinarian, a checker-up, a pusher whose chief function is to see that employees hew to the line. If a supervisor behaves mainly in this way, and if he has considerable influence, then he can be a substantial restraint on employees, and they are likely to be dissatisfied with him or even fearful of him.
4. On the other hand, if the supervisor has *little* power or influence, then neither his helpful behavior nor his restraining behavior will have much concrete effect on the employees. He cannot help them to get what they are after or restrain them substantially. Neither behavior will have any marked effect on their satisfaction. In fact, the more helpful he tries to be, the more we might expect to find some increase in *dis*satisfaction, because employees' hopes will have been aroused, only to be disappointed.

These four points lead us to expect something like the picture of relationships between supervisory behavior and employee satisfaction shown in Figure 1. If such a picture should emerge, we could say that the supervisor's influence "conditions" his leadership. That is, his amount of influence (high or low) determines whether his supervisory behavior will cause employee satisfaction to rise (the solid line) or to fall (the dotted line).

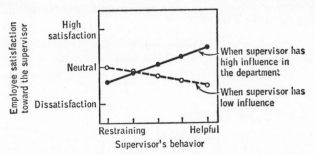

Figure 1. Theoretical Effect of Supervisor's Behavior on Employee Satisfaction.

## Installment No. 3: How Influence "Conditions" Leadership Behavior

For the third analysis of our study, to determine how the supervisor's influence "conditions" the effects of his leadership behavior, two kinds of supervisory behavior were selected: the degree to which he "takes sides with employees or with management" and the degree of his "social closeness" to employees. In general, it seems likely that the supervisor who sides with employees and is socially close to them will behave more in the "helpful" direction. And, in general, it seems likely that the supervisor who sides with management and who is socially distant from employees will behave more in the "restraining" direction.

We then computed statistical measures to find out how these supervisory behaviors seemed to affect various employee attitudes. A "positive" measure of relationship would indicate that employee satisfaction was higher under those supervisors who tended to take the employees' side and who were socially close to employees. A "negative" relationship would indicate the reverse: Employees were more dissatisfied under supervisors showing these behaviors.[1]

The results were, in general, pretty much in line with the theory. Data never fit a theory completely; there are too many other factors at work.

[1] A technical note: The strength of these positive or negative relationships was measured with product-moment correlations. Several employee attitudes were used, the main one being an index of employees' satisfaction with the way the supervisor himself was doing his job. The relationships were measured separately under influential and under noninfluential supervisors for each of seven different types of employees or work situations. That is, separate analyses were performed for white-collar *vs.* blue-collar occupations, men *vs.* women, small groups *vs.* large groups, and groups covered by a union contract *vs.* groups not so covered. Several statistical controls were used which need not be described here.

But note the striking correspondence between the theoretical diagram shown in Figure 1 and some of the actual results shown in Figure 2.

Figure 2 shows that under influential supervisors (solid line) an increase in "siding with employees" is accompanied by a general rise in employee

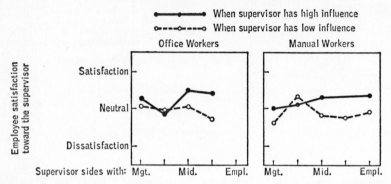

Figure 2.  Relationship of Supervisor's "Taking Sides" to Employee Satisfaction.

satisfaction. But under noninfluential supervisors (dotted line) the same behavior produces no rise but a slight drop in employee satisfaction.

This diagram shows only one aspect of the results. The complete picture is given in Figure 3. For the group of high-influence supervisors, we

```
              + = positive relationships (r = +0.06 or greater)
              0 = zero            "        (r = ±0.05 or less)
              − = negative        "        (r = −0.06 or greater)
High-influence supervisors    ++++++++++++++++++++000−−−−−−
Low-influence supervisors     ++++++++00000000−−−−−−−−−−−−
```

Figure 3.  All Relationships between Supervisory Behaviors and Employee Satisfactions.

obtained 28 measures of relationship between the supervisory behavior and various employee attitudes in different types of situations. For the low-influence supervisors, we obtained a parallel set of 28 measures. According to the theory, we should obtain generally positive relationships under high-influence supervisors but zero or negative relationships under low-influence supervisors.

Under high-influence supervisors, in 19 times out of 28 we find that "siding with employees" and "social closeness" are accompanied by some rise in employee satisfaction. (Seven of the positive correlations are large enough to be "statistically significant," a result which is 11 times better than chance.) But, under low-influence supervisors, these supervisory behaviors are accompanied by a rise in satisfaction only 8 times out of 28; a loss in satisfaction (negative effect) is the more common result.

All measures of relationship were modest in size. But the positive results under influential supervisors were sufficiently uniform that the total set may be regarded as highly trustworthy (or "statistically significant").

It seems fairly clear, then, that a supervisor's influence or power within the department does "condition" the way his supervisory behavior affects employee attitudes. It is plausible to conclude that *the supervisory behaviors of "siding with employees" and "social closeness to employees" will tend to raise employee satisfaction only if the supervisor has enough influence to make these behaviors pay off in terms of actual benefits for employees.*

## Light on Mystery of Installment No. 2

The contradictory effects which we discovered in the second analysis can be solved in part by these new findings, although—as always with social data—an explanation in terms of any single factor is never complete. Further analysis of the data showed that in this company's *small* groups the supervisors who sided with employees also tended to be the ones who had high influence and could get results when they attempted to do something. On the other hand, in this company's *large* work groups the supervisors who took the employees' side were generally the ones without influence; they could not follow up their helpful attempts with concrete gains for employees; as a result, employees were less satisfied than if their supervisors had maintained a neutral position. Facts such as these helped to clear up the mystery of our previous findings.

We do not know at the present time whether these facts about work-group size and supervisor's influence are true of other companies. We must be careful not to claim a general principle here before studying more companies.

## Implications for Administrators

According to these findings, if an influential supervisor attempts to help employees achieve their goals, his efforts will tend to succeed. Concrete results will be achieved, and therefore employee satisfaction will rise. But —according to the data—if a noninfluential supervisor tries to get the same results, his efforts may often fail. Employee expectations will be frustrated, and consequently their satisfactions will not rise and may even fall.

Such findings have several implications:

1. It may not be possible to give supervisors a universal set of rules on how to behave so as to maximize their employees' satisfaction. What each man should do or should not try to do will depend, among other things, on how much weight he carries within the organization. In general, the supervisor should probably not attempt to do more for his employees than he can reasonably hope to accomplish.

2. The same principle applies to the current emphasis on the training of first-line supervisors. If the supervisors lack the authority or the influence to put the training into practice, in a way that produces concrete changes, then perhaps we may question whether the training should be given at all. Training courses should urge the supervisor to introduce changes only in matters where he has considerable authority or where he has the real support of supervision at higher levels. Otherwise the result may only be frustration for himself and his group.[2]

3. Even further, it may in some cases be necessary to *increase* the amount of influence given to first-level supervisors—by increasing their voice in higher decisions, by delegating more autonomy to them. These are substantial changes, not to be suggested lightly. But it may be that many training courses cannot improve the effectiveness of supervisory leadership unless management is willing to give a larger share of influence to this supervisory level.

4. At the same time, it becomes essential to examine the effects of giving supervisors a larger voice, as many writers on administration are advising. How is this increased power to be used? It is a potential source of threat to employees as well as a benefit. Perhaps it should not be undertaken unless steps are taken simultaneously to make sure the increased power is used in helpful ways rather than in restraining and hindering ways.

5. And, finally, from the long-range standpoint of the science of management, it becomes clearer that "group leadership" and "organization" are not distinct concepts but are inseparably intertwined. The organization "conditions" the effects of leadership, and probably the reverse is true. An organization cannot be understood simply by breaking it up into small groups and studying them in isolation. Nor can we understand the way a leader relates to his group unless we also study how they both relate to the rest of the organization.

[2] This same conclusion about training is illustrated in an article by Monroe Berkowitz called "Education of Foremen Can Be Dangerous," in the March, 1952, issue of *Personnel*.

$$Supervisory\ and$$
$$Administrative\ Behavior^*$$

*Basil S. Georgopoulos*
*Floyd C. Mann*

## Supervisory Skills: Administrative, Human Relations, and Technical Skills

The preceding discussion of the concept of supervision has direct implications concerning the essential skills that an occupant of the generic office of supervisor must have. To perform the functions required to coordinate the activities of one organizational family with another, the supervisor must have *administrative competence.* To integrate organizational objectives with individual member needs, he must have *human relations competence.* And to accomplish his other assigned tasks, including the performance of concrete day-to-day work functions and specialized subobjectives, he must possess *technical competence.*

The marked division of labor and high degree of specialization that characterize hospitals, as well as other large-scale organizations, require that the occupants of supervisory positions have at least the minimum technical competence necessary to understand and direct the work being done within their respective organizational units. The higher the degree of specialization and differentiation, moreover, the greater the need for supervisors with technical competence is likely to be. *Technical skill,* or competence, as used here, refers to the ability to use pertinent knowledge, methods, techniques, and equipment necessary for the performance of specific tasks and activities, and for the direction of such performance. Fundamentally, it involves an understanding of, and proficiency in, a specific class of functions in the organization. This includes not only concrete motoric skills of doing things, however, but also the abstract orientations and basic frames of reference that are normally associated with particular professional roles and affiliations. The technical skills of a head nurse, for example, would encompass such highly specialized activities as giving intravenous injec-

* From *The Community General Hospital,* The Macmillan Company, New York, 1962, Chap. 9. Reprinted by permission.

tions, and such value orientations as implied in continuing to read, study, master new techniques, and generally keep up with the profession and improve her standing as a professional nurse. Technical skills are acquired through formal training in professional schools, informal on-the-job training, and combinations of academic and internship or apprenticeship programs. Once acquired, moreover, they tend to remain stable and are seldom lost.

Just as technical skills are primarily concerned with task-centered competence, human relations skills are concerned with the ability to work with other people effectively. In the case of supervisors, the other people involved are one's subordinates, superiors, and colleagues at the same organizational level, i.e., other supervisors. *Human relations skill,* then, refers to the ability to use pertinent knowledge and methods of working with people or through people. It includes an understanding of general principles of human behavior, particularly those principles which involve the regulation of interpersonal relations and human motivation, and the skillful utilization of this understanding in day-to-day interaction with others in the work situation.

The supervisor with human relations skills not only understands how the principles of behavior affect others but himself as well. Furthermore, these skills involve not only consideration and support for others and their problems, but also the ability of the supervisor to motivate his subordinates sufficiently so that they may perform their assigned tasks effectively, and the ability to integrate the goals of individuals with the objectives of the organization. The supervisor must be able to identify those needs of others which are central to their self-concept, and to relate these to organizational objectives in a manner that is psychologically meaningful and rewarding to them. At times, this will mean coordinating the goals of one's subordinates with those of people in higher levels; at other times, it will mean creating, modifying, or shifting either organizational or individual goals so that a balance or integration between the two may be attained. Basically, the present class of skills involves managing the emotional and motivational dimensions of interpersonal relations in an organization.

The human relations skills of a head nurse, for example, would include getting members of the nursing team to work together cooperatively; getting them to do the best they can as individuals; being available to discuss their problems; and helping them with their work when necessary or requested. They would also involve, on occasion, the development of the aspirations of her subordinates regarding the contribution they might make to the hospital and the larger community. The head nurse might also on occasion find herself in the position of vigorously defending the behavior of her subordinates before others, or trying to modify the actions of her superiors for the benefit of her work group. In general, it would be her function to build and maintain the loyalty and commitment of her subordinates to the hospital and its goals.

The third class of basic supervisory skills deals with administrative competence. *Administrative skill,* or competence, refers to the ability of the supervisor to think and act in terms of the total organizational system within which he operates—in terms of the organization as a system of people and physical objects, with its own image, structure, and process, which functions as a complex problem-solving arrangement for the purpose of attaining particular objectives. The emphasis here is on understanding and acting according to the objectives of the total organizational system, rather than on the basis of the goals and needs of one's immediate work group only. Administrative skills include such things as planning, programing, and organizing the work; assigning the right tasks to the right people; giving people the right amount of responsibility and authority; and coordinating the efforts and activities of different organizational members, levels, and departments. In short, administrative skill requires an ability to conceptualize and comprehend the organizational system as a whole, and to fit individual parts in the overall organizational frame. The administrative skills of a head nurse, for example, would involve an ability to organize effectively the work of the members of her nursing team, to relate nursing functions to medical activities, and even to coordinate work among different groups and shifts. They would also involve the ability to translate broad organizational aims into sets of specific tasks and processes that are capable of being implemented, and the ability to allocate resources and distribute people and work properly.

In summary, we have suggested three classes of essential skills that are normally required of supervisors and those in administrative positions in the organization—technical skills, human relations skills, and administrative skills.[1] Technical skills pertain to "know-how" competence regarding particular tasks for which the supervisor is responsible. Human relations skills concern the understanding of organizational members as people with their own problems and needs, or the understanding of the emotional and motivational dimensions in interpersonal relations. Administrative skills deal with the demands of the organization for unified activity and integration. Thus, the three kinds of skills respectively concern tasks, people, and organization.

[1] As early as 1953–54, Mann and Dent (21) found it necessary to distinguish between technical competence and human relations competence in a study of supervision. In subsequent studies, dealing with problems of supervision and automation, Mann and Hoffman (23) and Mann and Williams (24) found the distinction among technical, human relations, and administrative competence a fruitful one. Katz (19), in a study of the skills of effective administrators, also made a distinction among technical, human relations, and, what he terms conceptual, skills.

## The Supervisory Skill-Mix

While all supervisors, regardless of their level in the organization, must have some minimum technical skill, some minimum human relations skill, and some minimum administrative skill, not all of them are likely to be equally strong in these different skills. More importantly, what may be an effective combination of skills for supervisors at one organizational level may not be an effective skill-mix for supervisors at another level. The relative importance of each kind of supervisory skill is likely to vary markedly across organizational levels. At the lower levels of the organization, for example, we expect that technical and human relations skills are the most important. At intermediate levels, technical skills are likely to be less important and administrative skills more important. And at the top managerial and administrative levels, administrative skills are likely to be the most important. Human relations skills are probably important for supervisors at all levels but, in view of our earlier suggestion that the motivational problem is not as acute at the higher levels, they are likely to become comparatively less important as one moves up the hierarchy. Certainly, they are no substitute for either administrative competence at the top or technical competence at the bottom levels of the organization.

Theoretically, therefore, one may suggest a paradigm in which technical skills become less important and administrative skills more important for supervisors at each succeeding higher level in the organization, with human relations skills being about equally important for supervisors at all levels, but somewhat less crucial at the very top level. Figure 1 presents schematically our conception of the relative importance of the three kinds of supervisory skills for different levels of supervision. Elsewhere, Katz (19) has proposed a similar view concerning the relativity of the supervisory skill-mix at different levels in an organization.

In addition to the variations in skill-mix required at different organizational levels, there is typically a good deal of variation in skill requirements at different times. Early in the life of an organization, technical and human relations skills are probably essential; later, as the organization becomes more complex, administrative skills become increasingly crucial. Similarly, during periods of rapid change, technical skills are likely to become very important at higher organizational levels. With the initiation of reorganization, or when new technology is introduced in the system, upper-level supervisory personnel have to draw more heavily on their technical competence at the early stages. During such a period of transition, the problems faced by the organization are basically of a technical character, and their solution depends very greatly on thorough command of specialized knowledge and technical-analytical ability. But, in the latter stages of reorganization and change, human relations skills assume greater importance once again; after the technical difficulties have been overcome, the remaining organizational problems are frequently of the human relations variety.

Thus, it is not enough to think in terms of the combination of the three kinds of supervisory skills required at different organizational levels. It is also necessary to consider the time dimension—how their combination,

Relative importance of different supervisory skills

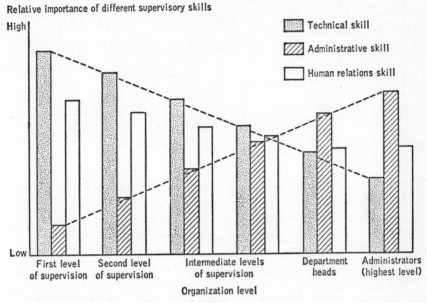

Figure 1

for a particular level, must vary over time. In this connection, on the basis of their findings from a study of the introduction of electronic data-processing equipment in an organization, Mann and Williams (24) point out that, over an extended period of change, different combinations of the three basic supervisory skills were required of different supervisory levels at the same time, and of the same supervisory level at different times.

## References

19. Katz, R. L.: "Skills of the Effective Administrator," *Harvard Business Rev.,* **33**:33–43, 1955.

21. Mann, F. C., and Dent, J. K.: "Appraisals of Supervisors and the Attitudes of their Employees in an Electric Power Company." Survey Research Center, 1954.

23. Mann, F. C., and Hoffman, L. R.: *Automation and the Worker: A Study of Social Change in Power Plants.* New York: Holt, 1960.

24. Mann, F. C., and Williams, L. K.: "Organizational Impact of White Collar Automation." In *Proceedings of Eleventh Annual Meeting of Industrial Relations Research Association,* Chicago, December 1958. Publication No. 22, 1959, 55–69.

# Leadership Practices in Relation to Productivity and Morale*†

*Robert L. Kahn*
*Daniel Katz*

In applying the principles discovered in laboratory studies to life situations, there is always the problem of the generality and meaningfulness of the findings. Can the more complex social situation be interpreted adequately in terms of the results of laboratory experiments? Will the use of the generalization from the group experiment be effective in the life situation, where the game is being played for higher stakes, and where people are playing for keeps? The direct study of natural groups and organizations may not necessarily challenge the validity of laboratory research, but it can demonstrate its importance or its triviality.

In a program of research on human relations in group organization, the Survey Research Center of the University of Michigan has attempted a direct attack upon the conditions and causes of worker productivity and worker morale through field studies, surveys and field experiments. In this program, the initial research was not planned around tight mathematical models of the hypothetico-deductive variety but was more empirically oriented, seeking to discover and explore those variables which assumed significant proportions in the industrial situations studied. Nevertheless, the

* From Dorwin Cartwright and Alvin Zander (eds.), *Group Dynamics, Research and Theory,* chapter 29, pages 554–570. Copyright © 1953, 1960, by Harper & Row, Publishers, Incorporated. This chapter was prepared especially for the Cartwright and Zander volume and is reprinted here by permission of the publishers.

† The findings and many of the interpretations are taken from several of the major studies in the program of human relations research conducted by the Survey Research Center of the University of Michigan. This program is supported by grants from the Office of Naval Research and the Rockefeller Foundation, and by contracts with the organizations in which the studies were conducted. The studies cited were directed by Gerald Gurin, Eugene Jacobson, Robert L. Kahn, Nathan Maccoby, Floyd C. Mann, Nancy C. Morse, and Donald C. Pelz. The results of these studies are presented more fully in the publications listed following this chapter.

contributions of the Lewinian school, the self-realization notions of Dewey and Rogers, and the realistic analyses of institutional structure by Allport and Mayo and Roethlisberger had a good deal to do with the directions of the research.

Field studies of this sort have the great advantage over laboratory situations of dealing directly with social realities and thus meeting the problem of applicability and generalization to social phenomena, provided they can deal with variables at some level of generality. They suffer, however, in comparison to laboratory experiments with respect to control in the identification and manipulation of variables. In the Human Relations Program, therefore, methodological emphasis was placed upon checks and controls in the field studies undertaken. Unquantified anthropological observation was replaced by standardized interviews with carefully defined samples of respondents. Impressionistic accounts of attitude and morale, as in the Hawthorne studies, were replaced with measures of workers' psychological responses. Effects of supervisory practices were not judged on the basis of what management assumed the results to be. Independently derived measures were employed in testing relationships between factors. For example, supervisory behavior was measured independently of its effects upon productivity and morale of workers. Interestingly enough, this is the first time such measurements have ever been taken in an effort to get at the functional relationships in an ongoing organization. Moreover, where productivity was taken as the dependent variable, supervisory practice as the independent variable, and morale as the intervening variable, the groups which were compared were equated on all the technological factors which could affect productivity.

Studies in this program of research have now been conducted in a variety of industrial situations, and in civilian and military agencies. These include the home office of an insurance company, maintenance-of-way section gangs on a railroad, an electric utility, an automotive manufacturer, a tractor company, an appliance manufacturer, and two agencies of the federal government. Some of the major research findings emerging from these projects are summarized in the following pages.

## Differentiation of Supervisory Role

The supervisor with the better productive record plays a more differentiated role than the supervisor with the poor productive record; that is, he does not perform the same functions as the rank and file worker, but assumes more of the functions traditionally associated with leadership. Foremen of railroad section gangs, for example, were found to differ with respect to the amount of time they spent in planning the work and performing special skilled tasks (Table 1). In general, the foremen with the better production records devoted more time to these aspects of their work, according to their own report. They were also perceived by their men as possessing superior planning ability (Table 2). Similarly, in a company manufacturing heavy agricultural and road-building equipment, both the foremen and the men of high producing sections evaluated the quality of planning as superior to that of most other groups.

**TABLE 1. Relation of What Foreman Reports Doing on the Job to Section Productivity (Section Gangs on a Railroad)**

|  | *Supervisory Duties* | | *Non-Supervisory Duties* | | | |
|---|---|---|---|---|---|---|
|  | *Planning; Skilled Tasks* | *Providing Materials to Men; Watching Men* | *Same Things Men Do* | *Keeping up Track* | *Number of Duties Mentioned\** | *N* |
| Foremen of high-producing sections | 42 | 41 | 8 | 7 | 98 | 36 |
|  | 83 | | 15 | | | |
| Foremen of low-producing sections | 25 | 42 | 15 | 14 | 96 | 36 |
|  | 67 | | 29 | | | |

\* The responses total more than 72 because many foremen gave more than one answer.

Another indication of the ability of the high-producing supervisor to differentiate his own function from that of the men is the amount of time which he gives to the work of actual supervision, as contrasted to the time allocated to activities which are not uniquely those of the supervisor. In the studies of clerical workers, railroad workers, and workers in heavy

**TABLE 2. Relation of Men's Perception of Foreman's Planning Ability to Section Productivity (Section Gangs on a Railroad)**

QUESTION: "HOW GOOD IS THE FOREMAN AT FIGURING WORK OUT AHEAD OF TIME?"

|  | *Very Good* | *Pretty Good* | *So-so and Not Very Good* | *Not Ascertained* | *Total* | *N* |
|---|---|---|---|---|---|---|
| Men in high-producing sections | 38% | 48% | 2% | 12% | 100% | 156 |
| Men in low-producing sections | 27% | 54% | 10% | 9% | 100% | 142 |

industry, the supervisors with the better production records gave a larger proportion of their time to supervisory functions, especially to the interpersonal aspects of their job. The supervisors of the lower-producing sections were more likely to spend their time in tasks which the men themselves were performing, or in the paper-work aspects of their jobs (Table 3).

The reverse side of this picture was also revealed in the railroad study, in which statements made by the section hands in low-producing sections indicated a tendency for an informal leader to arise in these sections. For example, in the low sections there was more frequently some one member

**TABLE 3. Relation of Time Spent in Supervision to Section Productivity (Sections in an insurance company; section gangs on a railroad; work groups in a tractor factory)**

QUESTIONS:

INSURANCE COMPANY—"WHAT PROPORTION OF YOUR TIME IS GIVEN TO SUPERVISORY MATTERS? WHAT PROPORTION TO OTHER DUTIES?"

RAILROAD—"HOW MUCH OF YOUR TIME DO YOU USUALLY SPEND IN SUPERVISING, AND HOW MUCH IN STRAIGHT PRODUCTION WORK?"

TRACTOR FACTORY—"HOW MUCH OF YOUR TIME DO YOU USUALLY SPEND IN SUPERVISING THE MEN, AND HOW MUCH IN OTHER THINGS LIKE PLANNING THE WORK, MAKING OUT REPORTS, AND DEALING WITH PEOPLE OUTSIDE YOUR SECTION?"

| *Section Productivity* | *50% or More of Time Spent in Supervising* | *Less than 50% of Time Spent in Supervising* | *Not Ascertained, or Can't Separate Functions* | *Total* | *N* |
|---|---|---|---|---|---|
| Insurance company | | | | | |
| High | 75% | 17% | 8% | 100% | 12 |
| Low | 33 | 59 | 8 | 100 | 12 |
| Railroad | | | | | |
| High | 55 | 31 | 14 | 100 | 36 |
| Low | 25 | 61 | 14 | 100 | 36 |
| Tractor factory | | | | | |
| 97–101% | 69 | 31 | 0 | 100 | 52 |
| 91–96% | 59 | 41 | 0 | 100 | 71 |
| 86–90% | 48 | 52 | 0 | 100 | 89 |
| 80–85% | 41 | 59 | 0 | 100 | 69 |
| 50–79% | 54 | 46 | 0 | 100 | 35 |

of the group who "spoke up for the men when they wanted something." Apparently the informal organization in the low groups compensated in some respects for the abdication or misdirected leadership of the foremen, but not without some losses in total effectiveness (Table 4).

The recognition by the supervisor of the importance of giving more time to his leadership role was also reflected in the morale findings. In the tractor company, for example, the men supervised by foremen who reported spending more than half their time in actual supervision not only had higher production records, but were more satisfied with the company than the men whose supervisors gave their time primarily to other aspects of the job.

Moreover, in the same company the men with the highest morale as measured in terms of satisfaction with job, supervisor, and company were those who perceived their supervisors as performing a number of broad, supportive functions. Almost all employees, of high or low morale, reported that their supervisors enforced the rules and kept production up,

**TABLE 4. Relation of Men's Perception of a Group Spokesman to Section Productivity (Section Gangs on a Railroad)**

QUESTION: "IS THERE SOME ONE MAN IN THE SECTION WHO SPEAKS UP FOR THE MEN WHEN THEY WANT SOMETHING?"

|  | Yes | No | Not Ascertained* | Total | N |
|---|---|---|---|---|---|
| Men in high-producing sections | 9% | 47% | 44% | 100% | 156 |
| Men in low-producing sections | 17% | 37% | 46% | 100% | 142 |

* Consists primarily of employees of whom this question was not asked.

but the high morale employees also reported that their supervisors performed such other functions as on-the-job training, recommending people for promotion and transfer, and communicating relevant information about the work and the company.

The differentiated role of the supervisor apparently affects the productivity of the group in two ways. The attention given to planning has a direct effect upon output in the coordination and organization of the tasks of the group. This is a type of skill of an engineering or institutional sort, in that the technical know-how of the supervisor is brought to bear upon the ordering of the work of the group on a long range basis. The second way in which the supervisor affects productivity is more indirect. He can increase or decrease the motivation of his employees to produce. These two abilities are not necessarily correlated in the same supervisors. But our evidence indicates that either the engineering skill or the human relations skill can increase the performance of the group. The relative importance of these two factors is determined in good part by the degree of freedom in the situation for the given skill to be effectively manifested. If the company is so tightly organized and so centrally controlled that the tasks of even the smallest work groups are prescribed, then the first-level supervisor with extremely high planning ability will not affect the productive process.

## Closeness of Supervision

A second major dimension which appears to discriminate between high- and low-producing supervisors is the closeness with which they supervise, or the degree to which they delegate authority. Although the high supervisors spend more time performing the supervisory functions, they do not supervise as closely as their low-producing colleagues. This general characteristic is reflected in a number of specific research findings. In the insurance study, low-producing supervisors were found to check up on their employees more frequently, to give them more detailed and more frequent work instructions, and in general to limit their freedom to do the work in their own way (Table 5). In the company manufacturing earth-moving equipment, the high-producing workers reported more often that they set their own pace on the job (Table 6).

**TABLE 5. Relation of Closeness of Supervision of Employees to Section Productivity (Sections in an Insurance Company)**

|  | Close Supervision | General Supervision | Not Ascertained | N |
|---|---|---|---|---|
| Heads of high-producing sections | 6 | 5 | 1 | 12 |
| Heads of low-producing sections | 11 | 1 | 0 | 12 |

NOTE.—The findings are based upon an over-all code which defines closeness of supervision as the degree to which the supervisor checks up on his employees frequently, gives them detailed and frequent instructions and, in general, limits the employees' freedom to do the work in their own way. This over-all code is derived from the supervisors' discussions of their jobs.

Closeness of supervision is an interesting example of the necessity for distinguishing between the engineering (or institutional) skill of the supervisor and his human relations skill in motivating people. Close supervision often is employed as an institutional device for insuring that workers fol-

**TABLE 6. Relation of Men's Perceptions of Pace-setting Factors to Individual Productivity (Employees in an Insurance Company)**

QUESTION: "WHAT IS THE MOST IMPORTANT IN SETTING THE PACE FOR YOUR WORK?"

| Employees with Productivity of: | Set Own Pace | Speed of Line Sets Pace | Speed of Machines, Condition of Tools, Set My Pace | Pressure for Production Sets Pace | Other, Unspecified and Not Ascertained | T | N |
|---|---|---|---|---|---|---|---|
| 100–119% | 46% | 14% | 17% | 9% | 14% | 100% | 327 |
| 90–99% | 38 | 12 | 27 | 12 | 11 | 100 | 762 |
| 80–89% | 39 | 11 | 27 | 10 | 13 | 100 | 452 |
| 70–79% | 38 | 11 | 27 | 9 | 15 | 100 | 269 |
| 40–69% | 37 | 5 | 31 | 7 | 20 | 100 | 275 |

low their job assignments correctly and assiduously. But this very practice also has negative morale and motivation implications, and some supervisors may give more freedom to their employees as a way of increasing their motivation. The greater freedom may produce positive results through the satisfaction that the individual has in participation and in self-determination. There is considerable evidence to support this interpretation in the research findings. In the tractor company studied, workers who perceived their foremen as supervising them less closely were better satisfied with their jobs and with the company.

In the same study, each worker was asked how much he had to say about the way his own job was done, and whether he would like to have more or less to say on this subject. Workers who reported having a lot to say about their own work wanted no less, and were relatively high on the three dimensions of morale—satisfaction with job, supervisor, and company. Workers who reported having little say about how their jobs should be done wanted more autonomy in this area, and were relatively dissatisfied with their jobs, their supervisors, and the company. Apparently, close supervision can interfere with the gratification of some strongly felt needs.

There is a great deal of evidence that this factor of closeness of supervision, which is very important, is by no means determined at the first level of supervision. Rather, the first-level supervisor tends to offer to his men the style of supervision which he experiences with his own supervisor. Or to put it another way, the style of supervision which is characteristic of first-level supervisors reflects in considerable degree the organizational climate which exists at higher levels in the management hierarchy. Among the many findings which bear out this interpretation are the following: In the insurance study the low-producing supervisors reported that they were under closer supervision from above than did the high-producing supervisors (Table 7). In the agricultural equipment factory, foremen of high-

**TABLE 7. Relation of Closeness of Supervision of Section Head by His Superior to Section Productivity (Section Heads in an Insurance Company)**

|  | Close or Fairly Close Supervision | Fairly General or Quite General Supervision | Not Ascertained | N |
|---|---|---|---|---|
| On high section heads | 2 | 9 | 1 | 12 |
| On low section heads | 8 | 4 | 0 | 12 |

NOTE.—Closeness of supervision is based on an over-all code, and was defined for coding purposes as the degree to which the section head was given freedom to handle his own problems by his superiors, as compared with the degree to which the superior was directly involved in running the section.

producing sections indicated relatively more freedom or scope of authority. They stated that they were able to plan their own work as much and as far ahead as they wanted to (Table 8). In the railroad study there was a tendency for the foremen of high-producing gangs to report relatively less pressure from above and to be more satisfied with the amount of authority which they had on their job, although these findings were not statistically significant.

There is an additional analysis which bears on the notion that supervisory behavior at the first level is conditioned in great degree by practices of higher management. The general hypothesis was that the relationships between the behavior of first-level supervisors and the attitudes of their

**TABLE 8. Relation of Foremen's Perception of Opportunity for Planning to Section Productivity (Foremen in a Tractor Factory)**

FOREMAN QUESTION: "ARE YOU ABLE TO PLAN YOUR WORK AHEAD AS MUCH AS YOU WOULD LIKE?"

| Foremen of Sections with Productivity of: | Can Plan Ahead as Much as Needed | Sometimes Have Trouble Planning Far Enough Ahead | Usually Can't or Hardly Ever Can Plan Ahead | Total | N |
|---|---|---|---|---|---|
| 97–101% | 37% | 42% | 21% | 100% | 52 |
| 91–96% | 51 | 32 | 17 | 100 | 71 |
| 86–90% | 29 | 41 | 30 | 100 | 89 |
| 80–85% | 29 | 46 | 25 | 100 | 69 |
| 50–79% | 14 | 40 | 46 | 100 | 35 |

employees are importantly conditioned by the organizational milieu in which the first-level supervisors are functioning, and particularly by the amount of their power or influence in the department—"their potential degree of control over the social environment in which their employees are functioning." In other words, the foreman who is given so little freedom or authority by his supervisors that he is unable to exert a meaningful influence on the environment in which he and his employees function will be ineffective in dealing with employees, regardless of his human relations skills. His intended supportive actions may even have a negative effect on employee attitudes, insofar as they encourage expectations which cannot be met by him. The data from this analysis of supervisors in a public utility in general support the hypothesis. Under high-influence supervisors, 19 of 28 correlations between supervisory practices and employee attitudes are positive, though small. Under low-influence supervisors, 20 out of 28 are zero or negative.

### Employee-Orientation

A third dimension of supervision which has been demonstrated to be consistently related to productivity is a syndrome of characteristics which can be called "employee-orientation." The employee-oriented supervisor, in contrast to the production-oriented or institution-oriented supervisor, gives major attention to creating employee motivation. The specific ways in which he does this may vary from situation to situation, but they contribute to a supportive personal relationship between himself and his work group members. Thus in the railroad study, the workers in high-producing groups more frequently characterized their foremen as taking a personal interest in them and their off-the-job problems. This finding was repeated in a study in heavy industry, in which the high-producing employees reported that their foremen took a personal interest in them. High-producing foremen also were more likely to say that the men wanted them to take a personal interest in them, whereas the low-producing foremen were more likely to have the perception that the men resented such a demonstration of interest. It is quite possible that this difference in perception is in part cause and in part effect. The low-producing foreman has a less satisfactory relationship with his employees and he may well be right in thinking that they want no more of the kind of relationship which he offers. At the same time, his conviction that they wish to minimize the relationship undoubtedly contributes to the psychological distance between him and the work group.

Even more consistent relationships were found in those behavior areas which not only reflect smooth interpersonal dealings, but also offer tangible evidence of the supportive intentions of the supervisor. Thus, in the railroad study the high-producing foremen were said by their men to be more understanding and less punitive when mistakes were made (Table 9). They were also more likely to groom employees for promotion by teaching them new things (Table 10).

**TABLE 9. Relation of Men's Perception of Foreman's Reaction to Bad Jobs to Section Productivity (Section Gangs on a Railroad)**

QUESTION: "WHAT DOES THE FOREMAN DO WHEN YOU DO A BAD JOB?"

|  | Foreman Punitive | Foreman Nonpunitive | Not Ascertained | Total | N |
|---|---|---|---|---|---|
| Men in high-producing sections | 35% | 54% | 11% | 100% | 156 |
| Men in low-producing sections | 50% | 36% | 14% | 100% | 142 |

In the insurance study, the high-producing supervisors were more employee-oriented and less production-oriented than their low-producing colleagues. The low supervisors emphasized production and technical aspects of the job, and tended to think of their employees as "people to get the work done," in contrast to emphasizing training people, taking an interest in employees, and considering them primarily as individual human beings. In the same study, the supervisors were asked the question, "Some people feel the job of supervisor is tough because they stand between the workers and management. Do you feel that this is a problem?" The high-producing supervisors were predominantly employee-identified, according to their own report. The low-producing supervisors were, for the most part, management-identified. This general statement was borne out by the supervisors' reactions to two aspects of company policy which at the time of the study constituted problems in morale or employee motivation. In both of these areas, the placement policy and the dining room setup, the high-

**TABLE 10. Relation of Ways Foreman Trains Men for Better Jobs to Section Productivity (Section Gangs on a Railroad)**

QUESTION: "IN WHAT WAY [DOES THE FOREMAN TRAIN MEN FOR BETTER JOBS]?"

|  | Teaches Men New Techniques and Duties | Teaches Men Better or Easier Ways of Doing Usual Jobs | Doesn't Train Men | Not Ascertained | Total | N |
|---|---|---|---|---|---|---|
| Men in high-producing sections | 29% | 21% | 33% | 17% | 100% | 156 |
| Men in low-producing sections | 17% | 24% | 44% | 15% | 100% | 142 |

producing supervisors were more critical and more aware of the situations as sources of employee disaffection than were the low-producing supervisors.

In the study of industrial workers, there was a whole cluster of findings which seems to fit this framework. The employees with highest production records were more likely to report a good over-all relationship with their foreman, in terms of the quality of his supervision, the way they got along with him, and the interest he took in them. In addition, they reported good communications with him; they said that the foreman let them know how they were doing, that he was easy to talk to, that it usually helped to talk over a problem with him, and that he took care of things right away (Table 11). This indicates both a supportive relationship and an effective role in the larger structure. It is perhaps a reflection of the importance of the supervisor's ability to understand and identify himself with the employees that, in this study, the foremen who had previously belonged to a labor organization had better production records than those who had not.

In this study, also, the employee-identification of the higher-producing supervisors was associated with a greater criticism of certain company policies, although at the same time high-producing supervisors were better satisfied with many aspects of their own jobs, and felt that their own superiors were well pleased with their work. But it was the high-producing foremen who in greater numbers felt that their own supervisors were doing less than a very good job, and were no more than fairly good at handling people,

**TABLE 11. Relation of Employee Perceptions of Supervisory Behavior to Productivity (Workers in a Tractor Factory)**

| | *Employees with Productivity of* | | | | |
|---|---|---|---|---|---|
| | 100–119% | 90–99% | 80–89% | 70–79% | 40–69% |
| *Over-all relationship with foreman** | | | | | |
| Better than most | 24% | 21% | 17% | 16% | 14% |
| About the same as most | 71 | 73 | 77 | 76 | 78 |
| Not as good as most | 4 | 5 | 5 | 7 | 7 |
| Not ascertained | 1 | 1 | 1 | 1 | 1 |
| Total | 100% | 100% | 100% | 100% | 100% |
| *Foreman interest in employee†* | | | | | |
| Great deal or quite a lot | 47% | 45% | 46% | 40% | 38% |
| Little or none | 50 | 54 | 52 | 59 | 61 |
| Not ascertained | 3 | 1 | 2 | 1 | 1 |
| Total | 100% | 100% | 100% | 100% | 100% |
| *Foreman communication to employee‡* | | | | | |
| Always or usually know | 59% | 60% | 54% | 49% | 55% |
| A lot of times I don't know or hardly every know | 39 | 39 | 45 | 50 | 45 |
| Not ascertained | 2 | 1 | 1 | 1 | 0 |
| Total | 100% | 100% | 100% | 100% | 100% |
| *Foreman accessibility for discussion§* | | | | | |
| Easy to talk to about most things | 78% | 76% | 78% | 67% | 70% |
| Hard to talk to about many things | 22 | 22 | 22 | 33 | 29 |
| Not ascertained | 0 | 2 | 0 | 0 | 1 |
| Total | 100% | 100% | 100% | 100% | 100% |
| *Foreman action following discussion‖* | | | | | |
| Usually or always does some good | 54% | 47% | 47% | 38% | 44% |
| Sometimes does some good | 30 | 34 | 35 | 40 | 33 |
| Usually does no good or hardly ever does any good | 16 | 18 | 16 | 22 | 22 |
| Not ascertained | 0 | 1 | 2 | 0 | 1 |
| Total | 100% | 100% | 100% | 100% | 100% |
| *Foreman promptness in taking action¶* | | | | | |
| Takes care of things right away | 55% | 52% | 51% | 43% | 52% |
| Sometimes takes care of things right away, sometimes doesn't | 28 | 30 | 28 | 32 | 27 |
| Lets things go | 16 | 17 | 20 | 25 | 20 |
| Not ascertained | 1 | 1 | 1 | 0 | 1 |
| Total | 100% | 100% | 100% | 100% | 100% |
| *Number* | 327 | 762 | 452 | 269 | 275 |

\* "On the whole, how would you say you get along with your foreman?"

† "How much interest does your foreman take in you on the job?" (Significant between .05 and .10 level.)

‡ "Does your foreman let you know how you're doing? Do you know where you stand with him?"

§ "If you have a problem you would like to talk over with your foreman how easy is it to talk to him?"

‖ "If you talk over a problem with your foreman, does it do any good?"

¶ "If there is something that needs to be taken care of, will your foreman do it right away or will he let it go?" (Significant between .05 and .10 level.)

A number of the supervisory characteristics which we have included in the concept of employee-orientation have important effects upon employee satisfaction as well as productivity. This is particularly true for the foreman's giving reasons for forthcoming changes on the job, demonstrating to employees that he holds other aspects of the work situation to be as important as high productivity, and that his concept of reasonable performance is not excessive. In the tractor company, these characteristics were related to job satisfaction, satisfaction with supervision, and satisfaction with the company as a whole.

A related finding appeared when each employee was asked who in the work situation took the greatest interest in him. The workers who felt that the foreman took the greatest interest in them also were getting the greatest psychological return from their employment in terms of satisfaction with job, supervisor, and company.

There is evidence that the quality of employee-orientation, like closeness of supervision, is in part determined by organizational characteristics and is not merely the reflection of personality traits.[1] For example, the tractor foremen who were reported by their men to make a practice of explaining in advance any changes in the job situation said that they were similarly treated by their own supervisors. The replication of supervisory behavior at successive echelons of large organizations is a phenomenon which deserves further study, particularly to reveal the motivational basis for such behavior and the environmental cues on which it depends.

## Group Relationships

The fourth factor which seems to be emerging as a major determinant of productivity in industrial situations involves relationships in the work group. Such a variable was tentatively identified in the insurance study. Employees in the higher-producing groups tended to express a more favorable evaluation of their section (work group) and of their division. This was based on over-all coded ratings of the interview content, and also on specific responses to the question, "How do you think your section compares with other sections in the company in getting a job done?" Several interpretations of this finding are possible. On the one hand it is conceivable that the employees in high-producing groups were simply reporting what they knew to be the objective fact—that their groups had superior work records. However, it is also possible that high involvement in the work group was the cause, and high productivity the effect. Finally, and perhaps most probably, there is the possibility that pride or involvement

[1] Research findings in this area are reported by Ralph M. Stogdill in "Studies in Naval Leadership, Part II," in Guetzkow, H. (Ed.), *Groups, leadership, and men.* Pittsburgh: Carnegie Press, 1951.

in the work group and productivity are interacting variables, and that an increase in either one tends to bring about an increase in the other (Table 12).

**TABLE 12. Relation of Employee Evaluation of Work Group to Section Productivity (Employees in an Insurance Company)**

|  | High Pride | Medium Pride | Low Pride | Total | N* |
|---|---|---|---|---|---|
| Employees in high-producing sections | 33% | 37% | 30% | 100% | 143 |
| Employees in low-producing sections | 10% | 41% | 49% | 100% | 142 |

NOTE.—Evaluation of work group is an index score obtained by summing coders' ratings of responses to the following items:

1. "How well do you think your section compares with other sections in the company in getting a job done?"
2. "How well do you think your division compares with other divisions in the company in getting a job done?"
3. An over-all coder rating of the respondent's degree of identification with his section; and
4. An over-all coder rating of the respondent's degree of identification with his division.

* There were 66 employees in high sections and 68 in low sections who could not be coded on one or more items of this index.

In the railroad study, both the men and the foremen in high-producing groups evaluated their group performances as better than most, even though they had no formal channels of communication through which to learn of the productivity of other groups.

In the factory manufacturing earth-moving equipment, this area was further explored. It was found that high-producing employees more often said that their groups were better than most others at putting out work. They also reported that they felt they were "really a part of their group," in contrast to the lower producers who were more likely to say that they were "included in some ways but not in others," or that they did not really feel that they were members of the group. Moreover, foremen of the higher-producing groups cited their sections as better than most in the way in which their men helped one another out on the job. Foremen of low-producing groups said their sections were not as good as most in this respect. Nor were these responses merely reflecting some general effect for the group (Table 13). There was no difference between high and low producers in the characteristics they ascribed to their groups in the areas of skill, know-how, education, and the like. All this tends to support the notion of team spirit or cohesiveness in the work group as a factor in productivity.

The relationships in the primary group are also important among the determinants of morale, especially satisfaction with the job and with the larger organization. Workers in the tractor company who reported that they really felt a part of their work group, and that they would prefer their present jobs to identical jobs in other groups, tended to be high in satisfaction with job and company (Table 14).

**TABLE 13. Relation of Employee Evaluation of Work Group to Productivity (Workers in a Tractor Factory)**

EMPLOYEE QUESTION: "WHEN IT COMES TO PUTTING OUT WORK, HOW DOES YOUR WORK GROUP COMPARE TO OTHERS?"

| Employees with Productivity of: | Better Than Most | The Same as Most | Not as Good as Most | Not Ascertained | Total | N |
|---|---|---|---|---|---|---|
| 100–119% | 33% | 63% | 2% | 2% | 100% | 327 |
| 90–99% | 32 | 65 | 2 | 1 | 100 | 762 |
| 80–89% | 28 | 67 | 3 | 2 | 100 | 452 |
| 70–79% | 26 | 67 | 7 | 0 | 100 | 269 |
| 40–69% | 21 | 67 | 11 | 1 | 100 | 275 |

Thus in the area of group relationships, as in others, we find that the twin criteria of productivity and morale have many determinants in common. This suggests again that the effect of supervisory behavior on motivation may be basic to understanding productivity differences. Yet the

**TABLE 14. Relation of Group Belongingness to Productivity (Workers in a Tractor Factory)**

EMPLOYEE QUESTION: "DO YOU FEEL YOU ARE REALLY A PART OF YOUR WORK GROUP?" (SIGNIFICANT BETWEEN .05 AND .10 LEVEL.)

| Employees with Productivity of: | Really a Part | Included in Most Ways | Included in Some Ways | Not Ascertained | Total | N |
|---|---|---|---|---|---|---|
| 100–119% | 58% | 24% | 10% | 8% | 100% | 327 |
| 90–99% | 56 | 29 | 10 | 5 | 100 | 762 |
| 80–89% | 51 | 31 | 13 | 5 | 100 | 452 |
| 70–79% | 52 | 28 | 10 | 10 | 100 | 269 |
| 40–69% | 46 | 31 | 15 | 8 | 100 | 275 |

coexistence of high morale and low productivity, or more frequently, low morale and high productivity, is sufficiently common so that no consistent relationship between productivity and morale has appeared in any of these research studies. One explanation of this discrepancy has already been suggested, namely, that the supervisor can increase productivity in two fairly independent ways: either through his engineering skill or through his ability to motivate his men. Another major explanation is that productivity can be increased in some instances by company practices involving negative sanctions which affect morale adversely.

It is possible also that the lack of a consistently high correlation between morale and productivity in these studies reflects the fact that we are dealing with only one measure of the over-all costs of production, namely, the amount at one point in time. If we were to include the costs of turnover, absence, and scrap loss, the correlation with morale might be higher. For example, in the case of a company with high production at a given point in time because of negative sanctions, the impression of over-all efficiency might change if we also had measures of turnover and quality of product.

## Conclusion

We have considered some research findings which suggest four classes of variables to be consistently related to the productivity of an organizational group and to the psychological returns which the group offers its members. These classes of variables—the supervisor's ability to play a differentiated role, the degree of delegation of authority or closeness of supervision, the quality of supportiveness or employee-orientation, and the amount of group cohesiveness—have been developed from a program of studies conducted in complex, ongoing organizations, the majority of them in business or industry.

In reviewing these research findings, one finds confirmation for much of the recent product of small group experimentation by Lewinian psychologists and others. Lewin's work on the decision-making process, the research of Lippitt and White on leadership climate and style, Bavelas' experiments with on-the-job autonomy in pace-setting, the Harwood project of Coch and French, the communications studies of Festinger and his colleagues—all offer results which are in substantial agreement with the findings reported here. Such agreement is especially significant in the light of the differences between most of the small group studies and the work of the Human Relations Program, in method, theory, and research site.

There is much in the experience of the program, however, which reinforces the ideas with which this chapter was begun—that it is necessary to study complex social situations and organizations directly, as well as to attempt laboratory abstractions of their most significant problems and characteristics. This is true not only because such studies facilitate generalization of research results (if they are not phenotypical relationships), but also because a direct grappling with the live organization tends to orient the researcher toward the most real and significant dimensions of organizational structure and function. The study of living organizations, particularly under conditions of change, suggests serious limitations in attempting to understand organizational change in terms of the primary group alone, and even more drastic difficulties in attempting to induce change by dealing only with the primary group. This wholistic emphasis upon the interrelationships in the total structure is of course consistent with the Lewinian point of view.

Primary work groups exist only in a larger organizational context, and many an unsuccessful industrial training program testifies to the almost insurmountable difficulties of producing change by means which fail to take adequate account of that context. To put it another way, the psychological field is an intervening construct and as such is not directly susceptible to manipulation; the field changes when the social psychological environment changes, and such alterations usually involve broad segments of the organization in addition to the group in which change is proposed. The awareness of industrial employees of these organizational characteristics is great. These results suggest that the full motivation of workers in a complex organizational system can be tapped only when some system of functional representation assures them of an element of control in the larger organization as well as the primary group.

## References

1. Jacobson, E., Kahn, R., Mann, F., & Morse, Nancy C. (Eds.): Human relations research in large organizations. *Journal of Social Issues,* 1951, **7,** No. 3.

2. Katz, D., & Kahn, R. L.: Human organization and worker motivation. In L. R. Tripp (Ed.), *Industrial productivity.* Madison, Wisconsin: Industrial Relations Research Association, 1951.

3. Katz, D., Kahn, R. L., Jacobson, E., Morse, Nancy C., & Campbell, A.: The Survey Research Center's ONR program. In H. Guetzkow (Ed.), *Groups, leadership and men.* Pittsburgh: Carnegie Press, 1951.

4. Katz, D., & Kahn, R. L.: Some recent findings in human relations research in industry. In G. E. Swanson, T. M. Newcomb, & E. L. Hartley (Eds.), *Readings in social psychology.* (Revised) New York: Holt, 1952.

5. Katz, D., Maccoby, N., Gurin, G., & Floor, Lucretia: *Productivity, supervision, and morale among railroad workers.* Ann Arbor, Mich.: Survey Research Center, 1951.

6. Katz, D., Maccoby, N., & Morse, Nancy C.: *Productivity, supervision and morale in an office situation. Part 1.* Ann Arbor, Mich.: Survey Research Center, 1951.

7. Pelz, D. C.: *Power and leadership in the first-line supervisor.* Ann Arbor, Mich.: Survey Research Center, 1951.

# Leadership and Supervision in Industry[*]

*Edwin A. Fleishman*
*Edwin F. Harris*
*Harold E. Burtt*

[*Leadership and Supervision in Industry*] describes a research study of the leadership of the first-line industrial supervisor. It notes how that leadership is influenced by a systematic training program for foremen and also by the leadership provided by the foreman's own boss. It determines the relationship of different foreman leadership patterns to the efficiency and morale of their work groups. The project was conducted under the supervision of the Personnel Research Board of the Ohio State University with the co-operation of the International Harvester Company.

There has been considerable interest during the last decade or so in "human relations" training for foremen. Reports have been published about projects in which foremen responded to some type of attitude questionnaire before and after training and did show progress in an understanding of human relations after such training. But these projects did not determine whether the effects were permanent, how they were influenced by the actual work situation in which a foreman operates, or the results such effects had on the over-all efficiency of the industrial enterprise. It was toward a study of these particular aspects that our project was directed.

Our research involved three principal phases. The first determined just what aspects of the foremen's leadership were important for our problem and then developed reliable instruments for measuring those aspects. The second phase used these instruments to determine what happened to the foremen's attitudes as a result of leadership training at a special school and, more important still, the nature of those attitudes and of his super-

* Based on chap. 9, "Summary for Non-Technical Readers," in Fleishman, Harris, and Burtt, *Leadership and Supervision in Industry,* Columbus, Ohio, Bureau of Educational Research, Ohio State University, 1955. Reprinted by permission of Ohio State University. For the present volume Professor Fleishman has re-edited the chapter and included some more recent work.

visory behavior when he returned to his plant. A further question was how his leadership attitudes and behavior were influenced by the type of leadership at the levels above him, or what we call the "leadership climate." The third phase related the different types of leadership to certain criteria of departmental and managerial performance, such as work group absenteeism, grievances, turnover, and accidents, as well as worker attitudes and foreman proficiency ratings.

The major part of the research was done at a motor-truck manufacturing plant, having five thousand employees, which is the largest factory in a city of eighty thousand. Other research data were obtained at the Company's Central School for supervisors in Chicago. This school provides an intensive two-weeks program for foremen sent in from the Company's various plants on a quota basis. The curriculum stresses heavily principles of human relations, but also has courses in Planning and Organizing, Economics, Effective Speaking, etc. Instructional methods include role-playing, visual aids, and group discussion, as well as the conventional lecture and textbook approach.

## Measuring Instruments

The first research phase, as indicated, was the development of devices for measuring leadership behavior and attitudes. The initial focus was on a form, Supervisory Behavior Description, which could be filled out by subordinates to describe their own foremen. It included items like, "He expresses appreciation when one of his men does a good job," or "He rules with an iron hand." For each item, the subordinate checked alternatives, such as *always, often, occasionally, seldom, never,* with reference to his foreman. These same items, with some slight changes in wording, could be used as a Foreman's Leadership Opinion Questionnaire in which the foreman himself indicated how he thought he *should* operate with his particular work group; for instance whether he should "rule with an iron hand" *always, often, occasionally, seldom,* or *never.*

Much research went into the development of these instruments. The first problem was what aspects or underlying factors of leadership we wanted to measure. We benefited here from the previous work of the Personnel Research Board. Originally there was a pool of 1,800 items about leader behavior but this was reduced to 150 on the basis of expert judgment of the staff. A group of three hundred Air Force crew members had answered the 150 items with reference to their commanders. These data then were analyzed to determine the underlying factors which were characteristic of leadership, as indicated by this questionnaire.[1]

The usual method is to get the correlation of each item with every other

[1] The detailed statistical procedure in this project will not be presented here but merely a general description of the method.

item, for instance, the extent to which those who "rule with an iron hand" also "criticize poor work," or whether those who "express appreciation of good work" likewise "accept suggestions for changes." There may be "negative" correlations, too, as when those who always rule with an iron hand never accept suggestions. It is possible to compute a correlation coefficient which may come out between +1.00 and −1.00 and tell the statistician just how close is the relation between any two items. Then a "factor analysis" of this array of intercorrelations is made. This technique assumes that the correlations between all the items may result from just a few underlying factors or dimensions of leadership. Although the analysis determines how many factors are necessary to explain these intercorrelations, we do not know what the factors are because they are just abstract. We do know, however, the "loading" of each item on each factor. For instance, the "iron hand" item might involve very little of the first factor, much of the second factor, and very little of the remaining factors. Then, if we look at the items that have high loadings on a given factor, we may be able to determine what that factor is and name it. In the present case it was necessary to use a modification of this method because of the prohibitively large number of items.

In the present instance, items with high positive loadings on the first factor involved behavior indicating a high degree of two-way communication, mutual trust, rapport and warmth between the leader and his group and more participation in decisions by the group; on the other hand, negative loadings were found for items suggesting authoritarian and impersonal behavior. This factor was identified as "consideration." The second factor had high loadings for items dealing with assigning of tasks, emphasis on production goals, defining channels of communication, and ways of getting the job done. This factor was identified as "initiating structure." Two minor factors were found but need not concern us here.

The next step was to adapt the questionnaire to industrial use. A scoring key was developed for each dimension of leadership which attached most significance to an item with high loading on a given factor and low loadings on the other factors. The questionnaire was then given to 100 foremen attending the Central School, who described their own boss. Starting with the Air Force scoring keys, a completely separate correlational and factor analysis was carried out. Accordingly the instrument was further revised, item by item, selecting items that had the highest correlation with the dimension they were supposed to represent and that were independent of the other dimensions. Some items were discarded. In this process, the two minor factors disappeared. The final result was a reliable instrument and scoring keys to measure "consideration" and "initiating structure," and to measure them quite independently in the industrial context. The keys gave different weights (4, 3, 2, 1, or 0) to the alternative answers (such as *always, often, sometimes, seldom,* and *never*) to each item. Thus, an "always" response to "rule with an iron hand" added zero to a supervisor's consideration score, while "never" would add 4. Total scores on consideration and structure were simply the sums of these item scores within each factor key.

The foregoing analysis dealt mainly with the Supervisory Behavior Description by which a person evaluated his boss. With some revision and item analysis the parallel instrument was devised, the Leadership Opinion Questionnaire, which indicated a supervisor's own attitudes.[2]

The fact that consideration and initiating structure correlate low to zero with each other is an important finding in its own right. This means they are complementary dimensions of leadership and not opposite poles of a single continuum. Supervisors may be high on both, low on both, or high on one and low on the other.

Subsequent use of these questionnaires to measure consideration and initiating structure in other phases of the research tended to indicate the adequacy of the instruments. There was, for instance, good agreement among different persons describing the same supervisor and high stability of estimates of foremen made on two occasions eleven months apart. The analysis just described may seem like a great amount of work, but it is scientifically justified. For if there are defects in the instrument, then those defects will show up in the results obtained with it. For example, a carpenter who used a yardstick 37 inches long would do a weird construction job. We feel that we really did get the "bugs" out of our questionnaires, and thus our results can be accepted with more confidence.

## Immediate Effects of Leadership Training

The next phase of the research used these instruments just described to determine how the leadership of the foreman is influenced by formal leadership training. The training in question was the Central School mentioned earlier. The Leadership Opinion Questionnaire was given to a group of foremen the day they entered the school and the day they finished the course two weeks later. It will be recalled that in this questionnaire the foreman indicated how frequently he *should* conform with whatever the item called for. The blanks were scored for consideration and initiating structure. The results were quite clear, with a general increase in consideration attitudes after training and a decrease in attitudes of initiating structure. . . .

Another way to show the trend would be to compare the average scores before and after training and to note the difference between the averages. In this connection, we must digress to make one statistical point. When

[2] The items in these two forms appear in the original book. The "Leadership Opinion Questionnaire" by Edwin A. Fleishman is available through Science Research Associates, 259 Erie Street, Chicago.

we have a difference between two averages, there is a possibility that it might be just accidental and not represent a real difference between the things we are measuring. This is especially apt to be the case if the scores contributing to an average are scattered rather than bunched near the average, and if we do not have very many scores in the average to begin with. The statistician has formulas which take account of the number of scores and how well they are bunched, and which yield an index that tells whether the difference between the averages is "significant." For instance, we often read that a difference is "significant at the one per cent level of confidence." This means that such a difference could occur less than one per cent of the time by chance. Our results, of course, were interpreted from this standpoint, and appropriate indexes appear in the main discussion.

To return to the discussion of the results, there was an increase in the average consideration score after training which was "significant," and there was likewise a significant decrease in the average initiating structure score. The changes appeared to be due to the training course. The data were further broken down according to foremen who were initially high or low (above or below average) in each dimension. It developed that the general increase in consideration after training was due primarily to changes in those who were initially low in this dimension. However, for initiating structure, both those initially high and low showed a significant decrease after training. Another important finding was the significant increases in the spread of scores after training. The training did not make the group more alike, but more different from one another in these attitudes.

## Permanent Effects of Leadership Training

The increase in consideration might have been expected because much of the program at the Central School was aimed at improved human relations. There was also less initiation of structure, which is surprising since "structure" subjects are also taught. But these results do not indicate what happens when the trained foreman gets back to his plant.

It was not possible to follow a group from school back to a plant because at any given Central School session there might be men from 17 different plants. It was possible, however, to get a comparable answer at the one factory available for our research by comparing foremen who had not been to Central School with foremen who had been there. Actually, we divided the latter into three carefully matched sub-samples, according to the time elapsed since their training—2 to 10 months, 11 to 19 months and 20 to 39 months. One possible source of error was checked at this point; namely, that those who were selected to attend the school might differ from the remainder in some other respect and even those selected early might differ from those selected later. However, no significant differences appeared among the groups in average age, education, years with the company, years as supervisor, or number of men supervised.

The members of these four groups, one untrained and three trained, were given the same Leadership Opinion Questionnaire as that used at Central School in order to measure their *attitudes* in the same two dimensions. It was also possible to get data on their leadership *behavior* by having several workers under each man fill out the form entitled Supervisory Behavior Description.

Gathering these data at the factory posed some administrative problems in the way of maintaining co-operation and safeguarding confidential information. The program was presented to plant officials as a project of Ohio State University parallel to some other leadership studies in progress. The research personnel spent some time around the plant, getting acquainted and being "seen." The foremen had an explanatory letter from the factory manager and were scheduled by the training director, who had good rapport with them. They were assured that no one in the company would see their individual answers. As to the workers, at least three under each foreman were selected at random. They did not write their names on their papers but merely wrote the name of the foreman they were rating, thus assuring anonymity. Several union stewards were included in the first session and co-operation appeared excellent.

We now had available for the four groups of foremen data on their own expressed leadership attitudes and on their leadership behavior as perceived by the workers under them. The next step was to compare the averages for the untrained and trained groups. This comparison showed little differences between the groups, except for a significant tendency for the most recently trained group to be *lower* in consideration behavior than the untrained group. There was a similar drop in consideration attitudes although it was not statistically significant. Moreover, there appeared to be some increases in initiating structure attitudes and behavior for some of the trained groups *versus* the untrained. The close correspondence between attitudes expressed by the foremen and the independent reports of their behavior made by their workers lent further support to the trends indicated.

The striking, and possibly disquieting, thing about all this is the discrepancy between the results of the questionnaire given the foremen at Chicago immediately after the two-weeks school and the results after the foremen's return to the plant. At the school, the men's attitudes change in the direction of more consideration, but the effect does not last. One explanation that occurs to us is that, while the course makes the foreman more concerned with human relations, the course also makes him more aware of his part as a member of management. He is singled out for this special training, and he participates without cost to himself in a program that is obviously expensive. Perhaps the human relations aspect persists long enough for the post-training questionnaire, but what the man takes back to his plant is a tendency to assume more of a leadership role. What is "right" and approved in training may be different from what is "right" in the plant. We shall see presently that the "climate" to which he returns is also a controlling factor.

The discrepancy between the results at Central School and at the plant indicate the danger of evaluating the outcome immediately after the training. There have been quite a few foreman-training projects in which the evaluation has been made this soon. The acid test is the ultimate conduct and attitudes of the foreman back in the work situation.

An additional evaluation of leadership training was made in connection with a "refresher" course which some of the foremen took. This was organized locally, had considerable similarity to the Chicago course, and lasted one week. Two groups of foremen were selected, all of whom had attended the Central School, but one group (experimental) had the local refresher and the other (control) did not. The groups were matched in that they had about the same average scores for consideration and initiating structure before the refresher course was given. The groups were also matched for age, education, years as supervisor, seniority, number of men supervised, and months since attending Central School. Some three months after the experimental group took the refresher course, both groups were evaluated again by the Supervisory Behavior and Leadership Opinion instruments. The differences between the groups were slight, and none of them were statistically significant. The trend, if any, was toward slightly more initiation of structure in the experimental group. Certainly the refresher course did nothing to reinforce the human-relations aspect.

## Leadership Climate

Up to this point, we have noted the discrepancy between the foreman's attitudes immediately after Central School and the attitudes and behavior back home. It is pertinent now to take a look at the home environment, or "climate" as we have called it. The situations to which the different foremen returned varied in leadership climate. Some foremen went back to a boss high in "consideration" and some to a boss low in consideration.

It was possible to measure climate by the instruments already developed, with slight modifications in some cases. Four types of data were used. The foreman's *boss* (General Foreman) filled out the usual Leadership Opinion Questionnaire regarding his own attitudes, telling essentially "How I should lead my foremen." He also filled out one as to "How I think my foremen should lead." Then the foreman filled out the schedule as to "How my supervisor actually leads," and again as to "What my boss expects of me." Each of these four schedules yielded scores on consideration and on initiating structure for the climate in which a foreman worked. However, it did not seem wise to average these four schedules into a single index of climate. They were used separately. On the basis of scores on a leadership-climate instrument, the foremen were divided into those with climates high (above average) in consideration and those low in consideration. This was done likewise for initiating structure. The same procedure was followed for the other three instruments. We then examined the leadership attitudes and behavior of the different foremen operating under these different "climates." The results showed that foremen who operated under leadership climates high in consideration scored significantly higher themselves in both consideration attitudes and behavior. In other words, a boss who was considerate tended to have foremen who believed and behaved that way. With reference to initiating structure, the trend was the same. In a climate high in initiating structure the foremen had higher initiating structure attitudes. Their behavior showed the same tendency although that trend was not statistically significant.

This was the general result of the analysis. But a further breakdown was made for the four matched groups mentioned earlier which differed in the length of time since they had attended Central School; one group had never attended. Curves were plotted for the high and low climates separately. At each point in time the results showed the day-to-day climate to be more important than whether or not the foreman had been to training. To a considerable extent, the specific training in human relations is wasted unless the environment in the plant is also strong in human relations.

We then became concerned in our analysis with what happens to a foreman emotionally, or otherwise, when he learns one point of view at school and then returns to a different "leadership climate" in the plant. We might expect that this experience would be frustrating. Accordingly, we developed a "conflict index" to investigate this point. The index was merely the discrepancy between the foreman's scores on the Leadership Opinion Questionnaire and on the Supervisory Behavior Description. If he felt one way but behaved otherwise, that presumably involved conflict. When we looked at these conflict indexes with reference to climate, it was apparent that there was more conflict on the part of the foremen who returned to a climate either low in consideration or high in initiation of structure. With the *untrained* foremen, however, the climate in which they operated made no difference as far as their own conflict index was concerned. Again we see the interaction of "climate" and training effects.

Another evaluation of the training was made in terms of an index of "leadership adequacy," the degree to which the foreman's behavior conformed with what his own men expected of him. The men had filled out a questionnaire with reference to "How you expect an ideal foreman to act," as well as a form describing the behavior of their own foreman. The difference between scores on these two instruments was the index of "leadership adequacy" used. A comparison of such indexes for trained and untrained foremen showed a tendency for the trained foremen to have higher leadership adequacy on the consideration dimension. No significant tendency was found on the initiation of structure dimension. Further analysis indicated that these results were due primarily to an increase in leadership adequacy for those who returned to climates high in consideration. This is just another indication of the importance of the supervisory climate on the training effects.

It was of passing interest to compare leadership attitudes at the different organizational levels quite apart from any of the other factors. Superintendents, general foremen, foremen, and workers had all filled out questionnaires which indicated their attitudes toward how work groups should be led. The workers were in favor of more consideration and less initiation of structure and differed significantly from the others in this respect. The foremen were intermediate between the workers and higher-level supervisors, but much closer to the latter. The higher up in the hierarchy the less consideration and more structure was expected of the foremen.

## Leadership and Effectiveness

Up to this point, we have said nothing about what is a desirable leadership pattern. One way to find out is to compare foremen with different degrees of consideration and initiating structure on independent criteria of their effectiveness and that of their work groups. For this, we need some indexes of the performance of each foreman's department or work group which we can relate to his leadership attitudes and behavior as measured by our instruments.

After some elimination we developed four objective criteria and two others which depended on some type of judgment or rating. The objective criteria were: absenteeism excluding legitimate absences, accidents that involved a trip to the dispensary, grievances that were actually filed, and employee turnover. These indexes were computed for each foreman's work group during the previous eleven-month period. A further indication of the effectiveness of the foremen was obtained from proficiency ratings made by plant management. Finally, we obtained an index of how well workers in each foreman's group liked working for that foreman.

Before correlating foreman leadership patterns with these various independent criteria, it was desirable to see whether any other variables were cutting across the criteria and influencing the results. For instance, if there was more absenteeism in a certain department, it might happen that the men were older, more of them were married, or the job was unusually hazardous so that the absenteeism was not related to poor leadership at all. The statistician calls such things "contaminating" variables. It was possible to analyze our four objective criteria from this standpoint. The items suspected of contamination were age, education, marital status, skill, seniority, method of pay, hazards, and pleasantness of the job. The last two were obtained from estimates by supervisors at higher levels. The statistical analysis was somewhat involved and will not be discussed here except to indicate that we noted the correlations between the suspected variables and criteria and then determined whether they had some underlying factors in common. The technique of factor analysis mentioned earlier was used. The ultimate goal was to eliminate these underlying "contaminating" factors. There is a straightforward technique (partial correlation) for doing this, once the factors are identified. The four objective criteria, absenteeism, accidents, grievances, and turnover, were "decontaminated" in so far as was statistically possible. Such treatment of the other criteria was not feasible.

We turn first to the relation between the leadership patterns of foremen and the proficiency ratings given them by higher management in the plant. The proficiency estimates were obtained using the "paired comparison" technique in which each rater compared each foreman with every other foreman an equal number of times. Each foreman's proficiency score was the number of times he was rated as more proficient. We found a high degree of agreement among different members of top management on how these foremen were ranked. For each foreman, then, we had a proficiency estimate, a consideration score, and a structuring score. Correlations were then computed. The first analysis was made by divisions. There were five divisions concerned with some aspect of production, and there were three (stores, inspection, and maintenance) that were essentially non-production divisions. An interesting difference between results for production and non-production divisions turned up. In the production divisions there was a significant positive correlation between proficiency and initiating structure, and a significant negative correlation with consideration. In other words, the foremen who were regarded by their supervisors as most proficient turned out to be those higher in "structure" and lower in "consideration." In the non-production divisions the relations tended to be reversed. Two divisions did not follow this trend for reasons which became apparent. One was a production division which at the time the data were collected was in the midst of a vigorous campaign to reduce the grievance rate, which was causing some alarm. The supervisors who rated foremen in that division were presumably a bit more sensitive at the time to considerate behavior on the part of the foremen. The other exception was a non-production division which, nevertheless, was under considerable pressure from a time schedule. In this respect it was much like a production division, and perhaps its foremen were rated accordingly. When this latter idea was followed up by having the divisions rated as to the "demandingness of time schedule," the non-production division just mentioned was under more pressure than some of the production divisions. It was simple to arrange all the divisions in the order of the demands of the time schedule and present the correlations between proficiency and leader behavior in that same order. The trend was rather obvious toward higher positive correlations between proficiency ratings and structure where there was more urgency. The correlations of proficiency with consideration went in the other direction; that is, in those divisions with more pressure the negative correlations between proficiency ratings and consideration became higher.

A further analysis was made by putting all the production divisions together and thus having a much larger number of foremen on which to figure correlations. The non-production divisions also were combined separately. With reference to the two exceptional divisions already mentioned, the one with the grievance campaign was dropped altogether and the other was placed with the production divisions, because, like them, it was operating under a demanding time schedule. When the correlations were computed as before, in the combined production divisions the trend was confirmed that the more proficient foremen (as rated by management) do more initiation of structure and are somewhat less considerate. In the combined non-production divisions the relations were not statistically significant, although the directions of the relations were just the opposite of what they were in the production divisions.

One other analysis related the urgency of a division's time schedule to the leadership behavior of its foremen. We had the eight divisions ranked in order as to this demandingness. We then averaged the consideration scores for all foremen in a division and likewise the structuring scores, so that we could rank the divisions with reference to considerate or structuring behavior of their foremen. When these ranks were compared or correlated, there was a clear-cut tendency for the divisions that were under the most pressure of time to have foremen who were most inclined toward initiating structure and *vice versa*. There was also a fairly marked tendency for the foremen in the most demanding divisions to operate with the least consideration.

Thus, the results of the various methods of analyzing the estimated efficiency of the foremen are clear in production divisions. The more efficient foremen, as rated by the boss, are inclined to show more initiation structure and less consideration. This trend is accentuated as the demandingness of the time schedule increases. In non-production divisions, this relation does not hold, and there is even a hint of rated efficiency going with consideration. But, if there is any underlying tendency of this sort, the pressure of deadlines certainly does not let it operate.

But what about the other criteria, the ones derived not from management's evaluation but from indexes derived from each foreman's work group? The index of how well workers liked working for a particular foreman used a laboriously developed "scaling technique" which we will not describe here. Suffice it to say that the relations between this index and foreman behavior were very clear. Foremen originally described high on consideration tended to be those for whom workers like to work. Workers tend not to like working for foremen high in structure, but this correlation was not nearly as high. It is clear that the kind of foreman liked by these workers is quite different from the kind rated "most proficient" by management.

The final evaluation of leadership behavior used the four objective criteria—absenteeism, accidents, grievances, and turnover. These are obviously related to industrial efficiency, although morale may be involved also. These criteria dealt, of course, with the behavior of work groups, but they may be a function of the conduct of the foremen in charge of those work groups The analysis involved the correlation of consideration and initiating structure as obtained from the Supervisory Behavior Description with the four criteria. We can say that every one of these criteria showed some relationship to at least one of these leadership dimensions in either the production or non-production departments or both. Without dealing with each of the sixteen separate correlations involved (two leadership dimensions x four criteria x four kinds of departments), we can summarize as follows. In general: high structure and low consideration tended to go with more absenteeism, accidents, grievances and turnover. There were no reversals of this picture, although some of the individual correlations were not significant. The highest relationships were those showing more absenteeism among workers with foremen low in consideration (in both production and non-production departments) and high grievances where initiating structure was high. Accidents were most marked in non-production departments having low consideration foremen and turnover was especially high in non-production departments with foremen emphasizing high structure.

The reader should keep in mind that low consideration does not necessarily follow from high structure. These were shown to be independent and many foremen exhibit a high degree of both kinds of behavior. Since the original study Fleishman and Harris[3] pursued this matter further using grievances and turnover as the primary criteria. These results clarify the earlier results. The main findings were that foremen with low consideration tend to have high turnover and grievances regardless of the amount of structuring done. However, high consideration foremen can increase structure without increasing turnover and grievances It was also shown in this later study that some of these relations are "curvilinear." That is, decreased consideration and increased structure have little relation to turnover and grievances until some critical point is reached Then there is a sharp rise in both turnover and grievances. In any case, it is clear that the group indexes produce a different picture of what is effective leader behavior than was derived from management ratings.

One final result is worth noting before further discussion. We found one

[3] Fleishman, E. A. and Harris, E. F., "Patterns of Leadership Behavior Related to Employee Grievances and Turnover." *Personnel Psychology,* 1962, **15,** 43–56.

group of foremen who were nominally foremen on the organization chart, but who were not perceived as the foremen of workers supposedly working for them. Consequently, we compared the Supervisory Behavior Descriptions of these foremen with those of foremen not by-passed. According to an analysis of separate items, the most discriminating ones showed that the foreman who was not by-passed stood behind his men when they were in trouble, encouraged both quantity and quality of production, explained the reasons for what he did, and took account of ideas presented by members of his work group. In general, these functional foremen were higher on both consideration and structure than the by-passed foremen.

## Conclusions

So where does that leave us in our effort to promote the best kind of leadership in industry, or anywhere else for that matter? For industrial, educational, and military leaders have a lot in common. It is probable that some of the psychological principles which we uncovered have implications outside the immediate situation in which we operated. Some of our findings may have a bearing on training in general, and on human-relations training in particular.

For one thing, after our experience with the school for foremen, we have some reservations about the conventional method of evaluating a training program. The immediate checkup at the end of the program is not the whole story. For instance, the final examination in an academic course is supposed to indicate whether the students have profited by the course, and, in a sense, they do profit by getting a mark on the registrar's record. But we are inclined to assume, further, that if they presently encounter some life situation where the material of that course will be useful, then the examination indicates how they will make out in that life situation. This looks to us like a mistaken assumption. While these foremen knew the answers immediately after their course at Central School, they did not carry out what they had learned when they got back to the plant. The immediate and the ultimate effects of training are not necessarily the same. Certainly we did not find it that way. If we are involved specifically in leadership training and rely entirely on an attitude questionnaire right after the training, we are certainly fooling ourselves.

With reference to training in human relations, our study yields one clear implication. Such training conducted in isolation from the practical situation falls short of its objective. It does not take much to upset whatever the training seemed to have accomplished. It is necessary to involve the social situation in which a person is going to operate. Our foremen developed a point of view in school but lost it on their return to the plant if their supervisor had a different point of view. What is socially correct in the school, and hence rewarded, may not be the same in the plant. The foreman "learns" two sets of attitudes, one for each situation. All this suggests that to improve social relations almost anywhere, it is important to work on the whole social setting. It is not possible to pull people out of this setting, tell or teach them some ideas, and then return them to the setting and consider everything fixed. In fact, if we are concerned with a supervisory hierarchy, it looks as if we should really begin working on the leadership attitudes *at the top,* so that the favorable leadership climate will spread down to the first-line supervisors, because certainly it will not spread up the line in the usual industrial organization. The powerful influence of "leadership climate" may be our most important finding. Leadership behavior is not a thing apart but is imbedded in a social setting. Besides, the foreman is actually being "trained" every day by the rewards and example provided by his own boss. We are apt to lose sight of the fact that this everyday kind of learning is more potent than a "one shot" training course. In this plant it was very clear that the kind of leadership management rated most proficient was very different from the training department's concept.

One result, not stressed earlier, was that the training did affect different people differently. We need to have more research into the personal and situational factors that interact with such training.

The criterion phase of our study, like the training phase, results in some contradictions. Employees like to work under a foreman whose leadership is high in consideration and lower in structuring. They are also less inclined toward absenteeism, labor grievances, turnover, and accidents. On the other hand, in production divisions, at least, the foreman who is more proficient in the eyes of higher-level supervisors turns out to emphasize initiating structure and low consideration. It looks like a conflict between productive efficiency, as judged by the boss, and effectiveness inferred from the worker's behavior. It is barely possible that the supervisors who rated the proficiency of the foremen were wrong. They may have been thinking primarily of production and attendant profits and hence have given high ratings to foremen who were high in initiation of structure. It may be that they were responding to a "stereotype" of how they thought an effective foreman "should" act. It should be noted that these same kinds of foremen tended to have more absenteeism, grievances, turnover, and accidents which would work against production and profits. If the supervisors had taken account of factors such as these, they might have tempered their enthusiasm for the high structure–low consideration type of foreman. Another thing that might help would be to decrease the urgency of time schedules. In the non-production divisions which did not work against deadlines, there was no problem. The foreman could exercise the kind of leadership his employees liked and still be seen as proficient by management. While this may seem a naive suggestion in view of the difficulties in changing modern production tempo, our results show another consequence of a pressure atmosphere in which "emergencies" are the rule instead of the exception.

Better production programming might resolve some of the conflicts revealed here. The finding of a low correlation between the two leadership dimensions shows that it is possible for supervisors to earn high scores in *both* consideration and initiating structure and many supervisors do. Some later research suggests that supervisors who are able to do this are more likely to "optimize" the various effectiveness criteria which may seem to be in conflict. The mechanism for this seems to be that consideration behavior, with its attendant rapport, keeps communication channels open and leads to an atmosphere of approval rather than threat. Subordinates are more apt to accept higher structure as supporting rather than threatening. However, more research is needed to clarify this.

We have drawn another disquieting generalization. The often stated proposal that good morale leads directly to increased efficiency needs to be qualified somewhat. Very often this is true, but it is advisable in the individual case to find out if it is that simple. To be sure, our concept of morale was limited to the techniques and indexes already described, and it was in production departments that we found the difficulties indicated. It would be interesting to explore the same problem using actual production units—this was not feasible in our assembly-line case—instead of estimated proficiency. And there might even be some "bugs," which we could not detect, in the estimates. But it did appear that the kind of leader the subordinates like best is not necessarily the one who is most proficient in getting results. Perhaps some of the things he does promote both morale and efficiency while other things help morale but hinder efficiency. It is well to watch both aspects simultaneously. Other concerns may find a situation similar to ours. It would thus be unwise to do a good job of building up morale and then relax on the assumption that a new day has dawned for the entire enterprise.

One final point with some possible generality deals with the actual role and responsibility of the applied scientist. He contributes, obviously, a lot of know-how, but his contribution may fall short of indicating what actually ought to be done. This is sometimes phrased to the effect that the scientist is concerned with means but some other agency must be concerned with ends. In our case, at least, we were able to determine some of the long-range effects of training, the importance of leadership climate, and the comparative effectiveness of the different leadership dimensions for different proficiency criteria. But, on the other hand, we were not close enough to the ultimate goals of the enterprise to determine what policy should be carried out with reference to first-line supervision. We had to return the problem to management. It may be like this in many other practical situations where the scientist discovers principles and how to predict the outcome of certain practices but is not in a position to decide long-range policy. To do this he would have to step out of character.

Nevertheless, such studies do raise questions about managerial values, policies, and goals. For example, the data show that in production departments, the leadership patterns of foremen rated proficient by plant management are also related to high turnover and grievances. What kind of leadership should we strive for in such departments? Such data may suggest a better definition of supervisory proficiency. They may also require an evaluation of managerial goals, short range as well as long range. Somebody will have to determine the relative importance of such goals for the industrial enterprise. Perhaps immediate efficiency may not be so important as a long-time balance between productivity and morale. That is the challenge.

# How to Choose a Leadership Pattern*

## Robert Tannenbaum
## Warren H. Schmidt

I put most problems into my group's hands and leave it to them to carry the ball from there. I serve merely as a catalyst, mirroring back the people's thoughts and feelings so that they can better understand them.

It's foolish to make decisions oneself on matters that affect people. I always talk things over with my subordinates, but I make it clear to them that I'm the one who has to have the final say.

Once I have decided on a course of action, I do my best to sell my ideas to my employees.

I'm being paid to lead. If I let a lot of other people make the decisions I should be making, then I'm not worth my salt.

I believe in getting things done. I can't waste time calling meetings. Someone has to call the shots around here, and I think it should be me.

Each of these statements represents a point of view about "good leadership." Considerable experience, factual data, and theoretical principles

* From *Harvard Business Review*, vol. 36, no. 2, pp. 95–101, March–April, 1958. Reprinted by permission of the *Harvard Business Review*.

could be cited to support each statement, even though they seem to be inconsistent when placed together. Such contradictions point up the dilemma in which the modern manager frequently finds himself.

### New Problem

The problem of how the modern manager can be "democratic" in his relations with subordinates and at the same time maintain the necessary authority and control in the organization for which he is responsible has come into focus increasingly in recent years.

Earlier in the century this problem was not so acutely felt. The successful executive was generally pictured as possessing intelligence, imagination, initiative, the capacity to make rapid (and generally wise) decisions, and the ability to inspire subordinates. People tended to think of the world as being divided into "leaders" and "followers."

*New focus.* Gradually, however, from the social sciences emerged the concept of "group dynamics" with its focus on *members* of the group rather than solely on the leader. Research efforts of social scientists underscored the importance of employee involvement and participation in decision making. Evidence began to challenge the efficiency of highly directive leadership, and increasing attention was paid to problems of motivation and human relations.

Through training laboratories in group development that sprang up across the country, many of the newer notions of leadership began to exert an impact. These training laboratories were carefully designed to give people a first-hand experience in full participation and decision making. The designated "leaders" deliberately attempted to reduce their own power and to make group members as responsible as possible for setting their own goals and methods within the laboratory experience.

It was perhaps inevitable that some of the people who attended the training laboratories regarded this kind of leadership as being truly "democratic" and went home with the determination to build fully participative decision making into their own organizations. Whenever their bosses made a decision without convening a staff meeting, they tended to perceive this as authoritarian behavior. The true symbol of democratic leadership to some was the meeting—and the less directed from the top, the more democratic it was.

Some of the more enthusiastic alumni of these training laboratories began to get the habit of categorizing leader behavior as "democratic" *or* "authoritarian." The boss who made too many decisions himself was thought of as an authoritarian, and his directive behavior was often attributed solely to his personality.

*New need.* The net result of the research findings and of the human relations training based upon them has been to call into question the stereotype of an effective leader. Consequently, the modern manager often finds himself in an uncomfortable state of mind.

Often he is not quite sure how to behave; there are times when he is torn between exerting "strong" leadership and "permissive" leadership Sometimes new knowledge pushes him in one direction ("I should really get the group to help make this decision"), but at the same time his experience pushes him in another direction ("I really understand the problem better than the group and therefore I should make the decision"). He is not sure when a group decision is really appropriate or when holding a staff meeting serves merely as a device for avoiding his own decision-making responsibility.

The purpose of our article is to suggest a framework which managers may find useful in grappling with this dilemma. First we shall look at the different patterns of leadership behavior that the manager can choose from in relating himself to his subordinates. Then we shall turn to some of the questions suggested by this range of patterns. For instance, how important is it for a manager's subordinates to know what type of leadership he is using in a situation? What factors should he consider in deciding on a leadership pattern? What difference do his long-run objectives make as compared to his immediate objectives?

## Range of Behavior

Figure 1 presents the continuum or range of possible leadership behavior available to a manager. Each type of action is related to the degree of authority used by the boss and to the amount of freedom available to his

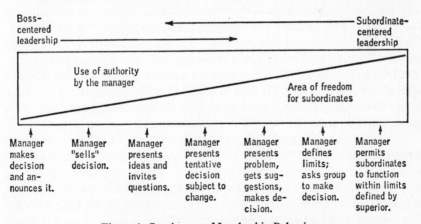

Figure 1. Continuum of Leadership Behavior.

subordinates in reaching decisions. The actions seen on the extreme left characterize the manager who maintains a high degree of control while those seen on the extreme right characterize the manager who releases a high degree of control. Neither extreme is absolute; authority and freedom are never without their limitations.

Now let us look more closely at each of the behavior points occurring along this continuum:

THE MANAGER MAKES THE DECISION AND ANNOUNCES IT. In this case the boss identifies a problem, considers alternative solutions, chooses one of them, and then reports this decision to his subordinates for implementation. He may or may not give consideration to what he believes his subordinates will think or feel about his decision; in any case, he provides no opportunity for them to participate directly in the decision-making process. Coercion may or may not be used or implied.

THE MANAGER "SELLS" HIS DECISION. Here the manager, as before, takes responsibility for identifying the problem and arriving at a decision. However, rather than simply announcing it, he takes the additional step of persuading his subordinates to accept it. In doing so, he recognizes the possibility of some resistance among those who will be faced with the decision, and seeks to reduce this resistance by indicating, for example, what the employees have to gain from his decision.

THE MANAGER PRESENTS HIS IDEAS, INVITES QUESTIONS. Here the boss who has arrived at a decision and who seeks acceptance of his ideas provides an opportunity for his subordinates to get a fuller explanation of his thinking and his intentions. After presenting the ideas, he invites questions so that his associates can better understand what he is trying to accomplish. This "give and take" also enables the manager and the subordinates to explore more fully the implications of the decision.

THE MANAGER PRESENTS A TENTATIVE DECISION SUBJECT TO CHANGE. This kind of behavior permits the subordinates to exert some influence on the decision. The initiative for identifying and diagnosing the problem remains with the boss. Before meeting with his staff, he has thought the problem through and arrived at a decision—but only a tentative one. Before finalizing it, he presents his proposed solution for the reaction of those who will be affected by it. He says in effect, "I'd like to hear what you have to say about this plan that I have developed. I'll appreciate your frank reactions, but will reserve for myself the final decision."

THE MANAGER PRESENTS THE PROBLEM, GETS SUGGESTIONS, AND THEN MAKES HIS DECISION. Up to this point the boss has come before the group with a solution of his own. Not so in this case. The subordinates now get the first chance to suggest solutions. The manager's initial role involves identifying the problem. He might, for example, say something of this sort: "We are faced with a number of complaints from newspapers and the general public on our service policy. What is wrong here? What ideas do you have for coming to grips with this problem?"

The function of the group becomes one of increasing the manager's repertory of possible solutions to the problem. The purpose is to capitalize on the knowledge and experience of those who are on the "firing line." From the expanded list of alternatives developed by the manager and his subordinates, the manager then selects the solution that he regards as most promising.[1]

THE MANAGER DEFINES THE LIMITS AND REQUESTS THE GROUP TO MAKE A DECISION. At this point the manager passes to the group (possibly including himself as a member) the right to make decisions. Before doing so, however, he defines the problem to be solved and the boundaries within which the decision must be made.

An example might be the handling of a parking problem at a plant. The boss decides that this is something that should be worked on by the people involved, so he calls them together and points up the existence of the problem. Then he tells them:

> There is the open field just north of the main plant which has been designated for additional employee parking. We can build underground or surface multilevel facilities as long as the cost does not exceed $100,000. Within these limits we are free to work out whatever solution makes sense to us. After we decide on a specific plan, the company will spend the available money in whatever way we indicate.

THE MANAGER PERMITS THE GROUP TO MAKE DECISIONS WITHIN PRE-SCRIBED LIMITS. This represents an extreme degree of group freedom only occasionally encountered in formal organizations, as, for instance, in many research groups. Here the team of managers or engineers undertakes the identification and diagnosis of the problem, develops alternative procedures for solving it, and decides on one or more of these alternative solutions. The only limits directly imposed on the group by the organization are those specified by the superior of the team's boss. If the boss participates in the decision-making process, he attempts to do so with no more authority than any other member of the group. He commits himself in advance to assist in implementing whatever decision the group makes.

## Key Questions

As the continuum in Figure 1 demonstrates, there are a number of alternative ways in which a manager can relate himself to the group or individuals he is supervising. At the extreme left of the range, the emphasis is on the manager—on what *he* is interested in, how *he* sees things, how *he* feels about them. As we move toward the subordinate-centered end of the continuum, however, the focus is increasingly on the subordinates—on what *they* are interested in, how *they* look at things, how *they* feel about them.

[1] For a fuller explanation of this approach, see Leo Moore, "Too Much Management, Too Little Change," HBR January–February 1956, p. 41.

When business leadership is regarded in this way, a number of questions arise. Let us take four of especial importance:

CAN A BOSS EVER RELINQUISH HIS RESPONSIBILITY BY DELEGATING IT TO SOMEONE ELSE? Our view is that the manager must expect to be held responsible by his superior for the quality of the decisions made, even though operationally these decisions may have been made on a group basis. He should, therefore, be ready to accept whatever risk is involved whenever he delegates decision-making power to his subordinates. Delegation is not a way of "passing the buck." Also, it should be emphasized that the amount of freedom the boss gives to his subordinates cannot be greater than the freedom which he himself has been given by his own superior.

SHOULD THE MANAGER PARTICIPATE WITH HIS SUBORDINATES ONCE HE HAS DELEGATED RESPONSIBILITY TO THEM? The manager should carefully think over this question and decide on his role prior to involving the subordinate group. He should ask if his presence will inhibit or facilitate the problem-solving process. There may be some instances when he should leave the group to let it solve the problem for itself. Typically, however, the boss has useful ideas to contribute, and should function as an additional member of the group. In the latter instance, it is important that he indicate clearly to the group that he sees himself in a *member* role rather than in an authority role.

HOW IMPORTANT IS IT FOR THE GROUP TO RECOGNIZE WHAT KIND OF LEADERSHIP BEHAVIOR THE BOSS IS USING? It makes a great deal of difference. Many relationship problems between boss and subordinate occur because the boss fails to make clear how he plans to use his authority. If, for example, he actually intends to make a certain decision himself, but the subordinate group gets the impression that he has delegated this authority, considerable confusion and resentment are likely to follow. Problems may also occur when the boss uses a "democratic" facade to conceal the fact that he has already made a decision which he hopes the group will accept as its own. The attempt to "make them think it was their idea in the first place" is a risky one. We believe that it is highly important for the manager to be honest and clear in describing what authority he is keeping and what role he is asking his subordinates to assume in solving a particular problem.

CAN YOU TELL HOW "DEMOCRATIC" A MANAGER IS BY THE NUMBER OF DECISIONS HIS SUBORDINATES MAKE? The sheer *number* of decisions is not an accurate index of the amount of freedom that a subordinate group enjoys. More important is the *significance* of the decisions which the boss entrusts to his subordinates. Obviously a decision on how to arrange desks is of an entirely different order from a decision involving the introduction of new electronic data-processing equipment. Even though the widest possible limits are given in dealing with the first issue, the group will sense no particular degree of responsibility. For a boss to permit the group to decide equipment policy, even within rather narrow limits, would reflect a greater degree of confidence in them on his part.

## Deciding How to Lead

Now let us turn from the types of leadership that are possible in a company situation to the question of what types are *practical* and *desirable*. What factors or forces should a manager consider in deciding how to manage? Three are of particular importance:

Forces in the manager.
Forces in the subordinates.
Forces in the situation.

We should like briefly to describe these elements and indicate how they might influence a manager's action in a decision-making situation.[2] The strength of each of them will, of course, vary from instance to instance, but the manager who is sensitive to them can better assess the problems which face him and determine which mode of leadership behavior is most appropriate for him.

*Forces in the manager.* The manager's behavior in any given instance will be influenced greatly by the many forces operating within his own personality. He will, of course, perceive his leadership problems in a unique way on the basis of his background, knowledge, and experience. Among the important internal forces affecting him will be the following:

1. HIS VALUE SYSTEM. How strongly does he feel that individuals should have a share in making the decisions which affect them? Or, how convinced is he that the official who is paid to assume responsibility should personally carry the burden of decision making? The strength of his convictions on questions like these will tend to move the manager to one end or the other of the continuum shown in Figure 1. His behavior will also be influenced by the relative importance that he attaches to organizational efficiency, personal growth of subordinates, and company profits.[3]

2. HIS CONFIDENCE IN HIS SUBORDINATES. Managers differ greatly in the amount of trust they have in other people generally, and this carries over to the particular employees they supervise at a given time. In viewing his particular group of subordinates, the manager is likely to consider their knowledge and competence with respect to the problem. A central question he might ask himself is: "Who is best qualified to deal with this problem?"

[2] See also Robert Tannenbaum and Fred Massarik, "Participation by Subordinates in the Managerial Decision-making Process," *Canadian Journal of Economics and Political Science,* August 1950, pp. 413–418. [Reprinted in this volume, pages 428–440.—Ed.]

[3] See Chris Argyris, "Top Management Dilemma: Company Needs vs. Individual Development," *Personnel,* September 1955, pp. 123–134.

Often he may, justifiably or not, have more confidence in his own capabilities than in those of his subordinates.

3. HIS OWN LEADERSHIP INCLINATIONS. There are some managers who seem to function more comfortably and naturally as highly directive leaders. Resolving problems and issuing orders come easily to them. Other managers seem to operate more comfortably in a team role, where they are continually sharing many of their functions with their subordinates.

4. HIS FEELINGS OF SECURITY IN AN UNCERTAIN SITUATION. The manager who releases control over the decision-making process thereby reduces the predictability of the outcome. Some managers have a greater need than others for predictability and stability in their environment. This "tolerance for ambiguity" is being viewed increasingly by psychologists as a key variable in a person's manner of dealing with problems.

The manager brings these and other highly personal variables to each situation he faces. If he can see them as forces which, consciously or unconsciously, influence his behavior, he can better understand what makes him prefer to act in a given way. And understanding this, he can often make himself more effective.

*Forces in the subordinate.* Before deciding how to lead a certain group, the manager will also want to consider a number of forces affecting his subordinates' behavior. He will want to remember that each employee, like himself, is influenced by many personality variables. In addition, each subordinate has a set of expectations about how the boss should act in relation to him (the phrase "expected behavior" is one we hear more and more often these days at discussions of leadership and teaching). The better the manager understands these factors, the more accurately he can determine what kind of behavior on his part will enable his subordinates to act most effectively.

Generally speaking, the manager can permit his subordinates greater freedom if the following essential conditions exist:

If the subordinates have relatively high needs for independence. (As we all know, people differ greatly in the amount of direction that they desire.)

If the subordinates have a readiness to assume responsibility for decision making. (Some see additional responsibility as a tribute to their ability; others see it as "passing the buck.")

If they have a relatively high tolerance for ambiguity. (Some employees prefer to have clear-cut directives given to them; others prefer a wider area of freedom.)

If they are interested in the problem and feel that it is important.

If they understand and identify with the goals of the organization.

If they have the necessary knowledge and experience to deal with the problem.

If they have learned to expect to share in decision making. (Persons who have come to expect strong leadership and are then suddenly confronted with the request to share more fully in decision making are often upset by this new experience. On the other hand, persons who have enjoyed a considerable amount of freedom resent the boss who begins to make all the decisions himself.)

The manager will probably tend to make fuller use of his own authority if the above conditions do *not* exist; at times there may be no realistic alternative to running a "one-man show."

The restrictive effect of many of the forces will, of course, be greatly modified by the general feeling of confidence which subordinates have in the boss. Where they have learned to respect and trust him, he is free to vary his behavior. He will feel certain that he will not be perceived as an authoritarian boss on those occasions when he makes decisions by himself. Similarly, he will not be seen as using staff meetings to avoid his decision-making responsibility. In a climate of mutual confidence and respect, people tend to feel less threatened by deviations from normal practice, which in turn makes possible a higher degree of flexibility in the whole relationship.

*Forces in the situation.* In addition to the forces which exist in the manager himself and in his subordinates, certain characteristics of the general situation will also affect the manager's behavior. Among the more critical environmental pressures that surround him are those which stem from the organization, the work group, the nature of the problem, and the pressures of time. Let us look briefly at each of these:

TYPE OF ORGANIZATION. Like individuals, organizations have values and traditions which inevitably influence the behavior of the people who work in them. The manager who is a newcomer to a company quickly discovers that certain kinds of behavior are approved while others are not. He also discovers that to deviate radically from what is generally accepted is likely to create problems for him.

These values and traditions are communicated in many ways—through job descriptions, policy pronouncements, and public statements by top executives. Some organizations, for example, hold to the notion that the desirable executive is one who is dynamic, imaginative, decisive, and persuasive. Other organizations put more emphasis upon the importance of the executive's ability to work effectively with people—his human relations skills. The fact that his superiors have a defined concept of what the good executive should be will very likely push the manager toward one end or the other of the behavioral range.

In addition to the above, the amount of employee participation is influenced by such variables as the size of the working units, their geographical distribution, and the degree of inter- and intra-organizational security required to attain company goals. For example, the wide geographical dispersion of an organization may preclude a practical system of participative decision making, even though this would otherwise be desirable. Similarly, the size of the working units or the need for keeping plans confidential may make it necessary for the boss to exercise more control than would otherwise be the case. Factors like these may limit considerably the manager's ability to function flexibly on the continuum.

GROUP EFFECTIVENESS. Before turning decision-making responsibility over to a subordinate group, the boss should consider how effectively its members work together as a unit.

One of the relevant factors here is the experience the group has had in working together. It can generally be expected that a group which has functioned for some time will have developed habits of cooperation and thus be able to tackle a problem more effectively than a new group. It can also be expected that a group of people with similar backgrounds and interests will work more quickly and easily than people with dissimilar backgrounds, because the communication problems are likely to be less complex.

The degree of confidence that the members have in their ability to solve problems as a group is also a key consideration. Finally, such group variables as cohesiveness, permissiveness, mutual acceptance, and commonality of purpose will exert subtle but powerful influence on the group's functioning.

THE PROBLEM ITSELF. The nature of the problem may determine what degree of authority should be delegated by the manager to his subordinates. Obviously he will ask himself whether they have the kind of knowledge which is needed. It is possible to do them a real disservice by assigning a problem that their experience does not equip them to handle.

Since the problems faced in large or growing industries increasingly require knowledge of specialists from many different fields, it might be inferred that the more complex a problem, the more anxious a manager will be to get some assistance in solving it. However, this is not always the case. There will be times when the very complexity of the problem calls for one person to work it out. For example, if the manager has most of the background and factual data relevant to a given issue, it may be easier for him to think it through himself than to take the time to fill in his staff on all the pertinent background information.

The key question to ask, of course, is: "Have I heard the ideas of everyone who has the necessary knowledge to make a significant contribution to the solution of this problem?"

THE PRESSURE OF TIME. This is perhaps the most clearly felt pressure on the manager (in spite of the fact that it may sometimes be imagined). The more that he feels the need for an immediate decision, the more difficult it is to involve other people. In organizations which are in a constant state of "crisis" and "crash programming" one is likely to find managers personally using a high degree of authority with relatively little delegation to subordinates. When the time pressure is less intense, however, it becomes much more possible to bring subordinates in on the decision-making process.

These, then, are the principal forces that impinge on the manager in any given instance and that tend to determine his tactical behavior in relation to his subordinates. In each case his behavior ideally will be that which makes possible the most effective attainment of his immediate goal within the limits facing him.

## Long-Run Strategy

As the manager works with his organization on the problems that come up day by day, his choice of a leadership pattern is usually limited. He must take account of the forces just described and, within the restrictions they impose on him, do the best that he can. But as he looks ahead months or even years, he can shift his thinking from tactics to large-scale strategy. No longer need he be fettered by all of the forces mentioned, for he can view many of them as variables over which he has some control. He can, for example, gain new insights or skills for himself, supply training for individual subordinates, and provide participative experiences for his employee group.

In trying to bring about a change in these variables, however, he is faced with a challenging question: At which point along the continuum *should* he act?

*Attaining objectives.* The answer depends largely on what he wants to accomplish. Let us suppose that he is interested in the same objectives that most modern managers seek to attain when they can shift their attention from the pressure of immediate assignments:

1. To raise the level of employee motivation.
2. To increase the readiness of subordinates to accept change.
3. To improve the quality of all managerial decisions.
4. To develop teamwork and morale.
5. To further the individual development of employees.

In recent years the manager has been deluged with a flow of advice on how best to achieve these longer-run objectives. It is little wonder that he is often both bewildered and annoyed. However, there are some guidelines which he can usefully follow in making a decision.

Most research and much of the experience of recent years give a strong factual basis to the theory that a fairly high degree of subordinate-centered behavior is associated with the accomplishment of the five purposes mentioned.[4] This does not mean that a manager should always leave all decisions to his assistants. To provide the individual or the group with greater freedom than they are ready for at any given time may very well tend to

[4] For example, see Warren H. Schmidt and Paul C. Buchanan, *Techniques that Produce Teamwork* (New London, Arthur C. Croft Publications, 1954); and Morris S. Viteles, *Motivation and Morale in Industry* (New York, W. W. Norton & Company, Inc., 1953).

generate anxieties and therefore inhibit rather than facilitate the attainment of desired objectives. But this should not keep the manager from making a continuing effort to confront his subordinates with the challenge of freedom.

## Conclusion

In summary, there are two implications in the basic thesis that we have been developing. The first is that the successful leader is one who is keenly aware of those forces which are most relevant to his behavior at any given time. He accurately understands himself, the individuals and group he is dealing with, and the company and broader social environment in which he operates. And certainly he is able to assess the present readiness for growth of his subordinates.

But this sensitivity or understanding is not enough, which brings us to the second implication. The successful leader is one who is able to behave appropriately in the light of these perceptions. If direction is in order, he is able to direct; if considerable participative freedom is called for, he is able to provide such freedom.

Thus, the successful manager of men can be primarily characterized neither as a strong leader nor as a permissive one. Rather, he is one who maintains a high batting average in accurately assessing the forces that determine what his most appropriate behavior at any given time should be and in actually being able to behave accordingly. Being both insightful and flexible, he is less likely to see the problems of leadership as a dilemma.

*Overcoming Resistance to Change**

Lester Coch
John R. P. French, Jr.

It has always been characteristic of American industry to change products and methods of doing jobs as often as competitive conditions or engineering progress dictates. This makes frequent changes in an individual's work necessary. In addition, the markedly greater turnover and absenteeism of recent years result in unbalanced production lines, which again makes for

* From *Human Relations*, vol. 1, no. 4, pp. 512–532, 1948. Reprinted by permission of Tavistock Publications and John R. P. French, Jr.

frequent shifting of individuals from one job to another. One of the most serious production problems faced at the Harwood Manufacturing Corporation has been the resistance of production workers to the necessary changes in methods and jobs. This resistance expressed itself in several ways, such as grievances about the piece rates that went with the new methods, high turnover, very low efficiency, restriction of output, and marked aggression against management. Despite these undesirable effects, it was necessary that changes in methods and jobs continue.

Efforts were made to solve this serious problem by the use of a special monetary allowance for transfers, by trying to enlist the cooperation and aid of the union, by making necessary layoffs on the basis of efficiency, etc. In all cases, these actions did little or nothing to overcome the resistance to change. On the basis of these data, it was felt that the pressing problem of resistance to change demanded further research for its solution. From the point of view of factory management, there were two purposes to the research: (*a*) Why do people resist change so strongly? and (*b*) What can be done to overcome this resistance?

Starting with a series of observations about the behavior of changed groups, the first step in the program was to devise a preliminary theory to account for the resistance to change. Then, on the basis of the theory, a real-life action experiment was devised and conducted within the context of the factory situation. Finally, the results of the experiment were interpreted in the light of the preliminary theory and the new data.

**Background**

The main plant of the Harwood Manufacturing Corporation, where the present research was done, is located in the small town of Marion, Virginia. The plant produces pajamas and, like most sewing plants, employs mostly women. The plant's population is about 500 women and 100 men. The workers are recruited from the rural, mountainous areas surrounding the town, and are usually employed without previous industrial experience. The average age of the workers is 23. The average education is eight years of grammar school.

The policies of the company in regard to labor relations are liberal and progressive. A high value has been placed on fair and open dealing with the employees and they are encouraged to take up any problems or grievances with the management at any time. Every effort is made to help foremen find effective solutions to their problems in human relations, using conferences and role-playing methods. Carefully planned orientation, designed to help overcome the discouragement and frustrations attending entrance upon the new and unfamiliar situation, is used. Plant-wide votes are conducted where possible to resolve problems affecting the whole working population. The company has invested both time and money in employee services such as industrial music, health services, lunchroom, and recreation programs. In the same spirit, the management has been conscious of the importance of public relations in the local community; they have supported, both financially and otherwise, any activity which would build up good will for the company. As a result of these policies, the company has enjoyed good labor relations since the day it commenced operations.

Harwood employees work on an individual incentive system. Piece rates are set by time study and are expressed in terms of units. One unit is equal to one minute of standard work: 60 units per hour equal the standard efficiency rating. Thus, if on a particular operation the piece rate for one dozen is 10 units, the operator would have to produce six dozen per hour to achieve the standard efficiency rating of 60 units per hour. The skill required to reach 60 units per hour is great. On some jobs, an average trainee may take 34 weeks to reach the skill level necessary to perform at 60 units per hour. Her first few weeks of work may be on an efficiency level of 5 to 20 units per hour.

The amount of pay received is directly proportional to the weekly average efficiency rating achieved. Thus, an operator with an average efficiency rating of 75 units per hour (25% more than standard) would receive 25% more than base pay. However, there are two minimum wages below which no operator may fall. The first is the plant-wide minimum, the hiring-in wage; the second is a minimum wage based on six months' employment and is 22% higher than the plant-wide minimum wage. Both minima are smaller than the base pay for 60 units per hour efficiency rating.

The rating of every piece worker is computed every day, and the results are published in a daily record of production which is shown to every operator. This daily record of production for each production line carries the names of all the operators on that line arranged in rank order of efficiency rating, with the highest rating girl at the top of the list. The supervisors speak to each operator each day about her unit ratings. Because of the above procedures, many operators do not claim credit for all the work done in a given day. Instead, they save a few of the piece rate tickets as a "cushion" against a rainy day when they may not feel well or may have a great amount of machine trouble.

When it is necessary to change an operator from one type of work to another, a transfer bonus is given. This bonus is so designed that the changed operator who relearns at an average rate will suffer no loss in earnings after change. Despite this allowance, the general attitudes toward job changes in the factory are markedly negative. Such expressions as, "When you make your units [standard production], they change your job," are all too frequent. Many operators refuse to change, preferring to quit.

## The Transfer Learning Curve

An analysis of the after-change relearning curves of several hundred experienced operators rating standard or better prior to change showed that

38% of the changed operators recovered to the standard unit rating of 60 units per hour. The othei 62% either became chronically substandard operators or quit during the relearning period.

The average relearning curve for those who recover to standard production on the simplest type of job in the plant is eight weeks long, and, when smoothed, provides the basis for the transfer bonus. The bonus is the percentage difference between this expected efficiency rating and the standard of 60 units per hour.

The relearning period for an experienced operator is longer than the learning period for a new operator. This is true despite the fact that the majority of transfers—the failures who never recover to standard—are omitted from the curve. However, changed operators rarely complain of "wanting to do it the old way" after the first week or two of change, and time and motion studies show few false moves after the first week of change. From this evidence it is deduced that proactive inhibition, or the interference of previous habits in learning the new skill, is either nonexistent or very slight after the first two weeks of change.

An analysis of the relearning curves for 41 experienced operators who were changed to very difficult jobs gives a comparison between the recovery rates for operators making standard or better prior to change, and those below standard prior to change. Both classes of operators dropped to a little below 30 units per hour and recovered at a very slow but similar rate. These curves show a general (though by no means universal) phenomenon: the efficiency rating prior to change does not indicate a faster or slower recovery rate after change.

## A Preliminary Theory of Resistance to Change

The fact that relearning after transfer to a new job is so often slower than initial learning on first entering the factory would indicate, on the face of it, that the resistance to change and the slow relearning is primarily a motivational problem. The similar recovery rates of skilled and unskilled operators tend to confirm the hypothesis that skill is a minor factor and motivation is the major determinant of the rate of recovery. Earlier experiments at Harwood by Alex Bavelas demonstrated this point conclusively. He found that the use of group decision techniques on operators who had just been transferred resulted in very marked increases in the rate of relearning, even though no skill training was given and there were no other changes in working conditions (3).

Interviews with operators who have been transferred to a new job reveal a common pattern of feelings and attitudes which are distinctly different from those of successful nontransfers. In addition to resentment against the management for transferring them, the employees typically show feelings of frustration, loss of hope of ever regaining their former level of production and status in the factory, feelings of failure, and a very low level of aspiration. In this respect, these transferred operators are similar to the chronically slow workers studied previously.

Earlier unpublished research at Harwood has shown that the nontransferred employees generally have an explicit goal of reaching and maintaining an efficiency rating of 60 units per hour. A questionnaire administered to several groups of operators indicated that a large majority of them accept as their goal the management's quota of 60 units per hour. This standard of production is the level of aspiration according to which the operators measure their own success or failure, and those who fall below standard lose status in the eyes of their fellow employees. Relatively few operators set a goal appreciably above 60 units per hour.

The actual production records confirm the effectiveness of this goal of standard production. The distribution of the total population of operators in accordance with their production levels is by no means a normal curve. Instead there is a very large number of operators who rate 60 to 63 units per hour, and relatively few operators who rate just above or just below this range. Thus we may conclude that:

*Proposition 1.* There is a force acting on the operator in the direction of achieving a production level of 60 units per hour or more. It is assumed that the strength of this driving force (acting on an operator below standard) increases as she gets nearer the goal—a typical goal gradient.

On the other hand, restraining forces operate to hinder or prevent her reaching this goal. These restraining forces consist, among other things, of the difficulty of the job in relation to the operator's level of skill. Other things being equal, the faster an operator is sewing the more difficult it is to increase her speed by a given amount. Thus we may conclude that:

*Proposition 2.* The strength of the restraining force hindering higher production increases with increasing level of production.

In line with previous studies, it is assumed that the conflict of these two opposing forces—the driving force corresponding to the goal of reaching 60 and the restraining force of the difficulty of the job—produces frustration. In such a conflict situation, the strength of frustration will depend on the strength of these forces. If the restraining force against increasing production is weak, then the frustration will be weak. But if the driving force toward higher production, i.e., the motivation is weak, then the frustration will also be weak. Probably both of the conflicting forces must be above a certain minimum strength before any frustration is produced, for all goal-directed activity involves some degree of conflict of this type; yet a person is not usually frustrated so long as he is making satisfactory progress toward his goal. Consequently we assume that:

*Proposition 3.* The strength of frustration is a function of the weaker of these two opposing forces, provided that the weaker force is stronger than a certain minimum necessary to produce frustration (3).

From Propositions 1, 2, and 3, we may derive that the strength of frustration (*a*) should be greater for operators who are below standard in production than for operators who have already achieved the goal of standard production; (*b*) should be greater for operators on difficult jobs than for operators on easy jobs; and (*c*) should increase with increasing efficiency rating below standard production. Previous research would suggest:

*Proposition 4.* One consequence of frustration is escape from the field (2).

An analysis of the effects of such frustration in the factory showed that it resulted, among other things, in high turnover and absenteeism. The rate of turnover for successful operators with efficiency ratings above standard was much lower than for unsuccessful operators. Likewise, operators on the more difficult jobs quit more frequently than those on the easier jobs. Presumably the effect of being transferred is a severe frustration which should result in similar attempts to escape from the field.

In line with this theory of frustration and the finding that job turnover is one resultant of frustration, an analysis was made of the turnover rate of transferred operators as compared with the rate among operators who had not been transferred recently. For the year September, 1946, to September, 1947, there were 198 operators who had not been transferred recently; that is, within the 34-week period allowed for relearning after transfer. There was a second group of 85 operators who had been transferred recently; that is, within the time allowed for relearning the new job. Each of these two groups was divided into seven classifications according to their unit rating at the time of quitting. For each classification the percentage turnover per month, based on the total number of employees in that classification, was computed.

The results are given in Figure 1. Both the levels of turnover and the form of the curves are strikingly different for the two groups. Among operators who have not been transferred recently the average turnover per month is about 4½%; among recent transfers the monthly turnover is nearly 12%. Consistent with the previous studies, both groups show a very marked drop in the turnover curve after an operator becomes a success by reaching 60 units per hour, or standard production. However, the form of the curves at lower unit ratings is markedly different for the two groups. The nontransferred operators show a gradually increasing rate of turnover up to a rating of 55 to 59 units per hour. The transferred operators, on the other hand, show a high peak at the lowest unit rating of 30 to 34 units per hour, decreasing sharply to a low point at 45 to 49 units per hour. Since most changed operators drop to a unit rating of around 30 units per hour when changed and then drop no further, it is obvious that the rate of turnover was highest for these operators just after they were changed and again much later just before they reached standard. Why?

It is assumed that the strength of frustration for an operator who has not been transferred gradually increases because both the driving force toward the goal of reaching 60 and the restraining force of the difficulty of the job increase with increasing unit rating. This is in line with Propositions 1, 2, and 3, above. For the transferred operator, on the other hand,

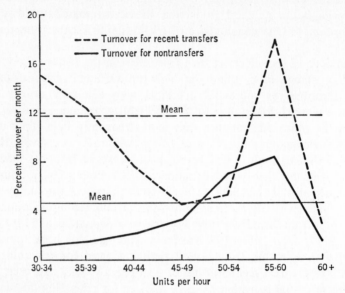

Figure 1. The rate of turnover at various levels of production for transfers as compared with nontransfers.

the frustration is greatest immediately after transfer when the contrast of her present status with her former status is most evident. At this point, the strength of the restraining forces is at a maximum because the difficulty is unusually great due to proactive inhibition. Then, as she overcomes the interference effects between the two jobs and learns the new job, the difficulty and the frustration gradually decrease and the rate of turnover declines until the operator reaches 45–49 units per hour. Then at higher levels of production the difficulty starts to increase again and the transferred operator shows the same peak in frustration and turnover at 55–59 units per hour.

Though our theory of frustration explains the forms of the two turnover curves in Figure 1, it seems hardly adequate to account for the markedly higher level of turnover for transfers as compared to nontransfers. On the basis of the difficulty of the job, it is especially difficult to explain the higher rate of turnover at 55–59 units per hour for transfers. Evidently, additional forces are operating.

Another factor which seems to affect recovery rates of changed operators is the amount of cohesiveness. Observations seem to indicate that a strong psychological subgroup with negative attitudes toward management will display the strongest resistance to change. On the other hand, changed groups with high cohesiveness and positive cooperative attitudes are the best relearners. Collections of individuals with little or no cohesiveness display some resistance to change, but not so strongly as the groups with high cohesiveness and negative attitudes toward management.

An analysis of turnover records for changed operators with high cohesiveness showed a 4% turnover rate per month at 30 to 34 units per hour, not significantly higher than in unchanged operators, but significantly lower than in changed operators with little or no cohesiveness. However, the acts of aggression are far more numerous among operators with high cohesiveness than among operators with little cohesiveness. Since both types of operators experience the same frustration as individuals but react to it so differently, it is assumed that the effect of the ingroup feeling is to set up a restraining force against leaving the group and perhaps even to set up driving forces toward staying in the group. In these circumstances, one would expect some alternative reaction to frustration rather than escape from the field. This alternative is aggression. Strong cohesiveness provides strength so that members dare to express aggression which would otherwise be suppressed.

One common result in a cohesive subgroup is the setting of a group standard concerning production. Where the attitudes toward management are antagonistic, this group standard may take the form of a definite restriction of production to a given level. This phenomenon of restriction is particularly likely to happen in a group that has been transferred to a job where a new piece rate has been set, for they have some hope that, if production never approaches the standard, the management may change the piece rate in their favor.

A group standard can exert extremely strong forces on an individual member of a small subgroup. That these forces can have a powerful effect on production is indicated in the production record of one presser during a period of 40 days:

### In the Group

| Days | Efficiency rating |
|------|-------------------|
| 1–3 | 46 |
| 4–6 | 52 |
| 7–9 | 53 |
| 10–12 | 56 |

### Scapegoating begins

| | |
|------|------|
| 13–16 | 55 |
| 17–20 | 48 |

*Becomes a single worker*

| | |
|---|---|
| 21–24 | 83 |
| 25–28 | 92 |
| 29–32 | 92 |
| 33–36 | 91 |
| 37–40 | 92 |

For the first 20 days she was working in a group of other pressers who were producing at the rate of about 50 units per hour. Starting on the 13th day, when she reached standard production and exceeded the production of the other members, she became a scapegoat of the group. During this time her production decreased toward the level of the remaining members of the group. After 20 days the group had to be broken up and all the other members were transferred to other jobs, leaving only the scapegoat operator. With the removal of the group, the group standard was no longer operative, and the production of the one remaining operator shot up from the level of about 45 to 96 units per hour in a period of four days. Her production stabilized at a level of about 92 and stayed there for the remainder of the 20 days. Thus it is clear that the motivational forces induced in the individual by a strong subgroup may be more powerful than those induced by management.

## The Experiments

On the basis of the preliminary theory that resistance to change is a combination of an individual reaction to frustration with strong group-induced forces, it seemed that the most appropriate methods for overcoming the resistance to change would be group methods. Consequently, an experiment was designed (Experiment I) employing three degrees of participation in handling groups to be transferred. The first variation, the control group, involved *no participation* by employees in planning the changes, though an explanation was given to them. The second variation involved *participation through representation* of the workers in designing the changes to be made in the jobs. The third variation consisted of *total participation* by all members of the group in designing the changes. Two experimental groups received the total participation treatment. The four experimental groups were roughly matched with respect to (*a*) the efficiency ratings of the groups before transfer; (*b*) the degree of change involved in the transfer; and (*c*) the amount of cohesiveness observed in the groups.

In no case was more than a minor change in the work routines and time allowances made. The no-participation group, 18 hand pressers, had formerly stacked their work in half-dozen lots on a flat piece of cardboard the size of the finished product. The new job called for stacking their work in half-dozen lots in a box the size of the finished product. The box was located in the same place the cardboard had been. An additional two minutes per dozen was allowed (by the time study) for this new part of the job. This represented a total change of 8.8%.

The group treated with participation through representation, 13 pajama folders, had formerly folded coats with prefolded pants. The new job called for the folding of coats with unfolded pants. An additional 1.8 minutes per dozen was allowed (by time study) for this new part of the job. This represented a total change of 9.4%.

The two total participation groups, consisting of eight and seven pajama examiners, respectively, had formerly clipped threads from the entire garment and examined every seam. The new job called for pulling only certain threads off and examining every seam. An average of 1.2 minutes per dozen was subtracted (by time study) from the total time on these two jobs. This represented a total job change of 8%.

The no-participation group of hand pressers went through the usual factory routine when they were changed. The production department modified the job, and the new piece rate was set. A group meeting was then held in which the group was told that the change was necessary because of competitive conditions, and that a new piece rate had been set. The new piece rate was thoroughly explained by the time-study man, questions were answered, and the meeting dismissed.

The group which participated through representatives was changed in a different manner. Before any changes took place, a group meeting was held with all the operators to be changed. The need for the change was presented as dramatically as possible, showing two identical garments produced in the factory; one was produced in 1946 and had sold for 100% more than its fellow in 1947. The group was asked to identify the cheaper one and could not do it. This demonstration effectively shared with the group the entire problem of the necessity of cost reduction. A general agreement was reached that a savings could be effected by removing the "frills" and "fancy" work from the garment without affecting the folders' opportunity to achieve a high efficiency rating. Management then presented a plan to set the new job and piece rate:

1. Make a check study of the job as it was being done.
2. Eliminate all unnecessary work.
3. Train several operators in the correct methods.
4. Set the piece rate by time studies on these specially trained operators.
5. Explain the new job and rate to all the operators.
6. Train all operators in the new method so they can reach a high rate of production within a short time.

The group approved this plan (though no formal group decision was reached), and chose the operators to be specially trained. A submeeting with the "special" operators was held immediately following the meeting with the entire group. They displayed a cooperative and interested attitude and immediately presented many good suggestions. This attitude carried over into the working out of the details of the new job, and when the new job and piece rates were set the "special" operators referred to the resultants as "our job," "our rate," etc. The new job and piece rates were presented at a second group meeting to all the operators involved. The "special" operators served to train the other operators on the new job.

The total participation groups went through much the same kind of meetings. The groups were smaller, and a more intimate atmosphere was established. The need for a change was once again made dramatically clear. The same general plan was presented by management. However, since the groups were small, all operators were chosen as "special" operators; that is, all operators were to participate directly in the designing of the new jobs, and all operators would be studied by the time-study man. It is interesting to observe that in the meetings with these two groups suggestions were immediately made in such quantity that the stenographer had great difficulty in recording them. The group approved of the plans, but again no formal group decision was reached.

**Results**

The results of the experiment are summarized in graphic form in Figure 2. The gaps in the production curves occur because these groups were paid on a time-work basis for a day or two. The no-participation group improved little beyond their early efficiency ratings. Resistance developed almost immediately after the change occurred. Marked expressions of aggression against management occurred, such as conflict with the methods engineer, expression of hostility against the supervisor, deliberate restriction of production, and lack of cooperation with the supervisor. There were 17% quits in the first 40 days. Grievances were filed about the piece rate, but when the rate was checked, it was found to be a little "loose."

The representation group showed an unusually good relearning curve. At the end of 14 days, the group averaged 61 units per hour. During the 14 days, the attitude was cooperative and permissive. They worked well with the methods engineer, the training staff, and the supervisor. (The supervisor was the same person in the cases of the first two groups.) There were no quits in this group in the first 40 days. This group might have presented a better learning record if work had not been scarce during the first seven days. There was one act of aggression against the supervisor recorded in the first 40 days. We should note that the three special representative operators recovered at about the same rate as the rest of their group.

The total participation groups recovered faster than the others. After a slight drop on the first day of change, the efficiency ratings returned to a prechange level and showed sustained progress thereafter to a level about 14% higher than the prechange level. No additional training was provided them after the second day. They worked well with their supervisors and no indications of aggression were observed from these groups. There were no quits in either of these groups in the first 40 days.

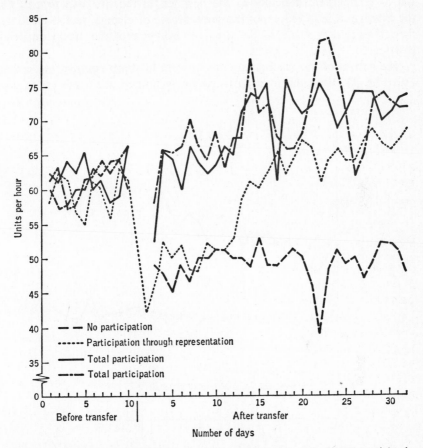

Figure 2. The effects of participation through representation and of total participation on recovery after an easy transfer.

(A fifth experimental group, composed of only two sewing operators, was transferred by the total participation technique. Their new job was one of the most difficult jobs in the factory, in contrast to the easy jobs for the other four experimental groups. As expected, the total participation technique again resulted in an unusually fast recovery rate and a final level of production well above the level before transfer.)

In the first experiment, the no-participation group made no progress after transfer for a period of 32 days. At the end of this period the group was broken up, and the individuals were reassigned to new jobs scattered throughout the factory. Two and a half months after their dispersal, the 13 remaining members of the original no-participation group were again brought together as a group for a second experiment (Experiment II).

This second experiment consisted of transferring the group to a new job, using the total participation technique. The new job was a pressing job of comparable difficulty to the new job in the first experiment. On the average, it involved about the same degree of change. In the meetings, no reference was made to the previous behavior of the group on being transferred.

The results of the second experiment were in sharp contrast to the first (see Fig. 3). With the total participation technique, the same group now

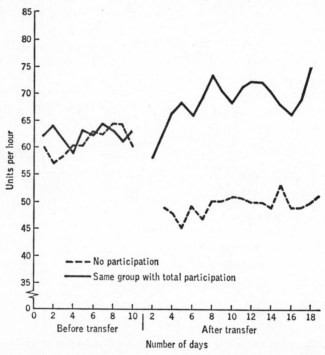

Figure 3. A comparison of the effect of no participation with the total participation procedure on the same group.

recovered rapidly to their previous efficiency rating and, like the other groups under this treatment, continued on beyond it to a new high level of production. There was no aggression or turnover in the group for 19 days after change, a marked modification of their previous behavior after transfer. Some anxiety concerning their seniority status was expressed, but this was resolved in a meeting of their elected delegate, the union business agent, and a management representative.

**Interpretation**

The purpose of this section is to explain the drop in production resulting from transfer, the differential recovery rates of the three experimental treatments, the increases beyond their former levels of production by the participating groups, and the differential rates of turnover and aggression.

The first experiment showed that the rate of recovery is directly proportional to the amount of participation, and that the rates of turnover and aggression are inversely proportional to the amount of participation. The second experiment demonstrated more conclusively that the results obtained depended on the experimental treatment rather than on personality factors like skill or aggressiveness, for identical individuals yielded markedly different results in the no-participation treatment as contrasted with the total-participation treatment.

Apparently total participation has the same type of effect as participation through representation, but the former has a stronger influence. In regard to recovery rates, this difference is not unequivocal because the experiment was unfortunately confounded. Right after transfer, the latter group had insufficient material to work on for a period of seven days. Hence, their slower recovery during this period is at least in part due to insufficient work. In succeeding days, however, there was an adequate supply of work and the differential recovery rate still persisted. Therefore, we are inclined to believe that participation through representation results in slower recovery than does total participation.

Before discussing the details of why participation produces high morale, we shall consider the nature of production levels. In examining the production records of hundreds of individuals and groups in this factory, one is struck by the constancy of the level of production. Though differences among individuals in efficiency rating are very large, nearly every experienced operator maintains a fairly steady level of production, given constant physical conditions. Frequently the given level will be maintained despite rather large changes in technical working conditions.

As Lewin has pointed out, this type of production can be viewed as a quasi-stationary process—in the on-going work the operator is forever sewing new garments, yet the level of the process remains relatively stationary (3). Thus there are constant characteristics of the production process permitting the establishment of general laws.

In studying production as a quasi-stationary equilibrium, we are concerned with two types of forces: (*a*) forces on production in a downward direction, and (*b*) forces on production in an upward direction. In this situation we are dealing with a variety of both upward forces tending to increase the level of production and downward forces tending to decrease the level of production. However, in the present experiment we have no method of measuring independently all of the component forces either downward or upward. These various component forces upward are combined into one resultant force upward, and the several downward component forces combine into one resultant force downward. We can infer a good deal about the relative strengths of these resultant forces.

Where we are dealing with a quasi-stationary equilibrium, the resultant forces upward and the forces downward are opposite in direction and equal in strength at the equilibrium level. Of course either resultant forces may fluctuate over a short period of time, so that the forces may not be equally balanced at a given moment. However, over a longer period of time, and on the average, the forces balance out. Fluctuations from the average occur, but there is a tendency to return to the average level.

Just before being transferred, all of the groups in both experiments had reached a stable equilibrium level at just above the standard production of 60 units per hour. This level was equal to the average efficiency rating for the entire factory during the period of the experiments. Since this production level remained constant, neither increasing nor decreasing, we may be sure that the strength of the resultant force upward was equal to the strength of the resultant force downward. This equilibrium of forces was maintained over the period of time when production was stationary at this level. But the forces changed markedly after transfer, and these new constellations of forces were distinctly different for the various experimental groups.

For the no-participation group the period after transfer is a quasi-stationary equilibrium at a lower level, and the forces do not change during

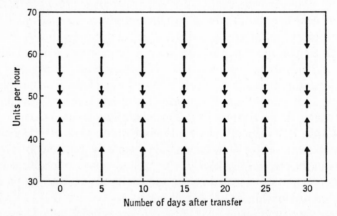

Figure 4. A schematic diagram of the quasi-stationary equilibrium for the no-participation group after transfer.

the period of 30 days. The resultant force upward remains equal to the resultant force downward, and the level of production remains constant. The force field for this group is represented schematically in Figure 4. Only the resultant forces are shown. The length of the vector represents the strength of the force, and the point of the arrow represents the point of application of the force, that is, the production level and the time at which the force applies. Thus the forces are equal and opposite only at the level of 50 units per hour. At higher levels of production the forces downward are greater than the forces upward, and at lower levels of production the forces upward are stronger than the forces downward. Thus there is a tendency for the equilibrium to be maintained at an efficiency rating of 50.

The situation for the other experimental groups after transfer can be viewed as a quasi-stationary equilibrium of a different type. Figure 5 gives

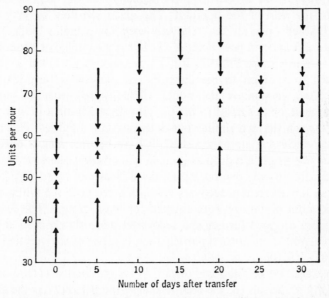

Figure 5. A schematic diagram of the quasi-stationary equilibrium for the experimental group after transfer.

a schematic diagram of the resultant forces for all the participation groups. At any given level of production, such as 50 units per hour or 60 units per hour, both the resultant forces upward and the resultant forces downward change over the period of 30 days. During this time the point of equilibrium, which starts at 50 units per hour, gradually rises until it reaches a level of over 70 units per hour after 30 days. Yet here again the equilibrium level has the character of a "central force field" where, at any point in the total field, the resultant of the upward and the downward forces is in the direction of the equilibrium level.

To understand how the differences among the experimental and the control treatments produced the differences in force fields represented in Figures 4 and 5, it is not sufficient to consider only the resultant forces. We must also look at the component forces for each resultant force.

There are three main component forces influencing production in a downward direction: (*a*) the difficulty of the job; (*b*) a force corresponding to avoidance of strain; and (*c*) a force corresponding to a group standard to restrict production to a given level. The resultant force upward in the direction of greater production is composed of three additional component forces: (*a*) the force corresponding to the goal of standard production; (*b*) a force corresponding to pressures induced by the management through supervision; and (*c*) a force corresponding to a group standard of competition. Let us examine each of these six component forces.

JOB DIFFICULTY. For all operators, the difficulty of the job is one of the forces downward on production. The difficulty of the job, of course, is relative to the skill of the operator. The given job may be very difficult for an unskilled operator but relatively easy for a highly skilled one. In the case of a transfer a new element of difficulty enters. For some time the new job is much more difficult, for the operator is unskilled at that particular job. In addition to the difficulty experienced by any learner, the transfer often encounters the added difficulty of proactive inhibition. Where the new job is similar to the old job, there will be a period of interference between the two similar but different skills required. For this reason a very efficient operator whose skills have become almost unconscious may suffer just as great a drop as a much less efficient operator. Except for the experiment on only two operators, the difficulty of these easy jobs does not explain the differential recovery rates, because both the initial difficulty and the amount of change were equated for these groups. The two operators probably dropped further and recovered more slowly than any of the other three groups under total participation because of the greater difficulty of the job.

STRAIN AVOIDANCE. The force toward lower production corresponding to the difficulty of the job (or the lack of skill of the person) has the character of a restraining force; that is, it acts to prevent locomotion rather than as a driving force causing locomotion. However, in all production there is a closely related driving force towards lower production, namely, "strain avoidance." We assume that working too hard and working too fast is an unpleasant strain; and corresponding to this negative valence there is a driving force in the opposite direction, namely, towards taking it easy or working slower. The higher the level of production the greater will be the strain and, other things being equal, the stronger will be the downward force of strain avoidance. Likewise, the greater the difficulty of the job, the stronger will be the force corresponding to strain avoidance. But the greater the operator's skill, the smaller will be the strain and the strength of the force of strain avoidance. Therefore:

*Proposition 5.* The

$$\text{strength of the force of strain avoidance} = \frac{\text{job difficulty} \times \text{production level}}{\text{skill of operator}}$$

The differential recovery rates of the three experimental groups in Experiment I cannot be explained by strain avoidance because job difficulty, production level, and operator skill were matched at the time immediately following transfer. Later, however, when the experimental treatments had produced a much higher level of production, these groups were subjected to an increased downward force of strain avoidance which was stronger than in the no-participation group in Experiment I. Evidently other forces were strong enough to overcome this force of strain avoidance.

THE GOAL OF STANDARD PRODUCTION. In considering the negative attitudes toward transfer and the resistance to being transferred, there are several important aspects of the complex goal of reaching and maintaining a level of 60 units per hour. For an operator producing below standard, this goal is attractive because it means success, high status in the eyes of her fellow employees, better pay, and job security. On the other hand, there is a strong force against remaining below standard because this lower level means failure, low status, low pay, and the danger of being fired. Thus it is clear that the upward force corresponding to the goal of standard production will indeed be strong for the transfer who has dropped below standard.

It is equally clear why any operator who accepts the stereotype about transfer shows such strong resistance to being changed. She sees herself as becoming a failure and losing status, pay, and perhaps the job itself. The result is a lowered level of aspiration and a weakened force toward the goal of standard production.

Just such a weakening of the force toward 60 units per hour seems to have occurred in the no-participation group in Experiment I. The participation treatments, on the other hand, seem to have involved the operators in designing the new job and setting the new piece rates in such a way that they did not lose hope of regaining the goal of standard production. Thus participation resulted in a stronger force toward higher production. However, this force alone can hardly account for the large differences in recovery rate between the no-participation group and the experimental groups; certainly it does not explain why the latter increased to a level so high above standard.

MANAGEMENT PRESSURE. On all operators below standard the management exerts a pressure for higher production. This pressure is no harsh and autocratic treatment involving threats; rather, it takes the form of persuasion and encouragement by the supervisors. They attempt to induce the low rating operator to improve her performance and to attain standard production.

Such an attempt to induce a psychological force on another person may have several results. In the first place the person may ignore the attempt of the inducing agent, in which case there is no induced force acting on the person. On the other hand, the attempt may succeed so that an induced force on the person exists. Other things being equal, whenever there is an induced force acting on a person, the person will locomote in the direction of the force. An induced force which depends on the power field of an inducing agent—some other individual or group—will cease to exist when the inducing power field is withdrawn. In this respect it is different from an "own" force which stems from a person's own needs and goals.

The reaction of a person to an effective induced force will vary depending, among other things, on the person's relation to the inducing agent. A force induced by a friend may be accepted in such a way that it acts more like an "own" force. An effective force induced by an enemy may be resisted and rejected so that the person complies unwillingly and shows signs of conflict and tension. Thus in addition to what might be called a "neutral" induced force, we also distinguish an *accepted* induced force and a *rejected* induced force. Naturally, the acceptance and the rejection of an induced force can vary in degree from zero (i.e., a neutral induced force) to very strong acceptance or rejection. To account for the difference in character between the acceptance and the rejection of an induced force, we make the following propositions:

*Proposition 6.* The acceptance of an induced force sets up additional "own" forces in the same direction.

*Proposition 7.* The rejection of an induced force sets up additional "own" forces in the opposite direction.

The grievances, aggression, and tension in the no-participation group in the first experiment indicate that they rejected the force toward higher production induced by the management. The group accepted the stereotype that transfer is a calamity, but the no-participation procedure did not convince them that the change was necessary, and they viewed the new job and the new piece rates set by management as arbitrary and unreasonable.

The other experimental groups, on the contrary, participated in designing the changes and setting the piece rates so that they spoke of the new job as "our job" and the new piece rates as "our rates." Thus they accepted the new situation and accepted the management-induced force toward higher production.

From the acceptance by the experimental groups and the rejection by the no-participation group of the management-induced forces, we may derive (by Props. 6 and 7 above) that the former had additional "own" forces toward higher production, whereas the latter had additional "own" forces toward lower production. This difference helps to explain the better recovery rate of the participation groups.

GROUP STANDARDS. Probably the most important force affecting the recovery under the no-participation procedure was a group standard, set by the group, restricting the level of production to 50 units per hour. Evidently this explicit agreement to restrict production is related to the group's rejection of the change and of the new job as arbitrary and unreasonable. Perhaps they had faint hopes of demonstrating that standard production could not be attained and thereby obtain a more favorable piece rate. In any case there was a definite group phenomenon which affected all the members of the group. We have already noted the striking example of the presser whose production was restricted in the group situation to about half the level she attained as an individual. In the no-participation group, we would also expect the group to induce strong forces on the members. The more a member deviates above the standard, the stronger would be the group-induced force to conform to the standard, for such deviations both negate any possibility of management's increasing the piece rate and at the same time expose the other members to increased pressure from management. Thus individual differences in levels of production should be sharply curtailed in this group after transfer.

An analysis was made, for all groups, of the individual differences within each group in levels of production. In Experiment I, the 40 days before change were compared with the 30 days after change; in Experiment II, the 10 days before change were compared to the 17 days after change. As a measure of variability, the standard deviation was calculated each day for each group. The average daily standard deviations before and after change were as follows:

| *Experiment I* | *Before Change* | *After Change* |
|---|---|---|
| No participation | 9.8 | 1.9 |
| Participation through representation | 9.7 | 3.8 |
| Total participation | 10.3 | 2.7 |
| Total participation | 9.9 | 2.4 |
| *Experiment II* | | |
| Total participation | 12.7 | 2.9 |

There is, indeed, a marked decrease in individual differences within the no-participation group after their first transfer. In fact, the restriction of production resulted in a lower variability than in any other group. Thus, we may conclude that the group standard at 50 units per hour set up strong group-induced forces which were important components in the central force field shown in Figure 4. It is now evident that for the no-participation group the quasi-stationary equilibrium after transfer has a steep gradient around the equilibrium level of 50 units per hour—the strength of forces increases rapidly above and below this level. It is also clear that the group standard to restrict production is a major reason for the lack of recovery in the no-participation group.

The table of variability also shows that the experimental treatments markedly reduced variability in the other four groups after transfer. In the group having participation by representation, this smallest reduction of variability was produced by a group standard of individual competition. Competition among members of the group was reported by the supervisor soon after transfer. This competition was a force toward higher production which resulted in good recovery to standard and continued progress beyond standard.

The total-participation groups showed a greater reduction in variability following transfer. These two groups were transferred on the same day. Group competition developed between the two groups, and this competition, which evidently resulted in stronger forces on the members than did the individual competition, was an effective group standard. The standard gradually moved to higher and higher levels of production, with the result that the groups not only reached but far exceeded their previous levels of production.

Probably a major determinant of the strength of these group standards is the cohesiveness of the group (1). Whether this power of the group over the members was used to increase or to decrease productivity seemed to depend upon the use of participation (4).

## Turnover and Aggression

Returning now to our preliminary theory of frustration, we can see several revisions. The difficulty of the job and its relation to skill and strain avoidance has been clarified in Proposition 5. It is now clear that the driving force toward 60 is a complex affair: it is partly a negative driving force corresponding to the negative valence of low pay, low status, failure, and job insecurity. Turnover results not only from the frustration produced by the conflict of these two forces, but also from a direct attempt to escape from the region of these negative valences. For the members of the no-participation group, the group standard to restrict production prevented escape by increasing production, so that quitting their jobs was the only remaining escape. In the participation groups, on the contrary, both the group standards and the additional own forces resulting from the acceptance of management-induced forces combined to make increasing production the distinguished path of escape from this region of negative valence.

In considering turnover as a form of escape from the field, it is not enough to look only at the psychological present; one must also consider the psychological future. The employee's decision to quit the job is rarely made exclusively on the basis of a momentary frustration or an undesirable present situation. She usually quits when she also sees the future as equally hopeless. The operator transferred by the usual factory procedure (including the no-participation group) has, in fact, a realistic view of the probability of continued failure because, as we have already noted, 62% of transfers do fail to recover to standard production. Thus, the higher rate of quitting for transfers as compared to nontransfers results from a more pessimistic view of the future.

The no-participation procedure had the effect for the members of setting up management as a hostile power field. They rejected the forces induced by this hostile power field, and group standards to restrict production developed within the group in opposition to management. In this conflict between the power field of management and the power field of the group, the group attempted to reduce the strength of the hostile power field relative to the strength of their own power field. This change was accomplished in three ways: (a) The group increased its own power by developing a more cohesive and well-disciplined group. (b) They secured "allies" by getting the backing of the union in filing a formal grievance about the new piece rate. (c) They attacked the hostile power field directly in the form of aggression against the supervisor, the time-study engineer, and the higher management. Thus the aggression was derived not only from individual frustration, but also from the conflict between two groups. Furthermore, this situation of group conflict both helped to define management as the frustrating agent and gave the members strength to express any aggressive impulses produced by frustration.

## Conclusions

It is possible for management to modify greatly or to remove completely group resistance to changes in methods of work and the ensuing piece rates. This change can be accomplished by the use of group meetings in which management effectively communicates the need for change and stimulates group participation in planning the changes.

For Harwood's management, and presumably for managements of other industries using an incentive system, this experiment has important implications in the field of labor relations. A majority of all grievances presented at Harwood have always stemmed from a change situation. By preventing or greatly modifying group resistance to change, this concomitant to change may well be greatly reduced. The reduction of such costly phenomena as turnover and slow relearning rates presents another distinct advantage.

Harwood's management has long felt that action research, such as the present experiment, is the only key to better labor-management relations. It is only by discovering the basic principles and applying them to the true causes of conflict that an intelligent, effective effort can be made to correct the undesirable effects of the conflict.

## References

1. Festinger, L., Back, K., Schachter, S., Kelley, H., & Thibaut, J.: *Theory and experiment in social communication.* Ann Arbor, Mich.: Institute for Social Research, 1950.

2. French, John R. P., Jr.: The behavior of organized and unorganized groups under conditions of frustration and fear. *University of Iowa Studies in Child Welfare,* 1944, **20,** 229–308.

3. Lewin, Kurt: Frontiers in group dynamics. *Human Relations,* 1947, **1,** 5–41.

4. Schachter, S., Ellertson, N., McBride, Dorothy, & Gregory, Doris: An experimental study of cohesiveness and productivity. *Human Relations,* 1951, **4,** 229–238.

# Participation by Subordinates in the Managerial Decision-making Process[*]

*Robert Tannenbaum*
*Fred Massarik*

## I. Introduction

The role of "participation" by individuals or groups in American culture in general and in industrial organizations specifically has been treated by many writers. Its implications for political theory as well as for a theory of human relations in formal organizations are numerous. However, in spite of this academic and extra-academic interest, a clear-cut, operational definition of the concept, or a precise set of hypotheses regarding its dynamics, has not been developed. While to do so will be the object of this paper, the treatment will not be completely operational. The development of appropriate methods of measurement is conceived as a next step that should follow the preliminary one of conceptual clarification undertaken in this paper.

A review of the literature indicates that three major approaches have been taken in dealing with "participation":

1. *The experiential approach.* This approach is exemplified by writers who in the course of their experience in enterprise work have obtained a "feel" for the role of participation in the decision-making process and have put down their experiences in article or book form.[1] Writings such as these

---

[*] From *Canadian Journal of Economics and Political Science,* 1950, pp. 408–418. Reprinted by permission of the authors and the Canadian Journal of Economics and Political Science.

[1] For example: H. H. Carey, "Consultative Supervision and Management" (*Personnel,* Mar., 1942); Alexander R. Heron, *Why Men Work* (Palo Alto, 1948); Eric A. Nicol, "Management through Consultative Supervision" (*Personnel Journal,* Nov., 1948); James C. Worthy, "Changing Concepts of the Personnel Function" (*Personnel,* Nov., 1948).

provide a set of insights and hunches whose verification in any systematic fashion has not been attempted. The actual referents from which these formulations are derived often are single sets of observations in a single or in a few enterprises—observations generally made in an uncontrolled fashion.

The experiential approach, operating outside the bounds of scientific method, nonetheless adds to scientific knowledge indirectly by providing the raw material from which hypotheses may be moulded. The precise structure of these hypotheses is not stated neatly by the experiential writers, but rather remains to be formulated.

2. *The conceptual, non-experimental approach.* This approach characterizes the writings of authors who are, essentially, academicians with strong theoretical backgrounds. It is typified by writings that deal with "conditions," "functions," and other abstractions, generally of a socio-psychological nature, that attempt to explain the dynamics of participation.[2] The conceptual, non-experimental approach at its best is the process of theory or hypothesis formulation. Ideally it lays the groundwork for actual testing and experimental work, but much of this type of technical literature so far published on participation lacks the clarity of conceptual definition necessary to make it useful as a basis for experimental work.

3. *The experimental approach.* This approach is found in the writings of authors who have seen fit to apply experimental techniques either to especially constructed social situations involving participation, or else in natural settings in which participational activities prevail.[3] With adequate controls and with a meaningful theoretical structure within which individual findings may be placed, this approach is doubtless the most fruitful. Ideally it indicates what will happen under specified sets of conditions and with what degree of probability. Unfortunately, up to now experimental work on the dynamics of participation in the decision-making process has been sporadic.[4]

The present paper is of the conceptual, non-experimental type. Participation in the decision-making process is conceived here as an instrument that may be used by the formal leadership of an enterprise in the pursuit of its goals. No attempt will be made to examine it from an ethical standpoint or in terms of its consistency within the frame of a democratic so-

---

[2] For example: Douglas McGregor, "Conditions for Effective Leadership in the Industrial Situation" (*Journal of Consulting Psychology,* vol. VIII, Mar.–Apr., 1944); Gordon W. Allport, "The Psychology of Participation" (*Psychological Review,* May, 1945).

[3] For the concept of the "natural experiment," see F. Stuart Chapin, *Experimental Designs in Sociological Research* (New York, 1947), and Ernest Greenwood, *Experimental Sociology* (New York, 1945).

[4] For a good summary of relevant experimental work, see Ronald Lippitt, "A Program of Experimentation on Group Functioning and Productivity" (in *Current Trends in Social Psychology,* Pittsburgh, 1948).

ciety, although it is by no means assumed that such considerations are less important than the ones set forward here.

## II. Definition of Participation

It is essential, in dealing with participation, to make clear the meaning which is to be attached to the concept. One must specify both who the participators are and in what they are participating. Too frequently in the available literature on the subject the reader must determine these matters for himself since no explicit statements bearing on them are made by the writers.

As already indicated, this paper is primarily concerned with participation as a managerial device. Attention is therefore focused on the subordinates of managers in enterprises as the participators. It is important to note that these subordinates may be either non-managers or managers.[5] If they are managers, they are subordinates of superior managers in the formal organization of the enterprise in addition to having subordinates who are responsible to them.

Because of space limitations, consideration of the participation of individuals as union members in specific activities of an enterprise is excluded from the scope of this paper. Suffice it to say here that in those cases where the participation of union members is direct and personal, the benefits to be derived by the enterprise are similar to those derived from participation within the superior-subordinate relationship. However, in those cases (which are the greatest in number) where the participation of the union member is indirect and impersonal, it is doubtful if such is the result. It is our conclusion that most of the statements which follow are relevant to the former cases.[6]

What then is the meaning of participation, and with what type of participation by subordinates are we here concerned? An individual participates in something when he takes a part or share in that thing. Since taking a part or sharing is always involved, participation takes place in a social context. Managerial subordinates in formal enterprises are responsible to their superiors for the performance of designated tasks. In such performance, they are participating in the production of the good or service of the enterprise. They also participate (share), through the receipt of wages or salaries, in the distribution of the total revenue received by the enterprise. These types of participation are common to all enterprises. But there is another type of participation which is much less frequently encountered,

[5] For definitions of these terms as used here, see Robert Tannenbaum, "The Manager Concept: A Rational Synthesis" (*Journal of Business,* Oct., 1949).

[6] In connexion with this discussion, it should be noted that when participation takes place within the superior-subordinate relationship, managers have primary control over the nature of the activity; when it takes place as part of the manager-union relationship, they may or may not, depending upon the relative power of the two parties.

although its use as a managerial device has, of recent years, grown rapidly in importance. This type involves participation by subordinates with their superiors in the managerial decision-making process.

Decisions are made by managers in order to organize, direct, or control responsible subordinates to the end that all service contributions be co-ordinated in the attainment of an enterprise purpose.[7] Since managers are those who accomplish results through subordinates, the latter are always directly and intimately affected by managerial decisions and therefore may have a considerable interest in them. Because of this possible interest, sub-ordinates may have a strong desire, particularly in a nation with deeply ingrained democratic traditions, to participate in the determination of mat-ters affecting them. It is of importance, therefore, to consider the form which such participation might assume.

Decision-making involves a conscious choice or selection of one behav-iour alternative from among a group of two or more behaviour alternatives.[8] Three steps are involved in the decision-making process. First, an individ-ual must become aware of as many as possible of those behaviour alterna-tives which are relevant to the decision to be made. Secondly, he must define each of these alternatives, a definition which involves a determina-tion of as many as possible of the consequences related to each alternative under consideration. Thirdly, the individual must exercise a choice between the alternatives, that is, make a decision.

In enterprises, managerial subordinates, as subordinates, can participate in the first two steps of the managerial decision-making process. They can-not participate in the third step. The actual choice between relevant alter-natives must be made or accepted by the manager who is responsible to his superior for the decision.[9] However, subordinates can provide and dis-cuss with their manager information with respect both to relevant alterna-tives and to the consequences attendant upon specific alternatives. In so doing they are participating in the managerial decision-making process.[10]

[7] See Tannenbaum, "The Manager Concept: A Rational Synthesis."

[8] This discussion of the decision-making process is based upon Robert Tannen-baum, "Managerial Decision-Making" (*Journal of Business*, Jan., 1950).

[9] In a democratic group, the choice can be made through a vote participated in by the rank and file. But, in such a case, the leader is organizationally responsible to the rank and file, and the members of the rank and file are not properly, in so far as the decision is concerned, subordinates of the leader.

Members of a democratic group, making the final choice in matters directly affect-ing them, may be more highly motivated as a result thereof than managerial sub-ordinates who are granted the right to participate only in the first two steps of the managerial decision-making process. For evidence of the motivational effects of group decision, see Kurt Lewin, "Group Decision and Social Change" (in T. M. Newcomb and E. L. Hartley (eds.), *Readings in Social Psychology*, New York, 1947.

[10] It is this type of participation that most writers, who deal with human relations in enterprises, have in mind when they use the concept. The following examples illustrate this contention: "One of the most important conditions of the subordinate's

The participation with which we are here concerned may take place in two different ways. First, it may involve interaction solely between a subordinate and his manager.[11] This would be the case where a worker originates a suggestion which he transmits to his boss. Secondly, it may involve interaction between a group of subordinates and their manager. This would be the case where a manager calls his subordinates together to discuss a common problem or to formulate a recommendation.[12]

## III. Possible Advantages of Participation as a Managerial Device

It becomes useful to inquire why managers might find it advantageous to use this device. In other words, what are the possible benefits which might accrue to an enterprise whose managers made it possible for subordinates to participate in the decision-making process? In providing an answer to this question, it is first necessary to indicate the criterion which would guide the managerial choice relating to the use of participation.

A manager of an enterprise (profit or nonprofit) who behaves rationally will attempt to make a selection from among alternatives related to any problem which will maximize results (the degree of attainment of a given

growth and development centers around his opportunities to express his ideas and to contribute his suggestions before his superiors take action on matters which involve him. Through participation of this kind he becomes more and more aware of his superiors' problems, and he obtains genuine satisfaction in knowing that his opinions and ideas are given consideration in the search for solutions" (D. McGregor, "Conditions for Effective Leadership in the Industrial Situation," p. 60); "I am not suggesting that we take over intact the apparatus of the democratic state. Business cannot be run by the ballot box. . . . We must develop other inventions, adapted to the special circumstances of business, which will give employees at all levels of our organizations a greater sense of personal participation and 'belonging' " (J. Worthy, "Changing Concepts of the Personnel Function," p. 175); "Action initiated by the responsible head to bring his subordinates into the picture on matters of mutual concern is not a sharing of prerogatives of authority. Rather, it is an extension of the opportunity of participation in the development of points of view and the assembly of facts upon which decisions are made" (H. Carey, "Consultative Supervision and Management," p. 288).

[11] The concept of interaction as used here is not restricted to direct person-to-person, two-way communication (as in the process of superior-subordinate discussion), but encompasses more indirect forms (such as, for example, written communication) as well.

[12] It may be observed that participation in the latter way, where there is communication between participators and where the act of participation is carried out through the medium of the group (as in cases of "group decision"), may often yield the more useful results. The level of derivable benefits may be higher than if participation had proceeded through channels in which there had been no inter-participator communication. Some factors important in this context are the following: (a) the feeling of "group belongingness" obtained by means of "action together" and (b) the role of norms, set as a result of group discussion, toward which behaviour will tend to gravitate.

end) at a given cost or which will attain given results at the lowest cost.[13] This is the criterion of rationality. Guided by this criterion, rational managers will find it advantageous to use participation whenever such use will lead to increased results at a given cost or to the attainment of given results at a lower cost.

There are many advantages which *may* stem from the use of participation as a managerial device. The following are the principal ones:

1. A higher rate of output and increased quality of product (including reduced spoilage and wastage) as a result of greater personal effort and attention on the part of subordinates.[14]

2. A reduction in turnover, absenteeism, and tardiness.

3. A reduction in the number of grievances and more peaceful manager-subordinate and manager-union relations.

4. A greater readiness to accept change.[15] When changes are arbitrarily introduced from above without explanation, subordinates tend to feel insecure and to take countermeasures aimed at a sabotage of the innovations. But when they have participated in the process leading to the decision, they have had an opportunity to be heard. They know what to expect and why, and they may desire the change. Blind resistance tends to become intelligent adaptation as insecurity is replaced by security.

5. Greater ease in the management of subordinates.[16] Fewer managers may be necessary, the need for close supervision may be reduced, and less disciplinary action may be called for. Subordinates who have participated in the process leading toward a determination of matters directly affecting them may have a greater sense of responsibility with respect to the performance of their assigned tasks and may be more willing to accept the authority of their superiors. All managers possess a given amount of formal authority delegated to them by their superiors. But formal authority is not necessarily the equivalent of effective authority. The real source of the authority possessed by an individual

---

[13] The term *cost* is here used in its highly precise form to refer to whatever must be given or sacrificed to attain an end. See "Price," *Webster's Dictionary of Synonyms*. The term *end* is broadly conceived to embrace whatever factors (monetary or nonmonetary) the managers themselves define as the formal ends of the enterprise.

[14] For examples, see Lippitt, "A Program of Experimentation on Group Functioning and Productivity"; John R. P. French, Jr., Arthur Kornhauser, and Alfred Marrow, "Conflict and Co-operation in Industry" (*Journal of Social Issues*, Feb., 1946); *Productivity, Supervision and Morale* (Survey Research Center Study no. 6, Ann Arbor, 1948).

[15] See, for example, Alex Bavelas, "Some Problems of Organizational Change" (*Journal of Social Issues*, Summer, 1948); Elliott Jacques, "Interpretive Group Discussion as a Method of Facilitating Social Change" (*Human Relations*, Aug., 1948); Lewin, "Group Decision and Social Change."

[16] See, for example, L. P. Bradford and R. Lippitt, "Building a Democratic Work Group" (*Personnel*, Nov., 1945); O. H. Mowrer, "Authoritarianism vs. 'Self-Government' in the Management of Children's Aggressive (Anti-Social) Reactions as a Preparation for Citizenship in a Democracy" (*Journal of Social Psychology*, Feb., 1939, pp. 121–126).

lies in the acceptance of its exercise by those who are subject to it. It is the subordinates of an individual who determine the authority which he may wield. Formal authority is, in effect, nominal authority. It becomes real only when it is accepted. Thus, to be effective, formal authority must coincide with authority determined by its acceptance. The latter defines the useful limits of the former.[17] The use of participation as a managerial device may result in a widening of these limits, reducing the amount of resistance to the exercise of formal authority and increasing the positive responses of subordinates to managerial directives.

6. The improved quality of managerial decisions. It is seldom if ever possible for managers to have knowledge of *all* alternatives and *all* consequences related to the decisions which they must make. Because of the existence of barriers to the upward flow of information in most enterprises, much valuable information possessed by subordinates never reaches their managers. Participation tends to break down the barriers, making the information available to managers. To the extent that such information alters the decisions which managers make, the quality of their decisions may thereby be improved.

These, then, are the principal advantages which *may* stem from the use of participation as a managerial device.[18] The conditions under which it *will* accomplish them—under which participation will lead to motivation —is the concern of the section which follows.

## IV. The Psychological Conditions of Effective Participation

All managers of an enterprise are faced with the problem of eliciting service contributions from their subordinates at a high level of quality and intensity. These service contributions are essential if the formal goals of the enterprise are to be attained. What induces subordinates to contribute their services? What motivates them?

A motivated individual is one who is striving to achieve a goal; his activity is goal-oriented.[19] But it should be stressed that motivation is only *potential* motion towards a goal. Whether or not the goal is reached depends not only upon the strength of the force in the direction of the goal, but also upon all other forces (both driving and restraining) in the given situation.[20] To illustrate, a person may be motivated to produce 200 units of an item per day, but the restraining force in the form of machine failure

---

[17] This concept of effective authority is expanded upon in Tannenbaum, "Managerial Decision-Making."

[18] These advantages will henceforth be referred to as enterprise advantages.

[19] A goal is defined as a result which, when achieved, has the power to reduce the tension of the organism that has caused the organism to seek it.

[20] Thus, motion in the direction of goals may be achieved not only by adding forces in the goal-direction, but also by reducing forces impeding such motion. See K. Lewin, "Frontiers in Group Dynamics" (*Human Relations*, vol. I, no. 1, 1947, pp. 26–27).

or a quarrel with the foreman may lead him to attain an output of only 150 units.

In enterprises, the goals towards which individuals strive may be of two kinds. They may be the formal goals of the enterprise, or they may be other goals which are complementary to the formal goals. The latter is the typical case. Individuals may strive for monetary reward, prestige, power, security, and the like; or they may strive for certain psychological gratifications through the very act of doing the job (that is, they work because they like their work). The primary reason why they contribute their services is to attain these latter goals. In attaining these desired goals, they make possible the attainment of the formal goals of the enterprise which to them are simply means to their own ends. In this sense, the desired goals and the formal goals are complementary.

In the former case, the goals desired by the individual and the formal goals are the same. The individual contributes his services primarily because such contribution makes possible the attainment of the formal goals of the enterprise which coincide with his own personal goals. To the extent that this coincidence of goals exists, the necessity for managers to provide complementary goals for subordinates is thereby lessened, and related costs are reduced. It is suggested that participation tends to bring about a coincidence of formal and personal goals.[21] It may be that through participation, the subordinate who formerly was moved to contribute his services only because he sought, for example, security and financial rewards, now comes to be moved additionally because he recognizes that the success of the enterprise in turn will enhance his own ability to satisfy his needs.[22]

Whether one conceives of participation as involving separate subordinates with their superiors or subordinates-in-groups with their superiors, in the final analysis one must not lose sight of the fact that the subordinate is a unique human being with a given personality. This implies that whether or not participation will bring forth the restructuring of his goal pattern (incorporating the formal goals within the scope of the personal goals)

---

[21] It must be noted that participation as used in this context is only one device which may lead to additional motivation by bringing about a coincidence of formal and personal goals. For example, some other devices that under certain conditions may result in motivational increases and their derivative benefits to the enterprise are permitting personal discretion to the person to be motivated and stimulation of a sense of pride of workmanship. In the former context, managers in all enterprises must always decide the amount of discretion to permit to subordinates. Many considerations naturally underlie this decision. For present purposes, it is important to emphasize that in many circumstances, the granting of considerable discretion may lead to substantial increases in motivation. Several devices may be used concurrently, and the dynamics of the devices themselves are interrelated. For example, use of discretion may bring about an enhanced pride-of-workmanship feeling.

[22] It must be recognized that typically goal configurations, rather than single goals, act as motivating agents.

will depend upon a set of dynamic psychological conditions, the primary ones of which are outlined below:

1. The subordinate must be capable of becoming psychologically involved in the participational activities. He must be free from "blockages" which may prevent him from re-arranging his particular goal pattern in the light of new experience. He must possess some minimum amount of intelligence so that he may grasp the meaning and implications of the thing being considered. He must be in touch with reality. If he responds to a dream world, any "real" developments, such as opportunities to take part in certain decision-making processes, may not penetrate without gross distortion and as a result miss their point.

2. The subordinate must favour participational activity. In other words, the person who believes that "the boss knows best" and that the decision-making process is none of his business is not likely to become strongly motivated if given an opportunity to participate. It is apparent that for personality types shaped intensely by an authoritarian system, opportunities for participation may be regarded as signs of weakness and leadership incompetence and on that basis may be rejected unequivocally.[23]

3. The subordinate must see the relevance to his personal life pattern of the thing being considered. When he realizes that through participation he may affect the course of his future in such a fashion as to increase its positive goal elements and to diminish the negative ones, he will become motivated. For example, a person who can see the relationship between "putting his two bits" into a discussion of a new way of using a stitching machine and the fact that this may mean greater job security and increased pay for himself may be motivated.

4. The subordinate must be able to express himself to his own satisfaction with respect to the thing being considered. He must be psychologically able to communicate; and, further, he must feel that he is making some sort of contribution. Of course, if he cannot communicate (owing to mental blocks, fear of being conspicuous, etc.), by definition he is not participating. If he does not feel that he is contributing, he may, instead of becoming motivated, come to feel inadequate and frustrated. This presupposes that not only is he articulate, but that he has a certain fund of knowledge on which to draw. Participation may fail if it involves considering matters that are quite outside the scope of experience of the participators.

All of the above conditions must be satisfied to some minimum extent. Beyond this requirement, however, the conditions may be mutually compensating, and a relatively low degree of one (although necessarily above the minimum) may be offset somewhat by an extremely high degree of another. For example, if a subordinate is unusually anxious to take part in

[23] For example, see A. H. Maslow, "The Authoritarian Character Structure" (in P. L. Harriman (ed.), *Twentieth Century Psychology*, New York, 1946). For more detailed treatments see the major works of Erich Fromm and Abram Kardiner.

participational activity (perhaps for reasons of prestige desires), he may come to be quite involved in the process of restructuring his goal pattern so that it will include some of the formal goals, even though he is not always certain as to whether or not he is really contributing anything worthwhile. Further, the relationships specified by the conditions are essentially dynamic. Opportunities for participation, reluctantly used at first, ultimately may lead to a change of mind and to their enthusiastic acceptance.[24]

It is apparent that individual differences are highly important in considering the effectiveness of participation as a motivational device; however, the "amount of participation opportunities" made possible by the managers is also a variable quantity. Thus, it is necessary to enquire what the limits to opportunities to participate are in terms of maximum results.

Common sense experience indicates that when some subordinates are given too many opportunities for participation, or too much leeway in participating, they may tend to flounder; they may find themselves unable to assimilate effectively the range of "thinking opportunities" with which they are faced.[25] On the other hand, if they are given little or no opportunity to take part in the decision-making process, by definition they will not come to be motivated by participational activity. For each individual, an amount of participation opportunities lying somewhere between these two extremes will result in a maximum amount of motivation. A hypothesis stemming from this formulation is that for effective operation of participation as a motivational device in a group situation, the members of the group must respond similarly to given amounts of participation, for wide divergences of response may bring forth social tensions and lack of team work within the group.

Of course, many factors act together to motivate an individual. Therefore, the usefulness of the conceptualization advanced depends upon the possibility of breaking down the total of motivational forces into those owing to participation and those owing to other factors. Experimental control methods, matching of cases, and similar devices may have to be utilized to make such an analysis possible. Whether or not the increment of motivation owing to participation is worthwhile depends to an important extent upon the level of intensity of motivation that prevailed previous to introduc-

[24] It should be stressed that "life spaces" of individuals (that is, their conceptions of themselves in relation to the totality of a physical and psychological environment) and their readiness for action in the light of these conceptions are never static. Constant change and "restructuring" take place, making for an essentially dynamic patterning of behaviour. For alternative definitions of the concept "life space" see Robert W. Leeper, *Lewin's Topological and Vector Psychology* (Eugene, 1943), p. 210.

[25] For the belief that "thinking" as a solution for the industrial problem of motivation is usable more effectively on the supervisory level, but less applicable on the "lower levels" of the organizational hierarchy, see Willard Tomlison; "Review of A. R. Heron, *Why Men Work*" (*Personnel Journal*, July–Aug., 1948, p. 122).

tion of the device of participation. No doubt, there are upper limits to intensity of motivation, and, if motivation has been strong all along, the effect of participation may not be very great.

## V. Extra-Participational Conditions for Effective Participation

Beyond the factors governing the relationship between participation and possible resultant motivation, certain conditions "outside" the individual must be considered by the managers in deciding whether or not this particular device is applicable.[26] It would be possible to distinguish a great number of such outside conditions that may determine whether or not the use of participation is feasible in a given situation. Those here indicated are suggestive rather than fully definitive. All are viewed with this question in mind: "Granting that participation may have certain beneficial effects, is it useful in a given instance if the ends of the enterprise are to be achieved?"

To answer this question affirmatively, the following conditions must be met:

1. *Time availability.* The final decision must not be of a too urgent nature.[27] If it is necessary to arrive at some sort of emergency decision rapidly, it is obvious that even though participation in the decision-making process may have a beneficial effect in some areas, slowness of decision may result in thwarting other goals of the enterprise or even may threaten the existence of the enterprise. Military decisions frequently are of this type.

2. *Rational economics.* The cost of participation in the decision-making process must not be so high that it will outweigh any positive values directly brought about by it. If it should require outlays which could be used more fruitfully in alternative activities (for example, buying more productive though expensive equipment), then investment in it would be ill-advised.

3. *Intra-plant strategy.*

a. *Subordinate security.* Giving the subordinates an opportunity to participate in the decision-making process must not bring with it any awareness on their part of unavoidable catastrophic events. For example, a subordinate who is made aware in the participation process that he will lose his job *regardless* of any decisions towards which he might contribute may experience a drop in motivation. Furthermore, to make it possible for the subordinate to be willing to participate, he must be given the feeling that no matter what he says or thinks his status or role in the plant setting will

---

[26] For analytical purposes, this article differentiates between conditions regarding the dynamics of participation as a psychological process and all conditions outside this psychological participation-to-motivation link. The latter category of conditions is treated under the present heading.

[27] See Chester I. Barnard, *Organization and Management* (Cambridge, 1948), p. 48.

not be affected adversely. This point has been made effectively in the available literature.[28]

*b. Manager-subordinate stability.* Giving subordinates an opportunity to participate in the decision-making process must not threaten seriously to undermine the formal authority of the managers of the enterprise. For example, in some cases managers may have good reasons to assume that participation may lead non-managers to doubt the competence of the formal leadership, or that serious crises would result were it to develop that the subordinates were right while the final managerial decision turned out to be in disagreement with them and incorrect.

4. *Inter-plant strategy.* Providing opportunities for participation must not open channels of communication to competing enterprises. "Leaks" of information to a competitor from subordinates who have participated in a given decision-making process must be avoided if participation is to be applicable.

5. *Provision for communication channels.* For participation to be effective, channels must be provided through which the employee may take part in the decision-making process. These channels must be available continuously and their use must be convenient and practical.[29]

6. *Education for participation.* For participation to be effective, efforts must be made to educate subordinates regarding its function and purpose in the over-all functioning of the enterprise.[30]

It must be stressed that the conditions stipulated in this section are dynamic in their own right and may be affected by the very process of participation as well as by other factors.

## VI. Effects of Participation as a Function of Time

An area of research that still remains relatively unexplored is that relating to the variation of the effects of participation with time. Some experimental studies have examined these effects in terms of increased productivity over a period of several weeks or months and found no appreciable reductions in productivity with time; while other evidence indicates that in some cases participation may have a sort of "shock" effect, leading to a surge of interest and increased motivation, with a subsequent decline.[31]

[28] See McGregor, "Conditions for Effective Leadership in the Industrial Situation," *passim.*

[29] For a rigorous mathematical treatment of channels of communication within groups see Alex Bavelas, "A Mathematical Model for Group Structures" (*Applied Anthropology,* Summer, 1948, pp. 16 ff.).

[30] See French, Kornhauser, and Marrow, "Conflict and Co-operation in Industry," p. 30.

[31] For evidence of no decline in the motivational effect of certain participational procedures in an industrial re-training situation after a relatively brief time period

Inadequate attention seems to have been given to this rather crucial question, and the present writers know of no studies that have traced the effects of participation (or other motivational devices) over periods as long as a year. However, on a priori grounds, and on the basis of experimental evidence, it would seem that, after an initial spurt, a plateau of beneficial effects will be attained, which finally will dissolve into a decline, unless additional managerial devices are skilfully employed.

# READINGS RELATED TO CHAPTER X

## Employee Attitudes and Employee Performance*

*Arthur H. Brayfield*
*Walter H. Crockett*

## Theoretical Considerations

*Morale as an explanatory concept in industrial psychology.* One principal generalization suffices to set up an expectation that morale should be related to absenteeism and turnover, namely, that organisms tend to avoid those situations which are punishing and to seek out situations that are rewarding. To the extent that worker dissatisfaction indicates that the individual is in a punishing situation, we should expect dissatisfied workers to be absent more often and to quit the job at a higher rate than individuals who are satisfied with their work. Since the general proposition about the effects of reward has received a great amount of verification in psychology, it is not strange that it has been carried to the analysis of absenteeism and turnover.

A plausible connection between satisfaction and performance on the job is less obvious. Let us consider specifically the possible relationship between satisfaction and productivity. Under conditions of marked dissatisfaction it is likely that low productivity may serve as a form of aggression which reflects worker hostility toward management. But the hypothesis that production should increase monotonically with increases in satisfaction apparently rests on the assumption that the worker will demonstrate his gratitude by increased output, or that the increased satisfaction frees certain

---

* From *Psychological Bulletin*, vol. 52, no. 5, pp. 415–422, 1955. Reprinted by permission of the American Psychological Association.

creative energies in the worker, or that the satisfied employee accepts management's goals, which include high production.

In any event, it is commonly hypothesized that, whatever the causes, increased satisfaction makes workers more motivated to produce. Given this condition, it should follow that increased productivity can be attained by increasing worker satisfaction. We are going to advance the proposition that the motivational structure of industrial workers is not so simple as is implied in this formula. We feel that research workers have erred by overlooking individual differences in motivations and perceptions because of their concern with discovering important and applicable generalizations. Most of what follows is an effort to point out areas in which differences between workmen may make a difference in their adjustment to the situation.

At the outset let us make it clear that we expect the relation between satisfaction and job performance to be one of concomitant variation rather than cause and effect. It makes sense to us to assume that individuals are motivated to achieve certain environmental goals and that the achievement of these goals results in satisfaction. Productivity is seldom a goal in itself but is more commonly a means to goal attainment. Therefore, as G. M. Mahoney has suggested,[1] we might expect high satisfaction and high productivity to occur together when productivity is perceived as a path to certain important goals and when these goals are achieved. Under other conditions, satisfaction and productivity might be unrelated or even negatively related. In the light of this consideration, we shall center our discussion on an analysis of industrial motivation as it relates specifically to employee satisfaction and to productivity.

For the sake of convenience we may distinguish between threats and rewards as incentives to productivity. Goode and Fowler (21) have described a factory in which morale and productivity were negatively related but productivity was kept high by the continuance of threats to workers. Here the essential workers—people with considerable skill—were marginal to the labor force because of their sex or because of physical handicaps. Since the plant was not unionized, it was possible for management to demand high productivity from these workers on threat of discharge. This meant that the workers, although most dissatisfied with their jobs, produced at a very high rate because of the difficulty they would face in finding another position should they be discharged.

There is little doubt that threat was widely used as a motivating device in our own society in the past and is presently used in more authoritarian societies. However, it is doubtful if any great amount of at least explicit threat is currently used by industries in this country in efforts to increase productivity or reduce absenteeism. First of all, considerable change has occurred in management philosophy over the past fifty years, and such

---

[1] G. M. Mahoney. Personal communication. March, 1953.

tactics are repugnant to many industrial concerns. Secondly, the growth of unions has virtually outlawed such tendencies except in small, semi-marginal industries which are not unionized.

Threats of discharge, then, probably do not operate as incentives unless the worker falls considerably below the mean in quantity and/or quality of output. For a number of reasons management has settled upon rewards for motivating workers to produce, including such tangible incentives as increased pay and promotion, as well as verbal and other symbolic recognition. Let us examine whether this system of rewards actually provides motivation for increased productivity by the worker.

It is a commonplace observation that motivation is not a simple concept. It is a problem which may be attacked at a number of different levels and from many theoretical points of view. Whatever their theoretical predilection, however, psychologists generally are agreed that human motivation is seldom directed only toward goals of physical well-being. Once a certain minimum level of living has been achieved, human behavior is directed largely toward some social goal or goals. Thus, in our own society, goals such as achievement, acceptance by others, dominance over others, and so on, probably are of as great concern to the average workman as the goals of finding sufficient food and shelter to keep body and psyche together.

We assume that social motives are of considerable importance in industry. We assume, further, that the goals an individual pursues will vary, depending upon the social systems within which he is behaving from time to time. Most industrial workers probably operate in a number of social systems. Katz and Kahn (33) suggest four such systems: first, the system of relations outside the plant; and, within the plant, the systems of relationship with fellow workers on the job, with members of the union, and with others in the company structure. We may ask whether job performance, and particularly productivity, is a path to goal achievement within these various sets of social relations.

OUTSIDE THE PLANT. It is often argued that any worker who is motivated to increase his status in the outside community should be motivated toward higher productivity within the plant. Productivity frequently leads directly to more money on the job, or involves movement to jobs with higher prestige or with authority over others. If productivity does result in such in-plant mobility, increased output may enable the individual to achieve a higher level of living, to increase his general status in the community, and to attempt such social mobility as he may desire. In this way productivity may serve as a path to the achievement of goals outside the plant.

The operation of this chain of relationships, however, depends not only upon the rewards given the high producer, but also upon the original motivation of the workman to increase his status position in the outside community. The amount of status motivation among production-line employees is open to question. Certainly the findings of Warner (57), Davis and Gardner (12), and others (6, 11, 13), indicate that there are systematic differences in the goals which are pursued in the different segments of our society. It is not impossible that a very large proportion of America's work force is only minimally motivated toward individual social achievement. The assumption that such a motivation does exist may reflect in considerable part a projection of certain middle-class aspirations onto working-class employees.

Furthermore, it is not unlikely that the reference group against which an individual workman evaluates his success may be only a segment of the community, rather than the community as a whole. An individual whose accomplishments are modest at best when compared with the range of possible accomplishments in the community may have a feeling of great accomplishment when he compares his achievements with those of others in his environment. If this is true, and if he desires to continue to operate within this segment of society, any further increase in rewards within the plant might lead to his exclusion from personally important groups outside the plant rather than to increased prestige in such groups.

Finally, there are many goals outside the industrial plant which may be socially rewarding to the individual and which require only minimal financial and occupational rewards inside the plant. Active participation in veterans' organizations, in churches, in recreational programs and similar activities may be and frequently are carried out by individuals at all positions in the industrial hierarchy. As a matter of fact, to the extent that the individual receives extensive social rewards from such activities he may have only slight interest in his work on the job, and he may continue to remain in industry only to maintain some minimum economic position while carrying out his outside functions. For such an individual, high productivity may lead to *no* important goals.

RELATIONS WITH OTHER WORKERS IN THE PLANT. The studies by Elton Mayo and his associates (43, 50, 51) introduced the work group into the analysis of industry, and a wealth of subsequent investigations have confirmed the importance of on-the-job groups. Throughout these studies has run the observation that members of the work group develop group standards of productivity and attempt to force these standards upon those workmen who deviate. Thus, in the Bank Wiring Room (51) it was the socially maladjusted individual, the deviant from the work group, who maintained a level of production above that of the group even though his native ability was considerably below that of many of the others.

Mathewson's (42) classic study of restriction of output among unorganized workers was an early demonstration of the operation of group norms.

Schachter and associates (52) have conducted an experiment which indicates that in cohesive groups an individual's productivity may be either raised or lowered, depending upon the kind of communications directed toward him by congenial co-workers. In an actual factory setting, Coch and French (8) presented existent groups with evidence that a change in job methods and in productivity was necessary if the factory was to remain in a favorable position relative to other, competing factories. These groups, through group discussion, arrived at a decision as to the proper job set up, and modified the group judgment of "fair" output markedly upward.

There is evidence, then, that the level of performance on the job frequently depends upon a group norm, and that performance level may be changed by changing the group norm in a direction desired by management. This change in the norm probably results from a conviction among the workers that higher production is in their own interest as well as management's, i.e., that their interests and management's interests coincide. This raises the perplexing question of whether, with regard to productivity, the interests of management and labor do, in fact, coincide.

Management, presumably, is interested in higher production as a way of reducing the ratio of cost to output, and thereby bettering management's financial and competitive position. In an expanding market, the argument goes, this makes possible the expansion of the company, increased wages, a larger labor force, and general prosperity not only for the corporation but for the employees as well.

The case may not be so attractive to the workers, especially when the market is not expanding and demand for the product is constant, nearly constant, or declining. In this event, higher productivity per worker means that fewer people are required for the same level of output, or that fewer hours are worked by the same number of workers. In either case, many workers may lose, rather than gain, by the increase in productivity. It may be argued that in normal times such individuals usually find fairly rapid employment in some other segment of the economy. However true this may be, from the viewpoint of the individual workman this involves a considerable disruption in working habits and in his social life in general, and is to be avoided wherever possible. Viewed in this light the interests of management and labor are inimical.

As psychologists we steer clear of such arguments. But we should be sensitive to the fact that the question is a debatable one, that a final decision will probably rest upon values rather than data, that each side is capable of convincing arguments, and that the perception of a certain inevitable conflict of interests between the two groups is honestly and intelligently held by many people. We should also recognize that any reduction in work force after a joint labor-management effort to increase productivity will likely be interpreted as resulting from the increased productivity, and may lead to a future avoidance not only of high productivity levels but also of labor-management cooperation.

At any rate, we often find that individual workers interpret higher productivity as counter to the interests of the employees. To the extent that this perception constitutes a group norm, such motives as are rewarded through the individual's social relationships with other workmen may be blocked by increased productivity. In such cases, productivity may serve as a path to certain goals, but as a block to social acceptance.

THE UNION STRUCTURE. One system of relationships of considerable importance in many industrial concerns is the union. In many companies much of what was said in the preceding section may be extended to refer also to the relations of the worker in the system of social relations within the union.

In some plants high productivity is not a deterrent to active union participation. Nevertheless, it probably is true that productivity is seldom a prerequisite for advancement within the union hierarchy. If the individual is oriented toward the union structure, it is unlikely that high productivity will serve as a path to such goals, whatever its effect on other goals he may pursue.

THE COMPANY STRUCTURE. We have indicated above that many of the worker's social motives outside the plant, as well as his desires for in-plant associations with fellow workmen and within the union, may be only slightly affected by increases in productivity and sometimes may be blocked by increased productivity. The apparent range of goals that a worker may have is so wide that productivity may be a path to only a few of them.

However, workers are often motivated toward goals within the plant such as turning out a quality product, higher wages, and promotion. Let us examine the relationship between satisfaction and productivity for workers who are motivated toward these in-plant goals.

At the start it is evident that productivity and quality are sometimes mutually exclusive. If the individual must concentrate on maintaining high quality work, speed of production probably plays a secondary role. Conversely, if he must emphasize speed, quality often must be reduced to some degree. The speed-quality dilemma is sometimes resolved by making the individual work units so routine and concerned with such minute changes in the material that increased speed will not affect the quality of the product. However, if a worker is more highly motivated when he is performing some meaningful job, the above procedure may be resolving one dilemma by raising another. At any rate, the artisan, motivated toward the goal of quality, may be highly satisfied with his job while turning out a very limited number of finished pieces per unit of time. If he is forced to increase productivity and lower in some measure the quality, we might expect his satisfaction to decrease. For such a person satisfaction and productivity would be negatively related.

Consider now the individual who is motivated toward higher wages and promotion. While these rewards may not be exclusively dependent upon job performance, at the same time productivity and other aspects of performance often are weighted heavily at promotion time in most companies.

In other words, productivity and other aspects of job performance constitute a path to the goal of promotion and wage increases.

Now it is likely that people with aspirations to change position in the company structure will often be quite dissatisfied with their present position in the company. Aspiration to move within a system implies not only a desire for some different position in the future, but some degree of dissatisfaction with the position one is presently occupying. The amount of dissatisfaction probably depends upon the length of time the individual has occupied this position. Thus, although productivity may be a path to the goal, failure to achieve the goal to date may result in dissatisfaction and the high producer may be less satisfied than the low producer.

Evidence sustaining this point of view is to be found in Katz and associates' (34) report of a large insurance company in which the best, most productive workers were also considerably more critical of company policy than were less productive workers. S. Lieberman reports a similar finding in a large appliance factory.[2] A year after all workers in the factory had filled out a questionnaire, Lieberman compared the earlier responses of those who had been promoted to foreman with a matched group of workers who were not promoted. Those promoted had been significantly less satisfied with company practices at the earlier time than had the control group.

Once again the question arises as to what is meant by satisfaction. It may be that extremely high satisfaction is indicative of a certain amount of complacency, a satisfaction with the job as it is, which may be only slightly related to job performance, if it is related at all. On the other hand, individuals who are highly motivated may perceive productivity as a path to their goals, but may also be more realistically critical of whatever deficiencies exist within the organization. They may feel, in addition, that their output is not being rewarded as rapidly as it deserves.

*Implications for future research.* We have arrived at two conclusions: first, that satisfaction with one's position in a network of relationships need not imply strong motivation to outstanding performance within that system, and, second, that productivity may be only peripherally related to many of the goals toward which the industrial worker is striving. We do not mean to imply that researchers should have known all along that their results would be positive only infrequently and in particular circumstances. We have been operating on the basis of hindsight and have attempted to spell out some of the factors which may have accounted for the failure of industrial investigators to find positive relationships in their data.

However, certain implications seem logical from the foregoing sections of this report. Foremost among these implications is the conclusion that it is time to question the strategic and ethical merits of selling to industrial concerns an assumed relationship between employee attitudes and employee performance. In the absence of more convincing evidence than is

[2] S. Lieberman. Personal communication. July 15, 1954.

now at hand with regard to the beneficial effects on job performance of high morale, we are led to the conclusion that we might better forego publicizing these alleged effects.

The emphasis on predicting job performance, and particularly productivity, rests upon the acceptance of certain values. That is, the many studies that have used productivity as the criterion to be predicted have been performed because productivity has direct economic value to industry, and, presumably, to society at large. But the fact that it has economic value does not mean that job performance is the only, or even the most important, aspect of organizational behavior. From the viewpoint of studying, analyzing, and understanding the industrial setting and individual reactions thereto, productivity and other aspects of job performance may be only one of several important factors. It would seem worthwhile to study the causes, correlates, and consequence of satisfaction, per se. It seems possible, for example, that conditions conducive to job satisfaction will have an effect on the quality of the workman drawn into the industry, the quality of job performance, and the harmony of labor-management relations. Such potential correlates, among others, merit exploration.

Another potentially fruitful approach involves studying the differential effect of particular kinds of management practices upon the attitudes and performances of workers with different motives, aspirations, and expectations. The appropriate questions may concern how, for particular workers, productivity comes to be perceived as instrumental to the achievement of some goals but not others, while for other workers a different perception develops.

The experimental approach has largely been neglected in this area of industrial research, yet the control of variables that it provides seems essential to the development and refinement of our knowledge in the area. Certainly, where experimentation has been used, as by Schachter and associates (52) and by Coch and French (8), the results have been both enlightening for the understanding of present problems and encouraging for its future application. As our concepts become increasingly precise, we may expect an increased use of experimentation both within the industrial setting and in the laboratory.

Perhaps the most significant conclusion to be drawn from this survey of the literature is that the industrial situation is a complex one. We have suggested that an analysis of the situation involves analysis not only of the individual's relation to the social system of the factory, the work group, and the union, but the community at large as well. It is important to know what motives exist among industrial workers, how they are reflected in the behavior of the workers, and how the motives develop and are modified within the framework of patterned social relationships in the plant and in the larger community.

We seem to have arrived at the position where the social scientist in the industrial setting must concern himself with a full-scale analysis of that situation. Pursuit of this goal should provide us with considerable intrinsic job satisfaction.

## References

6. Centers, R.: *The psychology of social classes*. Princeton: Princeton Univer. Press, 1949.

8. Coch, L., & French, J. R., Jr.: Overcoming resistance to change. *Hum. Relat.*, 1948, **1,** 512–532.

11. Davis, A.: *Social class influences upon learning*. Cambridge: Harvard Univer. Press, 1948.

12. Davis, A., Gardner, B. B., & Gardner, Mary R.: *Deep south: A social and anthropological study of caste and class*. Chicago: Univer. of Chicago Press, 1941.

13. Ericson, Martha C.: Social status and child rearing practices. In T. M. Newcomb & E. L. Hartley (Eds.), *Readings in social psychology*. New York: Holt, 1947. Pp. 494–501.

21. Goode, W. J., & Fowler, I.: Incentive factors in a low morale plant. *Amer. sociol. Rev.*, 1949, **14,** 618–624.

33. Katz, D., & Kahn, R. L.: Some recent findings in human relations research in industry. In G. E. Swanson, T. M. Newcomb & E. L. Hartley (Eds.), *Readings in social psychology*. New York: Holt, 1952. Pp. 650–665.

34. Katz, D., Maccoby, N., & Morse, Nancy: *Productivity, supervision and morale in an office situation*. Univer. of Michigan: Survey Research Center, 1950.

42. Mathewson, S. B.: *Restriction of output among unorganized workers*. New York: Viking Press, 1931.

43. Mayo, E.: *The social problems of an industrial civilization*. Cambridge: Graduate School of Business Administration, Harvard Univer., 1945.

50. Roethlisberger, F. J.: *Management and morale*. Cambridge: Harvard Univer. Press, 1943.

51. Roethlisberger, F. J., & Dickson, W. J.: *Management and the worker*. Cambridge: Harvard Univer. Press, 1939.

52. Schachter, S., Ellertson, N., McBride, D., & Gregory, D.: An experimental study of cohesiveness and productivity. *Hum. Relat.*, 1951, **4,** 229–238.

57. Warner, W. L., & Lunt, P. S.: *The social life of a modern community*. New Haven: Yale Univ. Press, 1941.

# Productivity and Job Satisfaction*

*Robert L. Kahn*

I did not select the topic of this paper, although I am glad to address my-self to it. My interest in doing so stems partly from the fact that a great deal of research on the determinants of productivity and job satisfaction has been done at the Survey Research Center. I have, however, a more personal reason for being interested in the Productivity and Satisfaction title: I am impressed to the point of fascination with the durability of the myth that productivity and job satisfaction are inseparable. I would like to begin by asserting, without qualification, that productivity and job sat-isfaction do not necessarily go together. The persistence with which man-agers and managerial consultants place them in juxtaposition is much more revealing of their own value structure, I believe, than it is indicative of anything in the empirical research data on organizations. If I am to back up this mildly iconoclastic assertion, I will have to ask you to rehearse with me some of the programmatic history of the Survey Research Center.

*First findings.* The work of the Survey Research Center in studying or-ganizations began in 1947 with a prospectus by Rensis Likert and Daniel Katz. The objectives of the program were described in some detail. For our present purposes, the following quotation is particularly appropriate: "Specifically, the objectives have to do with the conditions making for a high level of group functioning, and a high level of individual satisfaction of the group members." There is here no assertion that efficient function-ing can be achieved only through the achievement of high levels of satis-faction, but it is perhaps significant that the notions of satisfaction and productivity were linked together even at the beginning of the research. The earliest project in this research program was conducted in a life in-surance company, and it consisted of a systematic comparison of work groups which had been demonstrated to differ significantly in productivity, as measured by the accounting procedures of the company. The analysis plan was to determine what supervisory practices were associated with

* From *Personnel Psychology*, vol. 13, pp. 275–287, Autumn, 1960. Reprinted by permission of *Personnel Psychology*.

high and low levels of satisfaction, and with high and low levels of productivity.

Although satisfaction and productivity were both defined as dependent variables, there was also a clear intention to use satisfaction as an intervening variable. As Katz stated, "A second direction has been a consideration of psychological, dependent variables that affect performance. We have considered the satisfactions or morale dimensions, then, both as dependent variables to be predicted from other factors, and as a reflection of intervening variables which could help to predict productivity" (Katz, 1951).

In this early study, a number of systematic differences in leadership were found to be associated with differences in productivity. These are fully described in the monograph, *Productivity, Supervision, and Morale in an Office Situation,* by Katz, Maccoby, and Morse (Institute for Social Research, 1950). For example, high-producing supervisors were found to spend more time in actual supervisory activities, and less time in performing tasks similar to those done by their subordinates. They were supervised less closely, and were themselves less closely supervised by their own managers. They were judged by coders who read their interviews to be more employee-centered in their attitudes. The employees of high-producing supervisors were more likely to feel that their supervisors would defend their interests rather than those of management, if such a choice had to be made.

The behavior of supervisors proved to be no less important in explaining the satisfactions of employees than in explaining their productivity. In some respects, however, the determinants of satisfaction present a more complex problem. This is true in part because satisfaction itself is not a unitary concept. In recognition of this, three indexes of satisfaction were employed in the present study: One reflecting satisfaction with the company as a whole, one reflecting satisfaction with financial and job status, and one reflecting satisfaction with the job itself. A fourth index was, in fact, less a measure of satisfaction than a measure of the perceived performance of the work group.

Rather different patterns of factors were correlated with each of these indexes. For example, the major determinant of job satisfaction appears to be the type of work actually done by the employee. Among people doing high-level technical work, 58 per cent indicated a high degree of intrinsic job satisfaction. Among people doing repetitious clerical work, only 23 per cent recorded equally high satisfaction scores. The behavior of the supervisor, as measured by the attitudes and perceptions of his subordinates, was associated with all of the satisfaction indexes in some degree. The association was the strongest with respect to financial and job status satisfactions, and to over-all satisfactions with the company. The behavior of the supervisor appeared to be less related to intrinsic job satisfaction, and to attitudes toward the work group. The most important finding, however, for our present line of argument is that no significant relationships were discovered between any of the indexes of satisfaction and the productivity of the work group. In other words, employees in highly productive work groups were no more likely than employees in low-producing groups to be satisfied with their jobs and the company, or with their financial and status rewards.

The completion of the research in the insurance company left us with a number of unresolved questions, questions which were obvious candidates for attention in subsequent projects. One of these questions was the central issue around which this paper has been written: "Is there a relationship between satisfaction and productivity?" Other major questions included: "What is the cause and effect relationship underlying the correlations between the supervisor's tendency to delegate and the productivity of employees?" More specifically: "Does the granting of increased responsibility and autonomy by the supervisor produce higher motivation on the part of the employee, with subsequent gains in productivity?" Or, alternately: "Does the employee who demonstrates high productivity receive, as a consequence of that productivity, a more general and less detailed kind of supervision from his immediate superior?"

Another question requiring solution was the nature and reality of the dimension which had been identified in the insurance company study as "employee-centered—production-centered." Was a supervisor who tended to be production-centered necessarily less sensitive and less oriented to employee needs? Might not a supervisor be both employee-centered and production-centered?

Finally, the study in the insurance company left us with the question of how to interpret the single area of satisfaction which seemed to relate to productivity—satisfaction with the work group. Was the prideful response of the high-producing work groups a measure of the spirit and motivation which caused their higher productivity, or were the members of these high-producing groups merely reporting their accurate perception? Their groups were in fact better than others when it came to getting the job done.

*Riddles and replication.* The second study in this series of organizational researches on the determinants of productivity was done on a railroad, among maintenance-of-way workers. This study, which involved about 300 laborers and 72 foremen, was very similar in design to the study of clerical workers in the insurance company. It was similar, also, in research purpose: to investigate the relationships among supervisory behavior, employee satisfaction, and productivity. The major difference between the two studies lay in the drastic contrast in setting. Manual labor was studied in place of clerical work, middle-aged workers instead of young people just out of high school graduating classes, men instead of girls. In addition, the two studies differed in the availability of performance information to workers. In the insurance company, the employees had available management's records of their group performance. In the railroad situation, such data were not available to employees. In fact, it was necessary for us to obtain rankings from management in order to determine the relative efficiency of work groups. We were looking to this second study to serve as a partial validation of the earlier research findings, and to illuminate the area of satisfaction and productivity, which had been characterized by such unexpected results in the first study.

As a study in validation, the research on the railroad must be considered successful. As in the insurance company, the effective foreman on the railroad was able to differentiate his role from the role of the nonsupervisory employee. Compared to less successful supervisors, he spent more time planning the work, more time performing highly skilled tasks, and more time in actual supervision. As in the insurance company, the high-producing railroad foreman showed greater sensitivity to the needs of his employees. He was more employee-centered in this sense. He was, for example, more interested in the men's off-the-job problems, more helpful in training them for better jobs, more constructive and less punishing when mistakes were made. With respect to the area of delegation, the railroad study was less definitive than the study in the insurance company. There was, however, some validation of the earlier findings, especially in the tendency of high-producing supervisors to report themselves as under less pressure from their own superiors.

In the matter of productivity and satisfaction, the results of the railroad study were identical with those of the work in the insurance company. There was no systematic relationship between productivity and such morale variables as intrinsic job satisfaction, financial and job status satisfaction, and satisfaction with the company. In the matter of attitudes toward the work group as potential predictors of productivity, the railroad study goes somewhat beyond its predecessor, in that the employees were questioned not only about their evaluation of their work groups' performance, but also about their liking for the other men in the section, about their feeling that the men stick together well, and about their reactions to good or poor workers in their group. In none of these respects did the workers in high-producing groups differ from those in low-producing groups. The high-producing workers did differ, however, in their evaluation of their work groups' performance. Men in high-producing maintenance-of-way sections were more likely than men in low-producing sections to see their work group as superior to other groups. The question of causality in the relationship between productivity and attitudes toward the work group remains beyond the scope of this second study so far as a definitive answer is concerned. The fact, however, that the men in the high-producing groups did not evaluate their groups as superior in all respects, but only with respect to the accomplishment of work, certainly questions the earlier interpretation that some such factor as group pride is operating to increase the level of productivity. The more plausible interpretation seems to be that despite the absence of official information regarding productivity, the men were able to form accurate judgments with respect to the relative accomplishment of work groups, including their own.

There are perhaps two additional findings in the railroad study which should be mentioned as significant amplifications of the previous research. The first of these lies in the area of role differentiation. In the low-producing sections on the railroad, the men more often said that one man in the section tended to speak up in their behalf when they wanted something. A possible interpretation of this finding is that in situations where the formal leader does not fill the leadership role adequately, there is a tendency for an informal leader to arise. If the foreman does not differentiate his role sufficiently from that of his subordinates to provide leadership, the men will, in effect, "elect" a kind of substitute leader of their own.

The second finding in the railroad study, which goes somewhat beyond the previous research, lies in the content area of employee-centered supervision. The section hands on the railroad were asked what their foreman did when someone did a bad job. Answers to this question were coded as reflecting punitive or nonpunitive behavior on the part of foremen. Nonpunitive behavior was more characteristic of foremen of high-producing sections than of low-producing sections. A concern with penalties rather than remedies, and with the assignment of personal blame rather than the discovery of causes for mistakes, appeared to characterize the low-producing units.

*The end of an hypothesis.* With the completion of the second study in this series on the determinants of productivity, we found ourselves again with a failure of the expected relationship between morale or satisfaction and the productivity of work groups. We decided in the third study to make an all-out effort to eliminate as many as possible of the reasons for this failure. Accordingly, we wished to find a research situation in which the number of subjects would be very large so that it would be possible to hold constant a substantial number of other variables while looking at the relationship between morale and productivity. We wanted also to find a research situation in which the range of skills and kinds of work represented was very substantial. In addition, we hoped to find a situation in which objective measures of individual productivity were available. We thought that the group measures of productivity, which were all that we had to work with in the first two studies, might tend to obscure relationships between individually-held attitudes and individual consequences of those attitudes. All these requirements for a third study on the determinants of productivity were well met in a large midwestern cluster of factories manufacturing agricultural equipment and tractors.

A study was conducted in these factories, in which all of the approximately 20,000 employees were included. Of this number, approximately

6,000 were on jobs for which productivity standards had been established by time study, and for which daily productivity data were available. In this study we introduced a number of changes with respect to research design and analysis. We decided to explore further the characterization of supervisors as employee-centered or production-centered, and to learn more about the characteristics of work groups. (Problems of causality, for example in the relationship between delegation and productivity, we saw as being resolved in a different study of experimental design.)

In general, the findings in the tractor company repeated the findings of the two earlier studies. There were, however, some significant differences. In the matter of employee-centered supervision, for example, the high-producing employees in the tractor company more often reported, as expected, that their supervisors took a personal interest in them, that they got along with him well, that he let them know how they were doing on the job, that it was easy to talk to him about most things, and so on through the list of behaviors which we had categorized as employee-centered. However, the high-producing workers were also more likely to say that high production was important to their foremen, and that one of the ways in which their foremen supervised them was by seeing that production was kept up. If we put these two sets of findings together, they lead us to a re-interpretation of the relationship between employee-centered and production-centered supervision. In the studies in the insurance company and on the railroad, we had treated employee-centered and production-centered supervision as if they were the two opposite ends of a single continuum. We had assumed, in other words, that as a supervisor became more production-oriented, he must of necessity become less employee-oriented. The research data from the tractor company suggested instead that the quality of being production-centered and the quality of being employee-centered should be regarded as theoretically independent dimensions of supervision. Thus we may, for convenience, think of a four-celled table, with each cell representing a kind of supervision which combines differently the attributes of employee orientation and production orientation. The most successful supervisors in this scheme are those who combine employee-centered and production-centered qualities, working out their own creative way of synthesizing these two concerns. We can also discover supervisors who are interested in the employees and sensitive to their needs, but neglectful or even disinterested in the production goals of the organization. Our impressions are that this is a style of supervision which sometimes generates a superficial popularity among the men, although we would predict that in time this would be replaced by feelings of aimlessness and lack of accomplishment. The supervisor who emphasizes production to the detriment of employee requirements is, according to the data from the tractor company, less successful both with respect to the productivity of his group and the attitudes of his men. Finally, we can imagine a supervisor who is seriously interested neither in productivity nor in the employees. We have yet to do research on supervisors in this category, but observation suggests that there are in many organizations men in supervisory positions whose own needs are so overpowering that there is little supervisory energy left for investment in meeting either the needs of the employees or the requirements of the organization.

A clue to the way in which successful supervisors synthesize their interest in productivity and in the needs of employees was provided by the responses of foremen in the tractor company. In answering the question as to how interested their own supervisors, the general foremen, were in productivity, more foremen of high- than low-producing sections reported that their supervisors felt high production was *one* of the most important things on the job, but not *the* most important thing. The foremen of lower producing units, however, were more likely to report that their own supervisors either overemphasized the achievement of high production by acting as if it were *the* most important thing on the job, or underestimated the importance of high production by acting as if it were not among the more important things on the job.

Another of the areas which had been marked for further clarification in the tractor study was group influences on productivity. In the insurance study the interpretation had been offered that group pride was a factor in generating a high level of productivity, and that the statement of employees in high-producing groups that their work group excelled others was primarily a reflection of this pride. In the railroad study, it was pointed out that the apparently prideful evaluation of work group performance might be no more than an accurate perception of the group's accomplishment, and should not be interpreted as a definite causal factor. In the tractor company study, a number of questions were asked employees regarding the characteristics of their work groups, and their individual relationship to the group. The results were to replicate the findings of the earlier studies. The high-producing employees in the tractor company again told us that their work groups were better than others when it came to getting a job done. But high-producing employees were also more likely to say that they really felt a part of the groups in which they worked. Low-producing employees were more likely to report that they felt accepted in some respects, but not in others. In addition, high-producing employees were apparently more anchored to their work groups. They were more likely to say that they would resist transfer to another group or to another job, even if the job were the same in content and the same pay were being offered for it. Finally, the foremen of high-producing work groups reported that their sections were better than most others in the way in which the men helped each other out on the job. The effect of these several findings was to convince us that there were significant differences between high- and low-producing groups in their peer relationships. The statement, obtained in three studies from high-producing employees, that their groups excelled low-producing groups now seemed neither a dispassionate statement of group achievement nor in itself a cause of high productivity.

The nature of these group differences has been well analyzed by Stanley Seashore, who began by contrasting groups with respect to cohesiveness, or the attraction of the group for the individual. Seashore reasoned, following the experimental research of Leon Festinger and his associates, that the more cohesive group, being by definition the group with greater attraction for its members, would by virtue of that attraction have greater power over the individuals in it. Each person, since he valued more highly his membership in the group, would be more responsive to the group's demands on him. If this were true, we would expect that the major differences between high-cohesive and low-cohesive work groups would be visible in their relative uniformity of member behaviors; that is, in the closeness to which members conformed to the norms of the group. Differences between high-cohesive and low-cohesive groups should be most apparent, not in the level of productivity, but rather in the variance of productivity. We could imagine a highly cohesive group which would, for some set of reasons, have established a very high productivity norm. In such a group, we would predict that all group members would tend to conform closely to that high productivity norm. However, another group of equal cohesiveness might have a productivity norm which was markedly low. In this case, we would predict that the group members would be equally faithful in conforming to the low productivity norm. In both cases, the cohesiveness of the group would show in the variance of the productivity distribution, rather than in its level. The data bore out this approach very well, and Seashore was able to show in addition that the crucial considerations, in determining the level of the productivity norm in a highly cohesive group, involved the relation of the employees to management and union. Peer relationships in the industrial situation can be a force which either implements or frustrates the goals of the organization, depending upon the basic relationship which has been established between management, union, and employees.

With regard to the hypothesized relationship between productivity and satisfaction, an all-out effort was made in the tractor company study. A factor analysis was done to identify the components of satisfaction among the approximately 6,000 workers for whom individual productivity scores were available. Four identifiable factors resulted from this analysis and were labeled: Intrinsic job satisfaction, satisfaction with the company, satisfaction with supervision, and satisfaction with rewards and mobility opportunities. None of these factors was significantly related to the actual productivity of employees in the tractor factories.

For purposes of our present discussion, the completion of the study in the tractor company represents the end of a cycle. We decided that the evidence from these three studies was sufficiently powerful so that we should abandon, in our future research, the use of satisfaction or morale indexes as variables intervening between supervisory and organizational characteristics on the one hand, and productivity on the other. This, perhaps, is the major conclusion so far as the topic of this paper is concerned. There are, however, a number of others worth mentioning, perhaps because of their continuing influence.

They are as follows:

We dropped from our empirical research and from our theoretical formulations the concept of morale as a sum of satisfactions realized in the work situation. This we did on the grounds that the factor analysis had shown, and the results of the previous study also suggested, that the several dimensions of satisfaction were quite independent, both with respect to their determinants and in their consequences.

We recognize the necessity of developing alternative theoretical schemes to show the determinants of each dimension of satisfaction and of productivity in the work situation. A discussion of several such alternatives is beyond the scope of this paper, but has been attempted elsewhere by Basil Georgopoulos, Rensis Likert, Robert Kahn, and others.

It is necessary to consider the relative stability over time of different levels of satisfaction and productivity. For example, Likert has proposed that the combination of high productivity with low satisfaction may be difficult or impossible to maintain over a long period of time, because of the fact that such a combination reflects the consumption and deterioration of the human assets of the organization.

Related to the above point is the need to develop more adequate criteria of organizational effectiveness. The measures of productivity used in the three studies cited in this paper should be supplemented by measures of the costs of recruitment, training, turnover, and the like. Georgopoulos and Arnold Tannenbaum have proposed the definition of organizational effectiveness as "the extent to which an organization as a social system, given certain resources and means, fulfills its objectives without incapacitating its means and resources, and without placing undue strain upon its members."

But these questions and hunches wait their turn in the continuing programs of organizational studies. What can we say in the meantime about the applied value of what has already been done? We are convinced that the growing literature of empirical research in organizations, of which the studies I have cited are a small part, is heavy with implications of responsibility and opportunity for psychologists who interact with the leaders of organizations. There is a terrible gap between the complexities of organizational life and the patent-medicine remedies which are peddled unceasingly at management's doorstep. The psychologist, as staff member or as consultant, can help management avoid the dismal sequence of oversold devices, unrealistic expectations, and undiscriminating disillusionment. He can offer the assistance of what research has already learned, and the realistic comfort of knowing when decisions must still be based on managerial intuition.

## Reference

Katz, Daniel: "An Overview of the Human Relations Program." In Harold Guetzkow (Ed.), *Groups, Leadership, and Men.* New York: Carnegie Press, 1951.

# READINGS RELATED TO CHAPTER XI

## Motivation in Work Groups: A Tentative View*

*James V. Clark†*

This paper represents an attempt to examine a number of different researches in the field of organizational behavior and to see if their similarities can be highlighted and tentatively explained by the use of Maslow's need-hierarchy concept.[1]

A recent research experience of mine (so far published only in case form)[2] suggested for me that this process might be a useful way of generating new hypotheses and methods of measurement. The present paper is presented in the hope that others can be stimulated in the same way.

More specifically, this paper makes no claim that the answers concerning employee motivation and its determinants are all in. Neither does it claim that the questions generated by the examination of several researches from the point of view of the need-hierarchy concept are all presently researchable in a strict operational sense. Rather, the paper puts up what, for me, appears to be a potentially operational scheme for analyzing motivation and its organizational determinants. With such a scheme, it

* From *Human Organization*, vol. 19, no. 4, pp. 199–208, Winter 1960–1961. Reprinted by permission of the publisher, The Society for Applied Anthropology.

† James Clark is in the Graduate School of Business Administration, Harvard University, Boston, Massachusetts. For discussion and criticism, the author is grateful to his colleagues L. B. Barnes, R. L. Katz, P. R. Lawrence, and A. N. Turner.

[1] A. H. Maslow, *Motivation and Personality*, Harper and Bros., New York, 1954.
[2] "Century Co. (A)—(I)," Harvard Business School, EA-A 321–329.

appears possible to study a number of different organizations comparatively, an effort which the field of organizational behavior needs.

I do believe, therefore, that the use of this theory puts us in a somewhat
better position than that outlined in a recent research on worker motivation
by Herzberg *et al.*:*

> This concept [Maslow's need hierarchy] has led many people to feel that
> the worker can never be satisfied with his job. How are you going to solve
> the dilemma of trying to motivate workers who have a continuously revolv-
> ing set of needs? Since each individual may present at any one time a differ-
> ent scramble of his psychological need list, a systematic personnel practice
> hoping to cater to the most prepotent needs of its entire working force is de-
> feated by the nature of the probabilities. Forgetting for a moment the indi-
> vidual "need hierarchies," it can be argued that there is sufficient homoge-
> neity within various groups of employees to make for a relative similarity of
> "need hierarchies" within each group. Even so, the changes in prepotency
> for the group will occur, and personnel administration will have to keep up
> with them. For some who hold to this point of view personnel administration
> is reduced to the essential of labor-management bargaining. For others it
> means that personnel programs must be geared to be sensitive to the changes
> that are continually taking place in the needs of the employees. And since
> this can be done only by the supervisors, the training of supervisors in un-
> derstanding human motivation, the factors underlying it, and the therapeutic
> or manipulative skills with which to cope with it is the most essential ingre-
> dient to any industrial-relations program.[3]

As this paper will show, I am not opposed to sensitive first line administrators. However, other variables relating to satisfaction and productivity
will be highlighted and in such a way as to suggest that the development of
worker motivation is not a random scramble but is perhaps predictable,
with only a modicum of sensitivity to employee needs.

## The Need-hierarchy Model

Let us start with McGregor's summary of Maslow's concepts,† which is
concise and simply put.

As most readers are probably aware, Maslow views an individual's motivations not in terms of a series of drives, but rather in terms of a hierarchy,
certain "higher" needs becoming activated to the extent certain "lower"
ones become satisfied. McGregor summarized these as follows:[4]

* [See pages 104–109 of this volume.—Ed.]

† [See pages 83–103 and 188–191 of this volume.—Ed.]

[3] Frederick Herzberg, Bernard Mausner, and Barbara Bloch Snyderman, *The
Motivation to Work*, John Wiley & Sons, New York, 1959.

Douglas M. McGregor, 5th Anniversary Convocation, School of Industrial Management, Massachusetts Institute of Technology, Cambridge, Massachusetts.

## Physiological Needs

Man is a wanting animal—as soon as one of his needs is satisfied, another appears in its place. This process is unending. It continues from birth to death.

Man's needs are organized in a series of levels—a hierarchy of importance. At the lowest level, but pre-eminent in importance when they are thwarted, are his *physiological needs*. Man lives for bread alone, when there is no bread. Unless the circumstances are unusual, his needs for love, for status, for recognition are inoperative when his stomach has been empty for awhile. But when he eats regularly and adequately, hunger ceases to be an important motivation. The same is true of the other physiological needs of man—for rest, exercise, shelter, protection from the elements.

*A satisfied need is not a motivator of behavior!* This is a fact of profound significance that is regularly ignored in the conventional approach to the management of ["normal"] people. Consider your own need for air; Except as you are deprived of it, it has no appreciable motivating effect upon your behavior.

## Safety Needs

When the physiological needs are reasonably satisfied, needs at the next higher level begin to dominate man's behavior, to motivate him. These are called *safety needs*. They are needs for protection against danger, threat, deprivation. Some people mistakenly refer to these as needs for security. However, unless man is in a dependent relationship where he fears arbitrary deprivation, he does not demand security. The need is for the "fairest possible break." When he is confident of this he is more willing to take risks. But when he feels threatened or dependent, his greatest need is for guarantees, for protection, for security.

The fact needs little emphasis that, since every industrial employee is in a dependent relationship, safety needs may assume considerable importance. Arbitrary management actions, behavior which arouses uncertainty with respect to continued employment or which reflects favoritism or discrimination, unpredictable administration of policy—these can be powerful motivators of the safety needs in the employment relationship at *every level,* from worker to vice president.

## Social Needs

When man's physiological needs are satisfied and he is no longer fearful about his physical welfare, his *social needs* become important motivators of his behavior—needs for belonging, for association, for acceptance by his fellows, for giving and receiving friendship and love.

Management knows today of the existence of these needs, but it often assumes quite wrongly that they represent a threat to the organization. Many studies have demonstrated that the tightly knit, cohesive work group may, under proper conditions, be far more effective than an equal number of separate individuals in achieving organizational goals.

Yet management, fearing group hostility to its own objectives, often goes to considerable lengths to control and direct human efforts in ways that are inimical to the natural "groupiness" of human beings. When man's social needs—and perhaps his safety needs, too—are thus thwarted, he behaves in ways which tend to defeat organizational objectives. He becomes resistant, antagonistic, uncooperative. But this behavior is a consequence, not a cause.

### Ego Needs

Above the social needs—in the sense that they do not become motivators until lower needs are reasonably satisfied—are the needs of greater significance to management and to man himself. They are the *egoistic* needs, and they are of two kinds:

1. Those needs that relate to one's self-esteem—needs for self-confidence, for independence, for achievement, for competence, for knowledge.

2. Those needs that relate to one's reputation—needs for status, for recognition, for appreciation, for the deserved respect of one's fellows.

Unlike the lower needs, these are rarely satisfied; man seeks indefinitely for more satisfaction of these needs once they have become important to him. But they do not appear in any significant way until physiological, safety, and social needs are all reasonably satisfied.

The typical industrial organization offers few opportunities for the satisfaction of these egoistic needs to people at lower levels in the hierarchy. The conventional methods of organizing work, particularly in mass-production industries, give little heed to these aspects of human motivation. If the practices of scientific management were deliberately calculated to thwart these needs, they could hardly accomplish this purpose better than they do.

### Self-Fulfillment Needs

Finally—a capstone, as it were, on the hierarchy of man's needs—there are what we may call the needs for *self-fulfillment*. These are the needs for realizing one's own potentialities, for continued self-development, for being creative in the broadest sense of that term.

It is clear that the conditions of modern life give only limited opportunity for these relatively weak needs to obtain expression. The deprivation most people experience with respect to other lower-level needs diverts their energies into the struggle to satisfy those needs, and the needs for self-fulfillment remain dormant.

For purposes of initial explanation and simplicity, McGregor spoke in terms of separate steps or levels. Actually, Maslow suggests that these levels are interdependent and overlapping, each higher-need level emerging before the lower needs have been satisfied completely. In our society, most people tend to be partially satisfied in each need area and partially unsatisfied. However, most individuals tend to have higher satisfaction at the lower-need level than at higher-need levels. Maslow helps to explain this by picturing the average citizen as (for illustrative purposes) 85 per cent satisfied in his physiological needs, 70 per cent satisfied in his safety needs,

50 per cent in his belonging needs, 40 per cent in his egoistic needs, and 10 per cent in his self-fulfillment needs.

## Some Suggested Uniformities Among Different Researches

Figure 1 shows how the need-hierarchy concept might be utilized to relate and explain the findings of a number of different studies. In other words, it takes McGregor's generalization of Maslow's theory, attempts to relate it to some existing studies, and concludes that workers under this or that combination of environmental conditions behave *as if* they were motivated in such-and-such a fashion.

Before we turn to this figure, however, a word of caution is in order. This way of relating and thinking about different organizational behavior researches is by no means perfect. First of all, the propositions which follow from the need-hierarchy theory are extremely difficult to test in a research sense. Secondly, the variety of environmental and internal-system factors affecting work-group behavior cannot be categorized so as to make all known descriptions of work situations directly comparable from some one point of view. Finally, almost all researches leave out, or find uncontrollable, some variables that are necessary for complete comparability. Nevertheless, some available researches suggest uniformities consistent with the need-hierarchy concept.

Figure 1 shows how a number of different "givens" in a work-group's environment can prevent or frustrate an individual's opportunity for need satisfaction at different levels of the need hierarchy. The figure is based on the assumption that all individuals have a potential for activating all the needs on the need hierarchy. Likewise, the figure assumes that an individual does not necessarily suspend or forget his unrealized needs during his hours on the job. Actually, in industrial situations, there are few data to support the first assumption, many data to support the second. Therefore, the figure can usefully be regarded as a tentative explanation of how and why most people, or an "average worker," would most typically react under different conditions at work.

The extreme left-hand scale of the middle block of graphs in Figure 1 represents the various levels of the need hierarchy (exclusive of the physiological needs). (In Maslow's description of his need hierarchy, the status-prestige need and the self-esteem need are placed side by side above the membership need. They are placed one on top of the other here for graphic simplicity.)

The remaining columns of the middle block depict the pattern of an individual's need activation and satisfaction under a number of different external conditions. These patterns will be discussed in this paper in relation to certain researches. (It is not possible to show all possible combinations

**Conditions in the work group's environment**

| | (1) | (2) | (3) | (4) | (5) | (6) | (7) |
|---|---|---|---|---|---|---|---|
| | | | | | | | Company perceived as supportive |
| | | | | | Low perceived contribution opportunity | High perceived contribution opportunity | High perceived contribution opportunity |
| | | | | Production-centered leadership | Accommodative leadership | Accommodative leadership | Group-centered leadership |
| | | | Low-status congruence | High-status congruence | High-status congruence | High-status congruence | High-status congruence |
| | | Low interaction opportunity | High interaction opportunity | High interaction opportunity | High interaction opportunity | High interaction opportunity | High interaction opportunity |
| | Low employment security | High employment security | High employment security | High employment security | High employment security | High employment security | High employment security |

(Need activation)

**Needs**

Self-actualization
Status-prestige
Self-esteem
Membership
Safety

☐ Need not activated    ▨ Need activated but relatively satisfied    ▦ Need activated but relatively frustrated

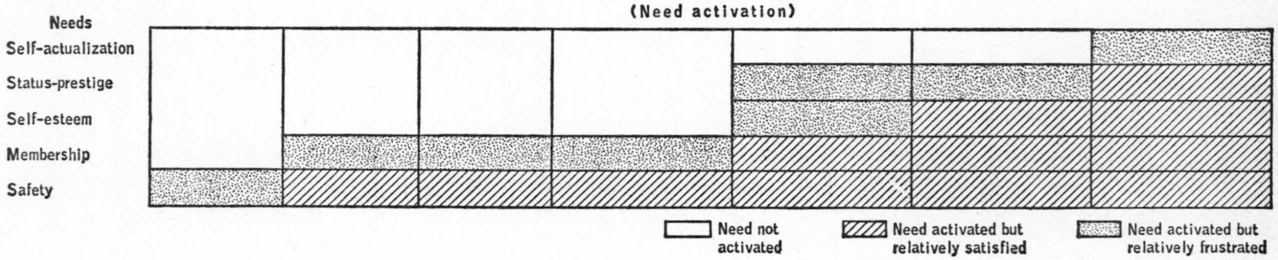

(Effects on productivity and turnover-absenteeism)

| | (1) | (2) | (3) | (4) | (5) | (6) | (7) |
|---|---|---|---|---|---|---|---|
| Productivity | High | Low | Low? | Low | Meets minimum requirements / Average | High | High |
| Turnover-abs. | Low | High | High | ? | Average | Low | Low |

Figure 1. Some Relations Between Conditions in the Work Group's Environment, Motivation, Satisfaction, Productivity, and Turnover-Absenteeism.

466

of external conditions: researches have not been conducted under such a wide variety of conditions.)

Across the bottom of the figure are two rows which show "productivity" and "turnover and absenteeism" for each column. These are by no means definitely established results but the researches examined in this paper often suggested certain tendencies in regard to these variables which are shown. Consequently, by beginning with human needs, we can move to the relationship between the satisfaction of these needs, external conditions, and productivity and turnover-absenteeism.

*Column 1* illustrates a situation in which employment security is extremely low. Such conditions might exist whenever alternative employment is unavailable (as in a depression) or is deemed by the workers to be not as desirable as present employment and where workers feel unprotected from a management which is perceived as arbitrary in its layoff and firing procedures.

Research by Goode and Fowler[5] in an automobile feeder plant illustrates this condition. In their study of a low morale, nonunion plant a small group of high service employees, for whom the job had become an absolute economic necessity, consistently produced according to management expectations. Turnover among other workers, for whom the job was less important, was high. They quit or were fired for not producing enough.

Interestingly enough, related situations were described some time ago, and were alluded to by Mitchell,[6] when he noted that the pace of work was slower in the flush times of 1900–1902 than it had been in the dull times of 1894–1896. He quoted a sample bit of testimony from the period. The superintendent of a company manufacturing electrical machinery said:

> Five years ago men did not restrict their output, union or non-union men, because they wanted to hold their jobs, and a man would do anything and all he was told to do. Now a man knows that all he has to do is to walk across the street and get another job at the same rate of pay. . . .

Obviously, a group's productivity does not always increase in depression times: it fell off in the bank-wiring room[7] shortly before the final layoffs. The suggestion being made here is that under employment conditions which an individual perceives as economically threatening *and* arbitrary (and such conditions probably exist most often in a depression), his higher needs cannot motivate. He is "stuck" on the safety level and his behavior can only work toward the immediate goal of economic survival. Under conditions of

[5] W. F. Goode and Irving Fowler, "Incentive Factors in a Low Morale Plant," *American Sociological Review,* XIV, No. 5 (1949).

[6] W. C. Mitchell, *Business Cycles and Their Causes,* University of California Press, Berkeley, Cal., 1941.

[7] F. J. Roethlisberger and W. J. Dickson, *Management and the Worker,* Harvard University Press, Cambridge, Mass., 1952.

this kind, financial rewards tend to be the primary incentives which motivate workers toward higher productivity.

*Frustrated membership needs.* Columns 2 through 4 all show situations in which membership needs are active, but frustrated. They are shown separately, because apparently they occur under different environmental conditions.

*Column 2* shows a situation where workers are less concerned with employment security, because they have it, but where the job technology imposes physical or spatial requirements where interaction is impossible or severely restricted. This condition reflects and is labelled "low interaction opportunity." Such conditions and their effects on satisfaction were described in two automobile assembly plant studies.

Walker and Guest[8] rated jobs according to their "mass production characteristics" (noise, repetitiveness, restricted opportunity for movement, etc.). Workers holding such jobs often reported social isolation to be an important reason for job dissatisfaction. Moreover, absenteeism and turnover (extremely high throughout the automotive industry) were nearly twice as high for persons whose jobs exhibited "extreme mass production characteristics."

Another study of automobile assembly workers by Jasinski[9] showed that the men resented not being able to follow conventional conversation patterns; looking at the listener, being able to pause for conversation, and to complete the "talk." A correlation was found between an individual's desire to talk on the job and his attitude towards his job: the higher the desire to talk, the less interesting the job.

It is possible that Van Zelst's study[10] of sociometrically restructured construction work groups may be illustrative of what happens when opportunities to interact are increased.

When men were allowed to work alongside others whom they themselves had chosen, turnover, labor cost and materials cost all dropped.

The inference can be drawn that these results occurred because membership level motivation was satisfied and higher needs became activated.

Another research, "The Case of the Changing Cage," [11] suggests what happens to a work group's productivity and satisfaction when interaction opportunities are suddenly lowered. (In this case, however, interaction opportunity was decreased by a combination of physical changes and another variable we will discuss later, leadership behavior.)

[8] Charles R. Walker and Robert H. Guest, *The Man on the Assembly Line*, Harvard University Press, Cambridge, Mass., 1952. [Reprinted in this volume, pages 218–238.—Ed.]

[9] Frank J. Jasinski, "Technological Delimitation of Reciprocal Relationships: A Study of Interaction Patterns in Industry," *Human Organization*, XV, No. 2 (1956).

[10] R. J. Van Zelst, "Sociometrically Selected Work Teams Increase Productivity," *Personnel Psychology*, V, No. 3 (1953).

[11] Cara B. Richards and Henry F. Dobyns, "Topography and Culture: The Case of the Changing Cage," *Human Organization*, XVI, No. 1 (1957).

Workers in a voucher-check filing unit in an insurance company worked together well, kept up with the work load and expressed feelings of satisfaction. Their work area was inside a wire cage surrounded by filing cabinets and boxes through which the group's supervisors could not see. For efficiency purposes, the cage was moved to a new area in which the filing cabinets were arranged so that supervisors could see into the cage and restrict worker interaction. The workers could no longer engage in social activities which had been important to them (games, chatting, eating, etc.). Their output declined drastically, the amount of time spent in nonwork activities increased substantially, and the workers expressed considerable dissatisfaction with the new setup.

In short, it appears that if there are any major physical or spatial technological factors which restrict opportunities for interaction (under conditions where safety-level needs are not primary) membership needs will be frustrated and, consequently, any higher-need levels will not be activated.

*Column 3* illustrates a situation in which safety-level considerations are relatively unimportant because they are satisfied, interaction opportunities are high, but where workers are placed in low-status congruence work groups.

The need-hierarchy explanation of this situation would be as follows safety needs are not active and membership needs are active but frustrated because social-status differences among persons in the work group are too large for the group to deal with effectively. Therefore no indications of higher-level needs are present. As a consequence, people would not see their work as something to which they could or should contribute. But why should low- or high-status congruence affect membership motivation?

In Zaleznik, Christensen, and Roethlisberger's recent study, a "theory of social certitude" was advanced to explain this on an individual level:

> In the condition of social certitude, the individual may be high, middle, or low in total status. But at whatever level, his status factors are well established. As a social entity, therefore, he can place himself and be placed readily in the structure of a group. People relate to him in terms of common expectations of behavior toward a person well established at his particular level of status. In turn, the individual knows what to expect from others. These expectations may or may not be functional for the group or the individual—there may be a more productive role for an individual than his status, well established as it is, allows him to play. Nevertheless, in a condition of social certitude the individual becomes "structured" into a group. Whether he is structured into the group at a high rank or low rank will depend on the level of the individual's total status.
>
> The condition of ambiguity, where the individual's status factors are out of line, provides no readily apparent social position for him. As an ambiguous social entity, the group has no clear expectations regarding behavior from or toward such an individual. On the one hand, being high in one or more dimensions of status seems to require the form of behavior associated with

a high status person. On the other hand, being simultaneously low in one or more dimensions of status seems to require behavior associated with a low status person. These mixed expectations create ambiguities and consequently anxiety in social relationships.[12]

This theory was advanced to explain why group members are attracted to or repelled by an *individual* whose status factors are out of line: some very high, some very low. Such an individual is ambiguous in relation to the group majority. The term "group-status congruence" refers to a collection of people who share similar status factors, even if the factors themselves may be out of line with one another for a given individual. In this kind of a situation, an individual who exhibits status factors different from the majority tends to be avoided by the majority even if his status factors are in line with one another. He is likely to be described by others as "not our class" or "not our kind of person." [13] The four combinations between an individual and his group (high group-status congruence, high individual-status congruence; high group-status congruence, low individual-status congruence, etc.) have not been studied as such. At the present time, loosely stated, it appears that if, under most conditions, an individual has status factors to some extent different from the majority of people in the small-group social structure to which he belongs, he will tend to be regarded as ambiguous by that majority, and hence will be regarded with anxiety.

Clark's supermarket research[14] was concerned with differences in group-status congruence between stores.

He found that groups with high group-status congruence (which he called "high status factors in common" groups) exhibited low turnover and low absenteeism, both indications of membership-need level satisfaction. Moreover, he further found that stores which had high-status congruent groups in them also tended to have higher labor efficiency ratings. In addition, he found that members of these groups tended to speak of their work as more satisfying.

Adams' bomber crew study[15] was somewhat similar.

He showed that crews with high group-status congruence tended to report feelings of satisfaction with group membership. However, Adams also showed that while crews with high-status congruence showed high technical

[12] A. Zaleznik, C. R. Christensen, and F. J. Roethlisberger, *The Motivation, Productivity and Satisfaction of Workers, A Prediction Study,* Harvard University Division of Research, Graduate School of Business Administration, Boston, Mass., 1958.

[13] James V. Clark, *Some Unconscious Assumptions Affecting Labor Efficiency in Eight Supermarkets* (unpublished D.B.A. thesis), Harvard Graduate School of Business Administration, 1958.

[14] *Ibid.*

[15] Stuart Adams, "Status Congruency as a Variable in Small Group Performance," *Social Forces,* XXXII, 16–22.

performance up to a point, beyond that point, as group status congruence increased, technical performance decreased.

Therefore, while Clark's and Adams' studies showed similar results in the relation between group-status congruence and membership satisfaction, their findings on group-status congruence and performance were less clear.[16] It is difficult to explain with confidence why Adams' highest technical performance groups were low-status congruent. Comparable data on social structure, motivation, satisfaction, and formal leadership might have provided clearer explanations.

Not only the possible difference between these two studies, but the findings of other researches in the general area of status and how people react to it, all indicate that not enough is known yet about this subject to offer inclusive explanations for work-group behavior. For example, Zaleznik's machine shop workers[17] had developed a social structure which offered its members at least a minimal level of satisfaction. In comparison to other studies, his workers could be said to have exhibited low individual and group-status congruence, although the congruence apparently was high enough for the group to form: it contained no Bolsheviks or Andaman Islanders. In short, the existing findings in this area suggest, but not conclusively, that under most industrial conditions, a group will be more cohesive to the extent to which its members exhibit individual and/or group-status congruence. (An important exception will be discussed under Column 7 of Figure 1.)

The remaining columns, 4 through 7, show those situations where neither technological restrictions on interaction, nor the given sentiments of workers (e.g., notions of member attraction stemming from status factors in common) are such as to prevent the formation of a satisfying social structure. Rather the constrictions on group development portrayed here stem largely from the behavior of the formal leader of the work group.

*Leadership behavior.* Since leadership is important here, it will be useful, before turning to the columns themselves, to describe roughly the leadership behavior under three different types.[18] The labels "accommodative," "production-centered," and "group-centered" will be briefly described, in that order.

The first, "accommodative," refers to situations where the leader's behav-

[16] However, the two studies do not necessarily contradict each other on this point, since Clark studied no stores with status-congruence measures as high as some of the bomber crews studied by Adams. Also, the two studies used different status factors, and different ways to measure group-status congruence. Clark's research is continuing in an attempt to test for lower labor efficiency under conditions of higher group-status congruence.

[17] A. Zaleznik, *Worker Satisfaction and Development,* Harvard University Division of Research, Graduate School of Business Administration, Boston, Mass., 1956.

[18] It is beyond the scope of this article to evaluate these labels or to offer a different classification scheme.

ior neither challenges a group, nor seriously violates its norms of how a leader should behave. The group's determination of its own work procedures is left alone. As a result, the formal leader does not seriously threaten the group's survival as a group.

This condition is a common one and was described in the following reports:

In the Whirlwind Corporation[19] a group of workers developed an improved tool capable of increasing their productivity on a certain item fifty per cent. Actually, they increased productivity ten per cent and used the remaining time to improve quality on some other products. A methods engineer was assigned to study the problem but the group withheld information about the tool from him. For some time, the foreman was aware of this but was "satisfied to let the men handle it their own way." He reasoned that at little expense he was able to get out production of high quality.

In Roy's research in a piecework machine shop[20] workers had an elaborate set of restriction-of-output activities. The foreman instructed new men in parts of this system. To one man he said:

Say, when you punch off day work onto piecework, you ought to have your piecework already started. Run a few, then punch off day work, and you'll have a good start. You've got to chisel a little around here to make money.

In the Century Company,[21] workers in one area (B) reported that their foreman left them completely alone and had for several years. Prior to that time, he had supervised the men closely but they had taught him not to, by telling him that they would refuse to work if he didn't let them alone.

Although the three situations above point to different degrees of foreman involvement in the group, the uniformity among them is that the leader has abdicated any influence in the setting of work procedures. The group determines its procedures. A variety of labels other than "accommodative" have been devised to describe such a foreman: "laissez-faire," "abdicratic," etc.

Other researches have pointed to the "production-centered" pattern of leadership behavior (and, moreover, suggested certain relations between such leadership and productivity).

In a study of productivity and leadership in an insurance company,[22]

[19] Paul Pigors and Charles H. Myers, *Personnel Administration, A Point of View and a Method,* McGraw-Hill Co., New York, 1956.

[20] Donald Roy, "Efficiency and the Fix: Informal Intergroup Relations in a Piecework Machine Shop," *American Journal of Sociology,* LX, No. 3 (1954).

[21] "Century Co. (A)—(I)," *op. cit.*

[22] Daniel Katz, N. Maccoby, and Nancy Morse, *Productivity, Supervision and Morale in an Office Situation,* Part I, Institute for Social Research, Ann Arbor, Mich., 1950.

certain leaders were characterized as seeing their job primarily in terms of methods, procedures, and standards of production. Called production-centered leaders, by the researchers, it was noted that such leaders headed seven out of ten low-producing sections.

In the Century Company (I) case,[23] one foreman said this about his idea of a good worker:

> A good man is a man who is reasonable. . . . He does what the company tells him he should do. He does not try to do what he thinks he should do, but he does what he is told.

The people working for this foreman had these kinds of things to say about him:

> Whenever my foreman sees a man sitting down, he comes up to him and gives him something to do. . . . I don't think he'll be happy until he sees everybody running around all the time. [Our] foreman shouldn't yell at a man in front of everybody or nail him down. . . . This makes friction and breaks down the group.

Borrowing the phrase from the above-mentioned insurance company research, the Century Company researchers labelled this foreman "production-centered."

This kind of leader is the direct opposite of the accommodative type, in that he allows the employees little or no influence in the setting-up of work procedures. Influence is supposed to move downward only according to such a supervisor. Although we are calling such a leader production-centered, others have described him as "authoritarian," "autocratic," and "task-centered."

"Group-centered" leadership was indicated in the same two studies.

In the insurance company,[24] "employee-centered leadership" referred to supervisors who saw their job primarily in terms of the organization, training, and motivation of subordinates. Such supervisors headed six of seven high-producing sections. The researchers said that:

> The supervisors of the high-producing sections . . . regard supervision as the most important part of their work. . . . Their method of supervision appears to be one of setting up certain general conditions for their employees and thus permitting their employees to work out the details of when and how the work will be handled.

In the Century Company case (I),[25] one foreman said this about his idea of a good worker:

[23] "Century Co. (A)—(I)," *op. cit.*
[24] Daniel Katz, N. Maccoby, and Nancy Morse, *op. cit.*
[25] "Century Co. (A)—(I)," *op. cit.*

In my estimation, a good furnace worker is a man who has confidence in himself. . . . A foreman should show confidence in his men, and this should be real confidence. I'm always ready to show confidence in a man, even though at first sight I might think he doesn't deserve it. What I do is give some directions to a man and then let him do his work without always being on his back. I want him to be free to do his work. . . . I realize that this requires a lot of talking on the part of the foreman. The men have to learn to trust their foreman. A foreman has to talk to his men to let himself be known by them. . . . Another thing, I like to tease the men, because it's one way for me to talk to them. It shows them I'm not dangerous.

The workers spoke about this foreman as follows:

Last week when ——— was our foreman we did not have any trouble. There were no complaints, no grievances, no beefs. It was hot and he understood that we were having more difficulty working at this temperature than at other times. After all, a man needs encouragement.

He knows how to run the men. I wish we could keep him for a long time. . . . We're not the only ones that have noticed he is good. Everywhere he has been in the company, people have been glad to work for him.

The researchers classified this foreman as "group-centered."

This kind of leader has been described as "democratic," "group-centered," "employee-centered," etc. In this paper, the group-centered label will be used. Regardless of the label, however, it can be seen that such a leader allows and encourages a *mutual* influence relationship with his men. Both the leader and his subordinates play a role in the setting-up of work procedures and the mutuality is made legitimate and encouraged by this kind of leader.

Returning to the Figure 1 diagram, *Column 4* shows the effects of the production-centered leadership condition in a situation where group formation potential is present. The behavior of a leader allowing low-influence opportunity, as described above, would tend to prevent a group from forming a satisfying relationship with each other and to its environment. Because workers are more consciously forced to attend to their work, their membership needs are frustrated.

The Century Company[26] cases showed two groups of furnace workers, both with equal numbers of high and low individually status-congruent people. Workers in furnace area "A" had a production-centered foreman and exhibited less social development, while workers in furnace area "B" had an accommodative foreman and showed more social development. The researchers made an attempt to assess motivation, also, and there was considerably lower indication of membership need activation in area A than in area B. Moreover, of those judged active at this need level in area A, the majority appeared frustrated.

[26] *Ibid.*

This study shows an instance in which membership needs were frustrated by a production-centered foreman: by holding workers rigidly to their required activities, he never permitted the social group to form, even though it was potentially capable of so forming. Incidentally, while accurate productivity data were not available for the two particular shift crews studied, area A as a whole (all four shift crews together) was producing much less than area B.

If production-centered leadership is introduced into a group that has already formed, however, there is some evidence to suggest that the group continues to function as a group: they unite around their hostility to management.

The "Case of the Changing Cage" [27] alluded to before illustrates this (although it contains no information about status congruence). The supervisor believed that he could better control output by looking into this cage and thereby reducing nonwork behavior. In the old cage, he could not see in, but in the new cage he could. The result, however, was the nonwork activities actually increased (although they were less visible: the group went underground).

Whether or not such a situation is indicative of frustrated membership needs is difficult to say. Perhaps it can be said, though, that this group was simply elaborating its membership needs: under this condition, the nonwork behavior offered the only *possibility* for need satisfaction.

Columns 1 through 4 have all illustrated how environmental conditions can restrict the development of social structure in work groups. In addition, they also illustrated motivational consequences at lower-need levels only. The remaining columns show situations in which there is indication that higher-need levels can become activated. Since, in a formal organization, people activated at these higher-need levels show a tendency to contribute their judgment and productiveness to the organization's task, the term "contributive motivation" may sometimes be a useful shorthand for all the need levels above the membership level. We shall use it occasionally in the rest of this paper.

*Column 5* shows two changes in comparison to Column 4. One, the satisfaction of membership needs, comes from the accommodative leader who, by not threatening the group too much, allows it to form and perpetuate itself. The second change is the frustration of the esteem needs, due to the introduction of a condition which might be labelled "low-perceived contribution opportunity." This refers to a worker's perception of a technological process as being predetermined for the most part. Here, except for the opportunity for an occasional change in setup, technology, etc., a member of a social group at work sees no continuing opportunity to contribute anything, to make a difference, to initiate, along with other members of this group, something useful on his environment. The Column

[27] Cara Richards and Henry Dobyns, *op. cit.*

five situation has often been described in organizational behavior research at the worker level because it is undoubtedly the most common. The self-esteem and status-prestige needs are released, because membership needs are relatively satisfied, but, since the workers' jobs prevent any satisfying feelings of group competence or mastery to emerge, and because the accommodative foreman has no concept of getting his group involved in setting up any of its own procedures, the esteem needs are frustrated. Typical comments of workers in such situations are:

A job is a job.
You have to work so it might as well be here as anywhere.
This job isn't bad: it's a nice bunch of guys but any moron could do the work [etc.].

It appears as if the "regulars" in the Zaleznik, Christensen, Roethlisberger prediction study[28] and the famous bank-wiring room workers[29] illustrate this column. Under such conditions, workers' productivity and satisfaction are determined mainly by their position in the social structure, since they are "stuck" on the membership level. Little, if any, opportunity for the satisfaction of contributive motivation exists.

*Column 6* differs from Column 5 in that it shows the satisfied self-esteem need under conditions of a high perceived contribution opportunity, but a frustrated status-prestige need (frustrated by the lack of recognition on the part of an accommodative foreman) which the worker would feel was justified by his competence. The accommodative leader allows a group to develop simply by not being around or bothering to impede it. His *not* being around or *not* understanding the forces which motivate productiveness (i.e., self-esteem around job competence) make him less likely to reward the work with verbal or economic recognition of these perceived skills.

This motivational pattern and these environmental conditions were seen in the previously referred to Century Company case.[30] Workers in one furnace area (B) were glad their foreman was not around to interfere with their nonwork activities and their exercising of skill and judgment in their work. However, they resented the fact that he did not *understand* the extent of their technical competence and hence could not reward them adequately when it came time for him to evaluate them.

Before leaving columns 1 through 6, which all illustrate one or another form of what Roethlisberger has called "frozen groups," [31] another condi-

---

[28] A. Zaleznik, C. R. Christensen, and F. J. Roethlisberger, *op. cit.*
[29] Where there is a suggestion (untested) that social structure was determined by individual status congruence. Cf. F. J. Roethlisberger and W. J. Dickson, *op. cit.*
[30] "Century Co. (A)—(I)," *op. cit.*
[31] A. Zaleznik, *op. cit.*

tion should be mentioned: "perception of company supportiveness." It has not been studied in enough situations to allow us to place it somewhere in columns 1 through 6; however two studies suggest its importance.

Seashore[32] found that high cohesive groups tended to produce significantly higher than average when they reported a high perception of company supportiveness and to produce significantly lower than average when they reported a low perception of company supportiveness.

In a piecework machine shop studied by Collins, *et al.,*[33] a work group had an elaborate system of output restriction. The accommodative foreman knew about and actively supported the system. The general superintendent, however, exerted much effort in an attempt to break it up. He told workers they should not accept group pressure to conform and that they were foolish and dishonest if they did. The men saw the overall company as being hostile toward them and went to considerable lengths to restrict output: they often finished their day's work in three or four hours, they had jigs and fixtures which increased their hourly productivity but which were unknown to management, etc.

*Column 7* shows a condition that has only recently been analytically studied on a continuing basis in industry. However, studies concerning group participation in the process of instituting technological change (e.g., the well-known relay assembly test room[34] and Coch and French[35] studies) might illustrate this situation for temporary periods where workers were involved in, and given recognition for, their ability to contribute to important organizational problems. Perhaps, too, the Lamson Company case[36] points to such a condition.

Skilled experience oil refinery workers were taken off their old job, given an extensive training course, and placed in a new tower. For several months they worked alongside the engineers who were installing and "debugging" the new and complicated equipment. Their suggestions were encouraged and accepted by the engineers and the men's behavior indicated they were highly satisfied with the experience.

Workers in such situations appear to be motivated at the higher need levels and to exist under maximal environmental conditions: they have a high opportunity to interact, a task to which they see a high opportunity to contribute and a leader who sets up a high opportunity for mutual influence between himself and his subordinates. Moreover, we can infer, too, that

[32] S. F. Seashore, *Group Cohesiveness in the Industrial Work Group,* Survey Research Center, University of Michigan, Ann Arbor, Mich., 1954. [Reprinted in this volume, pages 330–334.—Ed.]

[33] Orville Collins, Melville Dalton, and Donald Roy, "Restriction of Output and Social Cleavage in Industry," *Applied Anthropology,* V, No. 3 (1946).

[34] F. J. Roethlisberger and W. J. Dickson, *op. cit.*

[35] L. Coch and J. R. P. French, "Overcoming Resistance to Change," *Human Relations,* I, 512–532. [Reprinted in this volume, pages 406–428.—Ed.]

[36] "Lamson Co.," Harvard Business School, HP 318.

such workers would exist in an organizational environment which they saw as supportive. In addition, one study in an electronics factory (not yet published) suggests that the remaining environmental condition, high-status congruence, is a prerequisite for the motivation pattern seen in Column 7.

However, in a recently published research by Barnes[37] members of an engineering group exhibited low individual and group-status congruence, yet had high opportunity to interact, high opportunity for mutual influence and a high contribution opportunity. A few individuals, considered as a collection, had high group-status congruence, yet the social structure was not determined by this fact. Moreover, much of the group looked as if they might be exhibiting the need pattern seen in Column 7.

Barnes' research suggests, therefore, that, when all other conditions are met, a group's social behavior is not "frozen" by the status factors its members brought with them. If one is interested in the growth and development of individuals in an organization, Barnes' study points to a helpful situation.

## Summary and Conclusion

By carefully examining Figure 1 we have attempted to describe factors which both release and constrain different motivations in members of industrial work groups. In addition, we have shown how, according to Maslow's theory, relative satisfaction of certain needs may release other needs which alter the picture. Roughly, the following diagram illustrates this process, and is nothing more than a simplified restatement of Figure 1.

Incidentally, the similarity between Figure 2 and the small group con-

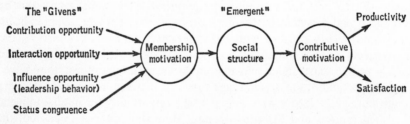

Figure 2

ceptual scheme of Homans'[38] is obvious. "Contribution opportunity" refers to the extent to which an individual's "required activities" are not so highly programmed that no room is left for the individual's contribution to them.

[37] Louis B. Barnes, *Organizational Systems and Engineering Groups,* Harvard University Division of Research, Graduate School of Business Administration, Boston, Massachusetts, 1960.

[38] George C. Homans, *The Human Group,* Harcourt, Brace & Co., New York, 1950.

"Interaction opportunity" refers to the extent to which an individual's "required interactions" do not limit him from getting together, on a social as well as task basis, with others. "Influence opportunity," a function of leadership behavior, has an effect on an individual's motivation because of the kinds of "given sentiments" most of us appear to have about leadership: when we are closely controlled or highly programmed, this violates our expectations of a satisfying superior-subordinate behavior. "Status congruence" refers to another large body of "given sentiments" most people seem to have: ideas about status and class which are widespread in our culture.

Any emergent small group behavior feeds back on the givens, however, as Homans and others have observed. And Figure 2 is oversimplified insofar as this feedback is not shown. Nevertheless, its importance is obvious, particularly if one must understand and/or deal with a group through time. For example, a foreman of a work group which, for various reasons, was producing too little might change his leadership behavior from accommodative to production-centered, thus, perhaps, frustrating membership and self-esteem needs. Another example of such feedback might exist in a group under a group-centered leader who allowed mutual influence opportunities and whose members were active at the membership and contributive levels. Conceivably, these members would see continuous contribution opportunities in their jobs, thereby releasing further contributive motivation. Another example, and one which a number of my colleagues at the Harvard Business School and myself hope to test specifically in a current project, is the possibility that the structure of a group operating on higher need levels will be less determined by the status congruence of its members than it was at an earlier time, when it was operating more at the membership level.

In conclusion, the obvious fact remains to be emphasized that better techniques for the measurement of need activation in workers must be developed before this broad-stroke explanatory theory can be refined, altered, or rejected in the organizational behavior area. Only one of the studies cited—and that not yet published except in case form[39]—made an explicit attempt to assess motivation in Maslow's terms.

Research takes time, though, and those of us concerned directly with the immediate here-and-now problems of executives cannot always wait for our own and others' patient and time-consuming testing of intriguing notions of potential utility to practicing administrators. And, it seems to me, an administrator *can* use this general way of thinking to predict, at least on a gross basis, that certain consequences are quite likely to follow from the "givens" in any situation. Such a prediction might be economically valuable to him. He might, for example, behave differently during a technological or organizational change than he would have if he were not aware of the suggested effects of low interaction opportunity and contribution potential

[39] "Century Co. (A)—(I)," *op. cit.*

on motivation, social structure and productivity, and satisfaction. Conversely, if he were experiencing severe problems of dissatisfaction in his work force, he might seek to understand them in terms of this theory, and thereby highlight some "givens" which might be changed: interaction opportunity, for example. Such a change might cut down grievances, or even avert a strike.

Hopefully, this paper may serve to stimulate some better ways of testing the utility of Maslow's concepts for the study of organizational behavior. Certainly we are in need of integrative and operational concepts that both form the basis for replicable and comparative research and offer some utility to the practicing administrator.

# An Integrating Principle
## and an Overview*

*Rensis Likert*

The managers whose performance is impressive appear to be fashioning a better system of management. [Earlier] two generalizations were stated based on the available research findings:

> The supervisors and managers in American industry and government who are achieving the highest productivity, lowest costs, least turnover and absence, and the highest levels of employee motivation and satisfaction display, on the average, a different pattern of leadership from those managers who are achieving less impressive results. The principles and practices of these high-producing managers are deviating in important ways from those called for by present-day management theories.

> The high-producing managers whose deviations from existing theory and practice are creating improved procedures have not yet integrated their deviant principles into a theory of management. Individually, they are often clearly aware of how a particular practice of theirs differs from generally accepted methods, but the magnitude, importance, and systematic nature of the differences when the total pattern is examined do not appear to be recognized.

* From *New Patterns of Management,* McGraw-Hill Book Company, Inc., New York, 1961, chap. 8, pp. 97–106. Reprinted by permission of the publisher.

Based upon the principles and practices of the managers who are achieving the best results, a newer theory of organization and management can be stated. An attempt will be made in this chapter to present briefly some of the over-all characteristics of such a theory and to formulate a general integrating principle which can be useful in attempts to apply it.

There is no doubt that further research and experimental testing of the theory in pilot operations will yield evidence pointing to modifications of many aspects of the newer theory suggested in this volume. Consequently, in reading this and subsequent chapters it will be well not to quarrel with the specific aspects of the newer theory as presented. These specifics are intended as stimulants for discussion and as encouragement for experimental field tests of the theory. It will be more profitable to seek to understand the newer theory's general basic character and, whenever a specific aspect or derivation appears to be in error, to formulate more valid derivations and propositions.

Research findings indicate that the general pattern of operations of the highest-producing managers tends to differ from that of the managers of mediocre and low-producing units by more often showing the following characteristics:

A preponderance of favorable attitudes on the part of each member of the organization toward all the other members, toward superiors, toward the work, toward the organization—toward all aspects of the job. These favorable attitudes toward others reflect a high level of mutual confidence and trust throughout the organization. The favorable attitudes toward the organization and the work are not those of easy complacency, but are the attitudes of identification with the organization and its objectives and a high sense of involvement in achieving them. As a consequence, the performance goals are high and dissatisfaction may occur whenever achievement falls short of the goals set.

This highly motivated, cooperative orientation toward the organization and its objectives is achieved by harnessing effectively all the major motivational forces which can exercise significant influence in an organizational setting and which, potentially, can be accompanied by cooperative and favorable attitudes. Reliance is not placed solely or fundamentally on the economic motive of buying a man's time and using control and authority as the organizing and coordinating principle of the organization. On the contrary, the following motives are all used fully and in such a way that they function in a cumulative and reinforcing manner and yield favorable attitudes:

The ego motives. These are referred to throughout . . . as the desire to achieve and maintain a sense of personal worth and importance. This desire manifests itself in many forms, depending upon the norms and values of the persons and groups involved. Thus, it is responsible for such motivational forces as the desire for growth and significant achievement in terms of one's own values and goals, i.e., self-fulfillment, as well as the desire for status, recognition, approval, acceptance, and power and the desire to undertake significant and important tasks.

The security motives.

Curiosity, creativity, and the desire for new experiences.

The economic motives.

By tapping all the motives which yield favorable and cooperative attitudes, maximum motivation oriented toward realizing the organization's goals as well as the needs of each member of the organization is achieved. The substantial decrements in motivational forces which occur when powerful motives are pulling in opposite directions are thereby avoided. These conflicting forces exist, of course, when hostile and resentful attitudes are present.

The organization consists of a tightly knit, effectively functioning social system. This social system is made up of interlocking work groups with a high degree of group loyalty among the members and favorable attitudes and trust between superiors and subordinates. Sensitivity to others and relatively high levels of skill in personal interaction and the functioning of groups are also present. These skills permit effective participation in decisions on common problems. Participation is used, for example, to establish organizational objectives which are a satisfactory integration of the needs and desires of all members of the organization and of persons functionally related to it. High levels of reciprocal influence occur, and high levels of total coordinated influence are achieved in the organization. Communication is efficient and effective. There is a flow from one part of the organization to another of all the relevant information important for each decision and action. The leadership in the organization has developed what might well be called a highly effective social system for interaction and mutual influence.

Measurements of organizational performance are used primarily for self-guidance rather than for superimposed control. To tap the motives which bring cooperative and favorable rather than hostile attitudes, participation and involvement in decisions is a habitual part of the leadership processes. This kind of decision-making, of course, calls for the full sharing of available measurements and information. Moreover, as it becomes evident in the decision-making process that additional information or measurements are needed, steps are taken to obtain them.

In achieving operations which are more often characterized by the above pattern of highly cooperative, well-coordinated activity, the highest producing managers use all the technical resources of the classical theories of management, such as time-and-motion study, budgeting, and financial controls. They use these resources at least as completely as do the low-producing managers, but in quite different ways. This difference in use arises from the differences in the motives which the high-producing, in contrast to the low-producing, managers believe are important in influencing human behavior.

The low-producing managers, in keeping with traditional practice, feel that the way to motivate and direct behavior is to exercise control through authority. Jobs are organized, methods are prescribed, standards are set, performance goals and budgets are established. Compliance with them is sought through the use of hierarchical and economic pressures.

The highest-producing managers feel, generally, that this manner of functioning does not produce the best results, that the resentment created by direct exercise of authority tends to limit its effectiveness. They have learned that better results can be achieved when a different motivational process is employed. As suggested above, they strive to use all those major motives which have the potentiality of yielding favorable and cooperative attitudes in such a way that favorable attitudes are, in fact, elicited and the motivational forces are mutually reinforcing. Motivational forces stemming from the economic motive are not then blunted by such other motivations as group goals which restrict the quantity or quality of output. The full strength of all economic, ego, and other motives is generated and put to use.

Widespread use of participation is one of the more important approaches employed by the high-producing managers in their efforts to get full benefit from the technical resources of the classical theories of management coupled with high levels of reinforcing motivation. This use of participation applies to all aspects of the job and work, as, for example, in setting work goals and budgets, controlling costs, organizing the work, etc.

In these and comparable ways, the high-producing managers make full use of the technical resources of the classical theories of management. They use these resources in such a manner, however, that favorable and cooperative attitudes are created and all members of the organization endeavor to pull concertedly toward commonly accepted goals which they have helped to establish.

This brief description of the pattern of management which is more often characteristic of the high-producing than of the low-producing managers points to what appears to be a critical difference. The high-producing managers have developed their organizations into highly coordinated, highly motivated, cooperative social systems. Under their leadership, the different motivational forces in each member of the organization have coalesced into a strong force aimed at accomplishing the mutually established objectives of the organization. This general pattern of highly motivated, cooperative members seems to be a central characteristic of the newer management system being developed by the highest-producing managers.

How do these high-producing managers build organizations which display this central characteristic? Is there any general approach or underlying principle which they rely upon in building highly motivated organizations? There seems to be, and clues as to the nature of the principle can be obtained by reexamining some of the [previous] materials. . . . The research findings show, for example, that those supervisors and managers whose pattern of leadership yields consistently favorable attitudes more often think of employees as "human beings rather than just as persons to get the work done." Consistently, in study after study, the data show that treating people as "human beings" rather than as "cogs in a machine" is a variable highly related to the attitudes and motivation of the subordinate at every level in the organization. . . .

The superiors who have the most favorable and cooperative attitudes in their work groups display the following characteristics:

The attitude and behavior of the superior toward the subordinate as a person, *as perceived by the subordinate,* is as follows:

He is supportive, friendly, and helpful rather than hostile. He is kind but firm, never threatening, genuinely interested in the well-being of subordinates and endeavors to treat people in a sensitive, considerate way. He is just, if not generous. He endeavors to serve the best interests of his employees as well as of the company.

He shows confidence in the integrity, ability, and motivations of subordinates rather than suspicion and distrust.

His confidence in subordinates leads him to have high expectations as to their level of performance. With confidence that he will not be disappointed, he expects much, not little. (This, again, is fundamentally a supportive rather than a critical or hostile relationship.)

He sees that each subordinate is well trained for his particular job. He endeavors also to help subordinates be promoted by training them for jobs at the next level. This involves giving them relevant experience and coaching whenever the opportunity offers.

He coaches and assists employees whose performance is below standard. In the case of a subordinate who is clearly misplaced and unable to do his job satisfactorily, he endeavors to find a position well suited to that employee's abilities and arranges to have the employee transferred to it.

The behavior of the superior in directing the work is characterized by such activity as:

Planning and scheduling the work to be done, training subordinates, supplying them with material and tools, initiating work activity, etc.

Providing adequate technical competence, particularly in those situations where the work has not been highly standardized.

The leader develops his subordinates into a working team with high group loyalty by using participation and the other kinds of group-leadership practices summarized [earlier].

## The Integrating Principle

These results and similar data from other studies (Argyris, 1957; March & Simon, 1958; Viteles, 1953) show that subordinates react favorably to experiences which they feel are supportive and contribute to their sense of importance and personal worth. Similarly, persons react unfavorably to experiences which are threatening and decrease or minimize their sense of dignity and personal worth. These findings are supported also by substantial research on personality development (Argyris, 1957; Rogers, 1942; Rogers, 1951) and group behavior (Cartwright & Zander, 1960). Each of us wants appreciation, recognition, influence, a feeling of accomplishment, and a feeling that people who are important to us believe in us and respect us. We want to feel that we have a place in the world.

This pattern of reaction appears to be universal and seems to be the basis for the general principle used by the high-producing managers in developing their highly motivated, cooperative organizations. These managers have discovered that the motivational forces acting in each member of an organization are most likely to be cumulative and reinforcing when the interactions between each individual and the others in the organization are of such a character that they convey to the individual a feeling of support and recognition for his importance and worth as a person. These managers, therefore, strive to have the interactions between the members of their organization of such a character that each member of the organization feels confident in his potentialities and believes that his abilities are being well used.

A second factor, however, is also important. As we have seen [previously], an individual's reaction to any situation is always a function not of the absolute character of the interaction, but of his perception of it. It is how he sees things that counts, not objective reality. Consequently, an individual member of an organization will always interpret an interaction between himself and the organization in terms of his background and culture, his experience and expectations. The pattern of supervision and the language used that might be effective with a railroad's maintenance-of-way crew, for example, would not be suitable in an office full of young women. A subordinate tends also to expect his superior to behave in ways consistent with the personality of the superior. All this means that each of us, as a subordinate or as a peer or as a superior, reacts in terms of his own particular background, experience, and expectations. In order, therefore, to have an interaction viewed as supportive, it is essential that it be of such a character that the individual himself, in the light of his experience and expectations, sees it as supportive. This provides the basis for stating the general principle which the high-producing managers seem to be using and which will be referred to as the *principle of supportive relationships*. This principle, which provides an invaluable guide in any attempt to apply the newer theory of management in a specific plant or organization, can be briefly stated: *The leadership and other processes of the organization must be such as to ensure a maximum probability that in all interactions and all relationships with the organization each member will, in the light of his background, values, and expectations, view the experience as supportive and one which builds and maintains his sense of personal worth and importance.*

### The Principle of Supportive Relationships as an Organizing Concept

This general principle provides a fundamental formula for obtaining the full potential of every major motive which can be constructively harnessed in a working situation. There is impressive evidence, for example, that economic motivations will be tapped more effectively when the conditions specified by the principle of supportive relationships are met (Katz & Kahn, 1951; Krulee, 1955). In addition, as motives are used in the ways called for by this general principle, the attitudes accompanying the motives will be favorable and the different motivational forces will be cumulative and reinforcing. Under these circumstances, the full power from each of the available motives will be added to that from the others to yield a maximum of coordinated, enthusiastic effort.

The principle of supportive relationships points to a dimension essential for the success of every organization, namely, that the mission of the organization be seen by its members as genuinely important. To be highly motivated, each member of the organization must feel that the organization's objectives are of significance and that his own particular task contributes in an indispensable manner to the organization's achievement of its objectives. He should see his role as difficult, important, and meaningful. This is necessary if the individual is to achieve and maintain a sense of personal worth and importance. When jobs do not meet this specification they should be reorganized so that they do. This is likely to require the participation of those involved in the work in a manner suggested in subsequent chapters.

The term "supportive" is used frequently in subsequent chapters and also is a key word in the principle of supportive relationships. Experiences, relationships, etc., are considered to be supportive when the individual involves sees the experience (in terms of his values, goals, expectations, and aspirations) as contributing to or maintaining his sense of personal worth and importance.

The principle of supportive relationships contains within it an important clue to its effective use. To apply this general principle, a superior must take into consideration the experience and expectations of each of his subordinates. In determining what these expectations are, he cannot rely solely on his observations and impressions. It helps the superior to try to put himself in his subordinate's shoes and endeavor to see things as the subordinate sees them, but this is not enough. Too often, the superior's estimates are wrong. He needs direct evidence if he is to know how the subordinate views things and to estimate the kinds of behavior and interaction which will be seen by the subordinate as supportive. The superior needs accurate information as to how his behavior is actually seen by the subordinate. Does the subordinate, in fact, perceive the superior's behavior as supportive?

There are two major ways to obtain this evidence. In a complex organization it can be found by the use of measurements of the intervening variables. . . . It can also be obtained by the development of work-group relationships, which not only facilitate but actually require, as part of the group building and maintenance functions, candid expressions by group members of their perceptions and reactions to the behavior of others. . . .

## The Central Role of the Work Group

An important theoretical derivation can be made from the principle of supportive relationships. This derivation is based directly on the desire to achieve and maintain a sense of personal worth, which is a central concept of the principle. The most important source of satisfaction for this desire is the response we get from the people we are close to, in whom we are interested, and whose approval and support we are eager to have. The face-to-face groups with whom we spend the bulk of our time are, consequently, the most important to us. Our work group is one in which we spend much of our time and one in which we are particularly eager to achieve and maintain a sense of personal worth. As a consequence, most persons are highly motivated to behave in ways consistent with the goals and values of their work group in order to obtain recognition, support, security, and favorable reactions from this group. It can be concluded, therefore, that *management will make full use of the potential capacities of its human resources only when each person in an organization is a member of one or more effectively functioning work groups that have a high degree of group loyalty, effective skills of interaction, and high performance goals.*

The full significance of this derivation becomes more evident when we examine the research findings that show how groups function when they are well knit and have effective interaction skills. Research shows, for example, that the greater the attraction and loyalty to the group, the more the individual is motivated (1) to accept the goals and decisions of the group; (2) to seek to influence the goals and decisions of the group so that they are consistent with his own experience and his own goals; (3) to communicate fully to the members of the group; (4) to welcome communication and influence attempts from the other members; (5) to behave so as to help implement the goals and decisions that are seen as most important to the group; and (6) to behave in ways calculated to receive support and favorable recognition from members of the group and especially from those who the individual feels are the more powerful and higher-status members (Cartwright & Zander, 1960). Groups which display a high level of member attraction to the group and high levels of the above characteristics will be referred to . . . as *highly effective groups*. These groups are described more fully [elsewhere].

As our theoretical derivation has indicated, an organization will function best when its personnel function not as individuals but as members of highly effective work groups with high performance goals. Consequently, management should deliberately endeavor to build these effective groups, linking them into an over-all organization by means of people who hold overlapping group membership (Figure 1). The superior in one group is a subordinate in the next group, and so on through the organization. If the work groups at each hierarchical level are well knit and effective, the linking process will be accomplished well. Staff as well as line should be characterized by this pattern of operation.

The dark lines in Figure 1 are intended to show that interaction occurs between individuals as well as in groups. The dark lines are omitted at the

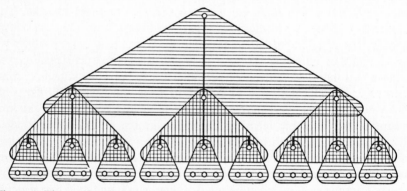

Figure 1. The overlapping group form of organization. Work groups vary in size as circumstances require although shown here as consisting of four persons.

lowest level in the chart in order to avoid complexity. Interaction between individuals occurs there, of course, just as it does at higher levels in the organization.

In most organizations, there are also various continuing and *ad hoc* committees, committees related to staff functions, etc., which should also become highly effective groups and thereby help further to tie the many parts of the organization together. These links are in addition to the linking provided by the overlapping members in the line organization. Throughout the organization, the supervisory process should develop and strengthen group functioning. This theoretically ideal organizational structure provides the framework for the management system called for by the newer theory.

## References

Argyris, C.: *Personality and Organization.* New York: Harper, 1957.

Cartwright, D., & Zander, A. (Eds.): *Group Dynamics: Research and Theory* (2d ed.). Evanston, Ill.: Row, Peterson, 1960.

Katz, D., & Kahn, R. L.: Human Organization and Worker Motivation. In L. Reed Tripp (Ed.), *Industrial Productivity.* Madison, Wis.: Industrial Relations Research Association, 1951, pp. 146–171.

Krulee, G. K.: The Scanlon Plan: Co-operation Through Participation. *J. Business, University of Chicago,* 1955, **28** (2), 100–113.

March, J. G., & Simon, H. A.: *Organizations.* New York: Wiley, 1958.

Rogers, C. R.: *Counseling and Psychotherapy.* Boston: Houghton Mifflin, 1942.

Rogers, C. R.: *Client-centered Therapy.* Boston: Houghton Mifflin, 1951.

Viteles, M. S.: *Motivation and Morale in Industry.* New York: Norton, 1953

# READINGS RELATED TO CHAPTER XII

## Personnel Management: Future Problems and Opportunities*

*Albert F. Watters*

The initial impetus for the development of the present concept of personnel management was supplied by the depression that began with the stock market crash in October, 1929. By the spring of 1933, nearly 13 million people—almost 23 per cent of the nation's labor force—were unemployed. The legislative action required to meet this critical situation culminated in the passage of the Wagner Act, with the concomitant pressures on industrial workers to organize into unions. Management thus found itself in a situation where it was required to bargain collectively with its unionized employees. Other new laws continued to come out of Washington at a rapid pace—laws that directly related to employer-employee relationships. The whole pattern of personnel administration in the Thirties centered on the issues arising from this kind of climate and the new ideal of collective bargaining.

These years were a time of struggle and strife, with businessmen trying to regain lost markets, workers seeking jobs, and labor unions fighting for recognition. The traditional concepts of craft unions were permanently altered as the new industrial unions came into being and organized themselves into new groupings that cut across individual company lines and exerted

* From *Personnel,* vol. 38, no. 1, pp. 53–59, January–February, 1961. Reprinted by permission of the American Management Association.

NOTE. This article has been adapted from the author's address at a recent seminar conducted by the Bureau of Industrial Relations of the University of Michigan.

their pressures on a nation-wide basis. During these years, employers were forced to acquire new knowledge and to develop new methods of dealing with their employees. The presence of unions was a major influence in this development.

With the advent of World War II, a whole new set of pressures and problems arose for the personnel manager. The era of labor plenty vanished overnight. To help meet the need for workers in the war industries, millions of women and older people entered the labor market, giving rise to new problems of job training. Because of the demand for war goods to support a global conflict, the personnel manager became preoccupied with the urgent priorities of production—and with production people.

At the end of 1945 the nation turned to the job of reconstruction and the transition back to a peacetime economy. For the personnel manager, this was a time when business turned again to consumer markets and some ten million men and women left the armed forces to seek civilian employment. Companies concentrated on filling the empty pipelines with consumer goods. The main concern was to step up consumer production. As the rush of pent-up consumer demand created new markets, the post-war boom got under way. Through the rest of the 1940's and the decade of the '50's, a burgeoning economy created jobs for millions of new workers. In this era of comparative peace and unparalleled prosperity, there was little need for radical change or innovation in personnel management.

## How Business Has Changed

Today, however, as we begin the decade of the 1960's, the business picture shows a number of important new factors that will exert a significant influence on the future of the personnel function. These new factors are visible on every hand—in the domestic political climate, in the international arena, in new methods of marketing and distribution, in the backdrop of modern union relations, and in the spectacular technological and educational advances that are changing our very lives.

On the domestic political scene, a new type of "Ivy League" politician is clearly in charge. The old-time "king-maker"—the big city political boss who could make or break a candidate through the traditional ward-and-precinct system of political control—has seen his power pass into the hands of men who, by comparison, are political newcomers.

Overseas, expanding populations and new middle-class markets in western Europe and Japan have created a business prosperity that rivals our own. As a result of lower production costs and technological advances, European and Japanese producers are invading our traditional overseas markets with quality goods at prices below ours and are making a serious bid for our domestic trade. American industry must therefore find new ways to make better goods at lower prices, both to protect the home market and to take advantage of foreign buying power by selling more goods overseas. There is also an urgent need for American business to invest in underdeveloped nations that are looking for a helping hand.

Here at home, shifts in the population centers and stringent business competition are radically altering methods of marketing and placing heavy emphasis on costs of distribution. Caught up in a period of unequaled competitive growth, with new products coming on the market at a constantly accelerating rate, business is spending record amounts for advertising in a strenuous effort to capture a larger share of the consumer dollar. In conjunction with our rapidly growing interests in overseas markets, these efforts are giving rise to an important type of managerial and marketing employee in the structure of many business organizations, both large and small.

The explosive growth of technological innovation, coupled with the rise in educational levels, constitutes another important influence upon management. The nation's workforce is expected to alter radically during the next ten years. We can expect to see marked changes in the types and numbers of jobs, in the levels at which they are positioned, in the skills they require, and in the kinds of people we employ, as compared with the past 30 years. With an increasing number of college and high school graduates, there will be a rise in the general educational level of the population. In five years, 40 per cent more young people will be completing high school; and the percentage of our youth in college will triple during the next generation. Future entrants into the job market will bring with them new points of view, new needs, and new expectations.

In the light of these new influences at work in business today, it is clear that personnel people must play a new role on the management team of the future. To do this, they must successfully meet three special problems.

## Personnel and the Management Team of the Future

First and foremost is the need for a broader concept of the job of personnel management. As I see it, our long-range objective should be to help management identify, select, utilize, develop, and compensate the kinds of people needed to achieve its over-all goals—people who will have the ingenuity and good judgment required to develop new business processes, the acumen to administer sound business programs, the necessary sensitivity to shifts in distribution patterns, and the ability to exact the maximum voluntary growth and productivity from each individual.

This calls for a work focus that is completely new to many personnel people. It requires them to understand and identify themselves with management's main objectives—profit and growth. And it means that they must be willing to be held accountable for results, for progress measured against specific objectives.

To the degree that they do this, they will at once be relating their efforts to the corporate cash register and will be embarking on a course of action that identifies itself with major management objectives. This in turn implies dealing in ideas and futures. It seems logical, therefore, to assume that a higher degree of *idea management* must become a part of the daily personnel job if personnel men are to earn and hold their place on tomorrow's management team.

Idea management—the second of our three key areas—stands in sharp contrast to procedure and program management, which in itself implies management of systems that are already in existence. In planning objectives related to profitability and growth, corporate management deals particularly with ideas and problems in terms of the future. Personnel managers must likewise deal more and more in concepts predicated on what lies ahead.

When we talk about idea management in a personnel sense, what do we mean? Two avenues in particular immediately occur to me:

*1. The need for new concepts of organization.* As we know, the military concept of line and staff organization has prevailed in American industry for many years. But there are encouraging signs that many managements are now willing to study and experiment with the new forms of organization required by changes in the general structure of the workforce. There is also evidence of an increasing readiness to organize job relationships and responsibilities in terms of agreed-upon end results, as well as to create a climate within the company in which individual goals can be achieved.

*2. The need for new concepts of motivation.* Motivation remains one of the important unexplored areas of profit opportunity for management. In a business system such as ours, in which managerial control is based on consent rather than coercion, motivation is of critical importance. There is a growing need to improve motivation through better management.

The third special problem area to which, I suggest, personnel men should direct particular attention in the years ahead revolves around the existence of *key employee groups* in our enterprises. Personnel people must identify these groups and distinguish the degree of impact that each group has on corporate growth and profitability. They must also direct their efforts in terms of the needs and expectations of these key employees.

## The Key Employee Groups

During much of the past 30 years, personnel management has been principally occupied with the problems of employees in large groups. As a matter of fact, the performance and value of the personnel function has often been evaluated on a purely quantitative basis—by the number of employees handled, the number of unions dealt with, the number and location of plants, the number of labor contracts successfully written, the number of strikes avoided, the number of grievances and arbitration cases successfully concluded, and so on. But today, mere numbers are no longer a valid basis for judging the constructiveness of the personnel function; the relative importance of the various segments of the workforce cannot be determined by the per-cent-of-payroll method. Today we face the emergence of certain key employee groups who *qualitatively* will account for a larger share of corporate profitability and growth.

The researcher, the engineer, the marketing specialist, the manager, the outside salesman are typical of these key people whose contributions to corporate growth and profitability far outweigh their numbers expressed as a percentage of payroll. They are the cutting edge of the workforce tool. Their needs must be considered from a different perspective than that traditionally taken with respect to mass groups of factory employees.

How are we to go about identifying these key groups? We can start by looking at the national picture—its projections for the future—and then reflect these forecasts against our own company needs.

At the moment, the semiskilled group is the largest in the labor force, numbering about 12 million persons, of whom more than one-fourth are women. This group has grown rapidly during the recent decades of industrial expansion, especially in manufacturing employment. Though automated processes are now taking over many operations formerly performed by these workers, further significant changes are expected in semiskilled jobs, particularly in manufacturing industries.

Another growing key group is the skilled workers, who are expected to total nearly 11 million by 1970—nearly 13 per cent of the working population. This increase will result from the technological advances of industry and the resulting needs for new and higher skills.

Professional workers are another key group. Today, the nation's white-collar workers already exceed the number of persons employed in manual occupations. During the next ten years, this trend will continue and accelerate. The fastest growth will occur among the professional and technical groups, especially engineers, scientists, and technicians, as well as among marketing and sales personnel. These will increase by 40 per cent to over 11 million workers, as opposed to an increase of about 18 per cent for the labor force as a whole.

In my own company,* out of a total workforce of 22,000, we have some 5,000 so-called key employees, who contribute much more to profitability than their numbers would indicate. By 1970, it seems likely that 30 per cent or more of our employees may be scientists and engineers, marketing specialists, and managers.

* [General Foods Corp.—ed.]

## The Cornerstones of New Policies

Once we have identified our key groups, we face the task of developing policies in line with their expectations and needs. In an era of high incomes, maximum employment, more leisure time, and a high level of education, employees look beyond monetary rewards for job satisfactions that lie in the opportunities we give the individual to use his own ideas and resources—to achieve maximum growth and self-development. These requirements, I suggest, will necessitate the development of new policies in four basic elements of the personnel function:

*1. Organization.* In organizing our work groups, we must move away from the rigid, formal patterns of the past toward a greater awareness of the dynamic relationships among people as the clue to greater organization potential. Key employees, especially, must be given the freedom to work at the highest capacities of which they are capable, and ways must be found to provide this freedom within the disciplines of the business organization. This may mean greater decentralization of authority and responsibility for end results—the development of teams with direct profit responsibility that at the same time operate *within* the formal framework of the multi-product organization. In our research laboratories, it may mean providing professional channels of advancement that parallel managerial channels in compensation and status. In the sales area, it may require a sharper distinction between selling and managing duties, and the establishment of job functions that will make fuller use of the initiative and creative potential of people in the selling organization.

*2. Selection.* There will be a need for better specifications for higher-level positions to serve as the basis for selection. Clearer definitions of the critical differences among jobs and the different abilities and skills required to fill them should produce sharper selection criteria against which candidates can be assessed.

Because of the higher investment per man for the key employee, as well as his greater potential for the company, selection procedures will have to be applied more carefully than ever before to provide as much relevant information as possible about individual candidates. More attention must be given to the particular business environment in which the higher-level employee will be working and the degree to which this environment is likely to be compatible with his own value system, experience, and interests as an individual.

*3. Development.* The key employee often needs more freedom to realize his full potential and make his maximum contribution. Study must therefore be directed at identifying, if possible, the processes and forces that contribute most to his development. Management must also work toward creating an environment in which people will be motivated to develop themselves. Our appraisal systems still need much study if they are to be effective as tools for future development as well as for the review of past performance. This calls for appraisals geared to the accomplishment of job objectives and to accountability for results. It thus requires the joint participation of supervisor and subordinate, for it is in the "supportive" relationship to which this participation contributes that both of them can reach an understanding of the end results to be achieved.

*4. Compensation.* Studies have shown that higher-level employees require broader types of compensation than purely monetary rewards. Challenging work, recognition for a job well done, a better environment, and opportunities for creativity and growth are among the incentives to maximum effort by key employees. We have known these things for years, but we have tended to overlook them. Now that the key employee is moving to the forefront, compensation systems offering broader appeals to his job needs are becoming more important.

Whereas the legendary figures of our industrial past were the geniuses of finance, technology, production—the Schwabs, the Edisons, and the Fords—the managerial genius of the future will be found among those who lead the way in maximizing the potential of our human resources. Through the development of policies that will motivate key employees, personnel men can make a major contribution to successful management—stimulating those people who contribute most to profitability and growth.

For the difference between what people can do and what they will do remains one of the great unexplored sources of corporate profits. How to stimulate the maximum contribution from those who have most to offer represents one of the most potentially rewarding challenges that lie before us.

# Human Asset Accounting*

*Rensis Likert*

Evidence was presented [in earlier chapters] for the necessity of including estimates of the current value of the human organization and of customer goodwill in all financial reports of a firm.

The absence of these estimates for each profit center and for the entire corporation is not due to a lack of interest on the part of the accounting profession (Hermanson, 1964). Cultural lag and the usual gaps in com-

---

* From *The Human Organization: Its Management and Value,* McGraw-Hill Book Company, New York, 1967, chap. 9, pp. 146–155. Reprinted by permission of the publisher.

munication among the relevant sciences are the culprits. To create human asset accounting and to make reasonably accurate estimates of its two dimensions—the current value of the human organization and customer goodwill—require close cooperation between accountants and social scientists highly competent in the measurement of the causal and intervening variables.

Such cooperation is now starting. It will require from five to ten years and many million dollars' worth of work to collect the data and to make the computations required before human asset accounting can become fully operational. Sophisticated measurement and accounting procedures should emerge from this work, enabling firms to incorporate in their financial reports reasonably accurate estimates of the current value of the human assets of an enterprise. These procedures will enable a firm not only to know the current value of these resources, but also what changes or trends are occurring from time to time in the magnitudes of these assets. In addition, it will be possible to prepare these estimates for each profit center of the firm and, where appropriate and useful, for any smaller unit within a firm.

Computing a firm's original investment in its human organization is a much simpler problem than estimating the current value of that investment. This is true for the company as a whole and for such units as profit centers, departments, and other subunits. There are several alternate methods for obtaining estimates of the original investment in the human side of an enterprise.

One way is to base these estimates on start-up costs. The problem in many ways is comparable to estimating a firm's current investment in machinery which it has built itself and continues to use for a period of time. The actual cost of building a machine can readily be computed. The human start-up costs of a new plant, unit, or department can be computed similarly, although the task of doing so is more complex and difficult. These start-up costs should include what it has cost to hire and train the personnel and to develop them into a coordinated organization operating in a reasonably satisfactory manner.

Start-up costs can be computed for various kinds of operations and for various-sized units. As these human investment costs become available enterprise, they can be used as a basis for estimating the magnitude of for the widely different kinds of operations performed by a particular the investment a firm has in its human organization—for the entire corporation or for any of its units.

A second way of estimating the magnitude of the investment in the human organization is to obtain data on the costs of hiring and training personnel for each of the many different kinds of positions in the company. The sum of these costs for every person in the firm usually will be substantial. It underestimates, however, the true investment in the human side of the enterprise, since it does not reflect the additional investment made during the period when the members of the firm were establishing effective cooperative working relationships[1] with one another. These cooperative working relationships might appropriately be called the synergistic component. To establish them takes an appreciable period of time and involves substantial costs.

This approach will require a tremendous amount of work if it is done for every kind of position and every member of the organization. The cost and effort of making these estimates can be reduced substantially by probability sampling. Efficient designs will yield estimates closely approximating those which would be obtained were all the jobs and all the positions examined.

## Estimating the Current Value of the Human Organization

Although computing a firm's investment in building its human organization or its customer goodwill may be difficult, obtaining reasonably accurate estimates of the *current* value of the human organization is a much more difficult and complex task. It is, moreover, much more important. For the reasons discussed at length in [other chapters], it is essential that reasonably accurate information be currently available to all levels of management as to changes and trends in the present value of its human organization. Managers and all other members of the organization and shareholders need to be kept correctly informed on these matters, since the health, profitability, and long-range survival of the enterprise depend upon sound decisions guided by measurements which reflect the current value of its human organization.

## Human Asset Accounting

Human assets, as used in this volume, refer both to the value of the productive capacity of a firm's human organization and to the value of its customer goodwill.

The productive capability of its human organization can be illustrated by thinking of two firms in the same business. Both are of the same size and have identical equipment and technology. One, however, produces more and earns more than the other, because its personnel is superior to the other's with regard to such variables as the following:

1. Level of intelligence and aptitudes
2. Level of training

[1] The nature of these relationships is described on pp. 183–185 of [Likert's] *New Patterns of Management.* [McGraw-Hill Book Company, New York, 1961].

3. Level of performance goals and motivation to achieve organizational success

4. Quality of leadership

5. Capacity to use differences for purposes of innovation and improvement, rather than allowing differences to develop into bitter, irreconcilable, interpersonal conflict

6. Quality of communication upward, downward, and laterally

7. Quality of decision making

8. Capacity to achieve cooperative teamwork versus competitive striving for personal success at the expense of organization

9. Quality of the control processes of organization and the levels of felt responsibility which exist

10. Capacity to achieve effective coordination

11. Capacity to use experience and measurements to guide decisions, improve operations, and introduce innovations

The difference in the economic value of the human organizations of these two firms would be reflected by the differences between them in present and future earnings, attributable to the differences in their human organizations. Similarly, differences in the value of customer goodwill would be reflected in the differences between them in the ease and costs of making sales, i.e., in the difference in the motivation among customers to buy the product of one firm, rather than that of the other.

Human asset accounting refers to activity devoted to attaching dollar estimates to the value of a firm's human organization and its customer goodwill. If able, well-trained personnel leave the firm, the human organization is worth less; if they join it, the firm's human assets are increased. If bickering, distrust, and irreconcilable conflict become greater, the human enterprise is worth less; if the capacity to use differences constructively and engage in cooperative teamwork improves, the human organization is a more valuable asset.

Since estimates of the current value of a firm's human organization are both necessary and difficult to obtain, it is highly desirable to use several alternate approaches in developing methods for making these estimates. The results from one approach can serve as a check on those obtained from the others. The initial estimates from any procedure, of course, are likely to have relatively large errors of estimate. As the methodology improves, two important developments will occur. The size of the errors will decrease, and the accuracy of estimating the magnitude of these errors will increase. The accuracy of human asset accounting will increase correspondingly.

The essential first step in developing procedures for applying human asset accounting to a firm's human organization is to undertake periodic measurements of the key causal and intervening variables. These measurements must be available over several years' time to provide the data for the needed computations. The data required for the initial computations should be collected at quite frequent intervals, quarterly or even more often.

The optimum frequency for the measurements will vary with the kind of work involved. The more nearly the work involves the total man, such as research and development (R&D) tasks, the shorter should be the intervals between successive measurements, for, as was mentioned in Chapter 5, the time lag between changes in the causal, intervening, and end-result variables is much less for such work than for work which is machine-paced. The sequence of developments . . . requires a shorter time interval for R&D and other complex tasks than for machine-paced or simple, repetitive tasks. Unfavorable attitudes lead much more rapidly to decreased productivity. A scientist who feels resentful toward his organization or manager rapidly becomes unproductive. With machine-paced and similar work, which usually employs only a part of the capabilities of the total man (e.g., hands), a longer period of time is required before the adverse effects of unfavorable reactions and attitudes manifest themselves in the forms of norms to restrict production, of increased grievances and similar developments, and, finally, in lower performance. For this kind of work, consequently, the intervals between periodic measurements can be longer than for professional and other complex work.

The total period of time required for the cycles . . . to reach reasonable equilibrium, of course, will vary also with the kind of work. The cycle reaches a stable relationship much more quickly with complex tasks than with machine-paced and simple, repetitive tasks. Complex tasks require less time to reach stable relationships; machine-paced and similar work require more time.[2]

The measurements of the causal and intervening variables should be obtained for the corporation as a whole and for each profit center or unit in the company for which productivity, costs, waste, and earnings can be computed. After these measurements have been made over a sufficient period of time for relatively stable relationships to develop or for the sequence of relationships to complete their full cycle, the necessary data will be available to relate the causal and intervening measurements to the earnings record. By using appropriate statistical procedures, relationships can be computed among the causal, intervening, and such end-result variables as costs and earnings. The resulting mathematical relationships will enable one to estimate the productive and earnings capability of any profit center, or smaller unit, based upon its present scores on the causal and intervening variables. These estimates of probable subse-

---

[2] The influence of different kinds of work upon the cycle of relationships among the causal, intervening, and end-result variables is discussed more fully in Chapter 6, *New Patterns of Management.*

quent productivity, costs, and earnings will reveal the earning power of the human organization *at the time* the causal and intervening variables were measured, even though the level of estimated subsequent earnings may not be achieved until much later. These estimates of probable subsequent productivity, costs, and earnings provide the basis for attaching to any profit center, unit, or total corporation a statement of the present value of its human organization.

Corporations which have a number of relatively comparable units, such as chain stores, will have a distinct advantage in using the method just suggested. The data from several comparable units will yield more reliable estimates by providing far more observations upon which to base calculations. Moreover, differences among the units can be used as well as changes for any particular unit over time. Based on these differences, computations can be made of the relation of earnings to each pattern of causal and intervening variables using, of course, optimum time intervals. By capitalizing the greater earnings of the better units, estimates of the present value of the human organization can be obtained.

It is probable that after sufficient research has been done and sufficient data and experience obtained, it will be feasible to do human asset accounting in much the same way that standard costs are now used to estimate the manufacturing costs of new products. Another use of standard estimates is the MTM (Methods-Time Measurement) process of setting a standard time for the performance of a particular task. Experience has shown that standard estimates can be used successfully in accounting and in industrial engineering. A comparable process should be equally successful in human asset accounting.

## Present Earnings May Yield Incorrect Estimate

Many corporations at present are making estimates of the current value of the human organization and of customer goodwill. This is done whenever a new firm or division is acquired. Every year there are a substantial number of acquisitions. In each instance, an appropriate value has to be placed on the acquired firm. The purchase price generally is substantially larger than the current value of the physical and financial assets and reflects allowances for both customer and employee goodwill. Both the firm which is acquired and the corporation acquiring it make these estimates in arriving at a fair price. An important factor in arriving at these estimates usually is the current and recent earnings of the acquired firm. This approach has to be used cautiously, however, since it contains a source of error which at times can be sizable. If the acquired firm has been using the approach to cost reduction based on personnel limitations, tightened budgets, and tighter standards and is at a point of high earnings but decreasing value of the human organization . . . , then an estimate of the value of the human assets based on current earnings is likely to be appreciably inflated.

### Estimating the Value of Customer Goodwill

Customer goodwill, like the value of the human organization, is an asset of substantial magnitude in most companies. The sizable costs in opening new markets or marketing new products demonstrate the magnitude of the current value of this asset in most companies.

This asset can vary appreciably from time to time, depending upon the behavior of the firm's management (a causal variable), the resulting motivation and behavior of the firm's personnel (intervening variables), and the corresponding price and quality of product and service provided to customers (end-result variables).

Cash income can be increased for a period of time by selling shoddy products and rendering poor service while charging the usual prices. This income should not be reported and treated as earnings in financial statements, however, since it is actually achieved by cashing in on the firm's customer loyalty. It represents a liquidation, often at a fraction of its value, of customer goodwill. Such "earnings" are as spurious and misleading as those derived from liquidating part of the firm's investment in its human organization.

Customer goodwill, as well as the value of the human organization, should be reflected at its present value in every financial statement. This can be done by drawing upon the methodological resources created by social-psychological research. The same basic concepts and methodology employed in estimating the current value of the human organization can be used to attach dollar amounts to the current value of customer goodwill. Favorable customer attitudes create motivational forces to buy a firm's products. One set of estimates of the current value of these motivational forces can be obtained by methods available for measuring the sales influence of advertising and marketing efforts. A method for obtaining the relevant measurements was published several years ago (Likert, 1936).

### Imbalance in Fiscal Management

In considering the desirability and expense of undertaking the work required for human asset accounting, it should be recognized that the present practice of treating, with great precision, a fraction of the firm's assets and completely ignoring assets of roughly the same or greater magnitude represents a serious imbalance. A firm's financial reports would be much more useful and appreciably more accurate if approximately the same level of accuracy were maintained in dealing with *all* of the firm's assets. The equity of the shareholders would be protected far better than at present if there were more balance in the accounting effort.

It is perfectly feasible for a company to establish a balanced effort in their accounting activities without an appreciable increase in their total accounting costs. This can be done by placing all accounting on a sample basis and using sample designs which yield estimates of acceptable accuracy. There would be a substantial reduction in the costs of the usual physical asset and financial asset accounting, and this saving could be used for human asset accounting, i.e., for obtaining estimates of the current value of the human organization and of customer goodwill.

This use of sampling methods in the accounting work would result in small sampling errors in the reports dealing with the physical and financial assets. At present, these reports usually contain no errors due to sampling, since a 100 percent sample is generally used. With sophisticated, weighted sampling designs, however, the sampling errors would be smaller than the other errors which arise from various assumptions, such as those used in handling depreciation and comparable problems.

The facts are clear. If sophisticated sampling methods were applied to physical and financial accounting, the maximum probable error would be so small as to be unimportant in its consequences. If sound sampling methods were used in conducting human asset accounting, physical asset accounting, and financial asset accounting, the errors due to sampling would be negligible, and a firm would have appreciably more accurate fiscal reports than at present. The sampling errors in such financial reports, on the average, would be only a fraction of the size of the errors which now occur in financial reports which are based on 100 percent sampling of the physical and financial assets and no sampling of the human assets.

### Interim Steps to Increase the Accuracy of Financial Reports

There is, of course, an interim problem to be dealt with. Even though a firm started tomorrow to do the research required to develop the necessary procedures for human asset accounting, several years would be required before it could be put into effect. In the meantime, however, corporate officers can take an important step which will enable them to safeguard company assets more completely and to improve appreciably the accuracy and adequacy of the information provided them.

The proposed step is to introduce the periodic measurement of the causal and intervening variables and *to have a record of these measurements made a part of every production and financial report*. This should be done for all fiscal and production reports, both those for profit centers and those for the entire corporation.

These measurements would help the board and the other managers of the firm to interpret more correctly the production and financial reports they receive. If there were no changes from one period to the next in the scores on the causal and intervening variables, the financial report could be considered essentially correct, insofar as any changes in the current value of the human organization are concerned. If, however, these measurements of the causal and intervening variables showed an unfavorable shift, then the financial report should be viewed as overstating the actual situation. Under such circumstances the report would reflect a more favorable picture than the actual facts and would include as earnings funds which were really derived from the liquidation of human assets. Conversely, if the measurements of the causal and intervening variables were to reflect a favorable shift, then the financial report would understate the real situation, since management actually would be doing a better job than the report revealed. The true earnings and changes in assets would be more favorable than the financial report showed.

The measurements of the causal and intervening variables can be used in this manner to assure that there are no serious mistakes in the interpretation of the financial and production reports for any unit, profit center, or the entire company. Managers of units which achieved part of their earnings or productivity by liquidating human assets would have their financial and production reports correspondingly discounted. On the other hand, managers who added to company assets by improving their human organization would have their performance records viewed as understating their total managerial performance. Changes in the size and composition of the labor force should be taken into consideration also.

Bankers making loans, investment houses, and others who are interested in the earnings and success of an enterprise should be just as interested as boards and senior officers in having these periodic measurements of the causal and intervening variables available. These data, as we have seen, are essential for the correct interpretation of production and fiscal data.

It is equally important to have similar periodic measurements of customer goodwill accompany financial reports and for the same reasons. These data should be interpreted and used in essentially the same way as the measurements of the causal and intervening variables.

As soon as corporate officers arrange to have the measurements of the causal and intervening variables and of customer goodwill as part of production and financial reports, enterprises will be managed more successfully. Better decisions will be made at all management levels, because these decisions will be based on more accurate facts. Senior officers and boards will not be misinformed, as they may be at present, concerning the management systems used by the managers who achieve the highest earnings year in and year out. With accurate information to guide its decisions, top management would not superimpose a System 2 manager on a System 4 operation and thereby destroy one of their most valuable assets.* The present management of large corporations whose previous managements have built great loyalty and high motivation committed to corporate success at all levels in the organization will not be able to show impressive but fictitious earnings over many years' time by progressively increasing the pressure and tightening the controls on their subordinate managers, supervisors, and nonsupervisory employees, i.e., shifting toward System 2 from System 3 or 4.

Frobably the most important improvement in fiscal management will be the profound changes which measurements of the human dimensions of an enterprise will bring in the generally accepted concepts of how a corporation or department should be managed to be financially most successful. The cold hard facts of accurate measurements will wipe out many of the erroneous concepts which are widely held today but which are based on incomplete accounting and short-run financial analyses of only a portion of a firm's total assets.

## The Opportunity Is Limited

The opportunity to use measurements of the causal and intervening variables during the interim period in the manner suggested will be affected by the management system of the firm and trends in this system. As was pointed out [earlier] cooperative motivation is necessary to obtain the most accurate measurements of the causal, intervening, and end-result variables over any period of time. A firm's capacity to use the interim steps suggested, therefore, will be influenced by its management system and the trends in this system. Companies which are using System 4 or are shifting toward it will have the cooperative motivation required for measurements to be accurate. Firms shifting toward System 1 or using System 1 or 2 will be unlikely to have such cooperative motivation.

Firms striving to use a science-based management system will have a distinct advantage over other companies in the adequacy and accuracy of the information made available to them to guide decisions and to evaluate results.

---

* [Likert's explanation of his Systems 1, 2, 3, and 4 appears in his "Table of Organizational and Performance Characteristics of Different Management Systems," pp. 14–24 in *The Human Organization,* chap. 2, "A Look at Management Systems."—Ed.]

# INDEX

Ability, 8
Accommodative leadership, 471
Accounting of human assets, 497–506
Adams, Stuart, 470
Administrative competence of supervisors, 359–363
Andrews, Frank, 52
Arensberg, Conrad M., 179
Argyris, Chris, 14, 24–25, 45, 52, 177
Asch, Solomon E., 33, 335
Aspiration, level of, 18, 145, 237, 360
Autocratic leadership, 39–40, 180

Barnes, Louis B., 478
Barrett, Dermott, 30, 290
Basic needs, 84
Bass, Bernard, 53
Bavelas, Alex, 30, 179, 290, 409
Bayton, J. A., 147
Bellows, Roger, 52
Bendix, Reinhard, 147
Bierstadt, Robert, 180
Blau, Peter M., 180
Blue-collar workers, 21, 61
Boss-centered leadership, 397
Brayfield, Arthur H., 51, 459
Brennan, Mal, 178
British Medical Council, 219
Brown, J. A. C., 32, 305
Burtt, Harold E., 380

Canter, R. R., 264
Carter, Launor, 181
Change, resistance to, 409
Christenson, C. R., 33, 469, 476
Chung, Kae H., 54
Clark, James V., 57, 461
Classical theory of organization, 23
Close supervision, 368
  definition of, 369
Coch, Lester, 43, 406, 477
Cohesiveness, 32, 189, 330, 413, 457
Collins, Orville, 489
Combination leadership, 39, 44, 406
Communication, 25, 30, 290, 297
  direction of, 298
  network of, 29, 178, 298
  one-way, 299
  two-way, 299

Consideration, 267, 382–386
Control, span of, 215
Crockett, Walter H., 51, 441
Cultural background, needs of individuals affected by, 19, 97–98, 150, 159–162, 209

Dartnell Corporation, 256
Davis, Allison, 20, 149
Davis, Keith, 42
Davis, Louis E., 28, 239
Democratic leadership, 39–40, 180, 396
Differentiation of supervisory role, 365–368
Drucker, Peter F., 20–21, 61, 164, 240

Educated worker, mobility of, 170
  organization of, 172
  productivity of, 168–169
Educational level, 61, 164–165, 493
  needs of individuals affected by, 20–21
  perceptions of individuals affected by, 138
  of underprivileged workers, 158
Egoistic needs, 13–15, 190, 464
Employee-oriented supervision, 40–41, 371, 455
Esteem needs, 91
Executives, needs of, 21
Experience, needs affected by, 21
  perceptions affected by, 141

Fiedler, Fred, 38
Fisher, Lloyd H., 1
Fleishman, Edwin A., 27, 40, 51, 181, 266, 380
Formal leadership, 177
Formal organization, 23, 25, 181
Fowler, Irving, 325, 467
Free-rein leadership, 39–40
French, John R. P., Jr., 43, 406, 477

Galbraith, J. Kenneth, 1
Gebhard, Mildred E., 146
General supervision, 40

507